Rhoda

A BIOGRAPHY

*"Comrade Kadalie,
You Are Out of Order!"*

For Mike!

Keep fighting the good fight!

Joel B. Pollak

UJ Press

Rhoda: 'Comrade Kadalie, You Are Out of Order!'
A biography

Published by UJ Press
University of Johannesburg
Library
Auckland Park Kingsway Campus
PO Box 524
Auckland Park
2006
https://ujonlinepress.uj.ac.za/

First published 2023

https://doi.org/10.36615/9781776413485

978-1-7764134-7-8 (Paperback)
978-1-7764134-8-5 (PDF)
978-1-7764134-9-2 (EPUB)
978-1-7764194-0-1 (XML)

This publication had been submitted to a rigorous double-blind peer-review process prior to publication and all recommendations by the reviewers were considered and implemented before publication.

Copy editor: Lauren Shapiro
Cover design: Hester Roets, UJ Graphic Design Studio
Typeset in 10/13pt Merriweather Light

Contents

For Julia

Julia Pollak (née Bertelsmann), Rhoda's daughter, with Rhoda at home in University Estate, Cape Town, after Rhoda received an honorary doctorate from the University of the Western Cape, 2007 (Courtesy Rhoda Kadalie)

Acknowledgments

This authorized biography was made possible through the gracious help of my mother-in-law, Rhoda Kadalie, who provided generous access to her files, letters, photographs, and extensive library of documents. She made time to sit with me for several hours of interviews from September through October 2021, to answer questions as they arose, and to offer innumerable clarifications. Rhoda also reviewed the first draft of the biography in December 2021, making corrections and additions, and contributing some of her own original vignettes, never before published.

Special thanks are also due to my wife —Rhoda's daughter, Julia — for her support and suggestions, as well as our children Maya, Alexander, and baby Amira, who allowed me to devote precious time to the completion of this biography during an exceptionally busy and difficult time in our lives. Thanks also to Judith Kadalie, Rhoda's sister, for her tireless care and support for Rhoda in the final weeks of her life, and to my parents, Raymond and Naomi Pollak, for helping with Rhoda's care as well. Maricel Abrahamson also cared for Amira during working hours, and accompanied our family to South Africa as we paid our respects to Rhoda after her passing.

In Johannesburg, Frances Jowell kindly granted me access to the Helen Suzman Papers at the Historical Papers Research Archive at the University of Witwatersrand Library, where Gabriele Mohale and the staff of the library provided extensive assistance. Zandile Myeka and the staff of the Nelson Mandela Foundation guided my research in the Jakes Gerwel Archive. Marc Lotter also made time to meet with me to offer his recollections of his work alongside Rhoda. Margot Bertelsmann provided invaluable insights into the background of Rhoda's in-laws, as well as help with proofreading. Thanks are due also to Shirley Resnick and the Resnick family for their hospitality.

In Cape Town, Anne and John Field reminisced about Rhoda's childhood in Mowbray, and provided an invaluable collection of photographs from her life's journey. I also met with several of Rhoda's close friends and colleagues, including Helen Zille, Terri Felix, Cyril Kern, and Chris Mingo, among others. In Stellenbosch, Justa Niemand provided access to some of Rhoda's correspondence with friends before Rhoda's emigration in 2018, and later helped connect me to Wikus van Zyl at the University of Johannesburg Press, whose partnership has been invaluable throughout the process of editing and publication. Further afield in the Western Cape, Edwena and Robert Goff hosted me at their home in

Somerset West; Ian Moodie guided me around the Molteno Brothers farm in Grabouw; and Betsie Ryke met me in Grabouw to describe Rhoda's assistance to her rural arts project. The staff of Harold Cressy High School graciously allowed me to tour the building after hours.

I spoke by telephone with Freddie Engelbrecht and Johnny Jansen in South Africa, and with Paul Curnow in Sydney, Australia. The Bundesarchiv in Germany assisted in confirming details about Rhoda's father-in-law, Werner Bertelsmann. Various friends and relatives of Rhoda provided insights and ideas, both formally and informally, as well as photographs. My own father-in-law, Richard Bertelsmann, also agreed to share some of his insights and his niece, Margot Bertelsmann Doherty, provided fascinating memoirs written by Rhoda's in-laws. Rhoda's niece, Robyn Russell, visited and read an early draft of the manuscript.

The staff of the University Library of California State University Northridge (CSUN) provided access to relevant periodicals and assistance in research. Lauren Shapiro in Johannesburg provided valuable edits to the submitted manuscript. Village Photo in Pacific Palisades, California, scanned and processed photographs for the book. Raymond Izaac of Digital Video & Film Lab in Santa Monica, California, converted Rhoda's old VHS tapes to digital format for review. Helmut Schulze of Rees Electronics provided a restored tape deck that could play decades-old interviews on cassette. The Buffalo City Municipality helped me indirectly: its Facebook postings about a memorial ceremony at the grave of Clements Kadalie in 2021 helped me locate the site.

Nicole Schoumer and Theo Schkolne provided informal advice and counsel throughout, and Pastor Robert Steiner of the Rondebosch United Church comforted Rhoda's family after she passed away in June 2022 and hosted a dignified memorial for her. Rabbi Boruch and Rebbetzin Rivka Rabinowitz provided spiritual and moral support, as did Rabbi Dovid and Rebbetzin Chana Shifra Tenenbaum; Rabbi Zushe and Rebbetzin Zisi Cunin; Rabbi Hirschy and Rebbetzin Elkie Zarchi; and Rabbi Osher and Rebbetzin Sarah Feldman; and Abigail Shrier, among many others.

There are many other people whose contributions to this book were crucial, including an anonymous reviewer who pointed out several gaps in an earlier draft. That prompted me to search for additional source material, and led to the fortuitous discovery of several boxes of documents that addressed many of the criticisms that had been raised. I am grateful to that reviewer, as well as to other readers and critics who have helped me along the way.

Finally, I am grateful to my colleagues at Breitbart News for their indulgence as I worked to complete this book in a busy news environment, with much work to do.

Editorial Note

This biography has been a labor of love. I wrote it for three reasons.

First, the personal: Rhoda Kadalie was my mother-in-law, and my close friend. We had a special bond, and through all the ups and downs of family life, we never lost sight of the deep love and respect we had for one another. Even before we knew that she had terminal cancer, I had thought about writing a biography that would provide a fitting tribute. With her grim diagnosis, we began a race against time.

Rhoda was able to work with me for several months; she even reviewed the first draft of the manuscript, and provided access to her documents and diaries. More of these became available after she passed away, when I discovered boxes that she had kept in temporary storage, awaiting a permanent home. She also connected me with people who would be able to shed light on key events in her life. Most were eager to be interviewed, though a few former colleagues could not be reached or did not respond. Given the sheer volume of material to analyze and digest, and the pressure of producing a biography while her memory remained fresh in the public mind, I hope that I have succeeded in telling her story.

Second, the historical: Rhoda Kadalie played a unique and important role in the South African story. She was on the front lines of the anti-apartheid struggle, and she changed the character of that struggle by bringing feminism into the broader liberation cause. What her grandfather, Clements Kadalie, did for the labor movement — shining a harsh light on racism — Rhoda did for the anti-apartheid movement with regard to women's issues. That made her a pioneer — and also, at times, a pariah. She was an internal, yet public, critic of the liberation movement, a role that she continued in the post-apartheid era. She was appointed by President Nelson Mandela to the new Human Rights Commission — and resigned, on principle, when she felt the institution was not fulfilling its constitutional duty. Through her non-profit foundation, Impumelelo ("Success"), she helped the government pursue its socioeconomic goals; through her opinion columns in the national press, she attacked that same government's illiberalism and corruption. At one point — as I shall relate in the pages to follow — she was secretly invited to lead the country's democratic opposition, but declined. Likewise, she refused to join the new "empowerment" elite, preferring to guard her integrity and independence. She championed the underdog in the new South Africa — the poor black masses, the besieged Afrikaner farmers, the disappointed Coloured minority, the frightened Jewish community. Through studying

Rhoda Kadalie's life and writings, we can better understand the hopes that drove the "struggle" — and the disappointments that have haunted the new South Africa. Her commitment to non-racialism and constitutional democracy also offers a path forward for a country that is, once more, in turmoil.

Third, the political: Rhoda Kadalie began as a revolutionary, became something of a liberal, and ended as a conservative — though she rarely used any of those terms to describe herself. Her shift from left to right was poorly understood by her critics, and indeed by many of her friends as well. But where some saw superficial discontinuities, for Rhoda there was a constant, underlying theme: the love of freedom. She was born in an era when freedom depended on overthrowing an unjust system; she became a national figure in South Africa by championing the liberal constitution that protected that hard-won freedom; and she later embraced conservative populism in the United States as the best way to protect freedom from a corrupt, oligarchic elite. Her life defies the idea that the legacy of the struggle against apartheid belongs to the political left alone. Rather, the principles of that movement were, and remain, universal; and suggest that justice requires a moral commitment from the "oppressed" as much as the "oppressor," not merely the self-negation of the latter.

Rhoda's approach to freedom was pragmatic, and ecumenical: it required the courage to oppose injustice, but also a willingness to accept a diversity of paths toward a common goal. Her philosophy reinforced one of the lessons I cherish from my own political experience: that while many of us are motivated by the desire to see change on a grand scale, the most profound changes are those that individuals make in their own lives, and the best system is one that enables each of us to do so in our own way.

That was also the lesson of Rhoda's academic success. She emerged from South Africa's segregated schools and pushed herself to excel. She thrived at the University of the Western Cape, where she gained a political education as well as an academic one. She went on to earn a master's degree at The Hague, and received several honorary doctorates. For all of that success, her intellectual journey was difficult, tearful, and often lonely. Rhoda learned — the hard way — that education is not only the most important commodity, but also one that cannot be distributed, or redistributed, without the individual effort of the student. Some may be born into more privilege than others, but even they are not spared the effort: there are no shortcuts to excellence. Rhoda demanded the highest standards from herself, and others.

Moreover, Rhoda consistently fought against corruption, regardless of partisan or ideological loyalty. She constructed a moral philosophy around that opposition to corruption, connecting personal decisions to broader principles in a way that gives the individual human being a way to improve their society — however marginally — by taking responsibility for their own moral choices. I wish to share Rhoda's ideas and her example with a world whose confidence in freedom, and in morality itself, seems shaken today.

This biography was largely completed before Rhoda Kadalie passed away on April 16, 2022. Therefore, it occasionally describes her using the present tense, since she was alive when it was written — and remains with us, in many ways.

Moreover, this biography is a work of scholarship, but it is aimed at a general audience, not just an academic one. And though it draws, at times, on academic sources, and follows academic conventions of citation, the style is journalistic. It is also, at times, deeply personal. It also includes several vignettes that are Rhoda's original, and hitherto unpublished, works. The text therefore has a heterogenous quality that, I hope, will enhance the reader's experience rather than complicating it. The original source material cited throughout this biography will, at the very least, prove invaluable to scholars as they strive to understand Rhoda Kadalie and the exciting, and at times tragic, era in which she lived.

The book also uses both American and South African spelling conventions; I have opted for the former, except when quoting works by other people, in which case I have preserved the latter. The exception is the word "Coloured," which I use to refer to South Africans of mixed race. The word is capitalized, except when quoting those who have chosen not to capitalize it.

Finally, in most cases when I have translated text from another language, I have relied on the assistance of Google Translate.

This biography aims to be comprehensive, but it will not be the final word on Rhoda Kadalie, whose life and ideas will continue to inspire those who knew her, and those who discover her in these pages. Rhoda was incredibly prolific, and while this biography aims to be comprehensive, it is likely that bits and pieces of her commentary will continue to surface in years to come — whether in published materials, or private notes and correspondence. It is my hope that future scholars will continue to explore her ideas as new material emerges, and new circumstances demonstrate the contemporary relevance of her ideas.

For those interested in honoring her life, Rhoda's memorial service, which was held in Cape Town in June 2022, is accessible on YouTube at https://www.youtube.com/watch?v=40A7iTBcoUo. And for those inclined to support her legacy, a scholarship has been endowed in her name to support the study of journalism at Hillsdale College in the United States. Contributions can be made at https://secured.hillsdale.edu/hillsdale/support-hillsdale-college; kindly specify "Rhoda Kadalie Endowed Journalism Scholarship" when donating.

I am too honest for my own good and I have often got into trouble,
but I don't regret it.
My driving force is justice. If something is just and true, I will fight for it.
I will not say the politically correct thing.[1]
– Rhoda Kadalie

---

1   Rhoda Kadalie, quoted in "Rhoda Kadalie: a strident voice for South Africa's oppressed." *Cape Argus*, 18 Apr. 1997.

Prologue

Smoke rose from the fires on campus in the late afternoon, as desks burned in lecture halls. A crowd of angry students surrounded the administration building, where the vice-chancellor and his aides were being effectively held hostage, unable to leave.

It was a familiar sight at the University of the Western Cape, in Bellville, near Cape Town, in the early 1990s, one of many riots that shook the politically volatile campus during the tumultuous transition from apartheid.

Suddenly, Rhoda Kadalie arrived onto the scene.

She stopped her car and hobbled out on crutches, having just come from the hospital, where she had endured an arthroscopy. Her daughter, Julia, then just a few years old, stared, wide-eyed at the chaos around her.

Seeing Rhoda, the "comrades" parted, stepping back deferentially.

"Oh, God, here comes Comrade Kadalie," one whispered fearfully.

Rhoda stood up as straight as she could, and addressed the mob.

"What the fuck do you think you're doing?" She demanded.

There was no response. Rhoda was a lecturer, but also an activist, a feminist with roots in the Black Consciousness movement, one of the few adults on campus who could still speak to the students with authority.

She turned and went inside, where she found her friend and colleague, Colin Bundy, standing nervously in his vice-chancellor's office. Though he, too, had marched against racism and segregation, he was the target of the students' ire — the nearest symbol of authority as they railed against the hated apartheid system, its impending demise only whetting their appetite for change. Next to him stood Nasima Badsha, a young academic star, terrified at what the crowd outside might do to them.

"Why are you scared of the students?" Rhoda demanded. "You can't give in to them."

The administrators shrugged nervously. This was different than the protests of the 1970s, when all the students had burned were their own neckties. This group was more radical, and unpredictable, the staff explained.

"Nonsense," Rhoda responded. She turned and hobbled back down to the entrance to the building, pausing at the doorway. The students, who had been chanting, quieted down.

"Release them," she scolded.

So they did, and Rhoda, wincing in pain, drove back to the hospital.

***

That is one of Julia's early memories of her mother, Rhoda Kadalie — a pioneering feminist, anti-apartheid activist, and human rights advocate who became an unlikely contrarian voice for both the South African opposition and the American conservative movement.

She is one of the most extraordinary and interesting political figures in South African history — and, indeed, the world.

A leader in the feminist movement within the broader black struggle against apartheid, Kadalie led the Gender Equity Unit at the University of the Western Cape — which describes itself today as a product of "radical black feminism"[2] — and pushed for the inclusion of women's rights in the emerging South African Constitution.

Appointed to the Human Rights Commission by then-President Nelson Mandela on an interim basis in 1995, and permanently in 1997, she became that body's most visible and accomplished member, before resigning in protest at the government's refusal to take the commission seriously, especially on socioeconomic rights.

She then created the Impumelelo Innovations Award Trust in 1999, an organization that identified and rewarded the country's most successful social development programs across a wide spectrum of issues, touching every aspect of South African life.

Taking up her pen as a newspaper columnist, she became one of the few public figures with "struggle" credentials who were willing to challenge the ruling African National Congress (ANC) in the early years of South Africa's democracy.

She became a leading voice against corruption, and she criticized the ANC's failure to deal with the HIV/Aids pandemic, its coddling of Zimbabwean dictator Robert Mugabe, and its culture of conformity under President Thabo Mbeki.

---

2   University of the Western Cape. "Gender Equity Unit Celebrates 25 Years Of Radical Black Feminism." 27 Sep. 2018. URL: https://www.uwc.ac.za/news-and- announcements/news/gender-equity-unit-celebrates-25-years-of-radical-black-feminism-554. Accessed on 7 Apr. 2022.

In one year's guide to "leading women," Rhoda was listed as an academic.[3] In the next she was listed as an expert on development.[4] Another listed her under "development and human rights," adding: "Rhoda Kadalie's work in human rights and social development is well respected in South Africa."[5] The *Mail & Guardian* listed her as a journalist in annual compendia of the year's best opinion columns. In truth, her career spanned all of these categories. And it was more than the sum of its parts.

By day, through Impumelelo, she helped the government pursue its development goals. By night, she was the government's most feared critic, taking on South Africa's obsequious media and corporate culture as well as the ruling party itself.

At one point, she was secretly offered the leadership of South Africa's main opposition party, the Democratic Alliance — and she turned it down, preferring the integrity of her principles to the compromises that partisan politics would require.

In addition, Rhoda emerged a strong advocate for the pro-Israel cause, against the overwhelming weight of elite South African opinion. She also emerged as a staunch defender of U.S. President Donald Trump, in whom she saw a kindred anti-establishment spirit.

Journalist Ed Herbst wrote, upon Rhoda's departure from South Africa to the U.S. in 2018, that she was "one of the country's most polemical political columnists," who, "[m]ore than anyone," had "flayed media hypocrisy" with a prescient view of the threats to South Africa's democratic experiment from an illiberal ruling party, its left-wing policies, and a culture of political correctness.[6]

She is also my mother-in-law, and my close friend.

***

I became friendly with Rhoda before I ever met her daughter, or knew she *had* a daughter.

---

3   "Rhoda Kadalie." *The Women's Directory: A Listing of Leading Women 1995-1996.* Cape Town: Femina, 1995. p. 10.

4   "Rhoda Kadalie." *The Women's Directory: A Listing of Leading Women 1996-1997.* Cape Town: Femina, 1996. p. 76.

5   "Rhoda Kadalie." *The Book of South African Women.* Johannesburg: Mail & Guardian, 2006. p. 166.

6   Ed Herbst. "'In djougevriet': Rhoda Kadalie leaves South Africa." *BizNews,* 7 Feb. 2018. URL: https://web.archive.org/web/20180207130610/ https://www.biznews.com/thought-leaders/2018/02/07/rhoda-kadalie-leaves-south-africa/. Accessed on 1 Jan. 2022.

In the early 2000s, I worked as the speechwriter for Tony Leon, the Leader of the Opposition in the South African parliament and the head of the foremost opposition party, the Democratic Alliance (DA).

I was born in South Africa, but grew up in Chicago, Illinois, proudly becoming a naturalized U.S. citizen with my parents in 1986. I returned to South Africa as a Rotary Foundation Ambassadorial Scholar in 2000, and stayed on to try my hand at freelance journalism, acting, and other pursuits. I became involved in South African political debates, primarily around foreign policy, and Leon offered me a job as his speechwriter in 2002. Like many who were involved in South African politics, I read Rhoda's weekly columns in the national *Business Day* newspaper. One day, after I was particularly impressed by something Rhoda had written, I approached Tony's secretary, the friendly yet formidable Sandy Slack, and asked for Rhoda's telephone number. She obliged, and I called Rhoda out of the blue.

I introduced myself, and congratulated Rhoda on her column. We had a pleasant conversation — the first of many, at regular intervals, for several years. We never met in person — at least, not yet — but developed a friendship based on our common concern for South Africa's democratic experiment, which had fascinated me as a young South African immigrant growing up in the U.S.

In late 2004, the chief of staff in Tony's office informed me that we were going to have an intern — a rare phenomenon in South Africa. Her name was Julia Bertelsmann, and she was one of the outstanding students in the province, who was headed to Harvard University the following year.

She also happened to be Rhoda Kadalie's daughter.

Julia was the emotional center of Rhoda's universe for many years. Through the country's political turmoil in the 1980s and 1990s; through the pain and bitterness of divorce; through financial ups and downs, Rhoda had fought to ensure that her only child — born "Coloured" in a segregated hospital — had the best chance to achieve success, to enjoy the best possible education in South Africa, and to take advantage of every opportunity the broader world could offer.

Julia was an award-winning student and an accomplished cellist by the time she came to Parliament, where she explored her passion for economic policy. Rhoda surreptitiously invited me to Julia's surprise 18th birthday party at the Mount Nelson Hotel, meeting me at the gate of Parliament to hand-deliver a parchment-colored scroll tied in a red ribbon.

It was the first time Rhoda and I had seen each other, and she smiled warmly at me. Little did I know that she would, in time, become a close part of my family — and I, of hers.

When Julia and I began to date, she invited me to her home for dinner — my first visit to Rhoda's place. They lived in a red duplex on a steep hill on the slopes of Devil's Peak, just beneath the busy highway known as De Waal Drive, or the M3 (now known as Philip Kgosana Drive), as it curved into the City Bowl area, the heart of Cape Town.

Their house had a sweeping view of the docks and the whitecaps of Table Bay. The neighborhood, known as University Estate, was adjacent to the vacant expanse of District Six, the diverse suburb that had been leveled by the apartheid government and where Rhoda had spent her early childhood.

No sooner had I arrived at the house than Rhoda turned on her stereo, full-blast, and produced several wooden musical instruments from underneath her glass coffee table — a marimba, a drum, and a sort of pan flute.

She and Julia started playing and pounding along, and I was evidently expected to do the same. I felt somewhat shy, but also delighted by this spontaneous expression of joy, and joined in wholeheartedly as Rhoda left the two of us to play while she attended to the dinner.

That was Rhoda's home: there was always room for music, and for fun.

It took courage for Rhoda to accept my relationship with Julia. I was not only older than her daughter: I was also American, and clearly an observant Jew. At the time, the ANC was circulating rumors that I must have been an Israeli spy: I simply "knew too much" about Israel. Later, I would learn that Minister of Intelligence Ronnie Kasrils — a "struggle" veteran whom Julia had once known as "Uncle Ronnie" — had taken his official car to her home to deliver a personal warning against developing a relationship with me.

Nevertheless, she welcomed me into her home. And later, she became part of ours. She was no typical mother-in-law; she was an intellectual partner as well. I learned so much from her that, looking back, it is hard to know where her ideas ended and mine began.

***

Rhoda is one of the few people with both the courage and the credibility to tackle the challenge that racism, and its proposed remedies, continue to pose for western civilization. She fought against apartheid; she strove to build a democratic society in its wake; and she resisted the excesses of the post-apartheid government.

On politics, Rhoda has rarely been wrong. In her many columns and in her book, *In Your Face* (2009)[7], she warned the African National Congress (ANC), the voters of South Africa, and the media alike that overlooking the liberation movement's transgressions would lead to its downfall. Many in the media who sucked up to the ruling elite despised her for her courage, and now admit that the ANC government has been almost as disastrous for South Africa as the end of apartheid had been good.

Iqbal Survé, the media entrepreneur who ambushed and took over the Independent Newspaper Group, served a summons for a defamation lawsuit upon Rhoda in 2015, claiming that she had "disturbed his mental tranquility" with her commentary. He later dropped the suit rather than face her in court and test the truth of her allegations.

Similarly, Rhoda predicted in 2015 that Donald Trump would win the U.S. presidency — when I, whose job it is to cover politics for a major international publication, was skeptical. "America needs a *skollie*[8], a disrupter who will right the ship," she quipped repeatedly.

Many of Rhoda's South African friends deserted her for supporting Trump's presidency, failing to understand that her close-up dalliance with the ANC alerted her to the penchant of revolutionary movements, throughout history, to destroy constitutional democracies.

Having worked with America's higher education institutions, and philanthropies such as the Ford Foundation and the Open Society Foundations, for over three decades, traveling to and from the U.S. almost every year, Rhoda fundamentally understood the political crossfires at work in the U.S.A. Her emigration to the "Land of the Free" in January 2018 was not an easy choice. A public persona in her own right, with roots deep in Cape Town's soil, she left saying, "I've done my national duty. South Africa devours one, and it's time to take a break."

Rhoda enjoyed American life, but found the United States cavalier about its constitutional democracy, careless about threats to the rule of law, deeply partisan in its politics, obsessed with race, and enmeshed in the politics of money and power.

America's movement away from liberalism, in the classical sense of the word, disturbs her.

***

---

7   Rhoda Kadalie. *In Your Face: Passionate Conversations about People and Politics.* Cape Town: NB Publishers, 2009.
8   Afrikaans slang for "gangster," or "rebel."

At that first dinner in her home, some 17 years ago, Rhoda — well-versed in the Bible, thanks her strict Christian upbringing — sought to provoke me by citing the Song of Songs: "I am black, but comely" (1:5).

When I think of Rhoda, other passages come to mind: the leadership of Deborah, who led the armies of Israel when no man had the courage to do so; or the story of Noah, who is described as a righteous man "in his generations" (Genesis 6:9).

The Jewish sages struggled with the latter passage. Some argued that Noah might not have been considered righteous had he lived in a different age. Others interpreted the passage to mean that Noah would have been even more righteous, had he been surrounded by good people instead of the corrupt society that was doomed to be destroyed in the Flood. The great 11th century scholar, Rabbi Solomon ben Isaac (Rashi), provided both explanations in his famous commentary.

There is another way, however, of understanding the passage. The Bible is pointing to the *character* of Noah's righteousness: that is, he contended *with his generation*. The society that surrounded him was entirely corrupt — not just in grotesque and obvious ways, but also in small ways. According to some commentators, people in Noah's time stole from each other constantly — taking tiny amounts, almost too small to be noticed. In so doing, they avoided punishment, but undermined the common bonds of trust throughout society.[9]

Noah refused to conform. Whether he was a righteous man in an absolute sense, the most important thing to know is that he stood, alone, against the immense social pressure of the evil society around him. It was not just *what* he stood for that made him righteous, but *how* he did so: he faced down generations. That courage made him worthy of salvation — and, in turn, saved humanity itself.

Such is the character of Rhoda Kadalie — a woman who was never afraid to stand alone. She fought injustice under apartheid, and again in the post-apartheid era. Though she could easily have shared in the spoils of the new South Africa, she turned down money and power and maintained her critical, independent voice, defending the values for which "the struggle" had been fought.

Rhoda saw corruption and mismanagement as problems that were systemic in nature, but which resulted from the bad moral choices of individuals. Conversely, she believes, every individual can make a small

---

9   Rabbi Rachel Isaacs. "Parashat Noach: How Societies Collapse." MyJewishLearning.com. URL: https://www.myjewishlearning.com/article/parashat-noach-how-societies-collapse/. Accessed on 18 Oct. 2022.

but important contribution by standing against the multitude and making the right choices. And, she believes, it is the duty of society to cultivate a diversity of voices, and to protect minorities — even minorities of one — because they might save society as a whole in an hour of need.

Noah built a great ark to ensure that there would be life after the Flood. Rhoda has built an ark of ideas and values, through her writings and her personal example of integrity and courage, that can help South Africa restore its hopes after it overcomes its present challenges. Her ideas also have broader relevance to the world in general, in particular to the United States, where she spent the last years of her life.

***

Rhoda moved in with us in January 2018, breezing through passport control at LAX airport with her green card in hand, and settling into what had been my eldest daughter's bedroom in our four-bedroom condo in Santa Monica. My daughter and son shared a room; I kept one bedroom as a study, working from home in the early mornings before heading to the company office in nearby Brentwood. Rhoda, a night owl, would stay up reading, working, or watching the news. At times, she would fetch our eldest daughter from the public school nearby, or volunteer at our son's day care.

For the most part, she was content to be Granny, and to enjoy her retirement. She had spent many years working in South Africa as an activist, an academic, a human rights commissioner, a columnist, and a leader in the non-profit world. She had taken care of her aging parents for years; once they passed away, there was little still tethering her to Cape Town. She had sold her home; the proceeds were not nearly enough to buy anything in L.A.'s pricey real estate market, so she simply invested the funds, and enjoyed caring for her grandchildren. She delighted in painting, dancing and playing with the children. It was Rhoda who taught them to throw and to catch, to play tennis, to ride scooters and balance bikes.

She cared for us, too. After returning from work, or from the gym, I would often find a meal that Rhoda had whipped up in the kitchen. Her cooking was exquisite: she specialized in the Cape Malay cuisine I had grown to love in South Africa. Though she found the strictures of the Jewish Sabbath irritating at first, when we did not answer the phone, she mastered the complicated dietary rules of a kosher home, and as long as I kept the groceries stocked, she kept the stove burning. She often brewed my favorite coffee for me; I was at her beck-and-call when she needed to look up an obscure fact, or wanted a painting hung on her wall, or piece of furniture moved.

With Rhoda's arrival, Julia and I felt free — for the first time — to leave home in the hours after the children went to bed and take strolls through the neighborhood in the evening, or to frequent local pubs together once or twice a week. We even managed the occasional romantic getaway together, for a night or so. And when my wife was away on her own, on her monthly reserve duty at the Navy, Rhoda and I made a good team, keeping the children entertained and the household in order until Mummy was done fixing helicopters. Other than writing the occasional column for the South African press, Rhoda took retired life easy.

There were occasional tensions, the inevitable result of three adults living together in a relatively small space. By late 2019, Julia had found a beautiful house in the hills of the Pacific Palisades, a posh, celebrity-heavy neighborhood that was, for the moment, bizarrely more affordable than Santa Monica simply because there was a larger inventory of homes on the market. We bought the house — a multi-level, ranch-style home next to the local school, with a swing set and a white picket fence, and a view of the mountains in one direction and the ocean in the other.

Rhoda had her own wing of the home, which allowed her to retreat into her own domain — and provided an escape for the children, when they wanted to evade bedtime or enjoy candy and other treats with which Granny Rhoda would indulge them.

When the coronavirus pandemic hit, just months after we moved in, we hunkered down together, enduring the health scares, financial stresses, and race riots that buffeted the country.

We also followed the 2020 presidential election closely. Watching the chaos unfold, from the inexplicable mandates of the COVID-19 pandemic, to the Black Lives Matter riots, to the controversies over the result of the November election, Rhoda became disillusioned with America's supposedly advanced democracy, as she continued publishing columns on American politics at Maroelamedia, an online Afrikaans news website. We often worked alongside one another, exchanging the latest news and political jokes, and we reviewed drafts of each other's writings. We commiserated over the latest political setbacks for the Republican Party, and delighted in the occasional success, or the latest outrageously funny controversy involving Donald Trump.

Despite the camaraderie of life in quarantine, living atop one another was at times a challenge. Julia and I could not work from our respective offices for many months during the COVID pandemic; Rhoda could not enjoy her usual diversions, such as attending the opera downtown.

With the birth of our third child, our second daughter, Rhoda began to look for a place of her own — and found one, a beautiful apartment down the street with sweeping views of the Santa Monica Bay, and a heated pool.

It was on the day she moved into her new home, September 15, that Rhoda arrived at the hospital, close to midnight, for her computed tomography (CT) scan.

The doctor phoned her early the next morning with the troubling news: it looked like cancer.

It happened to be Yom Kippur, the Day of Atonement in the Jewish faith. When I heard the news, I spoke to Rhoda. I apologized for all the disagreements we had ever had; we forgave each other. She smiled at me, warmly; her growing suspicions about her health had been confirmed, and she seemed almost fascinated by her predicament. Face-to-face with the prospect of death, she seemed to take comfort in the discovery that she felt unafraid.

I asked her if she wanted to travel anywhere, or do anything, with the time she still had. No, she said; she had seen and done it all. She asked me to pray — not for a cure, necessarily, but to avoid suffering, if possible. And though she was not afraid of dying, she would do what she could to stay alive.

Like all of her battles, Rhoda is prepared to fight to the end, even when the odds against her are overwhelming. This biography is a tribute to her enduring courage.

March 31, 2022

Timeline

1953:   Rhoda Kadalie born on 22 September in District Six to Pastor Fenner Christian and Joan Kadalie (née Francis)

1961:   Kadalie family moves from Bloemhof Flats to cottage at Municipal Wash House in Harriers Road, Mowbray

1970:   Kadalie family, with nine children, forcibly removed from Mowbray under the Group Areas Act

1971:   Rhoda matriculates from Harold Cressy High School, District Six

1975:   Rhoda graduates from the University of the Western Cape (UWC) with a Bachelor of Library Science degree

1976:   Soweto riots launch nationwide student protests against the apartheid regime

1978:   Rhoda graduates with Honours degree in anthropology at UWC

1981:   Rhoda meets Richard Bertelsmann and they begin dating

1982:   Rhoda and Richard marry in Namibia in December

1983:   Tricameral Parliament; launch of the United Democratic Front

1985:   Rhoda and Richard leave for Europe to begin studies; state of emergency in South Africa

1986:   Second state of emergency; Rhoda completes Masters degree in Development Studies at Institute for Social Studies at The Hague

1987:   Rhoda gives birth to Julia Inge on 21 February; Jakes Gerwel installed as UWC rector

1989:   Richard and Rhoda split after a fight in December

1990:   Nelson Mandela freed; anti-apartheid organizations unbanned; negotiations begin

1992:   Rhoda's divorce from Richard finalized in May

1993:   Rhoda founds the Gender Equity Unit at UWC; Amy Biehl murdered in Gugulethu

1994:   South Africa's first democratic elections on 27 April

1995:   President Nelson Mandela appoints Rhoda to interim Human Rights Commission

1996:   South Africa's new Constitution finalized

1997:   Rhoda resigns from Human Rights Commission, effective 31 December; begins writing columns for local publications, starting with the *Mail & Guardian*

1998: Rhoda chairs District Six Task Team within Commission on Restitution of Land Rights

1999: Rhoda launches Impumelelo Innovations Awards Trust; begins writing for *Business Day*; appointed to University of Cape Town council; receives honorary doctorate from Uppsala University; Thabo Mbeki elected President and Tony Leon elected Leader of the Opposition

2001: Rhoda delivers lecture in Grahamstown, "Silencing Critique," on ANC's authoritarianism

2004: Rhoda approached to take over Democratic Alliance; declines to enter politics

2005: Mbeki fires Deputy President Jacob Zuma for corruption; Rhoda delivers lecture on liberalism and opposition in honor of Helen Suzman; Julia leaves for Harvard

2006: Democratic Alliance defeats ANC in Cape Town; Helen Zille becomes mayor

2007: Rhoda receives honorary doctorate from UWC; resigns from UCT council in protest; appointed to lead Cape Town's street renaming committee

2009: Rhoda publishes collection of columns, *In Your Face*; receives honorary doctorate from Stellenbosch University, joins council; Zuma elected President; Julia graduates Harvard, marries

2010: Rhoda visits Israel for the first time with the South African Jewish Board of Deputies

2011: Pastor Kadalie passes away; Rhoda resigns from Stellenbosch council in protest

2012: First grandchild, Maya Hannah, born in Santa Monica, California, USA; Rhoda and Julia publish *The Politics of Pregnancy*

2015: Second grandchild, Alexander Caleb, born in August; Joan Kadalie passes away

2016: Rhoda sells University Estate home; predicts Donald Trump's victory in U.S. elections

2017: Cyril Ramaphosa takes over ANC, elevated to President following year

2018: Rhoda leaves South Africa for USA in January

2020: Rhoda shelters with family during pandemic; writes for Afrikaans-language Maroelamedia on Black Lives Matter riots and U.S. election

2021: Third grandchild, Amira Leah, born in July; Rhoda diagnosed with cancer in September

2022: Rhoda publishes final column in January; passes away 16 April in Los Angeles, California; memorialized in Cape Town; interred at Hollywood Forever cemetery

Chapter One:
Origins

*"When I tell people I am Clements Kadalie's direct granddaughter,
they say that, politically, I am a chip off the old block.
Not racially, but politically.
I find that interesting."*[1]

Rhoda Kadalie was born on September 22, 1953, in District Six, the third of Fenner and Joan Kadalie's nine children and the first of two daughters, sixteen years apart.

The Kadalie family lived in the Cape Town neighborhood known as District Six, a vibrant, racially diverse, and somewhat impoverished urban area at the foot of Table Mountain, uphill from the docks and adjacent to the city's central business district. District Six was the heart of the city's mixed-race, or "Coloured," culture, a melting pot where Christians and Muslims lived side-by-side, along with a few Jews and other European minorities.

Today, Capetonians regard the memory of District Six with much the same nostalgia that Americans think of the Harlem Renaissance as a creative, critical mass of people, and an oasis of cultural spontaneity.

Fenner Kadalie was fully part of the District Six scene. He was a jazz musician, and something of a playboy, making the rounds of the local nightclubs, a well-dressed young man and *bon vivant* in a vibrant time.

He met his wife, Joan, in that milieu. Her ancestry was typical of the mixed origins of much of the local population: her ancestors had been slaves, but included people from a variety of racial backgrounds. Her father was white; her mother was considered Coloured. Her family included both Christian and Muslim branches, with several sisters marrying Muslim men. Members of her family had had served in the British forces during the Boer War, and in the Royal Navy.

Joan was among the eldest of 13 children in her family, and grew to be a fashionable young woman. When she fell in love with the dashing musician, she expected the party to continue. Yet shortly before their marriage, Fenner experienced a religious conversion. He soon became a

---

1   Rhoda Kadalie, quoted by Ryland Fisher. *Race*. Auckland Park: Jacana Media, 2007. p. 57.

born-again Christian, and set aside his musical career in favor of the Bible and the pulpit.

Joan Kadalie (née Francis), cavorting in a two-piece bikini on the hood of a car, c. 1948 (Courtesy Rhoda Kadalie)

To Joan, Fenner's decision was a surprise, and at times burdensome. Though she came to embrace the role of a pastor's wife, and the two remained deeply in love, she was known to complain: "You're not the man I married." (To which he would occasionally retort, teasing her, "I only married half of you" — a reference to the weight she had gained since then.) Joan resisted quietly by retaining her taste for high fashion, frustrating her husband's newly modest tastes and meager budget.

Rhoda was equally a child of both parents. She absorbed deep religious convictions from her father, and a rebellious streak from her mother. As the eldest daughter — separated from her younger sister, Judith, by 16 years — she also bore a heavy burden of household responsibilities, though she recalled that she never felt inferior to her seven brothers.

"For sixteen years, I was the only daughter in a big family with seven brothers," she told an interviewer. "I think that my father valued me as much, if not more than my brothers because I was the only girl. Ours was not a patriarchal family – my father treated me with complete respect."[2]

Joan and Pastor Fenner Christian Kadalie, c. 1950
(Courtesy Rhoda Kadalie)

She also recalled her mother as being unusually assertive:

My mother was what I would call the complete feminist. She had to cope with so many sons, and had to compete with God and the church for my father's attention, so she became a fighter for her own rights very early on in her marriage. She taught my brothers that they were also expected to perform domestic chores and to be independent. There were no stereotypical gender roles in our family when I was growing up. My mother made it clear that she wasn't willing to be anyone's

---

2   "In Conversation: The personal remains political: Elaine Salo speaks with Rhoda Kadalie." *Feminist Africa*, No. 5 (2005). p. 112.

slave. She worked as well. She and my father asserted their rights and responsibilities as equal parents. My mother was one of thirteen siblings, and I think that she learned to assert herself because she came from an impoverished matrifocal household. This is typical of a culture of poverty.

Though Rhoda recalled wanting "a more subservient mother,"[3] like those of other children, she came, in time, to admire her strong character.

Ironically, it was Fenner, not Joan, who came from an activist family — one whose legacy continues to shape South Africa.

***

Fenner was one of several children of Clements Kadalie, one of the first black trade unionists in Africa, and one of the giants of South African history — indeed, of history on the entire African continent.

Historian Henry Dee, in an unpublished doctoral thesis, relates how Clements Kadalie "established black trade unionism as a political and economic force on the African continent, and in doing so transformed global ideas about race, class and worker organisation."[4]

Clements Kadalie, undated (Courtesy Rhoda Kadalie)

3   Ibid., p. 113.
4   Henry Dee (2020). Clements Kadalie, trade unionism, migration and race in Southern Africa, 1918-1930 [unpublished doctoral dissertation]. URL: https://era.ed.ac.uk/handle/1842/37022. Accessed on 3 Jan. 2022.

Clements Kadalie was born in the village of Chifira, in the Nkhata Bay district, a northern region of Nyasaland, a country known today as Malawi. The precise date of his birth is unknown, but he was christened on Easter Sunday in 1896.[5] He was the grandson of Chiweyu Wandodo, who was a chief of the Tonga people. The Tonga of Malawi, like the Polynesian ethnic group of the same name, have a lifestyle that is connected to the water, though that is where the resemblance ends. The group is small, and lives in northern Malawi, on the shores of Lake Malawi, one of several freshwater bodies in the Great Rift Valley. They are distinct from a similar ethnic group with the same name elsewhere in sub-Saharan Africa. They were deeply entwined in British imperial efforts in the region, both administrative and religious.

Clements Kadalie was originally christened as Lameck Koniwaka, Dee notes, and his family had adopted a surname, Muwamba, in the European style, by the late nineteenth century.[6] The new surname "Kadalie" apparently referred to his family's royal title, and was first adopted by his brother, Robert Victor, who preceded him in migrating to South Africa and may have taken his forenames from a diamond mine where he had worked in the Free State, one of the two Afrikaner republics.[7] Clements Kadalie used the same surname to fit in with his brother, with whom he lived in the Malay Quarter, or Bo Kaap, when he arrived in Cape Town.[8]

Clements Kadalie was not directly in line for the chieftainship, since it was passed from generation to generation along matrilineal lines; he "only held a distant claim to the family title," Dee observes.[9] The family's political power was somewhat displaced when a rival chief aligned more closely with the British; partly as a result, Dee notes, Chiweyu may have allowed the Watch Tower movement, an indigenous, syncretic Christian rival to the Scottish missions, to use his village as a base of operations.[10] The Watch Tower movement preached a philosophy of black separatism within the Christian faith — a direct challenge to the missionaries and British rule.[11]

These experiences in religious dissent may have prepared Clements Kadalie for a life of activism — and would echo, years later, in the

---

5   Dirk Hermann. "Rhoda Kadalie: van actives tot burgerlike ambassadeur." Maroelamedia, 17 Apr. 2022. Excerpt from Dirk Hermann. *Regstellende Trane*. Brandfort: AfriForum Uitgewers, 2013.
6   Dee, 74.
7   Ibid., 94.
8   Ibid., 91.
9   Ibid., 76.
10   Ibid., 80.
11   Ibid., 99.

iconoclasm of his granddaughter, who challenged established Christian doctrines on subjects such as same-sex relationships and abortion, but remained devoted to her faith.

Clements Kadalie was educated in the Scottish mission school system, and was trained as a teacher and theologian. He worked for some time at the Livingstonia Mission, but was dismissed for "misbehaviour," a charge that was relatively easy to incur, given the exacting standards of the missions.[12] He left Nyasaland in 1915 — "in quest of a higher civilised life," he later wrote[13] — and found his way via Southern Rhodesia (today's Zimbabwe) to South Africa, which was a magnet for labor from throughout the region. British authorities had initially imposed hut taxes on local populations, payable only through the currency earned by migrant labor on the gold mines of the Witwatersrand; later, educated immigrants like Kadalie came pursuing their own career ambitions.

Kadalie was a poor fit within the mining labor system, which had always been racially stratified and was becoming ever more so. Given his education, and his noble origins, he rejected the idea of adopting a subservient role relative to white men (and women) who were less literate than he, or simply prejudiced. At the Shamva Mines in Southern Rhodesia, for example, he recalled that a female typist "could not tolerate seeing me in the same office at my desk doing the same clerical work as herself."[14] He held several other short-lived clerical jobs, rejected a job offer as a police detective, and sought to join the British Army during the First World War. He settled, for a time, in Bulawayo, where he "organised some social activities among the African community," which were 'characterised as revolutionary by many people."[15] Following another quarrel with an employer — one of many confrontations with authority — Kadalie made his way southwest to join his brother in Cape Town, the cosmopolitan port city of the Cape Province within the new Union of South Africa, and a jewel within the Anglophonic sphere of influence.

Kadalie had already been influenced by the ideas of the American activist Marcus Garvey, who preached "Africa for the Africans." He was in touch with an organization of Nyasaland migrants called the Nyasaland Native National Congress (NNNC), which had been established in the gold mining region of the Transvaal to oppose discriminatory "pass laws" restricting the movement of black workers.

12   Ibid.
13   Clements Kadalie. *My Life and the ICU: The Autobiography of a Black Trade Unionist in South Africa.* London: Frank Cass, 1970. p. 33.
14   Ibid., 34.
15   Ibid., 35-6.

Clements Kadalie's first home in South Africa, where he stayed with his brother Robert Victor Kadalie, 6 Morris Street, Bo Kaap as viewed in February 2022

6 Morris Street, with Table Mountain in the background, as viewed in February 2022

But Kadalie did not agree with the NNNC's effort to advocate for Nyasaland emigrés separately from other black migrants, and to support the overall British imperial project.[16] He took a pan-African approach that "explicitly demanded rights (rather than simply 'justice'), and called for non-co-operation against church and state soon after his arrival in South Africa."

Though trained in theology, Kadalie, perhaps influenced by the Watch Tower movement, joined a growing body of black Christians who rejected "the paternal leadership of white missionaries." He would later claim not to have prayed since 1910, but when he married a Muslim widow, a Coloured woman named Johanna "Molly" Davidson, she converted to Christianity first.[17]

Molly Davidson, first wife of Clements Kadalie, c. 1960
(Courtesy Rhoda Kadalie)

---

16   Dee, 95–6.
17   Ibid., 97, 99.

After several more jobs, the seminal political event in Kadalie's life took place on what he later described in his memoir as "[o]ne beautiful morning," when he took leave from work for a few hours to greet a friend who was arriving by ship at the Cape Town docks.[18]

Kadalie recalled:

> *One Saturday afternoon during the influenza epidemic of 1918 I was in the company of two Nyasaland friends in Cape Town. We were strolling in Darling Street when the Cape Argus, the afternoon daily newspaper, was out in the streets for sale. I bought a copy of the paper, and as soon as I perused it, I began to inform my friends that the end of the [First World] war was in sight, for Sir Douglas Haig had launched his offensive in Flanders. Suddenly appeared a European constable, who pushed me off the pavement, assaulting me at the same time. I informed my friends of my intention to report the matter at police headquarters.*

Kadalie's African friends were unwilling to accompany him there, but a white man who had witnessed the assault gave Kadalie his business card and offered to corroborate his account of events.

When Kadalie arrived at the police station, he was confronted by a constable who interrogated him, rather than taking down the details of his complaint. "Where had I come from? Where had I obtained my education? I was probably to him unlike the ordinary African usually seen in Cape Town. I pressed my complaint, however, brushing aside these irrelevant questions."

Kadalie persisted until he received an apology from the sergeant in charge, who said that the constable had been affected by "overwork with the epidemic cases which were raging in the city." This did not satisfy Kadalie as an excuse, and the officer relented, promising to investigate further.

Then, later, Kadalie called on the man who had given him his contact information. He turned out to be A.F. Batty, a small-scale entrepreneur in the "cutlery business" who was also politically involved. He asked Kadalie to help him run for a parliamentary seat as a candidate from the small Democratic Labour Party (DLP) from the local Harbour constituency — this at a time when many black voters still had the franchise in the Cape. Kadalie joined Batty's election committee, but Batty was narrowly defeated.

After the election, Batty suggested that Kadalie consider organizing a trade union: "He informed me that he was satisfied I could be useful to my people if I could embark on trade union activities instead of politics.

---

18   Clements Kadalie, ibid. p. 37.

I readily agreed to his suggestion, although I anticipated difficulty in getting people together. We planned to invade the Cape Town docks, as the Harbour constituency fell in that area."

On January 17, 1919, Kadalie organized a meeting of dock workers — most of them Coloured, with about half a dozen "Africans" — with Batty presiding. They voted unanimously to form a union, with Kadalie as its general secretary. The Industrial and Commercial Union (ICU) — the country's first "non-European" trade union — was born.[19]

There is some controversy about this origin story, as related by Kadalie along the lines above. Batty later claimed, Dee notes, that he himself came up with the idea of founding the ICU, acting at the direction of the Cape Federation of Labor Unions, as part of an effort to recruit black voters to the DLP. Dee observes that a "white-only" organization called the "Industrial and Commercial Union" already existed in 1918 at the docks in Simonstown, a small naval station south of the city.[20]

Regardless of the ICU's origins, its ideas were radical within the context of the broader labor movement — including that part represented by Batty. As Dee notes, Kadalie and his contemporaries, inspired in part by Marcus Garvey, began asking "uncomfortable questions about the role of race" and "denounced white South African communists' prioritisation of class-before-race."[21] If the ICU had some help from white labor activists at its founding, it would not easily be controlled by them. Indeed, the relationship between Kadalie and Batty soon deteriorated, and they became opponents within the growing organization.

***

Before the end of the year, Clements Kadalie had organized the ICU's first strike. It was motivated by two goals. One was to support a strike by white workers against food exports to Europe while local prices were soaring. The other goal was to establish a minimum wage for non-white workers of six shillings per day.

After three weeks, with the union running short of money to compensate striking workers, Kadalie called off the protest, having achieved "some scanty increase in the wages of the dock labourers."[22] Making matters worse, he had been dismissed from his own regular job.

---

19   Ibid., 40.
20   Dee, 105–6.
21   Dee, 103.
22   Dee, 44.

But that freed Kadalie to devote his full energies to the movement. The following year, the ICU demanded a minimum wage — and succeeded, thanks to the eagerness of local cargo companies to avoid another strike.

The union began to grow in strength and numbers — and South African authorities began to take notice, even attempting to deport Kadalie from the country. But the fire had been lit, and began to spread across the country, as ICU branches opened up nationwide. The very name of the union was a catchy double-entendre, standing for the phrase "I See You," and suggesting that black workers were bearing witness to their mistreatment by white employers and the whole edifice of white supremacy in South Africa, "reversing the European gaze and turning white policing authority on itself," Dee notes.[23]

Kadalie, who had taken a course in public speaking to improve his leadership skills, gained renown as an orator. Through the ICU's newspaper, *The Workers' Herald*, he began to reach a wide audience, which included other future African leaders, who were interested in and inspired by Kadalie's example.

The union grew to over 100,000 members, and Kadalie became an internationally renowned figure, traveling to Europe and receiving invitations to visit the United States as well, though the latter were canceled over logistical difficulties.

As Dee notes, Kadalie nevertheless did manage to connect from afar with members of the black community in the U.S. "As a writer for *The Messenger* [a black socialist newspaper], Clements Kadalie was the only official South African correspondent of any US-based New Negro newspaper."[24] Through his dispatches, Kadalie helped black American readers understand their own struggle in a global context, alongside workers of all races. Had he been able to tour America, Kadalie's effect on the nascent civil rights movement may have been even greater.

South Africa's elite recognized that Kadalie was a legitimate and powerful political force. In 1926, he was the honored guest speaker at the inaugural meeting of a new private club, henceforth known as the 1926 Club, which brought the leaders of the Rand together in an informal setting to host provocative debates and discussions. (Rhoda Kadalie would be invited to address the club on its 80th anniversary, in 2006: the meeting's program noted that her grandfather had inaugurated the lecture series, eight decades before.[25])

---

23   Dee, 105.
24   Dee, 31.
25   The 1926 Club. "80th Anniversary Dinner." Program. 26 Sep. 2006.

Kadalie also visited Europe in 1927, including the United Kingdom, where he electrified debates about race and empire, and shocked white South African representatives to international labor conferences by presenting an alternative perspective that they had ignored or attempted to suppress. Though not everyone was impressed — some accusing him of drinking and womanizing — he had a profound effect on the labor movement in Europe, challenging its leaders to think about the interests and aspirations of black workers for the first time, especially in overseas colonies.

Dee notes: "Kadalie and the cause of black workers had a transformative impact on numerous British socialists, inspired black British leaders such as CLR James and George Padmore, and led to the creation of transnational connections that would be central to Britain's anti-colonial movement in the 1930s and 1940s."[26] Padmore would later call Kadalie "the uncrowned king of the black masses" — not just in South Africa, but worldwide.[27]

Moreover, Kadalie succeeded in building a mass movement despite constant hounding by the police. In a pattern that would later become familiar to anti-apartheid activists, he was monitored by police, banned from addressing public meetings, jailed for his activities, and prosecuted (though often acquitted). He fought the government of the day in court, winning many battles for free speech, however fleeting, decades before the apartheid government was to suppress opposition political activity. He did all of this largely independent of the relatively ineffective African National Congress (ANC), which he did not oppose but with which he had, at best, an arm's-length relationship.

Kadalie even faced up to antisemitism: in later years, as the ICU began to collapse, his own faction, the "Independent ICU," relied heavily on a Jewish benefactor, Philip Morris, who became a target for antisemitism in the broader labor movement.[28] Kadalie's relationship with Morris was a statement of defiance against a creeping prejudice on both left and right that was, within a few years, to have devastating consequences. The ICU, Dee notes, also organized female workers, making him one of the first labor leaders in the world to have "organised across divisions of ethnicity, race and sex" and to challenge "established notions of respectability and gender."[29]

---

26   Dee, 213.
27   George Padmore, quoted by Dee, 353.
28   Dee, 291.
29   Ibid, 383.

Toward the end of the 1920s, Kadalie's organization began to suffer organizational problems, including rivalries that sometimes reflected ethnic divisions. A breakaway Durban faction of the ICU, for example, driven in part by Zulu nationalism, foreshadowed tensions within the post-apartheid South African government, a century later. Kadalie was accused of mismanagement and corruption, with critics pointing to his large expense accounts. He had the habit, for example, of touring the country with a chauffeur, which was an important symbolic statement at a time when only white people owned cars, but cost a considerable sum of money to maintain.

Other labor leaders turned against him — so much so that when the Congress of South African Trade Unions (Cosatu) was launched in 1985, participants sang a song denouncing Kadalie — who had died decades before and had not been active in the labor movement for half a century.[30] In addition, Kadalie's personal problems took a toll on his family, as well as the union: he would eventually leave Molly for a lover, Eva Moorhead, who later became his second wife.

The ICU did not last. But it was a radical experiment. At the time, the South African trade union movement was strongest on the Witwatersrand, where white mine workers downed tools to demand racial segregation against black workers, whom they accused of being willing to work for lower wages. The idea of a trade union that specifically organized "non-white" workers was completely new. It was so radical that even organizations such as the African National Congress (ANC), founded to represent "Native" interests in 1912, had not yet adopted the ICU's tactics.

Clements Kadalie was not, therefore, merely the first black trade unionist in the country, but the first leader of a mass popular movement of black people against racial discrimination and white domination in South Africa. He was among the first such black leaders anywhere in the world.

Moreover, Kadalie rejected communism, a movement that would later have a profound influence in shaping the leadership of the anti-apartheid struggle and its ideological outlook. He called himself a socialist, and shared many of the communist ideals common to labor leaders in the 1920s, many of whom still saw the Soviet Union as an inspiration. But he criticized communists for their obsession with overthrowing capitalism — "making usual fruitless noise" — rather than helping workers achieve real, albeit incremental, progress.[31] Kadalie's ICU was a democratic labor movement that aimed to serve the economic interests of its members, and to eliminate racial segregation, but not to revolutionize society itself.

---

30 Dee, 397.
31 Clements Kadalie, quoted by Dee, 207.

Eventually, the ICU expelled its communist members — earning the enmity of the Communist Party, so much so that South Africa's communists were still indignant, nearly a century later, at Kadalie's decision to expel them, claiming he and the ICU had become "'good boys' and 'boss-class instruments'."[32] But in so doing, Kadalie also earned respect from members of the white liberal establishment, and enabled the union to be more effective in advocating for the interests of its workers, whose problems could not await a global proletarian revolution.

Kadalie also rejected a blunt, racial, African nationalism. He had been inspired by Garvey, but rejected the idea of racial exclusivity. Kadalie sought, and won, gestures of solidarity from white trade unions, while he remained steadfast in his opposition to racial segregation. Dee notes: "Kadalie himself fully endorsed the idea that the labour movement had to organise all workers, 'regardless of their colour or nationality', into a 'mass industrial organisation' in order to pull off successful strike action, exert political pressure, and radically transform the status quo." That was partly because he himself was an immigrant, and while he shared the skin color of many of the workers he was organizing, he did not fit into South Africa's various tribal or ethnic categories, which made him more sensitive to the need to transcend the politics of identity.

As such, Kadalie authored an idea of "blackness" that was inclusive of Coloured and Indian workers, as well as African immigrants like himself. In that way, he anticipated the later Black Consciousness ideas of Steve Biko in the 1970s, as Dee notes:

> [C]oloured ICU leaders such as James La Guma, John Gomas, James Thaele, Henry Tyamzashe and Samuel Dunn, and Indian ICU leaders such as Ralph de Norman – as well as Kadalie – dramatically challenged contemporary conceptions of race, rejecting the differences between Ccoloured, African and Indian workers. As recognized by Collis-Buthelezi, "the ICU was the first organization that actively sought and gained the participation of both Coloureds and Natives and tried to articulate a coherent and inclusive black identity". In doing so, it was a trade union – rather than a congress, party or association – that became the "first organization to name such an identity 'black' rather than 'coloured'." ICU leaders were never consistent in their descriptors of race, interchangeably talking about 'black', 'African', 'Bantu', 'non-European' and 'native' trade unionism. And in this sense, the ICU's

---

32   Blade Nzimande. "Nzimande on the ANC breakaway and its antecedents." PoliticsWeb, reprinted from Umsebenzi Online, 5 Nov 2008. URL: https://www.politicsweb.co.za/news-and-analysis/nzimande-on-the-anc-breakaway-and-its-antecedents. Accessed on 28 Mar. 2022.

*interwar notion of race consciousness was different from Steve Biko's
similarly heterogeneous but more specific idea of black consciousness in
the 1970s.*[33]

Moreover, Kadalie was pragmatic in his political strategy. In the 1920s, he
aligned with the National Party, led by the Afrikaner leader J.B.M. Hertzog,
as did other labor leaders, who saw the rise of the Afrikaner nationalists
as a chance to oust the pro-business, Anglophone government at the
time. Herzog, shrewdly, reached out to Kadalie in a letter, expressing
his condolences for the deaths of ICU members killed in a strike action.
The correspondence conferred legitimacy on Kadalie and the ICU, though
Kadalie was later to be disappointed when Hertzog backed new racial
discrimination laws.

Despite the ICU's eventual failure, and Kadalie's own isolation, he
had a lasting impact on South Africa and on the world.

In 1970s, historian Stanley Trapido characterized Kadalie as a man
ahead of his time, in an introduction to Kadalie's posthumous memoir:

*He created an organization which began with twenty-four members
and before it burnt itself out within the decade it laid claim to a hundred
thousand members. Inexperience, the lack of success, which bred factions
among the leaders and disillusion among its followers, together with
the hostility of White society and the State, led to its collapse. But in the
light of recent experience in Africa, it is apparent that Kadalie had the
misfortune to have been born in the wrong place at the wrong time. A
leader in tropical Africa who built an organization like the ICU after 1950
would have led his followers to an independence which a colonial power
would readily have conceded.*

Kadalie and the ICU faded from the political forefront. But while he did
not win freedom for black South Africans, he planted the seeds of future
activism — and pointed toward a new order that was neither communist,
nor nationalist, but liberal and social-democratic.

* * *

As bright a star as Kadalie shone across South Africa, his family — notably,
his children — resented his absence and his lifestyle. Fenner Kadalie, in
particular, disliked his father; his own religious conversion likely owed
something to his rejection of his father's libertine lifestyle.

---

33   Dee, 45. Footnotes omitted.

Rhoda Kadalie never even knew anything of her grandfather's pioneering career until she was in high (secondary) school in standard nine and ten (grades eleven and twelve). As she told an interviewer, "My father did not talk to us about my grandfather because he did not like his own father." She was informed about Clements Kadalie by her teachers: "I began high school at Harold Cressy High School [in District Six] and encountered teachers such as Helen Kies, who was a member of the Teachers League of South Africa. They admired my grandfather, Clements Kadalie. Helen Kies introduced me to the story of my grandfather."

Rhoda has likened Clements Kadalie to Allan Boesak, one of the leading figures in the United Democratic Front (UDF), an anti-apartheid organization founded in Cape Town during the 1980s, when the ANC was still banned. A brilliant, charismatic, and effective leader, Boesak's career was marred by personal scandals and allegations of corruption, which led to his conviction for fraud (he was later pardoned).

To Pastor Fenner Kadalie, his father was an example to avoid, not a model to emulate. Clements had named his son, born in Johannesburg in 1928, after British explorer David Livingstone — who had met Chief Chiweyu — and British socialist Fenner Brockway. To Clements Kadalie, who moved his family to back Cape Town when Fenner was two, those were great men to emulate.

But even those august names were a burden: the initials "FL" evoked the term "French Letter," which was an early twentieth-century slang term for "condom." In keeping with his newfound religious convictions, Fenner changed his middle name to "Christian."

And yet within Fenner Christian Kadalie's own career in the clergy, one could detect the same zeal for justice that once stirred Clements Kadalie to challenge the authority of an abusive white police officer. As Rhoda would later recall, what Clements Kadalie did as a "campaigner against the exploitation of black workers," Fenner Kadalie did in "building God's spiritual kingdom on earth."[34]

Soon after he had become a Christian believer, Kadalie became a missionary within District Six, leading the City Mission, an institution that catered specifically to the needs of Cape Town's poor. As Rhoda would later note in a tribute to her father at his funeral, "Under our dad's leadership the City Mission grew into an evangelical movement that incorporated social welfare issues."[35]

---

34   Rhoda Kadalie. "Funeral of Fenner Kadalie." Cape Town City Hall, Cape Town, 20 Jul. 2011.
35   Rhoda Kadalie. Ibid.

*The first four Kadalie children, including Rhoda (far left),
at City Mission, District Six, c. 1959 (Courtesy Rhoda Kadalie)*

In addition to religious worship, the City Mission ran a dining hall that offered discounted meals to the poor. Pastor Kadalie led one church in Smart Street and another in Constitution Street. After the era of forced removals, when his congregants were scattered across the townships of the Cape Flats, he ministered to them there, as well. He expanded the City Mission to the city's most notorious townships — including Manenberg, Mitchells Plain, and Bonteheuwel, where he founded a church in 1975.

Pastor Kadalie ministered to the great and the small — including the gangsters of District Six and, later, the Cape Flats. "[T]o thousands of people," Rhoda recalled, "he was one of the few real God-fearing men left in this country."[36] His devotion to the community often caused strains at home, Rhoda said: "I often felt sorry for my mother because it was hard for her to compete with a man who so loved God, the church, his wife and his children — in that order. As children we knew our place in that hierarchy but we knew we were loved by a love that was immeasurable."[37] He drilled his children in their knowledge of the Bible, and allowed them to criticize his sermons at home.

---

36 Ibid.
37 Ibid.

At his retirement celebration in 2004, Fenner Kadalie described his own journey, which was as much about service to the public as to the Lord:

> You could say it all began 56 years ago in 1948 in Smart Street, District Six, when I — and also my wife Joan — converted to the Lord Jesus Christ. We were later married in Aspelin Street City Mission in 1950. Our marriage office[r] was Robert Stewart, then the senior missionary of the City Mission. He died in 1956 and I received the calling to take over his work at Smart Street and also oversee Aspeling Street City Mission. For the next 25 years I ministered in the District Six area.
>
> Over this period of time, I gained true knowledge and experience of what it means to be a missionary in the service of the Lord. The work of the City Mission in District Six was much more than your weekly church services. It was a mission in keeping with the word of the Lord that says, "We are his workmanship created in Christ Jesus unto good works which God has before ordained that we should walk in them". This work involved so many elements: Your regular youth meetings and Bible classes; outreach meetings; open air services; cottage meetings; factory meetings; also burying the dead. It was not only about spiritual welfare, but also about compassion for the material plight of the poor and the destitute. The City Mission has always been practical.[38]

Pastor Kadalie became a familiar and beloved figure in the poor and crime-ridden townships to which the apartheid government had consigned the "non-white." Such was the respect he commanded even among criminals that he was considered untouchable as a target of crime. "Hey watch it, here comes the pastor!" Gangsters would shout when they saw him.[39]

When Pastor Kadalie was posthumously awarded the Order of Luthuli in Silver, one of South Africa's national honors, the citation noted:

> Rev Kadalie ran two churches in District Six, one in Smart Street and another in Constitution Street. Under Kadalie's leadership, the City Mission grew into an evangelical movement that incorporated social welfare issues, such as fighting against gangsterism and drugs, providing food and clothing to the poor, running social clubs for the youth and using the church as a centre for community development and social cohesion. As such, he was a community- and institution-builder par excellence.

---

38   Pastor Fenner Kadalie. Speech upon retirement, 2004.
39   Ibid.

The City Mission became the receptacle for all those excluded from the mainline churches – the marginal and the alienated. He conducted marriages, funerals, baptisms and burials to all who needed them regardless of their social standing. He broke up gang fights and enjoyed great respect from District Six's skollies [gangsters], who would shout: "Hey watch it, here comes the Pastor!"

The City Mission was hit hard by the Group Areas Act, 1950. From 1971 to 1979, Rev Kadalie saw his entire parish dispersed across the Cape Flats, brutally uprooted from a vibrant community that included 22 churches, schools, community halls, and a lively cultural, political and artistic life. Powerless against the apartheid state, and as a family itself a victim of the Group Areas Act, 1950, he refused to submit to the tyranny of the Act by following his parish members wherever they were scattered. He set up a City Mission in areas such as Bonteheuwel, Manenberg, Hanover Park and Heideveld [all Coloured townships].

In addition to his extensive church work, Rev Kadalie ran soup kitchens, distributing food to the poor in poverty-stricken areas such as the Flamingo Crescent informal settlement in Lansdowne, to the unemployed men at Kromboom, Lansdowne and Philippi Roads, for 40 years.

With funding from his brother, Dr Victor Kadalie, and sister-in-law, Dr Ruth Kadalie, he built and ran a crèche in Khayelitsha [the largest black township in Cape Town] for 15 years. This crèche provided employment to 19 people and cared for 250 children.

In 2004, a journalist was walking around the Cape Flats and saw a man distributing food, from his combi [minivan], to long queues of indigent people from all colours of the rainbow. She was astounded, interviewed him and discovered that he had been doing this for more than 30 years. This unsung hero was Rev Fenner Kadalie.[40]

A similar tribute, delivered at his retirement ceremony, had noted that Pastor Kadalie had turned down a salary increase from his congregation. And it added: "Modest to a fault, very few know that he is the youngest son [from the first wife] of the famous trade unionist Clements Kadalie, because he never speaks about it."

---

40   Office of the Presidency, South Africa. "Reverend Fenner Christian Kadalie (Posthumous)." Award citation, 2015. URL: http://www.thepresidency.gov.za/national-orders/recipient/reverend-fenner-christian-kadalie-posthumous. Accessed 24 Sep. 2021. Original emphasis.

His wife, Joan, upon accepting the Order of Luthuli on his behalf, recalled that Fenner Kadalie was so humble that she sometimes felt "embarrassed about what he had to do to serve the people." She noted that when she suggested cutting back on his activities, perhaps by serving food to the poor only in the winter months, "he told me that they are hungry every day. He didn't care who you were and what colour you were — he gave freely."[41]

Pastor Kadalie devoted himself to helping the poor directly, not through trade unionism or politics, which he avoided. But Rhoda remembered him quietly cultivating a sense of outrage at the apartheid government.

On May 31, 1961, when South Africa declared itself a republic and left the British commonwealth, and the Kadalie children came home from school with the government's orange-and-blue flags, their father scolded them. He also switched off the radio every time the national anthem of the white regime, *Die Stem* ("The Call"), was played.

Rhoda did not discover Clements Kadalie's story until years later. But his legacy, had been handed down to her, however quietly.

---

41   Joan Kadalie, quoted by Hazel Allies-Husselman. "Highest honor for Reverend Kadalie." *Athlone News*, 16 May 2012. p.6.

Chapter Two:
Childhood

*"My father taught me never to stand back for any man;
my brothers or anyone else. That's where my voice comes from."*[1]

Rhoda Kadalie began her life in District Six in its heyday. It was still a vibrant neighborhood, a commercial hub and racial melting pot, where members of different economic classes — from well-to-do shopkeepers and landlords, to beggars and gangsters and petty thieves — mixed in close quarters.

*Rhoda as an infant, District Six, circa 1954
(Courtesy Rhoda Kadalie)*

---

1 Rhoda Kadalie, quoted by Shanthini Naidoo. "Guaranteed Authentic."
   The Oprah Magazine, July 2007. pp. 103-4.

Today, District Six remains largely empty, a scar on Cape Town's landscape, an inadvertent monument to the apartheid government's determination to rid the city of its most integrated neighborhood. It fell under the hammer of the Group Areas Act of 1950, and the area was slowly demolished over several decades, with some 70,000 people forcibly removed to the wastelands of the Cape Flats. Only religious buildings — churches and mosques — were left standing.

Though the government tried to entice white residents to the neighborhood that it now called Zonnebloem ("sunflower"), which it had declared a whites-only area, few wanted, even during the apartheid era, to move into it.

Much of District Six *was* impoverished, even in its prime. But there were also middle-class families, and a thriving polyglot culture with its own traditions and aspirations. Thousands of residents worked at the city's port, or at its nearby factories; shopkeepers created a vibrant commercial district along the main road through the area, Hanover Street; and local entertainment flourished, in jazz music and in movie houses. There were criminals, and gangs, and brothels. But there were also churches, and mosques, and communities.

The flavor of life in District Six has been well-documented, and even recreated, in literature, drama, and film — even in a small replica neighborhood in the Grand West casino, on the Cape Flats. Rhoda, like many Capetonians, indulged a sense of bittersweet nostalgia for District Six — including that expressed by the late novelist Richard Rive, with whom Rhoda would later develop a friendship. Rive captured the mood of the neighborhood in the mid-1950s in his nostalgic novel, *'Buckingham Palace', District Six* (emphasis removed):

> *I remember those who used to live in District Six, those who lived in Caledon Street and Clifton Hill and busy Hanover Street. There are those of us who still remember the ripe, warm days. Some of us still romanticise and regret when our eyes travel beyond the dead bricks and split tree stumps and wind-tossed sand.*

> *When I was a boy and chirruping ten, a decade after the end of the Second World War ... I remember especially the weekends, which began with the bustle of Friday evenings when the women came home from the factories and the men came home late although they had been paid off early — and the feeling of well-being and plenty in our house on the upper left-hand side of Caledon Street near St. Mark's Church. We lived in the fourth in a row of five mouldy cottages called 'Buckingham Palace' by the locals. The first, 201, the one farthest from the church as if*

by design, was a bluepainted House of Pleasure called the 'Casbah'. In it lived Mary and The Girls.

...

Saturday mornings were brisk, for some men must work and all women must shop. And Hanover Street was crowded and the bazaars and fish-market did a roaring trade. There were groceries to buy on the book and clothes on hire-purchase.

...

And in the evenings we would stand in hushed doorways and tell stories about the legendary figures of District Six ... or show off about our prowess with the local girls, or just talk about the ways of white folks and how [early anti-apartheid activist] Cissie Gool was fighting for us and showing the white people a thing or two.

Echoes of that life still resound, in tiny pockets of Cape Town, such as the lower reaches of Woodstock, and Salt River, a largely Coloured neighborhood sandwiched between the docks and the bohemian student enclave of Observatory.

Local *klopse* — minstrel troupes dating to the 19th century — paraded down Hanover Street on New Year's Eve and on *Tweede Nuwe Jaar,* the second day of January, celebrated by generations of Coloureds as a day of respite from, and then emancipation from, slavery. To this day, the festival lives on, embraced by the city government and even commercialized with corporate sponsorships. It has drawn in communities from as far away as rural towns like Wellington. It was, sadly, canceled for two successive years during the coronavirus pandemic. And as for what District Six was like before apartheid and the era of forced removals, much has faded, living on only in literature, black-and-white photographs, museums, and memory.

Rhoda and her family were deeply enmeshed in the Coloured community — the majority in District Six. Like many Coloured families, they had a variety of ancestors, and both Christians and Muslims among their relatives. Their forebears came from Clements Kadalie's Central Africa — but also from the East Indies, and from Europe. Later, Rhoda would learn from a DNA test that she also carried a crucial genetic marker possessed by descendants of the Khoisan, the original indigenous population of the region, prior to the arrival of European explorers – and African migrants. She was, in every way, a daughter of Cape Town, both indigenous and cosmopolitan.

The Kadalie family lived in a large apartment complex in District Six known as Bloemhof Flats.[2] The buildings consisted of several multi-story towers, arranged around a central courtyard, surrounded by busy streets on all four sides.[3] Rhoda would later say it was her happiest home.

Rhoda's paternal grandmother, Molly Davidson, Clements Kadalie's former wife, lived in Bloemhof Flats as well, in an apartment near the entrance to the complex. She worked as a cleaner at St. Mark's Anglican Church — "referred to as a warden in the 1950s and 60s," Rhoda later recalled.[4] She used to bring Rhoda sweets, and offer words of wisdom. "She wasn't a sage, she was a granny," Rhoda recalled, "and a loving granny. We all loved her."[5]

Local historian Joe Schaffers, who was himself evicted from Bloemhof Flats during the era of forced removals, described the complex to visiting geographer Tom Slater:

> The Bloemhof Flats was a municipal housing complex in the District, a community within a community, and a place with its own civic energy via social organisations and sports and music associations. Joe met his wife Audrey there, who was also born and bred in Bloemhof. The block Joe and Audrey lived in after they got married was one of those in the complex that were bulldozed in the demolitions, replaced by a row of garages to serve the remaining buildings that were spruced up and gentrified by white residents, and the whole diminished complex was then renamed 'Skyways'.
>
> ...
>
> The entire Bloemhof community, as with the entire population of District Six, was scattered among different townships.[6]

To this day, the Skyways apartments still exist in Cape Town, one of the few surviving pieces of residential real estate from that era still in District Six.

2   See Willie Bester, *Bloemhof Flats*, oil on canvas. URL: http://bit. ly/3tkFjTm. Accessed 26 Sep. 2021.
3   See Katie Hold. "District Six Exhibit Bloemhof Flats." URL: https://www. flickr.com/photos/katieholt/9475864744/in/photostream/. Accessed 26 Sep. 2021.
4   Draft article for *Beeld*, 4 Oct. 2017. Personal files.
5   Rhoda Kadalie. Personal communication with the author. 31 Mar. 2022.
6   Tom Slater. "Joe Schaeffers' Honorary Doctorate." URL: https://blogs. ed.ac.uk/tomslater/joeschaffersdoctorate/. Accessed 26 Sep. 2021.

Rhoda visits Bloemhof Flats (Skyways), District Six, Cape Town, c. 1980
(Courtesy Rhoda Kadalie)

Rhoda attended St. Mark's Primary School, later recalling that it was where "my first teacher, Mrs. Devoux, loved me so much that school from then onwards became pure joy."[7] Most of her neighbors and friends were, like her, Coloured. She remembered one white man, a Mr Beukes, who was the caretaker of the local community center, and who would chase children off the *stoep* [veranda] of the building. The phrase "*swart gevaar*" ("black peril"), which had been used to frighten white voters into supporting the National Party in the historic 1948 elections, was appropriated by local children to spin frightful tales about local milkmen: "*Die milkie gaan jou vang!*" ("The milkman will catch you!"), they warned.[8]

Rhoda revisited her early childhood memories, nearly half a century later, in a visit to now-desolate District Six with BBC radio:

When I grew up in District Six, I remember a vibrancy, there were fish shops everywhere, bakeries. And then, of course, there was a

---

7   Draft article for *Beeld*, 4 Oct. 2017. Personal files. Ibid.
8   Rhoda Kadalie. Notes on "Political awareness at an early age." Personal files.

cosmopolitan community of Jewish landlords, Indian traders, Coloured intellectuals, everybody mixing and getting on very well. I cannot deny that there was quite a lot of slum degradation taking place because the government wanted to use the Slum Clearance Act to declare District Six a white area. And so they consciously allowed it to deteriorate. And you must remember ... in the seventies, this was a maze of streets with residential houses. My father's church was up on a hill, in a cobbled street called Smart Street. And when I was a little girl, I stood on the corner of the road, every Sunday night, and rang the brass bell for the parishioners to come to church. So I have fond memories of all the people who lived in that area. These are the only cottages in District Six that have not been demolished. They have had to — with the Group Areas Act in 1965 [see below], they were forced to sell their property. Many of them got next-to-nothing for it because they were forced to move. And then, when they sold, white people moved in. ... Where all these garages were, that was like a play pit, a huge play pit for all of the children in the neighborhood. Where that flat is, that was a community center, where we all did ballet, and singing lessons, and in winter everybody got soup, and toast, and God knows what. But every Christmas, they would have pageants, here in the middle, and everybody would attend: Muslim, Christian — anybody. It was the most intact, wonderful community. And that's all that I remember about my childhood. [9]

Though District Six held her happiest memories, Rhoda — like many Capetonians — still regarded the area with bitterness as well as nostalgia, decades later. But in the 1950s, the destruction of the community was still over the horizon.

The Kadalie family grew rapidly. Fenner and Joan welcomed their first son, David, in 1951; followed by Charles, born in 1952. Rhoda was born in 1953, followed by brothers Reuben in 1955, and Paul in 1957. More children were to come: Rhoda would later joke that South Africa did not have television until the 1970s, hence her parents' astonishing fertility.

***

When the Kadalie family left District Six, it was not because they were forcibly removed: rather, an opportunity arrived with a new job from the Cape Town municipality.

Fenner was placed in charge of municipal wash houses in the segregated town of Mowbray, a lower middle-class suburb southeast of

---

9   Rhoda Kadalie, on *BBC Women's Hour*. 27 Jun. 2002.

the city center. Today, Mowbray remains an important crossroads between the townships of the sand-swept Cape Flats, the plush white suburbs of the mountainous Cape Peninsula, and the bustling downtown area of the City Bowl.[10]

Fenner relaxes in the garden of the Mowbray Wash House
with Rhoda at his side, c. 1962 (Courtesy Rhoda Kadalie)

At the time, Mowbray was divided between white academics and professionals on the one hand, and poorer Coloured families, nestled behind St. Peter's Church. Few people had their own washing machines, and poorer families could not afford domestic help or private laundromats.

10   The *gaatjies*, the diminutive assistants who open the door and collect fares on the city's ubiquitous minibus taxis, often cry out "Mowbray *Kaap*!" to passersby as they head into town.

The municipal wash house in Harriers Road was an important amenity — and a meeting place for the community. Because it needed access to water, it was also at the boundary of the urban environment of the city proper, and the somewhat pastoral expanse of the Cape Flats. It primarily served the white households of the area, including those white families living around the Rondebosch Common, a large reserve beloved by locals for its natural vegetation and hiking trails. It also provided employment for a large workforce, who were predominately Coloured women.

As Rhoda would later write:

In 1961, when the Kadalies left Bloemhof Flats District Six, where they lived, it was not because of the Group Areas Act. It was because my father, Fenner Christian Kadalie, was promoted to Superintendent of the Cleansing Department in the City Council and was transferred to Harriers Road, to oversee the Mowbray municipal wash houses, the pound for stray animals, and other cleansing departments.

When we moved there, Black River Parkway [a prominent modern road] did not exist and that entire area consisted of rambling fields of grass. The pound stabled stray animals, especially from black areas such as Langa, used predominantly for lobola [brideprice].

As children we cut grass for the animals and enjoyed having them to look after. Some of the animals were wild, terrifying and uncontrollable. Others were stubborn, such as a donkey, which always managed to escape by digging deep holes under the stable gate. This donkey was a constant source of amusement to us, but a headache to my dad.[11]

The building was nearly destroyed by a fire in 1965, but remains standing today, though the expansive grounds now front onto the M5, a busy local highway, from which it is separated by a large, imposing fence.

11   Rhoda Kadalie. "Forced to move from home." *Cape Times*, 22 Jul. 2013. URL: http://bit.ly/3UEQNNs. Accessed on 26 Sep. 2021.

Rhoda outside the Mowbray Wash House, Mowbray, Cape Town, c. 1967
(Courtesy Rhoda Kadalie)

Rhoda's four youngest siblings would be born in Mowbray, including her brother Thomas, and her twin brothers Bruce and Patrick. Her only sister, Judith (Judy), was born on October 24, 1969 — the youngest of the nine Kadalie children, spanning 18 years. Rhoda would later recall that Thomas and Judy were both born at home, in the large Mowbray farmhouse that the family inhabited. She was especially excited by Judy's arrival, as she later recalled: "When my mother was pregnant for the 8th time, and 7 brothers later, I prayed for a sister every day. I was prepared to turn agnostic because with every pregnancy I prayed for a sister, but God thought otherwise and sent a boy. So when my dad announced a girl I was so overjoyed, I could barely contain myself."[12]

Rhoda with mother Joan and sister Judy, c. 1970 (Courtesy Rhoda Kadalie)

Her family made her a natural feminist. Rhoda would later recall that her father spoiled her, giving her seven brothers something of an inferiority complex. Her mother, Joan, was "very conventional," she later recalled, and no "feminist," in the political sense, but was "an assertive woman in

12   Rhoda Kadalie. Comment on Facebook, 23 Oct. 2021. URL: https://www. facebook.com/rhoda.kadalie/posts/10159931922165039. Accessed on 28 Mar. 2022.

her own rights."[13] She refused to do too much housework, demanding that the boys learn to cook, clean, and iron for themselves. "I resented that as a child," Rhoda said, "and I thought she was a bad mother but as I grew older I began to understand her sort of rebellion and I actually admire [her] today."

Rhoda wrote:

Here we grew up very happily, in a peaceful abode, with my father working next door and my mother working on and off as a machinist at the Ensign [clothing] factory.[14]

We all went to St Peter's Primary School, Mowbray, which was about a mile away, and bus fare was one big round cent. Because of the municipal wash houses, the grounds in front of our house were enormous and here my brothers had endless fun playing soccer and cricket. We could roam around freely, playing on the vast open spaces in front of us. Our childhood was idyllic, to say the least.[15]

Many of Rhoda's friends were from the surrounding neighborhood. Across from the school was a small mosque, where Muslim men gathered for prayer, especially on Fridays, responding to the call of the *azzan*, the call to prayer, from the *muezzin*. Rhoda's best friend was Yasmina, a Muslim girl who lived near the mosque. Through her, Rhoda learned much about life in the Muslim community, including the holidays and the cultural traditions.

Through the washhouse, Rhoda also encountered people from all walks of life. Professors, teachers, lawyers, and architects brought their laundry in on a daily basis, and many of them came to know Pastor Kadalie and his family. One client was a renowned pianist, who, while waiting for his laundry, would visit the Kadalie home to play the piano. He played the compositions of Franz Liszt and Edvard Grieg, as well as George Gershwin's *Rhapsody in Blue*, leaving the Kadalie children in awe. Decades later, Rhoda would recall, she attended his concerts at Cape Town City Hall with the Cape Philharmonic Orchestra.

---

13   Rhoda Kadalie. Unpublished interview with Melanie Walker, 27 Oct. 1994.

14   The factory, in Woodstock, was demolished around 2000. See: Stewart Harris, "Ensign clothing factory, Woodstock." Flickr, 21 Nov. 2011. URL: https://www.flickr.com/photos/myskygarden/6529717773.   Accessed on 26 Sep. 2021.

15   Rhoda Kadalie, *Cape Times* 2013, ibid.

Rhoda in the garden of the cottage at the Mowbray Wash House, c. 1970
(Courtesy Rhoda Kadalie)

Despite the idyllic surroundings, the anti-apartheid struggle had reached a point of crisis in South Africa. The Sharpeville Massacre of 1960 had set the country on a course for violent confrontation over apartheid.[16]

---

16   At Sharpeville, police in a township south of Johannesburg shot and killed dozens of peaceful black protesters who were demonstrating against the discriminatory "pass" laws. The event shocked the world, triggered a wave of emigration from the country, and convinced the ANC to begin a violent underground struggle against the state.

Racial tensions had become more intense in Cape Town, too — though not for everyone. Rhoda recalled:

> *We were the only coloured family in this area, and some neighbours were friendly while others watched us with great suspicion, but in the end we became friends. One of our neighbours was a magistrate by the name of Mr Frank. He always introduced himself, as "Frank by name and frank by nature".*

> *He loved my father, who was also a lay pastor in District Six, and always advised him which topics to include in his sermons, especially hire purchase, which he branded as the scourge of the poor. He raised his domestic worker's daughter Betty and I remember how amazed I was to hear a black girl my age speak impeccable English when mine was pretty lousy.*

> *...*

> *Another neighbour was Rev Crawford, the head of the Presbyterian Church, his wife (who was also called Rhoda) and their two children. He chatted to my father as a fellow pastor, but was often racist. The neighbours across the road, the Cruikshanks, (the husband was an architect) were very aloof and hardly greeted us until I saved their house from burning down.*

> *I came from school one day and saw the roof burning and shouted and shouted until they heard me. This was no mean feat as they had scary, loud dogs. My throat was hoarse, but the house was saved. I remember how disappointed I was when they just gave me a box of [embroidered] handkerchiefs as a gift, for what I considered to be a heroic deed.[17]*

One Dutch family, the De Lange household, who lived next to Rev. Crawford, only allowed Rhoda to play with their daughter once, and under strict supervision. When children from the nearby community of Black River, a Coloured settlement, raided the De Lange family orchard, they invariably blamed Rhoda's brothers, which enraged her parents.

Still, there was an overall atmosphere of tolerance, and the Kadalie children grew up relatively insulated from the disruptions taking place elsewhere in the city. But the peaceful yet troubled racial coexistence that Rhoda had known was soon to come to an abrupt end.

***

---

17   Rhoda Kadalie, *Cape Times* 2013, ibid.

South Africa had known racial discrimination in various forms for many decades before the arrival of apartheid. But the victory of the National Party in 1948 marked the arrival of a new and institutional form of racial segregation.

Ironically, the ideology of the National Party was itself rooted in an experience of repression and suffering. The British fought the fledgling Afrikaner republics in the Anglo-Boer War of 1899-1902 to seize control of South Africa's lucrative, capital-intensive gold and diamond industries. After the British overwhelmed the Boers ("farmers") in direct military confrontations, the Afrikaners took to guerrilla warfare.

In response, the British developed one of the most insidious weapons of the twentieth century: the concentration camp. To crush the remnants of Boer resistance, the British rounded up civilians — notably women, children, and the elderly — whom the guerrilla fighters had left at home, and burned their farms. Many Afrikaners died in the camps before the end of the war.

The experience of persecution created an enduring bitterness among the Afrikaner population that festered long after the Boer generals and statesmen negotiated favorable terms in the negotiations that led to the formation of the Union of South Africa in 1910.

Though South Africa fought on the side of the Allies in both the First and Second World Wars, significant portions of the Afrikaner population sided with Germany, as Britain's enemy. Prime Minister Jan Smuts, a former Boer general who was an architect of the United Nations, tried to satisfy Afrikaner aspirations within the template of a British-style parliamentary democracy. But in 1948, voters worried about the rising economic power and presence of black South Africans — the so-called "*swaart gevaar*," or "black peril" — rejected Smuts and his United Party in favor of D. F. Malan and the National Party.

The National Party's ideology of "*apartheid*" — an Afrikaans word meaning "separateness" — held that South Africa's diverse racial groups represented distinct nations, each with its own aspirations. This idea provided a convenient pseudo-moral justification for segregating the members of various races into separate areas, and ratifying the grossly unfair apportionment of land that had been undertaken in the early years of the Union. The National Party also gave religion, and the Dutch Reformed Church in particular, pride of place in national culture, and identified communism as a grave threat to the state, placing it — however uncomfortably — among the western nations.

Apartheid was rolled out in a series of laws. Several were particularly important — and notorious. The Population Registration Act of 1950, for example, required every South African to be classified by race, according to an assigned set of physical criteria that were said to be scientific, but which were often arbitrary.

A related law, the Prohibition of Mixed Marriages Act of 1949, prohibited marriage across the color line; it reinforced the Immorality Act of 1927, a law that predated apartheid, banning sex between white and black people. The Reservation of Separate Amenities Act of 1953 imposed segregation in public places, including on public transportation; the Bantu Education Act of 1953 condemned black South Africans to inferior training, for all but menial jobs; and the Suppression of Communism Act of 1950 gave the state the tools to suppress opposition by prohibiting certain public gatherings and even "banning" particular individuals from political activity.

Perhaps the most impactful law was the Group Areas Act of 1950, which divided South Africa into particular areas assigned to each racial group — usually the major four: white, African, Coloured, and Indian. When District Six was destroyed, the government was acting, in part, pursuant to the Group Areas Act, under which the largely Coloured neighborhood had been reclassified as white. Other urban neighborhoods throughout the country met the same fate: Sophiatown, a largely black neighborhood in central Johannesburg, had been a vibrant center of African modernity until it was destroyed and its residents forcibly removed to black townships.

In Cape Town, the Group Areas Act had not stopped at the boundaries of District Six. Other areas in the central area of the city or the near suburbs were also classified as white, despite the diversity of their populations. Not all of these areas suffered forced removals, which became increasingly unpopular in the face of local resistance and international criticism. But many did, and were changed forever.

Mowbray was one such area. And though Pastor Fenner Kadalie had moved there to pursue a civic duty to the municipal government, the apartheid regime soon wanted him, and his family, gone.

***

Rhoda noted that the area of Mowbray where her family lived was considered predominantly "white," though the washing house provided a window onto what was, in fact, a remarkably diverse area:

We were considered privileged by some as we lived in a "white area", on a big property, with endless space for our big family. We had a garden of orchards – every fruit tree one can imagine, there were enough bedrooms for the children, and as the only daughter for 16 years, I always had my own room while the boys shared rooms.

The wash house next door was an intriguing place. It was the predecessor to the laundry and Laundromats. Working class women, black and coloured, mostly Malay, hired washing facilities from my father, and white people would bring their washing to be laundered and ironed.

Soon we became part of this community of washerwomen and white clients who interacted with my parents and us as children. Among them were famous people, but the one we loved the most was a pianist who came into our house and rocked the piano with long concertos from Chopin to Lizst. Today, he and I frequent the same symphony concerts at the City Hall.

The washerwomen loved us and we them. We were the beneficiaries of their traditional fare during Ramadaan and Eid; we were invited to countless Muslim weddings and family events. They were part of the big family that surrounded us.[18]

Like several other "gray" areas of Cape Town that were formally reserved for whites, but managed to survive the apartheid era somewhat intact, Mowbray might have endured as a diverse, working-class community. However, politics intervened, as Rhoda recalled:

In 1970, my brothers were playing soccer with the white kids in the neighbourhood. It was election time and a National Party member, Mr Carr, was recruiting voters. He walked around, saw my brothers playing and inquired who they were. Within a matter of days we were issued with a Group Areas eviction order. My parents were distraught. With nine children they had no capital to buy a house big enough to accommodate their family.

The council led my father to believe that he was secure in his job and the house but could do nothing against the power of the apartheid state. The prospects of going to a council house on the Cape Flats such as [the Coloured townships] Bonteheuwel, Manenberg, or Hanover Park seemed too ghastly to contemplate, and it was the first time I saw my mother weep. The Cape Flats was vastly underdeveloped and to move from a homely idyllic environment into the unknown was scary for all of us.[19]

---

18   Rhoda Kadalie, *Cape Times*, ibid.
19   Ibid.

D.M. Carr was the National Party member of Parliament representing the industrial suburb of Maitland, several kilometers to the north. He was a passionate advocate of apartheid.

In a debate in 1968 in the all-white House of Assembly in Parliament about the creation of the separate Coloured Persons Representative Council, which would exclude them from representation in the white Parliament after Coloured voters had already been stripped of the franchise, Carr said:

During all the years that the Coloureds were on the Common Roll [of voters], it is undoubtedly true that they remained backward and illiterate. The vote was no good to them. Admittedly it was very useful to the [opposition] United Party on many occasions but to the Coloured people it was no use at all.

...

It is no good saying that the Coloured people speak English or Afrikaans and that they belong to the same churches as Whites. We know that they are different, and that they react differently and that they will always react differently when mixed together with Whites politically. ... We want a white Parliament. That is the unquestionable desire not only of Afrikaans speaking South Africans in the National Party, it is the desire of the vast majority of South Africans, right across the language line. It will redound to the credit and honour of the National Party that it was this Government which gave us a purely white South African Parliament. This act will stand as a monument to the present régime.

...

I am satisfied that the proposed new legislation will be a tremendous asset to the Coloured people because for the first time they will have a body consisting of a majority of elected members, a body which will be able to give us and the outside world the genuine voice of the Coloured man.[20]

---

20   D.M. Carr, quoted by Griffin Lerner. "Neither Black Nor White: Louisiana Creoles of Color, South African Coloureds and the Struggle for Identity, Nationhood, and Belonging." Thesis, University of North Carolina, 2015. URL: https://bit.ly/3UvcvmS; accessed 7 Mar. 2022. Quoting: Republic of South Africa, House of Assembly Debates, no. 4, 1968, col. 1366–8. URL: http://www.historicalpapers.wits.ac.za/inventories/inv_pdf0/A1132/A1132-C270-001-jpeg.pdf. Accessed on 7 Mar. 2022.

The 1970 general election was the first election for an exclusively white parliament, and Carr was campaigning for the National Party throughout the area. One day, as John Field remembers the incident, Carr was not canvassing for votes, but picking up his washing. He noticed the Kadalie boys and the Field boys playing soccer. The sight of Coloured and white boys playing together triggered his indignation. His intervention — and Fenner Kadalie's innocent reply, when asked who the mixed group of boys were — doomed the family and the local Coloured community to forced removal.

Rhoda recalled: "He was walking around, and he saw my brothers playing soccer with the white kids. He came to ask my father whose children are these, and the next day there were government officials with papers, telling us that we should leave."[21]

Rhoda also recalled that Carr's actions did not go over well with some of his white Afrikaner constituents. Joy Kelley, the Afrikaans-speaking wife of a missionary named Pat Kelley, knew Pastor Kadalie through her husband's Bible study group. When she learned about the forced removals, she apparently phoned Carr and excoriated him, calling him a "swine." Her outburst won the Kadalie family a temporary reprieve: unlike other families, they would not be evicted until they had found alternative accommodation.

The Mowbray removal took place, nevertheless — proceeding several years after the Civil Rights movement had already dismantled much of what remained of formal racial segregation in the United States; and just a few years after Robert F. Kennedy delivered his memorable address on racial equality at the University of Cape Town, just above Mowbray on the slopes of Table Mountain.[22]

Similar removals took place in other "white" suburbs of Cape Town. While the forced removals of District Six became iconic, the quieter removals in Mowbray, Sea Point, Claremont, and Newlands were no less traumatic for their victims.

For the Kadalie family, eviction and removal were not just political issues: they created an acute and deeply personal crisis, as the family had to find shelter, and wished to avoid the impoverished, windswept,

---

21   Rhoda Kadalie, on *BBC Women's Hour*. 27 Jun. 2002.
22   Robert F. Kennedy. "Day of Affirmation Address." University of Cape Town, Cape Town, South Africa. 6 Jun. 1966. URL: https://www.jfklibrary. org/learn/about-jfk/the-kennedy-family/robert-f-kennedy/robert-f-kennedy-speeches/day-of-affirmation-address-university-of-capetown-capetown-south-africa-june-6-1966. Accessed on 26 Sep. 2021.

crime-ridden public housing on the Cape Flats. Rhoda recalled in 2002: "I remember that my mother really sobbed the day she was told to leave her house. ... All kinds of mixed emotions. And I find, I find I'm often quite angry about it, even now."[23]

Fenner Kadalie managed to apply for a larger house in the Coloured township of Primrose Park, Rhoda wrote, with help "from an Afrikaner missionary [Pat Kelley] ... who happened to know a Member of Parliament [Carr]." And with that, "within a matter of months we were forcibly removed from Mowbray."

She recalled the emotional toll of the evictions:

For us it was a great time of upheaval from a secure, comfortable home to a smaller house, new neighbours, and strange surroundings.

...

While we were undergoing our upheaval, our maternal and paternal relatives, as well as my father's congregants, were all served eviction notices.

Over a period of ten years we witnessed all our people forcibly removed, trucks moving in and out of District Six, people not knowing where they were going, the bewilderment of social dislocation taking its toll on mothers, fathers, children, the elderly, the youth, the employed, the professionals, the traders, the owners, the poor and the marginalised.[24]

Before, she noted, the family had felt lucky, among a privileged few who could participate fully, if at times uncomfortably, in Cape Town. That comforting illusion was now shattered:

The Group Areas Act and all the other pieces of racist legislation that accompanied it, became the much-despised great leveller.

With this national scourge of forced removals, we were not special, as we always thought. We were part of the oppressed of South Africa.[25]

Despite their education, their faith, and their service to the government, the Kadalies were to be judged by their color. It was a lesson Rhoda would never forget.

---

23   Rhoda Kadalie, on *BBC Women's Hour*, 2002, ibid.
24   Ibid.
25   Ibid.

Chapter Three:
A Student of Politics

*"I went to five different schools because of the Group Areas Act. ...
under protest, [I] went to UWC, which in retrospect I don't regret,
because I think my political formation was achieved there."*[1]

Forced removals meant an abrupt interruption in the education of many
South African children. Many children found themselves isolated from
the older, more established schools they had formerly attended, and were
trapped by the inferior education provided by the apartheid system.

A few found ways to continue their education in the places they
left behind, if they were able to flout apartheid's racial boundaries and
make the heavy investments of time and money required. For the Kadalie
children, education remained a crucial lifeline, a link to the aspirations
they refused to give up simply because they had been evicted.

The Kadalie children were fortunate in that most of them were
able to attend primary school in Mowbray, before they were evicted, at a
local Anglican school, St. Peter's. It was owned by the St. Peter's church
abutting the school property, and was a small and intimate facility, led
by influential teachers. Some of those teachers left the country with the
enforcement of the apartheid government's Bantu Education Act of 1953,
and its extension into "non-white" universities and colleges in 1959.

Like other primary schools across South Africa — including public
schools — St. Peter's was highly regimented, with school uniforms, daily
prayers, and corporal punishment for even minor infractions. But the
teachers were devoted to ensuring that their pupils — called "learners"
in the politically correct jargon of post-apartheid South Africa, to soften
the inequality between educators and students — had the basic skills
necessary to survive, even in a racially segmented job market.

---

1   Rhoda Kadalie, quoted by Ryland Fisher. *Race*. Auckland Park: Jacana
     Media, 2007. pp. 20-21.

Rhoda and her siblings dressed for school at St. Peter's, Mowbray, c. 1962
(Courtesy Rhoda Kadalie)

Rhoda would later say that she was first exposed to the reality of apartheid when she attended St. Peter's — not inside the classroom, but on the way home:

> *I went to school in Mowbray at St. Peter's and walked down from St. Peter's home every day. And at Sawkins Road is a little park. And I played in this park every day, and sometimes met the little kids of the neighborhood and played with them. And suddenly, one day, there was a board up which said, "whites only." And I couldn't understand it. And I think it was very painful for my mother to explain to me what that meant. And so I found that very brutal. I would walk my white friends home, and their parents' would say, "How dare you call them by their name? You should call them, "Miss so-and-so." And I innocently said, "But they don't call me, 'Miss.'"[2]*

2   Rhoda Kadalie, on "Woman Today," SAfm, June 1996.

Prior to that, Rhoda said, she had no consciousness of race. "We grew up in a very sheltered home. ... We weren't really aware of race as such. Race meant, to us, the white caretaker in District Six, where we lived before, who chased the children away when they played on the *stoep* of the clinic, for example."

When the area around St. Peter's was declared a "white" area under the Group Areas Act, Rhoda, who had studied at St. Peter's through Standard 3 (5th grade), continued for two years at the Sydney Street Primary school in the Woodstock neighborhood, a neighborhood abutting the old District Six, stretching from the docks upward along the slopes of Devil's Peak, the distinctive hook-shaped massif to the east of Table Mountain.

Sydney Street was known then as a school for "half caste" children — "fair kids from mixed parentage who could pass for white," Rhoda recalled. Light-skinned children in Woodstock, especially from Walmer Estate — one of the most elite neighborhoods within the Coloured community — often managed to slip through the cracks in South Africa's segregated society. Being classified as white in official documents, or simply mistaken for being white, could open a whole world of opportunities that were denied to darker-skinned Coloured people of equal talents. It was not uncommon for two children of the same parents to attend different schools on the basis of appearance alone. Some of Rhoda's relatives gamed the system in this way.

Efforts to evade the arbitrary apartheid scheme of racial classifications led to some absurd results, documented in the government's annual report on cases of people who had applied for reclassification. Upon the use of various pseudoscientific tests, measuring the thickness of hair or the slope of shoulders, a handful of people who were originally declared to be part of one racial group were declared to be part of another. The report was demanded regularly in Parliament by the anti-apartheid stalwart Helen Suzman, causing some grim embarrassment, at home and abroad, to the government.

Rhoda, a diligent student, qualified to attend Sydney Street based on her grades alone, though she was relatively dark-skinned. When she arrived, having never met anyone there before, she was treated poorly by some of the teachers, as well as some of her classmates. Many, even those classified as Coloured themselves, had internalized the hierarchical racial outlook of South African society, which was reinforced with vigor by apartheid's intricate system of exclusions.

But Rhoda did not let the abuse deter her, and she studied diligently, as did her siblings, most of whom excelled in school. The Kadalie children also benefited from the encouragement of their next-door neighbors, a white couple named John and Anne Field. John was a professor of zoology at the University of Cape Town (UCT), and he and Anne took an interest in the bright, precocious Kadalie children, hiring Rhoda to help babysit their children — all of whom went on to lead successful lives.

The Fields were a liberal family, Rhoda recalled, opposed in principle to apartheid — partly due to the influence of John's mother, Sheila van der Horst, who was a prominent economist at UCT, specializing in the study of migrant labor, a staple of the South African economy that attracted much criticism. His father was Stanley Field, a well-known lawyer in Cape Town.

Together, the Fields formed a close and enduring bond with the Kadalie family. Rhoda recalled: "The Fields were very kind to my parents and donated several Volkswagen Combis to my father for his church work, which he did in his spare time."[3] Later, they would pay Rhoda's university tuition.

It was a friendship that would endure, long after the two families were forcibly separated by the apartheid regime.

Rhoda with the Fields family children, c. 1970
(Courtesy Rhoda Kadalie)

---

3   Rhoda Kadalie. "Forced to move from home." *Cape Times*, 22 Jul. 2013. Ibid.

At one point, years after the forced removals, when Rhoda was twenty-one years old, and still living at home, she showed up at the Fields' home after an argument with her parents and declared that she was moving in with them. Behind her was the little Volkswagen "Fun Bug" that she had been given for her birthday; on the back seat were all of her worldly possessions, tied in a sheet with a knot, in the style of the stereotypical hobo.

John agreed, on condition that her father be informed of her whereabouts. She agreed, and Professor Fields called Pastor Kadalie to let him know that Rhoda was staying with them. The arrangement continued, amiably, for seven months, until the familial dispute had run its course, and Rhoda returned home.

$$***$$

After completing Standard 5 [7th grade], Rhoda continued her studies at the Wesley Training College, a school for teachers. Wesley was founded in the early twentieth century in the industrial hub of Salt River,[4] a working-class and largely Coloured community originally settled by British laborers. The college, which is an ordinary public school today, is a large Cape Dutch-style school along one of the main industrial roads, across from the residential portion of Salt River, whose streets are named after great English literary figures, and whose skies resonate five times daily with the Muslim call to prayer from neighborhood mosques.

At the time, Wesley permitted students to attend for general studies up through Standard 8, or 10th grade. Students who continued into Standard 9 and the final year of high school, known as matriculation or "matric," would train specifically to be teachers. Rhoda, who had developed broader interests, wanted to apply to university. She had the support of her parents: "My parents were very conservative in most ways, but they never thought I should have less education because I was a girl," she later recalled.[5]

So she transferred schools again — this time, to Harold Cressy High School, which remained in District Six. Though the family had left District Six long ago, it was a logical choice, as Rhoda recalled later: "Our maternal and paternal relatives still lived in District Six so we lived across both

---

4   "Wesley Practising School." URL: https://wesleypractisingschool. wordpress.com/about-us/academics-2/. Accessed on 27 Sep. 2021.
5   Helen Suzman Foundation. "Interview with Rhoda Kadalie, Human Rights Activist." *Focus* 24, 2001. URL: https://hsf.org.za/publications/ focus/issue-24-fourth-quarter-2001/interview-with-rhoda-kadalie-human-rights-activist. Accessed on 27 Sep. 2021.

areas. My father had three parishes in District Six and we had a huge circle of friends, consisting of congregants, family, and neighbours."

Harold Cressy was also unique in that it catered specifically to Coloured students. The school was originally founded in 1951 as the Cape Town Secondary School, and was renamed in 1953 for Cressy, the first Coloured in South Africa to graduate with a Bachelor of Arts degree (from the University of Cape Town). Cressy had been a passionate advocate for education among black South Africans before his life was tragically cut short by pneumonia.[6]

The site on which the school had been built had previously housed a Jewish community school known as Hope Lodge Primary School.[7] Jewish immigrants had played a key role in developing District Six, and owned many of the buildings where Coloured residents lodged at the time of the forced removals. A disproportionate number of Jews were active in politics, trade unions, and the anti-apartheid movement as well.

Though the apartheid government wanted the school gone, Harold Cressy, along with nearby Trafalgar High School, resisted the pressure, in part by continuing to produce graduates who performed well on matriculation exams.[8]

Cressy was not only an excellent school; it was also a highly political one, whose left-wing outlook was sharpened in response to the confrontation with the apartheid government. Several teachers, and their families, were also involved in political activity. One of Rhoda's teachers was Helen Kies (née Abrahams), a member of the Teachers League of South Africa (TLSA). The TLSA was an organization of Coloured teachers that opposed racial segregation and apartheid. Kies was married to Benjamin Mason Kies, a prominent socialist, yet non-Stalinist, Coloured intellectual.[9] He would later be "banned" under the notorious Suppression

6   "Harold Cressy." URL: http://pzacad.pitzer.edu/NAM/newafrre/ writers/cressy/cressyS.htm. Accessed on 27 Sep. 2021.
7   "Harold Cressy High School: Heritage Impact Assessment." 28 May 2014. URL: https://sahris.sahra.org.za/sites/default/files/heritagereports/ Harold%20Cressy%20HIA.pdf. Accessed on 27 Sep. 2021.
8   "Trafalgar High School, Cape Town, marks 100 years." South African History Online. 13 Jan. 2012. URL: https://www.sahistory.org.za/archive/ trafalgar-high-school-cape-town-marks-100-years. Accessed on 27 Sep. 2021.
9   "Benjamin Magson Kies." South African History Online. URL: https:// www.sahistory.org.za/people/benjamin-magson-kies. Accessed on 27 Sep. 2021.

of Communism Act.[10] Helen Kies, too, was later imprisoned briefly for her political activity.

Rhoda would credit Helen Kies and other teachers for developing her political consciousness. It was Kies, she said, who first told her about her famous grandfather, Clements Kadalie, about whom her father had maintained a steadfast silence. "They worshipped my grandfather," she told an interviewer.[11] Through Kies and others, Rhoda learned about her family's political legacy — one of resistance to racism, and one of self-reliance, which eschewed communism on the left and racial nationalism on the right.

Her experience at Harold Cressy was more than a preparation for the matriculation exams she would need to pass to enroll at university: it was also a political education in the past and present of resistance to racial discrimination in South Africa.

By then, Rhoda had experienced the brutality of the apartheid regime personally: her own family's forced removal meant that she had to take the bus several miles to school: "I remember, how as a matric [final year of high school] pupil, travelling from Harold Cressy High to Primrose Park, I missed seeing trees, greenery and the mountain," she later recalled.[12]

In the District Six neighborhood surrounding the school, the forced removals continued. The stark reality of apartheid was impossible to ignore; it was literally right outside the classroom windows.

Harold Cressy marked the beginning of a political journey for Rhoda, one she would continue at university in the mid-1970s, when South Africa was quietly undergoing an intellectual ferment that would soon explode on the streets.

***

Rhoda faced a choice when she matriculated: she could apply to the University of Cape Town, the prestigious white institution just south of Harold Cressy on the windward slopes of Table Mountain; or she could apply to the University of the Western Cape, a relatively new institution for Coloured students.

Though the University of Cape Town (UCT) was for whites, it admitted a limited number of other students — Coloured, Indian, and African — with the permission of the apartheid government. Harold

10   "Helen Kies." South African History Online. URL: https://www.sahistory. org.za/people/helen-kies. Accessed on 27 Sep. 2021.
11   Rhoda Kadalie, quoted in Salo, ibid.
12   Rhoda Kadalie, *Cape Times*, ibid.

Cressy encouraged its students to apply there, rather than the Coloured option at the University of the Western Cape (UWC).

UWC had the stigma of segregation, and the apartheid philosophy of "separate development." Founded in 1960, UWC was also known as a "bush college" because it was established on the windy, sand-swept plain of the Cape Flats, where few people lived at the time (and where Cape Town's segregated Coloured and black townships were being established). As a new institution, and also as one that elite white students would never apply to attend (at least until decades later), UWC was also considered a second-class university, one frowned upon by the most upwardly mobile, talented and ambitious Coloured students.

Ciraj Rasool, a professor of African history who earned his Ph.D. at UWC, but who studied at UCT as an undergraduate, recalled how his parents regarded UWC in the early days:

> As much as a yearning for university studied on the lower reaches of Devil's Peak [i.e. at UCT] had been instilled in me, so scepticism and a suspicion had also been inculcated about the meaning and value of UWC. ... This was Coloured Representative Council[13] territory, close to where the CRC met and where many CRC members lived, and this area was thought to be in a vice grip of collaborationism, that old condition of false consciousness that made opportunists actively work with the institutions of their oppression. But as you drove a little further, and the signs pointed to UWC, the parental instruction was swift and resolute: "Look to your left, and do not look to the right!" For this was a "bush college," site not just of unequal education, but of inferior education, in a university specially created to produce compliance and mediocrity. And you were implored to look the other way for your own protection, in case you got tainted or infected by this condition.[14]

Rasool would later have cause to revisit this early impression — both on political and academic grounds. But at the time, the university was seen by critics as just one of many institutions created to educate separate racial groups and thus to reinforce apartheid's basic structure.

---

13   The Coloured Persons Representative Council was a limited legislative body created during the apartheid era.

14   Ciraj Rasool. "Full circle: concerning UWC's academic value." Premesh Lalu and Noëleen Murray, eds. *Becoming UWC: Reflections, pathways, and unmaking apartheid's legacy.* "Full circle: concerning UWC's academic value." Cape Town: Centre for Humanities Research (University of the Western Cape), 2012.

The apartheid government was not interested in creating an educated middle class or professional class among any of the "non-white" groups, except insofar as the graduates could be encouraged to serve their own racial groups, and to provide an economic and political buffer between a bourgeois white society and a potentially restive black population.

Rhoda knew all of that. And she rejected the more conventional career paths of Coloured girls — "to be a teacher, social worker, or nurse," she later recalled.[15] So she applied to UCT, hoping to study physical therapy, a discipline taught in the world-renowned medical school. She saw physical therapy as an alternative to what she regarded as the "typical" fields for Coloured women, such as teaching and social work.

But she changed her mind, as she later wrote: "UCT had a bizarre rule that applicants should include a photograph of themselves in a bathing costume,"[16] or at least a "full length photograph."[17] Rhoda regarded that rule as an indignity on a number of levels. It was partly a way of scrutinizing the race of applicants, according to the apartheid regime's criteria, which went well beyond simple skin color and often included hair, facial features, and even posture.

Moreover, the photograph was a way for university admissions officers to scrutinize the female bodies of applicants — something that Rhoda fiercely resented. She was not ashamed of her body: she was slender and pretty. But whether it was her Christian upbringing, or her early feminist instincts, Rhoda simply would not bring herself to comply with UCT's apparently sexist requirement. She wrote to UCT and contested the requirement, to no avail.

Several of Rhoda's friends have disputed her claim about the bathing costume, noting instead that Rhoda's decision was likely a result of apartheid exclusions. Under the Extension of University Education Act of 1964, "non-white" students could only apply to UCT if they were pursuing degrees that were not offered at UWC. At the time, these included medicine, architecture, and engineering. Rhoda had little interest in these fields, so she chose UWC. That, at least, is how the contrary story goes. Journalist-turned-politician, Helen Zille, who was once the public affairs director of UCT, disputed Rhoda's claim about the bathing costume — but Rhoda stuck to her guns.

---

15   Rhoda Kadalie. "Dear Rhoda." *From Me to Me: Letters to my 16 1/2-year-old self.* Auckland Park: Jacana, 2012. 121.
16   Ibid.
17   Rhoda Kadalie, quoted in *Beyond*, 2 Dec. 2010. URL: https://issuu.com/beyondpublishing/docs/issue09. Accessed on 6 Mar. 2022. p. 61.

Regardless, Rhoda applied to UWC instead, even though matriculants from Harold Cressy typically scorned "bush colleges." She registered for a four-year degree in Library Science — largely to differentiate herself from other Coloured female students, many of whom tended to study social work, teaching, and nursing. And she added two additional subjects, English and anthropology.

Rhoda's Bible study group at UWC, c. 1975 (Courtesy Rhoda Kadalie)

Her father, Pastor Kadalie, remained supportive — though he tried to discourage her from studying anthropology, afraid that the study of evolution would undermine Rhoda's faith. She "laughed him out of court," she recalled, and pressed ahead with her chosen course of study.

As it turned out, enrolling in UWC would turn out to be a more subversive decision than either Rhoda or her father could then understand. "I went to UWC under protest," she recalled later, "because at the time none of us liked the university. But for me, it was a blessing in disguise to go to the University of the Western Cape, because it politicized us very radically at the time to what was going on in the country.[18]

---

18   Rhoda Kadalie, "Woman Today," ibid.

Far from being an apartheid cog, UWC would emerge as a center of resistance. Ironically, while many of her classmates who enrolled in UCT faded into the landscape, UWC gave Rhoda her voice. "I would never have been as high-profile as I was, politically," had she not gone there, Rhoda said.[19]

***

UWC began as a tightly-controlled institution, founded in the aftermath of the Extension of University Education Act of 1959, which segregated higher education. It was run by the broader University of South Africa, a public institution that provided (and still provides) courses by correspondence. Its physical construction was overseen by the apartheid government's Public Works Department. As architect and scholar Noëleen Murray would later write:

> *As with many other newly designated Group Areas, UWC was built on land that was environmentally inferior to other parts of Cape Town. It was a treeless wetland area exposed to harsh winds and sun, known as the "bush", and later to become the Cape Flats Nature Reserve. The establishment of the Flats as a balkanised dumping ground for people after forced removals was also a function of the rapid growth of population, including continued migration to the city of people from small towns and rural areas in what was then the Cape Province.*

The faculty of UWC were predominantly white, with many coming from Afrikaans-speaking institutions. This was more than a means of educating the Coloured student population, many of whom spoke Afrikaans as a first language. It was also a deliberate attempt to ensure that UWC remained passive. As Rhoda would later note, the Broederbond ("Brotherhood"), a secret society of Afrikaner leaders, kept a close watch on UWC's development. Their goal, Rhoda recalled, was "mind control" — guiding the ideas of rising generations of Coloured professionals within the boundaries of the regime's philosophy of "Christian National Education," hoping to reinforce a docile mindset that would support the apartheid system rather than challenging it.[20]

Over time, the university began opening up positions for Coloured faculty and administrators, including Richard ("Dick") van der Ross, who was appointed to serve as the university's rector — its chief academic

---

19   Rhoda Kadalie. Personal communication with the author. 6 Mar. 2022.
20   Rhoda Kadalie. Personal communication with the author.

official — in 1975. Van der Ross was a fascinating, controversial, yet widely admired figure. Rhoda would later describe him as a "thoroughly decent man, prepared to work within the system, while changing it." Affectionately known as "Uncle Dick," he fought long and hard for the recognition of the Coloured people as a cultural group in their own right, with a unique history and historical experiences that set them apart from black Africans. That interest both conformed to, and challenged, the government's policy of "separate development."

After studying at Trafalgar High School in District Six, Van der Ross earned a Ph.D. in education at UCT, and worked both as a teacher and administrator in schools within the Coloured community. He also became politically active during the period of forced removals, protesting against the policy of the apartheid regime under the Group Areas Act.

Yet he also showed a willingness to work within the apartheid system. In 1958, the apartheid regime established the Department of Coloured Affairs,[21] and Van der Ross accepted an appointment within it as Assistant Planner of Education.[22] This made him the first Coloured person to work within the department — and, indeed, in any position under the apartheid regime. It was a position that allowed him to serve his own community — but at the moral price of working for a government whose racial policies he abhorred.

Much of Van der Ross's career, in academia and in politics, expressed similar contradictions. In 1969, he was among the founding members of the Labour Party, a specifically Coloured political party that formally opposed apartheid but participated in the regime's Coloured Persons Representative Council (CRC), a legislative body in appearance only. He participated in apartheid institutions, while opposing segregation; he served the Coloured community, while objecting to a system that had marked Coloured people out for dispossession and discrimination. In many ways, his career encapsulated the dilemmas facing Coloured people under apartheid — with which, to his credit, he wrestled constantly.

---

21   South African History Online. "The apartheid government establishes a Department for Coloured Affairs' (CAD)." URL: https://www.sahistory. org.za/dated-event/apartheid-government-establishes-department-coloured-affairs-cad. Accessed on 29 Sep. 2021.

22   Ibid. "On 17th November 1921 Professor Richard van der Ross was born in Plumstead, Cape Town." URL: https://www.sahistory.org.za/dated-event/17th-november-1921-professor-richard-van-der-ross-was-born-plumstead-cape-town. Accessed on 29 Sep. 2021.

Van der Ross had actually opposed the creation of UWC in 1960, but later joined it as a member of the faculty.[23] As rector, Van der Ross sought to transcend the contradictions at the heart of UWC by building its capacities and reputation as an academic institution. That meant attracting scholars to teach there, and building facilities to accommodate a growing student population, as well as research facilities. However odd a position UWC occupied within the apartheid system, Van der Ross and his Coloured colleagues were determined to ensure that the education they provided was, at least, a quality one.

Another important Coloured pioneer at UWC was Jakes Gerwel, who obtained a Bachelor of Arts degree and Honours (a year-long, post-B.A. degree) in Afrikaans, Dutch, and Sociology in the late 1960s. Gerwel also studied in Brussels, Belgium, and was appointed in 1972 to an entry-level position as a lecturer in Afrikaans and Dutch at UWC.[24]

Gerwel would later become one of Rhoda's colleagues, and among her closest friends, even sharing office space with her in UWC's Faculty of Arts building. He began to cause a political stir as he climbed through the academic ranks, challenging not only the apartheid system, but the role of UWC within it. He would eventually emerge as one of the most important academic influences on the anti-apartheid struggle, director-general, or chief of staff, to President Nelson Mandela in the first post-apartheid government.

Rhoda attended UWC during this tumultuous stage of its history. She found Library Science tedious, and was more drawn to anthropology and English. Increasingly, however, what was most interesting of all was what was going on outside the classroom, within student organizations, in the faculty lounge, and on the campus grounds.

A new intellectual movement known as Black Consciousness, led by medical student Steve Biko, was sweeping through the academic community, particularly among "non-white" students. Before long, it would have an impact on UWC, as well — and ignite the upheaval that ultimately brought the apartheid system crashing down.

---

23   Malcolm G. Scully, Paul Desruisseaux, and Helen Zille. "South Africa: The Crisis: the Campuses, and Some Messages for Americans." *Chronicle of Higher Education*, 11 Jun. 1986. p. 14.

24   The Jakes Gerwel Foundation. "Who was Jakes Gerwel?". URL: https://jgf.org.za/who-was-jakes-gerwel/. Accessed on 29 Sep. 2021.

Chapter Four:
Black Consciousness

"As a young, vocal black student, the lecturers quite liked me — this was the seventies at the height of intense political confrontation ... I actually raised the questions."[1]

In the late 1960s and early 1970s, the rest of the world was in turmoil. The Prague Spring brought Czechoslovakia a brief respite from communist repression — until the Soviet tanks rolled in. Riots nearly toppled the French government, and swept American cities in the wake of several political assassinations, as hippies created a global counterculture embracing peace and love.

South Africa, in contrast, was experiencing political stability — and stagnation — as the apartheid regime consolidated its power. Much of the anti-apartheid leadership had been sent to prison, driven into exile, or chased underground.

In 1961, The ANC had launched an "armed struggle" against apartheid through its new military wing, Umkhonto we Sizwe ("Spear of the Nation), also known as MK. But the apartheid regime caught Nelson Mandela and several other MK leaders in a sudden raid on their hideout at Lilliesleaf Farm, in Rivonia, near Johannesburg, in 1963. In 1964, Mandela and several of his ANC comrades were sentenced to life imprisonment and sent to Robben Island, off Cape Town's coast.

The ANC's rival, the Pan Africanist Congress (PAC), had also been suppressed. Its leader, Robert Sobukwe, was also imprisoned indefinitely on the infamous Robben Island after its armed wing, Poqo, carried out terrorist attacks.

Thus, even as the wrecking balls and bulldozers rolled across District Six, and the eviction notices were served to the Kadalie family and others in Mowbray, there was little political reaction. Apartheid had no serious domestic opposition, save for the lone dissent voiced by Helen Suzman and her Progressive Party, who were easily dismissed as English-speaking (and often Jewish) elitists from the posh Johannesburg suburb of Houghton.

---

1   Rhoda Kadalie. Unpublished interview with Melanie Walker. 27 Oct. 1994.

South Africa found itself increasingly isolated on the global stage. Many of its athletes and sports teams had been barred from legitimate international competition. International economic sanctions against South Africa began to advance. And the "brain drain" of skilled professionals that began after Sharpeville steadily increased.

Yet the country still exuded self-confidence and achievement. Dr. Christiaan Barnard performed the world's first heart transplant at Cape Town's Groote Schuur hospital. The South African economy boomed; in the early 1970s, the South African Rand was more valuable than the U.S. dollar.

Life in South Africa — for white South Africans, at least — was comfortable, and even idyllic, with many able to afford domestic servants and swimming pools. For "non-white" South Africans, there seemed to be little prospect of political or social change.

It was in that political vacuum that the Black Consciousness movement was born. By the early 1970s, one of the only organized sources of opposition to apartheid was the National Union of South African Students (NUSAS). The group, led by white students, was sympathetic to the cause of black activists. But in the mid-1960s, under increasing scrutiny from the apartheid government, it backed away from formal criticism of the regime. Even though it continued to conduct multi-racial activities, its black members grew frustrated with its quiescence. The white liberals of NUSAS would not challenge the white supremacist system.

In 1968, Steve Biko, then a student at Natal University's Non-European Medical School, founded the South African Students' Organisation (SASO) as an alternative to NUSAS. Unlike NUSAS, the new SASO was entirely black — and by "black," SASO included all "non-white" students. Historian R.W. Johnson notes:

> Though influenced by the American Black Power movement, Biko and his followers developed a peculiarly South African form of Black Consciousness, embracing African, Indian and Coloured students not only into one organisation but also into one self-definition, that they were all black. The ideology of Black Consciousness (BC, as it was known) was projected as the ideology of all non-white South Africans and consisted in asserting black values, black pride and a black challenge not only to the white apartheid state but also to the liberal views of many white sympathisers. BC purported to be non-racial but its appeal to a younger generation was often that it legitimated their rejection of all things white and insisted that they determined their own destiny.

...

Ironically, at first the government did not mind: convinced that its troubles came from white communists, it saw BC as a welcome counterweight — and even a partial affirmation of the need for separate black homelands. Moreover, the BC movement did not try to mount an organisational challenge: there were no mass demonstrations or protests and it did not even have a political programme. Its method lay simply in 'conscientising' its following through a network of classes throughout the country.[2]

Though its political influence had yet to be felt, Black Consciousness "spread like wildfire on the tribal college campuses, and from there it quickly reached the townships and the schools" Johnson notes. UWC was one such "tribal" campus, and Black Consciousness arrived just as young Rhoda Kadalie did.

***

UWC's role in the anti-apartheid struggle was perhaps inevitable, despite its origins as a separate, Coloured institution within the apartheid system. As UWC English professor Julia Martin would later write of the regime's plans for the campus:

In all their proud assertions, the authorities had somehow not anticipated that, in building an institution of education, they were creating the conditions in which people could actually become educated.

The other thing the planners did not foresee was that assembling a number of the oppressed together in one place would enable them to organise.[3]

The political awakening of UWC took place gradually — and, initially, outside the classroom. Gerwel recalled being introduced to Marxist ideas in the 1960s in small study groups.[4] In 1966, several UWC students boycotted the campus memorial service for Prime Minister Hendrik Verwoerd, who

---

2   R.W. Johnson. *South Africa: The First Man, the Last Nation.* Johannesburg: Jonathan Ball, 2004. 163-4.

3   Julia Martin. "An open space." Premesh Lalu and Noëleen Murray, eds. *Becoming UWC: Reflections, pathways, and unmaking apartheid's legacy.* "Full circle: concerning UWC's academic value." Cape Town: Centre for Humanities Research (University of the Western Cape), 2012. 26.

4   Premesh Lalu. "Campus: A discourse on the grounds of an apartheid university." Premesh Lalu and Noëleen Murray, eds. *Becoming UWC: Reflections, pathways, and unmaking apartheid's legacy.* "Full circle:

had been stabbed to death in Parliament by a deranged assassin.[5] In 1970, a student named Desmond Demas refused to obey the campus dress code, which required men to wear ties to lectures. The tie came to represent conformity and subservience to the apartheid regime's cultural dictates and its philosophy of Christian National Education, intent on churning out like-minded Coloureds who would support the status quo. Demas was expelled, provoking a successful protest in which students burned their ties,[6] or engaged in "imaginative fun" such as wearing ties with regular T-shirts.[7]

***

The changing racial politics of UWC were a challenge for Rhoda, and her classmates, to navigate. Throughout her life, Rhoda never thought of herself primarily in racial terms. When she became politically conscious, she rejected the label "Coloured" as a creation of the apartheid government to divide the population. She, like many who were influenced by Black Consciousness, preferred simply to be known as "black."

And yet she also knew that there was something real, and substantive, and worth celebrating in her uniquely Coloured identity — something the apartheid regime could not define, and the liberation movement could not wish away.

In private moments, she and her colleagues at UWC — who included some of the future luminaries of the post-apartheid institutional order — would joke about creating an entire field of academic study devoted to Coloured culture and identity (see Chapter 14). Much of it centered around food: trifle pudding at Christmas, late-night Gatsby sandwiches — curried meat on a submarine loaf, stuffed with potato chips and doused in sauces.

There was also the *Kaapse taal*, the Cape dialect of Afrikaans slang; the impossibly complex syncretism of intermarried Muslim and Christian communities; and the *klopse*, the hopelessly politically incorrect minstrels, parading gaily in blackface.

The Coloured people of South Africa are a small minority, and in some ways an accidental one, created by liaisons between European

concerning UWC's academic value." Cape Town: Centre for Humanities Research (University of the Western Cape), 2012. 40.

5   Heike Becker. "South African student protests, 1968 to 2016." *International Socialist Review* 111, Winter 2018-19. URL: https://isreview. org/issue/111/south-african-student-protests-1968-2016/index.html. Accessed on 30 Sep. 2021.

6   Lalu, ibid.

7   Becker, ibid.

settlers and indigenous herders, and by the cosmopolitan mix of slaves, sailors, and merchants at the Cape.

To be "Coloured" was to be both old, and new. The population traces its roots back centuries, before the arrival of Europeans in the mid-17th century, or the southward migration of African tribes who clashed with white settlers. Rhoda herself found, through a genetic analysis, that she was partly descended from the Khoisan people, the native "bushmen" of the Cape.

And yet in contemporary South Africa, new Coloured people can be generated over time. Under apartheid, any interracial coupling between a white and a black South African could produce a child that would be classified as Coloured by the regime.

The comedian Trevor Noah, who went on to stardom in the U.S., wrote in his memoir, *Born a Crime*, that since his father was white, and his mother Xhosa, their illicit liaison made him something else entirely — a Coloured. To this day, many South Africans still regard children who would be called "biracial" in the U.S. as Coloured.

Coloured culture has been, moreover, adaptive, and dynamic, appropriating elements of Western and African culture, as well as Islamic traditions and themes of popular culture. The minstrels of the *klopse*, for example, came about because of the popularity of traveling Wild West and vaudeville shows, arriving by ship in the late nineteenth and early twentieth centuries. The Coloured population adapted the vaudeville style to existing local celebrations such as *Tweede Neuwe Jaar*, the Second New Year, celebrating the emancipation from slavery under British rule in 1834.

Among the creations of Coloured culture was Afrikaans itself. The high language of white nationalism was actually a pidgin dialect, invented in the kitchens of the Cape, which enabled the members of a diverse population to communicate with one another. It was based on Dutch, but incorporated elements of English, African languages, and even Malaysian terms. It was first written down in Arabic, by Islamic teachers who had traveled from the Ottoman Empire and needed to learn the local jargon to instruct their congregants.

To be Coloured was, and is, to live in several different worlds, and embrace those contradictions.

Though there are other *mestizo* or creole communities worldwide, there are few other places in Africa to be Coloured. Even within South Africa, the community is poorly understood outside the Western and Northern Cape. Asserting Coloured identity within the context of the anti-apartheid struggle was difficult.

It was the emergence of SASO that ultimately electrified the campus. SASO and its philosophy of Black Consciousness not only represented an ideological challenge to apartheid at its core, they also rejected the apartheid government's elaborate distinctions among "non-white" groups. These had allowed the white minority to divide and rule, and co-opted some of the victims by granting them some privileges within the system.

In embracing Black Consciousness, Coloured activists could cut the Gordian knot that constrained the political choices of an earlier generation of academics, such as Richard van der Ross. They could join the anti-apartheid movement as equals, and even lead it.

UWC students brought SASO onto campus in defiance of the university administration. A student named Henry Isaacs, who was elected president of the officially recognized Student Representative Council (SRC), also was elected chair of SASO on campus. As Dr. Jean Swanson-Jacobs later explained:

> *The SRC was affiliated to South African Students' Organisation (Saso) and Henry was the president of both. The task of every Saso member was to "conscientise" as many people as possible — to make them aware that they were black, and that the labels of "coloured, Indian, and African" were racial tags intended to divide and rule the black majority.*[8]

The university would not recognize the SRC, and Isaacs would eventually be expelled and subjected to a "banning" order by the government, which made it unlawful for him to address public meetings. But a broader movement had arisen, confronting the UWC administration throughout 1972 and 1973 and issuing lists of demands, which included the hiring of a black rector, recruitment of more black faculty, and the equalization of pay among black and white staff. (The term "black" was used, not "Coloured.") By 1973, the students' manifesto declared: "We reject completely the idea of separate ethnic universities."[9]

The students' demands were rejected, leading to protests that forced administrators to call in the police and shut down the university.[10]

---

8   Jean Swanson-Jacobs. "Unsung hero helped transform UWC terrain." *Cape Times* 2 Oct. 2009. URL: https://www.pressreader.com/south-africa/cape-times/20091002/282428460238601. Accessed on 30 Sep. 2021.

9   Lalu, ibid. 46.

10   South African History Online. "Black Consciousness and student revolt in the Cape." URL: https://www.sahistory.org.za/article/black-consciousness-and-student-revolt-cape. Accessed on 30 Sep. 2021.

In June 1973, the university announced that campus would be closed to all students for a month, and that all who wished to continue their studies would have to re-apply for admission, "and undertake to endorse all rules and regulations of the University and to submit to the authority of the University Authorities."[11] The protests continued and spread, with black staff members rallying behind the students and the cause of a "fair and just South Africa" that was "totally free."[12]

Soon, the protest moved beyond the campus itself, with student leaders addressing a crowd of some 12,000 supporters in the Coloured township of Athlone. The rally included speakers who were a cross-section of the nascent anti-apartheid movement — including Chief Mangosuthu Buthelezi, who would later play a controversial role as leader of the KwaZulu tribal homeland, and of the Inkatha Freedom Party, a Zulu rival to the ANC.[13]

Buthelezi linked the struggles of students at UWC to the broader struggle against apartheid, providing a detailed history of discriminatory policies on Coloured education and describing it as an essential component of white minority rule. Reflecting on his own political activism at the University of Fort Hare, from which he had been expelled in 1950, Buthelezi addressed the student activists in the first person plural, and urged the authorities to forego any penalties against those who had participated in demonstrations:

> *If South African Society was not structured on Racism we would not be in the situation we are in today. Had policies pursued by all the White Regimes since 1652 [the date of Dutch arrival at the Cape] not been based on Racism we would not be experiencing this trouble our young people find themselves bogged in at the University of the Western Cape.*
>
> ...
>
> *The principle of Separate but Equal did not apply as Black Professors and Lecturers had to earn, "kaffir, coolie, and coon" [all pejorative terms] salaries, and their White Counterparts had to earn higher salaries which their White Skins and not qualifications earned them.*

11   University of the Western Cape Registrar. "Notice: Closure of University." 11 Jun. 1973. Jakes Gerwel Archives, Nelson Mandela Foundation.

12   Black Staff Association. "Statement by Black Staff Association Addressed to the Student Body." 12 Jun. 1973.

13   Ibid.

Rhoda: 'Comrade Kadalie, You Are Out of Order!'

We see the White man's hypocrisy in telling the World that he is establishing Black Universities when these are areas of a new type of Colonisation.

...

There is no doubt that the whole nature and style of running these Universities was influenced by the fact that they were for a voteless and therefore a voiceless people who had no means of effectualising their objections. It is obvious that it was an Educational system tailored by the powerful for the powerless done with the intention of ensuring that these Universities produced "good Kaffirs, Hottnots, and Coolies".

We hated this "benevolent despotism", but in the absence of anything else we had to use what was there, despite the simmering discontent within the Black Community.

Is it therefore surprising that young sensitive minds of our youth find this so sickening that they have expressed their indignation in such an unorthodox manner?

...

I think we should be grateful for the moderate protestations of Students despite all this provocative set-up in their so-called Universities. I wish to appeal to the powers-that-be to save these young people and this Country by acting reasonably in this particular case. ... What Students have done simmers in the heart of every Black man in South Africa, and the only thing they have done is to express it in a dramatic manner typical of Students throughout the world.[14]

The protests continued, with students and faculty uniting in demand that the students be reinstated.

Ultimately, the UWC administration backed off its demand that students reapply for admission, and appointed a commission of inquiry to evaluate students' grievances. The subsequent report said that students had been misled by SASO, and identified Gerwel as a key figure in the unrest, warning that he had embraced concepts of Black Consciousness in his writings.[15] But in a key concession, the administration appointed Van der Ross as the first Coloured rector.

---

14 Mangosuthu Buthelezi. Speech at Athlone Stadium, Athlone, Cape Town, South Africa. 8 Jul. 1973. Jakes Gerwel Archive, Nelson Mandela Foundation.
15 Lalu, ibid., 49.

The regime, Rhoda recalled, saw Van der Ross as an accommodating figure. True, he opposed apartheid; however, he was willing to work within the government system, leading the government to believe he could be co-opted. Many students resented him, for the same reason: he was vilified by radicals on campus, and treated with disdain. Yet Rhoda recalled: "He retained an autonomy and an authenticity that was often *dwars*" — i.e. contrarian.

Van der Ross attempted to explain what he acknowledged as the "crises" on UWC's campus:

In many ways, the University of the Western Cape is ideally situated for crises. It is exposed to all the problems which beset all universities, but some of these are accentuated by the fact that this is supposed to be the only university to serve the Coloured people. Now, the Coloured people are far from being a homogeneous group. There are wide differences in regard to geographic distribution, occupation, educational background, social class and ethnic origin. In the case of White South Africans, some of these differences are accommodated by the fact that their needs are catered for by eleven universities spread over the country, thus allowing students to satisfy their needs as to regional zone, language, social class, tradition of the institution or of the student's family, and even religion or political orientation. The student can choose an institution to suit his peculiar needs and so, hopefully, some of the crises which would stem from poor adaptation, do not arise.

But at the U.W.C. we gather them all together, urban and rural, English and Afrikaans, Catholic, Protestant and Muslim, middle-class and working class, the English-oriented Natalie and the South West African of German descent, those from well-equipped schools with highly qualified teachers and those from schools with much poorer offerings, those who have acquired relatively easy relationships with white people, and those who have never before communicated with Whites, those from a politically-enlightened background, and those who had never been introduced to the controversies of politics. Surely it would be strange if some hundreds of young people whose lives had been subjected to such diverse influences were to be put together, physically and mentally, and if there were to be no crises and no outward, visible demonstration of such crises.

...

Yet crises are not necessarily bad; indeed there are times when they become inevitable, and there are those who might hold that my very investiture here tonight is the outcome of a crisis. If only we could learn to resolve our crises by rational discussion rather than by violence, we might proceed more rapidly towards mutual understanding and general happiness. As a University, this would enable us to place the accent where it belongs, i.e. on people and their individual worth, and on scholarship. Basically, a university is a merit organization, not a democratic one in the sense that issues are decided by a show of hands. The properties of a triangle as taught in Mathematics, or the atomic weight of substances as taught in Chemistry are not decided at a mass meeting, yet it is another of those anomalies of life that material of a high level of objective appraisal is conveyed by and to human beings who are not all equally objective in their approach.[16]

A decade later, in 1985, after the country had erupted in protest against the apartheid regime, Van der Ross would give another lecture, reflecting on the challenge facing UWC in particular, and suggesting that the university should offer counsel to students, not lead them to the barricades:

The [nonconformist, activist group] would describe itself as radical political, often rejecting the motive of upward social mobility as being inimical to the cause of liberation. This, however, leads to great dilemmas, as the same students who will, on the one hand, act as though they deny that they wish to condone any features of "the system," will on the other hand, when the crisis has passed, seek to be part of the system once more, desiring participation in tests, re-writing of examinations missed, continuation of State and private sector bursaries, etc. etc.

...

We must not be insensitive to the ongoing political and economic questions, but neither must we assume the full responsibility for correcting the ills in those areas. We must not betray the youth, or the parents, by behaving in such a manner that we frustrate their desires of upward social mobility whilst enjoying the fruits of such mobility ourselves.

...

Let me give an example. Many of our students, influenced no doubt by many ideas gained inside or outside university, reject capitalism, say that they would prefer socialism, identify comfortable living and upward

---

16   Inaugural Address of Rector and Vice Chancellor of the University of the Western Cape R.E. van der Ross. City Hall, Cape Town. 3 Mar. 1975. Jakes Gerwel Archive, Nelson Mandela Foundation.

social mobility with capitalism, and therefore by association are left with grave dilemmas as to their own integrity, let alone the integrity of their lectures.

Surely our role should be, if we identify these dilemmas, to bring about some degree of help. ... If we have answers why not share them, together with the reasons therefor. If we have no answers, why not share the experience of searching for the answers, thereby creating an atmosphere of intellectual vigour and honesty.[17]

Decades later, Rhoda would praise Van der Ross for his emphasis on UWC's educational mission, focusing on the future of the students even as they fought for the future of the nation.[18]

Despite Van der Ross's efforts, radical storms continued to brew on campus, and activism continued to move in a more radical direction. One leaflet, calling on students to boycott classes in August 1975, declared in ALL CAPS:

BLACK STUDENTS, STRIKE NOW! STRIKE AND YOU WILL DESTROY BANTU AND INDIAN EDUCATION. COLOURED, BANTU AND INDIAN EDUCATION MOULDS US INTO SLAVES TO SERVE THE WHITES ... THROUGHOUT THE YEAR YOU MUST CONFRONT THE OPPRESSORS. ONLY THEN WILL YOU DESTROY SLAVE EDUCATION AND LIBERATE AZANIA [a radical name for an envisioned post-liberation South Africa]. ... NO WHITE WILL GIVE US LIBERATION. WHY WILL HE GIVE US LIBERATION IF IT IS TO HIS BENEFIT WE REMAIN SLAVES. MAKE THINGS BAD FOR HIM. IF YOU STRIKE YOU SCARE HIM. USE VIOLENCE! THAT WILL REALLY SCARE HIM. BURN HIS MANSIONS AND HIS FACTORIES AND INSTRUMENTS OF OPPRESSION (BARS, BOTTLE STORES). CRIPPLE THE ECONOMY. USE VIOLENCE BECAUSE HE USES VIOLENCE. ... IF ALL BOYCOTT THE SYSTEM CAN'T DO A THING. ALL MUST BOYCOTT MON 11 & 12 AUGUST. BOYCOTT CLASSES AND END OPPRESSION. DON'T LISTEN TO TEACHERS WHO TRY TO SCARE. DO YOU WANT TO PASS EXAMS AT THE COST OF FREEDOM? FREEDOM IS MORE VALUABLE THAN A SLAVE EDUCATION. ... REMEMBER IF YOU DON'T BOYCOTT BECAUSE OF EXAMS YOU SELL YOUR FREEDOM. THAT SLAVE CERTIFICATE MEANS NOTHING.

---

17   Richard van der Ross. "The Role of the University of the Western Cape in [the] South African Situation Today." Lecture, University of the Western Cape, Bellville, South Africa. 1 Mar. 1985.

18   Ibid.

PASS IT AROUND[19]

Students were also involved in political struggles off campus, such as resistance against the apartheid government's policy of forced removals, which were still ongoing. For example, they protested against the removal of a squatter camp along Modderdam road, the street alongside UWC's campus.[20] The sprawling settlement had been home to "Africans" who had been ejected from Cape Town for lack of a "pass"; it was demolished by two bulldozers in August 1977.[21]

In the spirit of Black Consciousness, overtures from students at the country's mainstream "white" universities were often met with disdain. In 1974, for example, student leaders at UWC considered a motion to reject an invitation from students at UCT to participate in a joint sporting and social event. The motion called the invitation "fraudulent, false-hearted and ignominious," and declared "that acceptance of such an invitation would militate directly against our deeply held philosophy of BLACK CONSCIOUSNESS as well as our conviction and principles."[22] The motion further mocked the alleged efforts of "liberal" institutions like UCT to conceal the brutality of apartheid with a veneer of multi-racial cooperation, declaring that "white students at UCT are trying to placate their guilt-ridden consciousness and also attempting to convince the outside world that BLACKS and whites are harmoniously living and playing together in South Africa." Concluding that "our Black experience has taught us that whites should be shunned and are not to be trusted," and that the "slave-slavemaster relationship between Blacks and whites in South Africa" meant that there could never be "meaningful dialogue" between the two sides until full political equality had been reached, the invitation was rejected with "utter contempt."

The UWC administration, with Van der Ross nominally at the helm, attempted to keep radical sentiments from overtaking the mundane task of providing an education to South Africa's future leaders. Occasionally,

19   Leaflet. Undated, 1975. Jakes Gerwel Archive, Nelson Mandela Foundation.
20   Rhoda Kadalie. "The wanton destruction of UWC." PoliticsWeb, 18 Nov. 2015. URL: https://www.politicsweb.co.za/news-and-analysis/the-wanton-destruction-of-uwc. Accessed on 17 Jun. 2022.
21   "Aerial view of Modderdam Road squatter camp, Cape Town." University of Cape Town Libraries Digital Collections. URL: https://digitalcollections.lib.uct.ac.za/collection/islandora-16836. Accessed on 17 Jun. 2022.
22   Motion, 1974. Jakes Gerwel Archive. Nelson Mandela Foundation. Original emphasis. I was not able to determine whether the motion passed.

van der Ross would even ban meetings on campus, hoping to keep boycott efforts at bay and to minimize disruption to classes.[23]

But events soon overtook both the university's and the government's ability to maintain control.

On June 16, 1976, a SASO-led, Black Consciousness-inspired protest in the black Johannesburg township of Soweto against a new government policy requiring Afrikaans to be used in elementary schools as the language of instruction led to the Soweto riots. South Africa would never be the same.

* * *

Rhoda arrived on campus in 1972 in the midst of all the political turmoil, which would come to define her academic experience — and her career.

Rhoda on the UWC campus, c. 1972 (Courtesy Rhoda Kadalie)

At first, Rhoda recalled, she was largely an observer, in the heady, early days of activism. She did not participate directly in SASO, nor in the

---

23   R.E. van der Ross. Memorandum. 20 Sep. 1977. Jakes Gerwel Archive, Nelson Mandela Foundation.

protests: "I was too young and a freshman," she recalled.[24] She was also "quite a conservative Christian," she later recalled, though she later was drawn to liberal theology.[25]

She was also exposed to feminism for the first time. She later recalled:

Feminism, to me, wasn't a Damascus Road, you know, where I suddenly saw the light. I came from a family of seven brothers. I'm the third eldest. And academically as a child I did very well which means that my brothers sort of had an inferiority complex towards me because I was [then] the only daughter, and a clever daughter, and so I didn't have to stand back. Because I was the only daughter, I was also spoilt rotten. ... [W]hen I came to university, feminism became an intellectual thing. At university ... I experienced discrimination unlike at home. And I think that was quite a revelation. I was always an outspoken person. I was always quite vociferous and the nice thing about being a student was I could debate with male students equally. I never saw myself as intellectually inferior as a woman — even though I was a woman, I liked being a woman.[26]

As her feminist identity was emerging, Rhoda began to participate in the anti-apartheid movement on campus, almost as a matter of course. "We all went to mass meetings, we were involved in our clubs debating the issues — liberation theology, revolution, or working within the system."[27]

Black Consciousness and SASO had created a space at UWC for those who were ongoing victims of the apartheid system to step outside of their experience, to examine it, and to challenge the foundations of the regime.

Rhoda's program of study in Library Science was, unlike many other South African disciplines, a four-year degree, rather than three. She completed the fifteen required courses, and graduated in 1975 with a Bachelor of Library Science (B.Lib.Sc), becoming the first member of the extended Kadalie family to graduate from university. Her degree qualified her to work in any academic institution around the globe.

Rhoda took the opportunity to travel after graduation, visiting Europe for six weeks as an exchange student in 1975 — the first of many overseas adventures, many undertaken in an academic context.[28] It was the first of what would become many trips abroad throughout her career.

---

24   Personal communication with the author.
25   Rhoda Kadalie. Unpublished interview with Melanie Walker, ibid.
26   Ibid.
27   Rhoda Kadalie, interview with Melanie Walker, ibid.
28   Rhoda Kadalie. Curriculum Vitae. 1992.

Fenner and Joan with Rhoda at a celebration for her 21st birthday, 1974
(Courtesy Rhoda Kadalie)

In 1979, Rhoda returned to Europe, visiting France, the Netherlands, and the United Kingdom. In addition to sightseeing, she spent time with South African anti-apartheid activists abroad, including trade unionist Ismail Meer. In England, she visited and traveled with the Field family, where John was enjoying a sabbatical year in Plymouth.

But while Rhoda loved to explore the world, the study of anthropology had caught Rhoda's attention — as it did many other South African students in the 1970s and 1980s.

Fenner and Joan with Rhoda at her graduation from UWC, 1975
(Courtesy Rhoda Kadalie)

Rhoda at the Anne Frank monument, Amsterdam, Netherlands, 1975
(Courtesy Rhoda Kadalie)

Rhoda enjoys an ice cream while visiting the Netherlands in 1979
(Courtesy Rhoda Kadalie)

She would later explain that anthropology gave her the tools to understand her own experience in South Africa, through the comparative study of others: "Anthropology, I think, is one of the disciplines that really forces you to look at other cultures in order to understand yourself."[29] As a lecturer, she would later challenge her students to examine their own prejudices — confronting her students, for example, with the idea that the African custom of "lobola," the cattle paid by a groom to the father of a bride, was not unique but bore some similarities to the practice, popular in the Coloured community, of providing a bride with a generous trousseau.

In South Africa's racially stratified society, anthropology also provided a means to cross the color lines — often in a subversive way. Scholars studying the cultures of South Africa's various communities could often witness firsthand what apartheid was doing to them, in a way few others were allowed to see. They were also able to document the emerging resistance to apartheid.

29 Rhoda Kadalie, "Woman Today," ibid.

UWC Anthropology Society, in Saldanha, Western Cape, c. 1975
(Courtesy Rhoda Kadalie)

Part of the subterfuge related to the ongoing change in the discipline of anthropology itself. South Africa was regarded as a global leader in biological or physical anthropology, thanks to the fact that many of the world's oldest hominid remains were found in the country. The renowned Dr. Philip Tobias of the University of the Witwatersrand was regarded as an international authority on the origins of the human species.

Social or cultural anthropology had emerged as a discipline through which to document the practices and beliefs of supposedly primitive peoples, who were often — as in Native American reservations — to be managed by government authorities. The apartheid regime was quite comfortable with anthropology — initially known as "*volkekunde*" in Afrikaans — in that mode, as such scholarship could reinforce racial and ethnic identity and difference, and thus the ideology of separate development.

As anthropologist John S. Sharp observed in 1981:

[I]n so far as South African volkekunde deals in more than descriptive ethnography, it assigns overwhelming explanatory power to the phenomenon of ethnicity, which it conceives in the narrowest, most rigid

terms possible. Ethnos theory starts with the proposition that mankind is divided into volke (nations, peoples) and that each volk has its own particular culture, which may change but always remains authentic to the group in question. The entity comprising a group and its culture is an ethnos, which, viewed over time and in relation to its physical and social environment, forms a life-process within which individuals exist. An individual is born into a particular volk; its members are socialized into its attendant culture; therefore they acquire a volkspersoonlikheid (a volk-personality). It follows that the most important influence on an individual's behaviour in any social context is his ethnos membership.[30]

This concept of anthropology was not uniform throughout South African academia — and it came under increasing scrutiny over time. Eventually, anthropologists began to see their work as giving voice to the people they studied, including their political reactions to government policies. It was no accident, for example, that musician Johnny Clegg, whose Zulu-infused rock challenged apartheid boundaries and was banned on South African radio in the 1980s, was also an academic anthropologist.

Anthropology became one of the most politically-conscious and left-wing disciplines, not just in South Africa but worldwide. In South Africa, anthropology provided a way to celebrate the country's diversity — and to push back against the brutal way in which that diversity was enforced by a state hierarchy.

Not that it was easy. Rhoda described her experience on campus as one of "culture shock." UWC was a campus, she would later say, designed for Coloured students — but run by the Broederbond. Faculty members were brought in from Afrikaans-speaking universities, and academic materials were often in Afrikaans — not the practical, everyday language she spoke fluently, and certainly not the local *Kaapse taal* dialect, but a complicated, scientific Afrikaans.

Rhoda recalled spending a great deal of effort in the early years of her university career translating Afrikaans texts into English so that she could understand them. In her psychology courses, she recalled, the word for "emotion" was not the familiar *"emosie,"* but rather the elaborate *"gemoedsaandoening"*; "perception" was not *"persepsie"* but *"gewaarwording."* The work was tough, but it gave her a renewed appreciation for the flexibility of Afrikaans, even as the language was becoming a political target.

30   John S. Sharp. "The Roots and Development of *Volkekunde* in South Africa." *Journal of Southern African Studies*, Vol. 8, No. 1, 1981. p. 19.

In addition to her formal studies, Rhoda began learning about other ideas that were not taught in class — and, indeed, which administrators hoped to suppress, or at least discourage. These included Black Consciousness and its various forms, such as liberation theology, which Rhoda and her student peers began to encounter in various Christian organizations on campus. Blackness, as a positive assertion against whiteness, became a hotly debated topic, engaging students for weeks with arguments that spilled over from lunch breaks and student groups, and eventually entered the classroom as well.

Students had a love-hate relationship with their lecturers. Some were out-and-out racists, while others considered their work at UWC to be like that of missionaries, "discovering Coloureds as humans," Rhoda later recalled. One academic, when asked why he wished to teach at UWC, was reported to have said: "*Ek stel belang in die kleurling as mens*" ("I am interested in the Coloured as a human being").

Rhoda found it difficult to despise such members of the faculty, many the epitome of politeness and humane condescension, who took seriously the task of educating the "natives." The head of *volkekunde*, Rhoda recalled, was one such teacher:

> He genuinely loved his class of 13, of which I was one. Regaling us day in and day out about the Zulus, the subjects of his fieldwork research, he wanted us to know how much he appreciated our views and learnt from us. Though he was often the object of ridicule by students, it was hard not to like him. One of my first essays moved him to tears, in which I disputed one of the readings in our anthropology textbook, which claimed that non-literate peoples resort to magic when they fail to understand the world around them. He inspired me to take a leading role in UWC's Anthropology Society, taking students on ethnographic excursions and to student conferences.[31]

Rhoda found that it was possible to learn from such professors, despite the fact that they indulged racial prejudices and were willing participants in a segregated educational system. They still had knowledge to impart, and Rhoda was determined to make the most of the opportunity.

After graduating with her Bachelor's degree, Rhoda pursued an Honours degree in anthropology at UWC, attending courses on a part-time basis while she worked as a student assistant in the university's anthropology department. She managed UWC's Anthropology Society, and

---

31   Rhoda Kadalie, personal communication with the author.

chaperoned students on trips to remote locations throughout the country, where they were participating in projects or conducting fieldwork.

She would later remember:

Proceeding to Honours in anthropology was a logical progression in my love for the subject and my subsequent appointment to Senior Lab Assistant in the Anthropology Department. Soon I started teaching first-years. The classes were huge, and included part-time classes at night as well for professionals who worked during the day.

This gave me lots of power and space to bring about change and transform the department from "volkekunde" to anthropology by demanding diversity in our roster of external examiners, who were mainly recruited from the Universities of Stellenbosch and Pretoria; we later added examiners from UCT and [liberal, English-speaking] Rhodes University in Grahamstown. The thrust of this change started with seminal debates about the cooptation of indigenous populations by colonialists using ethnography and fieldwork to gain access to the colonized across the globe, moving on to South Africa's own checkered history of volkekunde scholars advising the apartheid government about "homeland" policy based on reified notions of tribal cultures.

Those debates led Rhoda to work on a new book of keywords, helping to redefine the language of the discipline of anthropology in South Africa in a more inclusive way.

In the early days of her work, she was the only black student surrounded by white faculty — and, often, the only woman. "As a young anthropologist," she later recalled, "I took students on excursions and I was shocked by the sexual harassment which took place on those excursions. For example, I was young [and] black, and the males ... when they got drunk [they would confess] all of their fantasies about having an affair with a young lecturer. And I had to deal with that — it was, I think, quite daunting."[32]

After three years of combining work and study, Rhoda completed her Honours degree in 1977, graduating in 1978. She continued to work at UWC — this time, as a lecturer, joining the faculty and teaching a new generation of students, hoping to climb the academic ladder. She later described herself as a "token black woman," but found that she was

---

32   Rhoda Kadalie, interview with Melanie Walker, ibid.

also taken seriously "because of the questions black students are raising about anthropology."[33]

Rhoda became notorious for challenging her students to push their own boundaries. She would provoke debates in class: she began one lecture by declaring, "All men are rapists!", then challenging students to defend and oppose the claim. She assigned them unusual projects, such as interviewing political detainees.[34] She also confronted their own cultural stereotypes, making them debate topics that were culturally taboo, such as rape. She would later bring her daughter, Julia, to work with her, and breastfeed her during classes, declaring, "This is feminism in action." Her lectures were packed, and often boisterous. To male students, she was an enticing, at times infuriating, enigma; to female students, she was an inspiration.

"I wasn't proud of my own education," she recalled, "so I made sure that I challenged my students regularly. ... I didn't tolerate nonsense. I put a lot of effort into my teaching, and there were lots of students who didn't like me because I was impatient when they were slack."[35] But to many, she was their favorite lecturer, feared yet appreciated.

Soon, she experienced what she would call her "absolute" liberation as a woman: buying a car. Though still living at home, Rhoda had the freedom to come home when she wished — to work as hard as she wanted, and to date whomever she wanted.

She recalled later that she brought her feminist principles into her dating experiences. After she rebuffed one determined suitor, her mother insisted that Rhoda give him at least one date. She agreed, but on condition that she drive. "It went well," she remembered, "but then he wanted me to hang around late in evening and I said no, I'm going home at 9 p.m. and that's that. I dropped him off at home, and he phoned my mum the next day to say her daughter is really something else. I don't think guys expected that in those days!"[36]

But political unrest made teaching, learning, and social life difficult. Classes at UWC were frequently interrupted by confrontations between students and police. After the Soweto riots in 1976, UWC was caught up in nationwide student demonstrations that turned violent and destructive.

The Rector, Van der Ross, later recalled:

---

33   Ibid.
34   "Rhoda Kadalie: a strident voice for South Africa's oppressed," ibid.
35   Rhoda Kadalie, quoted by Sharon Sorour, p. 78, ibid.
36   Rhoda Kadalie, quoted by "Guaranteed Authentic." *The Oprah Magazine*, Jul. 2007. p. 103.

On our campus, the events of 1976 brought forth strong reverberations. Our student body reacted to the events which shook South Africa in a very direct manner. It could not have been otherwise.

...

It is important to note that the students' problems were not rooted in the University situation in the narrower, academic sense. They were protesting against something else, against the social order, against the political structure, against the economic arrangements in South African society. This is clearly shown by the fact that their first — and, I believe, sincere — reaction to the events following 16th June in Soweto was to ask for a period to hold a symposium so that they might "sort themselves out." This week was granted, and lectures were suspended, so that they might assess their own position in the South African situation.

Why, then, did the situation change from orderly discussion to campus protest, class boycotts, lecture disruption, and arson?[37]

After grappling with several possible explanations, Van der Ross expressed a hope for "constructive change." But tempers would not cool soon. And amid the thrill of the struggle, and the liveliness of political debate, there was also constant fear. Van der Ross himself received threats from students, which he revealed in a memorandum to the university in August 1976.[38]

The rector did his best to discourage boycotts and other disruptions, calling a proposed walkout in 1977 "a most serious transgression" that would "damage the students' academic and professional careers." While conceding that it was the "right" of students to protest, even by leaving classes, no student had the right "to compel other students to do so, to interfere with their studies, or to impose his will on those who wish to remain at university." It was to little avail: the protests continued, year after year, as long as apartheid remained in place.

***

---

37   R.E. van der Ross. "Campus Unrest 1976." *UWC News*, Nov. 1976. Jakes Gerwel Archive, Nelson Mandela Foundation.

38   Rector E.R. van der Ross. Memorandum. 18 Aug. 1976. Jakes Gerwel Archive, Nelson Mandela Foundation.

Vignette: "UWC Student Protests," by Rhoda Kadalie

In my 21-year career at UWC, I witnessed many protests, peaceful and violent. Often overcome with teargas, we brought to work our "struggle *takkies* [sneakers]." When comrades shouted "*hek toe*" ("march to the gate"), we knew the police were around.

One day, I saw armed police in our corridors in the Faculty of Arts and Philosophy. They were strutting past my office, reeking of vengeance. They were spoiling for a fight, as I overheard one of them say "*Vandag, gaan die bloed spat*" ("Today the blood is going to splat").

The students were incensed. The police filled with bloodlust. We just knew that shit would strike the fan in more ways than one.

Several senior academics gathered to avert a bloody confrontation. The police stood on one side with their guns cocked; the students on the other side, shouting "*Een boer, een moer*" ("One Afrikaner, one beating"); and "One man, one bullet." Both were a play on the liberation slogan, "One man, one vote."

It was tense. The academics appealed to the students to cool down, when suddenly mayhem ensued. I fled back to my office, took my car keys and drove to the gate.

At the gate, the students were throwing rocks and stones at the police. I promptly made a U-turn — and landed on the island with my Volkswagen Fun Bug. The students rushed to my car, shouting, "It's comrade Kadalie, help her!". In one fell swoop, they lifted my car, with me inside, off the island, and shoved me back onto campus.

When eventually I arrived home that evening, avoiding the melée, the telephone rang non-stop. Many wanted to know where I was, and sighed a sigh of relief that I was home safe. Why? Because all my colleagues who tried to intervene between students and police were arrested. They looked professorial in their formal teaching attire, and were easily identified in the crowd.

Dressed in a bright pink rain jacket and blue jeans, looking very much like a student, I escaped arrest.

In any case, the one thing I never wanted was to be arrested or be a martyr. I loved my bed more than a jail cell.

***

For the next phase of her career, Rhoda looked back up the mountainside. In 1979, she enrolled for a Master of Arts degree in anthropology at the University of Cape Town. There, she encountered a level of academic rigor and analytical debate for which she felt completely unprepared.

Rhoda and her Volkwagen "Fun Bug," c. 1982 (Courtesy Rhoda Kadalie)

Her academic adviser at UWC, the late Martin West, challenged her to do her best — but was often stern and unforgiving. He once took a 68-page research proposal she had written and tore it up in her face.

Rhoda recalled crying when she had to present her work to classmates — as did Mamphela Ramphele, a fellow graduate student. Ramphele was a well-known anti-apartheid activist who had two children with Steve Biko before he was murdered by apartheid police during his detention in 1977 (she had been pregnant with their second child at the time). Kadalie and Ramphele formed a lasting friendship as they faced a learning curve that was as steep as the slope that separated UCT from UWC on Table Mountain.

Rhoda chose to do her fieldwork in the town of Atlantis, a community built on sand dunes about 40 kilometers north of Cape Town. The town had been planned by the apartheid government as an economic hub for Coloureds. The regime hoped to develop a Coloured middle class, and offered incentives for businesses and factories to move there. It was an experiment in social engineering — one that Rhoda hoped to document. Her proposed title for her thesis was "Problems of Resettlement — Displacement and Survival in a newly-created Growth Point, viz. Atlantis."[39]

She would drive to Atlantis, often alone, in her Volkswagen Fun Bug, or in a university-owned van, in which she also slept. She enjoyed the support of the local population, many of whom had moved to Atlantis with high hopes, but who felt disillusioned after the companies that had moved there proved incapable of providing sustainable jobs.

Envisioned as a manufacturing center, Atlantis soon became a dormitory town, with residents commuting endlessly along sand-swept single-lane roads to menial jobs in Cape Town. Gangs moved into the area, as did alcohol, drugs, and crime. A newspaper clipping from 1979 that Rhoda kept in a diary reported that the provincial government had decided to conduct an inquiry into living conditions in the town after discovering that residents were abandoning the "city of hardship" at the rate of 25 per day.[40]

One night, while Rhoda was in Atlantis, a man attempted to break into her car — while she was in it. Rhoda took to staying overnight in a caravan on the grounds of the local Dutch Reformed Church parish for safety. After four months, she completed her fieldwork. But she struggled to complete her thesis.

In addition to academic challenges, Rhoda faced political ones. The violence at UWC — where Rhoda still worked while pursuing her M.A. in anthropology at UCT — constantly disrupted her schedule, making it impossible to balance work and study. Students had to be prepared to run from police, who would move in with batons, tear gas, Casspir armored vehicles, and rifles. The chaos and the constant commute back-and-forth between teaching at UWC and studying at UCT — crossing apartheid's battle lines in each direction — led Rhoda to abandon her UCT studies.

Still, her experience at UCT proved valuable. As she told an interviewer, "I learnt a hell of a lot ... because I realized that you're not angry when you're criticized. You're not hostile when you tell people

---

39   Rhoda Kadalie. Curriculum Vitae. 1992.
40   "Atlantis warship inquiry is ordered." *Cape Times*, 29 Jun. 1979.

their work is bad or when you raise questions ... I think UCT actually ... contributed to my growth, to my vocality, or my outspokenness."[41]

Her relationships with white colleagues began to change, as well:

The irony [was] that with white males in my department, as much as they were white males, and conventional, they began to treat me as an equal because I was stronger politically, stronger emotionally, and I was also fair to them in a very hostile environment because I could see their good points and I could see their bad points, and present them as human beings ... to my [black] colleagues.

...

I would call it the Broederbond campus, it was so bad, and [yet] because those whites who were nice people were apologetic about their existence, it gave us a lot of space to develop, to be vocal.[42]

At UWC, Rhoda began to insist on higher standards for students and staff, such as punctuality — and chafed at white faculty members who inflated the grades of black students out of empathy for their circumstances. She wanted to instill in her colleagues, black and white, a sense of the academic rigor to which she had been exposed at UCT.

As a result, she later recalled, "for a long time I was actually called a 'bourgeois, divisive feminist' by my own friends. And to me that was actually a compliment. I saw it as setting me apart from 'popular' culture." She credited her religious upbringing, which she described as Calvinist, for her emphasis on honesty and accountability.

Increasingly, Rhoda found herself between several worlds — one of the only people who could navigate South Africa's fractious society. As she later told an interviewer in 1994:

I've known the best of both worlds. I can understand that culture, where it's coming from, where the resentment lies, and I also understand the disgruntlement of Coloureds on this campus because it's part of that continuum of that whole culture ... I am very privileged to have grown up as the daughter of a township pastor with my roots in that stuff. I can laugh, I can be cynical, I can make fun. There is nobody who can make fun of Coloured people in their presence like my brother and I. And my hairdresser kills herself laughing ... because I was telling them, at an autobank [ATM] in a white area you always get notes which are

41   Rhoda Kadalie, interview with Melanie Walker, ibid.
42   Ibid.

81

crispy, in a Coloured area the notes are always dirty, filthy so obviously all the shit money goes there. That makes them crack up with laughter, deeply racist, nowhere in the world can you say that kind of thing. So that's being able to identify. I hang out with these larnie [fancy] whites all my life, live with them, marry them, divorce them, so my life is that contradiction and I can actually be non-racist, or human.[43]

Rhoda was among the few South Africans who could cross cultural and racial boundaries in a time of enforced divisions.

Rhoda participated in many protests, but avoided violent ones, where possible. Van der Ross tried to discourage faculty and students from participating in the unrest. One day, Rhoda had joined a protest inside the campus, marching toward the gates, when she noticed Van der Ross, who lived nearby, driving by in his blue Mercedes.

The next morning, he called her to his office. Rather than disciplining her, he offered her a drink and chastised her gently. While he understood the anger, he said, and felt like protesting himself, it was difficult enough to run the university in ordinary circumstances, hence on occasion he needed staff to work with him to maintain law and order on the campus.

The conversation cemented a friendship between them; Rhoda would attend all of Van der Ross's functions, even family events. Decades later, when he passed away in 2017, Rhoda recalled:

Unlike many university leaders who no longer distinguish between right and wrong, especially in times of turmoil, Prof Van der Ross never lost his moral compass despite the tumultuous 70s and early 80s. The Soweto Uprising and political upheavals that followed were not easy to navigate.

Between the stormy waters of a recalcitrant apartheid state and militant students, Vice-Chancellor Van der Ross acquitted himself with dignity and aplomb, using reason to argue that our methods of protest sometimes weakened our cause and were often counter-productive.

Rather than placate or appease students, he put himself on the front line of the Struggle as mediator, prepared to negotiate head-on with the apartheid government about the historical challenges facing the country. He was an active citizen, he was one of us, readily inserting himself as a participant into the mess of liberation, prioritising reason above anger to get his point across.

---

43   Rhoda Kadalie, interview with Melanie Walker, ibid.

Severely criticised by the increasingly militant factions of the student leadership, Van der Ross pointed out that regardless of the criticisms against him, UWC should be judged by the quality of the graduates who emerged from the institution. That, after all, is what a university is about.[44]

Regardless of Van der Ross's efforts to encourage a more productive approach to protest, the unrest continued.

On another occasion, Rhoda recalled, she was in her office in one of the faculty buildings when she heard a police officer walking down the hallway, who commented: *"Vandag gaan die bloed spat"* — "Today, the blood is going to splat" (see above).

Outside, roughly one hundred police had gathered near the university's canteen — there was no student center yet — and were facing off against a crowd of unruly students. A group of academics, Rhoda included, tried to intervene, but could not stop the inevitable chaos.

Rhoda returned to her office, then went home — after being rescued by several students when she drove her car onto a traffic island — learning only later that all of her faculty colleagues had been arrested, including Gerwel, social work lecturer Edna Van Harte, social work lecturer Jimmy Ellis, and others.

With chaos on campus and in the streets, Rhoda found it impossible to move up the academic ladder. If she wanted to advance her studies, she would have to leave South Africa.

---

44   Rhoda Kadalie, quoted in "Uncle Dick stood at the front line of the Struggle; Respected UWC rector Van der Ross was inspired by 'life of the mind'." *Cape Argus*, 23 Mar. 2018. p. 13.

Chapter Five:
Love

"I committed myself to my marriage
but there were racial problems between me and his family."[1]

In 1983, the South African Parliament passed the Constitution Act, which created the Tricameral Parliament — one house for whites, one for Coloureds, and one for Asians. The idea behind the Tricameral Parliament was to relieve some of the pressure — internal and external — for reform, while retaining white minority rule.

The result was to infuriate the far-right wing of the National Party, which split off to create the Conservative Party, without pacifying those who opposed apartheid. Notably, Africans — the majority of the country's population — were not directly represented in the Tricameral Parliament, which met for the first time in 1985.

The Tricameral Parliament provoked a new wave of protest in the country — and new anti-apartheid organizations. A new group, called the United Democratic Front (UDF), was launched at a large rally in Rocklands, a neighborhood in the Coloured township of Mitchell's Plain, on August 20, 1983. A multi-racial crowd of thousands attended the launch at the Rocklands Civic Centre, with people hanging from the rafters — and security police embedded in the audience, keeping a close watch.

Among those present were many UWC academics and activists, including Rhoda Kadalie.

In the coming years, the UDF would be a "front" in more ways than one: it would be the covert domestic representative of the African National Congress (ANC), which was still banned, its leaders in exile. The UDF brought together churches, labor unions, student organizations, and anti-apartheid activists in nationwide protests aimed at President P. W. Botha and the National Party.

The ANC, cheering — and, to some extent, directing — the unrest from abroad, called on South Africans to make the country "ungovernable."[2] The UDF was part of that project, leading a loose coalition called the Mass

---

1   Sharon Sorour. "Rhoda Kadalie: Born to Lead." *Femina*, Jun. 1996. p. 149.
2   Reader's Digest. "Tricameral Parliament. *Illustrated History of South Africa: The Real Story.* 3rd ed. Cape Town: Reader's Digest Association, 1994. 482.

Democratic Movement (MDM), which was also tied to the ANC, and which became a more formal organization after the government cracked down on the UDF in 1988.

The apartheid regime declared a state of emergency in 1985, arresting activists and in some cases assassinating them. It was a heady time, ripe with the expectation of progress — but riven by fear of violence and death.

And UWC was at the heart of it all. Not only had the unrest swept the campus, but the anti-apartheid movement had begun to draw some of its most important leaders from the UWC student body, from UWC alumni, and from the faculty itself. The UDF was a multi-racial — or, in South African terms, "non-racial" — organization, but its leadership, including radical cleric Allan Boesak, a UWC graduate, was disproportionately Coloured. With the advent of the UDF, the campus, on the front lines in the heart of the Cape Flats, became more connected to the "struggle" than ever.

**

Vignette: "Making History," by Rhoda Kadalie

After the 1976 uprisings, apartheid was being challenged from all quarters. School kids protested against mandatory Afrikaans. University students protested against segregated education. NGOs mobilised against forced removals and inferior housing. Feminists railed against subjugation. Activists opposed constant surveillance and harassment. Activists marched against segregated beaches. People rose up against apartheid laws such as the Separate Amenities Act, the Mixed marriages Act, the Group Areas Act, forced removals, the Pass Laws, migrant labour Laws, school segregation, and so on. The list was endless.

Struggle graffiti was everywhere:

"Lesbians Unite in Armed Snuggle"

"A Naartjie in our Sosatie" (Anarchy in our Society, a play on words: a naartjie is a tangerine and a sosatie is a kebab).

"Albie Sachs, the ANC's one-armed bandit" (This happened later, after Sachs, an anti-apartheid attorney and later Constitutional Court justice,

lost his arm in a car bombing [in 1988] by the apartheid government in Mozambique)

"Een Boer; een moer!"

Every sector was waging its own battle on its own turf until political leaders across a wide spectrum came together to pool their resources. The idea was to form an umbrella mass democratic movement, consisting of all non-governmental organizations (NGOs), community-based organizations (CBOs), faith-based organizations, grassroots movements, universities, and women's organizations against apartheid.

After much debate and negotiations with the ANC in exile, the movement was ready to unite around a common purpose. We would temporarily suspend our differences and fight the common enemy: apartheid and the National Party government.

Universities held conferences and debates; activists mobilized around all manner of issues; women's groups drew up charters fighting several issues simultaneously; and the underground movement flourished. The country was ripe for change. The air was thick with tension. Bombs exploded, churches were attacked, political leaders were banned, police ambushed students, and students retaliated with violence.

Thus came the great day to launch the United Democratic Front, August 1983 (see Chapter five). The launch took place in Mitchell's Plain. The hall was packed. People were hanging from the rafters and every space was occupied. In fact, for all intents and purposes, it was a safety hazard.

At some point, the security marshals called on people to obey safety standards and called on them to descend from the rafters. No one budged, at which point the masses became irritated and restless.

Suddenly, a voice from behind shouted *"Manne, manne, kom nou van die beams af, ons wil beginne history maak"* ("People, people, now come off the rafters, we will begin to make history").

The crowd guffawed with laughter, but that did the trick. History was made.

***

Rhoda enthusiastically joined the activities of the UDF. She participated in a UDF affiliate called the Mowbray Inter-Race Group; later, in 1988, she would lead the Women's Desk of the Western Province Council of Churches, which took a strong stand against apartheid.

A handful of white academics were drawn to UWC at the time. Some wanted to link up with the "struggle" where it was happening; a few were secretly members of the underground ANC. Others were motivated by a more general sense of altruism, wanting to do their part for the future of the country by teaching black and brown students. And a few were working as spies for the apartheid regime, which became increasingly alarmed at the political role UWC was playing: a state-run university within the apartheid system that was providing a platform for the anti-apartheid movement.

One of the white academics who appeared on campus in 1981 was a young German language lecturer named Richard Bertelsmann. He had a slight frame and a shock of long, blond hair; he wore bell-bottomed jeans and drove a Volkswagen. He was handsome, and dashing — and brilliant, fluent in several languages, including French. But he was also timid, and seemed out of place at UWC, overwhelmed by the chaos and violence that wracked the campus daily. Despite his apparently left-leaning convictions, some of Bertelsmann's faculty colleagues suspected he might be working for the apartheid regime, and so they avoided him.

Rhoda did not. She found herself drawn to the man, who stood out among other lecturers with his sincerity and somewhat naïve approach to life at UWC. She also pitied him: the rhetoric at UWC could be explicitly anti-white, especially among colleagues aligned with the Black Consciousness movement.

Though she herself had sworn she would never date a white man, Rhoda could not deny the attraction that began to develop between herself and the quirky blond language lecturer. They began dating, and soon began a passionate romance that would alarm their UWC colleagues — and Bertelsmann's rather conservative family.

Richard was born on July 31, 1953 in Windhoek, Namibia, when that territory was still known as South West Africa, and under the administration of the South African government.

The territory had once been a colonial possession of Germany — one of the few outposts of the limited German empire — until South Africa won the right to run it, thanks to the Treaty of Versailles in 1919, which rewarded Jan Smuts's decision to enter the conflict on the Allied side. The region retained a significant ethnic German population, which persists to this day, albeit among a small, white minority.

The Bertelsmann family had arrived in Windhoek far later than some of their German neighbors. They had, in fact, settled in the territory after the Second World War — though the family patriarch, Werner Bertelsmann, had long taken an interest in the fate of the German ethnolinguistic minority under foreign rule in South West Africa, as had many other Germans in the interwar period.

Werner, christened Werner Georg Julius Bertelsmann, was born and grew up in Kassel, near the center of contemporary Germany. The family had deep roots in Germany itself. They are related to the famous Bertelsmann publishing dynasty, and still own property close to the town of Kassel, near the center of contemporary Germany. They were scholars, and professionals; Richard's grandfather, for whom he was named, was a doctor who had — according to family lore — treated the Kaiser himself.

Dr. Richard Bertelsmann also developed an interest in South Africa, and sympathized with the Boers during the Anglo-Boer War — so much so that he traveled to assist in the war effort. As Werner's mother, Brigitte, later recalled:

> *His father had as a young doctor come out to South Africa with the Belgian Red Cross and installed a little field hospital outside the besieged Mafikeng, corresponded with [Robert] Baden-Powell, who was the English commander in the town [and later the founder of the Boy Scouts], and with [Afrikaner leader] Paul Kruger. ... Naturally his children became interested in South Africa after hearing their father tell of his experiences there.[3]*

Werner studied law at the University of Kiel. In his third year, he was chosen to be the first German exchange student at the University of Stellenbosch, east of Cape Town. He lived in the Dagbreek residence — which still exists — and used his school holidays to travel throughout the country. He became proficient in both English and Afrikaans. As his wife later put it: "Werner loved Germany — but he fell in love with South Africa and wanted to come out and live here for good after finishing his studies in Germany. But war broke out in 1939 and Werner was called up immediately."[4]

The Bertelsmann family had also been Nazis — members of the Party, fully supportive of the ideology of National Socialism, as well as its leaders. There was no question that Werner would serve in the German war effort. He was assigned to the Wehrmacht reserves in 1939 and 1940, then fought in the infantry accompanying a Panzer battalion, Kompanie Schützen-Regiment 8, according to German military archives. He was stationed in Nazi-occupied France and Norway before being sent to the Eastern Front. He was in the regular army, not the SS, which carried out

---

3   Speech by Brigitte Bertelsmann, Petersburg (Polokwane). Undated. Courtesy of Margot Bertelsmann.

4   Ibid.

most of the atrocities. According to German military archives, he was then transferred to the propaganda department, where his knowledge of foreign languages was deemed useful. He wrote scripts for broadcasts to the Allied countries to discourage support for the war. Specifically, he worked with three South Africans who were sympathetic to the Nazi cause, and who were later tried and convicted of treason in South Africa after the war.

Werner was also, according to family lore, the lone survivor of his combat unit. Some of his fellow soldiers had died in battle; others were felled by the grueling Russian winter, or by typhus. Werner would later credit his survival to his cigarette habit, though there is no known link between tobacco and immunity to the bacterial disease.

At some point after his grueling experiences on the front, Werner briefly found an easier assignment, thanks to the intervention of an uncle, who happened to be General Kurt Wolff, the officer in charge of all prisoner-of-war (POW) camps in Silesia. Wolff, a member of the pre-Nazi military establishment, would later be convicted by a war crimes tribunal of exposing British POWs to air raid attacks while they were performing forced labor at a fuel plant, resulting in the deaths of four British soldiers during an Allied bombing attack in 1944. In mitigation of sentence, the court heard testimony that Wolff had generally treated British prisoners well, and had quietly opposed the Third Reich, sympathizing with the failed attempt to assassinate Adolf Hitler on July 20, 1944. He was sentenced to seven years in prison, though he served roughly two years at Werl Prison in Germany.[5]

As Brigitte recalled, General Wolff had assigned Werner to a POW camp where South African POWs, captured at Tobruk during the North African campaign, were held. General Wolff hoped to use Werner's language skills to train the German guards — many of whom had no idea of the ethnic and linguistic differences among the South African POWs — and to talk to the prisoners themselves to hear their grievances. Brigitte noted:

They were very surprised to meet a German officer who could speak Afrikaans. The general complaints were that the different working groups were not allowed to meet. They wished to play rugby against each other; they wanted to form an orchestra but the instruments which were sent to them by the Red Cross were not dealt out; and they felt very concerned that the Afrikaans Predikant [minister in the Dutch Reformed

---

5   Phil Nix. "Wolff." Comment on "Generalleutnant Kurt Wolff." URL: https://forum.axishistory.com/viewtopic.php?t=10824. Accessed on 2 Aug. 2022.

Church] was not allowed to visit the different camps and that they had no church services while there were ministers among the prisoners.[6]

Assuaging General Wolff's concerns about possible collusion among the prisoners, Werner successfully pressed for them to be allowed to play rugby and to attend church.

On a return visit, Lieutenant Bertelsmann was greeted by grateful prisoners. As he later recalled:

To my surprise, General Wolff did do what I suggested, and afterwards he invited me to visit the same POWs again and make sure that they were now satisfied. I did this and I was struck by the great gratitude shown to me. One of those South Africans then said that he was so grateful that he wanted to give me something as a token of appreciation. I then said no, I certainly wouldn't accept a gift from a poor POW who had practically nothing himself, but he persisted and opened his cupboard and said, "Please, take something -- anything you like!" Then I saw an Afrikaans Bible there, something I had always wanted but which I could not afford in 1937 as a student in SA. I then ask if it will be difficult for the prisoner to get hold of a Bible again, and he says no, it is not a problem at all, and immediately he writes in the Bible "To Lieut Bertelsmann, With wishes of the best. J.A. Joubert, 4021 K.G. No. 76180, Breslau 14/4/44."[7]

It was an autograph that would later prove immensely valuable.

For her part, Brigitte was a medical student who would likely have become a doctor had her studies not been interrupted by the war. She had lived for a time in Dresden, and endured the massive firebombing of the city by the Allies in the closing months of the war, which left tens of thousands of civilians dead and much of the town in ruins.

Brigitte's family and the Bertelsmanns had been acquainted since 1928, and she and Werner met again in 1945, when he returned home and began teaching English to her sister, Herta, and other friends. She and Werner would henceforth refer to each other as "Billikins" and "Daddy," the nicknames they adopted during English conversation lessons. They were engaged on July 28, 1945. The marriage was postponed, given the dire circumstances of the defeated country, but Werner and Brigitte were permitted by both families to begin married life together until they were

---

6   Brigitte Bertelsmann, ibid.
7   Werner Bertelsmann, quoted by Brigitte Bertelsmann, ibid. Translated from the Afrikaans.

formally wed in 1946. In the interim, she became pregnant with their first son, Eberhard.

For the Bertelsmann family, as for many other Germans, the fall of the Third Reich was a deeply disorienting event. Werner, who spoke fluent English, found employment with the American occupation forces as part of the legal defense team at the Nuremberg trials, representing Nazi officials and German officers facing charges of war crimes. Upon applying to work as an attorney, he had to state the fact that he had been a member of the Nazi party; he had not, however, been part of the Abwehr, the German secret service, whose members were imprisoned without trial.

The Bertelsmanns, like many other German families, would claim that they knew little of what was happening to Jews in Germany and in Nazi-occupied Europe. Even if that had been true, the trials exposed the reality of the Nazi genocide to fellow Germans and the world.

Regardless, Werner's job was to represent his clients as best he could — and he did it well, much to the irritation of the U.S. Army Counterintelligence Corps (CIC) and its local chief, a man named Thomas Donlon. As Brigitte would later note:

> In court, Werner repeatedly had to cross-examine American witnesses for the prosecution who had mistreated his clients that the poor defendants were acquitted. (Most of the American judges were legal professionals...). This, of course, angered Werner's CIC (the other defense attorneys didn't have the moral courage to do the same for their clients and were too afraid of the CIC), and Donlon was angry and wanted revenge. He had the fixed idea that Werner must have been with the defense. If he could prove that to him, Werner would firstly have been subject to automatic arrest and secondly he could have been sentenced to a long prison term for so-called questionnaire falsification, because Werner had denied belonging to the counter-intelligence on all the questionnaires he had filled out.[8]

Brigitte's account of events is tinged with awkward sympathy for the Germans who had been sent by the U.S. to prison camps, or "concentration camps," as she called them, without irony. The Americans, understandably, had little sympathy for the Nazis, and none for those who participated in the war crimes of the Third Reich. But Werner was not among those who had committed the atrocities.

---

8   Brigitte Bertelsmann. "Das Wunder am Königstor." Undated memoir. Translated from the German. Courtesy of Margot Bertelsmann.

Donlon arrested Werner and interrogated him, but released him for lack of evidence. He would arrest him again, however, in 1946, when South African prosecutors came to Germany to interview witnesses in the treason trials of the three broadcasters for whom Werner had written propaganda material during the war. Though Werner had not been accused of any crime, Donlon used the investigation as a pretext to place him in solitary confinement in the local police station. He and Brigitte had only been married for five days.

As Werner later recalled:

I was placed in solitary confinement under the strictest security measures, and for three weeks I was interrogated on all aspects of my speech. In particular, the CIC agents hammered on the fact that I had access to prisoner of war camps during the war; for them it was already proof that I was connected to the secret service.[9]

A worried but determined Brigitte did all she could to intervene. She approached an American judge who liked and respected her husband; she went to Donlon's office with care packages for her husband. She remembered:

I went into Donlon's office daily (trembling inside, confident on the outside) and was given permission to give Werner something to eat and bring a letter to Werner each day. Of course, he didn't get the letters (and I always wrote them to suit Donlon's censorship). But we were able to tell each other something, because the prison officials – exposing themselves to great danger – found ways and means. ... On March 16, like every day, I packed Werner's basket. Of course, I kept imagining how agonizing solitary confinement must be because I had to, Werner wasn't allowed to speak to anyone and wasn't allowed to read anything either. But it occurred to me that internationally all prisoners should be allowed to have a Bible. So I fetched the Afrikaans Bible from Werner's room, which he had shown me earlier, so that while reading he would have foreign-language spiritual food and inspiration at the same time. I put them on top of the basket and when I got to police headquarters one of Donlon's men took it from me: "Give me that stuff, your husband is under interrogation!"[10]

---

9   Werner Bertelsmann, quoted by Brigitte Bertelsmann, speech in Petersburg, ibid. Translated from the Afrikaans.

10   Brigitte Bertelsmann, "Das Wunder," ibid.

Meanwhile, Donlon and two other colleagues were pressing Werner to admit that he had been in the Abwehr. As Werner would later relate:

> Three CIC agents yelled at me simultaneously, threatened to mistreat me, and particularly pounded on the fact that during the war I had had access to prisoner-of-war camps. This alone proves that I must have been with the Abwehr. What I stated about the purpose of my visits to the Silesian POW camps they simply declared to be lies. "How can you travel there?" I was shouted at: "Call just one witness!" I named General Wolff, followed by a sneer: "Ha, your own uncle and a war criminal himself. He's no witness for us! Call one of the South Africans!"[11]

Things looked bleak for Werner: he could easily have been interned with other suspects, some of whom did not survive the experience.

Then a "miracle" happened:

> But then I remembered the Bible, and I said, "Wait a minute – one of the South Africans wrote me his name," and I told him how I got the Bible. But I forgot that name too. "Of course," yelled the CIC agents, "and of course the Bible was lost in the war, you can't show it either!" "No," I said, "I lost a lot in the war, but the Bible must still be there, I've got it at home."

> And then the miracle happened: the door opened and a police officer brought in the basket of food that my wife was allowed to deliver for me every day and which was always examined by the CIC before it entered my cell. On top of that basket was the Bible that was just mentioned! I just said, "There's the Bible." The CIC agents were speechless, dumbstruck, then all three of them pounced on the book at once to see if the South African's name was in it.

> That was the end of the interrogation, I was never interrogated again, nor was I maltreated or sent to an internment camp, and two days later I was released. So I was able to resume my honeymoon and then my practice."

> I firmly believe that an angel guided my steps as I packed up the Bible and stood at that crucial moment.[12]

---

11   Werner Bertelsmann, quoted by Brigitte Bertelsmann, "Das Wunder,"
      ibid.
12   Ibid.

The Bertelsmanns never found the soldier, J.A. Joubert, whose inscription in the Bible had saved Werner. But they remained deeply grateful; for a family on the losing side, burdened by the stigma of Nazism, it was one of the few redemptive experiences of the war.

With the trials concluded, Werner and Brigitte tried to find a place for themselves in the new, postwar West Germany, with its postwar hardships and liberal ideals. When an opportunity arose for Werner to work as an attorney for a German company with interests in South West Africa, he seized the chance to move his family there. The country was among the most isolated places in the world, but the conservative cultural outlook of the German community — and the privileges enjoyed by the white residents — suited the Bertelsmann family's outlook.

A German-language website documenting important personages in Namibian history lists Werner Bertelsmann as follows:

> *From 1945 to 1951 Werner Bertelsmann practiced as a lawyer in Kassel, mainly as a defense lawyer before the military courts of the US occupation forces in West Germany. In 1951 he went to Johannesburg and Germiston as legal advisor to German companies. From 1952 to 1959 he was editor and later editor-in-chief of the "Allgemeine Zeitung" in Windhoek, then, from 1959 to 1961, as an official in the administration of South West Africa in the translation office of the Official Journal State information service in Pretoria and at the end of 1964 he was employed as managing director and research assistant at the Institute for Foreign Law at the University of South Africa.[13]*

His role at the *Allgemeine Zeitung* was a significant one: the paper was the only German-language paper to survive the First World War, and remains the country's oldest daily newspaper still in print.[14]

Werner went on to pursue an academic career, publishing a book, in German, in 1979 about the German minority in South West Africa, *Die Deutsche Sprachgruppe Südwestafrikas in Politik und Recht seit 1915* ("The German language group of South West Africa in politics and law since 1915").

---

13   "Werner Bertelsmann." Namibiana Buchdepot. URL: https://www. namibiana.de/namibia-information/who-is-who/autoren/infos-zur-person/werner-bertelsmann.html. Accessed 08 Jan. 2022. Translated from the German via Google Translate.

14   Adam Hartman. "Namibia: Namib Times Celebrates 50 Years." *The Namibian*, 8 Dec. 2008. URL: https://allafrica.com/stories/200812081045. html. Accessed 08 Jan. 2022.

Meanwhile, the family had relocated to Pretoria, in South Africa. Richard's eldest brother, Eberhard, followed his father's career path in the law, eventually becoming one of South Africa's most prominent judges, presiding over the fraud trial of Winnie Madikizela-Mandela, President Nelson Mandela's former wife (see Chapter 12). The middle brother, Helmut, became an educator and an author.

Richard was both the rebel and the baby of the family. His mother indulged him from an early age, making his bed and his breakfast — so much so that he reached adulthood without learning to fry an egg. Growing up in the shadow of his elder brothers' achievements, he attended what was then known as the Rand Afrikaans University (RAU) in Johannesburg, the conservative cross-town rival of the English-speaking University of the Witwatersrand.[15]

As he came of age, Richard took an interest in literature, theater, and rock 'n' roll. He went to Frankfurt to study German literature, and developed a keen interest in the left-wing Frankfurt School of philosophy, studying Heinrich Heine, Theodor Adorno, and Herbert Marcuse. He also delved into the writings of the French novelist Marcel Proust.

Richard rebelled against his parents, abhorring their Nazi past and rejecting their enduring racial beliefs. Once the blue-eyed, golden boy of the Bertelsmann family, he soon became the "black sheep," whose increasingly left-wing political and social views provoked his parents' disapproval — and led him to UWC.

***

Vignette: "Meeting Richie," by Rhoda Kadalie

In 1980, in the Faculty of Arts, we had a welcome session for new staff members. It was during a very "black consciousness" period in UWC history. And I noticed that some of my black colleagues weren't very welcoming.

Richie looked very lonely and un-welcomed. So I went to him and welcomed him. Soon after, my colleague in the office next door invited me to see a political play, *Call me Woman*, on campus and said she would invite a new colleague, who grew up with her to accompany us. It was Richie.

---

15   Today RAU has been incorporated into the University of Johannesburg.

The play was very poignant, about the effects of migrant labour and the Pass Laws on black women. As we walked back to our offices, Richie kept ingratiating himself to me, expressing his disgust with apartheid, etc etc. It increasingly irritated me, as I felt I did not need his approval. I invited them to my office for coffee and lunch, as we did not have a staff dining room at the time.

The conversation became less serious, and more fun. When he returned to his office, I told Ada, my colleague, "That's the kind of man I go for."

Soon after, Richie was in my office asking me whether I would accompany him to a Jimmy Cliff concert the next Friday. Richie came to fetch me, picnic basket and blanket in tow. As we sat on the lawn and the concert started, Richie covered us with a blanket, and suddenly I felt him holding my hand. I was a bit offended, and said nothing. The evening turned out to be most enjoyable.

Almost every week, he invited me to some or other event, concert, or theatre. And so it continued for almost a year. Unbeknown to me, Richie told his parents that he had met me, but his father did not approve. So he was engaged in a painful discussion with his father for months.

Ironically, his German relatives, who visited South Africa on occasion, really liked me. I used to cook for them in his flat, and I showed them around Cape Town with Richie, and we generally had much fun together.

The same camaraderie failed to develop with his South African family. After a year of courting, we decided to end the relationship. After much sadness, I went home crying.

The next day, Richie was at my door, saying that he had thought much about it and he decided "that many couples break up because they no longer love each other. We broke up because we love each other. Given all the political obstacles, let's just play it by ear, and take it one day at a time." He had many gifts, a LP record, plants and a book.

My parents liked Richie, although my dad was upset that he wasn't a Christian. We decided to defy everybody. And so we continued for three years, and decided to get married on 3rd December 1982 in Namibia, as it was illegal to marry in SA.

***

Richard and Rhoda's relationship was more than controversial. It was illegal.

The Immorality Act of 1927, passed before apartheid, already outlawed extramarital sex between members of different radical groups. The Prohibition of Mixed Marriages Act of 1949 was the first significant apartheid law, and it barred white South Africans from marrying South Africans of any other racial group. In 1950, an amendment to the Immorality Act made all sex illegal between blacks and whites.[16]

The goal was to reinforce racial identity; the effect was to make romantic love itself — a basic human emotion — illegal among people of different skin colors.

The law was no mere paper offense; it was enforced by the police, and there were several high-profile cases in the early years of apartheid. Racial taboo became linked to the shame of sexual scandal.

One historical digest summarized the Immorality Act at the height of apartheid: "Certainly, its implementation during its heyday in the 1960s was frequently marked by policemen, binoculars at the ready, hiding in trees to observe offending couples; late night raids; the checking of bedsheets and underclothes for signs of sexual intercourse; not to mention numerous shattered lives and frequent suicides".[17]

The irony was that South Africa's racial makeup would have been impossible without love, sex, and even marriage across racial lines. The Coloured population, for example, was created largely through relationships between white settlers or travelers at the Cape, and the indigenous population. The Afrikaans language itself is a hybrid that brought Dutch together with Arabic and indigenous elements — impossible without close racial mixing.

Richard's parents rejected the idea that their son would date a black or Coloured woman. As the relationship continued, and became more serious, they attempted to dissuade their son from marrying Rhoda.

In doing so, they used arguments that went further than apartheid's official ideology, and drew from their own past. If Richard and Rhoda had children, his father warned, they would be "genetically inferior."

Richard tried to ignore his family's protests, but they placed his relationship with Rhoda under incredible strain. He did not share their racial views, but he still loved his family and wished to please his parents, however difficult they were.

---

16   Reader's Digest. "Creating the apartheid society." *Illustrated History of South Africa: The Real Story.* 3rd ed. Cape Town: Reader's Digest Association, 1994. 375.
17   Ibid, 376.

But Pastor Kadalie was also reluctant to embrace Richard because the latter was open about his atheist beliefs. Though the Bertelsmann family were Lutherans, and had enjoyed traditional German Christmas celebrations and the like, Richard himself rejected Christianity, and all organized religion, as part of his general rejection of bourgeois society.

Rhoda, married to Richard, joins the Bertelsmann family — with Großmutter and Großvader (center) — during the holiday season, Pretoria, 1983
(Courtesy Rhoda Kadalie)

To Fenner Kadalie, the racial hierarchy of South African society was meaningless; he did not care what color Rhoda's boyfriends were. What was important was whether they were part of the church and whether they believed in God. To him, faith was the basic foundation of any marriage.

Rhoda found her father's views somewhat old-fashioned. However, she shared his conservatism in one respect: though courted by many suitors, she was still a virgin by the time she met Richard, believing that sex was best left to marriage, no matter how long it took to find a husband.

Rhoda recalled some of the difficulties she faced with her own family as the relationship with Richard developed in a 1994 interview:

Rhoda: 'Comrade Kadalie, You Are Out of Order!'

[I]t was taboo especially in coloured households when you have a boyfriend they don't get into your bedroom. By that time I was doing my honours [degree], working as a lab assistant, and my parents had built me a flat at the back of the house, and I said to them I am going to bring my boyfriend into my room ... and I could see they didn't like it. And I insisted on that, and I said to my parents, if you suspect me of sleeping with my boyfriend, I can do it in the car. ... To have your boyfriend in your room doesn't necessarily mean, you know, that you will have sex. So that one day, I was a young lecturer ... a lab assistant ... we had stacks of marking. Richie was in my room and I had lots of marking, and we were marking into the early hours of the morning. And I heard footsteps. I heard my father coming and he said, "Are you still there?" And I said, "Come in." And he was shocked that I immediately let him in, and he was equally shocked to see Richie sitting [on] that side of the room marking, and me [on] the other side of the room marking.[18]

The relationship also faced scrutiny from colleagues at UWC. Although the left-wing faculty were generally tolerant — or even welcoming — toward interracial relationships, Richard was viewed with skepticism by some of Rhoda's friends. He was not politically savvy enough to fit in among the activist members of the faculty.

For Rhoda and Richard, the opposition to their relationship created significant challenges. But it also brought them closer together. Dating often meant *Romeo and Juliet*-type escapades, such as evenings spent parked in Richard's car on the top of Signal Hill, the rounded promontory overlooking the city lights and the Atlantic Ocean.

One evening, a fog rolled in, leaving the lovers atop the hill, unsure of which way to drive back down. The wrong turn could lead them over the edge, tumbling down along the steep slope.

It was an apt metaphor for the challenge of navigating their forbidden relationship.

***

When Richard proposed to Rhoda in 1982, she gladly accepted. But she knew they could not marry in South Africa itself, where interracial marriage had been forbidden by law for decades.

So instead, the couple eloped to South West Africa (Namibia). The decision was as much a practical one as a religious one, as Rhoda told

18   Rhoda Kadalie, interview with Melanie Walker, ibid.

an interviewer in 1987.[19] Rather than leave the country altogether — as other mixed-race couples had done — they decided to marry and face the consequences. But the only country that would perform the marriage was South West Africa, where its own Mixed Marriages Act was repealed in 1978.

They headed north in December 1982. As Rhoda later recalled: "We decided to fly to Namibia for a weekend, marry, then come back, and move into our house." For the ceremony, Richard ditched his jeans for a smart tan suit; Rhoda wore a flowing white sundress. In their wedding photographs, they are smiling and happy, though alone — and perhaps *because* they were alone, finally able to express their love openly.

Not that the ceremony was particularly pleasant. Rhoda recalled:

> *The Mixed Marriage Act had been repealed in Namibia in 1978, but that didn't mean that the people there liked marrying us. The white magistrate didn't even look at us, and during the ceremony he asked, "Do you, Richard Bertelsmann, white man, marry Rhoda Kadalie, Coloured girl?" He tried to rub it under our noses that we were breaking the law in South Africa and that he hated having to marry us. I wanted to keep my maiden name for feminist reasons. But for political reasons I decided to adopt Richie's name to rub it under their noses that, "I am married, and you will have to accept it whether you like it or not."[20]*

Rather than being offended or disappointed by the ceremony, Rhoda recalled, the two newlyweds "burst out laughing" at the absurdity of it all.[21]

When they returned to South Africa, they moved into a small, semi-detached cottage in the bohemian suburb of Observatory, at 11 Willow Road. Though officially classified as a "White" area under the Group Areas Act, the neighborhood, which sits between Woodstock and Mowbray, was known colloquially as a "gray" area by the mid-1980s, meaning that the growing presence of black residents, while illegal, was tacitly tolerated.

19   Rhoda   Bertelsmann-Kadalie.   "Rhoda   Bertelsmann-Kadalie, interview by Diana Russell, South Africa, 1987." URL: https://search. alexanderstreet.com/preview/work/bibliographic_entity%7Cvideo_ work%7C3373700. Accessed on 3 Oct. 2021.

20   Rhoda Bertelsmann-Kadalie. "Marriage Across the Colour Bar." In Diana E.H. Russell. *Lives of Courage: Women for a New South Africa*. New York: Basic Books, 1989. 299.

21   Rhoda Berteslmann-Kadalie, interview by Diana Russell, ibid.

Rhoda and Richard Bertelsmann wed in Windhoek, Namibia, 1982
(Courtesy Rhoda Kadalie)

Chapter Five: Love

Richard recalled the process of moving in:

Because the Immorality Act had not yet been scrapped, Rhoda and I had to get married in Windhoek, Namibia, where apartheid laws no longer existed. However, because the Act was still on the statute book, and complaints from the public (e.g. neighbours etc.) could lead to prosecutions, it was important for us to enlist the tacit support, or at least tolerance, of our neighbours. So, after we had moved into our house in Observatory, I approached the neighbours, introduced myself and Rhoda, and expressed the hope that we would have good, friendly neighbourly relations.

I started with our next-door neighbour, Billy. Before Observatory became a haven for UCT students, it had been a white working class neighbourhood. Billy, a fairly large, grey-haired man, was clearly a remnant of Observatory's workers-class past. Squinting over my shoulder at Rhoda, he said: "Ag, man, don't worry, it's all right — we all mind our own business here. The two ladies next to you on the other side are lesbians, the guy next to us is a druggie, but don't worry — we all mind our own business here!"

I was too taken aback to ask him what his "business" was. It later turned out that his wife was an alcoholic. They had a dog that had the irritating habit of going on seemingly endless barking spells, and we could never work out what triggered these. Billy's reaction to these disturbances was to growl: "Butcher, one more sound and you're a dead dog!" Needless to say, he never punished the dog, far less killed him; it seems that they were caught up in what the French call a "folie à deux" - a madness two persons (or living beings) share.

The other anecdote I remember also had to do with our (strictly speaking) "illegal" status in a residential area officially classified as "whites only," though irreversible social and economic factors had already subverted this legal reality. One hot summer's day, when we had the front door open to allow some cooling draught into our house, a marked police car with a white cop and a black cop inside (both on the front seats, nogal [moreover]) stopped and stood in front of our house for what seemed an inordinately long time. Rhoda and I looked at these guys, waiting for them to approach us. Nothing happened. Eventually I said to Rhoda: "Check that mixed couple of cops. Should we report them?" After quite a

while, they drove away; it was obviously more fun (and less dangerous)
to intimidate a "mixed couple" than to round up hard-line criminals.[22]

Rhoda's memory of moving in was similar: as she remembered, their neighbor informed them: "Don't worry - your neighbours are either drunkards or dykes. You'll just fit in."[23]

Rhoda and Richard's first home in Observatory as viewed in February 2022

But the state security police had been informed of their marriage, and the newlywed couple was subjected to constant harassment. Rhoda later recalled:

After our return, the police drove up and down the street about five times
a day to intimidate us. They would stop at the gate and look at us but
not say anything. I remember one night we went to a party and came
home very late. We were sitting in the car kissing when a cop car parked
next to us. The cops looked at us, and we looked at them, and then we

22   Richard Bertelsmann. Personal communication with the author. 2 Sep. 2022.

23   "Rhoda Kadalie: a strident voice for South Africa's oppressed," ibid.

rolled down the window to say, "Hey, what's this all about?" but they left before we could question them.[24]

On another occasion, after Rhoda and Richard had been asked to babysit Allan Boesak's children, the police called them at home and demanded that Rhoda report to their offices to face an accusation of violating the Group Areas Act, the Mixed Marriages Act, and the Immorality Act. She refused, at first, but the officer persisted, and she went in with her husband for questioning. As Rhoda later recalled:

> *Richie speaks perfect Afrikaans, and their attitude was, "How could a sweet, innocent Afrikaner like you go wrong?" The police officer was shocked to learn that he had studied at the Rand Afrikaans University. Throughout the interview the officer ignored me. He didn't even look at me or address me, as if I didn't exist to him. He didn't recognize me as the wife of his man. But when they were finished with Richie, the sergeant looked at me and asked, "Do your friends recognize you as white or Coloured?" I said, "I have the kind of friends to whom that doesn't matter."*[25]

The officer gave them a form to fill out, which they never returned.

Richard, similarly, recalled:

> *[W]e received a letter from either the police of the Department of the Interior, or whatever they were called at the time, informing us that they had taken note that we had got married in Namibia, and that we had to report the the Wynberg police station. I don't know whether this is general international practice, but apparently the Namibian authorities were under some obligation to inform their South African counterparts of any South African citizens being born, getting married or having died in Namibia.*

> *With some trepidation, Rhoda and I drove to the Wynberg police station, where we were informed that we had to apply to some South African authority, probably the Department of the Interior or Home Affairs of whatever they were called at that stage, to have our marriage "legalised", or something to that effect. In reaction to this, I wrote them a letter, saying that we had got married and moved to Observatory because we did not recognise the State's authority to pronounce on the legality or illegality*

---

24   Rhoda Bertelsmann-Kadalie. "Marriage Across the Colour Bar," Ibid, 300.

25   Ibid, 300-1.

of a personal relationship such as a marriage. If we applied to have our marriage "legalised," it meant that we recognised the State's authority in this regard after all, which we found unacceptable, "yours sincerely."

If I remember correctly, we subsequently received some communication intended to outline the serious consequences of our attitude and conduct, for example that any children born out of this unrecognized marriage would be considered illegitimate, and that this would have serious consequences in the case of intestate inheritance, etc. etc. If I remember correctly, we ignored this letter.[26]

The case was eventually dropped, but the intimidation was constant. At one point, Richard approached the country's small, liberal opposition party, the Progressive Federal Party (PFP), made famous by Helen Suzman, for help:

I cannot remember whether that was it this stage or earlier, I sought (and found) protection from two other sources. At that stage, and particularly during the 1981 general election, I was quite active in my local (Cape Town, Gardens) constituency branch of the then-Progressive Federal Party (PFP); I did quite a lot of canvassing – I lived in a flat in Tamboerskloof at the time. And so, shortly before or after our wedding, I made an appointment to see PFP leader Frederick Van Zyl Slabbert and told him about our situation; he told me that I should not worry, and that we could rely on him if we experienced any official harassment. He said something in the line of: "If we don't help people in such cases, our opposition means nothing."

The other support we relied on was from the UWC authorities. Somehow I seem to remember that we got assurances from Jakes Gerwel, though the rector at that time (December 1982) must still have been Van der Ross. Anyhow, to an extent we relied on the calculation that, given the habitual political instability at UWC at the time, the authorities would consider it unnecessarily provocative to prosecute a "mixed couple" of UWC academics in terms of the Immorality Act. Regardless of how little-known or how well-known we may have been at UWC, and how popular or unpopular, the "activists" on campus would have regarded such a prosecution as a God-sent opportunity to start "mass action," with poster demonstrations at the main gate, chanting of slogans, boycotting of classes and (possibly) stoning of cars (whose drivers, needless to say,

26   Richard Bertelsmann. Personal communication with the author. 2 Sep. 2022.

had nothing to to with the matter). And so, quite rightly, we thought we were quite safe from prosecution.[27]

Ultimately, the apartheid government did not want to risk the negative publicity of enforcing its laws — but it wanted Rhoda and Richard to know that it was watching them, and it wanted them to be miserable.

***

Vignette: "Monitoring the Tricameral Elections," by Rhoda Kadalie

Just before the Tricameral Parliament elections in 1983, the ANC in exile issued a request to UWC academics to monitor the elections to assess how many coloured and Indian people would vote for this farce.

I monitored in Cape Town, my husband in Woodstock. In Cape Town there were more police than voters. And they monitored and harassed us. One officer approached me and asked me for my name. I had deliberately refused to take my ID with me, expecting all manner of shenanigans.

After hardly using my married surname for months, that day I decided to use my married name: "R. Bertelsmann," I said.

An hour later, the officer arrived again, asking me for my name. "R. Bertelsmann," I offered politely.

I noticed a puzzled look on his face but made nothing of it.

A few minutes later, a more senior police officer came and asked me for my name. "R. Bertelsmann", I replied.

"But there is another R. Bertelsmann, in Woodstock," he said.

I ignored him, and off he toddled.

Unbeknown to me, my husband was going through the same questioning in Woodstock. He too claimed to be R. Bertelsmann, which he is more authentically than me! Having checked on him multiple times, by this time, they must have thought the phrase was an ANC password.

---

27   Richard Bertelsmann. Personal communication with the author. 2 Sep. 2022.

One cop shouted at him, and banged his fist on the table; "Therrre is anotherrrrr R. Berrrrtelsmann in Cape Town. Arrre you lying to me."

"Well, officer," my husband replied, "she is my wife!"

"But she's colourrrred!"

"I told you she's my wife."

The next day, the police headquarters called to ask us to come in for questioning. This was the second time, but we ignored them and went about our business unperturbed.

It was a period of heightened political tension. My husband and I volunteered to look after Dr. and Mrs Allan Boesak's four children during their travels abroad. As leader of the World Alliance of Reformed Churches and the United Democratic Front, they were traveling all over the globe keeping the world abreast of repression, detention, and the hounding of activists in South Africa.

We stayed in their home for two weeks, caring for their kids, who were very young at the time, fully cognizant that their house was under surveillance, and the telephone tapped.

When the Boesaks returned, we went back to our home in Observatory. Soon after, we received a call from the police headquarters in Wynberg to come in for questioning.

This time they were serious, and we could not ignore them. So off we went.

"Good day, Mr. Bertelsmann", greeted the white police officers — ignoring me, because to greet me would mean they accepted this marriage, which in their view was illegal.

Thus started the interrogation.

Richie answered them in impeccable Afrikaans. Prior to that, they treated him as a lost German, who would, of course, marry a black, "so misguided are they."

They asked him about his life, where he grew up, where he studied, et cetera. They looked at him pitifully, thinking aloud, "How could such a sweet blonde, blue-eyed, Afrikaans-speaking boy go so wrong?"

After an hour, they turned to me, very hostile. "Werrre you always colourrred?"

I burst out laughing.

Super-annoyed, they tried again: "Arrre most of yourrrrr frrriends colourrrred or white?"

I responded arrogantly: "To me it doesn't matter what my friends are."

Thoroughly annoyed, they asked us to sign a declaration that we had violated the Mixed Marriages Act, the Immorality Act, and the Group Areas Act. On our lawyer's advice, we signed, "We were married 3 December 1982."

That was that, an act of defiance on our part.

They did not prosecute us, because the abolition of petty apartheid laws was under discussion in Parliament at the time. It suddenly occurred to me that the reasons for their racist questions to me were to assess whether or not I was racially re-classifiable, so I would be less of a public embarrassment and shut up.

Bottom line: while the abolition of petty apartheid laws was being discussed in Parliament, the police roundly harassed and intimidated people thought to be violating those pernicious laws.

***

Though they were never prosecuted, Rhoda and Richard faced continued, daily harassment. When the two of them went to a "White" beach, Rhoda was detained by two police officers while Richard was swimming in the ocean. Rhoda recalled — perhaps in an alternative version of Richard's anecdote, above — that one of the officers was Coloured. After Rhoda insisted they wait for her husband to return, they were shocked to see that he was white. The white officer observed that they were a mixed couple — to which Richard quipped: "So are you."

Rhoda and Richard had confronted racial boundaries when they decided to marry — but marriage did not end that struggle. Not even the repeal of the Mixed Marriages Act in 1985 ended the harassment. The only respite was in Europe — ironically, in Germany.

Chapter Six:
Europe

*"We were 30 feminists from different countries and I think that was
quite significant because for the first time my local feminist perspective
was given international affirmation and I realized I was in keeping
with the world and that I wasn't a maverick, you know,
the kind of stereotypical feminist they branded you."*[1]

In 1985, Rhoda and Richard left South Africa to study in Europe, where
both hoped to obtain their Master's degrees in Germany. They each took
a sabbatical from their teaching duties at UWC, where the protests and
violence had continued, making academic life difficult.

The fact that their marriage was illegal, and that they were living
in Observatory in defiance of the Group Areas Act, only added to the
stress. Europe represented an opportunity for each of them to add to their
academic credentials while enjoying a change of pace from the frantic,
everyday confrontations of life during the "struggle."

For Richard, the opportunity to study in Germany was an important
escape in two other ways. First, it was an opportunity for him to explore
his roots, to immerse himself in the language and the culture that he
had imbibed from a distance. Second, it was a chance to meet up with his
connections in Germany — aunts, cousins, and university friends.

Contemporary Germany was not the place that the Bertelsmann
family had left after the Second World War. It had become one of the most
liberal and tolerant societies in the world. Old prejudices occasionally still
emerged, but interracial marriage was not rejected.

For Rhoda, Europe offered what it had provided for decades
to black intellectuals, from the U.S. as well as South Africa: a sense of
perspective. Many of the writers and artists of the Harlem Renaissance
found it fascinating to study or work in Europe, particularly in France,
where the familiar western culture they knew was not suffused with
the same kind of racism they encountered at home. Though racism is a
doctrine with European origins, and reached its nadir in the 17th century
European slave trade, and again in Nazi Germany, contemporary Europe
was often a more tolerant place.

---

1   Rhoda Kadalie. Unpublished interview with Melanie Walker, 27 Oct.
     1994.

Rhoda and Richard in Munich, Germany, 1985 (Courtesy Rhoda Kadalie)

Europe in the 1980s was also particularly sympathetic to the anti-apartheid movement. Several countries in particular took an interest in supporting it, notably the Netherlands, which was faintly embarrassed by its historic association with Afrikaner nationalism.

In Eastern Europe, the Soviet Union and its satellites provided education, military training, and weapons to the ANC in exile. In Western Europe, the focus was on South African civil society, and several European governments provided funding to South African anti-apartheid organizations. Even in the United Kingdom, whose Conservative government opposed sanctions on South Africa, the anti-apartheid movement enjoyed widespread sympathy.

White South Africans backpacking through Europe often felt embarrassed or ashamed of their origins. But black South Africans were often welcomed eagerly and sympathetically. As Rhoda and Richie arrived in Germany, she later recalled, there was an article in the local press specifically about their marriage, and how difficult and controversial it had become in a South African context.[2]

---

2 Rhoda Bertelsmann-Kadalie. "Marriage Across the Colour Bar." In Diana E.H. Russell. *Lives of Courage: Women for a New South Africa.* New

Studying in Europe meant the opportunity to interact with other anti-apartheid activists who had left South Africa, whether voluntarily or otherwise. The ANC had a significant underground presence even in Western Europe, as did several other Third World liberation movements.

Rhoda also used her time in Europe to connect for the first time with a long-lost family member: namely, her father's half-brother, Victor Kadalie. Victor was the child of Clements Kadalie's second marriage, to the well-educated Eva Moorehead,[3] and he had become a doctor in Germany. He was also a member of the German Communist Party, and was active in supporting anti-apartheid causes. He also donated to Pastor Kadalie's charitable causes in Cape Town. His wife, Ruth, was equally committed to the communist cause, and worked extensively with the international trade union movement. She contributed funds to the nascent South African trade union movement, especially efforts to organize domestic workers — a project in which she would take a close interest for decades.

Meeting Rhoda for the first time, and observing her fierce anti-apartheid political convictions, Victor remarked that she seemed to have inherited his father's passion for justice. The two would develop an enduring connection that lasted for decades — though they discovered some sharp areas of difference. While Victor loved Rhoda's feistiness, on his regular visits to South Africa in the post-apartheid years, he would plead with her to tone down her criticism of the ruling African National Congress (ANC). He would concede some of her criticisms were correct, but disagreed with others — until he came around to her point of view in later years (see Chapter 12).

Rhoda and Richard also visited Victor's son, Khwezi, a committed communist and anti-apartheid activist who had been detained in South Africa during the Soweto riots in 1976. He had gone into exile, where he joined the ANC's armed wing, Umkhonto we Sizwe, and trained with the terrorists of the Palestine Liberation Organization.[4] He lived in Berlin at the time of Rhoda and Richard's visit, though he would later work for the ANC in London.

York: Basic Books, 1989. 299.

3   Cape Town Museum. "Clements Kadalie." URL: http://bit.ly/3tfjHbb. Accessed on 4 Oct. 2021.

4   Red Youth. "Red Salute to Comrade Khwezi Kadalie." 5 May 2014. URL: https://redyouthuk.wordpress.com/2014/05/31/red-salute-to-comrade-khwezi-kadalie/. Accessed on 17 Jun. 2022.

Above: Kwezi Kadalie; Below: Rhoda at the Berlin Wall, East Berlin,
German Democratic Republic, c. 1985 (Courtesy Rhoda Kadalie)

In August 1985, Rhoda and Richard joined Khwezi on a trip behind the Iron Curtain, to East Berlin. The experience opened Rhoda's eyes to the limits of the socialist utopia that she and fellow radicals had indulged on campus back home. She noted in her diary that the food in East Berlin was "dreadful," and that given the limited usefulness of the few East German Marks they had obtained, they decided to spend 25 Marks each on alcohol. "Richie and Kwezi [sic] drank themselves to a standstill — talking politics," she noted in her diary.[5]

Rhoda later recalled in a speech to students at the German International School in Cape Town:

[Khwezi] invited us to visit him in late 1985 in the trendy suburb of Kreuzberg. Having shed ourselves of all our Marxist leanings, we could not help hide our amusement as we entered his flat, to see a big red communist flag hanging from his dining-room wall above a bronze bust of Lenin. Without a hint of irony, he proudly showed off his communist paraphernalia, leaving my husband and I in a state of deep Unglaublichkeit [incredulity].

The next day he took us to East Germany. A frequent sojourner across the wall, he made our crossing of Checkpoint Charlie and our conversion of money into 25 German Marks, very easy. We were immediately struck by the gloomy Soviet landscape, the ominous socialist realist architecture, the uniform blocks of concrete flats, "distinctly lacking paint" to quote a comment on the internet.

Alexanderplatz, with its iconic Rote Rathaus, the Teacher's House and Congress Hall, and East German Palace of the Republic, with the iconic TV tower, (the first thing one sees), captured my interest as my cousin wove his political myths around the socialist realism architecture, almost charming in the oppression it represented.

Throughout the hours we spent there, my husband and cousin were engaged in explosive political arguments. The more Khwezi tried to convert us to socialism, the more my husband smashed every argument. Needless to say, soon we were followed around by the Stasi but pretended not to notice. As we prepared to return, Khwezi remembered that we had not spent our money, so he took us into the East German Palace of the Republic where they doused their political rage with 25 marks' worth of beers. The bored waiters failed to mitigate the long food queues with their lethargic service. While we waited Khwezi and Richard continued their

---

5   Rhoda Kadalie. Diary entry, 17 Aug. 1985.

fight while it was clear that the waiters enjoyed this exchange. When I got my hardly edible food, one waiter told me that he had understood the entire conversation and found it very interesting.

Needless to say, that experience opened my eyes to the realities of communism.[6]

Khwezi had been detained during the Soweto riots in 1976. Years later, Khwezi would return to a liberated South Africa; he is buried today in the ANC's Acre of Heroes in West Park Cemetery, in Johannesburg.

At first, Rhoda and Richard enjoyed being in Germany together. They traveled throughout the country, and through the rest of Europe, enjoying an extended honeymoon they never could have had in South Africa. Rhoda had studied some German at UWC already, and became even more proficient as she and Richard traveled through Europe. On occasion, she even addressed her parents in Cape Town as "Liebe Mutter, Lieber Vater" in letters home.[7]

But Rhoda struggled to navigate the German educational bureaucracy. While Richard was able to begin his studies in German language and literature without difficulty, Rhoda had trouble starting her academic program in Munich. The qualifications to begin coursework proved hopelessly complicated.[8] She tried attending some university lectures in Germany, but was not impressed. "The anthropology course here is not so good & after one bad lecture, I decided not to go any longer. A pity!" she wrote her parents.[9] She tried immersing herself in German culture and society — "visiting museums, attending interesting lectures, visiting other states," and earned a certificate for completing a German language course.[10] And though her conversational skills were good, she struggled with the task of studying in German. "The language proved far too difficult for me to transact my academic ambitions," she admitted years later.[11] After months of frustration, she told Richard that she had to try other options.

On a whim, Rhoda wrote to the Institute of Social Studies (ISS) in the Netherlands, a public policy university well known for its radicalism.

---

6   Rhoda Kadalie. "When the Wall Fell." Speech to German International School Cape Town. Cape Town, South Africa. 28 Apr. 2015.
7   Rhoda Kadalie. Letter to Fenner and Joan Kadalie. 2 Aug. 1985.
8   Rhoda Kadalie. Curriculum Vitae. Draft. 1992.
9   Rhoda Kadalie. Postcard to Fenner and Joan Kadalie. 17 May 1985.
10   Rhoda Kadalie. Curriculum Vitae. Draft. 1992.
11   Rhoda Kadalie. "When the Wall Fell." Ibid.

She asked whether the ISS had a place for her in its program, and whether financial assistance might be available.

To her surprise, she received a positive and enthusiastic reply almost immediately. She was accepted to study for a Master's degree in development studies, based at the ISS campus in The Hague, and also received a scholarship to cover her tuition and other costs. It was an opportunity she could not miss. She left Germany for Holland during the week, planning to reunite with Richard on weekends.

***

Rhoda arrived in The Hague in September 1985 to begin her studies at ISS, in pursuit of her Master's degree in Development Studies and the new field of Women's Studies.

She and Richard had scouted out the campus earlier that year, visiting in April. Rhoda wrote to her parents that The Hague was "a very beautiful city," but added: "The university here frightens me because it is very big & stretches over many streets."[12] Rhoda was also apprehensive about being away from her husband, who eventually decided to study in Cologne (Köln), closer to the Netherlands and to ISS, rather than in Munich.

At the time, ISS attracted would-be left-wing revolutionaries from around the world. Rhoda's program included 35 students, most of whom were political activists from Third World countries. Many, like her, were from Africa; seven were women from the South West Africa People's Organisation (SWAPO), the political movement aiming to achieve independence in Namibia. Others were from Latin America, Southeast Asia, and other points on the post-colonial map.

The school was housed in an old hotel, near the Madurodam, a miniature park popular among tourists. The building, with its ornate features, provided a stately backdrop to revolutionary discourses. Her courses included: "Contemporary Theories in feminism; feminist methodology; women and agrarian change; the effects of international capital on women; reproductive rights; women, mass media and applied communication; history of women's struggles; comparative labor relations."[13] She also studied development economics, and methodologies in women's studies.[14] The classes were informal, and discussion-oriented, with the students sharing insights from their various political struggles.

---

12   Rhoda Kadalie. Letter to Fenner and Joan Kadalie. 23 Apr. 1985.
13   Rhoda Kadalie. Curriculum Vitae. 1992.
14   Rhoda Kadalie. Curriculum Vitae. Draft. 1992.

As excited as she was about ISS, Rhoda also found it daunting. Money — or the lack thereof — was a constant source of stress. She and Richard were "exceptionally poor" in European terms, she later wrote.[15] They were only able to draw salaries from UWC through October 1985. Because she had applied late to ISS, she had also missed opportunities to apply for scholarships. The ISS recommended instead that she write to several local sponsors — which she did, though without luck. She was able to obtain a loan from UWC, but found that the South African Rand did not stretch very far. "Life is expensive in Europe," she wrote to her parents in August 1985, "and the Rand is now, more than ever, worth nothing. We [are] getting a raw deal and I'm glad that the blacks are giving the govt. hell!"[16]

At the suggestion of ISS, she applied for funding from a group called the Nederlands Zuid-Arikaanse Vereniging (NZAV), which offered her a scholarship. However, she was horrified to find that it had a "conservative" stance on the struggle in South Africa.[17] Fearing that NZAV would use her to boost its credibility by claiming it had "sponsored a radical black female student," Rhoda informed ISS that she was turning down the money. The administration at ISS was relieved: the fact that the NZAV had been on their list of potential sponsors had been an oversight, and politically embarrassing to them. They eagerly refunded Rhoda the money she had paid towards tuition thus far, and agreed to cover her future costs.

For Rhoda, the experience was a lesson in the importance of standing up for her beliefs. "It is incredible how the Lord undertook even respecting my political convictions," she wrote to her parents. "So now I have the freedom to think & feel politically like I always felt with ties to no one."[18]

Nonetheless, Rhoda found the coursework very challenging. "I have been going to bed at 2 a.m. every morning because of all the reading and writing," she wrote to her parents in late September.[19] The cold, rainy weather of northern Europe also dampened her spirits. And she was lonely, too: "I miss Richie terribly as much as he misses me — but we both realise that it is important to sacrifice in order to get done with our studies, even though it is very difficult for us both. I cannot help to have a lump in my throat every time he phones & that's not so often, ± 2x a week as it is very expensive to phone." On her third wedding anniversary, in 1985, Rhoda found herself alone in Holland, miserable without Richard; she took consolation in an unexpected telephone call from her parents and

---

15   Rhoda Kadalie. Letter to Fenner and Joan Kadalie. 27 May 1986.
16   Rhoda Kadalie. Letter to Fenner and Joan Kadalie. 2 Aug. 1985.
17   Rhoda Kadalie. Letter to Fenner and Joan Kadalie. 30 Sep. 1985.
18   Ibid.
19   Rhoda Kadalie. Letter to Fenner and Joan Kadalie. 30 Sep. 1985.

a letter from her husband, in which he professed his love: "Sweet music to my ears!!!" she wrote.[20]

The feeling of longing was mutual. Richard wrote to his in-laws — whom he addressed as "Mom" and "Dad" — in October 1985 that he had just seen Rhoda off at the train station after a brief visit, and that the "loneliness is worse after her departure."[21] He took comfort in the presence of his landlord's dog, who snoozed under his desk as he worked. And he was, after all, in somewhat familiar cultural surroundings. For Rhoda, alone in a country where she had no roots, the isolation was even more painful.

Rhoda's appearance also puzzled her peers: "*Die mense hier kan nie glo dat* ["The people here cannot believe that"] Coloureds in all shapes and sizes *kom nie*. So I have to explain why some are fair, some dark, some Indian-looking and so on." Though she "enjoyed" the fact that people could not guess her origins, it underscored the fact that she was alone abroad. In December 1985, she sent a postcard to her parents, lamenting that she had spent her wedding anniversary by herself, studying and doing laundry, cheered only by their phone call and by a letter from Richard.[22]

Rhoda also chose to live at a remove from the other students. She enjoyed their company at times, and learned a great deal from them. At one birthday party, she noted, the classmates spontaneously regaled one another with "freedom songs from their own countries."[23] At an academic conference on women's history, she joined her "sisters" in staging a disruptive protest against the failure to include scholars from from Africa and Asia. "This evoked a huge debate where all kinds of sentiments were aired ranging from racism to lesbianism," she recorded in her diary.[24] Later, she would help organize a boycott of classes to protest the appointment of a professor who had done some work for the Bantustan government of Transkei (in today's Eastern Cape province).

Still, she found her classmates to be a "strange bunch of self-centred women."[25] As she explained to her parents:

They form cliques. There is the Latin American clique, who thinks they are very smart, way-out and beautiful. Then the Asian clique who have enormous inferiority complexes. Accuse everybody of being bourgeois

20   Rhoda Kadalie. Postcard to Fenner and Joan Kadalie. 9 Dec. 1985.
21   Richard Bertelsmann. Letter to Fenner and Joan Kadalie. 27 Oct. 1985.
22   Rhoda Kadalie. Postcard to Fenner and Joan Kadalie. 9 Dec. 1985.
23   Rhoda Kadalie. Diary entry, 16 Jan. 1986.
24   Rhoda Kadalie. Diary entry, 26 Mar. 1986.
25   Rhoda Kadalie. Letter to Fenner and Joan Kadalie. 27 May 1986.

and upper class, especially if you dress like me. They don't like whites, but all wish to get a white boyfriend. Then there is the Ghana clique — who calls everybody in Europe racists etc. The Tanzanian group is boring and dumb — and all people like me who don't belong to a group are either too intellectual, too snobbish, too pro-white etc. So, in a way I have no friends in my class. The people I get on with most are also rejected by the class. A white Dutch anthropologist who worked in Chile for 10 years; a Sudanese girl, who now is beginning to become aware of the evils of Europe; and a Somalian woman who has a 10 yr old daughter. The Dutch woman stays in Leiden and has 2 children, so unfortunately, I cannot visit her or go out with her. The other 2 are very busy with their own lives. Most weekends I stay at home — studying. I don't go out at all.[26]

Some of her colleagues were overly "aggressive," Rhoda noted[27]; she also found some to be "not stimulating enough," telling her parents in another letter that they seemed to be in Holland "for one big *jol* [party]."[28] The ISS provided free accommodation, but she did not want to live in dormitories, nor in student "digs"; instead, she lived with a Dutch host family, whom she called "a great pleasure to be with." She also applied her anthropological and linguistic skills to soak in the fine detail of Dutch culture from within the confines of domestic life.

Among the few friends Rhoda described to her parents, Rhoda became something of a confidante. Amina, from Somalia, had fled her husband, who would not grant her a divorce. Rhoda's roommate, Tamadur, from Sudan, fell in love with a lecturer, and carried on a secret, torrid romance that ended in heartbreak when he broke off their relationship before they were set to be married in England, after graduation. She later told the sorry tale to Rhoda in a long, confessional letter — full of the curse words that Rhoda, steeped in Cape Town's colorful slang, had taught her.

Richard and Rhoda wrote to each other frequently, and spoke occasionally on the phone, in an effort to remain part of each other's lives. In one letter, Richard described attending an event organized by German anti-apartheid activists, gently mocking the effort, including a choir from Namibia that "sang perfectly false," as well as "poor poetry" that had been badly translated into German, and competing speeches by representatives of the various local political parties. He wrote in tender prose, reassuring Rhoda that their love would survive the pain of separation.[29] In writing

---

26 Ibid.
27 Rhoda Kadalie. Diary entry, 26 Mar. 1986.
28 Rhoda Kadalie. Letter to Fenner and Joan Kadalie. 7 Jan. 1986.
29 Cite letter.

to Rhoda's parents, Richard's tone was more detached; he dwelled extensively on intricate details of life around him. Yet he did make an effort to stay connected.

She would later lament that he wanted to stay in Germany rather than moving to Holland with her: "[H]e really loves Germany, which is a pity."[30] She felt that Germany, and Germans, had been "cursed" by their recent history. "Richie's mother makes me dislike them even more," she complained.[31] After spending the year-end holidays together in Holland, he returned to Germany in early January. Rhoda noted in her diary: "Richie left today while I went to ISS. Came home sad & lonely — to a telephone call from Richie and a nice warm letter waiting for me on the bed."[32] Two weeks later, she noted sadly: "Sobbed my heart out — missed Richie so much!"[33] The loneliness was occasionally interrupted by a letter from home including from her brother Bruce, who had begun to study at UCT and wrote to Rhoda seeking advice about life, academics and politics.

Still, Richard visited Rhoda frequently, usually on weekends. They savored Holland together, and the fact that they spoke Afrikaans made it easy for them to fit in. Though Afrikaans was being imposed on South African students by the apartheid regime, Rhoda and Richard enjoyed speaking it freely in Europe. Occasionally, she would visit him in Germany, as well — usually when he had family events. Rhoda found Richard's family in Germany more welcoming than his immediate family had been in South Africa. The liberalizing influences of postwar Germany left Richard's relatives in Europe with a different outlook. They also enjoyed life in Germany together, jogging around the Nymphenburg Palace, for example, and taking in other sights.

Rhoda's eyes were opened, too. Holland was a more egalitarian society, compared to the chauvinistic and patriarchal climate of South Africa. At the same time, Rhoda became aware of just how difficult conditions were for women elsewhere in Africa. Tamadur had been forced to undergo circumcision as a young girl; when she returned to Sudan, having been jilted by her European lover, she was shunned by those who believed that she could no longer marry a Muslim man. Rhoda had always had feminist instincts; in The Hague, she learned in detail just how difficult the plight of women could be.

---

30   Rhoda Kadalie. Letter to Fenner and Joan Kadalie. 7 Jan. 1986.
31   Ibid.
32   Rhoda Kadalie. Diary entry, 10 Jan. 1986.
33   Rhoda Kadalie. Diary entry, 23 Jan. 1986.

Rhoda and Richard at anti-apartheid protest outside South African embassy, The Hague, Netherlands, c. 1986 (Courtesy Rhoda Kadalie)

Though many of her classmates at ISS hoped to contribute to the liberation of their countries from colonialism, segregation, and poverty, Rhoda discovered that many had faced discrimination — and worse — within their own revolutionary movements. The women from SWAPO opened up to her, and revealed that many of them had been raped or assaulted by more senior leaders within the organization's camps. There was no mechanism for the victims to make accusations, or to take action; and if they appealed to the state to intervene, they would be accused of betraying the movement. They were victims of the regime — and the revolution.

For her thesis, Rhoda chose to write about the experiences of women under apartheid and within the struggle against it.[34] Titled *Structures and Struggles: The State and the Oppression of Women in South Africa*, the 109-page paper applied feminist and Marxist analyses to explain the experiences of women and the roles of various women's organizations in South Africa.

---

34   Rhoda Kadalie. *Structures and Struggles: The State and the Oppression of Women in South Africa*. Unpublished thesis. Institute of Social Studies, The Hague, Netherlands. Dec. 1986.

While women of every race and class experienced common oppression — "the responsibility of domestic labour and childcare ... the brunt of gender discrimination ... male violence and control .. [and] the sexual division of labor — that oppression was "qualitatively different for different groups" under the apartheid system, Rhoda wrote.

"[E]ven for white working class women," she observed, "political and economic conditions are far above those of coloured and Asian working class women, not to mention African women." The apartheid state managed and manipulated these differences for its own purposes. The one common experience of women across racial boundaries was "the fact that they constitute the reserve army of labour, the shock absorbers of the economy — drawn into the labour force in times of economic boom, and just as easily disposed of in times of economic recession."

In common with many other activists and intellectuals at the time, Rhoda believed that the end of apartheid would also mean the end of that capitalist system, at least in its peculiar South African form. However, she warned that "under socialism the struggle for women's liberation will still have to continue," and that "the abolition of capitalism, does not mean an automatic emancipation from male domination."

She did not think much of the work she had produced, which she felt was suited to a classroom project rather than a research paper. It was more a series of observations and descriptions than an attempt to answer an academic question with research or analysis.

But the project was a way for Rhoda to reflect on her own experiences — as an academic, and as a female activist within the anti-apartheid movement. Despite her fraught relationships with classmates, she had benefited from the insights they shared with her. She knew of women in South Africa who had experienced what the SWAPO women had, and she could never look at the struggle against apartheid in quite the same utopian way. In her thesis, she reached a conclusion that would guide her future work, and her writing: that for women, the struggle would continue past the moment of liberation.

Through her experience at ISS, Rhoda had begun to shape a new perspective on the struggle for freedom in South Africa. She was not merely a black activist, but also a feminist. More than that, however, she knew she could not simply be a revolutionary — not when that meant loyalty to the revolution above all else. She had to be a critic as well.

Rhoda celebrates the end of exams with classmates, Institute of Social Studies, The Hague, Netherlands, 1986 (Courtesy Rhoda Kadalie)

Rhoda began to think of herself as a different kind of activist — one that her colleagues in the Black Consciousness movement might have shunned: she began to see herself as something of a liberal, committed to individual freedom, beyond the categories imposed by the apartheid regime — and by its opponents.

***

Rhoda had another reason to reconsider her feelings about the anti-apartheid struggle — not the justice of the cause, but rather her interactions with the ANC underground that was ostensibly leading it.

She began to notice that some of her classmates at ISS were suddenly hostile toward her. There was one activist couple from Angola — the wife dark-skinned, the husband a doctrinaire white revolutionary — who seemed particularly aloof. The husband's claim to fame and to ANC insider status was that he had been a colleague of exiled activist Ruth First when she was killed in Mozambique by a mail bomb sent by the apartheid regime. Their attitude was noticeable enough that Richard picked up on it during one of his visits. But it was not the only bizarre interaction Rhoda had.

Another classmate, Bunie Sexwale, an ANC representative in the Netherlands,[35] turned cold toward Rhoda rather suddenly. Her lecturers had also become abrupt with her. Rhoda could not understand their behavior; it seemed, she recalled later, like a "Cold War that made no sense."

Eventually, Bunie called Rhoda and asked to meet with her the next day, February 6, 1986, in a private location, far from the campus, where no one would see or overhear them. She left no hint about what she wanted to discuss. Rhoda, suspicious, asked Richard, who was in town, to accompany her to the meeting.

At the rendezvous, Bunie informed Rhoda that the husband-and-wife activists had suspected that she, Rhoda, was an apartheid spy. Evidently, they had been spreading the rumor among others in the anti-apartheid movement.

"We followed you.," Bunie said, according to Rhoda, who also recalled being told that there had been talk of "necklacing" her.

"Necklacing" was a reference to the assassination of suspected informers within the movement. In the townships, these killings took the gruesome form of placing a tire around the neck of the intended victim, filling it with fuel, and setting it alight, burning the victim alive. Though "necklacing" was widely condemned, and shocked even those sympathetic to the anti-apartheid struggle, some activists defended it as the only way to deter spies and maintain revolutionary discipline.

Sexwale later recalled the discussion differently — that the activists who had made, and spread, the accusation that Rhoda was a spy "never said anything about wanting to kill her," but rather that she and Rhoda had discussed "the seriousness and danger of such accusations in the context of what was happening at the time re necklacing etc."[36] She and a fellow South African activist wanted to warn Rhoda for the sake of her own safety, she said, in case the same rumour had been spread back home by the time she returned.

Either way, Rhoda was stunned to hear she had been targeted by activists in the anti-apartheid struggle and suspected by her own classmates. The warning was all the more chilling because of Bunie's close association with the ANC hierarchy.

According to Rhoda, Bunie then explained that their intelligence network had investigated Rhoda thoroughly, following her through much

---

35 Nemato Change a Life. "Board of Governors." URL: https://www.matinyanafund.org.za/nsf-contact.htm. Accessed on 2 Sep. 2022.

36 Bunie Sexwale. Personal communication with the author. 22 Dec. 2022.

of her time in The Hague. Rhoda had drawn suspicion, Bunie explained, because she had previously visited Europe in a delegation from South Africa; because she chose to live separately from the other students, with a Dutch family; because she was seen in the company of a white man — her husband; and because she and Richard were overheard speaking Afrikaans together, which was interpreted as a sign of loyalty to the apartheid regime.

Their investigation had reached beyond the Netherlands, Rhoda recalled being told. They had even looked into Dr. Victor Kadalie and probed his background. It was there that the investigation apparently began to unravel. Victor had long been supportive of the anti-apartheid movement. His son, Khwezi, had helped smuggle weapons to the ANC in exile, and was briefly detained by the apartheid regime.[37] One of Rhoda's classmates at ISS, a black student whom she called Loyiso (which was not his real name), had been jailed with Khwezi and privately vouched for Rhoda — though, she later remembered, he had been jealous of her husband.

According to Rhoda, Bunie said there had been other clues that suggested Rhoda's innocence: "We realized that if you were a spy, you were a bad one, because you were not interested in us." Rhoda seemed to spend very little of her free time outside of class hanging out with the revolutionaries. Instead, when the activists tailed her, their own spies discovered that Rhoda had a curious habit of going to clothing stores and toy stores, looking through items for babies. Unbeknownst to them, Rhoda had stopped taking her birth control pill, and had begun thinking of motherhood. Her future child had perhaps saved her life.

Rhoda, while relieved and grateful that Bunie had confided in her, was terrified by the revelations, and felt utterly disgusted. She and Richard were still wrestling with what they had learned when Rhoda received a call from the principal of the ISS program. She went to his office, where he informed her that he had learned of the rumors, and reassured her that "he would put a stop to all this,"[38] and that all those involved had been disciplined. She was grateful, and resolved to complete her studies, but refused to have anything to do with many of her classmates.

She later recounted the ordeal to her parents:

T]he rumour was spread that I was a spy for the S.A. govt. A huge insult which left me speechless. Was spread by a white lecturer's black wife — jealous of me (so says the Rector) and she was soon put in her place, by

---

37   Red Youth. "Red Salute to Comrade Khwezi Kadalie." 31 May 2014. URL: https://redyouthuk.wordpress.com/2014/05/31/red-salute-to-comrade-khwezi-kadalie/. Accessed on 5 Oct 2021.
38   Rhoda Kadalie. Diary entry, 6 Feb. 1986.

others who were initially her friends. But who later came to tell me what was going on.[39]

The experience soured Rhoda on the activists — permanently. Just as the stories of her fellow women activists convinced her that she could not be a radical, the experience of being stalked by ANC members shook her trust in the anti-apartheid movement. She was still committed to change, but could never trust the "comrades" again. Later, she noted that she was still held in suspicion by some classmates as a "bourgeois intellectual" because she insisted on asking questions. She wrote in her diary in May 1986 that "many people in that institute are not only jealous, but also did not like one to intellectually engage in topics."[40]

Years later, the Angolan couple visited South Africa to attend a ceremony launching a memorial lecture in honor of Ruth First at UWC.[41] They were shocked when Rhoda was the first speaker. Rhoda noticed that they seemed deeply ashamed — perhaps remembering what they had done.

***

Rhoda continued to work on completing her Master's thesis, even after discovering that she was pregnant. Because she found it uncomfortable to sit down while working for long periods of time, she took to typing her drafts while standing up, her typewriter balanced precariously on the mantelpiece of her host family's hearth, just above her growing belly.

Eventually, she began to feel weak. She went to the hospital, where doctors advised her that she was working too hard, and that she was at risk of losing the baby unless she rested. So after finishing her thesis, she left for Germany, rejoining Richard.

Richard's family remained welcoming. While resting, Rhoda enjoyed spending time with them — and they with her. Later, Richard's German relatives visited South Africa, and they became particularly enamored of Rhoda's pineapple salad, which they pleaded with her to make for them every time they came to see the young couple.

But there was not much time left for the couple to spend in Germany, because Rhoda wanted to deliver the baby in South Africa, near familiar

39   Rhoda Kadalie. Letter to Fenner and Joan Kadalie. 27 May 1986. Original emphasis.
40   Rhoda Kadalie. Diary entry, 26 May 1986.
41   This lecture, or colloquium, appears to have taken place at UWC in August 1992.

surroundings and her own family. So she flew — eight months pregnant — back to Cape Town with Richard at the end of 1986. She had completed her Masters' degree; despite his studies, he had not.

In the time that she and Richard had been away, the unrest in South Africa had become more intense. The government had declared a state of emergency in July 1985, lifting it only seven months later, in March 1986. In that period, the government detained some 10,000 people without trial, provoking an international outcry. The regime imposed a new state of emergency in June 1986, in a bid to limit unrest ahead of the 10th anniversary of the Soweto riots.[42] Some of the apartheid laws had been removed, such as the Mixed Marriages Act. But other rules remained in force.

Rhoda, watching for afar, wrote in her diary that the news from South Africa was "very depressing." She added: "Both of us feel that we can't go back, at the same time there is a tug to be part of the struggle."[43] In a similar vein, Richard wrote to his in-laws:

It is with fear and trepidation that Rhoda and I switch on the radio these days or listen to the news on BBC International Service, for each time we expect to hear of more and greater destruction [in South Africa]; and yet we cannot restrain ourselves from trying to hear as much as possible. It is a very strange feeling to be so far away from home at such a time of crisis: we feel helpless, in a different way than you do, and we almost despise ourselves for the privilege of being away from it all, while others have to live with this daily emergency. Then again, it is such a relief to be physically away from it all, that we do fully enjoy the great privilege of being here. It is a constant change of mood, I suppose, which corresponds to the instability of the situation.[44]

The prospects for peaceful political change — or change of any kind — looked grim. As Rhoda later remarked to an interviewer:

When the level of struggle escalated in 1985, I was still overseas and I thought the time for revolution was at hand. Then when my friends or family came to visit, they'd still be the same. One friend said, "Rhoda, you're going to be a grandmother before you see change." Now that I'm back, I really feel like that is true. I saw a documentary on the military might of South Africa, and I am convinced that the government will fight

42   Alan Cowell. "State of Emergency Imposed Throughout South Africa; More than 1,000 Rounded Up." *New York Times*, 13 Jun. 1986, p. A1.
43   Rhoda Kadalie. Diary entry, 13 Jun. 1986.
44   Richard Bertelsmann. Letter to Joan and Fenner Kadalie. 27 Oct. 1985.

to the death before it changes. So I think I'll be one of the many who will not remain to tell the story.[45]

She had frequently written to her parents about how shocked she and Richard had been to hear news of violence from South Africa — both between the government and the liberation movement, and among South Africans themselves. Though Rhoda was amused at clashes between the ruling National Party and the neo-Nazi Afrikaner Weerstandsbeweging (AWB),[46] she was shocked by the violent deaths of UDF activists,[47] and murderous attacks within the black community. She was bitterly resentful of the Reagan administration in the U.S. and the Thatcher government in the United Kingdom for opposing sanctions on apartheid South Africa. She feared that civil war was inevitable — so much so that she wrote to her parents in late May 1986 that she was prepared to become pregnant to avoid becoming mired in politics when she returned to South Africa. "What makes me scared about coming back is that I **will** get involved. Therefore, I should rather try to fall pregnant, so that I could have an excuse not to be involved."[48] (She would give birth to her daughter, Julia, almost exactly nine months later.)

Behind the scenes, the apartheid government had already begun negotiating secretly with Nelson Mandela, who was still in prison. The state of emergency had convinced some reform-minded leaders within the National Party that change was inevitable. But on the surface, it appeared that the ANC and other liberation movements were crushed — silenced politically, defeated militarily. While much had changed, South Africa remained a racially divided society, reinforced by various forms of segregation, formal and otherwise.

On February 21, 1987, Rhoda gave birth at the Mowbray Maternity Hospital to a healthy baby girl. She had quietly hoped for a girl: "If you give me a boy, God, I'm sending him back," she recalled praying. She and Richard had debated several names — many of them in German — before settling on "Julia," simply because they liked it. They gave her the middle name "Inge," which had been the name of the daughter of the Dutch family that hosted Rhoda in The Hague.

---

45   Rhoda Bertelsmann-Kadalie. "Marriage Across the Colour Bar," Ibid, 306.
46   Rhoda Kadalie. Letter to Fenner and Joan Kadalie. 27 May 1986.
47   Rhoda Kadalie. Letter to Fenner and Joan Kadalie. 6 Jul. 1985.
48   Rhoda Kadalie. Letter to Fenner and Joan Kadalie. 27 May 1986. Original emphasis.

In keeping with the enduring system of racial segregation, Julia was born in the Coloured wing of the hospital, and was classified as Coloured on her birth certificate, a status that her white father had not diluted.

Rhoda later recalled: "When Julia was born, the nurses handed the baby to Richie and sent him downstairs to have the baby weighed, etc. When he returned to the ward where I was, they directed him to a ward for white women, when he told them that his wife was in another section!! Julia received her birth certificate later than normal because they weren't sure whether to classify her coloured or white even though their laws of race classification stipulated that the kid takes on the race of the mother."[49]

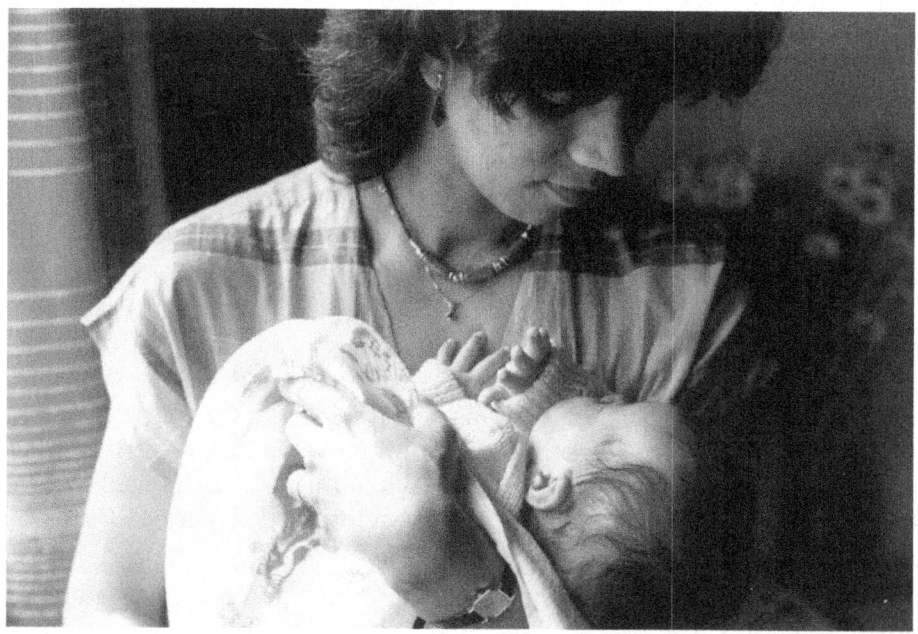

Rhoda holds newborn Julia Inge Bertelsmann, Observatory, Cape Town, 1987
(Courtesy Rhoda Kadalie)

Rhoda was determined to raise Julia in a feminist mode. Armed with her new Master's degree, she returned to teaching at UWC as soon as possible, and brought her baby with her to work. When she returned to her first faculty meeting with Julia bundled in a carrycot, Jakes Gerwel, who by then was the dean, stopped the meeting and demanded that Rhoda remove Julia's blankets so he could see her.

---

49   Personal communication with the author. 1 Feb. 2022.

"*Amandla*," he shouted from the podium, giving the familiar liberation salute, "she's Coloured!" The faculty burst into applause.

When Julia cried during lectures, Rhoda would simply open her blouse or dress and breastfeed her baby while teaching. That was not so unusual in an African context, where female breasts — at least in African communities — are often seen as functional rather than merely sexual. But it was unusual in a university setting, and among male-dominated faculty, no matter how radical their professed political persuasions. Rhoda used to say: "This course is about feminism in theory. Well, this is feminism in practice. If you don't like it, there's the door."[50]

The protests on campus continued, and Rhoda brought Julia to those, as well. While the state of emergency had suppressed some of the country's political unrest, it could not snuff out protest completely — and certainly not at UWC, whose faculty viewed themselves as the intellectual vanguard of the struggle.

Rhoda participated in protests — but also raised criticisms of the movement. She demanded that women be heard, declaring that "the struggle for national liberation itself has a gender context."[51] She challenged the idea that the struggle for freedom from racism could ignore women's struggle for equality.

She would soon face that struggle in a deeply personal way.

---

50   Personal communications with the author.
51   Ibid.

Chapter Seven:
Divorce

"People stigmatise divorce, but they should really stigmatise marriage — it's a completely dysfunctional institution."[1]

By 1987, Rhoda had every reason to feel optimistic about her family's future, even if the country's political situation seemed irresolvable.

She and Richard returned home from the hospital to their small semi-detached cottage in Observatory with their new baby. The terms of Rhoda's housing subsidy from UWC had prevented them from renting out the property while the young couple was in Europe. But the cottage had been well-kept by friends in the interim, and the suburb was still trendy, attracting young families and an eclectic mix of students, artists, and upwardly mobile people of every race.

Rhoda, Richard, and Julia at Julia's first birthday, Observatory, Cape Town, 1988 (Courtesy Rhoda Kadalie)

---

1   Sharon Sorour. "Rhoda Kadalie: Born to Lead." *Femina*, Jun. 1996. p. 78.

The Group Areas Act was still the law of the land, but it was essentially a dead letter in much of urban South Africa. The Immorality Act and the Mixed Marriages Act had been repealed, meaning that Rhoda and Richard no longer faced surveillance and arrest for the mere crime of being married, even though they still faced all kinds of other disadvantages. A growing number of religious schools were simply ignoring the government's racial boundaries and accepting black, Coloured, and Indian children, meaning that Julia would have more options than Rhoda had.

Most promising of all, Richard's family had begun to warm to Rhoda. She had enjoyed the time she spent with the extended Bertelsmann clan in Germany. Now, she could sense a thaw among Richard's South African family as well. His older brother, Helmut, had developed liberal ideas and was active in the Democratic Party, the descendant of Helen Suzman's anti-apartheid Progressive Party. Richard's nephews and nieces adored her. And even Werner Bertelsmann warmed to her. After his wife, Brigitte, was rather cold toward Rhoda during her first Christmas with the family, Werner intervened, asking her to include Rhoda in the family festivities.

Werner and Rhoda also had something in common: they both taught at "bush colleges." The Bertelsmann patriarch taught law at the University of the North, also known as "Turfloop," which the apartheid government had established specifically for black students in the northern Transvaal.[2] As at UWC, the state had assigned the most conservative faculty it could find to shape the minds of future black professionals — a strategy that Rhoda called "mind control." But even the most politically *verkramp* or recalcitrant professor could still care deeply for the education of his students. Rhoda and Werner bonded — tentatively — over shared academic values. They had continued to grow closer until his death on the 4th of July, 1984, from emphysema.

Rhoda hoped that her relationship with Richard's immediate family would continue to improve. However, even with some warmth, there were new tensions. Rhoda believed that "*Großmutter*" [Grandmother] Brigitte, as her family called her, had not reconciled herself to her son's marriage.

Several months into their sojourn in Europe, for example, Brigitte had arrived for a visit. That made everything worse: not only did Rhoda feel that Brigitte had ignored her, but Richard had seemed to ignore her, too, as he attended to his mother.

When she did address Rhoda, Großmutter advised her daughter-in-law to cut down on visits with Richard. After all, she said, "*Großvater und*

---

2   The area is known as Limpopo today; the university is called the University of Limpopo.

ich" — "Grandfather and I" — had been separated for a year during the war. What was a short separation during the academic term, compared to having a husband away in the Wehrmacht, fighting the Red Army on the Eastern Front?

Rhoda recounted Christmas spent with Richard in Germany in December 1985 with some bitterness, in a letter to her parents:

> *What I did not like was the way Richie's mother & her spinster sister regulated our lives. We were told when to get up, what time is lunch & told when to meet for supper. What's more they expected us to entertain Richie's eldest brother's 2 kids who accompanied the old lady to Germany. ... very sweet — but they like sitting in older people's company. Never did they leave Richie & me alone. Richie's mother is so possessive — Richie & I didn't see each other for 5 weeks & she expected us to be with her & them all the time. Also the old lady smokes 25 hrs a day — She never stops & she gets cross when I complain. ... When Richie complained that I found it bad & that he too doesn't like it she started becoming very bitchy & sarcastic towards me. ... What's more they all speak German & never once try to speak English.*
>
> *So I was thoroughly bored. I'm afraid that my relationship with my mother-in-law is finished. She tried to make me feel better when she saw that I was finished with her — but I find it hard to pretend. Of course, it makes Richie very sad because he thinks she's very wonderful & I think she isn't. She only has time for her own family & her own grandchildren. I hope that when I have a child that it is black & looks like me — so that she doesn't have to like it. It will be better for both me and the child. ... She also tries to make Richie think that I am difficult, so because he loves us both he is very divided & just becomes quiet when I nag about her. ... Also, she only tends to accept me for what I am when other people treat me well — but on her own I know she resents it that Richie married a darkie. Meanwhile she is rather dark herself — looks very much Turkish (that is bad in Germany) in blonde & blue-eyed Germany.[3]*

Rhoda's letter reflected the difficulty of navigating her relationship with her in-laws. She was conscious that she, too, was contributing to the difficulty, but what pained her most was her husband's inability to set protective boundaries around their marriage. Lacking the security of that intimacy, she confided her deeply personal thoughts to her own parents, half a world away.

---

3   Rhoda Kadalie. Letter to Fenner and Joan Kadalie. 7 Jan. 1986.

When Brigitte phoned Rhoda, by then alone in Holland, to say goodbye before she returned to South Africa from Germany, Rhoda became uncharacteristically emotional. "She was surprised," Rhoda noted in her diary, "but also teasingly said that she would phone my parents to say I was homesick. Or when Richie works on my nerves, she is sure that I am pleased to be without him." Rhoda was confused, and suspected that "Mutter" was simply trying to break up the marriage. "She is just so unfeeling," Rhoda concluded.

After Brigitte returned to South Africa, Rhoda and Richard endured a calamitous fight whose aftershocks would shake the marriage for years afterward. At first, Rhoda was unsure what had caused it. She noted in April 1986 that "Richie blew his top" unexpectedly during a discussion about Nicaragua — which was then the latest front in the Cold War between East and West.[4] "I lay in bed confused for 2 days over this sudden outburst," Rhoda wrote in her diary.[5] "Could it be because of the letter I wrote to his mother?" she wondered. Her suspicion was later to be confirmed.

In those days, when international telephone calls were prohibitively expensive, and air mail was the most efficient way to communicate overseas, Rhoda and Richard would tear open any letter that arrived from friends and family, sharing the words eagerly with each other. But on one occasion, Richard opened a letter from his mother and tried to hide it quietly away.

Rhoda was curious, and — in a decision she would later regret — she searched for the letter and read it. In it, Brigitte responded to her son's earlier reports of suffering with allergies from the pollen near Rhoda's residence in Holland. She warned that deeper medical issues might be a risk, and mentioned the new HIV/Aids virus. She suggested flippantly that it was common among black women, and that her son therefore ought to be careful in his dealings with Rhoda.

Furious, Rhoda wrote to her mother-in-law, defending herself; informing Brigitte that her letter had deeply disgusting, racist overtones; and telling her to stop trying to interfere with their marriage.

Richard soon heard from his mother about Rhoda's reply. In a letter that he later shared with Rhoda, Großmutter told her son that she had been deeply hurt by his wife's letter. She had never imagined, she said, that a private joke would cause so much trouble.

She was also upset that Rhoda had accused her of racism, and of trying to break up the marriage. "Our fundamental concerns about your

---

4   Rhoda Kadalie. Diary entry, 3 Apr. 1986.
5   Ibid.

marriage had and have nothing to do with Rhoda's personality," Brigitte wrote. "We were determined to treat your wife like our other daughters-in-law and to take them into the family after you were married." What happened before the marriage belonged to the past. "I always respected Rhoda as a person — her intelligence, her sense of humor and her ability to be a good woman to you. ... I had hoped that I and Rhoda would develop a friendship of our own."[6]

She recounted her past efforts to reconcile with Rhoda — despite perceived slights, such as Rhoda failing to wish her a good trip back to South Africa. Brigitte clearly felt that Rhoda had not appreciated her efforts — though, as her list of compliments included the fact that Rhoda could do dishes and laundry more quickly than she could, it was not hard to see why Rhoda might not have appreciated Großmutter's praises. In any event, Brigitte told Richard that she would not reply to Rhoda until she had apologized.

Instead of siding with Rhoda, Richard was furious at her — angry that she had invaded his privacy by reading his mother's letter, and angry that she had complicated his troubled relationship with his mother by taking her on directly herself. He kept his anger to himself until an "outburst" that Rhoda recalled in her diary, noting that when she called him to talk about it, "he was crying & put the phone down on me."[7]

The two of them argued over and over again about the issue. Richard could not bring himself to forgive Rhoda, or to understand her perspective. He could not defend his mother's views, but he also felt he could not oppose her openly. For weeks, they exchanged painful letters and shared anguished phone calls in which they aired their grievances from afar, frustrated with each other and themselves. At one point, Rhoda asked Richard if he wanted to continue their relationship. She noted his response: "He felt ambivalent toward me."[8]

Finally, in mid-April 1986, he visited Rhoda in Holland in an effort to reconcile. She noted a "[q]uiet, happy but sensitive reunion."[9] They avoided talking about the painful issues that had sparked their arguments — but then argued again after he returned to Germany. Richard wrote to her, asking her to write a letter of apology to Brigitte. Rhoda, exhausted by the argument, skipped class to visit him in Cologne "to solve this problem

6   Letter from "Großmutter" Brigitte Bertelsmann to Richard Bertelsmann, translated from the German, 28 Mar. 1986.
7   Rhoda Kadalie. Diary entry 7 Apr. 1986.
8   Rhoda Kadalie. Diary entry, 12 Apr. 1986.
9   Rhoda Kadalie. Diary entry, 18 Apr. 1986.

once & for all," she later recalled to her parents.[10] After a chilly greeting, their fight began anew:

> And then he started on how much I had hurt his mother; and that she really likes me; and that he can't be the same to me because I'm too stubborn to say sorry etc. etc. and so on & so on. Then I exploded, told him I wasn't married to his mother; that it was typical white dominance and that I will not say sorry unless he treats me better. After a long silence he got up and went for a walk. We went to sleep on 2 separate beds.

The following day, Rhoda began packing for her return to The Hague. Richard, seeing her preparing to leave, was suddenly apologetic. The two of them reconciled, and Rhoda agreed to swallow her pride and write a brief letter of apology to Brigitte — though Richard was nervous about what Rhoda would say.

"It was very heavy & difficult for me to write to his mother," she told her parents, "especially because I am convinced that I was not wrong & to say sorry when one is not sorry is for me the hardest thing to do. But since Richie appealed to my Christian & marital sense of love, I suppose this was the right thing to do." Richard also agreed to move nearer to the Netherlands, leaving Cologne for Mulheim, two hours closer, where he could stay with an aunt.

Großmutter acknowledged Rhoda's apology in a reply, but could not let the dispute rest.

To "find a basis for a renewed relationship of mutual respect and trust," Brigitte wrote, "I must insist that you explicitly take back your insulting accusations ... You called me heartless and put me on the same level with the South African government." She reminded Rhoda that she and her late husband had "allowed" her to address her as "Vater" and Mutter" on her first visit, as a sign that she had been accepted into the family.

The tensions between Rhoda and Richard had grown visible enough that Ruth Kadalie, Victor's wife in Germany, wrote to Rhoda before her departure from Europe in December 1986 to say that she regretted not having had the chance to advise Richard about the challenge of being in an interracial marriage.

---

10   Rhoda Kadalie. Letter to Fenner and Joan Kadalie. 16 May 1986.

She wrote:

I would have liked to tell him my personal experience and to discuss with him the fact, that there is no alternative than to live a life on the "black people's" side. According to my experience once cannot stand with one foot in the "white people's" side and with the other foot in the "black people's" side. You know what I mean. To be married to a black partner is not any longer an individual choice of love and affection[,] it is at the same time a political choice with all its consequences. One has no alternative than to also be "black" and to live a "black life," only then is one able to gain the necessary sensitiveness to share a black person's life with your partner in all respects and with all its aspects.

I would have liked to talk to Richie about this in detail in view of the birth of your child, because he has to share his child's experiences in life.[11]

Ruth saw the tension as fundamentally a political one. Whether politics was the primary factor or not, Richard felt torn between Rhoda's needs on the one hand, and his mother's demands on the other.

There were more weeks of tension, punctuated by moments of happiness. When Richard visited Rhoda in May 1986, their romance seemed to have been rekindled. "Richie arrived. Happy Reunion," Rhoda wrote in her diary on May 30, adding that she suspected that she had become pregnant: "Conception!!!?".[12] She confirmed that speculation with a pregnancy test in late June, and again in a formal examination in Germany in early July. Richard accompanied her to the latter, and "he was only too proud to be recognised as an equal partner in the whole deal," though he turned "pale green" owing to his "hospital phobia."[13] Rhoda was thrilled at the prospect of motherhood, and kept a photograph of her ultrasound in the pages of her diary, with the "body" and "head" labeled appropriately. Richard would continue to visit throughout her pregnancy, nursing her through morning sickness and a bout of the flu.

News of the reconciliation evidently reached South Africa. Rhoda's mother, Joan, wrote to the couple in early June 1986 — before the pregnancy had been confirmed: "[W]e are especially happy that things has turn [sic] out for the best between you and Richie just one of the many Bridges we have to cross. *Elke huis het n kruis* ["Every house has a cross"] sometimes

---

11   Ruth Kadalie. Letter to Rhoda Bertelsmann. 8 Dec. 1986.
12   Rhoda Kadalie. Diary entry, 30 May 1986.
13   Rhoda Kadalie. Diary entry, 2 Jul. 1986.

its good. [B]ecause it draws one closer to each other. My only regret is that you are so far from us it must have been terrible for you both."[14]

Tensions persisted, however. At times, Rhoda recorded her disappointment at Richard's prolonged absences: "Never gives me a second thought when I'm not around," she complained in her diary.[15] When he did call, she sometimes burst into tears; the subject of his mother continued to haunt and divide them. But he surprised her in late August with an early visit before her birthday, presenting her with the gift of a typewriter "& a little chocolate in a sweet box."[16] It would prove useful in the often lonely months ahead, as she worked on her thesis, struggling to beat academic deadlines and her baby's due date. Despite all the difficulties they had had, Rhoda noted that she "bawled" when he departed alone for South Africa in December 1986 — leaving her to work on finishing her thesis.

Though Rhoda and Richard would reunite happily in Cape Town, a gulf remained, leavened somewhat by the prospect of parenthood, and the renewed excitement of academics and activism.

***

Vignette: "The Great Confession," by Rhoda Kadalie

It was the late eighties. Dr. Allan Boesak was at the height of his political career. A speaker of note, he impressed the world with his oratory condemning the apartheid government in no uncertain terms.

Fêted across the world, he was held in high esteem by the anti-apartheid movement in Holland, Scandinavia, the United Kingdom, and America's Black Congressional Caucus, the Kennedys, and pop stars. Boesak himself became a celebrity. Money flowed into South Africa's liberation movement like water from all and sundry, meant to pay for defense lawyers, political prisoners and detainees, organizing the masses, and supporting indigent struggle leaders.

As noble as the struggle was, the air was thick with leadership hubris. Money disappeared into profligate lifestyles; leaders became unfaithful to their lovers and wives. As underground activity became a way of life,

---

14   Joan Kadalie. Letter to Rhoda and Richard Bertelsmann. 4 Jun. 1986.
15   Rhoda Kadalie. Diary entry, 18 Jul. 1986.
16   Rhoda Kadalie. Diary entry, 30 Aug. 1986.

the secretive world, while genuinely necessary in many cases, became an excuse for all manner of devious pursuits.

One fine day, as Boesak flew into Cape Town with Democratic Senator Ted Kennedy of Massachusetts, the headlines alleged that he was having an affair with a white woman, Di Scott, a secretary based at Cowley House in District Six.

There was great denial. "Boesak is being framed by the apartheid government," claimed the struggle leaders.

Boesak, who pretended to be loyal to his wife and children, denied the allegation the most. The "struggle" was in a tizz as more and more evidence surfaced. Activists gathered at his home, putting together hundreds and hundreds of t-shirts, emblazoned with slogans like "We stand by our leaders," or "*Ons staan met ons leiers*," in Afrikaans.

"As they lay with their lovers," my cynical husband, Richard, whispered wryly, witnessing the t-shirt-donning activists milling about the house.

Unable to evade the cameras and the media, Boesak decided to confess and apologize to the struggle and his wife, in that order. But it would be done in dramatic fashion, at the very hall in Mitchell's Plain where the United Democratic Front was launched. It was to be the Great Confession. The masses gathered from far and wide.

True to form, the brazen Boesak made a dramatic entry, wearing his bright red cassock, as people shouted "Boesak, Boesak, Boesak!"

My husband and I arrived a bit late, when there were no seats left, so we watched the saga from outside. As people chanted, "Boesak, Boesak, Boesak!", a *bergie* (homeless man) next to us, filled with the spirit, shouted "*Dis van lat jou broek sak, broek sak, broek sak, wat jy nou hier is*" ("It's from letting your pants sag, pants sag, pants sag, that you're here now").

Our evening was made. Boesak did not, in fact, confess, but it took the salt of the earth to know the truth.

***

The cottage in Observatory was small enough with just two adults living in it; with a new baby, it was almost claustrophobic.

One day, Rhoda and Richard took Julia to a beach. She went "berserk," as Rhoda would later recall, as soon as the family settled onto the sand: she had never seen an outdoor surface other than the little lawn in front of the cottage. The "towel-sized" front garden had left young Julia with little room to explore — and few parents in crime-ridden South Africa would take their children to the local park.

Rhoda's house in University Estate; today the home is painted gray
(Courtesy Rhoda Kadalie)

Rhoda's house, on the slopes of Devil's Peak, overlooked Woodstock below
and Table Bay beyond

So they began looking for a new home, and found one: a larger home on Fryde Street, a steep road in a neighborhood called Upper Woodstock, along the slope of Devil's Peak, above the main N2 highway and below the winding mountain road known as De Waal Drive. The house also had a separate apartment on the ground floor, with a bedroom and a kitchen.

The new house shook in the howling winds that whipped around the mountain in summertime. And wildfires, both seasonal and man-made, that burned across the fynbos of Table Mountain would occasionally threaten the neighborhood. But the home had a large back yard with lemon trees, and sweeping views of Table Bay. Rhoda, who had bought the house in Observatory, used the sale proceeds to help pay for the new house, though it had to be in Richard's name, in deference to the enduring labels of the Group Areas Act.

The first two years they spent in the house were the happiest of their lives together, Rhoda recalled. But Richard was quietly brooding, nursing wounded emotions that Rhoda could not detect.

His resentment began to emerge on a family trip to Pretoria, to visit the Bertelsmann clan. Julia, who was nearly two years old, felt unsettled by the long trip, and was difficult to manage. Rhoda tended to the child on her own, separate from the family; Richard barely checked on her.

Later, they were sitting with Richard's relatives, when his sister-in-law began to disparage Rhoda's education. The subtext, Rhoda felt, was jealousy — and race: Richard had returned from Europe without earning a degree. Already, in Europe, Rhoda had noted that he seemed more interested in reading and writing for his own interest than in his studies. Moreover, when he did work, "[h]e reads a lot and tries to be too thorough, that is why he does not get anywhere," she wrote to her parents.[17] His own family struggled to understand why she had managed to earn her qualification, while their relative, a native German speaker who in their view was far more intelligent than her, had failed.

There was another context as well: the Bertelsmanns had just suffered a tragic loss. Helmut's son, Tommy, had been riding his bicycle near his home when he was struck by a car and killed earlier that month. The family was devastated, and emotions were running high.

Rhoda mourned with the family, traveling for the funeral and noting in her diary that day — 21 December 1988 — that she had been moved by the service, and was "overwhelmed by grief." She also noted that Großmutter's reading from Isaiah 65 ("And I will rejoice with Jerusalem,

---

17   Rhoda Kadalie. Letter to Fenner and Joan Kadalie. 27 May 1986.

and I will exult with My people, and a sound of weeping or a sound of crying shall no longer be heard therein" 65:19) had been "memorable."[18]

Yet she and Großmutter encountered a familiar tension, and Rhoda felt that the Bertelsmanns were mocking her degree, telling her that development studies was not a real academic field. Rhoda, not wishing to rock the boat, stayed quiet. When she and Richard were alone together, she demanded to know why he had not stood up for her. "If you're such a strong feminist," he replied rhetorically, "why didn't you stand up for yourself?"

With that, Rhoda decided to return home. She took Julia to the airport and caught a flight back to Cape Town, leaving Richard to spend the Christmas and New Year's holidays with his family, alone. She felt that if she had met his relatives earlier, she never would have married him. And she resolved to have nothing to do with them: she had given up trying to build bridges.

In the airport, she noticed a forlorn-looking blond couple. "Is something wrong?" she asked them. They turned out to be an Austrian flight attendant and her husband, who had decided to visit Cape Town on a whim, but had discovered that all of the hotels were full for the holiday season, and that no rental cars were available.

"Well, you can stay with me," she said. She welcomed the disbelieving but excited couple into her home, and entertained them for several days, regaling them with stories about Cape Town — and unburdening her troubles. She told them about the ongoing fight with her husband, and they provided a sympathetic ear.

Suddenly, Richard returned. He behaved toward Rhoda as if there had never been a fight; the Austrian couple, who knew every detail, found themselves in an awkward position.

When the Austrian couple finally returned home, the tension between Rhoda and Richie returned. The entire winter holiday season had exposed lingering conflicts in the marriage. (Rhoda's diary on 23 December 1988 read: "Disaster through to January."[19])

Those tensions only deepened after Richard was given a share of a large inheritance from his parents. Just as her degree had made the Bertelsmann family in Pretoria uncomfortable, the fact that she had bought their first house in Observatory herself — without any inheritance whatsoever — also made them feel resentful.

---

18   Rhoda Kadalie. Diary entry, 21 Dec. 1988.
19   Rhoda Kadalie. Diary entry, 23 Dec. 1988.

When Richard finally had his own money, Rhoda told him she did not want any of it. He did buy her a car — a white Toyota to replace the Volkswagen "Fun Bug" that she had sold to cover some of their expenses in Europe. But she did not want to feel beholden to him, or to his family.

In August 1988, Rhoda discovered that she had an ectopic pregnancy, and had to be hospitalized. Her diary entry for 28 August read: "Got up with feeling of pain in left side of abdomen. Contacted doctor from 10 onwards. Reached him by 11:30. Went to doctor, examined me — & then had scan done. Operated immediately to remove ectopic pregnancy. Doctors kept saying that scan showed pregnancy sacs in uterus as well."[20]

Technically, it was a heterotopic pregnancy. The embryo that had apparently implanted in Rhoda's uterus failed to survive. She was hospitalized for several days, and was discharged on the first of September; she continued to suffer pain and infection for days afterward.

That loss was, perhaps, a sign of a marriage that was quickly approaching a crisis.

Yet the way it finally unraveled would be a shock to them both.

***

Life settled into a familiar pattern, amidst the chaos of the anti-apartheid struggle and the constant turmoil on campus. There were protests, prayers, and police raids, with courses frequently disrupted by riots, or by boycotts. A diary entry from 18 July 1988 read: "Nelson Mandela's 70th birthday. Everything banned! Police encircled Langa [a black township], UCT, UWC."[21] On 24 October, she wrote:

> *Cops stormed into campus. Threw teargas cannisters and grenades were fired into student rooms so that 3 bedrooms were set alight. 6 Casspirs [riot control vehicles] intimidatingly drove around campus — quite fed-up that students were not provocative enough & so provoked them by charging after them into buildings.*[22]

Alongside the violence, there were endless debates and discussions about the path forward, the prospects of political change, and what a post-apartheid South Africa might look like, including a future bill of rights. Rhoda participated in these, to the best of her ability, as she balanced politics, academia, and family life.

---

20   Ibid, diary entry 28 Aug. 1988. Original emphasis.
21   Rhoda Kadalie. Diary entry 18 Jul. 1988.
22   Ibid, diary entry 24 Oct. 1988.

Through it all, Richard and Rhoda — who used her husband's married name, Bertelsmann, at the time — managed to secure a housing subsidy for their home in University Estate. Julia grew quickly, and though she often seemed to be sick with colds and fevers, she learned to speak quickly. Rhoda spoke to her in English, and Richard in German. She loved books and music, and was happy in the home, which had a large back yard.

These years — 1987 through 1989 — would be the happiest of their marriage, despite lingering disagreements, and occasional ups and downs.

One evening in December 1989, Rhoda was at home, waiting for Richard to return from work. She had phoned him, asking him to buy a tablecloth, which she intended to give as a wedding present to one of his cousins in Germany.

She busied herself with chores. Outside, in the back yard, the family's heavily-pregnant cat was about to give birth, an event Richard had anticipated with curious interest. Marianne Thamm, a journalist who was living in the flat below the house, was in the kitchen with Rhoda.

When Richard came home, Rhoda was chatting with Marianne. Rhoda greeted her husband, but he walked right past her, intent on tending to the cat and her kittens. Rhoda quipped to Marianne: "You see, the kittens get more attention than me." Both laughed at what Rhoda believed had been an innocent remark; Marianne soon returned downstairs to the flat.

Richard appeared to ignore the remark, and spent some time tending to the cat in the garden, as Rhoda tidied drawers in Julia's room. He returned, suddenly, and approached Rhoda — and struck her in the face with his fist, sending her reeling to the floor. He hit her several more times, leaving her slumped against the chest of drawers, bleeding. Then he stormed out of the house, slamming a garbage can as he did so.

Julia, who was then two-and-a-half years old, suddenly noticed her mother in her wounded condition, and was frightened and confused. So, too, was Rhoda. "He smashed me up," she would later recall. "I was shocked."[23]

The surprise was about more than the fact that her slight, soft-spoken and gentle husband had attacked her. Here she was, an academic with a degree in women's studies, who had heard countless stories from abused women who had been beaten by their husbands — and now she, too, was a victim.

Richard had been quietly smoldering with rage over Rhoda's remark as he walked in the door. Rather than express his irritation in the moment,

---

23   Personal conversation with the author.

and verbally, he had let his anger fester. Ironically, as he tended delicately to the vulnerable, fragile kittens, he was furious with his wife.

Months of distance and frustration, which had built up since their time in Europe, and which had been exacerbated by family tensions, had culminated in a calamitous outburst of violence, which was completely out of character for the otherwise gentle Richard.

Rhoda called to Marianne for help. Marianne was livid to see Rhoda's injuries, and confronted Richard when he tried to return, swearing at him. He would never move back to the house on Fryde Street.

The shock was severe. Rhoda would recall in a draft letter to the court years later: "In December 1989 our marriage exploded over a minor incident (in fact) over a joke I had made. He beat me up so severely so much so that I had to see a doctor and stay home from work for 2 weeks. That sudden eruption was the end of my marriage."[24]

As she reeled from her injuries, Rhoda's feminist training took over. She knew she needed to have herself examined by a doctor — both to assess the damage, and to document what happened. Later, Richard would tell her that the doctor's report had made it impossible for him to reconcile with her: the fact that there was a record of his outburst made it much harder for him to imagine it could be overcome.

Not that Rhoda was too interested in reconciliation — at least, in her recollection. She decided that any man who would hit her did not deserve her. She was also concerned for her daughter — who adored her father, but who was so upset by what she had seen him do that she called him names in his absence — perhaps repeating what she, or Marianne, had said about him.

The unexpected violence meant the marriage was effectively over, despite the happiness that Rhoda felt they had begun to enjoy.

Richard agreed that the event marked the end of their relationship, although he remembered the cause rather differently:

The fatal event, as far as our marriage was concerned, was a telephone conversation Rhoda had with my mother, at a time when I had already moved out of the house. They had a difference of opinion, and I tried to explain what I took to be my mother's position. I was terribly conflicted, feeling enormous pressure and moral obligation to agree with each one of these conflicting positions. This angered Rhoda enormously, and she said (or "spat out", as "penny horrible" literature would put it) :

---

24   Rhoda Kadalie. Draft letter to the Supreme Court of Cape Town. Unsent. 30 Jul. 1995.

"Then go to your mother!" Despairing at her unwillingness or inability to understand my position, I totally lost it and hit her several times, until she ran to her bedroom (the "conversation" had taken place at her home's front door). For me, that was the end of our relationship. I don't know myself as a violent person, and I felt I could no longer be with someone who could drive me to such extremes. I also feared that she could / would abuse this experience at any possible future difference of opinion: "Watch out, you know you're a violent man, now calm down and accept what I say!" In a subsequent telephone conversation she did ask me to come back, but I refused, for the reasons given above.[25]

Richard felt that Rhoda had pushed him to extremes of behavior that he did not recognize in himself. Precisely because he regretted his violent outburst, he felt he could not return.

Apartheid's absurd racial legislation had not kept them apart. They had defied the regime, with all its might, despite the fact that it had spied on them and threatened them with arrest. They had stood up — for a time, at least — to the opposition of their respective families. They had made it through two years of a long-distance relationship in Europe, seeing each other only on weekends and holidays. They had survived the suspicion and surveillance of the ANC underground. In in the end, it was one unpredictable moment that irrevocably ended a marriage that had endured so many challenges.

Over time, Julia would repair her relationship with her father — with Rhoda's encouragement. Richard would take her to school daily, and the two developed a bond that extended through her teenage years.

***

The divorce was, at times, a bitter one, and was finalized in May 1992. They quarreled throughout: Rhoda noted in her diary in February 1991 that when she and Richard were both evacuated from Cape Town to the eastern suburb of Somerset West during one of the periodic brush fires that threatened residential neighborhoods on the slopes of Table Mountain, they had a "big fight" at a restaurant that "spoilt" the camaraderie of the evening.[26] Every family event provided a flashpoint, including Julia's birthday parties.

---

25   Richard Bertelsmann. Personal communication with the author. 2 Sep. 2022.

26   Rhoda Kadalie. Diary entry, 8 Feb. 1991

They tried marital counseling at first, and attended a few sessions together, until the marriage counselor did something that struck Rhoda as unusual. She called Rhoda one night, after a session, and advised her that the best thing for her to do would be to leave the relationship.

That did it for Rhoda. She decided to make the separation permanent — and fought long and hard for custody of Julia, for the house, and for the car.

Richard wanted to recover his share of the value of the house, if Rhoda were to live in it. Prior to the settlement of the divorce, he stopped paying the mortgage, meaning that unless Rhoda could obtain a housing subsidy from UWC, the bank could repossess the property. She ultimately agreed to take over the mortgage and to buy him out of his share. In the divorce agreement, approved by the provincial court, they also agreed that Rhoda would have custody of Julia, with Richard hosting Julia on designated weekends.

Richard informed Rhoda abruptly in July 1992 that he had decided to remarry. Rhoda came to believe that he had planned his new marriage long before the divorce had been settled.

Two years later, in 1994, Rhoda was surprised to receive a summons that she received from Richard's brother, Eberhard, an attorney in Pretoria who would later go on to become a judge. Eberhard notified Rhoda that she owed Richard tens of thousands of rands to make up the difference between what she had actually paid him (almost R30,000) and what she had agreed to pay him (R43,000) for his share of the house — plus interest.

Rhoda believed that Richard had borrowed money from Eberhard to buy a home with his new wife, and wanted to repay him with funds from Rhoda. The argument escalated to the point where Eberhard threatened to have the home seized by the local sheriff and to have Rhoda evicted from it. Rhoda noted in a diary entry in September 1992: "Put a poster on the front door — Judge Bertelsmann *se moer* ("Judge Bertelsmann's mother," an insult in Afrikaans slang).[27] Ultimately, a court decided in Rhoda's favor, and the matter was dropped, though Eberhard successfully appealed a court order to pay Rhoda's costs.

Rhoda would later explain the collapse of her marriage as the result of tensions with Richard's family — either because of racism, or simple personality conflicts:

Well, I was married to a white German man. And I never met his parents before because they opposed the marriage. But we loved each other, and

---

27   Rhoda Kadalie. Diary entry 26 Sep. 1992.

we left the country, we went to Namibia and got married. And it was only after my marriage that I met the family. And I was never sure that it was racism or in-law problems. I was always uncomfortable with that family. I'm a very easy person and I get on very well with people, and I have a huge circle of friends from all colours. And so that, for me, was the dilemma. [28]

Rhoda concluded: "And I think if I had met him, with his family, before we got married, I would never have married him."[29]

Richard would later recall:

I believe we were indeed very different: she outgoing and enterprising, I more reserved and reflective. I believe that I was also more accommodating and prepared to compromise, though (of course) opinions may differ on that. I do believe that opposites attract one another, at least initially, but after a while such a constellation causes tensions. ... I sometimes wondered if her attitude had been formed by her having been the only girl among six or seven brothers. [30]

Despite the lingering harsh feelings between them after the acrimonious divorce, and subsequent legal fights, Richard remained closely involved in Rhoda's and Julia's lives, with Rhoda's approval. They developed a routine: he would pick Julia up from school and drop her off every day. That allowed Julia to continue developing a close emotional bond with her father, which lasted through her school days.

At first, Rhoda enrolled Julia in St. Joseph's, a nearby Catholic school. Julia was miserable there, and made to feel unwelcome, since she had not been baptized. According to Rhoda, Julia was also subjected to teasing because of her skin color — and her mother's. She recalled "with anger and distress" that Julia, who was oblivious to racial distinctions, was mocked by other children for having a "black mummy."[31]

Rhoda searched for an alternative and found St. Cyprian's school for girls, an elite private Anglican school in the City Bowl area that began at the early grade level and continued through high school.

---

28   Rhoda Kadalie, "Woman Today," ibid.
29   Ibid.
30   Richard Bertelsmann. Personal communication with the author. 2 Sep. 2022.
31   Institute of Democracy in South Africa. "A necessary irritant?". *Democracy in Action*, Vol. 9 No. 7, 15 Dec. 1995. p. 10.

Richard objected: the tuition was expensive, and public schools were opening up to all races. But Rhoda insisted that Julia have the best education she possibly could. Somehow, she scraped together the money to pay — not just for school, but for cello lessons, and even for a horse in the countryside, which Julia insisted on learning to ride. Ironically, years later, once Rhoda could afford Julia's tuition, her daughter won a music scholarship that covered most of the costs.

Julia and Rhoda at home, preparing for the St. Cyprian's School matriculation ball, 2004 (Courtesy Rhoda Kadalie)

Richard's new wife, Jessica, was a radiography nurse by training, and the cousin of Franklin Sonn, one of the more intriguing personalities on the South African political landscape. A teacher by training, Franklin had been known as a moderate within the Coloured community before becoming more active in the anti-apartheid movement. He supported the ANC in the historic 1994 elections, which cost him a post on the board of South Africa's state broadcaster, but helped deliver the Coloured vote for the ANC in the Cape, thus earning himself a post as the first post-apartheid ambassador to the U.S.[32]

---

32   Staff reporter. "Who's tipped for payback postings." *Mail & Guardian* 2 Dec. 1994. URL: https://mg.co.za/article/1994-12-02-whos-tipped-for-payback-postings/. Accessed on 6 Oct. 2021.

Rhoda and Franklin had been friends for years. He would later become chair of the board of Impumelelo, the organization she founded to recognize excellence in social development programs (see Chapter 11). But she did not have much of a relationship with Jessica. Ironically, despite the difficult circumstances of the divorce, Rhoda and her family stepped in to care for Richard when he survived a near-fatal car accident in December 1999 on a trip to the wedding of his domestic worker's son in the rural Eastern Cape — an unusual journey for a white South African to take, and a risky proposition for anyone daring to board the long-distance minibus taxis, driven by overworked drivers on little to no sleep.

On returning from the wedding, the taxi in which Richard was riding suffered burst tires and skidded off the road.[33] The carnage was so severe that it made the national news. Six passengers were killed; Richard was among three survivors, and suffered a broken nose, injuries to his eyes, and acute memory loss. Rhoda's brother, who happened to be in the Eastern Cape, took it upon himself to find Richard in a public hospital and helped bring him back to Cape Town to recover.

The horror of his injuries and the precarious state of his health, as well as the miraculous fact of his survival, moved her to intervene. Rhoda noted in her diary on December 13, 1999: "Richie survived an accident in which 6 people died upon return from the wedding in Transkei. ... Asked [brother] Reuben to go — said the hospital was disgusting, smelly, & Richie was lying exposed."

***

Vignette: "Rescuing an Ex-husband", by Rhoda Kadalie

In December 1999, Richie came to see me to tell me that he was leaving for the Eastern Cape to attend his domestic worker's son's wedding. I asked him how he would be travelling and he told me that he would fly there and they would collect him in a combi.

My spontaneous response was: "*Jy soek kak*" (you are looking for shit, or trouble).

He reassured me that the combi was fully serviced, had new tires, etc etc. A few days after he left, I was driving to the university and heard

---

33   Rhoda Kadalie. Letter to Jurgen and Catherine Girgensohn. 4 Jan. 2000.

on the news that a combi had crashed in the Eastern Cape, perhaps near Cradock. Immediately, I switched off the radio, muttering to myself "I hope it's not Richie."

After work I went to a UCT Council meeting, and when I returned home, all the lights were on, and the front door was open. Knowing that Julia was alone at home, I panicked. It was Margot, Julia's cousin, who had come to tell her that Richie had been in a serious accident.

When I phoned Jessica, she didn't seem to know much, nor where Richie was hospitalized. I called a UCT professor, R. Kirsch, to help me find Richie. His friend was Minister Jay Naidoo's brother, who was in charge of the hospitals in the Eastern Cape, and immediately the brother snapped into action and traced Richie to a hospital in the Eastern Cape. He told me that Richie was in a serious condition, but would recover.

I suddenly remembered that my brother Reuben was working in the Eastern Cape for a stint for his company and called him. Reuben found Richie in some disgusting hospital in the province, in a ward with 20 others, lying half naked, his face smashed up and bandaged, with hardened blood under his fingernails. He said the ward was humid, with no air conditioning, and it reeked of blood and urine.

I called Jessica and gave her the news. Her response was that "now he would know the state of SA hospitals."

I was gobsmacked. Reuben was horrified to see the conditions under which Richie was being held, given that he had superior medical insurance. He said, "Rhoda if you were still married to him, you would instruct me to put him in the medical centre nearby." The point was, I was no longer married and could do nothing about it.

Jessica flew down three days later to see him. Richie's nose was broken, and he had facial injuries. Moreover, he had severe amnesia. All he spoke about was the traditional ritual slaughter of an ox at the wedding, which clearly made an impression on him: he loved animals and had found the spectacle unbearable.

Richie could not be transferred to Cape Town by plane as he needed to be stabilized, so the ambulance drove them for several hours to Vincent Pallotti hospital in Pinelands.

He was immediately put on a drip in a private ward. Upon our first visit, we found Richie lying half-naked, having ripped out the drip because he needed the toilet and the nurses did not hear him scream. He was too brain-damaged to know to use the call button.

Julia was traumatized to see him like that when again we found him half-naked the next day. I promptly went and bought him two pairs of pyjamas and a nail clipper, and cut his nails.

***

Richard recovered slowly from his injuries; he had acute memory loss and suffered hallucinations. Julia was distraught to see her father suffering. As Rhoda noted after Julia visited him in the hospital: "When I fetched her, she sobbed & sobbed telling me how she hated seeing her dad in his confused state. He was hungry, starving for hamburgers. Went to the phone & thought he was ordering hamburgers. So I went to Steers & bought him 2 big hamburgers. His face lit up when he saw them."[34]

Though their divorce had been bitter, Rhoda did her best to help him return, slowly, to his normal life. For years thereafter, she would keep track in her diary of the annual holiday season death toll on the country's roads, which became a topic of national concern.

After the divorce, Rhoda lost interest in marriage. For the first several years after Richard left, she virtually barred men from her home. She rented the apartment below her house to a series of women, including lesbian couples, and became one of the most vocal advocates for gay and lesbian rights in South Africa. At a lecture on feminist thought that she delivered to UCT's "Summer School" program, she received a standing ovation for arguing for the recognition of gay rights in South Africa's emerging new political order.

In later life, Rhoda would return to dating, though she developed few enduring love interests. Jakes Gerwel would occasionally send her flirtatious notes, though their relationship apparently never developed beyond a close friendship. The closest they came to something more was in the late 1980s and early 1990s, when Gerwel would send notes such as: "You'll never get remarried the way you manage to keep avoiding your main potential suitor. I've phoned, I've called personally...".[35]

On one occasion, Gerwel sent Rhoda a humorous placard, evidently purchased as a novelty, that read: "Notice of What Counts: Small-breasted women have big hearts." He attached a sticky note: "A heart as big as yours should have a place in it for me as well."[36] More typical was an email he sent her after missing a lunch date in January 2004: "You are

---

34   Rhoda Kadalie. Diary entry, 1 Jan. 2000.
35   Jakes Gerwel. Note to Rhoda Kadalie. 23 Mar 1990.
36   Jakes Gerwel. Note to Rhoda Kadalie. Undated (circa late 1980s early 1990s).

very special in my life; I am one of your most unapologetic fans; you are one of my oldest friends and most continuous and consistent friendships. … Rhoda, please forgive me. I love you and will never do such a dastardly thing to you deliberately."[37] He added: "Remember, women with small breasts have big hearts. Please be big-hearted and accept my apology and forgive me."

Rhoda commented that she was "no prude," noting that in the years after her marriage ended, she "had two red hot love affairs … which she enjoyed; she'll take them to her grave."[38] Still, she never allowed any relationship to go too far. In later years, she was often accompanied in public by philanthropist James MacGregor, a friend who served on the board of the Molteno Brothers Trust with her (see Chapter 17), and who shared many of her intellectual interests and cultural tastes. But their relationship was never intimate, or exclusive. She valued her independence too highly to allow a man to control any aspect of her life.

Rhoda with Joan and Fenner at her home in University Estate, c. 1993
(Courtesy Rhoda Kadalie)

---

37   Jakes Gerwel. Email to Rhoda Kadalie, 21 Jan. 2004.
38   Rhoda Kadalie. Personal communication with the author. 13 Mar. 2022.

Her divorce also challenged her to rethink some of her ideas about domestic violence, which is a widespread social phenomenon in South Africa. It was an important topic in sociology, criminology, and anthropology, and one she had discussed and debated with her students.

Men, Rhoda had believed, used domestic violence, particularly in black communities, to express their frustration with their social marginalization. Racism excluded them; capitalism exploited them. So physical dominance over women and children offered the temptation to assert some kind of control over their lives.

She still believed that to be true, and argued against the tendency of some feminists to target or demonize men and masculinity. Yet she now realized, from firsthand experience, that domestic violence was not merely a social phenomenon or a by-product of a bad system. It was also an independent evil, one that could emerge in any social context, white or black.

Moreover, Rhoda felt it was not enough to teach about violence against women: she set out to find solutions.

Chapter Eight:
Feminism

"I came [back] to UWC with an intellectual understanding of what I'd always believed in terms of my gut feelings. I could put substance to the oppressions [of] women, to the position of women nationally, locally, internationally. ... I became an activist because I think it's important that one deals with the issues which affect women on a day-to-day basis."[1]

By 1987, when Rhoda returned to the University of the Western Cape, the campus had reached a turning point. In the fall of 1985, four members of the administration had joined a group of 2,000 students in a march to the nearest police station to protest against the state of emergency and the detention of political dissidents.[2] Many students had boycotted their classes for half the year to express solidarity with boycotts by black high school students, a reflection of the fact that younger students had been in the vanguard of the struggle since 1976.[3] The political tension in the country as a whole had begun to affect UWC, as it had all campuses, especially the "bush" colleges.

Jakes Gerwel, one of the first black faculty members, and once criticized by the white administration for his role in the Black Consciousness movement, was named rector of the university, replacing the moderate Richard Van der Ross. He gave Van der Ross credit for allowing students to express themselves: "He has created the space for protest," he told the *Chronicle on Higher Education*, which devoted its June 1986 issue to the crisis on South Africa's campuses. "Like the true liberal that he is, although he did not always agree with what the students were saying, he listened to them. He changed the university from a place of authority to a place that caters to criticism and protest."[4]

---

1   Rhoda Kadalie. Unpublished interview with Melanie Walker, 27 Oct. 1994.
2   Scully et al., ibid., p. 13.
3   Ibid., p. 14.
4   Gerwel, quoted by Scully et al., ibid., p. 14.

UWC faculty, staff, and students join an anti-apartheid protest, c. 1985. Jakes Gerwel is in the front row, right of center (Courtesy Rhoda Kadalie)

Former UWC Chancellors Jakes Gerwel and Richard van der Ross flank Rhoda Kadalie after honorary doctoral ceremonies, Bellville, 2007 (Courtesy Rhoda Kadalie)

But the political mood had moved beyond liberalism and collegial debate. The anti-apartheid struggle had become about more than inclusion with whites on an equal basis in the same social institutions: it aimed at revolutionary change in the institutions themselves. Mamphela Ramphele, by then a professor of social anthropology at UCT, declared: "[The liberal universities] have always assumed that the system they have is the right one, and all you want is to have access to it. It isn't that way at all. We are challenging the very system."[5]

Not even UCT could stand aloof from the violence. In October 1986, anti-apartheid protesters violently disrupted lectures by Conor Cruise O'Brien, the former leader of the Irish anti-apartheid movement, who opposed an academic boycott against South African universities. Hundreds of students, many dressed in black,[6] rushed past university administrators and burst through security, forcing O'Brien to flee for his safety. The atmosphere on campuses throughout South Africa was one of increased radicalization and polarization.

At his inauguration, Gerwel delivered an address at which he declared that he would make UWC an "intellectual home for the Left."[7] Established as part of the apartheid system of separate development, the university had since achieved its emancipation from that system, he declared:

I saw, experienced, and participated in its growth and development over the years; I was privileged to share in the process of its emancipation — an emancipation from the academic and intellectual deprivedness of its origins as an ethnic college to being today intellectually one of the most exiting [sic] and charged institutions of higher learning in the country, daringly exploring new spaces and modes of academic and intellectual practice; emancipation from the political and ideological restrictiveness of its apartheid origins to being a place where the examination and pursuit also and particularly of progressive ideas are not only protected but actively encouraged.

But it was not enough, Gerwel said, for a university to have a commitment to "free scholarly discourse"; it also had to oppose apartheid. He continued:

5   Mamphela Ramphele, quoted by Scully et al., p. 6.
6   Helen Zille. "Student Disruptions Hit Lectures at Cape Town as S. African Universities React to U.S. Sanctions." *Chronicle of Higher Education*, 22 Oct. 1986. 39.
7   Jakes Gerwel. Inaugural address. 5 June 1987, University of the Western Cape, South Africa. URL: https://jgf.org.za/inaugural-address-by-jakes-gerwel-as-uwc-vice-chancellor-and-rector-5-june-1987/. Accessed on: 7 Oct. 2021.

I cannot in conscience, in Truth, educate, or lead education, toward the reproduction and maintenance of a social order which is undemocratic, discriminatory, exploitative and repressive and stands universally recognised as such. While a university may never have a corporate opinion our university, at least, can never condone or live comfortably with Apartheid in any of its mutations. And the democratic left stands as fundamental opposition to Apartheid in all its dehumanising aspects.

The university could not stand apart from the ongoing political struggles of the country, he argued: it had to participate in them. It would liberate itself — and, in so doing, catalyze the liberation of the country.

Chancellor Jakes Gerwel looks out over the UWC campus, c. 1990
(Courtesy Rhoda Kadalie)

Then-journalist Helen Zille — who would go on to lead the post-apartheid political opposition — placed Gerwel's extraordinary speech in context:

Professor Gerwel has been dean of the faculty of arts at U.W.C. for several years. He is set to assume leadership of the university at a time when many of its 7,000 students — the vast majority of whom are mixed-race — view themselves as an integral part of the liberation struggle in the country and are demanding that their university support them in that role. In the past year the students have used the campus as what they have called a "site of political struggle," and their political activism has often found expression in extended class boycotts to protest government policies and conditions in South Africa.

Richard E. van der Ross, the current rector, who will end his 11 years in the position at the end of 1986, has followed a policy of allowing students to express their political views and to stage protests on the campus. While some serious disruptions of academic activities have occurred, the policy has enabled the university to shake off its image as a "creature of apartheid" and shed the label of "bush college," the pejorative term often used here to describe universities created specifically for blacks.

Although the government has dropped racial qualifications for admission to universities in South Africa, students now are mobilizing as never before against apartheid in the society at large.[8]

But the goal, in Gerwel's view, could not merely be to end apartheid and establish a multi-racial, democratic political system. The "liberal anti-apartheid" orientation represented by Van der Ross, while appreciated, was insufficient.

Rather, Gerwel declared, the goal towards which UWC would strive was "*the social reorganization* of power and privilege" (original emphasis). He argued that in an environment where "every South African university has a dominant ideological orientation" — the Afrikaans-speaking institutions aligning with the nationalists, the English-speaking universities linked to liberalism and "big business" — UWC would align with the "under-represented, or not at all represented" forces of the "radical Left."

Gerwel added that this meant a new approach to the pursuit of "Truth" and "Science." Certainly opposition to apartheid was compatible with the pursuit of truth and science. But the broader reorganization of society meant challenging traditional notions of truth, and a "social reorganization of science."

He suggested that could be done while maintaining tolerance for intellectual criticism and debate "based on political and

---

8   Helen Zille. "Rector aims to turn South African University into 'Intellectual Home' of Left." *Chronicle of Higher Education*, 6 Aug. 1986. pp. 33-4.

ideological grounds," and that UWC could lead by example through its "democratic culture."[9]

That was a commitment that Rhoda, and some of her colleagues, would put to the test.

The African National Congress (ANC), to which Gerwel had become more closely aligned in the 1980s, had already shown authoritarian tendencies. Its military commanders, trained by the Soviet Union and its satellites, were committing their own human rights abuses, notably in the ANC's prison camp in Angola, known as Quattro. While the movement's leaders were increasingly pragmatic, exile had made the ANC leadership intolerant of internal dissent.

That intolerance was seen, for example, in the ANC's attitude toward feminism, which it initially rejected. As Rhoda later recalled:

> *According to BC [Black Consciousness], gender was not the primary issue. Even in the 1980s, when the UDF came into being, women's liberation was seen as divisive of national liberation.*
>
> *This belief was also dominant within the ANC. Yet at the same time, some women in the liberation movement were raising issues about women's rights. Within the ANC, they were fighting against sexual harassment in the ANC Quattro camps. A report was written about this issue, but wasn't released. ...*
>
> *I was part of the group who met with the ANC women in Harare in the early 1990s [1989]. There I learned that women in exile had written reports about sexual harassment, but that the ANC leadership stopped the release of these reports because they were embarrassed. ...*
>
> *There was a tendency within the ANC Women's League not to talk about feminist issues explicitly. When I raised these issues at the Harare meeting [in 1989], I was called "that little revolutionary."*[10]

When women protested the way they were treated by the ANC, or tried to talk about the prospect for women's rights in a future new South Africa, they were marginalized.

That intolerance was reflected in the struggle on UWC's campus as well.

***

9   Ibid.
10   Rhoda Kadalie, quoted in "In Conversation: The personal remains political: Elaine Salo speaks with Rhoda Kadalie." *Feminist Africa*

The radical academics and activists at UWC, the "intellectual home for the Left," who were committed to using the university to reorganize society, did not typically include women's rights in their calculations. Like the ANC abroad, they regarded feminism as an irritation at best — or, at worst, a point of leverage through which the apartheid regime could divide the movement, and undermine the struggle.

As Rhoda later recalled, early efforts to advocate for women at UWC met with "resistance":

> *There was a strange alliance between male students and some male staff members who tacitly agreed that while rape was brutal, women asked for it; that wanting to be equal has created all these problems for women, and that if women wanted to be educated, they should suffer the consequences should they try to take over matters which traditionally were the preserve of males. The debate was often acrimonious, but also encouraging because for the first time in our political history the students critically examined the notion of culture ... This was an exciting time on campus giving rise to some of the most creative initiatives at the university, and it was in this context and atmosphere that women's studies developed.[11]*

Ironically, it was UCT, not UWC, that first approached Rhoda to share her perspectives on feminism after she returned from the Netherlands in 1987. Rhoda prepared a week-long seminar for UCT's "Summer School" program on "contemporary debates in feminism," including the conflicts between liberal and Marxist feminists, as well as black feminism and "western versus third world feminism."[12]

Rhoda later recalled the UCT experience as a watershed moment for the participants, and for herself:

> *The participants who registered for the course ranged from interested mavericks to some of Cape Town's foremost feminists from a variety of women's organizations. Besides the impact and excitement that the course generated generally, lesbian women who attended confided that my lectures inspired them to come out of the closet for the first time. They also felt that as a black "straight" woman I was the first to break the silence around lesbian sexuality in public at a time when the intense homophobia which characterized the liberation movement at the time*

---

11   Rhoda Kadalie. "Women's Studies in South Africa: University of the Western Cape — A Case Study." 1993.

12   Rhoda Kadalie. "Women's Studies in South Africa," ibid.

made mention of the topic taboo. The reaction from black activist women was equally interesting as they now had moved away considerably from the old position that feminism was divisive and secondary to the liberation struggle, to criticizing openly the sexism of comrades within the liberation movement. Needless to say, the Summer School was significant in that topics which were formerly regarded as too sensitive were now opened up for debate and contestation in the public arena.[13]

UWC was still ill-disposed, structurally, toward feminism and the needs of women generally. The discussion of women's issues on campus was moribund: Rhoda described a summer workshop on feminist theory at UWC as being exceedingly boring. In her diary, she noted that an attempt to encourage men to take an interest "[e]nded in total chaos." She concluded at the end of the week: "What a relief to be finished — audience exhausted me. I found them, as well as did some of the lesbian women in the audience, very oppressive."[14]

But she did not give up, and she found Jakes Gerwel to be a crucial ally — even if he, too, would take some convincing. The new rector was, after all, representing not only UWC as an institution, but also the anti-apartheid movement, neither of which had been particularly hospitable to the feminist cause. Rhoda told an interviewer that she and other female colleagues had mocked Gerwel's inaugural speech: "We said, 'If this is the home of the left, then...', and we had, you know, we had puns on the intellectual left homeland [Bantustan], and the intellectual home of the leftovers, and stuff like that."[15]

What ultimately redeemed Gerwel and made him a unique partner was his openness to debate and his willingness to listen to criticism. Rhoda later recalled: "I was part of the Marxist Theory Seminar who disputed this acclamation [of Gerwel's] declaring the university a space for political and ideological contestation and that alignment with the ANC negated other political tendencies from enjoying equal legitimacy on the campus. This was an exciting time of debate, dialogue and discussion."[16]

While she was critical of Gerwel's inaugural declaration, it was also a challenge that inspired Rhoda to become more active in her advocacy for women on campus. She recalled:

13   Rhoda Kadalie, ibid.
14   Rhoda Kadalie. Diary. 22–23 January 1988.
15   Rhoda Kadalie, interview with Melanie Walker, ibid.
16   Rhoda Kadalie. "UWC Reunion October 2013." Draft. Personal files.

My activism was inspired by the very exciting degree I read at the Institute for Social Studies in The Netherlands in Development and Women's Studies during 1985–6. When I returned at the beginning of 1987, it gave shape and intellectual substance to my activism and provided me with new tools to comprehend the anti-apartheid context theoretically and experientially in all its complexity. "National Liberation first; Women's Liberation second" and "Women's Liberation is Divisive of the National Liberation Movement" were two slogans that got the feminists in the struggle all riled up. We were not prepared to accept that the abolition of apartheid meant male domination in general and black male domination in particular. The men needed racial solidarity with women to win the anti-apartheid struggle but somehow claimed that women's liberation was of secondary importance.

We furiously spearheaded awareness campaigns in all directions: reproductive rights, gay rights, equality campaigns, and rights against domestic and sexual violence [and] abuse. These were explosive times because black women were often called upon to demonstrate national solidarity with black men, when we knew that they often betrayed us within the private contexts of our lives. Thus started the navigation between the personal and the political in ways that often pit us against our male comrades. It was a painful journey but there were many men in the struggle who supported our campaigns and who encouraged us to give structure to our claims.[17]

The pressure from Rhoda and her feminist sisters on campus was complemented by appeals from international agencies who urged UWC to take up women's issues in a substantive way. Gerwel responded by asking six leading women on campus to form a commission to address issues facing women at UWC.

As Rhoda later recalled: "Simultaneous to all these happenings on campus, the rector [Gerwel] called upon the women staff to form a *Women's Commission (WC)* to address conditions of employment for women on campus. The first task was to review all service conditions in terms of gender, and to recommend reforms."[18] She added:

It was in this context that the Women's Commission, the Women's Studies initiatives, and anti-sexual harassment and anti-sexual violence campaigns started in 1987 on UWC's campus. The Women's

---

17   Rhoda Kadalie. "UWC Reunion," ibid.
18   Rhoda Kadalie. "Women's Studies in South Africa," ibid. Original emphasis.

Commission consisted of 6 women representing all constituencies on Campus. This unity across class, race and occupational divisions led to the achievement of absolutely radical achievements for women with regards to maternity and paternity leave (5 month fully paid leave); an anti-sexual harassment policy; housing subsidy for women; a crèche to support the child-care needs of staff; and even a non-sexist language policy unanimously adopted by Senate.[19]

It was, Rhoda said, "pioneering stuff" — though it was not always appreciated. When, decades later, a book was published documenting the history of UWC, she noted that the women's struggle had largely been omitted. "This oversight, again demonstrates how easily the struggles of women are made invisible, even though our interventions saved UWC lots of negative publicity in the media about sexual violence on the campus that was rapidly being obliterated through our systemic interventions."[20]

The fight for a sexual harassment policy in the late 1980s was a particularly important and difficult battle. It emerged from a tension between the feminist movement and the broader liberation struggle. As Rhoda later wrote:

This tension came to a head in the early eighties[21] when one of the student leaders raped a female student on campus and nothing was done to discipline the student concerned. A kangaroo court was set up in the residence by the political comrades of the alleged rapist, where the trial degenerated into a mudslinging match between the male comrades of the rapist and the feminist supporters of the victim. The outrage of the women students and staff compelled management to address sexual violence against women more seriously and formally.[22]

The university formed an anti-sexual harassment committee that recommended basic reforms, such as installing extra lighting on campus, and training security officers to deal with sexual harassment. UWC also created an "Ad Hoc Committee on the Handling of Reported Rapes on Campus" to review cases of sexual assault and to make policy recommendations. But Rhoda and her fellow activists felt that attitudes needed to change as well: "So we embarked on campus-wide campaigns through public debates, panel discussions, theater and movies to educate

---

19   Rhoda Kadalie, "UWC Reunion," Ibid.
20   Ibid.
21   Another source in Rhoda's files records the date as 1987.
22   Rhoda Kadalie. "Women's Studies in South Africa," ibid.

the campus community about sexual harassment and sexual violence as forms of political control against women."[23]

Rhoda helped lead the university's effort to develop a sexual harassment policy equal to the task. She conducted a thorough review of the academic literature on sexual harassment within academic institutions, gathered examples of sexual harassment policies at other universities — including both local institutions, such as the University of Cape Town, and universities abroad, such as the University of California, Berkeley. To ensure that the new policy would be accepted within UWC, Rhoda and her colleagues enlisted the input of a broad range of stakeholders: "It was agreed that the whole campus would collectively embark on the writing of a sexual harassment policy as an educational process to get all the sectors involved in discussions of definitions of sexual harassment and rape and in the formulation of appropriate formal and informal grievance and disciplinary procedures."[24] Rhoda held public meetings with different departments and even different student residences to solicit input.

There was, again, opposition: "Suddenly 'culture' was invoked by men to justify violence against women, and those who dared to equate racial discrimination with gender discrimination were vilified as 'pro-government spies', 'divisive', 'bourgeois' and 'frustrated lesbians'!"[25] But Rhoda continued working on the issue, and a new draft policy was presented to the campus in the latter half of 1990. Rhoda announced a series of campus discussions about the new policy, designed to solicit additional comment. "Representatives from all the university's constituencies recently wrote a working document on sexual harassment," she told the *University of the Western Cape Campus Bulletin* in August 1990. "There is not only racial oppression, but also oppression of women. Men should consider how they deal with women in public."[26] The final policy was adopted in 1991, and the Women's Studies Group set about promoting it with flyers, discussions, and campus events. A pamphlet titled "Breaking the Silence" was added to orientation materials for new students to educate them about UWC's new, robust policies on sexual harassment.

Notably, the new policy placed sexual harassment in the context of other forms of discrimination and abuse. The preamble to the policy began: "UWC will not condone harassment based on an individual's race, religion, ethnic origin, gender, sexual orientation, or physical

---

23   Rhoda Kadalie. "Women's Studies in South Africa," ibid.
24   Rhoda Kadalie. "Women's Studies in South Africa," ibid.
25   Rhoda Kadalie. "Women's Studies in South Africa," ibid.
26   Rhoda Kadalie, quoted in "Focus on sexual harassment." *University of the Western Cape Campus Bulletin*, Vol 2, No. 22. p. 1

handicap."[27] This successful effort to link women's rights to other rights would eventually be repeated in South Africa's new Constitution, several years later. The policy also included avenues for mediation and informal dispute resolution. And, crucially, the rights of those accused of sexual harassment were placed on equal footing: "The rights of complainants will be protected, as will the rights of those complained against."[28] Such guarantees emerged organically from a political culture in which activists were keenly aware of the rights of defendants, which were routinely abused by South Africa's apartheid justice system. These guarantees also ensured that the new policy would be accepted by men, who feared being targeted by false or unprovable accusations, as well as the women who expected to be the primary beneficiaries of the new procedures.

One success led to another, as the successful effort to develop UWC's sexual harassment policy was soon followed by other achievements:

> At the time a core group of young academics, some newly appointed and others who had just returned from studies abroad, felt the need to start a Women's Studies Group (WSG) to infuse a gender consciousness into the political discourse and curricula across the faculties.[29]

The Women's Studies Group, established in August 1987, did more than just "study"; it also took up women's causes on campus. A surviving copy of the minutes from the group's first formal workshop, on Sep. 19, 1987, records that about 60 people attended, and agreed to several core principles, as well as to meet again in December.[30]

Following that meeting, Rhoda sent a letter to Gerwel on behalf of the group -- evidently at his request — to address the "conditions of service of women employees."[31] In her letter, Rhoda summarized the history and aims of the Women's Studies Group:

> The Women's Studies Group (WSG) is an informal working group on UWC campus, started on 21 August 1987 to address issues concerning women in all spheres of university life. The main purpose of this group is to find effective ways of raising gender issues and gender consciousness in UWC

---

27   University of the Western Cape. "Policy and Procedure on Sexual Harassment." 1988.
28   Ibid.
29   Rhoda Kadalie. "Women's Studies in South Africa," ibid. Original emphasis.
30   Gender and Women's Studies Working Group. Newsletter. c. October 1987.
31   Rhoda Kadalie. Letter to Jakes Gerwel. 17 Dec. 1987.

*in the context of the struggle for democracy in S.A. The WSG is committed to the following **general principles**:*

- *to struggle together with other democratic [groups] for a non-racial democratic S.A. free of class domination and gender oppression*
- *we recognise that the burden of exploitation and oppression weighs most heavily on black working class women*
- *to share and make accessible resources on gender and women's issues*
- *to cooperate with community groups, unions and organizations*
- *to work in collective and democratic ways*

*The **specific aims** of the group are*

- *to coordinate needs and interests in order to form small working groups around specific areas of interest, such as, feminist theory, trade union education, women's health, women's organizations, rural women, etc etc.*
- *to integrate gender and women's issues into teaching programmes, courses, and research projects*
- *to learn to make resources and information on gender and women's issues accessible to groups*
- *to engage in debates and discussion on theoretical work that contributes to our understanding of gender and women's issues, and to make theoretical work accessible*
- *to challenge sexist practices in our workplaces, groups, organisations of which we are members*
- *to establish a resource centre*
- *to establish links with existing political organisations.*[32]

Rhoda informed Gerwel that the Women's Studies Group had already formed its own subsidiary "working groups" to address a variety of practical issues, such as child care and working conditions. She also asked that he enlist the assistance of other campus institutions, creating a wide network of input and support for the new women's initiatives. She concluded: "I feel privileged that you ask my advice on this issue, and we hope to hear from you soon so that we can get down to some serious business!!". She would later recall that Gerwel had encouraged Rhoda "to institutionalize our feminist concerns through formal structures around

---

32   Ibid. Original emphasis.

policies and practices that would visibly improve the position of women at university."[33]

The "serious business" soon began, and Rhoda and her sisters, working together with Gerwel, completely overhauled UWC's approach to women's issues. As she later recalled:

All over the campus gender study groups were being formed; seminars were held on the race, class, gender debate amongst women in South Africa, and in the Arts and Humanities there was a growing visibility of "women and gender" in the disciplines and research projects in the university. International Women's Day (8th March) and National Women's Day (9th August) were used to raise public awareness around the history of women's struggles nationally and internationally and to focus on the achievements of women throughout the centuries. The Women's Commission also encouraged women to talk about the more subtle forms of discrimination they were experiencing with regards to promotion, staff development, job interviews, research grants, conditions of leave, and so on. From the discussions it became clear that there was a desperate need to develop formal affirmative action mechanisms, which would more adequately address all the issues raised by women.[34]

Crucially, Rhoda also ordered UWC's first collection of feminist books for the campus library, creating a resource that would endure through the decades.[35] Thanks to Rhoda and her colleagues, women at UWC achieved enormous progress in an extraordinarily short span of time — from the late 1980s to the early 1990s. And they did it all on a volunteer basis, performing tasks for which senior administrative staff were typically responsible at universities abroad.

But women still faced difficulties in the classroom — even on a politically conscious campus:

While teaching anthropology, I also was aware of how women at the university, academics and staff, were discriminated against. And also how women students were regarded as not equal to male students in a variety of ways. Now, the University of the Western Cape was a very politicized university. It openly aligned itself with the Mass Democratic

---

33 Rhoda Kadalie. "Tribute to Jakes Gerwel on his 60th birthday." In *Professor Jakes Gerwel: 60 years, marking time....* Commemorative book. 2006. p. 27.

34 Rhoda Kadalie. "Women's Studies in South Africa," ibid. Original emphasis.

35 Rhoda Kadalie. Letter to the Personnel Manager. 21 Jul. 1992.

Movement. And the student leadership was 110% committed to the struggle for democracy. But gender discrimination was not equated with racial discrimination. So in the discourse, racial discrimination gained primacy, while gender discrimination was treated as divisive of the liberation movement.[36]

Rhoda attempted to challenge these attitudes, both inside and outside the classroom. She confronted male students, for example, with the similarities between what some of them said about the "natural" inequality of the sexes with what Hendrik Verwoerd, one of the ideological architects of apartheid, had said about the "natural" inequality of black and white. That, she said, "jolted" many into reality.

She also delighted in provoking outrage, and debate, as one interviewer noted:

She once began a class, for instance, by asserting that "all men are rapists". Predictably "the class went berserk" and a furious debate ensued.

"We concluded," Kadalie recalls, "that as long as men rape women and other men who do not identify with the rape say nothing, they are acquiescing in the act. They are actually supporters of that act. One man rapes on behalf of all men because a lot of progressive men who do not rape do nothing about the fact that their brothers rape. I said, when you men who are against rape, march against it and condemn it, then I shall no longer call you rapists," and she laughs.[37]

Rhoda also later recalled that she had been "put off" by the way in which black female activists in the U.S struggled to oppose the abuse of women within the American the civil rights movement. That, she said, made her sensitive to similar problems at UWC:

I wondered how we could be defending "our men" at a place like UWC, where women were being sexually harassed and beaten across the breasts if they did not take part in class boycotts. The male students would say that women had no right to complain – they should consider it a privilege to suffer for the struggle. They said that women's rights should be sacrificed in the name of a unified struggle. I and some of my women colleagues at UWC were outraged by this, and said so. We were promptly labelled bourgeois Western feminists by some of our

36   Rhoda Kadalie, on "Woman Today," SAfm, June 1996.
37   Institute of Democracy in South Africa. "A necessary irritant?". *Democracy in Action*, Vol. 9 No. 7, 15 Dec. 1995. p. 10.

male comrades. Being labelled in this manner did not stop me from complaining about the harassment that women were subjected to on campus and in the residences, as well as the number of rapes that were occurring. The rector of the campus at the time [Gerwel] said that rape was endemic to our society, and that the university administration could not call in the apartheid police for rape, only for murder. I asked why were they distinguishing between crimes of gender and other crimes? Why privilege murder over rape? They were both serious crimes.

The struggle for women's rights to be recognised as human rights was devalued all the time in the name of the anti-apartheid struggle. In the UDF, the argument was "We can't let the enemy know that some of us are committing gender-based crimes of violence." This was similar to those who were pushing the womanist position in the US, using the issue of racial solidarity – " we can't let the white man know".[38]

Far from weakening the anti-apartheid movement, Rhoda argued, the inclusion of women's issues strengthened it. Conversely, excluding women's issues — and tolerating the abuse of women within the movement — weakened the struggle, she claimed. The struggles against racism and sexism were one.

In 1991, writing in the journal of the Black Sash, an anti-apartheid women's organization, she related an incident that had, no doubt, been shared with her by Namibian colleagues:

A few months before Namibia gained independence, a Swapo mass rally was held in Rehoboth. As usual, the meeting started with a revolutionary exchange of slogans between chairperson and audience. This is how it went:

Speaker: A vote for Swapo ...

Audience ... is a vote for democracy!

Speaker: A vote for Swapo ...

Audience: ... is a vote for freedom!

Speaker: A vote for Swapo ...

Audience: ... is a vote for equal rights!

Speaker: A vote for Swapo ...

Audience: ... is a vote for women's rights!

---

38   Rhoda Kadalie, Ibid.

A macho voice rose above the audience, shouting, "Not a fuck! Now you're going too far!"[39]

"Unless we see these two systems as equally evil and interlocking," she continued, "the abolition of apartheid will merely mean that a white patriarchal government will be replaced by a black patriarchal one. And this is certainly not the vision I, as an ANC Women's League member, have for the new South Africa." Liberating women would require men to give up male domination, just as liberating South Africa from racism would require whites to abandon white supremacy. She predicted that equality for women would be even more challenging, given that relations between men and women were complicated by love and family relationships, and that "subordination is made more tolerable if exercised under the guise of love." [40]

Rhoda understood the reluctance of many within the anti-apartheid struggle — including women — to embrace the feminist cause. As she would later reflect in an essay on feminism, published in 1995 — just after the country's first democratic elections:

Publicly, black women have blamed apartheid for robbing black men of their dignity. For many black women, the abolition of apartheid has thus meant the restoration of male pride, dignity and masculinity to black men. This partly explains why, for a long time, the democratic movement tended to see the liberation of women as being secondary to and contingent upon national liberation.

...

The battle against apartheid often deflected attention away from gender oppression. The publicity given to racial oppression protected the left male activist as an oppressor of women. Furthermore, his most powerful arguments appealed to tradition and culture and denied that feminism was an authentic voice within the community.[41]

Rhoda's answer, in part, was to argue that the anti-apartheid struggle had been a struggle for women's rights from the beginning — that "struggles since 1913 [when the Native Land Act was passed, limiting black land

---

39   Rhoda Kadalie. "Racism and sexism: an unholy alliance." *SASH*, Sep. 1991. p. 9.
40   Ibid.
41   Rhoda Kadalie. "The F-word." *Agenda*, No. 205 (1995). pp. 74-75.

ownership] have been largely feminist in context."[42] She noted that many of the ANC's most important campaigns in the early- to mid-20th century had been "bread-and-butter concerns" affecting women, and that women had led many of the protests.

Rhoda also believed that women within the academy had a special role — both to develop the intellectual foundations for feminism within the broader democratic movement, and to struggle for equality within their own institutions. She had returned from Europe with a sense of affirmation in her instincts about the poor treatment of women in the academy, and a new ability to connect the struggles of women in South Africa to the struggles of women globally. But she was also frustrated in her ability to convey the insights of her experience in Europe to her colleagues. She channeled that frustration into organizing.

She later recalled in an interview that her early experiences involved protests — such as a plan to spread diapers over the vice-chancellor's floor to protest for child care benefits — as well as intellectual activism. "[M]any of us who had studied overseas, the young products of this university, came back and we were enlightened, we all came back Frankfurt School converts, or radical unreconstructed Marxists, or whatever. And we formed the Women's Studies Group, and I remember our first WSG meeting ... people for the first time spoke about gender issues in academic terms, in intellectual terms, and that was exciting."[43]

Rhoda also became increasingly involved in women's issues at UWC through her academic work — both in academic debates on campus, and in the administrative duties she took on, which included adjudicating accusations of sexual assault on campus.

She discovered that violence against women was not only a serious problem on campus, but that it was widely accepted — including by many women themselves. As she later recalled:

I sat on the student tribunal where these cases were heard. Some of the male students would defend their acts of rape by arguing, "Oh she comes from my home village. Now that she is here at university, she has become so uppity, that's why I beat her up."

However, some of the women were also complicit in condoning these acts of violence. They would brag about being beaten up, saying that this was proof that "he owns me, he loves me". The message that was going out placed women in a double bind: violence against women meant men's

---

42   Ibid., p. 74.
43   Rhoda Kadalie, interview with Melanie Walker, ibid.

ownership of them. These men were effectively saying, "We beat those we value and treasure." This also explains why some women found this interpersonal violence acceptable. This is why people tolerate gender-based violence.

Also, many of these women experienced gender equality for the first time when they came to university. After examinations, when the results were posted on the noticeboards, some of the women who achieved the highest marks would erase their results. They did not want the fact that they were often better students than the men to become public.

We used the undergraduate classroom to raise gender awareness amongst our students. So, for example, students would engage with the nature-nurture debate on gender issues by asking whether all men are born rapists. (Laughter.) Similarly, we asked whether Lorena Bobbitt's act of cutting off a man's penis was equal to men's rape of women. When the UDF was founded (and most of our students were members), it raised all sorts of race and gender contradictions for them, which we discussed openly in class.[44]

Rhoda noted, as she had in Europe, that women who were involved with the "struggle," alongside idealistic men, also experienced sexual harassment and rape. And when she confronted students and faculty about the problem, she was often told that it was the norm, or a culturally accepted practice, particularly for African students. However, when she challenged men about their attitudes, she found them willing to change. "I found that the African male students became my biggest allies in the struggle against sexism," she recalled.[45] She also challenged women in the student residences to be more assertive in standing up for themselves.

The task was difficult, and almost Sisyphean, at times, as each new year brought turnover and whole new cohort of students to confront. Rhoda never gave up. "I was kind of a missionary," she recalled. "And I used to say, I never want to be like Dad when I am older. But I'm exactly like him around the issue of gender equality."[46] Students responded to her because she seemed genuinely interested in their welfare — which was all too rare. "I think there are many academics there who do not take an interest in the real life of students," she said. "I was horrified when I discovered that some of my students study by candlelight."[47]

44   Ibid.
45   Rhoda Kadalie, on "Woman Today," SAfm, June 1996.
46   Ibid.
47   Ibid.

While she was able to stimulate debate and greater consciousness about gender equality among students and peers, Rhoda believed that the university needed to do more for women — both for the safety of women on campus, and the equality of women on the faculty. She was determined that women's rights would not be shunted aside by the anti-apartheid struggle, especially on a campus with revolutionary aspirations.

Too often, she recalled, women's issues were "hijacked" by those who called themselves "progressive" — some of whom, she said, used the label as an excuse for laziness, or intolerance. "I saw myself as very much part of a progressive core and also not part of it because of the Stalinism, populism, and I always felt that as an academic we should insist on being critical. ... And I felt very strongly that the day I am denied in an academic institution the right to be critical, I shall leave. And I think that's a space which I created for myself, which people began to respect, because whereas a few years before I was called a bourgeois feminist, a few years later, everyone asked me to write papers around this."[48]

Rhoda began to stand up for herself, and other women on campus, more aggressively. In one meeting of the faculty senate, she stood up to a condescending dean by simply showing him her middle finger.[49]

Femina magazine, which profiled her in 1996, described her as both a "[f]iery zealot," a "[f]ree spirit," and a "troublemaker" who showed a "blatant disregard for authority," especially when that authority was grounded in "male insecurity."[50] Another interviewer noted: "Some describe Kadalie as arrogant, judgmental and unpredictable."[51] She delighted in standing up to men and male authority — playing their own game against them, she argued.

Rhoda explained her confrontational approach: "I think I'm difficult because I don't like hypocrisy. I don't like pretense. I don't like authoritarianism. I don't toe the line, also. I'm notorious for not being politically correct." Universities, she said, no matter how "progressive," were often male-dominated and hostile to change. She wasn't having it: "I cut through the crap."[52]

***

48   Rhoda Kadalie, interview with Melanie Walker, ibid.
49   Sharon Sorour. "Rhoda Kadalie: Born to Lead." *Femina*, Jun. 1996. p. 74.
50   Ibid.
51   Institute of Democracy in South Africa. "A necessary irritant?". *Democracy in Action*, Vol. 9 No. 7, 15 Dec. 1995. p. 10.
52   Rhoda Kadalie, on "Woman Today," SAfm, June 1996.

Vignette: "Lorena Bobbitt," by Rhoda Kadalie

At the height of our struggle for women's rights on campus, a story in the news caught my attention. It enraged as much has it engaged debate. Lorena Bobbitt, an abused woman, sliced off the penis of her husband, John Wayne, in 1993 in Virginia, USA. She used an 8-inch carving knife, escaped in her car, and flung the severed member into a field along the way. She had had enough of domestic and sexual abuse.

Engaged at the same time as the Gender Equity Officer at UWC, in extensive anti-sexual violence work on the campus, I had an idea. At a time when the liberation movement's credo was "national liberation first, then women's liberation," I decided to use this incident to educate the students about violence against women, and to insist that women's struggle will not be subordinate to the national liberation struggle.

Liberation leaders, both men and women, believed that national liberation deserved primacy over equality with women. They believed falsely that men contributed more than women to the fight for liberation — a belief roundly contradicted by ANC scholar, Tom Lodge, who said that throughout history women were more vociferous in their demands for racial equality than men, as exemplified by the many Defiance Campaigns led by women since 1913.

Feminists who believed that the national liberation movement itself was gendered were pilloried as reactionary, especially on campus, where the student leadership considered themselves the "vanguard" of the struggle – an aggrandizement that covered a multitude of sins. Student leaders felt, by virtue of their vanguardism, that they were indeed immune from prosecution for sexually assaulting women students. And the more these misdemeanors surfaced in the residences, the more the imperative to bludgeon women into silence at a time when sexual assault was also rife in the trade union and liberation movements.

Many women were complicit, calling those of us who exposed the rot "bourgeois feminists" to silence us. And the more intense our fight, the more the male comrades undermined us.

So the Bobbitt amputation was a timely opportunity.

I decided to organize a mass debate around the topic: "Is Rape Equal to Penis Amputation?". To add spice to the event, I asked the loquacious Professor Kader Asmal to chair the debate. Asmal was one of the most vocal advocates of women's empowerment on campus, who assisted me in drawing up our gender equity policy.

The crowds gathered. There was excitement in the air. The speakers presented their arguments, and questions followed. Needless to say, there was much laughter, a happy diversion from the last kickings of the apartheid dead horse.

Male chauvinists revealed their true colors in their condemnation of Lorena Bobbitt. Women rejoiced, calling upon their comrades to make sacrifices in the fight against violence against women.

Most vocal were the male comrades, the so-called Vanguard of the Liberation Movement. "We can never equate rape with such a heinous act"; "Women should not be encouraged to take the law into their own hands"; "Male genitals are necessary for procreation, and that is an act of extreme violence." Women retorted that rape symbolized the severing of the women's inner sanctum and that it was the ultimate form of violence.

Kader Asmal railed against the male students who insisted that the penis was necessary for procreation, arguing that women could now procreate via artificial insemination. An irate comrade shouted, "What is that, Comrade Asmal? Never heard of it!"

The audience shrieked with laughter as Asmal explained, in didactic terms, what artificial insemination and *in vitro* fertilization meant, mindful that most African male students came from the townships and the rural areas, where such topics were never discussed.

"Hai, *suka* (Xhosa for "get lost")," shouted the student, "Comrade Asmal is out of Odder!"

***

In 1991, UWC formed a committee called the Gender Policy Task Group (GPTG) to consider all of the ongoing activities on campus focused on women's issues. The GPTG made several recommendations, including that UWC adopt a formal gender policy; create a "Gender Equity Unit"; appoint a Gender Coordinator; and develop a curriculum in women's studies.[53] These recommendations attracted interest from international donors, and in 1993, the Gender Equity Unit (GEU) was launched as an institution within UWC specifically devoted to women's issues on campus. It was the outgrowth of everything that Rhoda and her colleagues had struggled to achieve over the previous years, and had the blessing of UWC rector Jakes Gerwel.

---

53   Rhoda Kadalie. "Women's Studies in South Africa," ibid.

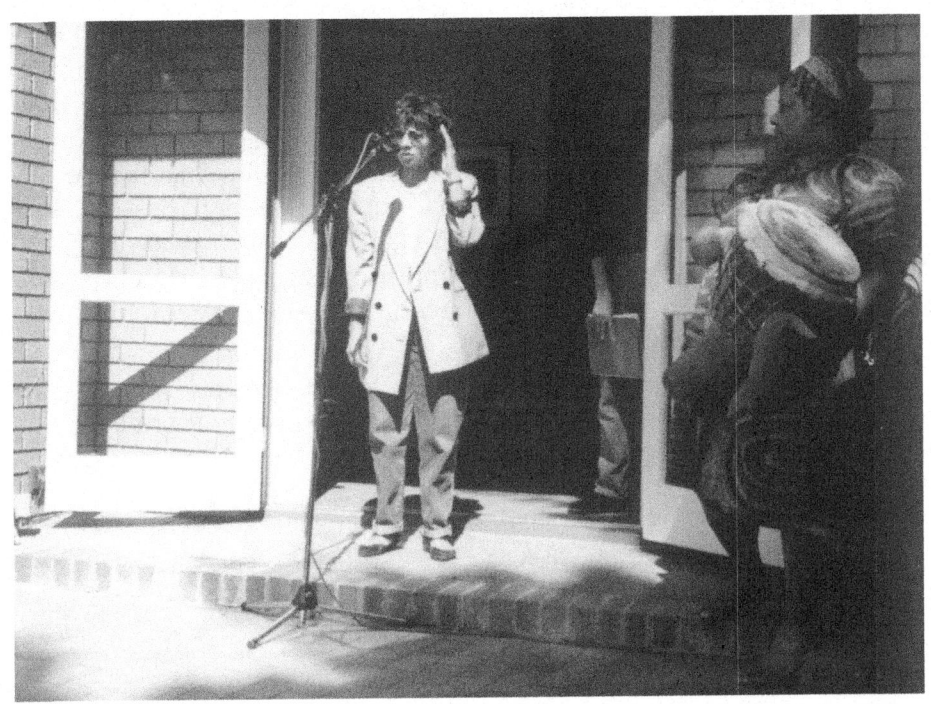

Rhoda at the opening of, and in the offices of, the UWC Gender Equity Unit, 1993 (Courtesy Rhoda Kadalie)

Rhoda applied for the advertised position of "Gender Co-ordinator" and was appointed to direct the GEU in 1992, effective on 1 January 1993, with the title of Gender Coordinator in the Gender Policy and Action Programme.[54] The seed funding was provided by the Ford Foundation in the United States — an institution to which Rhoda would later turn for future projects. It was the first project of its kind in South Africa — and the continent.[55] In her application letter, Rhoda noted that she was, by 1992, "the longest standing member of the [anthropology] department," and that she had played a role in changing what had once been a "narrow-minded" part of the university.[56]

Immediately, the GEU began to push for changes on campus. One of the most urgent issues was the physical safety of female students. As Rhoda later recalled:

My job was to set up infrastructure to protect female students against sexual harassment and violence.

I marshalled resources at a very high level to make this a reality, the first being to have the Gender Equity Unit (GEU) recognised as a senate body with multi-stakeholder representation on the campus.

My job was to win over the male leadership and top management to help us fight all forms of violence against women. Initiatives of the GEU included the establishment of a gender-representative tribunal; tracking cases of violence against women and prosecuting offenders.

Our primary goal was to remove stumbling blocks that hamper the advancement of all women on the campus. On one occasion, I visited all heads of departments to win support for our cause.

In the science faculty, I was told repeatedly that female students achieved the highest grades, but were reluctant to pursue postgraduate study. Many female students said working in the labs after hours was "life-threatening".

54   UWC Personnel Department. Letter to Rhoda Kadalie. 27 Nov. 1992.
55   Chris Barron. "Obituary: Rhoda Kadalie fought for women's rights and against state incompetence." *Business Day*, 18 Apr. 2022. URL: https://www.businesslive.co.za/bd/national/2022-04-18-obituary-rhoda-kadalie-fought-for-womens-rights-and-against-state-incompetence/. Accessed on 20 Apr. 2022.
56   Rhoda Kadalie. Letter to the Personnel Manager. 21 Jul. 1992.

> *Walking to their residences after dark killed their desire to continue
> studying. These fears were compounded by other cultural factors – inter
> alia, that there were few role models for women in the sciences.*[57]

Journalist Chris Barron, reflecting on Rhoda's advocacy for women on
campus, would write: "The whole culture at UWC was as at all SA campuses
patriarchal and entrenched."[58] He noted that she faced "considerable
pushback from those who believed that the only struggle that mattered
was against racism and apartheid," and that women's issues were
tangential at best.

Yet while she encountered some prejudice and institutional inertia,
Rhoda found some of the male faculty and administrators eager to help.
For example, she worked together with Professor Kader Asmal — later,
Minister of Education in the post-apartheid era — to create a gender
policy for UWC as a whole. Gerwel continued to be supportive: when Rhoda
demanded an entire building for the GEU, not just an office, he obliged.
"The unit opened its doors in 1993 and became a haven for abused and
sexually harassed women, not least lesbians whose rights she was also one
of the first in the country to champion," Barron observed.[59]

The GEU also developed a policy for UWC on the use of gender-
neutral language, and compiled racial and gender statistics about UWC's
staff.[60] Rhoda then began to monitor appointment committees to ensure
that women were able to compete on a level playing field. She wrote new
guidelines to help the university avoid "sexist questions about a woman's
marital or maternal status" during job and promotion interviews.[61] In
one case, Rhoda later recalled, she pushed for the university to allow a
secretary time for study leave, which her boss had initially denied, but
which later allowed her to become an academic in her own right.

The GEU began using its new status to highlight entrenched,
"systemic" discrimination; to foster debates about gender policy and
ideology; and to challenge the male-dominated status quo. As a recent
history of the institution noted:

---

57 Rhoda Kadalie. "How to reform the snake pits our campuses have become
for women." *The Citizen*, 6 Oct. 2017. URL: https://www.citizen.co.za/
news/opinion/1679031/keep-women-safe-on-campus/. Accessed on
13 Apr. 2022.
58 Barron, ibid.
59 Barron, ibid.
60 Sharon Sorour, p. 78, ibid.
61 Ibid.

The Gender Equity Unit staff started to hold countless public debates, forced the student disciplinary committees to change, conducted awareness raising workshops, educated and trained student leadership and hosted extensive conscientising programmes in the residences to transform the gender hostile climate on campus.[62]

The results were almost immediate. The GEU pushed successfully for the establishment of a crèche (day care) on campus. It also created a Gender Equity Tribunal, to hear complaints of sexual harassment against faculty and students. The GEU also expanded academic opportunities for women, creating a Women's Study Programme, a Women's Winter School, and a Women's Student Centre. A new Women's Commission monitored gender discrimination in employment, at UWC and beyond; a Gender Policy Task Force took up the specific task fo developing affirmative action policies for women.[63] Before the GEU, few women had been awarded scholarships to study overseas. Rhoda was among the few exceptions — and used the GEU to open the door of opportunity to other women as well. And a new publication, the *Women's Bulletin*, kept the campus informed about all of these advances, while also publishing articles and commentary to raise awareness about women's issues in South Africa, especially violence against women.

Rhoda noted the core achievements of the GEU as follows:

From 1993 to 1995 we set up a post-graduate Women and Gender Studies Interdiscipliary Program; we produced a quarterly Women's Bulletin and sexual harassment resource booklets (also translated into a black language); and designed policy guidelines for gender policy, non-sexist language and sexual harassment. On an on-going basis the GEU increasingly took on a political function holding affirmative action workshops, training women students to do gender-awareness training of students in the residences and assisting with training for [an] orientation program on sexuality, sexual harassment and formal and informal grievance and disciplinary procedures. Later the office took on an additional function as OMBUDS office where women brought whatever grievances they had, real or perceived, within the university for mediation, which we then channeled through the appropriate structures for resolution. In this way the university began challenging

---

62   Gender Equity Unit. "History of the Gender Equity Unit." URL: https://www.facebook.com/GenderEquityUnit/. Accessed on 8 Oct. 2021.

63   Rhoda Kadalie. "Editorial." *Women's Bulletin*, University of the Western Cape, Vol. 1 No. 1. Apr. 1992.

discrimination and its embeddedness within the culture of the university in a more systemic way.[64]

All of this was achieved during South Africa's political transition to democracy. It did not await the arrival of a new political dispensation, or new government; it was the result of the effort of women themselves, beyond the state, a lesson Rhoda would remember and emphasize. Decades later, UWC would honor their efforts, noting Rhoda's work alongside that of "Jean Benjamin ... Zenariah Barends, Zelda Holtzman, Daphne Williams, Lynette Maart, Febe Potgieter and Cheryl Carolus."[65]

Through the GEU, UWC had set an example for the rest of South Africa's tertiary institutions to follow:

> *By the mid-nineties UWC had the best maternity benefits in the country — 5 months fully paid leave and 7 days paternity leave for men; housing subsidies for married women; chief invigilation duties for women; and an educare centre for children of staff. The unit also developed a Sexual Harassment Policy; a Gender Policy and a Non-Sexist Language Policy. Resource booklets on sexual harassment were developed and distributed. Ad hominem promotion was granted to women academics and they for the first time had equitable access to study leave and research funding. A Women's and Gender Studies Programme was also established.*
>
> *Women students formed a volunteer group, called Kopanang, and began to raise gender awareness amongst students. UWC became the centre for women and gender awareness raising in the country well in advance of the post-apartheid liberal language framework and rhetoric.*

The Kopanang group in particular provided one of the first vehicles for lesbian students to become politically active on campus.[66]

Thanks to the success of the GEU, Rhoda recalled, she was appointed to the university's Human Resources Committee, which dealt with personnel issues in general. Her success in overturning many decisions to discipline faculty, and her role in investigating claims of misconduct, was

64 Rhoda Kadalie. "Women's Studies in South Africa," ibid.
65 University of the Western Cape. "Women's rights are everybody's rights." *Three-sixt-e: Alumni e-Newsletter.* Issue 11, Dec. 2014. p. 9.
66 Mary Hames. "Lesbian students in the academy: Invisible, assimilated, or ignored?". In Seth Matebeni, et al. *Queer in Africa: LGBTQI Identities, Citizenship, and Activism.* p. 138.

so widely respected that men began approaching the GEU when they, too, felt they had been treated unfairly by the university hierarchy.[67]

In addition to advocating for women within the academy, the GEU supported efforts to develop a curriculum for women — both on and off campus. As she wrote in 1995:

Many community organisations which have been involved in gender awareness programs realise that they now need to go beyond the feminist activism mode. Since the [1994] elections they have requested advice, guidance and expertise from academic feminists to assist them in formulating new ideas and visions.

At the University of the Western Cape, the Gender Equity Unit took these challenges on board by holding a Women's Studies Winter School which catered particularly for women in community organisations, non-governmental organisations (NGOs), teachers and the corporate sector. Courses offered were contemporary feminist theory, gender and development, gender and sport, women's rights, sexual harassment and women's health. Due to its overwhelming success, we have decided to institutionalise the school as an annual event. The Gender Equity Unit also offers an Inter-disciplinary honours and M. Phil programme in Women's Studies to cater for the needs and interests of those who want to pursue post-graduate research and scholarship around women and gender. [68]

There was widespread recognition throughout South Africa of what Rhoda had accomplished. Rhoda would be described by *Femina* magazine in 1996 as having "almost single-handedly quashed sexism at the University of the Western Cape."[69] Her effort inspired women to demand change — not just on campus, but in politics, in the boardrooms of private companies, and in everyday social interactions.

***

---

67   Rhoda Kadalie, interview with Melanie Walker, ibid.
68   Rhoda Kadalie. "The F-word," p. 77.
69   Sharon Sorour, p. 74, ibid.

Vignette: "Tales from the Gender Equity Tribunal," by Rhoda Kadalie

Our campaign to advance the position of women at UWC meant a total transformation of the campus culture. Structural and educational reform backed up by suitable policies and implementation, made up the whole package. One such innovation was the formation of a gender-sensitive tribunal dedicated to dealing with gender discrimination seriously.

The tribunal board consisted of the deputy vice chancellor, Professor Jaap Durand; a law professor; and women representing several constituencies. It was here that gender discrimination in all its pernicious forms was revealed.

"Peeping Tom"

Tom (not his real name) appeared before the tribunal. Women students alleged that he had been caught several times in the women's bathrooms behind the shower curtains. He clearly had a history of peeping at women from behind these curtains. Before we ascertain guilt, we usually request the student's grades as a mitigating factor. Tom was a straight A student, in ... wait for it ... Theology! We doubled the sentence!

"Dagga-smoking student"

A campus security officer lodged a complaint against a student who was smoking dope in his residence room. The rather disheveled student denied it vehemently, against the officer's clear evidence of remnants found in his trashcan and from other student witnesses.

Feeling cornered, the student explained that he was smoking a herb grown in his rural village. Tribunal members asked for the name of the herb. Cleverly, the student gave some long Xhosa word, knowing that none of us would have a clue what it was. We asked him to write down the name of the herb, so he panicked and admitted it was dagga: "I used it coz it helped me write poetry and be creative."

Before sentencing the student, we asked for his grades. He had straight A's in English and fared equally well in his other subjects. I declared there and then that dope should be made mandatory for all students!

The guy got off on a warning. Needless to say, this was one of our more pleasant student cases.

"I *klapped* her because in my village she knew her place"

A good-looking student appeared before us for repeatedly assaulting his girlfriend. When we asked him why he kept doing it, he responded: "We are from the same village. We attended the same school and now we are here together at UWC. I beat and *klapped* her because she is uppity. At home in our village, she knew her place; here at UWC, she thinks she's better than me because her grades are better than mine. So, I had to beat her to remind her where she comes from."

"Admin couple"

After returning from a conference abroad, my secretary approached me with a concerned look on her face. "I am not sure about the details of this case, but some things don't add up. I know you cannot be admitted to the jury for this case, but can you please ask the chairman if you could sit in on the case and advise."

A young administration officer was rather depressed, so her boyfriend, a senior student, took her on a long drive. She did not return after lunchtime, so colleagues called her parents to inquire about her whereabouts. The parents, who had no clue, immediately concluded that she was with her boyfriend, of whom they did not approve.

When she arrived home, pretending to be back from work, they confronted her, inquiring where they were and whether they had sex. The woman did not lie, so the parents accused him of having raped their daughter. They promptly lodged a case with the police and the university. During the hearing, I could see the administrative officer at pains to accuse the guy, whom she clearly loved, of the heinous crime of rape.

I had so feminized my tribunal that they were prepared to find the student guilty. The tribunal chair was a Tanzanian professor who did not understand certain details of the complaint simply because he did not understand geographical logistics. The woman claimed that she urged her boyfriend to return home as it was dark already, and they needed to be home by 6:00 p.m. But it was summer, and it does not get dark until around 8:00 p.m. Malmesbury is an hour's drive from Cape Town, and she got that detail wrong of how long the drive back home was.

The saddest part of the whole story was that this couple loved each other, against their parents' wishes. They both claimed to be "born again" Christians, so sex before marriage was forbidden in her household. When her mother asked whether she had had sex, she admitted to it, and her parents compelled her to claim rape, when in fact it was consensual sex between two people who loved each other.

When I pointed out all the irregularities in her testimony vis-à-vis her boyfriend's solid testimony, he was acquitted.

Tania, my secretary who was Australian, very bright, and who had been in Cape Town for a while, was vindicated for her doubts, while she couldn't make complete sense of the saga.

Feminizing the Tribunal did not mean finding against men, regardless. It meant applying the rule of law, without fear or favor. When we fail to do that, we weaken the fight for gender equality.

***

Rhoda soon became widely known as one of the most assertive and effective feminists in the country. Some of her views were radical: "The time has come to break down the traditionally patriarchal family unit to construct a new one," she declared in 1996. "It's not only the site where we learn dominant gender-power relationships and how to control one another in a destructive way, for many it's also a site of oppression."[70] On marriage, she quipped: "People stigmatize divorce, but they should really stigmatize marriage — it's a completely dysfunctional institution."

She was never quite anti-male: "I really like men," she said. However, she added: "I hate myself for liking them."[71]

Rhoda was also actively involved in the debate around abortion, taking the position that it ought to be guaranteed to women as part of the basic right to bodily integrity — at least during the first trimester of pregnancy. This view was controversial in South Africa, still a conservative society; it was even controversial among ANC women. But Rhoda saw it as an essential component of the liberation of women for whom sex and contraception were not matters of choice.

"I'm 150 percent pro-abortion," she said in 1996. "Women have had abortions for centuries and in a country like ours where many women don't have a choice when it comes to contraception, they have a right to abortion if they choose it."[72]

Rhoda often found herself arguing against religious conservatives, notably the Rev. Kenneth Meshoe, later the founder and leader of the African Christian Democratic Party (ACDP), who cited Christian prohibitions against abortion. In response, Rhoda developed Christian arguments in favor of abortion rights. Her main point was that given the coercive nature

---

70   Rhoda Kadalie, quoted by Sharon Sorour, p. 78, ibid.
71   Ibid.
72   Ibid.

of sex in many South African communities, and the horrific conditions in which illegal abortions were being performed, it was an act of mercy and salvation to rescue vulnerable women from harm. Otherwise, they would be subjected to unwanted sex and pregnancy; exploited by "quack" doctors; and possibly left maimed for life.

During a 1996 debate over South Africa's first legislation legalizing abortion, the Choice in Termination of Pregnancy Act, Rhoda told Parliament in a public hearing: "The anti-abortionists are not so much pro-life as they are pro-vengeance ... my advice to those who are against abortion is don't have one, but don't deny others their right to have one. The very essence of our democracy is the freedom of each religious group to teach and preach ... to attempt to impose on women a particular morality based on sectarian beliefs goes beyond the legitimate role of religion in our political life."[73]

At one point, Rhoda organized an abortion for a young colleague, whose life would have been damaged immeasurably had she continued with the pregnancy. She had already had one child, and a second, so soon after the first, would have made it impossible for her to work her way out of difficult economic circumstances. Today, the woman Rhoda helped has a job in politics, owns a house and a car, and has been able to put her son through school successfully, as a single parent.

Rhoda's support for abortion did not mean that she rejected her religious principles. On the contrary, her faith remained deeply important to her, and she was proud to have come from a "conservative coloured family where I learnt good values and sound Christian principles."[74] But she adopted a liberal, even radical approach to fundamental Christian concepts: "The Bible, to me, is not about rules and regulations, it's about discovering life and God, through Mary, children and the elements of nature. ... I see God as mysterious and powerful, but also as feminine."[75]

In an op-ed in 2000, Rhoda developed her argument for abortion rights, grounded in her reading of Biblical texts and principles:

From a conscience point of view, the Government should challenge the prevailing religious viewpoint that abortion is murder and that those who are pro-choice are murderers.

...

---

73   Rhoda Kadalie, quoted by Gaye Davis. "It's Christians versus Christians Over Abortion Bill." *Mail & Guardian*, 18 Oct. 1996.
74   Sorour, p. 79, ibid.
75   Ibid.

Old Testament law is very clear: if you cause the death of a foetus, you pay a fine; if you cause the death of a woman, you lose your own life. In those days a foetus was not considered to be a person.

If "person" were defined as beginning at conception, abortion would, indeed, be the crime of murder. Women's bodies, their rights and health would be subordinated to the protection of the embryo. No abortion would be permitted for any reason, including rape and incest. Each miscarriage would have to be investigated, the legal consequences of which would be catastrophic.

Equally ludicrous, if we accept the argument that life begins at conception, we have to accept that life begins before conception, in that the sperm and the ovum are alive long before they get together in the moment of fertilization.

An acorn is not an oak; a seed is not a carrot; an embryo is not a human being. Nowhere in the Bible is the embryo or foetus given the status of a human being. Personhood does not begin at conception. Personhood begins when the baby takes its first breath; that is when God infuses the baby with a soul.

Genesis 2:7: "And the Lord formed man out of the dust of the ground, and breathed into his nostrils the breath of life, and man became a living soul."

So when an infant breathes its first breath the soul enters its body and it achieves the status of a person, and its birthday is celebrated from then on, not conception.[76]

Rhoda speculated that the true motivation of pro-life activists was not "reverence for life," since they seemed to disregard the life of the mother, but rather "revenge" for the "sin" of premarital or extramarital sex. But she did not consider the question of late-term or partial-birth abortion, which was not then an issue in South Africa.

Rhoda's views would shift considerably after she arrived in the U.S. in 2018, when pro-choice activists began pushing for legislation guaranteeing abortion rights up to the moment of birth. She was somewhat shocked, and eventually came to believe that given great advancements in reproductive technology, abortion was morally problematic after the

---

76 Rhoda Kadalie. "The biblical argument for abortion." *Cape Argus*, 27 Jun. 2000. 16.

first trimester, and that late-term abortion was, in fact, murder, given alternatives such as adoption.

Similarly, Rhoda also came to believe that the pro-life movement was a just cause, motivated at least in part by the desire to defend freedom of religion and conscience against policies that force taxpayers to subsidize practices to which many people of faith have deep moral objections. She began to criticize openly the work of Planned Parenthood in running what she considered an abortion industry — profiting from the plight of poor black women, opposing restrictions even on late-term abortions, and promoting the Democratic Party to ensure that they continued to receive state funding in perpetuity.

All that, however, was in the distant future.

While at UWC in the 1990s, Rhoda began pushing for new programs and institutions aimed at protecting women from abuse, and creating equal opportunities for women in the academy.

Robert Goff, one of the administrators at UWC who had worked with Rhoda on establishing a sexual harassment policy and disciplinary processes, recalled that she was far ahead of her time, focusing on women's rights in the 1980s at a time when most people were focused elsewhere. "She was out-and-out a pioneer," he said. "She was not a quiet person, not diplomatic. She was fierce — but respectful."[77]

Fellow academic Wilmot James, who would later go on to be a leader within the post-apartheid opposition, said that Rhoda "tend[ed] to be quite tempestuous and fiery." But he added: "A lot of people, myself included, tend to be diplomatic and cautious with others, but Rhoda gets to the heart of the matter immediately and there are times when this is necessary and valuable."[78]

Her assertive approach yielded results — and advances for women. As Rhoda later told interviewer Elaine Salo:

We were the first university campus in South Africa to develop a sexual harassment policy. At UWC, I was part of a group of women who identified women's rights as human rights on campus. We examined the social position on women on campus closely – we wanted equal rights for women, so we set out to develop an anti-rape and sexual harassment policy, we won maternity and paternity benefits for academics, and a gendered housing subsidy policy that provided academic women with the same resources with which to obtain housing as their male colleagues.

---

77   Robert Goff. Interview with the author. 25 Feb. 2022.
78   Rhoda Kadalie, quoted by Sharon Sorour, p. 79, ibid.

I was able to push for these issues because I was nominated to a number of governing committees at UWC, as well as the senate. I was able to obtain an intimate working knowledge of how the university was governed, about the networks and the people who sat on these committees. So I was able to work with colleagues on these bodies, and lobby for improving the status of women on campus. On the academic front, we also pushed for the promotion of women in the academic hierarchy. At the time, I think there was a single white woman professor on campus.

After we raised these issues, many opportunities opened up for women to improve their academic qualifications, or to take time off and do research, write and publish at universities abroad, such as in the US and in the Netherlands.[79]

Robert Goff noted that at one of the first meetings to discuss UWC's sexual harassment policy, Rhoda delivered a blistering attack on the administration over the condescending language with which it referred to women on campus. "She put them in their place," he recalled, and the meeting ended after a few short minutes.

Gerwel would prove to be an important ally throughout the process. Though reluctant to adopt some of Rhoda's bolder ideas, such as a public campaign against rape on campus (see below), he supported her efforts. As Edwena Goff (née Le Cordeur), who worked as Gerwel's executive assistant (and later married Robert Goff), recalled, Gerwel was a careful and strategic player, both at UWC and, later, within the Mandela administration. Rhoda was one of the many future South African leaders whom he cultivated within his orbit — and she was the only one who could walk into his office unannounced. The two had a close personal friendship, one that Rhoda carefully negotiated by diligently paying respect to Gerwel's wife, Phoebe. Gerwel, who opened UWC to students classified by the apartheid government as "African," was not afraid to rock the boat to enact institutional change, but also knew how to do so without triggering a backlash.

Rhoda discovered that elevating women within the university sometimes required more than just changing the rules of the institution. It also meant building connections among female academics, offering each other mutual support and encouragement. She recalled:

I remember being invited to bring five black women academics to a conference in Utrecht to present papers. We read each other's drafts and

---

79   Rhoda Kadalie, quoted by Elaine Salo, ibid.

edited them in preparation for the conference. Desiree Daniels' paper focused on women in the labour movement,[80] Desiree Lewis wrote about black women in South African literature, Yvonne Mokgoro wrote about gender and the law in South Africa, while my own paper dealt with the issue of sexual harassment and rape on the university campus. Our papers were very well received at the conference. I remember [Renée Römkens], one of the discussants, remarking about the fact that we insisted that sexual violence be looked at in relation to poverty. In Holland, they explained sexual violence in terms of psychoanalysis. At the conference we married the two positions and thought creatively about how sexual violence could be analysed through the dual lenses of psychoanalysis and socio-economic factors. The conference proceedings were published in a volume edited by [Renée Römkens].[81]

The conference took place in December 1993, and opened doors to more conferences and academic opportunities, including visits from American scholars to South Africa. Rhoda forged links to the University of Utrecht, Netherlands, and to the University of Missouri in the United States, which would help UWC develop its own women's studies curriculum. South Africa's isolation, thanks in part (perhaps ironically) to the cultural and academic boycotts of the anti-apartheid struggle, meant that the field of women's studies was virtually unknown in the country before the 1990s. "Furthermore," she later explained, "feminism was highly suspect during the struggles of the sixties, seventies and early eighties, and to entertain the idea of introducing feminist studies into universities at the time would have earned us the pejorative epithet of elitism!"[82] Rhoda pressed for women's studies to be expanded and institutionalized at UWC, and launched an annual Women's Studies Winter School to reach a wider range of students and professionals who were interested in the subject but did not want to devote their careers to it.

---

80 Daniels is listed in the poster for the event as lecturing jointly with Nazeema Mohamed of UWC on "The gendered nature of political violence in South Africa." Universiteit Utrecht. "Southern Africa: Women's Perspectives." Poster. 1–3 Dec. 1993.

81 Ibid. A similar conference took place at the University of the Western Cape from 13–15 January 1997, with Römkens, then at Utrecht University, in attendance. Römkens commented: "South Africa's feminism, whether in or outside academia, is the living and fascinating example of a fragmented, often contradictory collection of interests and identities where social class, race and gender intersect in the most complex ways." (Renée Römkens. "Gender and Colonialism." *European Journal of Women's Studies*, Vol. 4, Iss. 3 (Aug. 1, 1997). pp. 398–400.

82 Rhoda Kadalie. "Women's Studies in South Africa," ibid.

As much as Rhoda learned from discussions with international scholars and activists, Rhoda drew on her anthropological training to challenge the cultural assumptions of her First World counterparts. She once told the story of "a western white woman anthropologist who came to her country and said proudly that her husband didn't give any cattle to marry her because her country didn't sell women. An African woman responded, maybe you aren't worth anything."[83]

Rhoda at a women's workshop in Uganda, 1990 (Courtesy Rhoda Kadalie)

But there were also setbacks, and university administrators — even those at the forefront of the struggle against apartheid — were often reluctant to accede to Rhoda's requests. She told Salo:

> *The university rector at the time [Gerwel] was reluctant to provide support for a campaign against rape. He said that the university could not afford the bad publicity if we had a public anti-rape campaign. He said that already the university was being seen in the media as lowering*

---

83 Carol Anne Douglas. "Workshop: Women's Studies in International Perspective." *Off Our Backs*, Vol. 26 No. 8, 1996. p. 7.

academic standards (because of its open admissions policy and anti-apartheid stance).[84]

Gerwel eventually changed his mind, and championed Rhoda's efforts.

Some anti-apartheid activists continued to argue that the aggressive pursuit of women's interests would divide the anti-apartheid movement. Women's issues were associated with white, bourgeois feminists who were accused of being more concerned with their own privileges than in the fundamental problem of racism, as enshrined in the apartheid system. Rhoda noted: "The anti-rape campaign was seen as being too closely associated with white liberalism, so the politicisation of the personal, ethical issues fell by the wayside."[85]

Still, Rhoda and her colleagues made progress:

One of the gains of our activism at UWC was that gender awareness was mainstreamed. So, for example, gender became part of courses in Sociology and Anthropology taught by women like [Elaine Salo] and Diana Gibson; and in languages and literature spearheaded by Miki Flockemann, Desiree Lewis, and Christelle Stander; in adult education programmes where Professor Shirley Walters drove it; it was part of the coursework in the Economics faculty, with work done by women like Cheryl Hendrick; Sandy Liebenberg was doing gender work in the Community Law Centre; Anne Marie Wolpe took it up in the Education Policy Unit; and Desiree Daniels in labour studies.

Rhoda saw women's studies not just as a way to critique other fields, but also one that could produce its own independent forms of knowledge. More than individual academic careers, Rhoda aimed to improve the lives of women throughout UWC — and beyond. "[W]omen form a powerful basis for change," she wrote, "and universities provide a challenging context for feminist social engineering to take place."[86]

***

In a country whose various cultures, regardless of race, were deeply paternalistic and chauvinistic, Rhoda's work began to change the lives and outlook of millions of people, male and female, on and off campus. By 1994, she was able to declare: "We have made major advances [at UWC]

84   Ibid.
85   Ibid.
86   Rhoda Kadalie. "Women's Studies in South Africa," ibid.

regarding women's rights. Men are no longer automatically defined as the breadwinners, which means married women staff finally can apply for housing loans." She noted, however, that she was still dealing with a case at the Gender Equity Unit "where a woman was incorrectly told by a personnel officer that she wasn't eligible" for the loans.[87]

Through her feminist advocacy, Rhoda became seen by many colleagues — black and white, male and female — as a voice for them against established hierarchies. She stood up to white racism on behalf of black colleagues — yet also stood up for women of all colors when against men, black and white, who often aligned to protect their privileges and private academic preserves from female intrusion.

"What I did at UWC was to watch the men in power and use the same ploys they did, to subvert and undermine their authority. But at the same time I provided them with the facts that proved injustices existed," she recalled later.[88]

Male faculty members who had experienced problems with the UWC administration began approaching the Gender Equity Unit for help, because Rhoda was there. Rhoda found that mildly irritating: "The very men who didn't like me for my feminism used me for my courage," she told the *Cape Argus* in 1997.[89] "A lot of men are crippled by ambition. They won't rock the boat for fear of jeopardising their career. I don't give a shit about rising to the top. My driving concern is the truth."

Those whom Rhoda helped through the GEU went on to a variety of illustrious careers, in every part of South African life. "I see the 'products' everywhere in the country," she recalled in 2010, noting the many examples of "powerful women whom she mentored and who are now working successfully in major organisations."[90]

She extended her growing influence beyond academia. Rhoda applied the feminist lens to her Christian faith, which she cherished, but whose institutions upheld the prevailing hierarchies of an unjust society, even if it had officially opposed apartheid.

In an essay submitted to a 1991 anthology on women's role in the church in Southern Africa, Rhoda recounted her public criticism in 1989 of the Anglican Church for its refusal, at the time, to ordain women as priests.

---

87   Rhoda Kadalie, quoted by Arlene Getz. "In S. Africa, women emerge from apartheid's shadow." *St. Petersburg Times*, 28 Aug. 1994. p. 22A.
88   "Rhoda Kadalie: a strident voice for South Africa's oppressed," ibid.
89   Ibid.
90   Rhoda Kadalie. Quoted by Estelle Neethling. "South Africa's humanitarian lodestar." *Leadership*, Ed. 207, August 2010. p. 16.

(The church ordained women for the first time in 1994.[91]) She noted that she had felt "anger and resentment" toward the church at the time:

> *It was not so much the refusal to ordain women that infuriated me, as it was the denial of the existence of women and their contribution in the church. The vote against the ordination of women by synod signified, once again, that the Anglican Church, which was so committed to the eradication of apartheid, was not so serious about the sin of sexism.[92]*

She continued, describing her own sense of personal alienation from the church, which complicated an enduring faith:

> *On a more personal note, the failure to address the needs of women in the church partly explains my own negative attitude towards the church. As a pastor's daughter, I virtually grew up in the church, and by the time I reached my mid-twenties, I was punch-drunk from listening Sunday-in-Sunday-out to three-point Bible-punching sermons, spewed forth with boring regularity, warning people to either turn or burn. I stopped going to church simply because "God the Ogre" did not appeal to me any longer. I was convinced that I was being robbed of a God who was something other than authoritarian, legalistic and punitive. I started exploring the Bible for myself and joined a Bible study group with other similarly disillusioned young people. As my relationship with God grew more intimate, it suddenly dawned on me that my growing disinterest in the church was a reaction to, what I now consider to be, blasphemous presentations of God in most sermons: an all-male God ministering to an all-male congregation! That the majority of people in the church were women only minimally affected the kind of ministry that was delivered by the church. The church failed to get involved with specific problems women were experiencing in their communities, such as divorce, alimony, contraception, abortion, childcare, domestic violence, child abuse, marital relationships and gender inequality, to mention but a few. The church was often clueless as to how to deal with these issues, and would resort to spiritualizing these aspects of life so as to avoid confronting these problems.*

91   John Darton. "After 460 Years, The Anglicans Ordain Women." *New York Times*, 13 Mar. 1994. URL: https://www.nytimes.com/1994/03/13/world/after-460-years-the-anglicans-ordain-women.html. Accessed on 7 Mar. 2022.

92   Rhoda Kadalie. "Epilogue." *Women Hold Up Half the Sky: Women in the Church in Southern Africa*. Pietermaritzburg: Cluster Publications, 1991. p. 391.

The God I began to discover was the God I occasionally caught glimpses of in the church. It was a God who could be likened unto the seas, the rain, the wind and the sun; it was a loving compassionate, kind and caring God, concerned with all of creation. It was, indeed, the God of the oppressed, the poor, the exploited and the down-trodden. As a woman, I had a sneaking suspicion that God, too, often felt marginalized within the church, which often uncritically reflects the broader society of which it is a part. Societal norms and values are often played out in the church with easy resonance. It is, therefore, no problem for the church to express itself in racist, sexist, legalistic, materialistic and competitive terms, and to present God as sanctioning these attitudes in very subtle, and sometimes not so subtle ways, especially when it comes to the oppression of women.[93]

Rhoda decided that the sexism of the church was not a religious norm or tradition, but an aberration, a form of blasphemy against the true meaning of Scripture:

In the context of an extremely hostile anti-woman culture, Jesus challenged men and women directly out of their socio-cultural stereotypes into a culture of wholeness by defying the laws and customs of the society which kept women in a position of subordination. Jesus keeps on challenging us to extract truths about women from the cultural contexts within which they lived, to show us that it was not so much the customs, but the messages through which they were conveyed. His relationship with the woman of Samaria, his appearance to Mary Magdalene after his resurrection, and his violation of taboos on ritual purity, all clearly point to his rejection of the notion of women as second-class citizens. In all of his dealings with women he brought wholeness to them. This is the wholeness I began to discover in my personal relationship with and explorations of God.[94]

Rhoda did not confine these insights to obscure academic texts: she shared them far and wide. In 1997, for example, she told the *Cape Argus*, the afternoon paper of Cape Town: "I think the way the church often depicts God — as male and white — is blasphemous. God doesn't identify with

---

93   Ibid., 392–393.
94   Ibid.

patriarchy or sexual violence."[95] As she later elaborated: "God is not male or female and is therefore 'gender neutral' without meaning to be."[96]

Edwena Goff recalled the stir that Rhoda caused when, as an invited speaker at the Cape Peninsula University of Technology, she gave an address challenging the gender and identity of God. She enjoyed pushing the boundaries of her audiences, both in person and in print, and provoking them to ask questions that would challenge established patterns of hierarchy and conformity.

Rhoda was, at times, ambivalent in her attitude toward religion. Yet she enjoyed attending services at the Rondebosch United Church, especially following the arrival of Dr. Robert Steiner, a young German theologian whose optimistic outlook and informal style — he wore jeans under his pastoral robes — suited Rhoda's own tastes. Robert, like Rhoda, loved traditional hymns, but spoke about contemporary themes, and added African marimbas to the music of the old organ in the century-old stone church.

Pastor Robert Steiner with Rhoda, c. 2017 (Courtesy Rhoda Kadalie)

95   "Rhoda Kadalie: a strident voice for South Africa's oppressed," ibid.
96   Rhoda Kadalie, quoted by George Claasen and Frits Gaum. "Bekendes for die Groot Debat." *Sarie*, April 2012. Translated from the Afrikaans via Google Translate. p. 60.

In Rondebosch, Rhoda found the community of Christian believers she had been seeking since her youth. As she told *Sarie* magazine in 2012: "I am a regular churchgoer because I want to be part of a Christian community that debates with God on the issues of the day. He is greater than our limited field of experience and the perspective keeps me humble."[97] Rhoda struggled with some aspects of her faith — and to her, the struggle was the point. "It is the mystery that God is that fascinates me the most," she said. "In my quest to understand God, I discover something new daily. For example, I do not understand at all why God created women to have to endure physical misery - menstruation, childbirth, menopause, you name it. I argue with God daily about this."[98]

On occasion, Rhoda was invited to act as a lay preacher — usually on holidays, such as Good Friday. One Easter, she delivered a sermon about the Biblical figure of Zaccheus, a tax collector whose story is told in the Gospel of Luke (19: 1-10). Short in stature, hated by his community of Jericho, Zaccheus was addressed by Jesus on a visit to the city, after Zaccheus had climbed a tree to watch the prophet pass through. Jesus told Zaccheus that he would visit him, which caused some grumbling among the townspeople, but inspired Zaccheus to contribute generously to the poor and to restore fourfold the wealth of those he had cheated.

Rhoda found a way to make the story relevant to South Africa's contemporary political dilemmas:

> *JESUS seeks out the excluded, the sick, the marginalized, the alienated, the rich and the poor!*
>
> *JESUS INVITES even CORRUPT POLITICIANS — a species we love to hate — whom we believe have no right to redemption because of their self-serving predilections. ... This story speaks directly to us as MINISTRY TO THOSE WE DESPISE AND REJECT ... May this message grant us the grace to develop more empathy with those on the other side of the rails and see in them the potential to embrace the transformative power of Jesus, Our Lord and Maker.*[99]

In admitting that even corrupt politicians were capable of redemption, at least in God's eyes, Rhoda was challenging her own, often uncompromising, stance.

---

97   Rhoda Kadalie, *Sarie*, ibid.
98   Ibid.
99   Rhoda Kadalie. "The Story of Zaccheus: The Trials of the Unobserved Life." Sermon as prepared for delivery. Rondebosch United Church, Rondebosch, South Africa. 2015 (?). pp. 3-4, 8. Original emphasis.

Rhoda: 'Comrade Kadalie, You Are Out of Order!'

Later, in 2016, Rhoda would urge the Dutch Reformed Church to accept gay marriage — a position at odds with her growing audience of conservative supporters. In an article in the Afrikaans newspaper *Beeld*, she drew once again on her religious beliefs, as well as her constitutional values, to make her argument:

> From a sociological point of view, marriage in South Africa, takes on a multiplicity of forms. Through divorce, children live across a variety of family forms. Polygamous marriages in African and Muslim communities add to the mix. I know of many same sex marriages within which children are raised extremely well. I also know of others where marriages have broken up causing the same amount of trauma as those within heterosexual marital arrangements.
>
> ...
>
> In South Africa, the Constitution is pre-eminent and the Bill of Rights provides for equality and non-discrimination on the basis of race, sex, gender, class, sexual orientation, and marital status, amongst others. The Synod would do well to engage with the Bill of Rights versus what they consider to be Biblical precepts. As a Christian, I see no contradiction between the Bill of Rights and what the Bible's key figure, Jesus, commands us to do. Just as Jesus defied the cultural and patriarchal order of the day, regarding gender relations, by talking to the Samaritan woman at the well, by touching the garment of a bleeding woman, and by asking a woman to spread the news that he had risen from the dead (an act that was contrary to the culture at the time), just so He would have defied the DRC Synod in support of same sex marriages.
>
> I can understand people who cannot and will not accept same sex marriages. They must just not make their prejudices mine or legal to suit their bigotries. I am convinced that the nature of the marriage would have been of least concern to Jesus, but He would have been concerned about whether or not love and care prevailed within those relationships and families as he was about every other societal arrangement.[100]

At the same time that she challenged prevailing traditional notions of race, gender, and tradition, she urged her colleagues at UWC to move beyond an

---

100   Rhoda Kadalie. "Same sex marriage and the DRC Synod - time to get with the programme." Post on Facebook, reprinted from *Beeld*, translated from the Afrikaans, 23 Nov. 2016. URL: https://www.facebook.com/rhoda.kadalie/posts/10154882703665039

obsession with politics, including the politics of gender solidarity, and to focus on academic excellence rather than identity politics.

When approached to join a black women's research forum, for example, she declined. "I said, I think the last thing I think we need on this campus is for black women to come together and talk about how to support each other. Why don't they just get down and write ... why don't you learn from these [white] women, and I think more than ever we need to interact [with them] in order to learn these skills. ... I think the criticism against me is that I haven't [supported] those meetings, the women want a big meeting, but it's a meeting to gripe." [101]

Ironically, Edwena Goff recalled, the toughest opposition to Rhoda came from fellow women in the academy. The campaign for women's rights on campus had involved educating men, some of whom came from cultures where physical violence against adult women was socially acceptable. But the effort involved educating women as well as men — and many women, however highly educated and accomplished, had been raised to accept patriarchal norms of behavior, including violence.

There was also, Edwena Goff recalled, some jealousy and resentment toward Rhoda among female colleagues. Men tended to be more confrontational when debating Rhoda; women tended to complain behind her back.[102]

In that vein, while Rhoda was credited with founding the GEU, and for its subsequent success, her role there was to be somewhat short-lived, thanks to behind-the-scenes maneuverings and the internal politics of the emerging post-apartheid order.

In the 1980s, Gerwel had begun traveling abroad to make contact with the ANC in exile. The ANC leadership, in turn, hoped that Gerwel would help it prepare for the task of governing, once political change came to South Africa. These meetings became more frequent and more public over time: Rhoda, too, participated in some of them.

Gerwel became an important conduit for the ANC to identify potential members of a future post-apartheid administration. In addition, the ANC wanted to find roles for its exiled leaders within existing institutions in South Africa.

That task became particularly urgent after February 2, 1990, when newly-installed President F. W. De Klerk — thought to be a conservative figure within the National Party — gave an historic address in Parliament,

101   Rhoda Kadalie, interview with Melanie Walker, ibid.
102   Edwena Goff. Interview 25 Feb. 2022.

announcing that apartheid would be reformed, that the ANC had been unbanned, and that Nelson Mandela would be released from prison.[103]

The speech electrified South Africa and shocked the world. While the future remained uncertain, it was clear that change was finally coming to South Africa.

The unbanning of the ANC meant the return of exiles and their families. And Gerwel was asked to find a role for Anne Marie Wolpe, the wife of Harold Wolpe, a communist who was arrested in 1963 with Nelson Mandela, but escaped to the United Kingdom.

Gerwel placed Wolpe at the GEU, effectively sidelining Rhoda. It was a bitter irony: Rhoda had been attacked as a supposed ally of white bourgeois feminists, and now she was being replaced by a white bourgeois feminist.

While she was diplomatic about her replacement, Rhoda later recalled with some bitterness:

> I knew UWC intimately; I sat on all the university governing committees; I was the only black woman to have a seat on the university senate at the time. I knew all the members and could use my networks to lobby for issues such as improving the conditions of employment for academic women. Some of the white women who took over the Women and Gender Studies programme after me were professional academics and did not come from an activist back-ground. They were newcomers to politics. Many of them had no resonance with grassroots peoples' issues.

But Rhoda was headed for much bigger things.

---

103   F. W. De Klerk. Speech at the Opening of Parliament. 2 Feb. 1990. URL: https://omalley.nelsonmandela.org/omalley/index.php/site/q/03lv020 39/04lv02103/05lv02104/06lv02105.htm. Accessed on 8 Oct. 2021.

Chapter Nine:
Democracy

"The 27th April 1994 elections meant turning our back on the past and charting a new course with our new constitution as a guide forward. Unlike many of my comrades, I did not expect miracles and wonders, having observed the ANC in all their dubious glory in exile when I studied abroad."[1]

F. W. de Klerk's historic speech at the opening of Parliament in 1990 did not bring an immediate end to apartheid. The release of Nelson Mandela on February 11, 1990; the unbanning of the ANC and other anti-apartheid organizations; and the repeal of many apartheid-era laws and regulations was only the beginning of a long process of negotiation.

It was to be a process fraught with fear and danger. Negotiations were frequently interrupted by terrorism, assassinations, and ethnic violence. Some left-wing extremists were still committed to overthrowing the government by force; some right-wing extremists were determined to use violence to stop the negotiations.

Rhoda jokingly used to say, "When Mandela is released, I don't want to be there," simply because of the euphoria that she believed would explode across the country. What she did not expect was how accurate her prediction would be.

Mandela's release was a moment of intense excitement — and chaos. Though much of the country — and the world — was jubilant at the sight of him walking free, he delivered a speech on the Grand Parade in Cape Town that repeated many of the ANC's most radical pledges. There were even violent skirmishes at the edge of the crowd.

Having just endured her divorce, Rhoda decided to spend a few days in the quiet coastal town of George, at her eldest brother's house. Mandela's release was announced while she was there. As she watched on television as frantic crowds gathered on the Grand Parade in front of the Cape Town City Hall, and waited impatiently for hours for Mandela to appear, Rhoda was pleased to be watching the event from a distance.

---

1   Rhoda Kadalie. "I did not know that we would mess up so badly." PoliticsWeb, 31 Dec. 2014. Reprinted from *Die Burger*. URL: https://www. politicsweb.co.za/opinion/i-did-not-know-that-we-would-mess-up-so-badly. Accessed on 10 Oct. 2021.

Despite his strident speech, Mandela soon announced a key step: the suspension of the so-called "armed struggle." The ANC would — at least temporarily — lay down its weapons, as would the apartheid government. The shared understanding between De Klerk and Mandela was that neither side would use force to pursue its aims. The negotiations would be open to all political organizations that accepted that basic rule.

The negotiations were also to be made public, in a forum called the Convention for a Democratic South Africa (Codesa). Though some of the most important talks were happening behind the scenes, the fact that a multiparty forum existed at which all segments of South African society were represented — at least, those that had agreed to shun violence — built public support for peace.

The talks were an opportunity for South Africans to make their voices heard about the kind of new political institutions they wished to build. The country would have a new constitution; the question was how it would work, and what rights it would enshrine.

Rhoda was involved in many of the discussions about women's rights, including under the auspices of the Institute for a Democratic Alternative in South Africa (Idasa). She had met with leading ANC women in Harare, at a 1989 conference hosted by Jennifer Boraine — the wife of anti-apartheid cleric-turned-politician Alex Boraine — and Sally Mugabe, the first lady of Zimbabwe. Boraine led a delegation of several high-profile South African women to meet with ANC women in exile, among them future Speaker of Parliament Frene Ginwala; Ruth Mompati; Gertrude Shope; Brigitte Mbandla; and many others. It was to be the first of several such conferences on the position of women in a future South Africa, unburdened by apartheid.

The reception, Rhoda would later recall, was warm and welcoming, and the participants debated hot-button issues for several days, including: military conscription; the prospects for the armed struggle; equality for women in the broader context of racial equality; and abortion and sexual violence. Rhoda later recalled in 2016:

> The topics were mostly about women and the defence force – the connecting point between white women who sent their boys to the border to fight to retain apartheid and black women whose sons and daughters were in the ANC's armed struggle Umkhonto We Sizwe. Most of the women we met there became members of Mandela's cabinet or were ambassadors in the new SA. I wrote a speech for one of them for her maiden speech. So I got to know them well, even the current speaker Baleka Mbete.[2]

---

2   Rhoda Kadalie. "History questionnaire." 21 Mar. 2016. Personal files.

Rhoda participates in discussions at the Idasa conference in Harare, Zimbabwe, 1989 (Courtesy Rhoda Kadalie)

Women on opposite sides of the political spectrum debated vigorously, interrupted by performances from singer Jennifer Ferguson during recesses, which helped break down racial and political barriers.

For the South African women, many of whom were meeting ANC activists for the first time, the event was eye-opening. "These ANC women are … so human!" one participant exclaimed, according to a contemporaneous account in Idasa's newsletter.[3] For the white participants in particular, the accounts of the ANC activists were revelatory. "It became apparent that some white delegates [from South Africa] were unaware of the full extent of repression and South Africa's involvement in destabilisation activities in neighboring countries," the *Weekly Mail* reported.[4]

But the ANC exiles also lacked a sense of perspective on how much South Africa had changed in the 1980s — and that even greater changes were around the corner. "When we left it was clear that the ANC women in exile had no idea that liberation was imminent," Rhoda later recalled, noting how Mompati had bade her a tearful farewell: "Goodbye, my little revolutionary." She, and her comrades, had no idea that her return would be imminent.

Rhoda's conversations with women in the ANC, however productive, also revealed that the party was reluctant to highlight issues of specific interest to women, such as abortion. Rhoda saw the right to abortion as a matter of "bodily integrity" (see Chapter 8).[5] She later lamented, "There was a rise of feminist consciousness within the ANC. Yet even at CODESA, a woman like Frene Ginwala didn't want the right to abortion enshrined in a new Constitution."[6] (The new South African constitution did, ultimately, include "the right to bodily and psychological integrity," with specific reference to the right "to make decisions concerning reproduction."[7])

Rhoda played an active role in other efforts to promote women's rights, including the Women's National Coalition (WNC), a new, post-1994 organization chaired by activist and future ANC parliamentarian Pregs Govender.[8] The WNC sought to increase women's voice within the

---

3   Ronel Scheffer. "Women take up the challenge." *Democracy in Action*, April 1989. p. 1.

4   "The Women's Trek." *Weekly Mail*, editorial. 28 Apr. 1989. p. 17.

5   Rhoda Kadalie, quoted in "In Conversation: The personal remains political: Elaine Salo speaks with Rhoda Kadalie." *Feminist Africa*. 114. Rhoda later told me that she did not imagine that late-term abortions should be legal, because of the clear viability of the unborn child.

6   Rhoda Kadalie, quoted in Salo, 114.

7   Constitution of South Africa, Chapter 2 § 12(2).

8   Amy Biehl, 1993, ibid. p. 5.

multiparty negotiations, as the new Constitution took shape, and as the outgoing parliament attempted to catch up by passing a number of laws promoting women's equality.

The WNC also launched a review of the "Women's Charter," a document first adopted by the Federation of South African Women (FSAW) in 1954.[9] The review process produced a final document, the "Women's Charter for Effective Equality." As Rhoda noted in 1992:

> [T]he Women's Charter for Effective Equality, designed to convey to the new government the concerns of women in their everyday lives and launched by the Women's National Coalition just a few months before the elections, is the product of intense discussions held over two years by ninety-two organizations, including major political parties, religious groups, trade unions, cultural and social interest groups, and business and professional women's associations, to convey to the new government the concerns of women in their everyday lives. The Charter is a holistic, comprehensive document consisting of twelve articles covering every aspect of women's live[s].[10]

The new charter demanded "effective change in our status and material conditions in the future South Africa."[11] Though the charter was non-binding, one observer had argued that the process of drafting it had "significant effects on the negotiations for a new Constitution, particularly with respect to women's representation and with respect to ensuring that women's interests are protected by the Bill of Rights."[12]

Rhoda was among the leading voices for women's rights — particularly those of black women — in the new South Africa. In 1991, she told South African television: "Women are saying, we want to be regarded as equals in our own right. We want to be considered when it comes to land, the economy, property, and marriage. And within marriage, women don't just want to just be the dependents. They want to have equal rights

---

9 South African History Online. "The Women's Charter." 1954. URL: https://www.sahistory.org.za/article/womens-charter. Accessed on 28 May 2022.

10 Rhoda Kadalie. "Constitutional Equality: The Implication for Women in South Africa." *Social Politics: International Studies in Gender, State & Society*, Vol. 2, No. 2, 1995. p. 209.

11 "Women's Charter for Effective Equality." 1994. URL: http://www.kznhealth.gov.za/womenscharter.pdf. Accessed on 28 May 2022.

12 Shireen Hassim, quoted by The Constitution Hill Trust. "The 1994 Women's Charter for Effective Equality." URL: https://ourconstitution.constitutionhill.org.za/14-the-1994-womens-charter-for-effective-equality/. Accessed on 28 May 2022.

within marriage."[13] She was also, however, critical of the anti-apartheid movement: "Women are saying, more and more, we want to have our struggle to be regarded as integral to the national liberation struggle. It's not secondary. We are fighting as equals, and to say we are secondary is not to recognize the contribution we're making. "[14]

Rhoda understood the gravity of the task that lay ahead: "The challenge facing us now in the post-election period will be to bring these constitutional rights in line with how women live currently in SA, knowing full well that the position of black women is dismal, to say the least."[15]

In the sudden flowering of political debate, Rhoda took up a unique position. She agreed with the newly unbanned ANC that the country needed radical political change, particularly with regard to women's issues and the "patriarchy." But she disagreed with many of her colleagues on the left that socialism was the only viable alternative. Nor would she accept the quaint notion that African society offered equality to women prior to the arrival of white European settlement.

In 1990, in a review of an anthology of essays on the history of women in southern Africa up to 1945, she pushed back against the left's claim that it was capitalism that had introduced the oppression of women:

> *The oppression of women is not unique to capitalistic societies, but predates it ... and has persisted in socialist countries despite the fact that socialist programmes have been designed to improve the position of women. ... Yes, African women may have been better off in precolonial society, but women were still subordinated by men under that system. All forms of patriarchy, whatever the class or race, need to be abolished if women seriously want to be recognised as human beings, now and in the future.*[16]

These skirmishes on the left were more than academic: they were also crucial in the ongoing debate about what the future institutional structure of South Africa would be.

Rhoda began to feel a sense of unease about the role that the ANC was playing. It had long been the leading liberation movement, but much of its leadership had been in exile or in prison during the 1970s and 1980s,

---

13 Rhoda Kadalie, quoted in *Agenda*, South African Broadcasting Corporation. May 1991.
14 Ibid.
15 Rhoda Kadalie, "Women in the New South Africa," Ibid. p. 210.
16 Rhoda Kadalie. "Review: Women and Gender in Southern Africa to 1945." *SASH*, Sep. 1990. p. 44.

when grassroots activists from the United Democratic Front had done the difficult work of persuading white South Africa to change and preparing for a post-apartheid institutional future.

Rhoda supported the ANC in general: she noted, with approval, that Mandela told De Klerk "where to get off" during one particularly tense moment in negotiations in December 1991.[17] And yet she noted in alarm that much of the country's leadership, including its academic leaders, seemed to defer unduly to the ANC. In 1991, she boycotted UWC's graduation, at which outgoing ANC leader Oliver Tambo was awarded an honorary doctorate. She noted in her diary that she had "decided not to attend as protest against ANC members being given Honorary Docs for several years in a row. Couldn't bear to witness another occasion of boasting when UWC could least afford to brag about its image."[18]

Rhoda was also directly affected by the violence that rocked the country as political change loomed. In September 1992, she noted in her diary that a friend had phoned "to say that men in residences ... were threatening to harm all feminists involved with feminist work on campus," which Rhoda knew meant her, among others.[19] In addition to such threats, and racial conflict, and terrorism by extremist groups right and left, there was factional fighting, and talk of a "third force" — a government-backed militia fomenting "black-on-black" violence in the townships and the rural areas. There was also a rise in crime, and vigilantism, as institutional order broke down. Rhoda noted in her diary on 18 October 1991: "UWC students take the law into their own hands & physically abused 2 suspects off the street so badly that Bishop Tutu & [anti-apartheid theologian Jaap] Durand had to be brought in to save the youth."[20]

Amy Biehl was a bright young 26-year-old American student, a Fulbright scholar from Southern California who had come to South Africa to study the country's ongoing democratic transition firsthand. Like many liberal-minded Americans, she had supported the anti-apartheid movement and was enthusiastic about South Africa's movement toward full democracy.

Biehl took up her scholarship at the University of the Western Cape, where she became involved in several anti-apartheid organizations, and Rhoda became one of her mentors and advisors. She worked closely with a number of academics and organizations on campus. She also frequently

---

17   Rhoda Kadalie. Diary entry, 20 Dec. 1991.
18   Rhoda Kadalie. Diary entry, 25 Oct. 1991.
19   Rhoda Kadalie. Diary entry, 7 Sep. 1991.
20   Rhoda Kadalie. Diary entry, 18 Oct. 1991.

offered to babysit Rhoda's young daughter, Julia, and became close to the family.

Rhoda recalled:

[Biehl] got involved in anti-apartheid orgs on UWC campus and worked with returned exiles on women and democracy, women, the law and customary rights, the abortion debates, domestic violence etc.

During this time, Amy played as hard as she studied. She was a student par excellence, but loved dancing, going to clubs, running marathons and the beach.

Soon she had friends all over Cape Town and in the black townships.

About three months into her stay, frustrated that the activists could not help her academically, she found me and by then I had treated her as just another American groupie on the campus.

I said "sure" and proceeded to correct her paper with a red pen and advised her whom to consult – I gave her a list of difficult tasks – whom to consult, whom to interview, which materials to consult, introductions to key figures.

Amy stood there with her blue eyes as big as saucers because I was the first person who actually took her work seriously and who could give her intellectual guidance.

Soon she trusted me and I became her mentor, also a mother figure, and could guide her into the vagaries of cultural life in SA.[21]

As part of her work, Biehl monitored the Codesa negotiations. "She kept me posted about debates during Codesa," Rhoda later recalled, noting that Biehl focused on emerging debates about abortion. "Many ANC members and other parties had misgivings about the word abortion; even Frene Ginwala was against it, hence the ultimate decision to use words like 'bodily integrity.' It would appease the vocal Jewish, Christian and Muslim religious constituencies. After much debate Codesa settled on the following phrasing [for the Bill of Rights in the interim constitution]: 'Everyone has the right to bodily and psychological integrity, which includes the right to make decisions concerning reproduction; to security in and control over

---

21   Rhoda Kadalie. Speech to Amy Biehl Foundation. Draft. 16 May 2017. Personal files.

their body; and not to be subjected to medical or scientific experiments without their informed consent.'"[22]

On August 25, 1993, Biehl was just two days away from returning to the U.S. to complete her Ph.D. at Rutgers University. She remained as devoted to her work in Cape Town as ever. Rhoda noted: Towards the end of her stay in August 1993, she was given many farewell parties; one by future Minister of Justice Dullah Omar, who really loved her and he was very effusive about her at a party he hosted to the point of embarrassing Amy who could not deal with too much praise."[23]

But with violence raging around the country, Rhoda advised Biehl to stay out of the townships. The mood was precarious, as Rhoda noted: "The ANC had called for Operation Barcelona, to make the townships ungovernable as a demonstration to the apartheid government that they were calling the shots when in fact the ANC was very weak vis national party [sic]."[24] Radical groups such as the Pan Africanist Congress (PAC) were still doing their best to undermine the negotiations.

"The day before her departure," Rhoda recalled, "she called me at home and kept telling me how difficult it was for her to leave — that 'my heart is here – I find it difficult to leave, and that I shall definitely be back for the first democratic elections.' Again I asked her to promise that she would not go into the townships."[25] Drivers passing by on the N1 highway, the northern commuter route to the Afrikaans-speaking suburbs, were being pelted with rocks.

In a fateful decision, Biehl agreed to drive three colleagues home to the black township of Gugulethu. Amy wanted to keep her promise to Rhoda. But, as Rhoda related, "her three friends were hitching a lift for an hour and no one stopped. They went back to campus and pleaded with Amy for a lift. She told them that she had promised not to go into the township but since they were desperate she emphatically said, I will just drop you on the outskirts of the township."[26]

As she tried to leave, she became stuck in traffic, and encountered an angry mob of PAC activists who had left a meeting. She was murdered, Rhoda said, "because she was white and represented apartheid to the marauding thugs."[27]

---

22   Personal communication with the author. 1 Feb. 2022.
23   Rhoda Kadalie. Speech to Amy Biehl Foundation, 2017. Ibid.
24   Ibid.
25   Ibid.
26   Ibid.
27   Ibid.

Rhoda: 'Comrade Kadalie, You Are Out of Order!'

The *Los Angeles Times* reported:

Biehl had been driving three black colleagues back to their township Wednesday when their car was surrounded by dozens of black youths. The mob pelted the car with stones before pulling Biehl from the driver's seat and hitting her in the face with a brick. She was then stabbed in the head.

...

When one of the youths at the mob scene was asked why Biehl had been singled out, he reportedly replied, "Because she is a settler," meaning she was white. Witnesses said the alleged attackers also shouted the PAC [sic] slogan, "One Settler, One Bullet."

During Thursday's memorial service, Evarson Orange, one of the passengers in the car, recalled that Biehl laid her head in his lap after the attack and eventually collapsed in his arms. The passengers then carried her back to the car and tried to rush her to the police station. She died shortly after arriving at police headquarters.[28]

Rhoda was quoted in the *Times* article:

Rhoda Kadalie, head of the university's gender program, said Biehl considered herself fortunate that she had not been a victim of violence but confided she feared she might lose her life in South Africa.

"I warned her about going into the townships, and she would dismiss me as a nagging old woman," Kadalie said. "Amy had a premonition that she would die.... She kept on saying how lucky she was that nothing had happened to her all the time she was here but it was all too good to be true. She had a feeling that something would happen before she left."

Biehl had been scheduled to return to Newport Beach on Saturday before heading to New Jersey to attend Rutgers University.

Speaking with Biehl's parents by telephone Thursday, Kadalie told them their daughter showed no fear when the stoning began.

28 Anthony Hazlitt Heard and Mark Platte. "Friends Mourn Victim of South African Mob; Slaying: Newport Woman's Death Rocks University Where She Studied. Two Black Youths Are Arrested." *Los Angeles Times*, 27 Aug. 1993. p. A1. Also quoted in the article was future U.S. ambassador to Russia Michael McFaul, who had known Biehl at Stanford University. He would later go on to be one of the foremost critics of President Donald Trump, whom Rhoda would support.

"She was always surrounded by loving and committed black people, never thinking for a moment that she could come to symbolize the enemy," Kadalie said.[29]

Rhoda had repeated premonitions. A year later, she would recall: "I told her often enough, 'Amy, you do things that I would never do.' She would go into the township. She would go clubbing with them. She would go partying with them. And, I mean, every day, I would warn her and say, 'Amy, you know, I wouldn't go in there,' and she'd dismiss me as a nagging old woman, you know?". Biehl also had premonitions, according to Rhoda. She recalled Biehl's sense, in her final week in South Africa, that something bad might happen: "She said it Sunday, she said it Monday and she said it two hours to me before she died."[30]

Biehl's death shocked the nation. Friends and colleagues held a memorial service at UWC the following day, where mourners sang the struggle song "Senzenina?", or "What Have We Done?".[31] Rhoda was one of the speakers. She had been up the entire night, crying: "I can't do this speech, but I'm going to," she began. She delivered a forceful and composed address, noting Biehl's devotion to the anti-apartheid struggle and the ANC in particular. Rhoda blamed the apartheid system for creating the climate of violence in which Biehl had been murdered, while also condemning the murderers, and warning black South Africans to set aside their anger about the past:

I'm haunted by what went through her mind as she was being beaten to death. On behalf of the Women's Alliance and the Gender Equity Unit, we express our absolute revulsion at the brutal way in which she was attacked and killed. Through a series of cold-blooded murders in our country, we've been made aware of all the monsters created and produced by this South African apartheid government, monsters which are now devouring each other so that the Nationalist Party looks so clean next to the others. Unless we stop and reflect on the past, the future will be too ghastly to contemplate, and we will descend into an abyss of anarchy and barbarism.[32]

---

29   Rhoda Kadalie, quoted in Heard and Platte, ibid.
30   Rhoda Kadalie, quoted in Barbara Walters. "The Amy Biehl Story." *Turning Point*, ABC News. 20 Apr. 1994.
31   Ibid.
32   Rhoda Kadalie. Eulogy for Amy Biehl. University of the Western Cape, Bellville, Cape Town. 26 Aug. 1993.

Afterwards, a throng of about 300 protesters marched to the police station in Gugulethu, holding signs that read "Amy Fought for Women's Rights," and "Comrades Come in All Colours."[33]

Rhoda devoted the lead story in the September 1993 issue of the UWC *Women's Bulletin*, the newsletter of the Gender Equity Unit, to Biehl. Several colleagues offered tributes and obituaries. Rhoda, described as Biehl's "mentor and friend," included an excerpt from a recommendation she had written for Biehl's Ph.D. studies:

> *Her research interests took [sic] her across the country and brought her into contact with women across the racial, regional and class divides in South Africa. In her field work, Amy demonstrated a remarkable capacity to understand and be sensitive to the issues which affect women generally, and black women in particular in this country, and in the process she has acquired a large circle of friends, mostly from the black community. In the course of gathering data, she has written several reports on conferences attended as well as several position papers, inviting debate from feminists involved in various organisations. The papers and reports produced by Amy have become invaluable resources for the Gender Project of the Community Law Centre, as well as the Gender Equity Unit at UWC.*[34]

Sadly, Biehl would never have the opportunity Rhoda had helped her secure.

For decades, Rhoda kept notes of condolence and consolation that poured in from around the world, expressing sympathy for Amy Biehl's death. One such anguished note, from a member of the Black Sash organization, described her murder as something like a Christian sacrifice, and tried to place it in the context of the ongoing violence of the apartheid system and the struggle against it: "Everyone under the sun must bless this Amy Biehl, true child of God, a shining star in the firmament. Her life, endeavors, joy, and death have touched us all — even her murderers. We are all linked up in the tragedy of apartheid, and the tragedies it spawns yet."[35]

---

33   Ibid.
34   Rhoda Kadalie. "In Remembrance of Amy." Excerpt from referee's report recommending Amy Biehl's application for doctoral studies. *Women's Bulletin*, Gender Equity Unit, University of the Western Cape. Sep. 1993.
35   Brian and Amy Sneddon. Letter to Rhoda Kadalie. 27 Aug. 1993.

Rhoda and Julia with Linda Biehl, mother of Amy Biehl, c. 1994

Biehl's positive contributions to South Africa would live on, both in the research she completed, and in the work of a charitable foundation her parents, Peter and Linda, established in her name. Rhoda would later credit Biehl for contributing to the inclusion of women's rights in the South African Constitution, as the *San Jose Mercury News* reported in 1995:

> *Kadalie said feminists helping to hammer out a new constitution are turning to Biehl's treatises on the rights guaranteed to women in the constitutions of Canada, Namibia, Zimbabwe and Australia, said Kadalie. While Biehl was doing this work, "we didn't even think about that issue," said Kadalie, a mentor of Biehl's at the largely black university. Now, she added, "every day I use this little booklet Amy wrote on (governmental) structures for women in the new South Africa. And my heart breaks. . . .*
>
> *"It's a very exciting time and I can just see Amy's little eyes glistening if she'd seen all of these things come to fruition."[36]*

"While we do lament her loss, she is very much alive," Rhoda said. She would continue to teach her students using Biehl's work: Rhoda's course reader for a course in "Women and Politics" at UWC included a paper by Biehl about women's role in South Africa's transition to democracy.

---

36   Marilyn Lewis. "Even in Death, Amy Biehl Makes Imprint on South Africa." *San Jose Mercury News*, 8 Jun. 1995. p. 1A.

Biehl had noted how women had pressed successfully for increased representation at multiparty negotiations, despite being all but excluded from what began as an all-male process. She had also noted a number of substantive issues of concern to women, including domestic violence. In one passage, she concluded: "[T]here appears to be a lack of recognition among the male peace negotiators that women are in fact victims of the political violence." Those words turned out, tragically, to be prophetic.[37]

Four men were eventually convicted of Biehl's murder. They were later granted amnesty by South Africa's Truth and Reconciliation Commission, and reconciled with the Biehl family. Rhoda praised the Biehls for their magnanimity, calling it an example of "amazing grace," and a "gift from God." She also praised their philanthropic work in their daughter's name.[38] Rhoda herself, however, could never forgive the murderers. After hearing their testimony in 1997, Rhoda — who was, by then, a member of South Africa's Human Rights Commission — still believed that their crime was "racially motivated" and not "politically motivated," and therefore ineligible for amnesty. She told the *Chicago Tribune*: "I would argue that the crime was racially motivated, not politically motivated. I think what Amy's parents are doing is very generous, and Amy is smiling down on them right now. But as a friend, I cannot accept amnesty."[39]

Later, when the Truth and Reconciliation Commission granted amnesty to Biehl's killers, Rhoda was adamant that it had been the wrong decision. Calling Biehl's killing a "barbaric, racially motivated murder of the most primal sort," she said: "Giving amnesty to an undisciplined and violent mob has serious repercussions for the rule of law. The amnesty committee is sending a message to street gangs that they also are not responsible for their actions. ... "Targeting a military installation is one thing. Attacking a church, or a bar, or dragging an innocent woman out of her vehicle, that crosses a sacred boundary. The truth commission's decisions have been disturbing and irresponsible."[40]

Biehl's fate was seen for years by many white South Africans as a warning about the dangers of reaching out across the old apartheid

---

37   Amy Biehl. "Dislodging the Boulder: South African Women and Democratic Transformation." In Stephen J. Stedman. *South Africa: The Political Economy of Transformation*. Boulder, Colorado: Lynne Rienner, 1994. Draft, 1993. p. 17.

38   Rhoda Kadalie. Quoted in Leslie Stahl. "Amy's Story." *60 Minutes*. 17 Jan. 1999.

39   Hugh Dellios. "Seeking Amnesty, 4 S. Africans Admit Killing Amy Biehl in 1993." *Chicago Tribune*, 9 Jul. 1997. p. 8.

40   Rhoda Kadalie, quoted by Jonny Steinberg. "Amnesty for Biehl's killers draws support and anger." *Business Day*, 29 Jul. 1998.

boundaries. (Biehl's murder also left a lingering sense of fear among Americans, too. When I arrived in Cape Town, seven years later, in a group of Rotary Ambassadorial scholars, those Americans among us who frequently visited the townships tended to avoid Gugulethu, with Biehl's memory in mind.) Black South Africans, while enthusiastic about the advent of non-racial democracy, were similarly worried about the explosion of violence. The same year Biehl was murdered, Chris Hani, the leader of the South African Communist Party (SACP), was assassinated by a right-wing extremist who had immigrated to South Africa. His death convinced many South Africans that the country was on the brink of civil war. There were stories of a "third force," backed by the regime, stoking "black-on-black" violence in rural areas.

With Mangosuthu Buthelezi's Inkatha Freedom Party (IFP) still withholding support for the negotiations into early 1994, there was a real danger that the talks would collapse and the country descend into chaos.

***

On April 27, 1994, South Africans of all races went to the polls together for the first time.

The country's first-ever multi-racial (or, in South African parlance, non-racial) elections were cause for celebration, locally and internationally. Long lines snaked for miles at some voting stations, as people waited patiently to cast their ballots. They had waited for decades; they were prepared to wait a few hours more.

There was little violence; the day was peaceful. Many voters were jubilant as they went to vote, feeling for the first time that they were citizens of their own country.

Rhoda later recalled:

I was 41 when I could vote for the first time. I remember that day so well, when I took my 7-year-old daughter with me to Wesley Training College (WTC) in Salt River, to make my cross against the iconic logo of the ANC. Julia understood the significance of that day, finding it hard to believe that her mother was excluded from the political process for 23 years of her life simply because of the colour of her skin. In her little mind, she also knew that we had paved the way for her to be able to vote when she would turn 18.[41]

---

41   Rhoda Kadalie. "I did not know that we would mess up so badly." PoliticsWeb, ibid.

Rhoda votes for the first time, April 27, 1994 (Courtesy Rhoda Kadalie)

Voters cast ballots for both the national and provincial legislatures, which had been expanded from four to nine. The national legislature would operate as more than a parliament; it would convene as a constitutional assembly, to negotiate the final draft of the constitution, after the election was conducted under an interim version. The ballots were simple: they listed the parties, plus their symbols, with portraits of their leaders, so that voters who could not read could still recognize the alternatives, and make their "X." The ballots were then counted by hand.

The outcome was never truly in doubt: it was clear that the ANC would win the election. The question was how well the opposition parties would fare. The National Party held out hope that it could provide strong opposition to Mandela's party, whose policies still worried many South Africans. The Inkatha Freedom Party rallied Zulu voters around fears that they were about to be dominated by the Xhosa-led ANC. The liberal Democratic Party, the descendant of Helen Suzman's Progressive Party, found that its moderate, reform-minded message was crowded out in the din of ethnic, racial, and nationalist appeals.

Ultimately, the ANC won more than 62% of the vote — enough to dominate the government, though short of the two-thirds threshold that would have allowed it to amend the constitution virtually at will (checked only by the power of the new Constitutional Court, which asserted the right to review constitutional amendments for their conformity with constitutional principles). The National Party won over 20%, which allowed it a strong voice, but fell far short of what De Klerk had hoped. The Democratic Party finished a distant fifth, winning less than 2% of the vote; it seemed doomed to obscurity.

The provincial results gave the opposition parties greater hope. In KwaZulu-Natal, the Inkatha Freedom Party won a slim majority. In the Western Cape, the National Party won over 50% of the vote, buoyed in part by strong support from the Coloured electorate. Though some Coloured voters had backed the ANC, many feared that they would be second-class citizens in the new order, dominated by black majority, just as they had been in the previous one, ruled by a white minority. Elsewhere, the ANC won seven out of nine provincial governments — and hoped, one day, to rule the others.

Rhoda cast her own vote for the ANC, the party of which she was a card-carrying member. While exhilarated at the experience of voting, Rhoda was skeptical of the ANC's prospects once in office, and did not share in the general euphoria about its victory. She recalled in 2014, twenty years later:

> [H]aving studied Marxism, Leninism, Feminism, labour and global economics, liberation movements and post-colonial societies at the radical Institute for Social Studies in Holland, I just knew that the road ahead would not be as hunky dory as many ordinary people, academics, and the business elite were wont to believe – many who dumped me for asking critical questions since day one of our democracy.[42]

She concluded: "I knew we would f...ck up. I just did not know that we would f...ck up so badly." But she was willing to give the new government a chance, and participated in the shaping of the new constitution.

***

The new government took office on May 10, 1994, with Nelson Mandela inaugurated as President. The National Party had agreed to join the ANC in a governing coalition, which was to be known as the Government of National Unity — both for the sake of stability through the transition to a new government, and (less admirably) with the hope of clinging to vestiges of power. De Klerk was to serve as deputy president under Mandela, along with Thabo Mbeki, a cerebral exile who had outmaneuvered Cyril

---

42   Ibid.

Ramaphosa, a trade union leader, to win the post of deputy leader within the ANC.

The new national legislature convened a constitutional committee that was to hammer out the remaining details over the course of the year. In 1995, a process of public participation began, in which organizations and individual citizens were invited to contribute their ideas to the new constitution — and to raise their objections about provisions in the interim document, or proposals that had been made by other parties. The process was contentious, but peaceful, as the country settled into its new political reality, still uncertain about the future but savoring Mandela's charisma — "Madiba magic" — and enjoying a return to the international community.

Rhoda participated in the debates around the new constitution. She was particularly vocal about women's rights, but also advocated for a variety of other new rights, as well as checks and balances on the power of the new government. She argued for strong protections against discrimination on the basis of sex, including pregnancy. She also argued for the rights of gays and lesbians to be free from discrimination (the question of marriage was later settled by the Constitutional Court). These were ideas well ahead of their time, more forward-thinking than the state of civil liberties in most developed countries.

A year later, in a speech at a Gender Equity Unit event, she noted that the 1994 elections had not only been "a victory for the liberation movements," but also "brought about a new dispensation for women who have been the backbone of the liberation struggle since 1913." She enumerated the victories that women had secured in the interim constitution: "Due to pressure from the women's movement, the [interim] Constitution adopted in January 1994 ensures equality regardless of race, gender and sexual orientation and also makes provision for the Commission on Gender Equality to ensure that the rights of women will be respected and implemented under a new government." These rights, she said, would also be bolstered by the Women's Charter.

Rhoda also noted that "an added victory was won when, at the eleventh hour at the multiparty negotiations, women overturned the recommendations of traditional leaders that customary law be exempt from the Bill of Rights." Traditional leaders had been compensated for that compromise by other provisions of the Constitution ensuring that indigenous law would be recognized by South African courts. However, rural women would no longer be subject to the absolute authority of tribal chiefs.

The final version of the constitution was finally adopted by the National Assembly, certified by the Constitutional Court, and promulgated by President Mandela in late 1996. The document stunned and delighted the international community. It included the broadest range of protections against discrimination yet seen in any constitutional document in the world.

Rhoda was effusive in her praise of the guarantees that the new Constitution provided for women, and also praised the ruling ANC for its efforts. "Women have achieved a lot with the drawing up of the interim Constitution," she said in 1994. "And the ANC's (Mandela's African National Congress) Bill of Rights is the most progressive rights declaration in the world on questions such as family law."[43]

The Bill of Rights to which she referred is contained in Chapter 2 of the new Constitution, which states in its ninth section, on equality:

1. *Everyone is equal before the law and has the right to equal protection and benefit of the law.*

2. *Equality includes the full and equal enjoyment of all rights and freedoms. To promote the achievement of equality, legislative and other measures designed to protect or advance persons, or categories of persons, disadvantaged by unfair discrimination may be taken.*

3. *The state may not unfairly discriminate directly or indirectly against anyone on one or more grounds, including race, gender, sex, pregnancy, marital status, ethnic or social origin, colour, sexual orientation, age, disability, religion, conscience, belief, culture, language and birth.*

4. *No person may unfairly discriminate directly or indirectly against anyone on one or more grounds in terms of subsection (3). National legislation must be enacted to prevent or prohibit unfair discrimination.*

5. *Discrimination on one or more of the grounds listed in subsection (3) is unfair unless it is established that the discrimination is fair.*[44]

While optimistic, Rhoda was also realistic about the challenge of putting these rights into practice. "It's easy to lobby and picket," she said. "But it's

---

43   Rhoda Kadalie, quoted by Arlene Getz, Ibid.
44   Constitute Project. "South Africa's Constitution of 1996 with Amendments Through 2012." URL: https://www.constituteproject.org/constitution/South_Africa_2012.pdf?lang=en. Accessed on 10 Oct. 2021.

going to be much more difficult to redraft the laws which still discriminate against women."[45]

Separately, Rhoda warned that the new Constitution had not resolved the challenge facing women's rights in South Africa. Rather, it had simply created a new terrain for struggle. "The challenge facing South African women in this postelection period is to bring these constitutional rights into line with women's everyday lives, fully knowing that the position of black women is dismal, to say the least."[46] She argued for more than mere formal equality: "[C]itizenship should include more than just constitutional rights for women." South Africa had to find a way to address the material hardships that were the legacy of colonialism and apartheid.

And the task was great — not least because the new government did not seem to take women's issues seriously. "Will the needs of women be overlooked in the new South Africa? Already, there are signs of male chauvinism, similar to the old order, being entrenched in many areas," she warned.[47] She noted that while one-third of parliamentary seats were occupied by women, few of the most powerful positions in government were held by women. She told the Voice of America's French-language broadcast that women had put solidarity with their party ahead of solidarity with fellow women. Although female parliamentarians had already had an impact on the institution — creating a day care in the building, for example, and making their voice heard in committee hearings — they had yet to assert real political power.[48]

Moreover — repeating an insight she had first articulated in her M.A. thesis a decade before — she noted: "Lessons from socialist and even advanced capitalist countries have shown that there is not an automatic relationship between legislation and social change."

It would not merely be enough, Rhoda argued, to dismantle discriminatory laws and practices that held women back. "We must question the patriarchal nature of the state," she wrote, and pursue a "radical restructuring in the gender division of labor," right down to the household level." This was an ambitious goal, one that would require "coercive" labor policies.[49]

That argument represented Rhoda at her most radical. But while she hoped to use the moment of political change to take down "patriarchy" in

---

45   Ibid.
46   Rhoda Kadalie. "Constitutional Equality," 1995, ibid. p. 210.
47   Ibid., p. 214.
48   Rhoda Kadalie, quoted by Voice of America. *Femmes d'Afrique*. 25 Oct. 1994.
49   Rhoda Kadalie. "Constitutional Equality," 1995, ibid. p. 221.

South African society, she also explicitly doubted the capacity of the state alone to make changes in women's lives.

She was also discouraged by the "state of disarray" of the women's movement in the aftermath of the 1994 elections.[50] She observed in 1995:

The ANC Women's League, which constitutes quite a major sector of this movement, is weak and deeply divided by a power struggle for the leadership; the Women's National Coalition also suffers from a crisis of leadership with two key members of its national executive now serving in parliament; and meetings convened to discuss the setting up of national machinery for the Commission on Gender Equality reveal that there is further turmoil within the ranks. We are floundering about trying to articulate a programme of action that will take us beyond the equality provisions in the interim Constitution.

Rhoda recommended that women "go back to our roots and recapture some of the energy and courage displayed by women who in the first half of the twentieth century challenge structures that kept them in subordination." She warned that divisions within the women's movement seemed to be an obstacle to progress, lamenting "the inability of South African women to deal adequately with conflict and difference, especially those embedded in the specifics of race, culture, ethnicity and religion." While women seemed able to overcome such differences in the past, that seemed harder to do in the absence of the common enemy provided by the apartheid regime.

For years, long before the end of apartheid, Rhoda had participated in public observances of Women's Day, on August 9, a holiday celebrated by the anti-apartheid movement to mark the anniversary of the Women's March against pass laws in 1956. In a 1996 forum to mark Women's Day, which had become a national public holiday, she warned that while "throughout history, since 1913, black women in South Africa used their sexuality, their sisterhood, their loyalty to men, their disdain of men to assert their right to democracy," once democracy had arrived, it had made women all but "invisible" to the country's new leadership.[51] She declared that she looked forward to the day when "Women's Day would no longer be needed: "I think it's for men to make Women's Day redundant. ... the time has come for men to grant equality to women." While defending affirmative action policies as a necessary corrective to misogynistic prejudices, she added: "It was said of [Israeli prime minister] Golda Meir

---

50   Rhoda Kadalie. "Where's the Rock?" *Southern African Review of Books.* May/June 1995.

51   Rhoda Kadalie, quoted on "Women's Day." SAfm radio, 9 Aug. 1996.

she was the best man in the Cabinet ... and I'm still looking to a future where we can say that that person is the best for the job, regardless of the gender."

She quipped: "Women who want to be equal to men lack ambition. I don't want to be equal to men — they've been bad examples. I want transformed men and women. Both men and women need to change. ... Every chauvinist has a mother." The goal, Rhoda said, was a society in which "the one isn't dominant over the other."[52] But that society seemed a long way off, even after the first democratic elections.

Her skepticism partly reflected the limits of the new Constitution itself. When it came to redressing inequalities, the text of the Constitution provided for measures to be taken, such as affirmative action policies, that would redress past discrimination. But theoretically at least, the constitution set limits to such actions, on the basis of "fairness." Effectively, that meant the courts would have to decide the limits of affirmative action. On the fraught issue of land reform, which would remain a racial flashpoint for years, the Constitution theoretically permitted expropriation without compensation. But at the same time, it strove to protect property rights. This created an ambivalence that was probably necessary for the compromise that ushered in parliamentary democracy, but it made resolving the issue difficult.

The Bill of Rights also included such idealistic notions as a right to "human dignity." It aimed to prevent the abuses of the past, stipulating the right "a. not to be deprived of freedom arbitrarily or without just cause; b. not to be detained without trial; c. to be free from all forms of violence from either public or private sources; d. not to be tortured in any way; and e. not to be treated or punished in a cruel, inhuman or degrading way." The new constitution also included a right to freedom of expression — although, given South Africa's precarious social tensions, that right was limited by a provision barring "advocacy of hatred."

Perhaps most controversial of all, the new constitution included socioeconomic rights — a right to housing, a right to food, a right to education, a right to health care, and even a right to a clean environment. These rights, critics warned, were not justiciable — that is, they could not be enforced by the courts, if the government lacked the capacity to provide them. To deal with that problem, the constitution noted that such rights were subject to "progressive realisation" — i.e. they would be enforceable over time.

---

52   Ibid.

The result was that South Africa's new government was locked into policies that relied on the state to play the leading role. That would constrain future debates about how to improve the lives of the poor. For the moment, however, it provided millions of South Africans hope for a better life.

***

South Africa's new leaders prided themselves on the new rights that they had established in their constitution. But they wanted to guarantee that those rights were observed. The power and legitimacy of the Constitutional Court had not yet been established, and there was concern that the new government would abuse its parliamentary and executive powers, just as the apartheid regime had done.

Under the old order, the majority party expanded the powers of Parliament such that it dominated both the executive and the judiciary. To prevent that from happening again, the new constitution provided for several "independent" state institutions.

These institutions were described in Chapter 9 of the constitution, and they included several "state institutions supporting constitutional democracy":

- **Public Protector**: The new constitution sought to prevent corruption by creating a special office to investigate the government itself, outside of the purview of the justice ministry or the police. The Public Protector, nominated for a seven-year term, would serve for longer than any particular five-years parliament. He or she could not initiate prosecutions, and could not investigate court decisions. But the office was given the power "to take appropriate remedial action" if misconduct was found, and was required to make reports of its inquiries public.

- **South African Human Rights Commission**: This was to provide general oversight of the government's fulfillment of the rights enumerated in the new constitution, as well as the promotion of a culture of human rights in the country more generally. It was given the power "a. to investigate and to report on the observance of human rights; b. to take steps to secure appropriate redress where human rights have been violated; c. to carry out research; and d. to educate." It also had the responsibility to demand that government departments provide annual reports on their progress towards fulfilling the constitution's socioeconomic rights.

- **Commission for the Promotion and Protection of the Rights of Cultural, Religious and Linguistic Communities**: White apartheid had forcibly separated South Africans of different races, and reinforced existing ethnic and linguistic divisions. The fact was that many South Africans cared deeply about their individual identities. That was as true of members of black tribal groups as it was of many Afrikaners, who had seen white minority rule as the only way to prevent their subjugation and assimilation. The new constitution sought to assuage those fears, and protect the prerogatives of traditional leaders, through a commission that could review the government's compliance with constitutional guarantees to these communities.
- **Commission for Gender Equality**: This institution was an indirect result of Rhoda's work at UWC, which had inspired other women to press for guarantees of gender equality. Though its mandate was somewhat amorphous — it had the power "to monitor, investigate, research, educate, lobby, advise and report on issues concerning gender equality" — its inclusion was seen as an important symbolic victory for feminists, who had struggled to be heard.
- **Auditor-General**: This office was to provide independent financial oversight of every government agency. The idea was to prevent some of the abuses of the past — such as the Information Scandal, in which the apartheid regime diverted funds to create a sympathetic newspaper, *The Citizen* — as well as future corruption. In a nation whose financial system was world-class, despite its underdeveloped state, the Auditor-General enjoyed particular prestige.
- **Electoral Commission**: Unlike the United States, where the rules for elections are set by politicians at the state level and only loosely overseen by the federal government and the courts, the electoral commission was to be independent of political interference, and administer all elections — national, provincial, and municipal.

In late 1995, as the constitution was being finalized, Rhoda received a call from Nelson Mandela's office: she was to be appointed to the South African Human Rights Commission. Nominated by her old friend and colleague, Jakes Gerwel, she was to be one of 11 commissioners, who had been chosen from among 85 nominees. The appointment was richly deserved: it came in recognition of her achievements at UWC in establishing the Gender Equity Unit, as well as her contribution to the anti-apartheid cause more generally.

Rhoda with President Nelson Mandela, UWC, Bellville, 1999
(Courtesy Rhoda Kadalie)

Letters and faxes congratulating Rhoda poured in from friends, colleagues, and fellow activists. Gerwel was jokingly said to have lamented "the departure [from UWC] of a person whose role had been to be difficult, uncomfortable and irritating."[53] Rhoda commented: "The gist of what he said was that I was a necessary irritant. I found that a compliment because, if I hadn't played that role, the university could have sat back and ignored the fact that women academics, staff and students had particular rights which the institution needed to respect." She left behind a UWC with a culture of "consciousness around gender issues," and with "one of the best student courts in the country."[54]

Rhoda was to be one of 11 members on the commission, chaired by theologian Dr. Barney Pityana, an anti-apartheid cleric in the Anglican Church who had spent sixteen years in exile. The other commissioners had similar "struggle" credentials. Notably, one of Rhoda's colleagues was Helen Suzman, who had retired from politics in 1989 but who still retained a prominent place in South African public life and enjoyed unimpeachable moral stature.

With Mandela's blessing, Rhoda would put her skills to use and principles into practice. Or so she hoped.

53   Jakes Gerwel, quoted by Institute of Democracy in South Africa. "A necessary irritant?". *Democracy in Action*, Vol. 9 No. 7, 15 Dec. 1995. p. 10. The quote is indirect, not verbatim.
54   Rhoda Kadalie, quoted by Institute of Democracy in South Africa, ibid.

Chapter Ten:
Human Rights

"During Mandela's reign and my stint at the Human Rights Commission there was much opportunity for women to engage in a new political discourse ... This sense of opportunity and freedom was short-lived."[1]

Rhoda took up her position on the South African Human Rights Commission (SAHRC) with excitement and enthusiasm. She was among 11 commissioners in total, each of whom was assigned specific oversight over one or more of South Africa's nine provinces.

Idasa applauded Rhoda's appointment, noting:

Apart from her activist credentials, Kadalie brings another kind of experience to this crucial work — long years of humiliation, hardship and oppression shared with millions of other black South Africans. Her family was forcibly removed from District Six [sic],[2] near Cape Town, in terms of the notorious Group Areas Act, for example; she was derided for her curly hair and dark skin for her school for "half-castes" in Woodstock; she got married in Namibia, away from family and friends, because the man she loved was white.[3]

Idasa noted that the SAHRC already faced credibility problems, because of a "flawed nomination process" that allowed members of the National Party, which had governed under apartheid, to join other parties in choosing the commissioners. Rhoda was prepared to look beyond that, arguing that while members of the old regime had to bear responsibility for what it had done, "these very people, who now have committed themselves to a human rights culture, are publicly saying that they come from such a history and are now prepared to start afresh."[4]

---

1   Rhoda Kadalie. *In Your Face: Passionate Conversations About People and Politics.* Cape Town: Tafelberg, 2009. p. 8.

2   The Kadalie family left District Six several years before the forced removals began, but was forcibly removed from Mowbray.

3   Institute of Democracy in South Africa. "A necessary irritant?". *Democracy in Action*, Vol. 9 No. 7, 15 Dec. 1995. p. 10.

4   Rhoda Kadalie, quoted by Institute of Democracy in South Africa, ibid. p. 11.

Rhoda was also given a specifically geographic mandate, "responsible for human rights monitoring in the Western and Northern Cape."[5] That happened to be the region of the country with the largest Coloured population. Though she did not have a specifically racial mandate, it was understood that Rhoda's inclusion was to provide additional protection for that community. Other commissioners were assigned one each, sometimes sharing responsibility for a single province. Rhoda was also assigned two committee chairmanships — one on Government and Parliamentary Liaison, and one on International Coordination. Only one other commissioner had two chairmanships.

Rhoda with fellow Human Rights Commissioner Helen Suzman (center), and staff members, including Paul Curnow (top left), Cape Town, c. 1998 (Courtesy Rhoda Kadalie)

The Commission's first task was to explain what it was, and what the new Constitution meant to ordinary South Africans. A 13-page pamphlet

5   South African Human Rights Commission. "The Chairperson, Deputy Chairperson, Commissioners and CEO of the South African Human Rights Commission." 1996. URL: https://www.sahrc.org.za/files/Commissioners%20and%20CEO%20Term%201-2.pdf. Accessed on 10 Oct. 2021.

from the commission attempted to summarize the rights provided by the new Constitution, as well as what the Human Rights Commission would do to enforce them. "Some problems happen between two people, others between people and the government, and some may be with an employer. Whoever your problem is with, if it involves your human rights, we will try to help you work it out."[6] The pamphlet listed Rhoda's name among the commissioners.[7]

The Commission was plagued from the outset with many logistical problems. For one thing, its budget was tiny — some R6.4 million (or about $1 million), far less than other government departments, and less than ten percent of what the Truth and Reconciliation Commission was allocated.[8] That money had to be stretched among many different officials: "We have a secretariat, we have a chief executive officer, and we have four heads of departments — we have a legal and investigations department, we have a research department, we have an education and training department, and we have a finance and admin[istration] department. But those departments themselves are very limited in their resources." The commission wanted to incorporate a human rights curriculum within South Africa's emerging new school curricula, but they only had two staff members to design materials. And finding good legal staff for the commission was difficult: "If we want to attract good lawyers, we have to pay."[9]

Though she had initially been a strident supporter of the Gender Commission, saying it was necessary in a country plagued by the "structural subordination of women,"[10] Rhoda came to believe that it was "an expensive exercise" to have so many Chapter 9 institutions competing for the same limited budget space. She added: "The Gender Commission is a complete duplicate of the Human Rights Commission ... I think we should have had a gender commissioner within the Human Rights Commission."[11] When one commissioner resigned, it took eight months to find a replacement.

6   South African Human Rights Commission. "South African Human Rights Commission: What You Need to Know; Protecting You, Protecting Your Rights." Pamphlet. 1997.

7   Oddly, the pamphlet listed Dr. Max Coleman as the commissioner for the Northern Cape, but that province actually fell under Rhoda's responsibilities. Later, she also temporarily oversaw the Free State as well.

8   Rhoda Kadalie, on *The Law Report*. SAfm, 11 Nov. 1996.

9   Ibid.

10   Institute of Democracy in South Africa, ibid. p. 11.

11   Ibid.

Despite these challenges, Rhoda was determined to pursue her responsibilities with vigor. Apart from attending obligatory planning sessions in Johannesburg, where the Human Rights Commission was based, Rhoda was allowed to operate from separate offices in Cape Town. She worked from home for nearly a year, while the other commissioners occupied plush offices in the Johannesburg suburb of Houghton.

Rhoda created a three-pronged strategy. First, she invited the public to lodge complaints about alleged human rights abuses directly with her office. Second, she decided to visit key state institutions personally, to introduce herself and the work of the commission. Third, she sought to forge partnerships with non-governmental organizations (NGOs) that would conduct research on human rights issues and help educate the public about the Bill of Rights and the commission itself.

Most of the other commissioners did not like the idea of allowing the public to lodge complaints directly. But Rhoda wanted to create a public complaints mechanism to learn more about the public's view of what human rights violations were; to work out a regular system for complaints to the commission; and to prepare the commission to follow up complaints with investigations and reports.

Her strategy bore fruit almost immediately, as it made her office the most visible face of the HRC. She received hundreds of complaints, about half of which were outside the commission's jurisdiction, leaving many legitimate issues to investigate. She explained the process:

> We encourage people to do written complaints — as you know, legal cases need reliable data. But we also have a big population which is non-literate and illiterate. So we encourage them to come to the offices and we take a statement under oath. We then consider is it a bona fide violation of a fundamental right. If it is, and if it's serious, we consider it. ... We then — cases that are not in our jurisdiction, we refer ... [to] whatever appropriate body exists.[12]

The committee had the power to initiate legal proceedings, including hearings. It could subpoena witnesses, and even seize documents, with judicial warrants. But Rhoda preferred mediation to confrontation: "Mediation is nice because through the process you educate the public. And I think, if we were heavy-handed, we wouldn't be a good commission. And I have found that many people change after they actually know

---

12   Ibid.

what the Bill of Rights are, and what people's rights mean, because they're human."[13]

The commission's proceedings were open to the public — yet here, too, Rhoda stressed that public hearings should be used sparingly. While it might be useful to present a "test case" of human rights to "educate the public," she noted: "Unlike the Truth Commission, we often cannot seek publicity. ... Confidentiality is central to our work. And if you don't keep things confidential, you often jeopardize your chances of resolving the case."[14]

Rhoda and the other commissioners also had legislative duties, monitoring pending bills in Parliament to ensure that they complied with the Bill of Rights and with international treaties. In addition, the commission's own investigations and hearings could, in theory, culminate in suggestions for legislation. Rhoda noted that, given the decades of apartheid statutes still on the books, the commission had to be "proactive" in seeking out laws to be rewritten.[15]

Above all these duties, Rhoda became known for interacting with the public about human rights issues. She familiarized herself directly with the most common forms of abuse experienced by South Africans on an everyday basis. And her office was inundated with hundreds of calls and human rights complaints, leading to scores of investigations on everything from school discipline to discrimination by the military against married female soldiers.

She later recalled:

An ordinary member of the working class, a domestic worker, will phone me up and tell me that her 'madam' has discriminated against her. There was a black woman who worked for a medical company where a doctor's wallet got lost and he immediately accused her of stealing it. Security guards came in and they strip-searched her to look for this wallet. But this woman came to me because she knew her rights. It is empowering when people know their rights and act on them. This is what I find encouraging about South Africa today.[16]

Paul Curnow, who was a newly-graduated attorney from Australia who had married a South African, joined Rhoda's staff as a volunteer, before

---

13   Ibid.
14   Ibid.
15   *Law Report*, ibid.
16   Rhoda Kadalie, quoted by Ryland Fisher. *Race*. Auckland Park: Jacana Media, 2007. p. 125.

Rhoda managed to secure him a stipend with the help of a grant from the Australian government. Now an established lawyer in Sydney with a practice focusing on environmental law, Curnow recalled that his early duties consisted of fielding calls, letters, and complaints that flooded Rhoda's office.[17] Most of the commission's responses simply involved writing letters on behalf of people with grievances, but some required further investigation — and revealed a country still grappling with the abuses of its past, and the lingering inequalities of the present.

As such, Rhoda was soon involved in several well-publicized cases that both drew attention to the lingering problems with human rights in South Africa, and educated the public about the values the new constitutional order wished to promote.

One celebrated case invoked a racist remark by an emergency dispatcher from the Cape Ambulance Rescue Service, who had referred to a suicidal black man as a "*dom* [stupid] darkie." As the *Sunday Times* summarized the case:

> When Themba Mbane called the ambulance service emergency number, 10777, after his brother had drunk battery acid earlier this month, he expected help.
>
> Instead he got a response which left him shocked.
>
> A transcript of the conversation which the commission has in its possession — Cape Metro [municipal government] has a copy — reveals that the operator called Mbane a "dom darkie" and said it appeared his brother wanted to die "so why disturb him?".[18]

Rhoda personally served an order on the chief of ambulance services, demanding that he identify the operator. It was, the *Times* noted, "the first time the commission has had to resort to serving an order of compliance since coming into existence."

Later, the HRC investigated and found that Mbane had tried calling the emergency number five times; and that the operator, a man named Windsor Sass, had allegedly hung up on Mbane several times. In his defense, Sass argued that he had mistaken Mbane's call for a prank. Still, the racist language riled the HRC, which wanted to send a message that such rhetoric was no longer acceptable from public employees in

---

17   Paul Curnow. Personal communication with the author. 25 Mar. 2022.
18   Yvette van Breda. "Ambulance racism furore: Legal action taken after operator calls caller a 'dom darkie'." *Sunday Times*, 29 Jun. 1997.

South Africa. It issued a finding that the operator "acted in a racist and humiliating manner."[19]

Rhoda also took up a number of cases involving children and teenagers. In one case, she investigated reports of abuse at a children's shelter in Stellenbosch, the capital of the Western Cape's wine country.[20] In September 1997, she spoke out, as a member of the commission, against a lenient sentence that had been given to a man convicted of raping and killing a five-year-old girl: "I see a recurring pattern that people are not being given high enough jail sentences for crimes of murder, sexual violence and rape. People are getting fed up. ... The state should send out a strong message that it's not okay to attack children." She recommended a life sentence without the possibility of parole.[21]

In yet another case, an 18-year-old pupil named Mandelsizwe Lufele, who had grown up in a shack and considered himself a Rastafarian, complained that his school was requiring him to cut off his dreadlocks before he could register to take final exams. Lufele claimed that the school was violating his right to religious expression. The Human Rights Commission, through Rhoda, intervened, and the school backed down without a court battle.[22] The case was only one of several involving Rastafarians, one of whom was a policeman who also wanted to grow dreadlocks.

Rhoda also assisted another student who had been barred from his school's matric dance — the South African equivalent of the "prom" — because he had come in traditional African attire rather than Western formal dress. And she ensured that the HRC intervened on behalf of a student whose house had been searched by a teacher who accused the pupil of stealing a set of keys. She also defended a student who had been expelled from a college in Natal for falling pregnant.

Rhoda took a particular interest in the so-called "places of safety" for children, institutions established to care for children who were victims of abuse, juvenile offenders, or chronic truants from school. These places were, in fact, often dangerous for children, who were subjected to deprivation and to physical abuse by fellow inhabitants. Together with interns Paul Curnow and Jesse Goichman, Rhoda conducted an investigation for the SAHRC, whose findings were presented to the Western

---

19   Human Rights Commission, quoted by Lindsay Barnes. "'Dom darkie' ambulance slur slammed in report." *Cape Argus*, 24 Jul. 1997.

20   Lindsay Barnes. "I quit, says 'unhappy' rights chief." *Cape Argus*, 23 Jul. 1997.

21   Rhoda Kadalie, quoted by Lindsay Barnes and Beauregard Tromp. "'Jail child-killer for life'." *Cape Argus*, 16 Sep. 1997.

22   Yvette van Breda. "Dreadlock victory: Matric pupil wins human rights battle to keep his hairstyle." *Sunday Times*, 15 June 1999.

Cape Department of Welfare. Rhoda reported that one place of safety known as Lindelani, Stellenbosch, was "worse than any of the prisons visited in the Western Cape." Citing the provisions of the country's new Bill of Rights, Rhoda reminded the provincial authorities of the need to build a "human rights culture" in the places of safety, and made several concrete recommendations for physical improvements to the facilities, as well as for the retraining of staff and for monitoring by outside institutions.[23]

Rhoda often weighed in publicly on human rights abuses that attracted the country's attention. But she resisted knee-jerk responses. In 1997, a woman named Nomboniso Gasa claimed to have been raped by a white man on Robben Island, which had, by then, been converted from a prison into a museum. The police investigated, but failed to find any solid leads.[24] Rhoda suspected that Gasa's story was not what it seemed, and was critical of the way that Gasa pursued the case — for example, her apparent delay in seeing a doctor as soon as possible for a forensic examination. The two exchanged letters privately, in which Gasa accused Rhoda of trying to "discredit" her[25]; Rhoda advised Gasa to "take time to heal" but also noted, sadly, that there was a "due legal process" that had to be followed.[26] When the police closed their inquiry later that year, Rhoda publicly defended their decision to do so — against protests by the Commission on Gender Equality and feminists who were adamant that Gasa deserved to be believed, as a purported victim.[27] (Today, Gasa maintains that she was indeed raped on the island, and blames police for a botched investigation.[28])

As antisemitism became a more dangerous threat to South Africa's small Jewish community, with the rise of a radical Islamic extremist minority, Rhoda spoke out stridently against anti-Jewish prejudice and violence. In July 1997, a group of anti-Israel demonstrators marched to the Israeli consulate in Cape Town, chanting "One Zionist, one bullet"

23   Rhoda Kadalie et al. "Meeting with the Department of Welfare on Places of Safety for Children." Memorandum, 9 Dec. 1997.

24   Staff Reporter. "Gasa: The rape was only the start of her nightmare." *Mail & Guardian*, 4 Apr. 1997. URL: https://mg.co.za/article/1997-04-04-gasa-the-rape-was-only-the-start-of-her-nightmare/. Accessed on 8 Jul. 2022.

25   Nomboniso Gasa. Letter to Rhoda Kadalie. 16 Mar. 1997.

26   Rhoda Kadalie. Letter to Nomboniso Gasa. 23 Mar. 1997.

27   Lindsay Barnes. "Anger As Island Rape Case Closed." *Cape Argus*, 20 Oct. 1997.

28   "EFF distances itself from tweet about activist's rape." News24.com, 9 Feb. 2015. URL: https://www.news24.com/news24/eff-distances-itself-from-tweet-about-activists-rape-20150209. Accessed on 8 Jul. 2022.

and "Death to Israel"— slogans that Rhoda said were "irresponsible and openly incite racial hatred and violence."[29] The violence was more than theoretical: a Jewish home in the suburb of Newlands was bombed, and there were bomb threats to other Jewish institutions, including a nursing home, which Rhoda condemned as "obviously racist and anti-Semitic."[30]

Her role on the HRC also allowed her to speak out on other prominent issues related to human rights. When a court ruled that gays had the right to consensual sex in private, overturning a conviction for sodomy, Rhoda joined other gay rights activists in hailing the ruling. "Western Cape Human Rights Commissioner Ms Rhoda Kadalie said the ruling was a great victory for the gay liberation movement," the *Cape Times* reported.[31]

She also took up the cause of victims for whom the public had little sympathy. These included homeless people, including children, who began taking up residence on the streets of Cape Town, at times harassing tourists and passersby for money or food. An informal poll by the *Cape Argus* in 1997 found that some 99% of readers believed that "vagrants and street children should be removed" by police.[32] Despite public support for vigorous police action, Rhoda and the HRC took up the cause of homeless people and children who said they had been arrested for no reason. The HRC, at Rhoda's direction, worked with police, church groups, and community organizations to coordinate a more humane and effective approach — one that did not criminalize homeless people merely for being on the street.

***

Rhoda took a particular interest in the tactics of the police, and the conditions of South Africa's prisons. Law enforcement in South Africa was often a brutal, and primitive, affair. The primary task of the police had been to enforce apartheid's racial boundaries and to suppress political dissent. Little attention had been paid to ordinary crime prevention, or investigation; moreover, a significant proportion of the police were functionally illiterate.

Meanwhile, South Africa was experiencing a shocking rise in crime. The murder rate had risen dramatically since the end of apartheid, peaking

---

29   Rhoda Kadalie, quoted by Staff Reporter. "Racist attack condemned." *Sowetan*, 16 Jul. 1997.
30   Rhoda Kadalie, quoted by Lisa Templeton. "Muslim leaders slam attack on Jewish home." *Cape Times*, 15 Jul. 1997. p. 3.
31   Lisa Templeton. "Adult gay sex is not a crime, court rules." *Cape Times*, 5 Aug. 1995.
32   Editorial board. "People of the streets." *Cape Argus*, 25 Aug. 1997.

in the years of political transition, against a background of political violence and institutional change.

Rhoda defended victims of crime, a growing but largely neglected group of South Africans whose voices the government preferred to ignore. She was particularly adamant about bringing an end to rape — and on insisting that men take responsibility for educating each other.[33] At the same time, she tried to open dialogues with Cape Town's gang leaders, who offered their help in de-escalating the violence in the city and had been ignored by other branches of government. The issue became particularly acute in the late 1990s as a new Islamic group called People Against Gangsterism and Drugs (PAGAD) began taking the law into its own hands, assassinating gang leaders and suspected criminals. Within a few years, PAGAD had been infiltrated by Islamic terrorists who carried out a series of bombings throughout the city before being shut down by police. The HRC spoke out openly against PAGAD's vigilantism.[34]

The crime wave placed increased pressure on the police to act. But they were ill-equipped to do so; they were sometimes victims of crime themselves. Many South African police stations hired private security firms to protect them from criminals who saw the facilities as inviting targets for robbery, given the weapons stockpiled there, and the drugs and cash often stored as evidence.

That, in turn, meant that police were often inclined to be brutal in their methods. The death penalty was banned in the new South Africa, having lost much of its legitimacy after the apartheid regime used it against political opponents. So police often took the law into their own hands, killing suspects in confrontations rather than risk the possibility that the justice system would simply release them back onto the street.

Rhoda was adamantly opposed to the death penalty: she criticized the premier of the Western Cape at the time, who called for a referendum on the subject, calling it "gross political opportunism." She argued: "The death penalty does not stamp out crime and it has not done so anywhere in the world where it has been or is being practiced, and it does not deter more effectively than any other punishments."[35] The real problem, she said, was the continued failure of the criminal justice system, from a failure to investigate crimes, to the overcrowding of prisons.

---

33   Lindsay Barnes. "Bear witness against crime, women urged." *Cape Argus*, 28 Aug. 1997.
34   "Rights group slams Pagad." *Cape Times*, 28 Aug. 1996.
35   Rhoda Kadalie. "Kriel out for votes with death penalty poll bid." Letter to *Cape Times*, 29 Oct. 1997.

There was also police corruption at every level — from high-ranking officials who developed lucrative relationships with crime syndicates, to low-level officers who hustled bribes from prostitutes and drug dealers.

Rhoda had plenty of experience dodging the apartheid police — the spies on her street, the riot crews on campus. She soon encountered the rot in the post-apartheid police force in an unexpected fashion.

One evening, she was driving with Julia in the coastal Cape Town neighborhood of Sea Point when she had a minor car accident. When they went to the Sea Point police station to report the crash for insurance purposes, Rhoda was shocked to see officers parading a string of prostitutes, one after the other, into holding cells.

When she asked what was going on, one of the officers laughingly said that they were simply waiting for the pimps to show up and pay cash to have the women released. Furious at the obvious exploitation of these vulnerable women, Rhoda introduced herself as a human rights commissioner and took the issue to the top of police management.

Rhoda also received a formal complaint from members of the public regarding a type of baton that security officers at the University of the Western Cape had begun using — or abusing — in crowd control during continued protests on campus. The device looked somewhat like an ordinary nightstick or club: it was long and black, with a black handle. But it functioned as a stun gun, shooting a high-voltage current that was used to intimidate members of the public — or to torture detainees in holding cells.

Rhoda recalled:

I had just been appointed Human Rights Commissioner in 1995. A senior black woman student came to my office to lodge a complaint that UWC officials had used stun batons on students when the university suddenly announced a shift in the admissions schedule to hours earlier. The students stampeded fearing that they might lose an admission. University officials then used the stun batons on students, men and women alike. Some women fainted.

Upon investigation the university authorities refused to respond to my requests. Forgetting that I had many admirers in the administration, university officials in the administration leaked information to me that there was a cache of armaments from the old apartheid days, consisting, inter alia, of stun batons, used to control the students.

My report went viral internationally, and was even commented upon by Amnesty International. Needless to say, the university was pissed off with me, but they promised to confiscate the cache.[36]

It was a small step toward progress, under difficult circumstances. In appreciation for her work, the students gave her a gift: a framed stun baton, encased in glass. She hung it in the entrance of her Woodstock home, where it hovered whimsically above her guests, among the paintings and Africana that had already been mounted on the pastel pink walls.

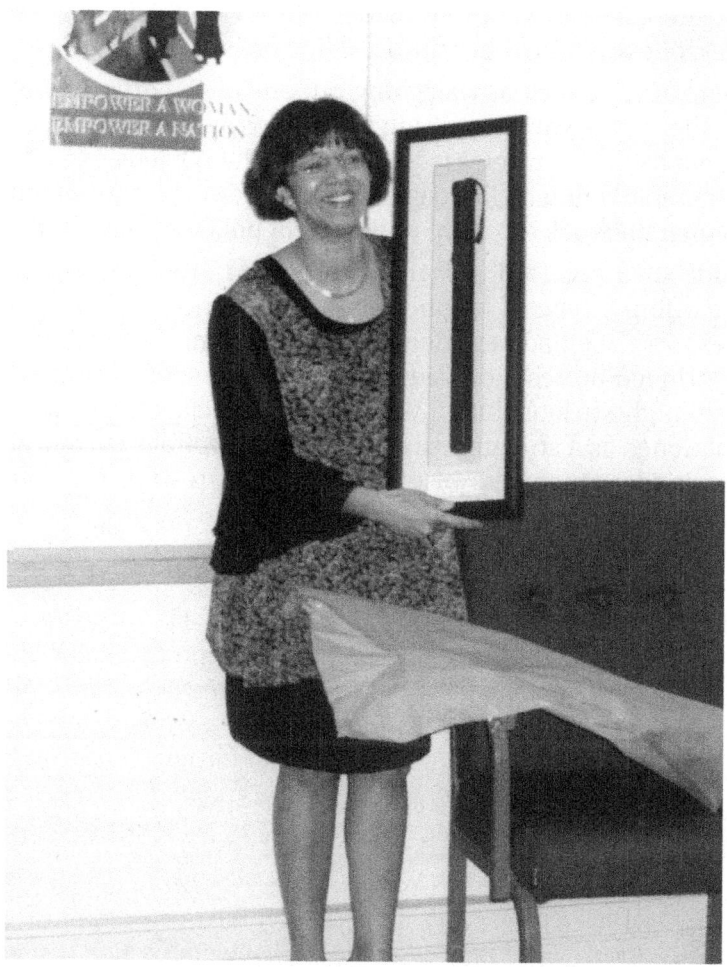

Rhoda receives a stun baton in appreciation for her work on behalf of student protesters, c. 1998 (Courtesy Rhoda Kadalie)

---

36   Personal communication with the author. Feb. 1.

Surprisingly, Rhoda found that the police were willing to work with her. She held meetings with Leon Wessels, who had been the police commissioner in the old regime. He enjoyed the fact that she spoke with him in Afrikaans, and the two of them exchanged compliments: "With that tie," she once joked, "you and I will rule the world." He invited her to address recruits at South Africa's police academies, and introduced her to his colleagues: "With that *tannie* [auntie], we'll work well together," he said.

Rhoda worked with the South African Police Service (SAPS), the national police force (municipal police forces did not yet exist; local police stations were branches of the national agency). She was adamant that the abuse of force had to be stopped; at the same time, she had an appreciation for the difficult job the police had to do in handling an overwhelming crime wave.

Through patient work with the police hierarchy, old and new, Rhoda was able to introduce educational materials and training practices that taught officers the basic principles of the country's new culture of human rights.

***

Another topic on which Rhoda developed a close interest was prison reform. The apartheid-era prisons were notoriously crowded; they were in an even worse state in the new South Africa, with arrests and convictions running high. Prisoners awaiting trial — some of whom were young and naïve — were often held together with hardened criminals, and often for months at a time.

Moreover, the prisons were largely run by large syndicates known as the "number gangs." These had a history dating back decades, to the early years of the South African penitentiary system. But they became even more notorious in the midst of South Africa's crime wave.

Of particular note were the gangs known as the 26, 27, and 28 gangs, each of which required inmates to commit particular crimes to gain acceptance. The 26s required theft; the 28s, murder. Prisoners who failed to join a gang were often targeted by those who had done so.

In such circumstances, prisons were not places for correction or rehabilitation, for most inmates. Instead, they were places where prisoners were subject to grotesque abuses, and where first-time offenders were trained to be hardened, violent criminals.

Moreover, through corruption in the prison service, gang leaders and drug kingpins were able to rule their empires outside the prison from inside. For many criminals, the boundaries between life behind bars and life outside — often in impoverished circumstances — became so blurred as to be almost nonexistent.

Rhoda took up the cause of prison reform out of a realization that many who were inside the system were victims of it. Apartheid had previously made even mundane economic activities, such as owning multiple businesses, illegal for black South Africans. In addition, the glaring inequalities of South African life were a constant temptation to crime, especially for the uneducated masses.

As a member of the South African Human Rights Commission, Rhoda had unique and unfettered access to prisons whose very name, in the very recent past, had triggered dread in the hearts of many South Africans. She made several visits to prisons in the Cape region and elsewhere, inspecting conditions directly.

As with the police, she found that administrators were eager to cooperate with her, and opened up facilities for her to inspect, including the notorious Pollsmoor Prison, where Mandela had been held for several years. One of her allies in reforming the prison was Freddie Engelbrecht, who was the area manager for the prison service, in charge of Pollsmoor and several other prisons. Another was Johnny Jansen, the head of the maximum security facilities at Pollsmoor, which was among South Africa's largest such facilities.

Engelbrecht and Jansen seized the opportunity to work with Rhoda to turn Pollsmoor into a correctional facility, rather than just a place where criminals victimized each other. She organized training in basic human rights principles for the prison wardens, and was invited in return to charitable functions with prison officials, including auctions of art made by some of the prisoners.

Engelbrecht recalled meeting Rhoda for the first time. He and Jansen decided to be straightforward with her about the problems at Pollsmoor, sensing that she would see through any attempt to sugarcoat the reality about conditions. "We were very scared of her," he recalled. "We tried to speak the truth but not hide anything because she knew she would find out and then be very disappointed in us."[37] They earned her trust, and began a close working relationship.

Jansen later recalled:

Rhoda Kadalie was one of those people I will never forget, I will be honest. What impressed me at the time was her vision. She had quite a

---

37   Freddie Engelbrecht. Personal communication with the author, 14 Mar. 2022.

clear vision for human rights in South Africa, and in prisons in particular. She was part of the political struggle, in which I was also a part, when we fought the apartheid system — she was also an activist during those days. And [her] becoming the human rights commissioner was one of the best things that could have happened to prisons, not just in the Western Cape province but in South Africa ... I was very fortunate to cross roads with her at the time, because my vision and Rhoda's vision coincided.[38]

He added that Rhoda's support for reform in the prisons was "not just in words": "She came to the prison and to be involved in activities at the prison, and it was any time of the day and any time of the night." During searches of prison cells at night, Jansen recalled, he would call Rhoda at 2:00 or 3:00 in the morning to supervise the guards' behavior to ensure it conformed with human rights standards. She would immediately drive to the prison, roughly half an hour from her home.

The young Paul Curnow was deeply impressed by Rhoda's work in the prisons. She could speak to the wardens in Afrikaans, and communicate with prisoners in the local Cape Flats dialect. And she was fearless: "We would walk through the cells, and she'd do prison inspections, and talk to the wardens and prisoners, and she'd be there with all the gang members, with all the tattoos, making them laugh."

In 1997, there was public outrage when some prisoners at Pollsmoor were assaulted and robbed by prison guards armed with shotguns. Engelbrecht recalled that he "called the provincial commissioner, [and] asked for [an] emergency support team around the Western Cape to search the facility." President Nelson Mandela himself, who had once been imprisoned at Pollsmoor, visited the facility and ordered an inquiry.

Engelbrecht feared that he and Jansen would be set up as the fall guys for the problems at the prison, partly because of their role in the wardens' labor union, the Police and Prisons Civil Rights Union (Popcru), which had been established in 1989, just before the end of apartheid. He believed that Sipho Mzimela, the Minister of Correctional Services, "wanted to dismiss them, needed to find somebody that [the government] can blame." In Parliament, Limpho Hani, the widow of the late South African Communist Party leader Chris Hani, was the chair of the relevant portfolio committee, and she "accused us of wanting to undermine the government of the day," Engelbrecht recalled.

Rhoda, who trusted Engelbrecht and Jansen, intervened: "She saved us, our careers, and she protected us." She also urged that the report into

---

38   Johnny Jansen. Personal communication with the author. 14 Mar 2022.

the incidents at the prison not be delayed: "I appeal to the president and the commission of inquiry to release the findings as soon as possible so that the process is not hampered in the prison."[39]

In her tenure on the HRC, Rhoda visited every prison in the Western Cape and the Northern Cape. As Rhoda would later recall, the prisoners were often exceedingly polite as they detailed their grievances. She was usually the first woman that many of the male inmates had seen in years; when she brought a female intern along with her, some of the men would thank her effusively for the sight.

After months of investigation, the Human Rights Commission produced a report, largely written by Rhoda. The introduction explained:

Questions have been asked as to why the Commission seems to have prioritised prisons. Criticism has been levelled at the Commission on the basis that there was not likely to be anything new that would come out of any inquiry the Commission might undertake. We decided to undertake the inquiry for the following reasons:

The prison population in South Africa was so disproportionately high that the maintenance of prison services was a major drain on national resources; Something needed to be done to address the culture of crime in prisons and the excessive recidivism which characterises our prison system.

The history of South Africa was such that the people most affected by a dysfunctional and malfunctioning prison system were those who had also been victims of apartheid. It was important both to take account of the legacy of apartheid that is responsible for our swelling prison population and to take steps to develop a different calibre of prison system that would be consistent with our new Constitution and with international norms and standards.

We believe that a humane and compassionate prison system is ultimately not only consistent with our Constitution but will ensure the preservation of human dignity to many who have lost all hope in humanity and have violated the rights and humanity of others.[40]

---

39   Rhoda Kadalie, quoted by Jermaine Craig. "Prisoners angry over probe, says Ndungane." *Cape Argus*, 7 Aug. 1997.
40   South African Human Rights Commission. "Report of the National Prisons Project of the South African Human Rights Commission." 1997. URL: https://www.sahrc.org.za/home/21/files/Reports/The%20 Nationals%20Prisons%20Project%20of%20SAHRC.1998.pdf. Accessed on 11 Oct. 2021. 3-4.

The report included several pages of straightforward recommendations for improving the prisons, from improving the quality of food, to involving the private sector in developing skills training programs for inmates. It also called for investigations of alleged corruption and criminality among officials in the prison system, and a retraining of personnel to educate them in the rights-oriented values of the new South Africa.

The report concluded:

> *The challenge of developing a human rights culture is a formidable one facing our society. In responding to such a challenge we cannot exclude any constituency from enjoying and laying claim to the protections and benefits that our Constitution has to offer.*
>
> ...
>
> *The correctional system has an important role to play in contributing to 'maintaining and protecting a just, peaceful and safe society'.[41]*

The report asserted that prisoners, too, had rights — not a popular view in the midst of a crime wave — and that upholding their rights was crucial to the entire edifice of human rights in the new South Africa.

Rhoda's report was considered so thorough and so powerful that President Mandela instructed Minister Mzimela to continue to inspect the prisons. Whether that meant any prospect for change was unclear, but she had gone above and beyond in the performance of her duties.

Moreover, Rhoda had built a relationship with the warders. "We basically became friends," Engelbrecht explained, "and then she really got involved in Pollsmoor with social innovations." Rhoda encouraged prisoners to work in various capacities in the prison — a hair salon, for example, or in a vegetable garden that would then donate the food the inmates had harvested. She also supported new programs such as an effort to call in young offenders and scare them off in terms of committing crimes, and say they shouldn't come there." She also supported the prison employees when they challenged the ANC's aggressive affirmative action policies, which had the effect of preventing the hiring and promotion of Coloured warders so that local prisons could meet national, "African" demographic targets.

"Rhoda played a major role, she changed our mindsets," Engelbrecht concluded. "She guided us in terms of how to treat a person, despite the fact that a person was sentenced and committed a crime.

---

41   Ibid, 50–51.

"She is, for me, like Madiba and Tutu — that stature, as a woman who stands up for what is right and what is just. And that, for me, is one of the major things that said to me this is a person to have a relationship with, to learn from, a teacher, a mentor, an amazing person — especially because everything at that time was *deurmekaar* [disorderly]."

Even as she defended the rights of prisoners, Rhoda devoted attention to the rights of victims of crime, as well — especially women. In 1997, she was invited to address the handover of an evaluation of the Wynberg Sexual Offences Court, a new specialized court to deal specifically with rape and other crimes, whose primary victims were female. The court had been established during the transition from apartheid to democracy by the attorney general of the Western Cape, after public outrage at the mishandling of rape cases in local magistrates' courts. [42]

In her remarks, Rhoda noted the problem of the "secondary victimisation" of rape survivors, who were often stigmatized and who were often humiliated by the insensitivity of the judicial system. Rhoda noted the human rights training that police had received, partly at her instigation, as well as the fact that the new Constitution included guarantees of the "freedom and security of the person." In keeping with her academic training, she noted the need for careful, expert evaluation of the Wynberg court as the pilot project before the model it created could be replicated in other provinces. She promised that the Human Rights Commission would "monitor on an ongoing basis government's commitment to addressing the human rights of women." [43]

In keeping with that commitment, Rhoda returned to UWC in December 1996 to open a special facility, the Women and Human Rights Documentation Centre, which served as a library and resource center for women's rights. A newsletter recalled the event: "We were delighted to have Ms. Rhoda Kadalie of the South African Human Rights Commission deliver the guest speech at the reception. She highlighted the important role of the Center as a resource in research, advocacy and lobbying aimed at advancing the equal status and development of women in South Africa." [44]

***

42   Sharon Stanton et al. *Improved Justice for Survivors of Sexual Violence? Adult survivors' experiences of the Wynberg Sexual Offenses Court and associated services.* Cape Town: Rape Crisis Cape Town, 1997. p. 1.

43   Rhoda Kadalie. Notes for a speech on the evaluation of the Wynberg Sexual Offenses Court. 9 Aug. 1997.

44   Sandy Liebenberg, et al. *Women & Human Rights Documentation Centre,* Vol. 1, No. 1, April 1997. p. 1.

Rhoda's work was rewarded by the response of the South African public. She noted in 1996, while still an interim commissioner, that she had been welcomed "with open arms" by farm workers. "Consistent complaints were racism on the farms, unfair labour practices — in some instances farm children are exploited for child labor, farm workers are whipped by farmers."[45] Despite their initial reticence, she expected to be welcomed, eventually, by farmers as well — just as the prison warders and magistrates had eventually seen the value of her interventions. At first, she recalled, judges "were quite offended and defensive" by the commission's criticisms. But they soon welcomed complaints about racism in the criminal justice system.[46]

Despite the hard work that Rhoda put into the reform of prisons, women's rights, and other matters, she was troubled by the Human Rights Commission's apparent lack of focus. As she would later note, during the institution's formative years, when there was a unique opportunity to establish its influence, the members of the commission spent more time debating office furniture than discussing human rights.

The report on prisons, which Rhoda had painstakingly prepared, was gratefully accepted by the commission, Mandela, and Mzimela — and promptly shelved. Little was done to follow up on its recommendations, in Parliament or elsewhere; South African prisons remained decrepit and corrupt.

Curnow recalled: "I think it's fair to say she ruffled quite a few feathers in the HRC. She did a great job of making these people in positions of government authority aware of what their obligations were in terms of the Bill of Rights ... There was always a bit of internal tension between her and Barney Pityana ... some of that played into the politics of the day." There was concern, he recalled, that Rhoda's efforts were beginning to make the new ANC government "look bad."

Despite its idealistic beginnings, the Human Rights Commission had begun to run into the ANC's hierarchical culture — as well as a particular policy that it had applied to the commission, and to all other institutions, public and private. That policy was known as "cadre deployment."

Under this strategy, which began under the Mandela administration, the ANC would seek to place its loyalists in every possible organization that it did not control. (The ANC referred to these party members as "cadres," a term common in the communist world, which describes a group of trained operatives who carry out the party's mission.)

---

45   Rhoda Kadalie, *Law Report*, ibid.
46   Ibid.

The "cadre deployment" had several goals. One was to extend the ruling party's power beyond the legislative and executive branches of the government, and into the judiciary, academia, the media, unions, and corporate boardrooms. The latter were particularly important: party members who had been "empowered" with billions of rands in company shares could ensure that some of that wealth was kicked back into ANC coffers, especially around election season.

Another goal was to carry out the ANC's management philosophy, which it referred to as "democratic centralism" — a Marxist-Leninist concept, which retained formal "democracy" while arrogating all real power to a closed circle of trusted leaders.

In theory, the new South African Constitution — which the ANC had championed —created a strong set of checks and balances, including the Chapter 9 institutions. Practically, the effect of cadre deployment was to undermine the independence of those institutions and make them instruments of the ruling party, rather than restraints on its power. Tony Leon, a young and pugnacious liberal who took over the leadership of the Democratic Party after 1994, called cadre deployment a "programme to destroy the proper distinction between party and state" that "strikes at the very heart of our democracy."[47] (In 2022, a state commission of inquiry finally declared cadre deployment unconstitutional.)

Later, during the presidency of Jacob Zuma, the ANC's policy of cadre deployment became the vehicle that outside interests, led by the Gupta family of Indian-South African entrepreneurs, achieved "state capture," controlling key government positions and policies. Rhoda would write in 2017 that cadre deployment had "single-handedly destroyed the institutions of democracy and the economy."[48] Two decades before, what cadre deployment meant for the Human Rights Commission was that it would tend to focus its attention and effort only on those human rights issues that best suited the political interests and ideological predilections of the ruling ANC.

And to the ANC, the main human rights issue in South Africa was racism — not racism in general, but the lingering racism of apartheid, both in the presumed attitudes of white South Africans and the unequal distribution of wealth that the transition to democracy had left largely

---

47   Tony Leon. Quoted in "ANC provokes opponents by planning to extend its power." *The Irish Times*, 3 Aug. 1999. URL: https://www.irishtimes.com/news/anc-provokes-opponents-by-planning-to-extend-its-power-1.213003. Accessed on 11 Oct. 2021.
48   Rhoda Kadalie. Draft article for *Beeld*. 5 Jul. 2017. Personal papers.

intact. Though Mandela had embraced racial reconciliation, his party strained to fight its former battles.

In July 1997, in advance of the ANC's 50th national conference, the party produced a draft strategy document that outlined the party's approach to race and politics in post-apartheid South Africa. According to the ANC, the country's new constitutional democracy was only a temporary compromise, which the party would use to alter the "balance of forces" in its favor. A "government based on the will of the people" was only part of the "National Democratic Revolution." A truly "united, non-racial, non-sexist and democratic society" would require the "transformation" of South Africa to remove inherited racial economic inequalities.

The ANC saw "the existing public service, including the security forces, the judiciary and parastatals" as obstacles to that transformation. So, too, were "the majority of public servants, especially at senior level, the captains of industry, and editorial rooms in most of the media," which allegedly "shared the perspectives of the former government or its white opposition."[49]

The strategy of cadre deployment was developed to counter these supposed elements of the old regime. Moreover, in the ANC's view, to embrace abstract principles of human rights in an unequal society was to allow the formerly privileged minority to entrench its power.

Hence the ANC's attitude toward the Human Rights Commission. The ruling party did not want to be constrained by the principles and institutions in the constitution, unless they could be used as tools to "transform" society and to increase the ANC's own power.

The job of the Human Rights Commission was therefore not to hold the new government accountable, but to flatter it — and to seek out vestiges of racism in South African society.

As Rhoda would later write: "[T]he only time the Human Rights Commission seems to find its *raison d'être* is when racism rears its ugly head."[50]

***

Rhoda agreed that racism remained a problem in South Africa — but argued that it was not the only problem, or even the most important one.

---

49   African National Congress. "Draft Strategy and Tactics of the African National Congress." *Umrabulo*, Special Addition, July 1997. URL: https://www.anc1912.org.za/wp-content/uploads/2021/07/Umrabulo-Issue-4-Special-Edition-1997.pdf. Accessed on 11 Oct. 2021.

50   Rhoda Kadalie. "Video uproar betrays culture of double standards." *Business Day*, 13 Mar. 2008.

As she would later write, in September 2000: "This obsession with race and racism is nothing but a cover-up for non-delivery in the public sector and a means of obscuring issues of national importance."[51]

She observed that the Human Rights Commission was highly selective in its investigations of racism, pursuing alleged racists in the media and the private sector while leaving the state and its institutions, now governed predominantly by the ANC, largely unexamined:

> While the role of the commission is to monitor socio-economic rights, it has decided to prioritise racism, because it is incapable of doing precisely that. The focus on race and not discrimination is also very telling.
>
> Should the commission focus on investigating discrimination and take matters to court, it would be able to set precedents that would set human rights standards and prevent such violations from taking place again.
>
> It would also discover that the state and its institutions are often the biggest violators of human rights — as I discovered in my job as a human rights commissioner. For example, by investigating a complaint of racism against the ambulance services in Cape Town, we discovered that they were routinely racist in denying services to black areas.
>
> What our investigation enabled us to do, with the cooperation of the ambulance authorities, was to conduct training workshops in human rights with the ambulance personnel who operated the telephones.
>
> Similarly, a complaint of discrimination against an HIV-positive woman who applied for a job in correctional services indicated that the department did pre-employment testing on the woman without her consent. [52]
>
> I can cite many examples of discrimination that were lodged before the commission that they often failed to investigate properly and successfully because of incompetence. My reports on racism on the farms in the Northern Cape were simply not followed up.

For more than two years, Rhoda wrestled with what she perceived as the incompetence, inertia, and political bias of the Human Rights Commission. "She was more willing to take matters on, and more willing to be vocal

---

51   Rhoda Kadalie. "The racism debate obscures other issues." *Mail & Guardian*, 1 to 7 Sep. 2000. URL: https://mg.co.za/article/2000-09-01-the-racism-debate-obscures-other-issues/. Accessed on 11 Oct. 2021.
52   Ibid.

... than perhaps the rest of the commissioners," Curnow recalled. "In meetings, she would just call a spade a spade, whether it was a government department or the private sector. She was never rude or antagonistic or aggressive, but people were uncomfortable."

She did see some improvements: In August 1997, Pityana followed her example and began leading an HRC delegation, which included Rhoda, to make direct visits to the provincial governments "in order to acquaint himself with human rights issues," the *Diamond Fields Advertiser* reported.[53] As part of her regional focus, Rhoda also visited the Northern Cape to investigate the living conditions of the Khoisan people, the so-called "Bushmen," who had been languishing in poverty.

Rhoda and Human Rights Commission chair Dr. Barney Pityana (left) with San leader and The Gods Must Be Crazy actor David Kruiper (second from left) on a delegation to the Northern Cape, 1997 (Courtesy Rhoda Kadalie)

Rhoda was proud of the effort, which brought Pityana to the Northern Cape to meet with communities of Khoisan people, colloquially known as "Bushmen," traditional hunters and gatherers of the Northern Cape. Though they had gained global notoriety through films such as *The Gods*

---

53   "Courtesy Call." *Diamond Fields Advertiser*, 27 Aug. 1997. p. 3.

Must Be Crazy, they received little benefit from the films' success and remained impoverished, far from economic opportunities. Many had been denied their ancestral land rights; others were mired in alcoholism and other maladies.

The community had bought land on which to settle, but the provincial government, run by the ANC, had prevented them from doing so, forcing them to live in an encampment for several years. The ANC premier (or governor) of the province allegedly said that "Bushmen" were "citizens of a lesser standard" and wanted the prime land to be reserved for members of the larger Tswana ethnic group.[54]

Curnow recalled the sense of adventure as Rhoda convened town hall meetings in the Northern Cape Town of Upington, and allowed the Khoisan people to air their grievances in public for the first time, achieving a sense of dignity that had long eluded them, under the old regime and the new.

As passionate as Rhoda was about these causes, she continued to be frustrated by the way the commission was run. She noted that the post-apartheid government had created so many additional commissions on human rights issues that a hypothetical black, disabled, pregnant woman would not know whom to approach — the Human Rights Commission, the Commission on Gender Equality, the Disability Board, or any number of other boards, numbering some 16 in total. And for all of its public, performative commitment to human rights, Rhoda felt, the ANC's commitment to human rights principles rarely went beyond rhetoric.

Pityana agreed with some of her criticisms: indeed, he complained that the government seemed indifferent to the commission's work, and that the institution was underfunded and understaffed. But he seemed unable, or unwilling, to tackle the problem at its source: the fact that the ANC expected the HRC, like other nominally independent institutions, to carry out its agenda, not to hold it in check.

Finally, in July 1997, Rhoda resigned, effective at year's end. She did so after writing to President Mandela, urging him to appoint a committee in Parliament to oversee the commission.[55] And she left Pityana with a list of "constructive" suggestions to improve the commission's performance. But it was clear that she lacked confidence that the institution could find its direction again.

---

54 Paul Olivier. "Top officials demand end to 'camp of shame'." *Sunday Argus*, 14-15 Jun. 1997.
55 Gaye Davis. "Reasons why I had to leave." *Mail & Guardian*, 8 Aug. 1997. URL: https://mg.co.za/article/1997-08-08-reasons-why-i-had-to-leave/. Accessed on 11 Oct. 2021.

In her letter to Pityana, Rhoda explained:

My resignation from the SAHRC on the 17th July 1997 was prompted by a series of events over the past few months which make me doubt that the institution will ever improve unless drastic measures are taken to remedy the situation. Personality conflicts, bad management, divisions between staff and commissioners seem to have become endemic to the institution, and as a consequence have led to a spate of resignations over recent months.

...

In my opinion, much of the service (not all) we render is mediocre and many in the HRC seem happy just to toddle along, producing shoddy work because they get away with it. This is exemplified by shifting deadlines, postponements, lack of commitment and work of poor quality. The taxpayer deserves more. The public needs value for money. An increase in the budget will do little to ameliorate the situation. We need to get our house in order first before we can even hope to address our constitutional mandate effectively.[56]

Rhoda provided a list of detailed complaints and constructive suggestions, taking up three pages. Whether Pityana took them up or not, she herself was done with the commission.

The *Mail & Guardian* reported at the time:

[Kadalie] told the M&G the commission was "like a horse with two heads", each pulling in different directions: "The staff feel we don't have a vision they can plug into, while from the commissioners' point of view, the staff are a law unto themselves and call the tune."

Personality clashes were "endemic" and had led to the resignation of almost one-third of the commission's staff in the 18 months it has been operating.

Too little had been done to keep good staff, said Kadalie, while a "bad employment policy" had created "pockets of incompetence and mediocrity" in key positions.

The commission, led by Barney Pityana, has blamed much of its difficulties on its funding. Kadalie said the commission did need to have

---

56   Rhoda Kadalie. Letter to Dr. Barney Pityana. 28 Jul. 1997. Wits Helen Suzman archive.

its budget increased, but said "more money will not address questions around management".

…

In the letter to Mandela, Kadalie says she had made "several attempts to bring the problems of the commission to the attention of the deputy president and other key persons in government, to no avail". She lists the frustrations that forced her to resign a job that put her "at the cutting edge" of human rights work.

- *A fundamental difference of opinion over the focus of the commission.*

- *Lack of good management and leadership.*

- *Personality conflicts.*

- *"Pockets of incompetence and mediocrity in key positions" owing to a "bad employment policy".*

…

Kadalie said that the commission, instead of trying to be "all things to all people", should focus on three key areas: building up its legal department (a complaints registrar had yet to be appointed); socio-economic rights; and national projects concerning the rights of farmworkers, children at risk and the elderly.

She had written a "constructive letter" to Pityana, spelling out her proposals, but at a subsequent meeting with commissioners he said he disagreed with her. "I was not satisfied with that response to my letter, and that's why I am definitely going to go," she said.

Her decision was described by the media as a "shock move."[57] "I love this job and I didn't want to do it (resign)," she told one local newspaper. "It's a very effective office with very limited resources. I want this job but under better conditions. I'm not happy with the way the organization is managed."[58] At one point, she revealed that the commission was almost bankrupt, with barely enough money to pay staff salaries.[59]

Pityana wrote to Rhoda in September, notifying her that the Commission wished to express its "regret" at her resignation, and that

---

57   Barnes, "I quit," 1997, ibid.
58   Ibid.
59   Rhoda Kadalie, quoted by Lindsay Barnes. "Kadalie leaves a storm in her wake." *Cape Argus*, 2 Dec. 1997.

"various efforts aimed at persuading" her to "reconsider ... have not been successful." Pityana added a bitter complaint that Rhoda's resignation "was handled in a most unfortunate manner," citing her letter to President Mandela and her comments to the media. He also pushed back against several "threats" he claimed Rhoda had made against the commission, as well as the suggestion that it be subjected to more direct oversight by a parliamentary committee.[60]

The drama did not end there. Rhoda indicated that she would be willing to reconsider her resignation, and eventually took the Human Rights Commission to the Commission on Conciliation, Mediation & Arbitration (CCMA), a forum typically used to resolve labor disputes. She enlisted the services of attorneys from Sonnenberg Hoffman and Galombik, who noted that Pityana had asked her in December 1997 to reconsider her resignation, and she had agreed.

However, owing to the fact that Parliament had closed for the holidays, a letter informing Parliament that she had rescinded her resignation was not received until January 1998, past the moment when the resignation took effect on December 31. Pityana wrote to the secretary of Parliament urging it to recognize that she was still a member of the commission.[61] Legally, however, there was nothing Parliament could do. Pityana then told Rhoda in late January that she would have to leave after all. Despite the attempted intervention of several human rights activists and organizations, Rhoda's resignation was final.

Years later, Pityana tried to claim that Rhoda left "in 2000 [sic]" because she "had no respect for her colleagues," adding that she "was divisive and largely struggled to work collegially." He also complained that she aired her differences with the commission in open meetings, rather than behind closed doors, and quarreled with fellow commissioners over "minor infringements."[62]

But her resignation was not the last: several other commissioners and staff resigned as well in subsequent months — notably, Helen Suzman herself, whose departure in late 1998 would be a further blow to the prestige of the institution. Suzman resigned shortly after a controversy in which the Human Rights Commission bizarrely sided against 11 immigrant doctors who had been denied the opportunity to engage in private practice.

---

60   Barney Pityana. Letter to Rhoda Kadalie. 24 Sep. 1997.
61   Barney Pityana. Letter to S. G. Mfenyana. 14 Jan. 1998.
62   Barney Pityana. "Rhoda Kadalie was fierce and had a mind of her own, like it or not." *Sunday Times*, 20 Apr. 2022. URL: https://www.timeslive.co.za/sunday-times-daily/opinion-and-analysis/2022-04-20-rhoda-kadalie-was-fierce-and-had-a-mind-of-her-own-like-it-or-not/. Accessed on 25 Apr. 2022.

Suzman issued a dissenting statement, which the commission tried to suppress.

In a brief letter to President Nelson Mandela, Suzman announced her resignation, without giving further explanation. In response to a letter from Human Rights Commission Deputy Chairperson Shirley Mabusela, however, Suzman was more explicit about her rationale:

I have to admit I was surprised to learn that you consider that "the respect and high esteem" I enjoyed across the political spectrum helped establish the reputation of the Commission, as I must tell you that I often felt during my three years on the Commission, that I was being side-lined that very little use was made of whatever special attributes I have. However, the experience was certainly educative, and some of it actually enjoyable.[63]

Suzman's disappointment with the commission was also clear from her remarks to the media. "I don't feel I'm serving any purpose," she told David Beresford of the *Mail & Guardian*. "They need somebody younger and possibly less cynical."[64]

It was Rhoda's resignation, however, that set off the initial alarm bells about poor management at the Human Rights Commission. The public and the media reacted in disbelief and outrage to the news. Jansen, who had worked with Rhoda in reforming Pollsmoor Prison, lamented: "She is the most competent, committed and principled person. It is a bad reflection on South Africa if the commission cannot solve its problems."[65] He still felt that way, years later: "I was quite close with her, I was very fortunate to be close with her, such a dynamic woman at the time — she was a great loss, I would say ... not just for correctional services but for the country."[66] Dene Smuts, a member of the opposition Democratic Party (later the Democratic Alliance), said that "Ms Kadalie had brought flair and energy to a difficult and ill-defined job, and had succeeded in stimulating fruitful debate on human rights issues in the Western Cape."[67]

63 Helen Suzman. Letter to Shirley Mabusela. 19 Jan. 1999. Helen Suzman Archive, Wits University.
64 David Beresford. "Resignation of Suzman another blow for HRC." *Mail & Guardian*, 9 Oct. 1998. p. 8.
65 John Jansen, quoted by Lindsay Barnes. "Kadalie leaves storm in her wake." *Cape Argus*, 2 Dec. 1997.
66 Personal communication with the author, 14 Mar. 2022.
67 Political Correspondent. "DP seeks urgent talks as rights chief resigns." *Cape Argus*, 24 Jul. 1997.

The lead editorial in the *Cape Argus*, Cape Town's main afternoon newspaper, called her resignation a "wake-up call," adding that she had enjoyed "considerable success":

Since her appointment in 1995 [sic] she has tackled her job as custodian and promoter of human rights with commitment and vigour, taking on issues as diverse as the "dom darkie" incident, the abuse of convicts in prisons and the Welfare Department's places of safety for children.

She has been where few have dared to venture, providing human rights training for police and sitting down for four days with 100 Correctional Services heads to inculcate a human rights culture in prisons.

...

Her resignation has disappointed all who came in contact with her work, not least those prison heads, one of whom described her quitting as "one hell of a setback for human rights."

It is hoped the commission management hears the warning bells and gets its house in order.[68]

The *Cape Times* agreed, noting that Rhoda "has played an active and highly visible role in promoting the cause of human rights and drawing public attention to any sign of their erosion ... Her resignation from the commission therefore represents a considerable loss."[69] The *Times* added that if Rhoda's allegations of mismanagement by Pityana were true, he should resign. "The commissioners, and particularly the chairman, are extremely well remunerated with taxpayers' money, and if some do not perform effectively, or prevent others from doing so, they should be replaced."[70]

Rhoda later recalled that she gave up a "fat pay cheque" by resigning, but that she felt she had no other choice: "Kadalie simply could not countenance the way in which the SAHRC's commissioners kowtowed to the government while collecting overblown salaries. She quips, with a hint of ruefulness: "If I'd stayed, my house would have been paid off long ago. But I said to myself, 'I'd rather be poor!'"[71]

---

68   Editorial board. "Wake-up call for Rights Commission." *Cape Argus*, 4 Dec. 1997.
69   Editorial board. "Human rights loss." *Cape Times*, 3 Dec. 1997.
70   Ibid.
71   Neethling, August 2010. Ibid.

Later, Rhoda escalated her criticism of the HRC, calling on Pityana to resign in December 1997. "She said the commission was poorly managed and its leadership lacked vision," the *Argus* reported. "Furthermore, the commission was virtually bankrupt." She also accused Pityana of being an "absent chairman" who had a "tendency to overrule decisions" by the rest of the commission.[72]

Pityana and the commission defended themselves by arguing that Rhoda could have raised her concerns internally, and that it was finalizing a "national action plan" on human rights. "[W]e are delivering on our mandate to protect and promote human rights," the HRC said in a statement.[73]

Rhoda had no idea what she would do next: she had given up a lucrative salary, with no alternative job. A decade later, she even considered rejoining the HRC, interviewing for a vacancy on the commission. A parliamentary committee chose former ANC member of Parliament Pregs Govender instead.[74]

Soon, however, Rhoda would find her own path to pursuing South Africa's promise.

72 Rhoda Kadalie, quoted by Lindsay Barnes. "Kadalie leaves storm in her wake." *Cape Argus*, 2 Dec. 1997.

73 Lindsay Barnes. "Kadalie call on Pityana to resign rejected." *Cape Argus*, 10 Dec. 1997.

74 Parliamentary Monitoring Group. "Vacancy for Human Rights Commissioner: Interviews, Deliberations and Finalisation." Committee report, 11 Nov. 2008. URL: https://pmg.org.za/committee-meeting/9731/. Accessed on 13 Apr. 2022.

Chapter 11:
Impumelelo

*"I have the best job in SA. Rewarding social innovation and best
practice I get to see the best SA has to offer across
the racial and cultural divide."[1]*

The years of South Africa's transition saw many old institutions dismantled
— but also provided opportunities to build new institutions. These included
institutions outside government that would provide the foundation for a
new, democratic civil society, and the research and leadership necessary
to support the government's ambitious goals of economic development.

There had already been many philanthropies, foundations, and
foreign governments who had contributed to the anti-apartheid struggle.
In the years after Nelson Mandela's release, as the country's negotiations
stumbled forward, more support began pouring in from those who wished
to help South Africa succeed.

One of the earliest and most important organizations was the
Institute for Democratic Alternatives in South Africa (Idasa), later known
as the Institute for Democracy in South Africa. It was co-founded by
parliamentarian Frederik van Zyl Slabbert and Methodist cleric-turned
politician Alex Boraine. Both had been members of the Progressive Federal
Party (PFP).[2] In 1986, Van Zyl Slabbert resigned from Parliament, declaring
that there was no possibility for ending apartheid through the country's
representative institutions at the time. While that was a moral blow to his
colleagues, others were inspired to look beyond politics: Boraine resigned
with him.

Idasa would go on to organize events intended to guide the country
toward a post-apartheid future. The most significant of these was a
meeting in Dakar, Senegal, in 1987 between Afrikaner intellectuals and
leaders of the banned ANC in exile. The enduring memory of the meeting is
that of a pipe-smoking Thabo Mbeki, who charmed his counterparts with
his use of the Afrikaans language, his academic credentials from the United
Kingdom, and his moderate temperament. The meeting convinced many

---

1   Rhoda Kadalie. Comment on Facebook, 10 Mar. 2016. URL: https://www.
    facebook.com/rhoda.kadalie/posts/10154114554645039.
2   The PFP grew out of the Progressive Party, and would later become the
    Democratic Party (DP), which became today's Democratic Alliance (DA).

of the Afrikaners who participated that the ANC was a viable negotiation partner in building a new political order.

Boraine would go on to serve as deputy chair of South Africa's Truth and Reconciliation Commission (TRC), the country's effort to confront the evils of its apartheid past. The TRC was based on past "truth commissions" in Latin America, notably in Chile and Argentina, which had been established to expose the way that authoritarian regimes had abused human rights, including through the torture and "disappearance" of political dissidents. Those who testified at these commissions were offered the possibility of amnesty for their crimes, provided that they made full confessions.

South Africa's TRC took the crucial step of applying the same standard of human rights to the anti-apartheid movement as it did to the apartheid government. In so doing, it exposed many of the abuses that the ANC and other liberation movements had committed themselves. Some ANC leaders argued that the "right" side of the struggle could not be judged as harshly as the "wrong" side. But Boraine, and others, notably TRC chair Archbishop Desmond Tutu, defended the idea that the ends did not justify the means.

In the wake of its success, the TRC inspired many successor organizations, devoted to human rights and racial reconciliation. Idasa also shifted to a new role after 1994, monitoring the progress of South Africa's new democracy. Rhoda was eventually appointed to serve on Idasa's board of trustees.[3] There were many other new institutions, such as the Helen Suzman Foundation (HZF), a liberal think tank founded in 1993; the Institute for Justice and Reconciliation (IJR), founded in 2000; and many others.

Into the mix stepped billionaire philanthropist George Soros, who began taking a keen interest in South Africa's democratic transition in 1993.

Soros was born in Hungary and had survived the Holocaust, albeit in somewhat controversial circumstances: he and his father had sold the property of deported Jews. Soros made a fortune in currency trading, infamously betting against the British pound and forcing its devaluation in 1992. As controversial as his business activities were at times, Soros gained respect through his support for democratic causes and the principle of the "open society," inspired by his youthful interest in philosopher Karl Popper.

---

3   "Rhoda Kadalie." *The Women's Directory: A Listing of Leading Women 1995–1996.* Cape Town: Femina, 1995. p. 10.

In the late 1970s, Soros created a charitable foundation, the Open Society Fund, which later became the Open Society Foundations (OSF). Ironically, his first efforts were in South Africa, where he donated funds for scholarships to support black students at the University of Cape Town. But he was disappointed with the effort — particularly at how "hostile" the black students were. He also felt that the apartheid regime would not yield, and he felt taken for granted by those he was trying to support in the struggle against it: "There was an imaginary pot of gold in the middle of the room and the participants were discussing ways in which it could be divided; that was not what I had in mind," he later said.[4]

He did support some successful projects. For example, he met the iconic Dr. Nthato Motlana, a black physician from Soweto who made it his mission to train other black doctors through a joint American–South African effort called Medical Education for South African Blacks (MESAB). Motlana met Soros and offered to guide him around the township, though he had no idea who Soros was. He showed the billionaire around various projects being run by non-governmental organizations in Soweto, as well as his own work with MESAB. Soros had been so impressed that he pledged R3 million — about $500,000 at the time — to MESAB.

But overall, Soros was disappointed. "I must admit that I gave up on South Africa," he recalled.[5] Soros then turned back toward his native Eastern Europe, helping countries that were emerging from Soviet domination.

It was only when South Africa began moving toward a democratic political transition that Soros decided to focus on the country once again. In 1987, Soros funded the Dakar conference, at the request of Van Zyl Slabbert and Boraine.[6] Soros also brought South Africa's emerging leaders to other countries so they could learn from international best practices. He also continued his support for projects that aimed to build a strong civil society and help economic development in the country's neglected black areas.

Ultimately, Van Zyl Slabbert and Boraine helped Soros select South African luminaries to join them in establishing the Open Society Foundation for South Africa (OSF-SA). These included Mamphela Ramphele, the deputy vice-chancellor of the University of Cape Town (UCT); Helen Zille,

---

4   George Soros. "The Concept of Open Society." Lecture, Johannesburg. 14 Dec. 1994. pp. 4-5.

5   Ibid.

6   Open Society Foundations. "Celebrating 25 Years of Grant Making in South Africa." URL: https://25.osf.org.za/timeline/van-zyl-and-boraine/. Accessed on 17 Jan. 2022.

who was the former public affairs director of UCT; Fikile Bam, a lawyer and former Robben Island prisoner, who would later become a prominent judge; Tony Heard, the former editor of the *Cape Times*; Peter Sullivan, the editor of the *Sunday Times*; G.T. Ferreira, a banker with Rand Merchant Bank; Professor Mike Savage, formerly of the UCT sociology department; and Rhoda Kadalie. The foundation was chaired by Fikile Bam's sister, Brigalia Bam, who would later go on to chair South Africa's Independent Electoral Commission for more than a decade.[7]

Similarly, Soros met with Professor Jakes Gerwel, then the vice chancellor of UWC, who suggested that he wanted to establish a school of government to prepare a cohort of civil servants for a post-apartheid administration. Soros pledged R3 million to Gerwel's project as well.

Rhoda came to know Soros during this time, both through her work on OSF-SA and her overseas trips. Years later, she would vehemently criticize his role in funding left-wing protests and politicians in the U.S. and elsewhere. But in the early 1990s, as he focused on post-communist and post-conflict societies, his influence was generally perceived as beneficent.

Rhoda and other board members found many of their journeys with Soros to be eye-opening. She recalled one visit to Eastern Europe with Soros:

> In the 1990s, financier George Soros took the board of the Open Society, of which I was a member, to some countries in eastern Europe "to see for ourselves". The last bit of socialist conscience I had dissipated after walking the streets of Poland, Hungary, Yugoslavia and Ukraine and seeing empty shops and listening to stories of rampant corruption, media suppression, inferior health-care systems and ineffectual industries, all made worse by the growing class and gender inequality. This was an eye-opener and broke down all the Marxist claptrap I had imbibed as a young social anthropology and sociology student.[8]

Rhoda felt, initially, that Soros was a positive influence on South Africa's emerging democracy; she grew more skeptical later. But in the short term, she became concerned that Soros was being manipulated by Van Zyl Slabbert and Boraine, who acted as gatekeepers to the billionaire

---

7 Seán Morrow. "Ideas and advocacy of Brigalia Bam still vibrant today." World Council of Churches, 20 Jun. 2018. URL: https://www.oikoumene. org/news/ideas-and-advocacy-of-brigalia-bam-still-vibrant-today. Accessed on 18 Mar. 2022.

8 Rhoda Kadalie. "SA's big-mouth communists offer no real solutions." *Business Day*, 26 Jul. 2007. p. 13.

(and his money). Gerwel, who had been tapped to serve in Mandela's new administration, was anticipating a grant from Soros for his new institute, but Van Zyl Slabbert and Boraine had insisted that all of Soros's donations flow through Idasa.

Rhoda intervened directly with Soros — remonstrating with him in his car on the way to the theater in Buenos Aires — and he agreed to fund Gerwel's project directly rather than through intermediaries. It was a favor that Gerwel never forgot.

It was also not the last time that Soros would find himself being manipulated by power brokers in South Africa. In 1997, Wilmot James, who was by then the chief executive of Idasa, wrote to OSF-SA requesting additional funding, noting that more attention would have to be paid to defending democracy as Nelson Mandela retired from politics and Thabo Mbeki took over the ANC and, eventually, the presidency. The letter was leaked to President Mbeki — not surprisingly, perhaps, given that several of OSF-SA's board members at the time were also advisers to the president. After these potential conflicts of interest emerged, Soros dismissed the entire board in late 2000, and replaced it.[9]

***

In 1999, Idasa advertised that it had received a grant for a new project that would identify and promote successful, innovative private-public partnerships throughout South Africa. The aim was to help the South African government achieve its development goals by tapping into the expertise of the private sector, both for-profit and non-profit.

Such partnerships were necessary because the new administration simply lacked the capacity to deliver results on its own. Even if the civil service had remained at full strength, it had never been designed to serve South Africa's entire population. The post-apartheid civil service had even less capacity, as it struggled with institutional change, staff retirements, and aggressive affirmative action mandates.

The funding for the project was to come from a variety of sources, including the Open Society Foundation; the Ford Foundation in the United States; the local Human Sciences Research Council, and the government of the Netherlands.[10] At the time, Rhoda was between jobs. She had resigned from the Human Rights Commission in 1997 on principle. In

---

9   Barry Streek. "Soros sacks South African foundation board." *Mail & Guardian*, 10 Nov. 2000.
10   "Delivery Organisations Queue Up To Receive Their Rewards." *Mail & Guardian*, 12 Nov. 1999.

1998, she headed up the District Six Task Team within the Commission on Restitution of Land Rights, under the auspices of the government's Department of Land Affairs. Within a year, Rhoda had set up a commission to address roughly 2,000 lingering land claims from those who had been victims of forced removals from District Six under apartheid, recruiting more claimants than had been on the lists before her arrival.[11]

Resolving the land claims in District Six was an immense challenge. "It's not just about giving land back," Rhoda later recalled.[12] The difficult part was "to prove that people have been racially dispossessed," and therefore entitled to restitution.

Chris Mingo, who worked as a researcher and administrator with Rhoda at the land claims commission, recalled the difficult conditions under which she began her work.[13] The institution had no offices, and no computers, meeting for the first several months in a board room. As journalist Chris Barron later noted: "[A] year later not a cent of a promised R1.7m [about $300,000 at the time] budget for her nine-member unit crowded into a supposedly temporary room had materialised. There was no money for pens and no computers. When computers arrived they had no software or were broken."[14] Rhoda turned to the U.S. Agency for International Development (USAID) for funding, and soon she was able to move the commission to offices in the Customs House building. But the commission said she could not raise outside funds, and had to pay what she had raised already for District Six into the commission's overall budget.[15]

Even with funding, the task of researching land claims was still daunting. Using the archaic methods of research available at the time, it took the commission from three to six months to investigate a single claim. One aging bureaucrat was the only person who seemed to know how to do the research, Mingo recalled, and he jealously guarded that information from other staff.

There was also the pressure of public expectations. As Rhoda later recalled: "Many of the communities ... felt that it was God returning me to provide land. Can you imagine how frightened I was by that kind of burden, that Divine instruction to come back and give land. But you know,

---

11   Barron, "Obituary," ibid.
12   Rhoda Kadalie, on British Broadcasting Corporation (BBC). "South Africans Talking." Radio special, 2 Aug. 1998.
13   Chris Mingo. Interview 2 Mar. 2022.
14   Barron, ibid.
15   Barron, ibid.

land restitution was a complicated process, and so we have had to educate ourselves about the Act, and then educate the public."[16]

Rhoda hired additional staff, and came up with a proposal so radical, yet so simple, that it was puzzling no one had thought of it before: she simply laid a map of new land claims over the old map of District Six property. That simplified the process, such that the commission was able to cut research times, completing up to 16 claims per month. Rhoda also organized community meetings on land claims to allow the public to offer feedback. To assist with restitution, she raised funds from the private sector and mobilized communities through the department's education programs to educate people about their rights under the Land Restitution Act of 1994.

Rhoda works at the land claims commission, overlaying maps of District Six, c. 1998 (Courtesy Rhoda Kadalie)

Precisely because she was so efficient, Mingo recalled, the ANC government began to view her efforts with suspicion, and threw up new obstacles to her progress. Moreover, Rhoda became caught in the crossfire between

---

16   Rhoda Kadalie, on British Broadcasting Corporation (BBC). "Women's Hour." 27 Jun. 2002.

various public interest groups that had organized to take advantage of the restitution process, and stymied by the general ineptitude of the government in responding to the public. When she began to encounter death threats, Rhoda resigned the position in 1998, after serving for a year.

The Idasa grant was a perfect opportunity: the timing could not have been better.

In 1999, Rhoda was working temporarily for Idasa after resigning from her post at the Human Rights Commission. It was then that Idasa's in-house economist, Warren Krafchik, put together a comprehensive proposal for identifying innovative practices in development in South Africa. Rhoda's job would be to implement the proposal as a sub-project within Idasa. Her first test was to set up a constitution for the new organization, and a "secretariat" of personnel roles, including a researcher, an evaluator, and a secretary. She also recruited a number of interns — a rare practice in South Africa, where internships are uncommon — to train for the roles the organization would need as it expanded, and to keep costs low.

Rhoda began hiring qualified researchers to evaluate projects according to a set of objective criteria, including the financial management of potential awardees, and the ability of individual projects to measure their success through the use of relevant indicators. Not only would the grants support successful projects, but over time, the organization could build up a database of successful projects, and develop a set of best practices in a variety of policy areas that could be used by the government. She also hired Mingo, who had spent a year working on budget management at Idasa. Bored with the technical details of his Idasa job, Mingo relished the idea of working directly with communities again, and with Rhoda.

Called "Impumelelo" — the Xhosa word for "success" — Rhoda's new organization drew on her detailed, expert knowledge of development studies, as well as her familiarity with the needs of the communities that were in greatest need of assistance. Her experience with UWC and the Gender Equity Unit gave her the necessary administrative experience to make the project a success; her service on the Human Rights Commission, and her subsequent resignation on principle, had given her unique credibility and a reputation for integrity. She set about appointing a board to oversee the project: one of its members was Helen Suzman, Rhoda's former colleague from the Human Rights Commission. Rhoda also included several other prominent South African women on the board, such that she was later to joke that if someone bombed a board meeting, they would eliminate every feminist in the country.[17]

The initial funding for the Impumelelo Innovations Award Trust was R3 million — roughly $500,000, in dollar terms. It was enough to hire a small staff of researchers and administrators, and pay herself a salary, in addition to funding the organizations that were due to receive awards. But unlike many other organizations in South Africa that had become somewhat decadent as they basked in the euphoria of the early Mandela years, Rhoda ran a frugal operation at Impumelelo.

Rhoda made the most of her connections in the new government to give Impumelelo the best chance of success. She launched her new program in Parliament, with the keynote address being provided by Minister of Finance Trevor Manuel. Manuel, a rabble-rousing union organizer on the Cape Flats in the struggle years, had risen rapidly through ANC ranks while maintaining a reputation for competence. International investors regarded him as a safe pair of hands for South Africa's economy, which enhanced his growing domestic stature, though his Coloured background was rumored to have kept him from contention for even higher office.

Other ANC officials, including those close to Mandela's successor, Thabo Mbeki, also supported the project. The first awards ceremony, for example, which was also hosted in Parliament, featured a keynote address from Essop Pahad, whose official title was "Minister in the Presidency," and who played the role of a gatekeeper and a political enforcer within the Mbeki administration and the ANC ranks. The fact that Pahad endorsed the project meant that even though Impumelelo was politically independent, ANC leaders were encouraged to work with it. After all, it was highlighting the best results that the government had achieved, albeit through private-public partnerships. Its success could only help the ANC deliver on its 1994 campaign pledge of "A better life for all."

The support of the ruling party was all the more significant, given that some of the best and most effective government policies were being implemented by the two provinces largely run by the opposition: the Western Cape and the Inkatha Freedom Party. The ANC had taken control of the Western Cape in 1999, but did so in a coalition with the New National Party (NNP) — De Klerk's attempt at a reboot, after he left the Government of National Unity in 1998 and returned to the opposition benches. Impumelelo offered a rare chance to put partisanship aside, and reward what worked.

* * *

---

17   Rhoda Kadalie. Remarks at Impumelelo 5th anniversary awards ceremony. University of the Western Cape, Bellville, Cape Town. 2004.

Impumelelo strove to become, as its 2010 mission statement put it, a platform to "showcase exceptional models of social innovation and facilitate networks of best practice to enhance the quality of public service."[18] It conceived of the problems of service delivery as being caused by a lack of knowledge about best practices. Through experimentation, it sought to discover what those best practices were.

Impumelelo's method was simple, but unusual, in that the use of any kind of evaluation system and objective criteria for assessing the success (or failure) of development projects was rare. The organization would put out a call for grant award applications, then evaluate the filings it received. The projects could be run by the government, by non-governmental organizations (NGOs), or by the private sector, but they had to involve the government as a partner in some way. The idea was to promote the best government policies, which could be replicated across the country.

Upon receiving applications, Rhoda's team of trained researchers would then fan out across the country over several months to conduct site visits and speak to personnel on the ground. Their subsequent reports would be the basis for evaluating which projects were to receive awards — and also created an opportunity for Impumelelo to provide feedback and suggestions.

In the first year of the Impumelelo awards program in 1999, the organization received 175 applications. Over half were run by NGOs or the private sectors; the rest were government projects. After an initial evaluation, 100 projects qualified for the shortlist. The *Mail & Guardian* described some of the entries:

> *The 100 shortlisted projects range from the Stepping Stones One Stop Youth Justice Centre in the Eastern Cape, to the Bekkersdal Flagship job creation programme in Beaufort West, to the Mapila Hydroponics Community Co-op in the Northern Province.*

> *The Stepping Stones project, for instance, in a former coloured area in Port Elizabeth, consists of a police station, youth court and counselling services in one location. It aims to confront the problem of "youth at risk" by diverting delinquent youth from prison, if possible, and counselling them. Courts are open at weekends and social workers are on call 24 hours a day.*

> *The Mapila Community Co-operative was started by a diesel mechanic in the Venda region, who persuaded landholders in his community*

---

18   Impumelelo Social Innovations Centre. Business Plan, 2010. p. 3.

to consolidate their land to start an intensive farming project which provides jobs and income to villagers, mainly women.

The initiator, Mavhungu Mukwevho, did not just start a simple food garden, but introduced advanced cultivation methods (hydroponics) producing strawberries for export and vegetables for local markets, including sales to Woolworths.

Says Kadalie: "Across the country, the nature of innovative government-funded community projects reflects the massive challenges facing South Africa's poor. It is heartening to know that the government is working together with ordinary South Africans to find creative solutions.

"The focus is particularly on the reduction of poverty in South Africa and on best practices that improve the quality of life of the poor. We seek to identify creative problem-solving projects, which exist in partnership with the government, and to document, broadcast and celebrate these projects in order to share elements of their success nationwide."

There were eventually 15 winners, with the successful projects awarded R700,000 each — about $100,000 at the time, in dollar terms. The award winners enjoyed publicity and recognition, which could help them to raise even more money and expand their operations. Impumelelo also awarded certificates of recognition to those projects that had not yet met the organization's standards, but which were making progress.

Over time, Rhoda observed that the applicants were "better and better every year."[19] And Rhoda hoped that the awardees would inspire the government to copy and expand models that had worked. When the Zibambele Road Maintenance System, a project of the opposition-controlled provincial government of KwaZulu-Natal, won in 2000 for a project assigning female-headed households a stretch of road to maintain and repair,[20] the hope was that the national government would fund similar projects elsewhere.

But Impumelelo was more than a funding project, or a public policy laboratory. It changed the lives of those whom it supported.

19   Rhoda Kadalie, quoted by Sue Segar. "Projects provide models for developing SA; Finalists present good news stories." *Cape Argus*, 12 Oct. 2013. p. 13.
20   "In Praise of Workers for the Poor." *Mail & Guardian*, 22 Feb. 2002.

Rhoda with Impumelelo Award Winner Soil for Life, 2016
(Courtesy Rhoda Kadalie)

Rhoda described the impact of Impumelelo on one successful project after a visit in 2008:

> *I was invited to attend the Western Cape education department's launch of a solar-powered computer laboratory in Bernardino Heights High School, in Kraaifontein, driven by a project called Khanya. It won an Impumelelo award for excellence in education in 2006, and is an initiative that installs computers in schools across the province, particularly in disadvantaged communities. Khanya also trains teachers in computer literacy and in curriculum development.*
>
> *...*
>
> *BUT this column is not about Khanya. It is about the equally praiseworthy Bernardino Heights High School, led by the visionary Henry Alexander. Sandwiched between the informal settlements of Wallacedene and Kraaifontein, it serves Scottsdene, North Pine, the informal settlements of Wallacedene and Bloekombos, and farming areas such as Bottelary, Backsberg, Klapmuts and Klipheuwel.*
>
> *Founded in 1988, this school is a model of excellence. It is immaculately clean, the small garden is beautiful, and the pupils are happy. They love*

their school; and more than that, they love their principal. Taking us from computer lab to computer lab, from electronic white-boarded classroom to classroom, Alexander's passion for holistic education is palpable. Modestly, he tells me that the success of the school is the involvement of parents in every grade, active community involvement and the commitment of teachers and parents. While he has comprehensive burglar-proofing at the school, vandalism has decreased due to the confidence the community has in this school.

Hosting 1400 pupils and 45 teachers, the pass rate on average is 95%, and his current challenge, he says, is to motivate his 230 grade 12 pupils to seek higher education. All the grade 12 girls I spoke to had plans to study at university, their ambitions ranging from tourism to engineering. The pupils were visibly proud of their school, well behaved and joyful. While music is not a school subject, the school band entertained the audience throughout the celebrations.[21]

Similar stories emerged everywhere Impumelelo was involved. In 2012, a local newspaper reported with breathless excitement that two projects in the small college town of Grahamstown had won Impumelelo Awards:

Champagne corks popped at the Impumelelo Awards for Social Innovation on Thursday night when the Amaphiko Township Dance Project won a coveted platinum prize and a groundbreaking community school that has given hundreds of marginalised students a second chance scooped gold for their efforts.

What makes the achievements of the two projects even more remarkable is the fact there were only 16 awards up for grabs across the whole country.

Started in Rhini township in 1993 by renowned theatre and dance stalwart Janet Buckland, Amaphiko provides hope and a better future to 200 disadvantaged children through formal dance training.

A year younger than Amaphiko, the matric school [project] started with the dawn of South African democracy by the internationally acclaimed Grahamstown Area Distress Relief Association (Gadra), which has operated from the City of Saints since the 1950s.

Run for nine months a year by Gadra Education, the intensive life skills at the Matric School (GMS) has helped hundreds of first-time failure matric

---

21   Rhoda Kadalie. "Bright Heights of hope in the gloom." *Business Day*, 14 Aug. 2008. p. 11.

candidates make more meaningful contributions in fields as diverse as the hospitality industry, banking, law, the arts and business.

The school's impressive 90% plus pass rate since it started and Amaphiko's life-changing dance empowerment were officially recognised at a glittering function at the Baxter Theatre by Finance Minister Pravin Gordhan.

Excited GMS director Dr Ashley Westaway yesterday said the awards were a fitting testament to the vibrancy and relevance of civil society in Grahamstown.[22]

Rhoda delighted in discovering projects that had been overlooked by politicians and the media, or that dealt with overlooked needs and issues. One project, for example, enlisted private companies to donate money to provide tampons and pads to local secondary schools so that girls, many of whom were too poor to afford sanitary products, did not have to stay home when they were menstruating. The result of the project was that the attendance rate rose to 90% in schools that were assisted.[23] Through Impumelelo, Rhoda breathed life into the Constitution's Bill of Rights. She was motivated by the idea of championing the underdog — the forgotten South Africans who had taken their destiny into their own hands, often against incredible odds.

Sometimes Rhoda developed enduring relationships with Impumelelo award-winners that transcended the funding of the projects themselves. That was the case for Balu Nivison, a professional dancer who put her skills to use in an arts and leadership project called Indoni. She first met Rhoda at a lecture hosted by the Union of Jewish Women, and was "blown away" by Rhoda's fresh, forthright perspective on South Africa. She applied for funding from Impumelelo, winning a grant and coaching her dancers to perform at Impumelelo's events.

It was a success story — until tragedy struck: one of the young performers, a talented opera singer named Yanda, who had carried the hopes of his whole family, was murdered in a dispute over a pair of sunglasses shortly after returning from the group's visit to Australia. Nivison was distraught, and turned to Rhoda for help. Rhoda published an op-ed about the student's death, and nominated Nivison to speak about her experience at a special event, organized by the Union of Jewish Women, devoted to "Women of Courage." Nivison was one of five women

---

22   David Macgregor. "By the people, for the people." *Daily Dispatch*, 8 Sep. 2012.
23   Neethling, August 2010. p. 18.

honored at the event, including the daughter of the late Chris Hani, the South African Communist Party leader who had been assassinated shortly before the end of apartheid.

When Nivison struggled to prepare a speech for the occasion, Rhoda visited her at her apartment in the seaside village of Kalk Bay to urge her to tell the story of her student's death so that it would not be in vain, and would inspire donors to continue supporting her arts academy. Nivison took her advice, recalling later: "I also spoke about my own journey as a Jewish woman in service and my lineage. I come from a long line of incredible women activists and community workers — my mother, grandmother, and great-grandmother." Because Rhoda knew her mother, she added, her connection with Rhoda was "even more special and precious," and the speech was a success.

"She was fearless — and loving, kind, warm, unshakeable," Nivison recalled.[24] Rhoda also stood by her when the project was wracked by internal squabbles, and the two became close friends, referring to each other by pet names: "Rhodaaaa"; "Comradia"; or "Womandla" (a slogan that seems to have been coined by the Black Sash, in a feminist play on the struggle slogan, "Amandla!", or "Power!").[25] When Nivison lost her mother to cancer, years later, Rhoda was a crucial source of emotional support. Such was the personal connection many Impumelelo awardees felt to Rhoda.

But there was more to the project than sentiment: there was also valuable data. Over the years, Impumelelo compiled a unique database on development projects — one that included information about government policy, but which went further than the government could or would. Rhoda's team was learning, firsthand, what worked in development, and what did not. The value of that knowledge, in a field characterized by good intentions but poor results, was immense.

24   Balu Nivison. Interview 28 Feb. 2022.
25   Patricia Davison. "On display." *SASH*, Vol. 37 No. 3, May 1995. p. 41. The slogan was on a T-shirt designed by Gus Ferguson.

Rhoda conducts an Impumelelo visit to a water project in Wellington, Western Cape, c. 2016 (Courtesy Rhoda Kadalie)

Impumelelo began publishing a series of pamphlets, *Impumelelo Case Studies*, that compiled examples of best practices within each policy area. The pamphlets described various successful development projects, and then summarized the overall lessons that had been learned. Some examples include the following:

Housing: There was immense pressure on the ANC to provide housing to the poor, but the homes built by the government under the Reconstruction and Development Programme — known as "RDP houses" or "Mandela matchboxes" — were tiny, and few in number relative to the demand. Impumelelo discovered that housing projects were more successful when they were planned in coordination with local communities; where they were more flexible in their design and in their methods of procuring building materials and labor; where help from technical experts was made available; and where residents were able to feel a greater sense of personal ownership.

Environment: South Africa is a country rich in natural resources, attracting tourism as well as extractive industries. Historically, concern about environmental policy had been a concern of the wealthy, white elite, who frequented the country's game reserves and developed an interest in hiking and other outdoor leisure activities. But there was a growing realization that environmental issues touched many other aspects of life. Impumelelo's case studies confirmed that the most successful environmental projects were those that took socioeconomic concerns into account and provided economic benefits to impoverished local communities rather than simply focusing on the preservation of the natural world.

HIV/Aids: This area of policy had become the most acute and controversial in post-apartheid South Africa by the early 2000s. The end of apartheid opened the country to the world; with new opportunities, however, came new challenges, such as the HIV/Aids pandemic. The disease spread rapidly among South Africans, given the relative lack of sexual education; the propensity of men — especially migrant workers — to have multiple sexual partners; and the country's enduring Victorian social mores, which discouraged leaders from speaking openly about sex. In the vacuum, conspiracy theories filled the void — even at the highest levels of government.

Given the delayed response — and outright obstruction — at the national level (see Chapter 12), the non-profit sector took the lead in South Africa's response to the pandemic. Impumelelo's research into these efforts showed that targeted interventions were helpful in preventing transmission in particular niches of society, such as mother-to-child transmission, and in delivering medicines and treatment as well. The willingness of local community leaders to speak openly about the threat of the pandemic was also crucial. Impumelelo observed that one missing element of HIV/Aids policy — even outside government — was a reluctance to educate South Africans about risky sexual behaviors.

Water: South Africa is largely an arid country. Its economic hub, centered around Johannesburg, relies on water collected in dams from mountain snows, especially in the landlocked country of Lesotho. Its agricultural heartland depends on seasonal rains — summer thunderstorms in the north, winter rains in the Cape. Though the national government would notoriously fail to invest in large-scale water infrastructure, leading to near-catastrophic droughts, Impumelelo learned that small-scale water projects aimed at bringing clean water to poor communities were improving as engineers began working closely with those communities and consulting them, rather than planning projects on a purely technical basis.

Crime: The crime wave became one of the most urgent and painful issues facing the new South Africa. Impumelelo worked hard to show examples of police working hand-in-hand with non-governmental organizations and with local communities — often doing so for the first time. While noting carefully that there was no substitute for determined government efforts to fight crime and corruption, and improving the professionalism of police, Impumelelo noted that there were rare examples of excellence and improvement, especially where local governments had taken more responsibility for public safety, rather than leaving it to the national police force alone.

***

Impumelelo quickly became one of the most respected non-governmental organizations in South Africa. Every year, the list of award winners was eagerly anticipated, with successful projects earning valuable media attention and praise from government officials that could then be used in appeals to donors to raise additional funds.

The awards ceremonies were prominent events, with project leaders brought to Cape Town from across the country. Some, from isolated rural areas, had never been to big cities before. The scene was always one of happiness, excitement, and hope, with community volunteers rubbing shoulders with celebrities and senior government officials.

The events were quintessentially Rhoda — ordinary people treated like celebrities, local musicians — especially opera singers — performing for the guests, prominent speakers with substantive ideas to share, and a touch of hilarity. The Impumelelo awards ceremonies were elegant, but humble: there were no expensive dinners, just refreshments in the hallway, well-lit auditoriums, and carefully-produced programs describing the winners and their projects. But they were the hottest ticket in town for those who cared — or wanted to be seen caring — about the country's development.

At Impumelelo, Rhoda found a unique niche — one that fulfilled an important function in South Africa's emerging democracy, and that provided her an opportunity to put her skills and training to use. At Impumelelo, she was able to give life to the socioeconomic rights of the new constitution, which had been celebrated by the international media and lauded by admiring law professors, but which otherwise were little more than ornaments. While the South African Human Rights Commission busied itself with priorities of political interest, such as probes into supposed racism in the media, Rhoda focused on getting things done.

It helped, of course, that there was money involved, and that Rhoda was handing it out. Impumelelo did not run the projects it funded; it was a gateway to funding, and to a broader donor base, for many projects. But Rhoda's organization gave more than money or publicity to the projects it supported. It also introduced the idea that progress toward socioeconomic rights should be measured and evaluated in a professional, impartial way. That was a stark contrast to most government programs, launched with great fanfare and good intentions, then lost in a fog of administrative wrangling, with money wasted or missing.

Impumelelo also provided a unique working environment for its employees. Rhoda hired talented but inexperienced young South Africans, many of whom came from disadvantaged backgrounds, and turned them into world-class professionals.

Terri Felix, who had just matriculated from Northlink College near Bellville when Rhoda hired her as an intern at Impumelelo, recalled that Rhoda had changed her life.[26] Rhoda was "strict, but matronly," and their relationship became less that of employer and employee, a more that of a mother and daughter. In addition to teaching administrative skills to Felix and other staff, Rhoda encouraged them to read more widely, and tried to expose them to new experiences. After work one day, Felix recalled, Rhoda took her to High Tea at the posh Mount Nelson Hotel, where tea was as much a cultural ritual as a refreshment. "She opened a world to me," Felix recalled.

Both Felix and full-time Impumelelo staffer Chris Mingo, whom she had hired away from Idasa, recalled their work with Rhoda as among the most important and enjoyable professional experiences of their lives. "I grew so much," Mingo said, noting that Rhoda had inspired him not only as an employee but in his family life.[27] Seeing how Rhoda was raising Julia — especially inculcating a love of books, and music — inspired Felix and Mingo to do the same with their children.

Rhoda also encouraged staff to air their views publicly. "There were no bad vibes in the office," Felix said. "You could say what you want." When Felix fell pregnant and decided to leave Impumelelo to raise her son as a single mother, Rhoda — a divorced mother herself — continued to offer advice for years. "I only did what she suggested later in life," Felix recalled ruefully.[28] She continued to seek Rhoda's advice throughout many adventures and misadventures, at home and abroad.

Rhoda urged employees to pursue their career ambitions. On one occasion, she found it difficult to turn away three applicants for a job as Impumelelo's website administrator — especially Gary, a "working class township boy with basic education in web development," who

---

26   Terri Felix. Interview 23 Feb. 2022.

27   Chris Mingo. Interview 2 Mar. 2022.

28   Terri Felix, ibid.

"astounded us with his understanding of website construction."[29] She decided, "irresponsibly," to hire all three of them, in addition to the actual website administrator.

Soon, she discovered that one of them was fascinated with the public bus system, and had sketched, on his own, a series of ideas for upgrading its website. It so happened that Rhoda knew the CEO of the bus company, and arranged for her employee to present his ideas directly to the board. She recalled the CEO's astonishment:

> "Wie sou kon dink dat so a bus-bevokte laaitie van die Cape Flats sulke bree kennis van die company sou he?" ["Who would have thought that such a bus-obsessed boy from the Cape Flats would have such broad knowledge of the company?"] the boss and I commented. "Gee hierdie kind 'n drie maande kontrak en dan sien ons watter diens hy vir ons kan lewer" ["Give this child a three-month contract and then we will see what service he can provide us"].[30]

Rhoda was able to arrange for Gary to work for the bus company, including a laptop and a stipend funded by philanthropists she roped into the project.

At Impumelelo, Rhoda was a tough and demanding boss, applying tough love to whip her team into shape. But they deeply appreciated what she taught them. Mingo said that he learned how to think critically, and how to write clearly, thanks to Rhoda's mentorship. "She played a huge role in my professional development," he recalled. He absorbed Rhoda's habit of speaking directly, and at times undiplomatically, when something was wrong.

Mingo also recalled that Rhoda often sought opportunities for her staff members to travel, and to gain new skills and experiences. She brought them along to international conferences, exposing them to new countries and cultures. These trips were no mere junkets: Mingo recalled that Rhoda and her staff would arrive for meetings with donors armed with PowerPoint slides, case studies, and data. Many of the other international organizations funded by the same programs were woefully underprepared, by contrast: Rhoda's Brazilian counterparts were "waffling," Mingo recalled with amusement.

Rhoda's international donors — including Soros — were delighted with her progress. She also developed a close relationship with the Ford

29   Rhoda Kadalie. "There is hope." PoliticsWeb, 21 Dec 2011. URL: https://www.politicsweb.co.za/news-and-analysis/there-is-hope. Accessed on 26 Mar. 2022.
30   Ibid.

Foundation in particular. Known in the U.S. for its left-wing bent, Ford found in Impumelelo a worthy, well-managed institution that people of all political persuasions, in South Africa and beyond, could celebrate.

That is not to say it was easy. Rhoda was constantly frustrated by the fact that Idasa initially controlled the flow of funding. For reasons Rhoda could never understand, the money went from the donors to Idasa, rather than directly to Impumelelo. Rhoda would then ask Idasa for money for the awards, and for operating expenses, and report back as to how it had been spent. But Impumelelo — despite its growing reputation for good management — never handled any of its own donor funds. Instead, Rhoda later noted, the money from overseas donors headed into the "black hole" of Idasa's accounts: she never managed a cent of it. She nevertheless insisted upon the funds that were due to Impumelelo, and kept a close accounting.

Sometimes, Rhoda's careful and forensic record-keeping created problems for her with donors. When she discovered inefficiencies and problems within the international organizations that were funding Impumelelo, she raised her objections — and irritated powerful people. She was "her own worst enemy," Mingo recalled, noting that her penchant for criticism and her insistence on accountability from everyone — including her donors — meant that she often found herself marginalized, excluded from meetings, events, and relationships.

Over time, Rhoda found she had to raise her own funds for Impumelelo. The initial seed capital had come from a group of donors, including Soros, and the Ford Foundation had stepped into a leading role for several years as well. But eventually, those sources of funding began to recede. George Soros's Open Society Foundation became more reluctant to fund Impumelelo, for reasons that Rhoda could not understand.[31] Privately, Rhoda suspected the motivation was political: Soros was increasingly committed to left-wing causes of which Rhoda had become more critical. But the Ford Foundation, too, told Rhoda that she had to develop local sources of funding. That, after all, had been one of the original goals of the funding: to enable the project to become self-sustaining, within its own funding networks. Rhoda had to turn to captains of South African industry for support. To her surprise, many of them were proud to contribute.

Over time, Rhoda raised close to R60 million from South African donors to disburse to various projects, wooing corporations to sponsor awards, and to play an active role in helping non-profit organizations replicate their successes to create "multiplier effects" across the country. By 2010, the organization still had a budget of nearly R3.5 million (about

---

31   Rhoda Kadalie. Letter to Isaac Shongwe. 19 May 2014. Personal files.

$500,000 in 2010 terms) — nearly R4.7 million (about $650,000) if the awards evening, a biannual event, was included.[32]

She was less successful at convincing the South African government to learn from Impumelelo's successes. After years spent identifying the best practices in various fields of socioeconomic development, captured in vibrant magazines and pamphlets that summarized the lessons learned, Rhoda found that the government was often uninterested. That was less true in the opposition-governed Western Cape, where provincial authorities were eager to break from the ANC's statist policies and try new solutions. Indeed, the Western Cape came to dominate the award winners: "[T]he Western Cape has consistently been one of the provinces that generates the most award winners every year," Rhoda observed in 2008.[33] She would later opine that if there was hope for South Africa, it was in the country's federalist structure, which allowed opposition parties to depart locally from the ruling party's failing national policies.[34]

There were also iconic projects developed at the local government level that were innovative, highly structured, and successful. These included the Mariannhill Landfill management program in Durban, which aimed to rehabilitate the environment while also generating organic gas for use in power generation. The project was described by an observer in 2011:

> The vision of the Mariannhill landfill model is to design a conservation area upon completion of the landfill.
>
> As an active site now it accepts on a daily basis 450 tons of waste and serves as an important natural corridor for species migration. Surprisingly stench free, there is a hiking trail, a Buddhist meditation bench and an array of endangered species on site.
>
> Environmentalists have come on board to work with the Mariannhill management to make this possible.
>
> The good news, however, is the income generated by this project for the province and the 6MW that is generated to supply 3 000 households with electricity.

---

32   Impumelelo business plan, ibid.
33   Rhoda Kadalie. "Western Cape tops awards for NPO, public sector initiatives." *Cape Times*, 19 May 2008. p. 5.
34   Rhoda Kadalie, quoted by Ryland Fisher. *Race*. Auckland Park: Jacana Media, 2007. p. 236.

In addition, Durban now reaps R46 million a year in carbon credits.[35]

Other success stories included a water sanitation program in the eThekwini (Durban) municipality; the Meulwater Treatment Works in the Western Cape Town of Paarl; and others.

These projects created "best practices" that the Impumelelo team worked hard to inspire other provincial and local governments to replicate. But the national government was less interested. While ANC officials were happy to speak at Impumelelo's events, they were reluctant to implement its ideas.

Thus it was that Rhoda began fighting a new battle: in the media.

---

35   Devi Rajab. "Moan about failures, but celebrate successes; If we complain when things go wrong we must also shine a light on the things that we or the government get right." *The Mercury*, 29 Nov. 2011, p. 11.

Chapter 12:
Columnist

*"Inspiration seldom responds creatively to deadlines but the scramble
for a column the night before deadline is saved so often by the
unscrupulous politician who, in the nick of time, determines one's
script. ... [M]ost of my columns are sheer gut responses to a government
that has failed to live up to the promises so easily made
during election time."[1]*

Rhoda had never been shy to speak out — whether against the apartheid regime, the university hierarchy, or the commissars of the liberation movement. "Comrade Kadalie, you are out of order!" she recalled being told by student leaders at an anti-apartheid protest at the UWC auditorium.

Therefore it was almost natural that she begin writing a regular column in South African newspapers, breaking stories of government corruption, building a loyal following, and developing a reputation for taking on the most powerful people in the new South Africa. It was as a columnist that Rhoda became a household name.

Rhoda's writing career began long before she was appointed to the Human Rights Commission. She wrote occasionally for a variety of newspapers and magazines, including the English-language dailies of the Independent Media group, and the weekly *Mail & Guardian* (see below). She also wrote for a variety of political publications and magazines, commenting on current events.

Strangely, writing did not come easily to Rhoda, at first. Though she was a diligent student, she had not learned to organize her thoughts on paper in an effective way until well into her academic career.

Her relationship with Richard was a turning point: he loved languages, and came from a family steeped in German literature. In the heyday of their relationship, Richard would edit Rhoda's writing, pointing out where she could have made a point more clearly. (Ironically, she would finish her Master's thesis, and he would not.)

Rhoda recalled the years of her struggles with writing, when she would spend days on a single page. Even well into her career as a columnist, she found writing very difficult, and would labor into the night as she

---

1   Rhoda Kadalie. *In Your Face: Passionate Conversations About People and Politics.* Cape Town: Tafelberg, 2009. p. 7.

worked to meet the next day's deadline — not because she had left the work to the last minute, but because she found the work required intense concentration. She developed the work habits of a night owl: only the silence and darkness of the quietest hours allowed her to focus on what she was trying to say.

But she loved doing it.

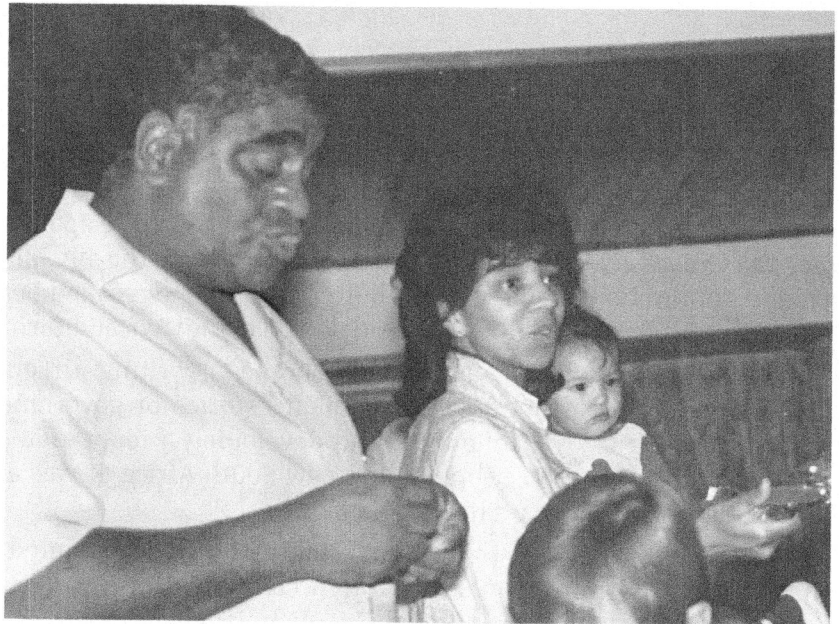

Rhoda, holding Julia, with celebrated novelist Richard Rive, c. 1988
(Courtesy Rhoda Kadalie)

Writing her columns became Rhoda's way of urging the ANC to do better — and urging the media, and the voters, to hold the government accountable. While she still had high hopes for South African democracy, she observed that "we are better at erecting a façade than an actual democracy, and behind the façade the rot is spreading."[2] She was determined to stop the rot by exposing it to sunlight.

Rhoda's first columns appeared in the *Mail & Guardian*, a weekly newspaper that had a reputation for highbrow content, despite its tabloid format. The *M&G* was the descendant of the *Rand Daily Mail*, a liberal newspaper that had been critical of apartheid, and which was eventually driven out of business by the regime's aggressive censorship. In the new South Africa, the *M&G* sought to continue the muckraking investigative

2   Barron, "Obituary," ibid.

journalism of its predecessor, while preserving a left-of-center editorial line sympathetic to the new government's objectives. Its opinion pages became a forum for criticizing the ANC — from the left.

In one of her earliest columns for the *M&G* in 1997, Rhoda — still prominently aligned with the ANC — wrote about the fact that the ANC Women's League had reelected President Mandela's estranged former wife, Winnie Madikizela-Mandela, as its president.

Winnie Mandela had once been a revered heroine of the anti-apartheid struggle. Week in and week out, police would toss all of her belongings out of the home to which she had been banished in the remote town of Brandtfort, as her husband languished in prison on Robben Island. When she tried to receive visitors, they were often blocked or taken to court.[3]

But during the unrest of the 1980s, Winnie Mandela became notorious for her role in leading a violent organization in Soweto, the Mandela United Football Club, which tortured and killed suspected informants and collaborators. The Truth and Reconciliation Commission would ultimately expose her role in these human rights abuses. In the new South Africa, she drew criticism for her lavish lifestyle, and was eventually convicted of fraud, though she would avoid serving time in jail. (In a curious irony, the judge in Winnie Mandela's fraud trial was Eberhard Bertelsmann, Rhoda's former brother-in-law.)

Winnie Mandela tried to reinvent herself as a populist leader, campaigning against the South African elite, whose white members had managed to hold onto most of their wealth as millions still languished in poverty. But it was clear, by 1997, that she was a deeply problematic leader, and Rhoda was outraged that the ANC Women's League chose her to continue serving as its president.

In her *M&G* op-ed, Rhoda — who was, by then, a member of the Human Rights Commission, wrote: "The re-election of Winnie Madikizela-Mandela as president of the African National Congress Women's League is more a reflection of the weakness of the organisation than it is a victory for the women's movement. ... She used her self-inflicted poverty to identify with the people of South Africa. She threatened to shut up the press should they continue to vilify her, she declared that the salvation of the people lies in her hands, as only she can lead them to the promised land. ... Is such rhetoric not the death knell of an organisation made ineffectual and

---

3   "Winnie Mandela is banished to Brandfort." South African History Online. URL: https://www.sahistory.org.za/dated-event/winnie-mandela-banished-brandfort. Accessed on 18 Mar. 2022.

weak by constant allegations of financial mismanagement, a cut-throat leadership battle and no clear programme of action?"[4]

Rhoda continued to develop her voice. In April 1999, Rhoda — newly freed from her responsibilities at the Human Rights Commission — offered her thoughts about the fraud conviction and prison sentence handed down to cleric and former UDF leader Allan Boesak. Rhoda argued that Boesak deserved his punishment, honoring his past contributions to the anti-apartheid struggle, but noting the character flaws that had led to his corruption. She also observed: "There was a way in which apartheid forced greatness on all of us, and Boesak's ego was ready bait for this.[5] In that comment, it was clear that Rhoda had begun to look beyond the moral framework of the anti-apartheid struggle, and to judge South Africa by the standards of any other democratic society.

Later in April 1999, with South Africa's second fully democratic elections looming, Rhoda wrote an op-ed in the *Sowetan*, titled "They may kiss babies, but beware." Speaking to a largely black readership, Rhoda advised South Africans to demand more from political leaders than simply plaudits about the past:

We should be wary of politicians who suddenly kiss babies and the elderly but whose welfare policies are against this sector of society; politicians who shake hands with all and sundry but refuse to meet with those who request meetings; politicians who stride smiling into shopping malls but who are inaccessible at crucial times; politicians who visit squatter camps and the rural areas but who are never seen again until the next election and politicians who woo women voters but who are intrinsically sexist.

Politicians should be subjected to close scrutiny before we decide to vote for them. Elections should be taken seriously because it is the most crucial

4   Rhoda Kadalie. "Women's League is dying." *Mail & Guardian*, 9 May 1997. By 2001, Rhoda would feel vindicated in her assessment of the ANC Women's League's prospects, declaring: "They are not even a player in the ruling party. They are completely invisible as a pressure group." (Rhoda Kadalie, quoted by "Wake-Up Call for Dormant ANCWL." Sowetan, 12 Oct. 2001.) Later, in 2007, when the Women's League voted to back Jacob Zuma, with his murky history with women, Rhoda would declare forthrightly: "The ANC Women's League is useless, moribund, dead, finish and *klaar* [clear]!" (Rhoda Kadalie. "ANC Women's League lets our women down." Letter to the editor. Cape Argus, 30 Nov. 2007. p. 22.) Her rather muted criticism in 1997, offered from within the ruling party, only hinted at the more strident voice that Rhoda would develop in her subsequent writing.

5   Rhoda Kadalie. "What you sow, you shall reap." *Mail & Guardian*, 2 Apr. 1999.

opportunity given to the electorate to hold politicians accountable. It is the clarion call for the electorate to exercise their democratic right to assess Government performance and to make choices.

On balance, many politicians are found wanting so the electorate should look at the different parties' manifestos to see how they hope to address human rights concerns.

The Aids epidemic, sexual violence against women and children, crime, job creation, unemployment, health care and housing are key indicators of measurement. Ask politicians to give concrete proposals how and in what time period they will address these concerns and judge them accordingly.[6]

...

Don't vote for those who are against corruption but who do not suspend those close to them who are corrupt. Don't vote for those who feel entitled to big salaries but never volunteer to take a cut in salary or live simply so that others can simply live. Vote for a clean, accountable and transparent government which will give priority to the needs of black women, children and the poor.[7]

While Rhoda targeted "politicians," South Africans do not generally vote for particular candidates, outside of local government elections. But by urging her readers to hold politicians accountable, Rhoda was hinting that they ought to look at parties beyond the ANC.

***

Rhoda was soon invited to write for the prestigious *Business Day*, the country's only weekday national newspaper published in English (most others were regional, or weekly). While the paper focused on industry and finance, it maintained a lively editorial and opinion page. If the *M&G* was proudly on the left, the *Business Day*, with its business-oriented readership leaned somewhat to the right — though its editors, like the business community itself, were often eager to appease the ANC, where possible.

In 1999, Alan Fine, a well-known journalist with the *Business Day*, visited Rhoda's office in the Idasa building to spar with her about politics. Fine was concerned that Rhoda was too blunt in her criticism of the ruling

---

6   Rhoda Kadalie. "They may kiss babies, but beware." *Sowetan*, 28 Apr. 1999.
7   Ibid.

party. After a long debate and discussion, he was so impressed by Rhoda's perspective that he offered to suggest to the editor-in-chief, Peter Bruce, that she be offered a bi-weekly column. Soon after, Bruce called to invite Rhoda to write a "no holds barred" column in the *Business Day*. Thus began her long association with the paper.

It was a natural fit: after her resignation from the Human Rights Commission, she had a unique public profile, which generated even more interest in her columns. Her reputation for integrity, her experiences in government, and her knowledge of the inner workings of the ruling party, gave her unique insights into politics and policy debates.

Rhoda's forté was exposing the hypocrisy of the ANC — even as she worked, through Impumelelo, to help the government achieve its development objectives.

In 2004, for example, in criticizing the way the ANC had reduced Parliament's independent power, making it effectively an arm of the executive branch and the ruling party, Rhoda reminisced:

In the heady days of apartheid, our African National Congress Woodstock branch was quite active. It was a motley crowd of ANC hacks, old unity movement types, Trotskyites, and so on. The one thing we all had in common, was our abhorrence of apartheid.

On one occasion, we were asked to elect a delegate to represent our branch at an impending ANC national conference. A very loyal activist was elected. At a subsequent meeting some who considered him too much of a renegade ("workerist", "Trot" — epithets hurled at those who dared to question the conventional wisdom of the party) objected to his election and proposed reversing the vote. The hacks invoked, against all logic, an array of Stalinist ploys to overturn the decision. After two hours of fierce debate, I left the meeting in protest.

A creeping sense of déjà vu came over me as I witnessed the recent fiasco in the National Council of Provinces (NCOP) [formally, the upper chamber of Parliament]. After the controversial encounter between President Thabo Mbeki and Democratic Alliance (DA) MP Ryan Coetzee [see below], the DA's Juanita Terblanche proposed a motion condemning Mbeki's reluctance to address the crime of rape against women and children; it was adopted unanimously by the dozy MPs. Subsequent attempts to reverse the decision once again reduced Parliament to the circus it has become. Days later, when they realised what they had done, and under great pressure allegedly from the executive, the NCOP reversed this decision.

*This incident is one of many that herald the decline of an institution that
had a hope of being a real people's Parliament.*

...

*Under Mbeki's leadership, Parliament has become a lame duck and a
rubber stamp for the executive, to whom it has become beholden on
most matters.*[8]

The ascent of Thabo Mbeki, who took over the leadership of the ANC from
Nelson Mandela in 1997, and succeeded him as president in the 1999
elections, gave new urgency to Rhoda's writing, as South Africa entered
a dangerous era of illiberal politics, quite different from the feel-good
"Rainbow Nation" era of the post-1994 transition.

Mbeki was respected, at home and abroad, for his intellectual
pedigree. He was the somewhat estranged son of the writer and ANC
luminary Govan Mbeki, who — like Mandela — had been imprisoned on
Robben Island; indeed, he was considered a rival to Mandela himself. But
his children felt abandoned; many armchair psychologists would later
conclude that Mbeki's cold personality was the result of that experience.

Unusually for a would-be revolutionary, Thabo Mbeki held a degree
in economics from the University of Sussex in the United Kingdom, during
his exile from the country. His pipe-smoking habit, immaculate English
syntax, and fluent Afrikaans impressed white intellectuals in the old
regime, and foreign investors in the new. He also impressed Rhoda when
she first encountered him upon his return from exile. She was impressed,
she wrote in her diary in 1991, with Mbeki's "true diplomatic" demeanor
upon encountering a militant group of youth activists in a town hall
meeting in the Woodstock neighborhood of Cape Town.[9]

In 1998, with Mbeki already beginning to assume many of then-
President Mandela's duties, Rhoda was optimistic about Mbeki's future
presidency, because he was seen as more focused on the actual tasks of
governing. The popular cartoonist Jonathan Shapiro (known as "Zapiro")
dubbed Mbeki "Mr. Delivery," which was also the name of a popular food
delivery service.

Rhoda had high hopes for Mbeki at first. When he was inaugurated
in June 1999, Rhoda noted in her diary: "Mbeki's speech was beautifully

---

8   Rhoda Kadalie. "Supine MPs blow chance for people's Parliament."
     Business Day, 25 Nov. 2004. Published in Rhoda Kadalie. *In Your Face*.
     Cape Town: Tafelberg, 2009. pp. 122–4.
9   Rhoda Kadalie. Diary entry, 15 Jan. 1991.

crafted, drawing on Setswana imagery & the [C]omrades marathon.[10] [First Lady] Zanele Mbeki dressed modestly and stylishly in a lemon outfit."[11] She noted in a letter to friend abroad in early 2000: "Mbeki drives his cabinet and they seem to be more productive under his governance than under Mandela's."[12] She also told a BBC audience:

> It was important that we had a president like President Mandela, who embodies forgiveness and reconciliation because of his past. But I think also because he's become an international cult figure, it often blinds us to the problems of this country. The problems of unemployment, of education, of child care, of housing. And I think that a person like Thabo Mbeki, because he doesn't come with that aura, has to, head-on, tackle those issues. We will not be mesmerized by the nice words, and the cult status of a president like Mandela. ... to the point of irritation, I might add. And I think that with Thabo Mbeki, he would have to take on the challenges of crime, of unemployment, of poverty, of housing, and we will see issues for what they are. I think at the moment, we tend to forgive President Mandela. We are soft on the man because he is so mesmerising. And I think we're not going to be as soft on Thabo Mbeki.[13]

Mbeki's economic knowledge, genteel habits, and technocratic managerial style seemed well-suited to the role that South Africans wanted him to play.

However, the erudite Mbeki had also been trained in the hierarchical, Stalinist political tradition in which the organization's leaders had been steeped during the years of exile. Mbeki and his cohort practiced the Leninist model of "democratic centralism," where decisions were ultimately controlled by a small group of insiders. They were also deeply suspicious of dissent, and constantly on guard for infiltration. These habits may have been well-suited to an underground resistance movement. They translated poorly, however, into the freewheeling politics of a young democracy — one whose local leaders had fought for the right to engage in vigorous debate.

Much of the populist left distrusted Mbeki because he was seen as the primary mover behind the ANC's fiscally conservative Growth, Employment, and Redistribution (GEAR) policy, which had replaced the more socialist Reconstruction and Development Programme (RDP),

---

10   An annual ultramarathon between the KwaZulu-Natal cities of Durban and Pietermaritzburg
11   Rhoda Kadalie. Diary entry, 16 Jun. 1999.
12   Rhoda Kadalie. Letter to Jurgen and Catherine Girgensohn. 4 Jan. 2000.
13   Rhoda Kadalie. "South Africans Talking," ibid.

and sought to keep inflation and deficits low in the hope of enticing foreign investment.

But Mbeki soon ignited controversy on all sides by embracing a dissident theory on the HIV/Aids pandemic — one that claimed poverty, not a virus, caused the immune deficiency at the heart of the disease. Worse, Mbeki enforced that dogma — and few in the ANC dared to challenge him.

* * *

Mbeki's denialism had actually begun years earlier, when, as Deputy President, he began pushing a domestic pseudo-treatment called "Virodene" as an alternative to expensive anti-retroviral drugs produced by western pharmaceutical companies.

The South African government succeeded in convincing the drug manufacturers to provide anti-Aids medication cheaply to the Third World. But Mbeki persisted with odd theories about the HIV/Aids pandemic.

The idea that poverty was the cause, and not a virus, suited Mbeki's economic worldview, which combined fiscal conservatism with the socialist idea that the wealthy had a moral obligation to redistribute wealth to the poor.

Mbeki's reluctance to pursue HIV/Aids as the public health emergency it was had already become apparent by the time the coastal city of Durban hosted a massive international Aids conference in July 2000. The scientists and activists who descended on South Africa hoped to nudge him toward a more proactive stance. They were sorely disappointed. As journalist Chris McGreal noted: "Not long after the 2000 Durban Aids conference, Mbeki's office issued a statement accusing those who wanted the government to provide anti-retroviral drugs in public hospitals of trying to poison black people. 'Our people are being used as guinea pigs and conned into using dangerous and toxic drugs,' it read, describing this as an onslaught 'reminiscent of the biological warfare of the apartheid era.'"[14]

Worse, McGreal noted, "In September 2000, Mbeki told the South African parliament that HIV and Aids numbers were not nearly so serious as scientists claimed. ... He ordered the health minister – Manto Tshabalala-Msimang – to consider a cut in the Aids budget."[15]

Mbeki also claimed that the scientific orthodoxy on HIV/Aids was racist. Specifically, he opposed the idea that the virus was spread through

---

14   Chris McGreal. "Special Report: Thabo Mbeki's catastrophe." *Prospect*, 21 Feb. 2002.

15   Ibid.

unprotected heterosexual encounters, saying that it was motivated by primitive racist notions of uncontrollable African sexuality.

Mbeki's denialism damaged public health in two ways. One was to confuse the public about how HIV was transmitted, thus aiding its spread. The other was to restrict access to a drug called nevirapine, which helped HIV-positive expectant mothers prevent their children from contracting the virus. Mbeki's government was reluctant to provide it, and discouraged doctors from prescribing it.

Making matters even worse, Mbeki appointed Dr. Manto Tshabalala-Msimang, a Soviet-trained physician, to be the country's Minister of Health. She began promoting an indigenous African alternative to antiretroviral drugs — a combination of olive oil, African potatoes, garlic, lemon, and beetroot — to boost immunity. Mbeki stood by her, even after she became the object of domestic ridicule and international condemnation, the face of South Africa's failure to grapple with HIV/Aids.

Despite his intellectual credentials, and his penchant for charming the former white elite and the leaders of the industrialized world, Mbeki seemed to see the HIV/Aids pandemic in crude racial terms. And few in his own party dared to speak out against him.

Rhoda was the rare exception. She began leading public criticism of Mbeki and Tshabalala-Msimang. In an open letter to the *Sunday Independent* in September 2001, she declared: "People are dying in the thousands. This is not what I fought for. ... I travel abroad to conferences often. Before, we could bask in [Nelson] Mandela's reflected glory. Now I have to explain Mbeki as whites used to have to explain apartheid."[16]

She called on Tshabalala-Msimang to resign: "We have a genocide on our hands and you and your cohorts have been unwilling to listen to the experts," she said. "If the president is making it impossible to do your work effectively, why not resign with dignity in defiance of someone who is taking the country down with him?".[17]

Rhoda also began writing a series of columns in the *Business Day* attacking the denialist posture of the ANC government. In one column in 2002, "Tshabalala-Msimang gives women a bad name," she wrote:

---

16   Rhoda Kadalie, quoted by Jon Jeter. "Political Resistance in S. Africa Blocks Wide Use of HIV Drugs." *Washington Post*, 1 Oct. 2001. URL: https://www.washingtonpost.com/archive/politics/2001/10/01/political-resistance-in-s-africa-blocks-wide-use-of-hiv-drugs/c7d8e959-27ef-4784-8e5b-5c18003ed664/. Accessed on 20 Mar. 2022.
17   Rhoda Kadalie, quoted by Chris McGreal. "Aids will kill 700,000 South Africans a year." *Guardian*, 17 Oct. 2001. p. 16.

By now, I would have expected the women in Parliament, in the cabinet and in senior public positions, to be convulsed by the utterances of the minister and to have called for her head.

That they are not vociferous about the AIDS pandemic, and most notably its effects on women, exemplifies how powerful the party list system is in silencing women.

...

Young women in particular are most affected by the disease. HIV/AIDS burdens women in ways peculiar to their gender.

As the main nurturers and caregivers of the family the responsibility to care for the sick and dying becomes mainly theirs.

More seriously, women as citizens in their own right are directly affected by the disease themselves, with the spectre of death hanging over their heads, knowing they will leave many orphans behind, with very little prospect of care.

Many are the family's sole breadwinners and with poverty becoming increasingly feminised, the state has an extra responsibility to ease the burden of women. The health minister has not risen to the challenge.

Under such circumstances how can we tolerate a minister who denies that HIV causes AIDS? How can we allow her to persecute those who dare to follow internationally recognized scientific prescriptions for the prevention, treatment and care of the disease?

...

In any civilised democracy, the health minister would have been given the boot. Why should a woman like her be thrust upon us?[18]

Rhoda continued to attack Mbeki's denialism and to excoriate Tshabalala-Msimang's policies in her columns. She also joined tens of thousands of demonstrators in the streets of Cape Town in 2003 in a march, led by a new organization called the Treatment Action Campaign, to demand that Mbeki provide antiretroviral drugs to pregnant mothers, and reverse his denialist policies. She recalled the experience in another *Business Day* column:

---

18   Rhoda Kadalie. "Tshabalala-Msimang gives women a bad name." *Business Day*, 26 Jul. 2002. Published in Rhoda Kadalie. *In Your Face.* pp. 92-4.

Rhoda: 'Comrade Kadalie, You Are Out of Order!'

[B]eing part of the Treatment Action Campaign (TAC) march of 30,000 people on February 14 2003 was my opposition to a government that does not give a damn about the people who voted it into power.

...

Feelings of déjà vu, as we marched down roads regularly trudged before 1994 to protest at the apartheid regime, enveloped us. We were toyi-toying[19] along the same roads against our democratically-elected government.

...

For me it was a march against a recalcitrant stubborn government that has come to betray the people who put it into power. It is about a government that has become a law unto itself because of its majority power, and secure in the knowledge that its alliance partners will give it legitimacy no matter what it does.[20]

Rhoda was among the first within the ANC's orbit to speak out against Mbeki and his HIV/Aids policies. Many senior members of the ANC realized that the president was leading the country down a dangerous path, but few spoke out publicly, instead sharing their concerns privately and hoping for change.

One such was Rhoda's own uncle, Dr. Victor Kadalie. He had retired from his medical practice in Haren Ems, Germany, where he had been well-known. He bought an apartment in Durban, in the hope of spending some time in South Africa doing voluntary medical work. He wanted to contribute to the country that had given him so much in his earlier years, but which he had lost due to his political beliefs and his cross-racial marriage. His son, Khwezi, had by then obtained a post in the ANC-run Gauteng provincial government; he complained to his father about Rhoda's columns, which were a source of embarrassment to him as he moved within ruling party circles.

Dr. Kadalie contacted his old comrade, Dr. Tshabalala-Msimang. Dr. Kadalie had helped support Tshabalala-Msimang in exile, bestowing his largesse when she was, like many ANC activists, living in relative poverty in exile. Tshabalala-Msimang agreed to meet with him at her offices in

---

19   A protest dance involving high knee lifts.
20   Rhoda Kadalie. "HIV sufferers still left out in the cold." *Business Day*, 26 Feb. 2003. Published in Rhoda Kadalie. *In Your Face*. Cape Town: Tafelberg, 2009. pp. 180-1.

Pretoria. But she never turned up, nor did she apologize for failing to make the meeting, which infuriated Victor.

Soon afterward, Rhoda recalled, Victor admitted to her that he had witnessed the dishevelment of the ANC in exile, and had excused it because of the conditions in which the movement had been forced to operate. But having seen the rot up close in government, he encouraged Rhoda to keep writing her criticisms.

She would later recall: "Victor died of a broken heart having sacrificed country, finances, and family for the ANC, yet he received nothing in return when in fact he only wanted to volunteer his services for the country he loved."[21]

Years later, when Tshabalala-Msimang died in 2009, the ANC government, then under the leadership of President Jacob Zuma, chose to honor her, Rhoda pushed back vehemently: "[W]hen it comes to Manto, the ANC will never admit defeat. ... As liberation leaders they have perfected the art of the divine right to rule, a doctrine supposedly so contrary to their socialist beliefs. They have the divine right to determine who is a hero; who deserves the higher orders of the land; who deserves state funerals, and who deserves to die.[22]

* * *

The task of criticism in the Mbeki era was made more difficult by the president's repeated habit of ascribing racist motivations to his detractors. His tactics became particularly ugly during the debate over HIV/Aids.

In October 2004, Mbeki used his weekly essay in the ANC's online newsletter, *ANC Today*, to attack the views of an unnamed white female journalist, Charlene Smith. Smith had published a newspaper article titled "Rape has become a sickening way of life in our land." In it, she argued that the HIV/Aids pandemic in South Africa was exacerbated by "men's attitude toward women." Without mentioning any race, or any particular culture, Smith had said that the country was afflicted by "a culture in which rape is endemic and has become a prime means of transmitting disease."[23]

Mbeki took issue with Smith's argument in a graphic manner:

In simple language she was saying that African traditions, indigenous religions and culture prescribe and institutionalise rape. The

---

21   Personal communication with the author. 1 Feb. 2022.
22   Rhoda Kadalie. *Die Burger*, 24 Dec. 2009.
23   Charlene Smith. "Rape has become a sickening way of life in our land." *Sunday Independent*, 2004.

"internationally recognised expert" was saying that our cultures, traditions and religions as Africans inherently make every African man a potential rapist.

Given this view, which defines the African people as barbaric savages, it should come as no surprise that she writes that, "South Africa has the highest rates of rape in the world, according to Interpol." To her, this assertion would have been obviously correct, because, after all, we are an African country, and therefore have the men [been] conditioned by African culture, tradition and religion to commit rape.

Mbeki went on to dismiss fears of crime in South Africa as a "psychosis" produced by the "psychological residue of apartheid":

For them our new democracy feels fraught with threats. They must continuously find negative superlatives to convey the story that South Africa is the world capital of all the negative things that affect all humanity.

In this situation, fear of crime becomes the concentrated expression of fear about their survival in a sea of black savages, which they fuel by entertaining the mythology that whites are the primary targets merely because of their race.[24]

This blunt attack on a journalist, from the office of the country's president, caused consternation in Parliament, where the opposition Democratic Alliance demanded that Mbeki explain himself. Ryan Coetzee, a close aide to DA leader Tony Leon, used the quarterly occasion of President's Question Time to pose several pointed queries to Mbeki about his views on HIV/Aids and rape.

Mbeki responded with more of the same racial vitriol, accusing Coetzee of trying to stir up a "televised debate that will help some people in our country to perpetuate the very dangerous pretence that racism in our country died with the holding of our first democratic elections ten years ago."[25] He added: "I will not keep quiet while others whose minds have been corrupted by the disease of racism accuse us, the black people

24   Thabo Mbeki. "When is good news bad news?" *ANC Today*, Vol. 4 No. 39, 1–7 Oct. 2004. URL: https://web.archive.org/web/20041208223522/ http://www.anc.org.za/ancdocs/anctoday/2004/at39.htm. Accessed on 20 Jan. 2022.
25   Thabo Mbeki, quoted by Tony Leon. *On the Contrary: Leading the Opposition in a Democratic South Africa.* Johannesburg: Jonathan Ball, 2008. 348.

of South Africa, Africa and the world, as being, by virtue of our Africanness and skin color — lazy, liars, foul-smelling, diseased, corrupt, violent, amoral, sexually depraved, animalistic, savage — and rapist."

Mbeki was so adamant in his response, and so proud of it, that he later had it reprinted in *ANC Today*, dripping with graphic racial and sexual innuendo. Mbeki concluded: "I would like to assure the Honourable Coetzee that the millions of Africans in our country, in Africa and the world did not fight against apartheid racism and white domination to create space for them to continue to be subjected to dehumanising, demeaning and insulting racism.[26]

As Tony Leon would observe: "For [Mbeki], there was no debate about HIV/AIDS; there was only a never-ending, never-yielding debate on race."

But Rhoda pushed back — and paid Mbeki in his own currency. In a column titled "What we black women ought to tell this president," she said:

> *The scourge of violence against women is not the prerogative of any ethnic group. In all groups men rely on patriarchal culture, religion and tradition to justify treating women as chattels and second-class citizens. This attitude has come a long way.*
>
> *...*
>
> *So what [Charlene] Smith says is unmitigated fact. To accuse her of saying, 'African traditions, indigenous religions and culture prescribe and institutionalize rape' and implying that 'African men are inherently potential rapists and barbaric savages' when no such evidence exists is libellous and irresponsible.*
>
> *Such far-fetched rubbish I have not heard in a long time. Racist interpretations of innocent statements such as hers smack of obsession at best and paranoia at worst. They resemble the incantations of a rabid African nationalist, not of someone described by the media as an intellectual.*
>
> *Surely this kind of response is out of kilter with the office of the president and enough to strike the fear of God into the hearts of any ordinary citizens who dare to voice their opinions? If a puny little white activist*

---

26   Thabo Mbeki, quoted in "Dislodging Stereotypes." *ANC Today*, Vol. 4, No. 42, 22-28 Oct. 2004. URL: https://web.archive.org/web/20041223175236/http://www.anc.org.za/ancdocs/anctoday/2004/at42.htm. Accessed on 20 Jan. 2022.

is capable of sending the president into continual fits of rage, what does this say of Mbeki?

...

Maybe we black women should start telling the president most black men treat black women badly, as borne out by the startling evidence of domestic violence, default on maintenance, sexual offenses and the criminal courts of the land.

...

Yes, Mr. President, most of these men are black — they violate not because they are black but because the majority of men in this country are black.

Mr. President, I suggest you undergo some serious antiracism training so that you can identify the sin when you see it. Lashing out at activists who dare to call abuse by its regular name weakens you and not them. Why are you selectively vociferous about some matters and not others? Why do you not similarly trumpet the promotion of safe sex, antiretroviral medicines and sympathy for those infected with HIV?

...

Your presidential letters are obsessed with your own notions of race and what it means to be African and how others, mainly whites, misinterpret this 'sacrosanct idea' that only you, Thabo Mbeki, understand.[27]

In an interview with the *New York Times*, Rhoda explained: "I think it is unbecoming of the president to single out a citizen for castigation. If we are going to brag that we are the rainbow nation, then people have a right to say what they think."

She added that while Mbeki was obsessing over race and sexuality, "this country is being depopulated of its young women."[28]

She acknowledged that racism was still a problem: she even agreed with the ANC that much criticism of the new government was racist. But that, she believed, did not excuse its failures to deliver on its promises.

27   Rhoda Kadalie. "What we black women ought to tell this president." *Business Day*, 28 Oct. 2004. URL: https://allafrica.com/stories/200410280338.html. Accessed on 20 Jan. 2022.
28   Rhoda Kadalie, quoted by Sharon Lafraniere. "After Apartheid: Heated Words About Rape and Race." *New York Times*, 24 Nov. 2004. p. 4.

Her sentiments echoed those of Treatment Action Campaign leader Zackie Achmat, a gay Muslim who defused accusations of racism by accepting their premise: "Someone says to me, 'You are racist' ... My response is usually that does not excuse your incompetence, laziness, sexism, or homophobia."[29]

Rhoda's approach was similar. "When people criticise this government, I am convinced that they are racists," she said provocatively, "but what I am sad about is that we prove these racists to be correct."[30]

***

Mbeki's racial filter on the HIV/Aids crisis also applied to the crisis in Zimbabwe, South Africa's northern neighbor, where President Robert Mugabe was still clinging to power after decades.

In 2000, Mugabe's party, the Zimbabwe African National Union – Popular Front (ZANU-PF), suffered a setback when it lost a constitutional referendum to expand his presidential powers. A new opposition, the Movement for Democratic Change (MDC), led by trade unionist Morgan Tsvangirai, began to pose a political challenge.

In response, Mugabe launched a program of "land reform" targeting Zimbabwe's white commercial farmers. Many were driven off their land, which was supposed to be redistributed to "veterans" of Zimbabwe's liberation war, but which largely ended up with ZANU-PF loyalists. The country, once a net food exporter, began to starve. Meanwhile, Mugabe continued to crack down on the opposition, arresting dissidents, silencing the press, and rigging elections.

Mbeki refused to criticize Mugabe, who cast his actions as righteous opposition to racist neo-colonialism. Instead, Mbeki pursued what he called "quiet diplomacy," which allowed Mugabe to continue destroying his country.

As these events unfolded, Mbeki faced no criticism or opposition from within his own party. No ANC office-holder, high or low, dared to question his complicity in Zimbabwe's collapse, though Cosatu belatedly rallied to the cause of the MDC, with which it shared a bond through the shared enterprise of trade unionism. (Mbeki's obeisance to Mugabe was such that he would continue to praise the dictator, and proclaim his

---

29   Zackie Achmat, quoted in Elaine Salo et al. "Black Gays & Mugabes." *Chimurenga*, Vol. 4 (2003). p. 27.

30   Rhoda Kadalie, quoted by Ryland Fisher. *Race*. Auckland Park: Jacana Media, 2007. p. 194.

regime to be a legitimate expression of the democratic will of ordinary Zimbabweans, long after Mbeki himself had retired.[31])

Rhoda was one of the few public intellectuals with "struggle" credentials who dared to speak out against Mbeki's policy — what she called "our president's unqualified support for Zimbabwean dictator Robert Mugabe and his ruthless reign of terror."[32] She did not blame Mbeki alone: to her, the Zimbabwe crisis was not just a failure of African solidarity politics, but also the racist condescension of Western governments, particularly the United Kingdom and the United States. She wrote in 2003:

Why do world leaders from western countries, in particular, tolerate dictators simply because they are black? Colonial guilt and its corollary racial oppression have become so entrenched that both sides have been unable to snap out of what have become continental pathologies. Why do they think we should make do with lower standards of democracy that they would not dare suggest to their electorates? Do they not have a greater duty to ensure that democracy works in Africa because of colonisation?[33]

As the ANC continued to coddle the Mugabe regime — famously declining to arrest Zimbabwean First Lady Grace Mugabe after she assaulted a model in a hotel while on a shopping trip to Johannesburg in 2017 — Rhoda continued to criticize the South African governments' foreign policy, particularly on Zimbabe, and suggested that its contempt for human rights abroad reflected its failure to uphold the values of the new Constitution at home:

While the Mugabes live the high life, buying property abroad, frequenting the best hospitals, sending their kids to the best private education institutions, their citizens are languishing in abject poverty.

This moral code is what the ANC supports against its own constitutional democratic state and the rule of law. The ANC's support for violence against women is confirmed by granting diplomatic immunity to

---

31   Rhoda Kadalie. "Mugabe: What is Thabo Mbeki smoking?". PoliticsWeb, reprinted from *Die Burger*, translated from the Afrikaans, 14 Aug. 2013. URL: https://www.politicsweb.co.za/news-and-analysis/mugabe-what-is-thabo-mbeki-smoking. Accessed on 28 Mar. 2022.
32   Rhoda Kadalie. "Hard-won freedom must not remain a paper tiger." *Business Day*, 13 Dec. 2002. Published in Rhoda Kadalie. *In Your Face*. Cape Town: Tafelberg, 2009. p. 170
33   Rhoda Kadalie. *Business Day*, 22 May 2003.

Grace Mugabe, who is nothing but a thug, a shrew, a skollie, in Cape Flats parlance.[34]

Few others, in the early 2000s, dared to criticize Mbeki's policies — least of all if they were ANC members in good standing. One member of Parliament, Pregs Govender, became more critical of the Mbeki government after she resigned in opposition to a corrupt foreign arms deal that cost the country untold billions of rands, and embroiled the ANC in corruption.

But few others spoke out. They were afraid of retaliation by Mbeki, who held the party in ideological thrall and controlled access to plum appointments, government contracts, and "black economic empowerment" opportunities in the corporate world.

Rhoda was furious, and her indignation at the erosion of South Africa's hard-won democratic culture motivated her columns. As she later wrote:

Under President Mbeki's erratic rule, a time of political unease, many comrades who fought for democracy and freedom shut up in the face of those who rewarded the acquiescent with position and patronage. Those of us who refused to be silent became the enemy. ... I then veered into writing about everything and anything that smacked of political opportunism, government ineptitude, and corruption. All over the place people succumbed to political pressure for silence, urged to be forever grateful to the ANC for ushering in our liberation, no matter how corrupt and self-serving public officials were. With others, I, too became targeted by former political allies, for simply appropriating the right to criticise government.

...

And so, like sheep, we feared being called 'racist,' 'right-wing,' 'a sellout,' 'disloyal,' 'a traitor' and 'unpatriotic.' These epithets were so powerful that many were prepared to sacrifice the truth. Even academics feared to ply their trade in public, lest they be construed as reactionary.

...

34 Rhoda Kadalie. "SA weeps as Grace, the 'skollie' goes free." *The Citizen,* 25 Aug. 2017. URL: https://www.citizen.co.za/news/opinion/1625987/ sa-weeps-as-grace-the-skollie-goes-free/. Accessed on 13 Apr. 2022.

Rhoda: 'Comrade Kadalie, You Are Out of Order!'

Whereas my feminist voice had been nurtured and cultivated during the struggle and by the struggle, I was suddenly expected to shut up after 1999.[35]

But Rhoda would not "shut up" — even when she found herself, at times, the lone voice of opposition.

---

35   Rhoda Kadalie. *In Your Face*, p. 8. 10-11.

Chapter 13:
Contrarian

*"I asked the BBC how they got to hear of me and they said they were
looking for an opinionated, cocky, arrogant, black South African
and the people said 'Rhoda Kadalie.'"[1]*

Rhoda had unique credibility to criticize the post-apartheid government.
She had suffered under apartheid, and resisted it. Her organization,
Impumelelo, was actually trying to help the government succeed. She
had fought for black liberation, and for women's liberation; she was also
a Kadalie, and her grandfather had fought bravely for civil rights long
before the ANC had become a political force.

Through her pen, she would continue to fight for the vision of a
"Rainbow Nation" — and for Clements Kadalie's vision of a free people,
beholden neither to radical socialists on the left nor racial nationalists on
the right.

The mood in post-apartheid South Africa, despite all of the country's
challenges, was euphoric at first. The nation, once a pariah, was the
darling of the world. President Nelson Mandela — known affectionately
by his clan name, Madiba — was a global icon. And South African sports
teams enjoyed a string of remarkable successes, winning the Rugby World
Cup in 1995 and the Africa Cup of Nations soccer tournament in 1996. At
the closing ceremonies of the 1996 Summer Olympics in Atlanta, the new
South African flag was the last to be hoisted, following the gold medal
victory of marathoner Josia Thugwane.

South African musicians and artists returned to the world stage, as
cultural boycotts ended and the world delighted in South Africa's diverse
cultural offerings. Vicky Sampson's song "Afrikan Dream" was ubiquitous
on local radio: "In my African dream, there's a new tomorrow/My African
dream, is a dream that we can follow."

That celebratory mood, however, was accompanied by political
conformity. Few South Africans, black or white, dared to criticize the new
government, which claimed — rightly or wrongly — to have brought about
the era of liberation. To speak out against that government's failings was
a sign of racist whinging, if you were white; or ingratitude, if you were

---

1   Rhoda Kadalie, quoted by Ryland Fisher. *Race*. Auckland Park: Jacana
     Media, 2007. p. 56.

black. A political debate that had once been vigorous became suffocated by political correctness. Groupthink and self-censorship took root.

Rhoda was among those who dared to raise their voices, saying what few others within the ANC were bold enough to say in public.

When she began writing occasional columns for the *Mail & Guardian* in the late 1990s, the paper was provoking the wrath of the ruling party by devoting resources to cutting-edge investigative journalism about the new government — including allegations of corruption and mismanagement.

One of the new South Africa's first major scandals was a notorious arms deal, in which the Mandela administration bypassed South Africa's respected domestic arms industry and bought foreign weapons at high prices, amid promises that the manufacturers would create new jobs in the country.

The arrangement was criticized as unnecessary and expensive, and was suspected of being corrupt. The ANC managed to undermine several investigations into the deal, including Parliament's own, suggesting the potential for wider corruption in the future.

The ANC chafed at coverage of the arms deal, and resented the criticism that it had begun to receive from the *M&G* and other media outlets. It began to argue that the South African media was part of a white backlash against its agenda — despite the fact that the media was predominantly liberal, and broadly supported the ANC's agenda. If anything, the media were dismissive of the political opposition.

In 2000, the Human Rights Commission began holding hearings into supposed racism in the country's newsrooms. The proceedings had a show trial atmosphere, as editors — many of whom were white — had to defend themselves, cheered on by the ANC.

Rhoda took on the institution from which she had resigned, blasting it as a "handmaiden" of the Mbeki administration. She wrote:

> *Is the lesson of Zimbabwe not imminent enough? Or is Mbeki following Robert Mugabe's example to achieve his not-so-hidden agenda? Mugabe also used race as a rallying point before his country's election to intimidate his opposition. ...*
>
> *More worrying and equally astounding is the support Mbeki gets for his political agenda from his forever-faithful handmaidens, the Human Rights Commission and the SABC[2] — institutions that should be*

---

2   South African Broadcasting Corporation, the state-owned broadcaster.

independent of the government and whose duty it is to serve the entire public without fear or favour.

This obsession with race is nothing but a cover-up for non-delivery in the public sector and a means of obscuring issues of national importance. While the public is clamoring for solutions to crime, sexual violence, AIDS, poverty, corruption and job creation, the government is dabbling with race and racism.

What's more, money is made available for these futile exercises while there is virtually no money for development. While the role of the commission is to monitor socioeconomic rights, it has decided to prioritise racism.

...

Barney Pityana and his colleagues have reduced the Human Rights Commission to a race industry where his "black consciousness" hang-ups seem to play themselves out in public.[3]

It was not that Rhoda believed there was no racism in the media. On the contrary, she told an interviewer later that the media, dominated by white men, "are racist in the way they report things, in the way they represent issues and the way they relegate certain stories to the back of the newspaper."[4] But she saw the attempt to use the Human Rights Commission as an effort by the ANC to silence criticism.

In a separate letter to the *M&G*,[5] Rhoda urged editors to "[I]gnore the subpoena from this discredited organization," slamming Pityana and the Human Rights Commission for having become the "self-proclaimed thought police,"[6] and calling the subpoenas "a gross violation of freedom of expression and an attempt to prescribe to the press what they should be thinking and writing."[7]

---

3   Rhoda Kadalie. "The racism debate obscures other issues." *Mail & Guardian*, 1 to 7 Sep. 2000.

4   Rhoda Kadalie, quoted by Ryland Fisher. *Race*. Auckland Park: Jacana Media, 2007. p. 179.

5   Evidence wa ka Ngobeni. "Sheena Duncan Quits Over Racism Probe." *Mail & Guardian*, 25 Feb. 2000.

6   Rhoda Kadalie, quoted by Hans Moleman. "Racistische meetlat voor pers Z-Afrika." De Volkskrant, 19 Feb. 2000. p. 4. Translated from the Dutch via Google Translate.

7   Chris McGreal. "Racism inquiry calls F T editor; Foreign media could face South African hearings." *Guardian*, 21 Feb. 2000. p. 13.

International journalists agreed — especially after the British *Financial Times* was subpoenaed over a 1996 article that documented the role of radical Islam in PAGAD, provoking criticism from the Media Review Network, a radical Muslim organization devoted to what it perceived as negative portrayals of Muslims in the South African media, as well as demonizing Israel.[8] The World Association of Newspapers urged President Mbeki to intervene and cancel the subpoenas (he did not).[9]

Later, when Pityana avoided responding to criticism of the media inquiry while on a trip abroad, she told the *Mail & Guardian* that Parliament should censure the Human Rights Commission "for bringing the country into disrepute at a time when (President Thabo) Mbeki's government image is extremely positive nationally and internationally," which was still true at the time; the HIV/Aids debacle had not yet turned him into an international pariah. She added: "Perhaps the commission should start earning their keep by doing what they have been appointed to do, that is, to protect and promote human rights in South Africa, and that includes the human rights of the media, too!"[10]

Despite the unease that many journalists felt, Rhoda was one of the few voices in the media who took on the racism hearings directly. Many were grateful for her stance. Professor Keyan Tomaselli of the University of Natal Centre for Cultural and Media Studies wrote to her to commend her for her courage in speaking out, noting that while the issue of racism in the media was a legitimate one, the methodology that was being used by the commission was dressed in "psychobabble" that had brought "cultural studies into disrepute."[11]

In later years, the threat to press freedom would be far more direct. In 2010, the Zuma–led ANC began pushing for a Protection of Information Bill, which would allow the government wide discretion to declare information about public affairs to be "secret," and to punish its publication. These powers would have echoed the censorship of the apartheid regime, and Rhoda and others raised the alarm about the pending legislation. She wrote:

Silencing criticism is the hallmark of liberation leaders who govern for too long and who use the state's resources to enrich themselves.

---

8   Rhoda Kadalie, quoted by Chris McGreal, ibid.
9   Bronwen Roberts. "Malaise croissant autour d'auditions de medias sur le racisme." Agence France Presse. 21 Feb. 2000.
10 Rhoda Kadalie, quoted by Evidence wa ka Ngobeni. "Kadalie Takes Another Swing At 'Curiously Invisible' Pityana." *Mail & Guardian*, 25 Feb. 2000.
11 Keyan Tomaselli. Letter to Rhoda Kadalie. 28 Feb. 2000.

Critics of the bill have argued that it undermines democracy by allowing ministers to classify any information, to the point of refusing to acknowledge that it even exists, in order to protect what the government perceives to be in the national interest and national security.

As liberation leaders increasingly come to mirror their former oppressors through undemocratic practices, corruption, moral turpitude, dereliction of duty and failure to deliver, the first line of defence is to shut down the media. The very media that gave them succour and publicity when they were denied a voice becomes the enemy of the state as soon as the state becomes the enemy of the people.

The notion of the national interest has always been invoked by liberation leaders the further removed they become from the nation. The more entrenched politicians become in their profligate lifestyles, the more they view and mistake their own vested interests for the national interest. The less they act on our behalf the more they pretend to speak on our behalf.[12]

Eventually, after intense local opposition and international attention, the idea was scrapped. But the threat to press freedom never disappeared — and it was sharpened by the media's own obeisance to political correctness.

***

A consistent theme developed in Rhoda's writing: she spoke out against the ANC's attempt to silence dissent, both internally and in debates within broader South African society. And she urged fellow South Africans to be more outspoken.

In 2001, she delivered a lecture at the Grahamstown Arts Festival titled "Silencing Critique," which was later published as a journal article. She warned that South Africa's young democracy was susceptible to the same undemocratic impulses that had appeared in Zimbabwe to the north over the previous 18 months:

Victory over colonisation meant no criticism of Mugabe and Zanu PF, for at least twenty years, during which time Mugabe entrenched and consolidated his power base with patronage, cronyism, corruption, the marginalization of independent and critical voices and the use of the race card whenever it suited them.

---

12   Rhoda Kadalie. "Liberation leaders now act like their oppressors." *Business Day*, 21 Sep. 2010.

Rhoda: 'Comrade Kadalie, You Are Out of Order!'

Much the same thing can happen in this country, in milder and subtler ways, when we cease to be vigilant.[13]

She attacked "white guilt," which she said made white South Africans "bend over blackwards." She declared: "A truly democratic society requires of whites to appropriate that freedom on an equal basis with black people regardless. Self-censorship, like repressive laws and practices, not only silences journalists, but also victimises ordinary citizens by depriving them/us of our right to full information."[14]

Few were quite so courageous. Rhoda's background allowed her to be outspoken on issues from which many South Africans — including journalists — shied away, for fear of being called racist, if they were white, or fear of being ostracized by the ANC leadership if they were black.

She was willing to be a contrarian — *the* contrarian — in an age of conformity.

For example, Rhoda gave voice to the fears shared by South Africans of all races about violent crime, a topic that made many in the media uncomfortable, though the subject could hardly be avoided. The ruling ANC often dismissed those fears as the "whingeing" of the disgruntled racist white minority.[15] But as a black anti-apartheid activist who had championed the cause of prison reform as a member of the Human Rights Commission, Rhoda could not be so easily ignored.

She often drew attention to the fact that many of the victims of crime were women, and children, particularly in black communities — the most vulnerable members of South African society, for whom the fight for democracy had been waged. "Bludgeoned to numbness by the constant reporting of the most heinous of crimes perpetrated against females, as a country we seem clueless about addressing the problem," she wrote in 2017.[16] And when white farmers — the "producers of food security" —

13   Rhoda Kadalie. "Silencing Critique." *Pretexts: literary and cultural studies*, Vol. 10, No. 2, 2001. p. 219. Based on a lecture at the Grahamstown Arts Festival, 6 Jul. 2001.
14   Ibid., p. 224.
15   Rory Carroll. "South Africans told to stop 'whingeing' about crime." *Guardian*, 20 Jun. 2006. URL: https://www.theguardian.com/world/2006/jun/21/southafrica.rorycarroll. Accessed on 9 Mar. 2022.
16   Rhoda Kadalie. "Women's safety in SA? Oh, please." *The Citizen*, 4 Aug. 2017. URL: https://www.citizen.co.za/news/opinion/1598264/government-is-clueless-when-it-comes-to-womens-safety/. Accessed on 13 Apr. 2022.

were singled out for attack, she noted, "their wives are often brutalised by the most vicious attacks imaginable."[17]

She also wrote:

> *I must admit it is hard as a woman to listen to the news. Violence against women and children abounds. South Africa's rapists and murderers are equal opportunity violators – two- and three-year-old girls, young women, pregnant women, grandmothers and farmers' wives are all victims of the misogyny that lies deep within the psyche of South African offenders.*
>
> ...
>
> *Despite the existence of an ANC Women's League, the Gender Commission and women's ministry, nothing of significance is done to stem the tide of violence against women.*[18]

The crime wave had many causes: centuries of violent conflicts, the brutality of apartheid, staggering economic inequality, and institutional chaos, to name a few. Rhoda traced the problem to a decline in the rule of law — first under apartheid, and then under the post-apartheid government:

> *Criminologists and psychologists are wracking their brains to try and understand why we are so lawless. But the answer is really simple. Our defiance stems from a national psyche nurtured by a corrupt state under both apartheid and ANC majority rule. Shaped by apartheid, our psyche has deteriorated under ANC rule – a political party that embodies no respect for the rule of law and which has cultivated an ethos that has systematically destroyed constitutional bodies designed to uphold the rule of law.*[19]

Rhoda also highlighted more immediate causes, such as lenient government policies, corruption in the ANC, and mismanagement within the South African Police Services (SAPS), a force that had previously been

17   Ibid.
18   Rhoda Kadalie. "The destruction of women's lives continues unabated." *The Citizen*, 19 May 2017. URL: https://www.citizen.co.za/news/opinion/1518467/the-destruction-of-womens-lives-continues-unabated/. Accessed on 13 Apr. 2022.
19   Rhoda Kadalie. "Why are we so lawless?". PoliticsWeb, reprinted from *Die Burger*, translated from the Afrikaans, 18 Jan. 2011. URL: https://www.politicsweb.co.za/news-and-analysis/why-are-we-so-lawless. Accessed on 28 Mar. 2022.

used to patrol the racial and political boundaries of apartheid, rather than to investigate and prevent crime.

Already, in 2003, she had written that President Mbeki and the ANC had failed to tackle the problem:

A few weeks before National Women's Day, eight-year-old Sasha-Lee Crook was snatched from her home. She was found dead, mutilated beyond recognition, on a vacant piece of land near her home. The police did not do the most basic of investigations.

...

Why do we as citizens accept this? Why do we accept the current state of affairs as a quiet admission that government is incapable of protecting its citizens? Surely we should demand more? Surely an economy cannot flourish if its base is not protected. Word that hundreds of prisoners are to be released adds to the despair, not because they should not be released but because petty criminals often become murderers. In this country offenders kill for five rands, for a cellphone or a handbag.

...

Lack of governance in this country is palpable. Public sector delivery is weak, crime is rampant and poverty due to extremely high levels of unemployment plague[s] this new democracy. The African National Congress (ANC) government should take control and start governing.

The president and deputy president need to fly around the world less and get to grips with the needs of citizens and the seriousness of the situation and tackle the criminal justice system with all the commitment it deserves. Or else national police commissioner, Jackie Selebi, should admit the problem is too big for him and do something drastic.[20]

Rhoda concluded her column as only she could: "As someone who strongly supported the ANC government, I suddenly realise that if I emigrate it will not be because blacks are governing this country. It will be because blacks are not governing."

Beyond pointing out the problem, Rhoda urged the government to adopt solutions. To restore faith in the criminal justice system, she said, and to deter future criminals, South Africa should set up a system of "community courts": "The courts would not only benefit victims and

---

20   Rhoda Kadalie. ""President must get to grips with crime." *Business Day*, 14 Aug. 2003.

deal with perpetrators effectively, but will serve as an education tool and deterrent at community level for those who think that killing sprees are fun."[21]

But the government showed little interest in ordinary policing, much less judicial innovation. Rhoda eventually concluded that political corruption was the most important factor enabling violent crime. In 2009, she wrote: "[O]ur law makers in Parliament are the worst law breakers. Rotten to the core, they are to blame for the crime in this country, and no one is more articulate about this than prisoners, gangsters and drug lords."[22]

She often returned to one scandal in particular, known as Travelgate, in which scores of members of Parliament — not just from the ANC — were found in 2004 to have abused vouchers intended for them to travel back and forth to their home communities.[23] Instead of punishing the offenders, the ANC's parliamentary leaders attempted to cover up the scandal, firing financial officer Harry Charlton and prosecuting a small proportion of those implicated.[24] To Rhoda, and many others, Travelgate was further evidence that the entire institution of Parliament had become corrupt.

As Rhoda wrote for *Die Burger* in one of her first columns for that Afrikaans newspaper, in 2011:

Remember the Travelgate Scandal. It exposed how corrupt the inner sanctum of Parliament was. Instead of firing the implicated MPs, Speakers Frene Ginwala and Baleka Mbete, kept the lid on this sordid saga, knowing full well that should all those implicated be charged, the dissolution of Parliament would in all likelihood have been a possibility. Add to that, Baleka Mbete, former Deputy Speaker of Parliament, who was found guilty of obtaining a car license fraudulently. For her sins, she

21 Rhoda Kadalie. "Women abuse: here's a plan." *The Citizen*, 1 Dec. 2017. URL: https://www.citizen.co.za/news/opinion/1745834/women-abuse-heres-a-plan/. Accessed on 13 Apr. 2022.

22 Rhoda Kadalie. "Why so much is rotten in the state of SA today." *Business Day*, 8 Oct. 2009.

23 Andrew Meldrum. "40 accused in South African MPs' fraud case." *Guardian*, 23 Jan. 2005. URL: https://www.theguardian.com/world/2005/jan/24/southafrica.andrewmeldrum. Accessed on 25 Mar. 2002.

24 Andisiwe Makinana. "Appeal victory for fired Travelgate whistleblower." *Sunday Argus*, 17 Sep. 2011. URL: https://www.pressreader.com/south-africa/weekend-argus-saturday-edition/20110917/281698316474838. Accessed on 25 Mar. 2022.

was promoted to Speaker of Parliament, while her whistleblower, John Muller died in penury and obscurity.[25]

Rhoda believed that corrupt behavior by South Africa's new leaders not only set a bad example for the rest of the country, but actively covered up links between senior government officials and the crime wave terrorizing ordinary people -- and events tended to prove her right. Just a few years after she challenged police commissioner Jackie Selebi to take drastic action, he would be investigated for corruption involving ties to organized crime. He was eventually convicted in 2010, confirming Rhoda's suspicion that crime was rampant in the streets because of corruption at the top.

Many political commentators were reluctant to write about violent crime, partly because it was simply so traumatic, and partly because doing so would embarrass the new government. (One notable exception was journalist Jonny Steinberg, who wrote about crime and punishment in post-apartheid South Africa in scholarly detail.) Rhoda challenged the taboo, writing openly about her own personal experiences with crime, as well as experiences related to her by others.

In 2013, for example, she wrote:

Many years ago I was a witness to the murder of my neighbour by a young white South African man. I mention his race because this was pivotal to the cavalier way the police dealt with this case.

Apart from botching the basic forensics, they released the guy on bail and soon he escaped. Years later he was caught in a major drug bust. I was called in as a witness and he was eventually sentenced to a long term in jail but while he was on the run, this incompetence caused the family much pain and anger.

When my laptop was stolen in September 2012 in the Waterfront, the CCTV footage that recorded it all was not even manned. Worse, the surveillance cameras are not even connected to SAPS in the Waterfront. The police refused to look at the footage immediately after the theft. They did so the next day, by which time the suspects had disappeared with the laptop.

...

25   Rhoda Kadalie. "Why are we so lawless?" PoliticsWeb, reprinted from *Die Burger*, 18 Jan. 2011. URL: https://www.politicsweb.co.za/news-and-analysis/why-are-we-so-lawless. Accessed on 26 Mar. 2022.

The sheer incompetence with a simple case like mine is mind-boggling and bodes ill for the more complex cases of murder and armed robbery. Spend a day in court, and it becomes clear why we have so many repeat offenders, high rates of bail, and even higher rates of recidivism.

...

Police incompetence is shrouded in bureaucracy and red tape when more than half of them are barely literate and qualified to do their work. That is why private security firms have become more popular than the police and exceed them in numbers by nearly 75%.

This incompetence results in seriously low conviction rates. ... [T]he question arises whether the R40bn of the total budget spent on the police, is value for money?[26]

Already, by 2006, Rhoda had seen so much crime, and heard so many horror stories, that her views on the death penalty had changed — from opposition to cautious support — and she argued that South Africa's ruling class was allowing crime to flourish because of its own corruption:

We cannot explain these evil crimes in terms of our past even though apartheid did play a role in brutalising people in ways we shall never know. Nor can we blame it all on poverty because many countries with similar and worse poverty do not have the levels of crime we see here. So what is going on here?

...

Many politicians are perceived by criminals to have become instantly wealthy. The criminals reckon that politicians do not have to be educated or work hard to be rich, so why can't we do the same? They are not role models, and so through crime and drug trafficking we gangsters can also live rich. What we see in townships is the glamourisation of crime, and many have told me that what they earn through real work is pocket money compared with the money they get through crime.

Government has failed to act and set boundaries for criminals, so criminals use their anger and criminality in a pseudopolitical context to

---

26   Rhoda Kadalie. "South Africa's embarrassing criminal justice system." PoliticsWeb, reprinted from *Die Burger*, translated from the Afrikaans, 27 Feb. 2013. URL: https://www.politicsweb.co.za/news-and-analysis/south-africas-embarrassing-criminal-justice-system. Accessed on 28 Mar. 2022.

continually test the limits of a weak justice system and its boundaries, which are extremely malleable and elastic.

...

Prison has no effect. With a rape culture that is endemic parole is often threatening to the public and should be feared. That is why people are calling for the death penalty.

As someone who has opposed the death penalty all my life — through columns and speeches and letters to the editor — I am beginning to rethink my firm conviction on this matter, only insofar as SA is concerned. The only way we will be safe is when those who take life are denied the right to life as the only means to reassure the public that murder will not be tolerated. Further, government has repeatedly pardoned criminals with heinous track records, some of whom committed even more horrendous crimes on their release only to be sent back to prison again.

...

Government is not interventionist enough. In fact, the tolerance of white-collar crime and the growth of the corruption industry among political "gangsters" sets the context for gangsters who constantly explore ways to buck the system.

Before 1994 we robustly sang, "We shall overcome." Today it more appropriately means, "Ons sal iets oor kom" ["Something will befall us"], if we do not do something drastic soon.[27]

But Rhoda did not just hold the government responsible for crime: she began to speak out against the fear and complacency of South Africans in accepting shoddy governance, on crime and other matters.

For example, she said, the media were complicit in neglecting the crime wave: "[W]e lack crime reporters as we had in the old days to keep a microscope on the findings of the courts and on the conviction rates. When judges, magistrates, prosecutors, investigating officers and detectives know their work is hidden from public gaze, they too become a law unto themselves and unaccountable as I witnessed in court."[28]

---

27   Rhoda Kadalie. "Evil depth of SA's crime calls for drastic measures." *Business Day*, 4 May 2006. Published in Rhoda Kadalie. *In Your Face*. Cape Town: Tafelberg, 2009. pp. 165–7.
28   Rhoda Kadalie. "SA's criminal justice system stinks." PoliticsWeb, reprinted from *Die Burger*, translated from the Afrikaans, 10 Oct. 2012.

The complacency of the media in tackling crime was reflected throughout the political class, Rhoda said, including among many who had supported the struggle against apartheid. For example, she wrote, violent crime against women was so rampant that "[b]eing a woman in this country is life-threatening, despite the president's lip service to gender equality. Women and girl children constantly have to look over their shoulders."[29] But feminists, and journalists, were muted: "All the activism around gender equality and sexual equality that was part of the liberation rah-rah has now evaporated now that the ANC is in power. And what I find very troubling is the self-censorship among women in the struggle."[30]

The fight against that self-censorship, among activists and in the media, soon became Rhoda's focus.

* * *

One of Rhoda's most frequent targets was the South African Broadcasting Corporation (SABC), which offered fawning coverage of the ANC, while dismissing the DA and other opposition parties.

The SABC was supposed to be politically neutral, but its news division had once functioned as a mouthpiece for the apartheid regime, and the ANC seemed eager to use it to the same effect.

Rhoda took the lead among South African pundits in pointing out the SABC's bias and conflicts of interest.

In 2003, for example, she took on SABC board member Dr. Thabane Vincent Maphai after he wrote an incendiary article in the newsletter of the left-leaning Institute for Justice and Reconciliation equating Democratic Alliance leader Tony Leon — an opponent of apartheid — with apartheid-era leader P.W. Botha.[31] Maphai had also tried to link Leon, a Jew, with the neo-Nazi Afrikaner Weerstandsbeweging organization.

URL: https://www.politicsweb.co.za/news-and-analysis/sas-criminal-justice-system-stinks. Accessed on 28 Mar. 2022.

29   Rhoda Kadalie. "Now the media thinks it can silence 'whingers'." *Business Day*, 13 Jul. 2006. p. 11.

30   Rhoda Kadalie, quoted by UN Integrated Regional Information Networks. "Sexual Assault Hidden in Culture of Silence." Africa News, 2 Mar. 2006.

31   Vincent Maphai. "The ANC Misses a Trick." *The SA Reconciliation Barometer*. Vol. 1, Iss. 3. Institute for Justice and Reconciliation, Cape Town. Oct. 2003. URL: https://web.archive.org/web/20041117084905/http://www.ijr.org.za/barometer/single%20A4%20.pdf. Accessed on 7 Mar. 2022.

In her response, she noted wryly that Maphai had, at least, proven "SABC Board member Thami Mazwai's suggestion that objectivity is a myth, correct."[32] Maphai then sent a hateful e-mail to Rhoda: "As a former friend, I thought you needed help. ... I have known you to be an empty tin which constantly make [sic] a great deal of noise. ... It is time for you to shut up now, take a breather and try to fill something into your empty head."[33]

Rhoda regarded the email as a trophy, and shared it with amused and delighted friends. She had only just begun.

In May 2005, Rhoda criticized SABC head of news Snuki Zikalala for admitting — at a celebration of World Press Freedom Day — that the state broadcaster was "not neutral" in its political coverage.[34] The SABC's communications department attempted to defend itself, writing a letter to the editor of the *Business Day* to rebut her accusation that the SABC newsroom was staffed with "sycophantic party apparatchiks whose sinecures come courtesy of government's redeployment policy."[35]

But Rhoda would have the last laugh.

On August 9, 2005, during celebrations for National Women's Day, the SABC reported that Deputy President Phumzile Mlambo-Ngcuka had addressed a mass meeting of ANC activists in Johannesburg. Mlambo-Ngcuka had only recently been appointed to her post, after Mbeki had summarily dismissed Jacob Zuma over allegations of corruption, provoking a backlash from the party's left-wing factions.

When Rhoda flipped the TV channel to e.TV (now known as eNCA), the only private broadcast television network in the country, she saw news coverage of exactly the same event. But unlike the SABC, e.TV's news broadcast showed footage of the crowd in Johannesburg booing the deputy president vociferously.

Rhoda immediately wrote a *Business Day* column which praised e News, noting that, without it, the SABC's omission would have gone unnoticed. The SABC responded immediately, claiming that it had no reporter at the event at the time the booing took place.

---

32   Rhoda Kadalie. "'Embedded' Media Runs Gauntlet of Credibility." *Business Day.* 4 Dec. 2003.
33   Thabani Vincent Maphai. Email, 5 Dec. 2003. Helen Suzman Archive.
34   Snuki Zikalala, quoted in "DA takes aim at 'biased' SABC." Independent Online, 5 May 2005. URL: https://www.iol.co.za/news/south-africa/da-takes-aim-at-biased-sabc-240421. Accessed on 21 Mar 2022.
35   Rhoda Kadalie, quoted by General Manager: SABC Corporate Communications. "Adjust your set." *Business Day*, 31 May 2005. p. 12.

The next day, e News showed extended footage of the event that indicated clearly that the SABC did, indeed, have a reporter at the event when the deputy president was booed.

Rhoda's exposé of the discrepancy between the networks' reporting led to the SABC apologizing to the public and firing a senior communications director.[36] In a statement, the SABC apologized "unreservedly" to viewers "for not airing the footage," adding that it "further wishes to assure viewers that its editorial autonomy and integrity does not prevent it from airing negative footage even when it involves senior government officials."

But the SABC kept digging. It claimed that it did not have the footage of the deputy president being booed because its freelance cameraman, Sonjay Singh, had arrived late to the event. Footage from e.TV then clearly showed him at the event.

Zikalala then claimed that the cameraman felt that the booing had been "irrelevant" and had not filmed it.[37] However, Singh angrily disagreed: "I did my work and everything is on tape," he protested to the *Rapport* newspaper.[38] An internal SABC investigation blamed the cameraman, and fired him.[39] Singh responded by admitting he had only sent the SABC 15 minutes of footage, but protested that his work had never been questioned by the editors before.[40]

Rhoda reported in her column a year later: "In response to the investigation launched by the new [SABC] CEO, Dali Mpofu, the news editor, Amrit Manga, suggested that perhaps cameraman Sonjay Singh had not raised the issue because of his perception that news inimical to the interests of the ANC was frowned upon and would not be favourably received."[41]

---

36   South African Press Association. "SABC apologises to the public." 18 Aug. 2005. URL: https://www.news24.com/news24/sabc-apologises-to-the-public-20050818. Accessed on 19 Jan. 2022.

37   Zikalala, quoted by ibid.

38   Sonjay Singh, quoted by "Cameraman could sue SABC." News24.com, 28 Aug. 2005. URL:https://www.news24.com/News24/Cameraman-could-sue-SABC-20050828. Accessed on 21 Mar. 2022.

39   Donwald Pressly. "Cameraman blamed in SABC bias probe." *Mail & Guardian*, 5 Sep. 2005. URL: https://mg.co.za/article/2005-09-05-cameraman-blamed-in-sabc-bias-probe/. Accessed on 21 Mar. 2022.

40   Wendy Jasson da Costa. "SABC tarnished my reputation, says cameraman." Independent Online, 6 Sep. 2005. URL: https://www.iol.co.za/news/politics/sabc-tarnished-my-reputation-says-cameraman-252767. Accessed on 21 Mar. 2022.

41   Rhoda Kadalie. "Obedient SABC seems content to can democracy." *Business Day*, 15 Jun. 2006. p. 13.

Regardless, the reputation of the SABC as a ruling party mouthpiece had been confirmed.

Rhoda continued to criticize the SABC's obsequious behavior, such as censoring a documentary about the president in 2006 that the ANC apparently feared would be unflattering. Later, Pippa Green, the former head of SABC radio news, who had once pushed back against Rhoda's criticisms, claimed that Zikalala had censored pundits known to be independent from the ANC — including the president's own brother, Moeletsi Mbeki, who emerged as a critic of the ruling party's approach to business.[42]

In a 2007 column, as the country was gripped by "service delivery" protests, often violent confrontations between disgruntled local residents and municipal officials, Rhoda blamed the SABC for failing to inform the citizens of South Africa's new democracy. "When the state contributes to the national dumbing down of the public and uses its media to keep the public ignorant, it shouldn't be surprised when the public riots in reaction to poor service delivery."[43]

Her battles with the SABC continued for years. In 2010, she accused the SABC of failing adequately to cover major national scandals, such as the arms deal and electricity blackouts, simply because they would cause embarrassment to the ANC.[44] And in the Zuma era, she noted that the SABC had made a seamless transition from protecting Mbeki to protecting his successor "through the usual censorship by omission and the broadcasting sabotage of opposition parties."[45]

The SABC tried to dismiss her criticism. But it failed: Rhoda's cynical view of the SABC became conventional wisdom. As she quipped during one exchange: "No one ever refutes any of the allegations I make, because they are so obviously true."[46]

***

42   Rhoda Kadalie. "Secrets and lies: time for Zikalala to take the stand." *Business Day*, 29 Jun. 2006. p. 11.
43   Rhoda Kadalie. "Dumbed-down SABC still its ANC master's voice." *Business Day*, 19 Apr. 2007. p. 13.
44   Rhoda Kadalie. "Mokoetle's record bodes ill for change at the SABC." *Business Day*, 28 Jan. 2010.
45   Rhoda Kadalie. "Bad news for poor as SABC freefall continues." *Business Day*, 15 Jun. 2010.
46   Rhoda Kadalie. "Denials are useless." Letter to the editor. *Business Day*, 7 Jul. 2009.

Yet Rhoda did not criticize the SABC alone. She felt that the South African media as a whole were unfair to the opposition. Knowing that the ruling ANC held them in suspicion, journalists and editors often went to great pains to praise minor ANC successes, while inflating the DA's flaws.

Race also played a role. The fact that most journalists in the media establishment were still white meant that some labored under the burden of historical guilt, and did not want to be seen as hostile to a black-led government. This meant that even when they criticized the ANC, they often took a harsher attitude towards the opposition — especially the DA, whose leadership was predominantly white.

Rhoda was having none of it: she had no patience for white guilt, any more than black sycophancy.

In a column in September 2005, titled "Where are journalists to speak truth to power?", Rhoda argued: "While the media decries Robert Mugabe's tyrannical treatment of the Zimbabwean opposition party, the Movement for Democratic Change, it does the same with its disdain for opposition as though criticism is its prerogative alone. ... The media needs to speak truth to power at all times, even about those it dislikes!"[47]

She followed up, months later, with an even sharper column, titled "Smug white journalists strangers to democracy." She declared: "There is nothing more irritating than smug white journalists who call the opposition smug, yet they alone claim the right to criticise. What journalists in SA need is a basic course in Politics 101."[48]

On one occasion, Rhoda wrote a letter to the editor of her own newspaper, disputing *Business Day* editor-in-chief Peter Bruce's suggestion that Patricia de Lille, who is Coloured, take over the leadership of the opposition DA from Tony Leon. "It is like saying Peter Bruce should not be editor because he is white," she wrote provocatively. "We have a new constitutional democracy where anyone is allowed to be leader. Many smaller parties have black leaders, but they did not do as well as the DA with its white leader."

"Frankly," she added, "given the mismanagement of this economy à la Eskom [the state-owned electricity company] and the recent fuel crisis, I am beginning to prefer my oppressors to be white."[49] She added that criticism of Leon's combative personality was "rubbish," as she had

---

47   Rhoda Kadalie. "Where are journalists to speak truth to power?". *Business Day*, 1 Sep. 2005. p. 15.
48   Rhoda Kadalie. "Smug white journalists strangers to democracy." *Business Day*, 26 Jan. 2006. p. 9.
49   Rhoda Kadalie. "Media destroyers." *Business Day*, 8 Mar. 2006. p. 12.

confirmed by meeting him in person: "He is well read, throws a good party and is nice and irreverent."

Later, in 2011, she castigated white journalists for criticizing Afriforum, a group representing Afrikaners. She wrote, with a touch of the raunchy rhetoric that occasionally marked her prose:

> Journalists write superficially about complex issues and they often lack the courage to take on politically incorrect stances. They will go out of their way to attack white people who take up a cause to defend their rights but will retreat when black people violate the rights of others.
>
> The "woundedness of black people" has become sacrosanct - the untouchable political G-spot! And, if you want any kudos as a white person, then attack your own. This is what the Home for All Campaign and the Wealth Tax debate were all about? The good whites versus the bad whites; the coconuts versus the nuts! And, God forbid if you are conservative, the wrath of Marx will be unleashed upon you as though conservatism is a sin.
>
> In essence, white people are too easily considered not worthy of constitutional rights and the ones who often negate their rights are other whites - the gate-keepers who appropriate the right to judge.[50]

Such commentary was rare enough from white writers, if it appeared at all. The fact that Rhoda, as a black woman, often stood for the rights of ordinary white South Africans — against the political correctness of white elites, and did so in stark terms — was stunning.

Rhoda also criticised the South African media for hyping left-wing claims of white racism in post-apartheid South Africa. Racism existed, of course, but the media seemed to be obsessed with finding it:

> Race baiting has become a national sport. It's as though there are appointed vigilantes watching for any sign of racism to pounce on the offender in order to bring him/her down. We have seen many such cases where white people, in particular, have been targeted for either uttering stupid comments or posting inappropriate comments on social media.
>
> It is not as though white people are the only culprits. Black people regularly post and carry banners with equally vulgar racist comments

---

50   Rhoda Kadalie. "Whites and the 'woundedness' of blacks." PoliticsWeb, reprinted and translated from *Die Burger*, 11 Oct. 2011. URL: https://www. politicsweb.co.za/news-and-analysis/whites-and-the-woundedness-of-blacks. Accessed on 26 Mar. 2022.

against whites, preambled by the F-word. And for as long as the belief exists within the political sphere that "blacks can't be racist" such one-sided abuse will continue.[51]

Instead of promoting outrage and sensationalism, Rhoda argued, the media in a post-conflict society had a duty to encourage tolerance: "The media must actively work towards creating a climate where freedom of expression and free speech, and even the right to offend, become central to political discourse."

Rhoda contended that the establishment media were not only hostile to the political opposition, but to any news that might cast the ANC in a bad light, especially about crime. She argued that the media should, if anything, be partial to the opposition, because both shared the responsibility to hold the government accountable:

We are a gullible nation. We allow politicians to treat us like dirt, and that is why they have no respect for us, the citizenry.

...

[T]here are many editors and journalists, mostly white, who find it difficult to criticise incompetent ANC ministers unconditionally. When they do, they have to cast aspersions on the opposition or white people who, according to them, invariably criticise "to score points", or who are "unusefully hysterical", or who "with the fearful and pessimistic haplessly combine" forces to trash government for their own ends. Increasingly, it is becoming dangerous to be right when government is wrong, as Voltaire warned a long time ago, yet the media keeps putting brakes on our right to be right instead of encouraging us to be bold about our civic rights.

The local media needs basic lessons in democracy, one of which is its duty to hold government accountable. This central function it holds in tandem with the opposition.

...

The taxpaying public has a right to moan when government fails to deliver or abuses taxpayers' money. We have a right to demonstrate

---

51   Rhoda Kadalie. "A media responsible for fuelling racial tension must be held accountable." *The Citizen*, 3 Feb. 2017. URL: https://www.citizen.co.za/news/opinion/1416153/a-media-responsible-for-fueling-racial-tension-must-be-held-accountable/. Accessed on 13 Apr. 2022.

and picket peacefully and to present petitions until government can no longer stand us. We even have a right to expect the media to assist in this regard![52]

Rhoda reserved particular contempt for the elite group of political "analysts" who were frequently quoted by journalists and featured in panel discussions on television and radio, and who almost always supported the ANC's worldview. Despite their various academic degrees and intellectual pretensions, they often failed, Rhoda believed, to understand or explain South African politics, and simply parroted the ANC's party line.

Sometimes corruption, not conformity, was the problem. In 2005, Rhoda alleged that two senior journalists who worked for the Independent Newspapers group had been paid by failing Western Cape Premier Ebrahim Rasool of the ANC. In 2010, it emerged that those suspicions had been correct. She blasted Chris Whitfield, editor of the *Cape Times*, for claiming ignorance of the scheme — and cited many of the letters to the editor she had written over the years, alleging that the paper was biased in favor of the ANC and against the DA. "The whole matter stinks ... These journalists alone are not to blame for the bias; the whole Independent Group is embedded [in the ANC]," she wrote in a *Business Day* column — and included years of her complaints to Whitfield about the paper's alleged pro-ANC tilt.[53] Rhoda also outed a fellow *Business Day* columnist for plagiarism, following a tip from a member of the public, and conducting her own investigation. In so doing, she embarrassed her own editors, but to her, the principle of intellectual honesty was paramount.

Rhoda eventually was appointed to the *M&G* board of directors. But her penchant for criticizing the left made her an uncomfortable fit for the newspaper's audience. She also became disillusioned by efforts to purchase the newspaper. In 2002, she opposed an effort by the president's brother, Moeletsi Mbeki, to buy it.[54] She later resigned from the board over concerns that the eventual purchase of the paper by Zimbabwean businessman Trevor Ncube in 2002 was beset by financial irregularities.

When new tabloid newspapers emerged in South Africa that had a more populist editorial line, Rhoda celebrated their arrival. "The tabloids are a reaction against politically correct newspapers," she declared,

---

52   Rhoda Kadalie. *Business Day*, 13 Jul. 2006. p. 11, ibid.
53   Rhoda Kadalie. "Stench of secrecy in spin scandal." *Business Day*, 13 Jul. 2010.
54   "Sale of Mail & Guardian newspaper falls through." Africa Analysis. 12 Jul. 2002.

approvingly.[55] "Rags" like the *Daily Sun* were brash, they were crude — and they were loyal to their readers, not to politicians. Rhoda, like many South Africans, also enjoyed the humor and audacity of the tabloids' political coverage as a welcome antidote to the stultifying self-righteousness and bias of the center-left, struggle-era media establishment. The headlines were not just catchy, but factual, she said.[56] She praised the new arrivals for bringing the general public into otherwise esoteric political debates.

Rhoda celebrates a headline in the tabloid Daily Sun criticizing then-Western Cape ANC leader and premier Ebrahim Rasool, c. 2006
(Courtesy Rhoda Kadalie)

---

55   Rhoda Kadalie, quoted by Rian Malan. "The Great White Hyena; Rian Malan on the Boer whose racy tabloid has challenged South African pieties by championing such traditional values as witchcraft." *The Spectator (UK)*, 17 Dec. 2005. pp. 36-7.

56   Rhoda Kadalie. "Role of the Tabloids in SA." Lecture, Semester at Sea. 14 Sep. 2005.

Rhoda also celebrated writers who, like herself, were willing to go against the grain, such as Thando Mgqolozana, who wrote critically about Xhosa circumcision rituals; Niq Mhlongo, who wrote about South African soccer fans' restless search for patriotism in the post-apartheid era; and Henriette Rose-Innes, who wrote about the discovery that her family had bought a home once owned by a Coloured family who had been forcibly removed from it. "We owe it to this generation of writers," Rhoda said, "who through honesty, courage and valiance are prepared to "skin themselves alive" and, in so doing, take off the skin of previous generations of oppressors and liberators, in order to forge a new future for themselves and future generations."[57]

***

Rhoda often punctured political correctness with irreverent humor in her columns. In 2006, when a group of Mbeki-aligned African nationalist intellectuals floated the idea of creating a "Native Club," Rhoda mocked the idea with an imagined dialogue in one of her columns:

Hi. I'm Rhoda Kadalie and I should like to apply for membership of the Native Club.

Your credentials, please?

I am short, black, and female.

You qualify on short and female, but not on black. Are you black as in ANC black? Or as in UDF black?

UDF black.

Sorry, the latter does not apply.

Why not?

There is too much rainbow in that black. To qualify for this club you need to be black black.

How do you determine that? Do you use the pencil test[58], the nose test, or the head test?

---

57   Rhoda Kadalie. "Blooming writers give us hope for the future." *Business Day*, 27 Jul. 2020.

58   The "pencil test" was a notorious apartheid-era test of racial identity: if a pencil placed in the hair would fall out, that individual was not "African."

No, those tests were used under apartheid.

Which tests do you use now?

The Native Club admits only those who can write, spell, and think.

Oh, I thought race was central.

No, you need only write what we tell you to write, then you'll be admitted. You see, that is what is meant by black.

Oh, now I understand — you mean black consciousness. But Steve Biko's motto was 'I write what I like', even though he was the leader of the Black Consciousness movement.

Yes, but he was black and unconscious — that is why he was never in the ANC![59]

Rhoda used this imaginary dialogue to puncture post-apartheid taboos about race, a frequent theme in her writing (see Chapter 14). The shocking hilarity of this racial farce was compounded by the fact that it appeared in the *Business Day*, the normally stoic, high-brow paper read by South Africa's elite and followed closely by overseas observers. (It was, for example, the only South African daily available in the reading room of the Harvard Business School library.)

Rhoda concluded: "The Natives are restless again, and this after ten years of democracy." Describing herself as a "coconut intellectual," using a pejorative term sometimes used for Coloured people who were perceived as acting too "white," she mocked the Native Club's racial essentialism, noting that it reflected the racial obsessions of the apartheid regime and the closed community of ideas that many of us gave up a long time ago."[60]

---

59 Rhoda Kadalie. "A coconut knocks on the door of the Native Club." *Business Day*, 1 Jun. 2006. In Rhoda Kadalie. *In Your Face.* p. 26.

60 Rhoda offered more serious criticism elsewhere, noting that the Native Club was unlikely to address the supposed intellectual vacuum in South Africa because it failed to address the causes of that vacuum, "which I believe include self-censorship; using the race card to discredit people who raise debates; and the tyranny of political correctness that has come to characterise political culture." She also noted that it was too close to President Mbeki to be of much use: "If the club remains in its current state, I would not count on its commitment to unbiased and unfettered debate. Such a commitment can only be credible if the club insists on political independence." She added: "If its main objectives are to create a national environment open to debate, and to develop a critical consciousness that will save us from a life of cultural limbo, then fostering a South Africanness that is isolated from advancements in the

Some of the jokes that Rhoda shared with colleagues and friends were even funnier, but too provocative to print. When an ANC-aligned judge, Siraj Desai, was accused of rape on a trip to India, he maintained that he had only had consensual sex — albeit with a woman he admitted was not his wife. The controversy was handled with utmost seriousness in the English-language press, but in the Coloured community, with its tradition of satirical *moppie* songs, the judge became the target of ridicule. Rhoda picked up one ditty at her local hair salon: "*Jy maai wat jy saai, as jy rond, rond naai in Mumbai*" — "You reap what you sow, as you fuck around, fuck around in Mumbai" — all of which, of course, rhymed with "Desai."

Rhoda's intolerance for political correctness meant that her columns often generated huge responses in the forms of letters to the editor — both from her grateful fans, and from irritated ruling party spokespeople.

Typical of the former was a letter in 2005 titled simply "Viva Kadalie!"[61]. Another letter the same week began: "Yet again Rhoda Kadalie hit the nail on the head."[62] One fan hoped she would seek high office: "Rhoda Kadalie for president! Her articles are brilliant and make so much sense. If only the 'powers that be' could think like her, SA would be a better place for all of us, all colours and creeds!"[63] The year before, the *Business Day* published a piece of fan mail under the headline: "Kadalie has balls."[64]

Critics accused her of being a "self-appointed warden of our democracy,"[65] or "a serial whinger who needs to come down from her high horse,"[66] and being a closet DA supporter. "Has anyone heard Rhoda Kadalie ... say anything positive or glowing about state achievements, of which I can assure you, there are many?" one reader complained.[67] One angry reader even accused DA leader Tony Leon of having disguised

global world will only set us back. ... If it is about opening our minds to the developments in the progressive world and is indeed about self-examination and self-reflection, then we are on our way to a truly open society." Rhoda Kadalie, quoted by Tom Levin. "New club triggers race tensions." African Business, Aug./Sep. 2006. p. 48

61 Arnold Muscat. "Viva Kadalie!" Letter to the editor. *Business Day*, 14 Nov. 2005. p. 10.
62 T.A. Cropper. "ANC hogwash." Letter to the editor. *Business Day*, 15 Nov. 2005. p. 14.
63 Jean Hickson. "Vote for Kadalie!". Letter to the editor. *Business Day*, 9 Mar. 2007. p. 14.
64 T.A. Cropper. "Kadalie has balls." Letter to the editor. *Business Day*, 26 Feb. 2004.
65 Themba Khumalo. "Who's a stranger to democracy?". Later to the editor. *Business Day*, 27 Jan. 2006. p. 8.
66 Patrick Mkwanazi. "Talk is cheap." Letter to the editor. *Business Day*, 14 Aug. 2006. p. 12.
67 Brian Venter. "Same old story." *Business Day*, 17 Oct. 2006. p. 10.

himself as Rhoda Kadalie for the purposes of publishing his ideas under a pseudonym.[68]

Some of her critics also tried to ostracize her socially. At an event at the American consulate in Cape Town, she recalled, several South African speakers, including Desai, were eager to dissociate themselves from her views after she criticized the country's affirmative action policies. That was the sort of criticism that rankled Rhoda the most: "They personalized the issue, which made me mad. I said that I found it strange that my colleagues could dissociate themselves from me, when I had empirically verifiable evidence and could prove what I had said."[69] She saw their public criticism as an example of hypocrisy: "You find many of the old comrades who will talk about racial politics behind closed doors and in public will say something else."[70] It was that kind of political correctness, she believed, that bedeviled South African politics and prevented the country from correcting course.

In addition to voicing her politically incorrect, but widely-shared, opinions, Rhoda also began to break news stories. At times, what Rhoda said was so controversial — yet also correct — that her commentaries became news stories in themselves. She had established herself as an independent voice, and had extensive contacts within the ruling party. Distressed whistleblowers began approaching her with tips, which she would then follow up with her own quiet investigations. She was also able to connect the dots for readers between one corruption scandal and the next, explaining details that were otherwise impenetrable.

Many of Rhoda's early insights into the flaws of the post-apartheid government have become, by now, widely acknowledged. But Rhoda was among the first pundits to give voice to the disappointment of millions of South Africans, black and white, for whom the first democratic elections in 1994 had been a moment of pride and hope — and who had watched in horror as the ANC created a "ruling kleptocracy"[71] that defied Mandela's exceptional example of racial reconciliation and constitutional deference.

In 2002, reacting to a new national marketing campaign called "Proudly South African," she wrote:

---

68   Phumlani Manikivana. "Window to open." Letter to the editor. *Business Day*, 28 Apr. 2006. p. 10.

69   Rhoda Kadalie, quoted by Ryland Fisher. *Race*. Auckland Park: Jacana Media, 2007. pp. 235-6.

70   Ibid.

71   Rhoda Kadalie. "A party at war with itself and its own people." *Business Day*, 7 Sep. 2010.

Rhoda: 'Comrade Kadalie, You Are Out of Order!'

When I studied at the Institute for Social Studies in the Netherlands in the mid-1980s, cultural events were the order of the day.

A Middle Eastern, Asian, West African, or Latin American evening would bring out some of the most flamboyant cultural outfits, unusual foods, and exotic dances to an audience eager to compete in displays of culinary largesse and acts of patriotism to assuage their longing for home.

The South Africans, on the other hand, had nothing to be patriotic about as the television serially transmitted images of apartheid atrocities at home.

We were the pariahs of the world and I envied the spontaneous flag-waving of my fellow students, feelings that so often eluded me in my young adult life.

My first pangs of patriotism surged forth in February 1990 when Nelson Mandela regally and victoriously walked out of prison to a jubilant crowd, all wanting to own a part of him.

The second such experience was after April 1994 — when voters flocked to the first SA general election open to all — at a conference I addressed in the US as a free South African. Basking in the reflected glory of Madiba [Mandela's clan name, a term of endearment] abroad was the feeling I so longed for when fellow institute students proudly regaled us with their cultural practices.

The third burst of pride was the day in 1996 when the constitution was adopted, and Deputy President Thabo Mbeki made his "I am an African" speech.[72]

---

72   One of Mbeki's few celebrated, and unifying, speeches: "I am an African. I owe my being to the hills and the valleys, the mountains and the glades, the rivers, the deserts, the trees, the flowers, the seas and the ever-changing seasons that define the face of our native land. ... I am the grandchild of the warrior men and women that Hintsa and Sekhukhune led, the patriots that Cetshwayo and Mphephu took to battle, the soldiers Moshoeshoe and Ngungunyane taught never to dishonour the cause of freedom. ... I am the grandchild who lays fresh flowers on the Boer graves at St Helena and the Bahamas, who sees in the mind's eye and suffers the suffering of a simple peasant folk, death, concentration camps, destroyed homesteads, a dream in ruins. ... This thing that we have done today, in this small corner of a great continent that has contributed so decisively to the evolution of humanity says that Africa reaffirms that she is continuing her rise from the ashes. Whatever the setbacks of the moment, nothing can stop us now! Whatever the difficulties, Africa shall be at peace! However improbable it may sound

Chapter 13: Contrarian

My patriotism, regrettably, has been short-lived.

The burgeoning poverty, the rapid increase in HIV infection rates, escalating crime, widespread abuse of children and women, unacceptably high unemployment rates, and endless cash-in-transit heists leave very little to be proud of despite statements claiming that crime has stabilised — a new government euphemism for minimal improvement.

Government is fast extinguishing the pride most of us had due to its failure to deliver in the areas that matter.

...

We have become virtual prisoners in our own homes. Living behind high walls, electronic gates, and burglar alarms has come to be considered normal. Those who do not have these facilities are thrown to the wolves.

...

Provision of effective basic services to the public is what should make us Proudly South African. I will feel proud of my country when trains and buses arrive on time. I will feel proud if I can walk the streets at night. I will feel proud if the hospitals are equipped to deal with the illnesses of the majority.

...

A Proudly South African campaign that mobilises relevant government departments to deliver effective public services would be more palatable than one that encourages a narrow parochialism. Endless summits, bosberaads [retreats] and conferences will not deliver the goods. Implementation, enforcement and actual monitoring of policies and plans of action are what will make South Africa a country to be proud of.

Our pride should be earned. A government that manages to revitalise the all too transient feelings of patriotism I experienced on [sic] April 1994 will get my vote.

Government is fast extinguishing the pride most of us had, because of its failure to deliver in the areas that matter.[73]

---

to the sceptics, Africa will prosper!" Thabo Mbeki. "I Am an African." Speech in the Parliament of South Africa. 8 May 1996. URL: https://soweto.co.za/html/i_iamafrican.htm. Accessed on 9 Mar. 2022.

73   Rhoda Kadalie. "Patriotism soured by dashed expectations." *Business Day*, 4 Oct. 2002. Published in Rhoda Kadalie. *In Your Face.* Cape Town: Tafelberg, 2009. pp. 76-8.

Rhoda: 'Comrade Kadalie, You Are Out of Order!'

It became increasingly clear, to Rhoda and to others, that the government's failures in service delivery were not merely a problem of the lack of administrative capacity, but were an outcome of the country's political stagnation. And at the root of that stagnation lay the age-old problem of race — which the ANC refused to transcend.

Chapter 14:
Race and Gender

"I always rejected the notion of being coloured and embraced the slogan of non-racialism quite easily. But in the post-apartheid South Africa I am quite politically disillusioned around race, because I am told by the ruling party, in various ways, once again, that I am coloured.

"Now I celebrate my marginality, because one can be what one wants to be in a racially divided landscape. One can appropriate the right to be whatever one wants to be and not subscribe to the racial labels that are forced upon us in a society that is racist."[1]

Rhoda was one of the few black public figures who rejected identity politics and the often anti-white racial obsessions of South Africa's new political and media elite.

That is not to say that she believed white South Africans should be let off the hook for apartheid. In 1998, after she left the Human Rights Commission, she declared that white South Africans had a special duty to contribute, materially and politically, to the building of a new South Africa, and that they should be grateful for the way the struggle against apartheid ended. She told the BBC radio on a panel discussion recorded in front of a live audience in South Africa:

> I think that a lot of white South Africans should be challenged and asked, are you prepared to contribute to a wealth tax? Like in Cuba, for example? "Each one, teach one"? Are white people prepared to give of their resources, their skills, and privileges they have had, and push it back into underdeveloped black South Africa? I think white people should be grateful for the transformation of this country in the peaceful way that it happened, because for many white South Africans, very little has changed. They can continue to live the way that they do, they go to the same schools — they just have to share with black people, which they didn't do before; it's the first time that they have to stand in the queue because of affirmative action; and I think white people should be gracious about that. And show the world that they are grateful for a

---

1   Rhoda Kadalie, quoted by Ryland Fisher. *Race*. Auckland Park: Jacana Media, 2007. p. 56.

peaceful transition, because if you look at elsewhere in Africa, people are crossing borders with their goods on their heads. And that didn't happen in South Africa. ... The white political leadership has an important role to play in building a truly democratic South Africa.[2]

She added that some of the lingering racial divisions that the Truth and Reconciliation Commission had exposed in South African society were worth acknowledging. Apartheid had created "structural racial discrimination," she said, and "all whites benefited, whether they wanted to or not." While painful, "those divisions are important for us to recognize before we can work with each other and live with each other," she concluded.

Likewise, Rhoda never lost her concern about bigotry of the old-fashioned, anti-black sort. She repeatedly criticized white racial attitudes, and spoke out against institutional prejudices that were hangovers from the apartheid era. She criticized the casual racism she still experienced as a black woman in the new South Africa. More than a decade into South Africa's new democracy, she told one interviewer:

I can regale you with a hundred and one stories. You go into shops and immediately the antennae of the security are alerted and they watch you. You get that all the time. I go into a dance shop in Dean Street in Newlands [an affluent suburb in Cape Town], and the shop assistants won't even look up. A white woman will come in and they will immediately ask to help her. The assumption is you cannot afford to shop there. I have to deal with this kind of racism all the time.[3]

Rhoda also spoke out against other ingrained prejudices, such as discrimination against gays and lesbians. She was featured in a documentary produced by gay rights advocates in 2003, declaring:

I think the church has to realize, quickly, that gays are a big part of the church community. They have needs like everybody else, they work, they want children, they want to marry, they want to live together. And from that point of view, gays are equal to everybody else. And I think homophobia is a sin. And the essence of Christianity is not to discriminate, is to love. And I think the command to love your neighbor as yourself is about loving across the barriers, and we haven't been very good at that.

...

---

2   Rhoda Kadalie, "South Africans Talking." Ibid.
3   Rhoda Kadalie, quoted by Ryland Fisher, ibid. p. 22.

Gay people are as human as everybody else. And when gays are excommunicated from the church, and excluded, you exclude the body of Christ from its own body.[4]

Rhoda also signed a joint statement by several public figures in 1997 to urge the Dutch Reformed Church, which had once provided the theological foundation for Afrikaner nationalism, to become more accepting toward gay and lesbian members.[5]

In December 2004, she spoke out against the use of racial profiling to screen blood donations, a practice that came to light when the South African National Blood Transfusion Service had destroyed some blood units from black and Coloured donors, citing higher rates of HIV infection in those populations. "I think that before they consider racial profiling as a means to determine risk, they should make sure they have a screening process which is equal and accurate in place," she said.[6] She emphasized that there was also an acute need for blood ahead of the Christmas holiday season, when South Africa's roads were heavily-traveled and accidents were common.

Later, despite her many criticisms of President Jacob Zuma, especially his philandering, Rhoda drew the line at crude attacks on his sexuality. In 2012, when the cartoonist Jonathan Shapiro, whose pen name is "Zapiro," drew Zuma as a penis, Rhoda wrote:

What is it with white male artists and cartoonists, especially, Zapiro, and their obsession with Jacob Zuma's sexuality? None of them has ever gone that far with white racist oppressors.

They forget that serial monogamy and philandering are as rife in white SA, from businessmen, university academics to politicians? Have we forgotten about those married men in high places who skipped the border to sleep with black women in the homelands when they made it illegal?

Need I remind these white obsessive artists – the only thing that is truly non-racial is patriarchy and many of them are no better than Zuma? By

4   Rhoda Kadalie, quoted in *Created in the Image of God.* Judith Kotze, director. IAM Video, Sep. 2003.
5   Karen Breytenbach. "Church called on to accept gays." *The Mercury*, 29 May 2007. p.5.
6   Rhoda Kadalie, quoted by "Blood: It's Science Vs. Politics." *Cape Argus*, 6 Dec. 2004.

Rhoda: 'Comrade Kadalie, You Are Out of Order!'

the way I believe in absolute freedom of expression; I just want you to examine your own depravities for a change![7]

Zapiro was not alone; artist Brett Murray had painted a portrait of Zuma, called *The Spear*. Loosely based on a similar portrait of Vladimir Lenin, the portrait was unremarkable except that Murray had added a depiction of Zuma's exposed genitals. Rhoda called the painting "gratuitous," and in a debate on the letters page of the *Cape Times*, she concluded: "Just be honest and acknowledge that the media plays along with this kind of deep and subliminal racism. White SA, take a hard look at yourself."[8] (However, she also mocked the media's obsession with the painting, when South Africa had much more urgent priorities, such as persistent poverty among black children: "The SPEAR is indeed mightier than the pen," she quipped.[9])

But unlike many others who spoke and wrote about white racism, Rhoda's intolerance of racism was non-racial: she applied the same standard regardless of who was the target of discrimination.

In 2008, for example, when a black official defended using the derogatory term "kaffir" to describe another black person, Rhoda insisted that racial language either had to be tolerated for everyone, or no one. "It's a problem with us black people: we call each other 'k*****' etc.[10] I hear it in the corridors at my workplace, calling whites 'boer' or 'honky.' I hear my domestic worker talking about whites, I hear coloureds talking about blacks. We joke about it. But when the tables are turned, when a white person is 'racist,' we cry foul, we go berserk."[11]

In 2017, Rhoda defended Democratic Alliance leader Mmusi Maimane — of whom she was otherwise deeply critical (see Chapter 16) — when he was attacked by an ANC rival (the minister and deputy minister of police, no less) for being married to a white woman. She called the criticism "disgraceful tribal patriarchal superiority against a fellow black man who dared to step outside the bounds."[12]

---

7   Rhoda Kadalie. Letter to the editor. *Cape Times*, 25 May 2012. p. 10.
8   Rhoda Kadalie. Letter to the editor. *Cape Times*, 30 May 2012. p. 10.
9   Rhoda Kadalie. "Another week spent not worrying about what really matters." PoliticsWeb, reprinted and translated from *Die Burger*, 5 Jun. 2012. URL: https://www.politicsweb.co.za/news-and-analysis/another-week-spent-not-worrying-about-what-really-. Accessed on 26 Mar. 2022.
10   "Kaffir," a word that derives from the Arabic term for "infidel," is a pejorative racial epithet in South Africa, the equivalent of the "n-word" in the U.S.
11   Rhoda Kadalie, quoted by Murray Williams. "2010 boss Irvin slammed for using 'K-word' insult." *Cape Argus*, 20 Feb. 2008. p. 6.
12   Rhoda Kadalie. Draft column for *The Citizen*. 2 Jun. 2017. Personal files.

Rhoda rejected the "hypocrisy" of banning racist language only when it was used by whites. She criticized radical African nationalist Julius Malema, for example, who was expelled from the ANC and formed his own Economic Freedom Fighters (EFF) party, for singing the inflammatory song, "Shoot the farmer, Shoot the Boer." The song, popularized during the anti-apartheid struggle, was considered hate speech under South Africa's new constitution. Rhoda spoke out against Malema's use of the song, especially in light of the large number of farm murders.

Rhoda also spoke out against the spate of farm murders generally — one of the few black public intellectuals to do so. To her, the racial motivation in such killings was unmistakable — and the irony that killing farmers hurt black South Africans as well. "As valid as the food security threats are, the more serious aspect of the heinous slaughter of fellow South Africans is a negation of their humanity and their right to life as any other human being, employer or producer of goods," she wrote in *The Citizen* in 2017.[13] "In fact, I would hazard a guess that farmers provide more for their workers than any other employer in the country – houses, clinics, schools and work. I bet the results of such a study would surprise us."

Writing in an Afrikaans newspaper in 2011, she said: "Justifying these wrongs in the name of apartheid gives carte blanche to yesterday's liberators to become tomorrow's oppressors."[14] Though she did not indulge alarmist claims of white "genocide," Rhoda pushed back against the idea that farm murders were simply ordinary crimes, and argued in 2015 that there was evidence that some were "racially motivated purges":

I have written extensively on both but the brutal murders of over 3000 farmers since 1994, many of the victims either shot point blank, stabbed, or their spouses mutilated with unspeakable cruelty, points to a deeper motive.

The obliteration of farmers is not just about robbery and common assault; it perhaps is also about revenge for land dispossession. What these murderous thugs do not realize is that they are also eradicating the producers of food who have come to exemplify the apartheid past.

---

13   Rhoda Kadalie. "The brutal purging of our farmers must come to an end." *The Citizen*, 17 Mar. 2017. URL: https://www.citizen.co.za/news/opinion/1459997/the-brutal-purging-of-our-farmers-must-come-to-an-end/. Accessed on 13 Apr. 2022.

14   Rhoda Kadalie, quoted by Celia W. Dugger. "Hate or free speech?; South Africa riveted by trial of populist youth leader Julius Malema." *New York Times*, 30 Apr. 2011. p. A6.

The evil of these deeds can be traced back to how they understand the word "boere" with its double entendre. It can mean farmers on the one hand, or it may connote conservative Afrikaners, whom these murderers consider to be responsible for dispossession. A collapse of these two meanings often inspires hatred against people they assume are responsible for their lack of power.

...

The state's denial that farm murders [are] not genocide and that the murder and brutal attacks on foreign shopkeepers are not xenophobic have to do with something far more sinister than is obvious. It is the shame to admit that black people can also be racist; that racism and racial discrimination is not only a "white thing"; it also a "black thing" and that we are capable of racism, often more heinous. It resurrects the history of tribal and internecine warfare reminiscent of pre-colonial conflict in the southern African regions, not to speak of the whole of Africa.

To label these very specific transgressions "criminality" is to let the police and the state off the hook. It allows them to ignore the seriousness of the crime and negate the communities' specific attempts to protect themselves as SAPS has done with the Commandoes [a volunteer police force, disbanded by President Mbeki] in the rural areas.

It also means government does not have to set aside dedicated forces to eradicate the underlying causes and investigate the overt and covert forms of racism that incite the murder of a class of hard-working people who do not wait for handouts from government, but who know that they must work to move ahead.[15]

Rhoda also rejected the idea that brutality against black farm workers explained, or justified, the murder of white farmers. "True, some farmers treat their workers badly, as do domestic employers, business employers, NGO employers and media employers," she acknowledged.[16] But that had to be offset against "how many jobs are created by the agricultural sector;

---

15   Rhoda Kadalie. "Racism is racism." PoliticsWeb, reprinted from *Die Burger* and translated from the Afrikaans, 28 Jan. 2015. URL: https://www.politicsweb.co.za/opinion/racism-is-racism. Accessed on 26 Mar. 2022.

16   Rhoda Kadalie. "Don't blame whites for black racism." PoliticsWeb, reprinted from *Die Burger*, translated from the Afrikaans, 16 Mar. 2011. URL: https://www.politicsweb.co.za/news-and-analysis/dont-blame-whites-for-black-racism. Accessed on 28 Mar. 2022.

how many farmers pay their workers a living wage; how many farmers provide schools, health-care, social work and housing to their workers."

Rhoda later developed ties to AfriForum, a self-described "civil rights" organization representing Afrikaners and rural communities, which invited Rhoda to speak to its members on occasion. In 2017, she spoke at the launch of AfriForum's "anti-racism unit," which sought to represent the interests of white South Africans against unfair discrimination. She "emphasised in her presentation that race is increasingly being used as a political weapon in South Africa," according to an AfriForum summary of the event.[17]

When Archbishop Desmond Tutu suggested that white South Africans be taxed as a form of reparations for apartheid, Rhoda dismissed the idea as "racist," "irresponsible," and "obscene."[18] She also pointed out the specifically ethnic nature of the criticism often aimed at farmers: "Shockingly the venom is reserved for Afrikaans-speaking farmers, while English-speaking farmers are very easily let off the hook."[19]

In 2008, when four students at the University of the Free State created a racist spoof, mocking the attempted integration of four elderly black staff members into the campus community, the condemnation was universal.[20] But Rhoda pointed out that similar racist acts by other groups were ignored:

Equally, at many predominantly black universities, racial segregation at residences is the order of the day, but nobody speaks about that because it is assumed here that freedom of association is a right. Do you remember the coloured man who moved into Khayelitsha and was hounded out by blacks for daring to go and live in a black area? And how many hundreds of Somalis in the Western Cape have been killed by other black people for simply being successful business people? Where are the headlines about this? Where is the Human Rights Commission when it comes to taking

---

17   AfriForum. "AfriForum Launches Anti-racism Unit." 11 Sep. 2017. URL: https://afriforum.co.za/en/afriforum-launches-anti-racism-unit/. Accessed on 19 Oct. 2022.

18   Rhoda Kadalie, quoted by "Weighing up atonement and reconciliation a taxing affair." *Cape Argus*, 3 Sep. 2011.

19   Rhoda Kadalie. "Kudos to those who supported the #BlackMonday protests." *The Citizen*, 3 Nov. 2017, URL: https://www.citizen.co.za/news/opinion/1714456/kudos-to-those-who-supported-the-blackmonday-protests/. Accessed on 13 Apr. 2022.

20   Staff Reporter. "Racist video surfaces at the University of the Free State." *Mail & Guardian*, 26 Feb. 2008. URL: https://mg.co.za/article/2008-02-26-racist-video-surfaces-at-the-university-of-free-state/. Accessed on 22 Mar. 2022.

up these plights? It shouts sanctimoniously from the rooftops that whites should apologise for apartheid 14 years into our democracy, as though this video has once again given it a reason for existing.[21]

In 2016, Rhoda mocked South Africa's knee-jerk response to accusations of racism when a supposed "blackface" incident at Stellenbosch University turned out to be "purpleface."[22] A duo of visiting American students attended a costume party dressed as purple space aliens. They were accused of attempting to dress in blackface to mock black people; though they were innocent, they apologized.

Rhoda summarized the chaotic controversy:

The self-appointed thought police, the Open Stellenbosch Collective, does not wait to condemn. With the help of the university authorities, it is turning our students into cringing curs, forcing them to apologise even for the colour purple that showed up a shade darker, on their selfie. Worse, when the executioners realised their charges were misplaced, it apologised to the students.

But then, not wanting to look weak among its peers, it retracted its apology, claiming it was not consensual and that "the picture should be considered within the context of heated racial debate at the university recently, and was, therefore, still 'blackface' ".[23]

The result, Rhoda said, was that students were being taught to censor themselves — at the very universities that ought to have encouraged free expression. Racism was real, but political correctness undermined the mission of universities to be "centres of learning," she argued.[24]

Rhoda was also scathing in her criticism of the xenophobia that erupted in riots across South Africa, whose primary target was African immigrants from other countries, notably Somalia. Black South Africans often blamed immigrants for taking jobs at lower wages than locals would accept. Moreover, in the wake of apartheid's suppression of black entrepreneurship, many immigrants from other parts of the continent

---

21   Rhoda Kadalie. "Video uproar betrays culture of double standards." *Business Day*, 13 Mar. 2008. p. 15.
22   Paul Herman. "Stellenbosch 'blackface' incident was actually purple-face." News24, 8 Feb. 2016. URL: http://bit.ly/3A3YaWH. Accessed on 6 Jul. 2022.
23   Rhoda Kadalie. "Black faces leave faces red." *The Citizen*, 12 Feb. 2016. URL: https://www.pressreader.com/south-africa/the-citizen-kzn/20160212/281788513109711. Accessed on 6 Jul. 2022.
24   Ibid.

also brought with them a greater familiarity with entrepreneurship — legitimate and otherwise. They often built wealth more rapidly than many locals, still struggling with poverty, were able.

While condemning the violence, Rhoda placed the blame squarely on the ANC's mismanagement and exploitation of racial divisions:

> *[Locals] see rising unemployment, the housing crisis and dire poverty as direct threats to their survival and retaliate against those closest to them, but who are considered "other".*

> *...*

> *All kinds of reasons have been proffered for the xenophobia, but no one dares to explore the deeper psychological stuff that is going on here. And it has to do with our inability to deal with the race question constructively. Not so long ago, I said President Thabo Mbeki's inability to deal with Robert Mugabe was because he has not dealt with his "inner Zimbabwe". An obsession with race has been the defining feature of his rule, and his design of an African renaissance was a poor attempt at dealing with the legacy of racial discrimination. It became his excuse for the mismanagement of SA; for blaming reports of corruption on the white media; for castigating those concerned about HIV/AIDS as being obsessed with black male sexuality; and for shutting up complaints about crime as an elitist preoccupation.*

> *...*

> *This one-sided portrayal of victimisation perpetuates and feeds into the "woundedness" of black people and breeds an entitlement often lacking in refugees and immigrants. It breeds an ethos in victims that they can never be wrong and, given the circumstances, are "owed" a livelihood. And when refugees and foreigners leave their countries for whatever reasons and come here and make it, it challenges the victim status quo. The lesson these outsiders teach us - not to depend on the government and not to expect handouts - goes against the inclination of those done hard by to find a solution to deprivation. This in no way justifies the government's lack of responsibility towards the poor, the alienated and the deprived, but it does mean that if this entire society is to be healed from years of racial discrimination, the government, political parties and civic organisations should take the lead in minimising the kind of conflict*

that arises in situations of dire poverty, uncontrolled immigration and competition for scarce resources, such as jobs and housing.[25]

More starkly, she commented on Facebook: "Othering black Africans is the worst kind of racism on the planet. Black South Africans seem to be selective against whom they mark, protest, destroy and kill. That makes it even more disgusting."[26]

She also noted that many Afrikaners had responded positively to the challenge of the new South Africa by contributing whatever they could to the new society — often quietly and without thanks. She was invited to speak to the Afrikaanse Christelike Vrouevereniging (ACVV), a women's group, in 2013, and wrote:

Now 109 years old, and its origins rooted in the horrors of the Anglo-Boer War, the ACVV is a far cry from its conservative Afrikaner roots, involved today in probably some of the most difficult services required by this country. Guided by their vision statement – together in service of the community – they run protection services for children and their families; day care for children; services to older persons and persons with disability. This organisation is a paragon of accountability, exceptional financial and project management, and boasts over 5000 volunteers who address the needs of the SA's most vulnerable. It is a truly democratic organisation operating in 570 communities in cities and rural areas including the Western Cape, the Northern Cape, the Eastern Cape and part of the North West.

...

Lest we think we can stereotype these organisations as "fuddy duddy Christian nationalists" those epithets will ricochet in the direction of those whose prejudices keep them ignorant. The ACVV is "with the programme" to echo SA's youth; they are energetic, and full of the joys of serving South Africa in the areas that are the least rewarding and often the most gruelling. They persevere because they witness transformation daily in the lives of children, mothers and grandmothers whom society has discarded.[27]

---

25   Rhoda Kadalie. "'Victim' psychology finds expression in attacks." *Business Day*, 22 May 2008. p. 13.
26   Rhoda Kadalie. Post on Facebook, 18 Apr. 2015. URL: https://www.facebook.com/rhoda.kadalie/posts/10153363982610039. Accessed on 28 Mar. 2022.
27   Rhoda Kadalie. Draft article for *The Citizen*, 6 Sep. 2013. Personal files.

Rhoda believed that Afrikaners, too, deserved protection against racism — what she called "*Boerehaat*," meaning hatred of the Boer.[28]

Rhoda remained sensitive to issues of race, and the reality of racism. Fundamentally, however, she believed South Africa had to set it aside. "In a global world of cross-cultural and transglobal relationships and intermarriage, race as a defining feature becomes all the more ludicrous," she wrote in 2017. "In my family, the lineages are so mixed that we are best described as mongrel! We belong to the wide world where race will increasingly be of no consequence."[29]

***

Rhoda grew increasingly impatient with the ANC's policies of racial redistribution, such as affirmative action, which prioritized black South Africans in hiring, university admissions, and government contracts.

In the 1990s, as head of the Gender Equity Unit (GEU) at UWC, Rhoda had pressed for affirmative action policies to help women in the academy. A GEU publication stated: "**Affirmative Action measures are necessary to make equal opportunity a reality** for historically excluded groups, eg. black people and women."[30] Notably, it specified: "Affirmative action should take place at the selection and recruitment stage only. Thereafter all employees should be developed and promoted on merit." The GEU supported internal promotions within UWC that would elevate black and female candidates to "positions formerly colonised by white men."[31]

While Rhoda initially supported affirmative action, she believed that there was a specific way to do it properly, offering beneficiaries training and support. She also opposed making race and gender the main criteria for appointing people to jobs, or admitting students to coveted places at university. She told the BBC in front of a live audience in 1998:

I think affirmative action is necessary. In fact, it's a constitutional provision. Because the majority of people have been excluded from access to jobs and housing and so on and so forth. But I think its implementation so far has been wrong. Hence there is a lot of antagonism towards affirmative action. I myself have been a victim of the bad implementation

---

28   Rhoda Kadalie, "Kudos," 2017, ibid.
29   Rhoda Kadalie. "The perils of racial stereotyping." *The Citizen*, 23 Jun. 2017. URL: https://www.citizen.co.za/news/opinion/1549683/perils-racial-stereotyping/. Accessed on 13 Apr. 2002.
30   Gender Equity Unit. "Affirmative Action for Women at UWC." Pamphlet. Undated. Original emphasis.
31   Ibid.

of affirmative action, where blacks are appointed and women are appointed because they are black and women, and not because they are black and skilled, black and qualified. And so what happens is, when you appoint blacks because they are black, and you appoint women because they are women, you set them up for failure when they are not qualified. And so I have had to witness many of my comrades fail, because they were appointed as blacks and women and not as qualified blacks and on the basis of merit. And so I think we need to do a lot of work with regards to affirmative action in this country and the way we implement it.[32]

Characteristically, Rhoda had also studied affirmative action policies to such a degree that she could rattle off the contemporary best practices within the field: "With affirmative action goes eight other things, which I think in our companies, in our universities, we are extremely weak at. Eight other things: selection, recruitment, training, staff development, mentoring, induction, monitoring, and so forth. And I just see us concentrating on the appointment of blacks and women for that sake."[33]

She later acknowledged that she herself had been something of an affirmative action appointee as a black woman on the Human Rights Council.[34] "They had to have a balance of race and gender. So I won't discount that," she said. "But I never see myself as an affirmative action appointment, because I think I can compete with the best in the world." Affirmative action, at its best, would identify talented and qualified people who would otherwise be overlooked because of bias, and would provide them training and support to help them succeed.

She noted that the ANC frequently used affirmative action as a cover for appointing unqualified apparatchiks to key posts. In a commentary on the ANC's destruction of the National Youth Commission, she wrote:

[T]his phrase "lack of capacity" has developed a life of its own, a euphemism for the appointment of unskilled, unqualified, and incompetent people under the guise of affirmative action. By their own admission, these highly salaried, BMW-driving youth lack the qualifications to do their jobs. It has become commonplace for government to employ underqualified people, often political appointees, to top jobs, but then employ consultants, researchers and academics to

32   Rhoda Kadalie, "South Africans Talking," ibid.
33   Ibid.
34   Rhoda Kadalie, interview with Business Network Radio. 11 Jun. 2013. URL: https://www.youtube.com/watch?v=YB6YIo6luqw. Accessed on 28 Apr. 2022.

do their work for them. Countless houses could have been provided with the money these institutions have wasted.

...

The country cannot continue on this path, and has to find a better way to implement affirmative action. Government has to acknowledge that political appointments are not the same thing as affirmative action.

Second, affirmative action is not about redress, because we cannot make up for the travesties of apartheid but we can adopt measures to make equal opportunity a reality for those discriminated against.

Affirmative action should not exclude white people but should create a balance between what is needed and who is the best person to do the job. So if I were the president, I would employ rather than alienate skilled whites precisely so they can make up for the past – those with the best skills and privileged education should contribute to rebuilding SA by using the skills that advantaged them.

Third, affirmative action means appointing on the basis of merit, skills and qualifications of those formerly excluded. It does not ever mean getting rid of incumbents, no matter what their race, gender, or ethnicity.

For affirmative action to succeed, it has to go hand in hand with relevant selection and recruitment procedures; proper induction of new employees; continuing training and development of staff; transformation of the organisational culture; establishing special training programmes; and periodically setting goals and timetables for achieving diversity.

"Lack of capacity" is the result of policies based solely on race, gender or disability, and is responsible for municipalities collapsing and the decline of efficient services to the poor.

Affirmative action is a human–rights violation when unskilled people are foisted upon the poor, who need effective service delivery most.[35]

Rhoda placed affirmative action in the context of a culture of entitlement among South African youth. She noted in 2009 that under Jacob Zuma, the ruling party's youth organizations had become politically emboldened and deeply corrupt: "[Y]oung, vacuous millionaires are being bred, who think that conspicuous consumption is the highest level of achievement,"

---

35   Rhoda Kadalie. "Poor excuse for failure develops a life of its own." *Business Day*, 24 Aug. 2006. p. 19.

she wrote.[36] She contrasted them to the ANC leaders of previous generations, who worked hard to gain an education. "Given the calibre of these leaders, many would have excelled at governing this country."[37] The ethos of rewarding identity, rather than achievement, had produced a new generation incapable of leading, she argued.

Later, Rhoda became sharply critical of the way the ANC applied affirmative action to skilled and technical posts. When the state-owned electricity company, Eskom, began suffering regular blackouts and imposing "load-shedding" on its consumers, Rhoda noted the toll that years of affirmative action appointments had taken on the company. While the ANC stacked Eskom and other state-owned enterprises with party loyalists as executives, it had driven out skilled engineers who happened to be the wrong color. She wrote:

> A lesson the ANC refuses to learn is that it is in the fields of technology and science that affirmative action will become our greatest risk: if an under-qualified doctor performs a heart transplant, the patient will surely die; an inexperienced pilot may cause a fatal accident; the poorly trained engineer's bridge will surely collapse, and the ill-equipped technician is not able to man a machine that needs specialised knowledge. It is as simple as that.
>
> ...
>
> Eskom is a failure because the people who run it are not suitably qualified. Worse, they have been protected by a president and ministers, equally guilty of a gross dereliction of duty.[38]

Rhoda would later return to the point:

> I have said this before and I will say it again – the poor application of affirmative action has human rights implications when those who are in charge of dispensing basic public services, are unqualified to do so. Affirmative action is entirely compatible with merit, skills and qualifications. When there is a dearth of suitably qualified black people,

36   Rhoda Kadalie. "ANC elders' lessons for the young and vacuous." *Business Day*, 19 Nov. 2009.

37   Ibid.

38   Rhoda Kadalie. "The price of the misuse of power: Stressing transformation at the expense of delivery is just one of the ANC's manifold failures, writes Rhoda Kadalie." *Cape Argus*, 29 Jan. 2008. p. 17.

then we must, of necessity, appoint others, regardless of colour, with the requisite skills to provide for the needs of the public![39]

If she were running the country, Rhoda explained in one interview, she would appoint black engineers — but if none could be found to do the job, she would appoint white engineers. "White people were privileged under apartheid, and therefore we should use them to use their privilege to build the new South Africa. We shouldn't be punitive, because white people are equal under the law, as everybody else."[40]

Over time, Rhoda also became increasingly intolerant of the spread of incompetence throughout the civil service and even private companies, which she blamed on overly aggressive affirmative action policies. In one example, she noted: "Another case of affirmative action gone mad is Telkom [the state-owned telephone company]. Not só long ago I phoned inquiries for the number of Chubb Alarms. The operator asked me to spell the name as he never heard of Chubb before. I proceeded to explain that it was a burglar alarm company like ADT, at which point he asked me to spell that too!"[41]

In a draft essay (or lecture) on whether a "pot of gold" might still be found at the end of the "Rainbow Nation," Rhoda pointed out that there were black South Africans, too, who felt "they have been left behind by affirmative action," given that overall economic inequality had only grown since the policy's adoption.[42] She elaborated: "The ANC's model of affirmative action did not favour blacks at the expense of whites. Rather, its narrow interpretation and implementation enriched only a small group of political cronies at the expense of *everybody* else — whites, blacks, coloured and Indians — with the poor hardest hit."

She was also outspoken about the degree to which affirmative action often hurt Coloured South Africans — many of whom considered themselves "black," but who were not seen as such by the ANC once it had gained power. One of the most tragic victims in Rhoda's life was Dick van der Ross. She noted a conversation with Van der Ross in her diary:

---

39   Rhoda Kadalie. "Eskom and the ANC's gargantuan AA failure." PoliticsWeb, reprinted from *Die Burger* and translated from the Afrikaans, 12 Feb. 2015. URL: https://www.politicsweb.co.za/opinion/eskom-and-the-ancs-gargantuan-aa-failure. Accessed on 28 Mar. 2022. Original emphasis.
40   Rhoda Kadalie, interview with Business Network Radio, ibid.
41   Rhoda Kadalie. Draft lecture on affirmative action. Undated. Jan. 2007.
42   Rhoda Kadalie. "The Rainbow Nation — Is There a Pot of Gold?" Essay, or lecture, draft. Circa 2007. Found in Rhoda Kadalie's papers. It is unclear whether, or where, it was published or delivered.

Rhoda: 'Comrade Kadalie, You Are Out of Order!'

He told me how coloured leaders including Jakes met him after he retired from UWC to tell him he would be Chancellor. A few weeks later, they rescinded this decision telling him it should be a black man, and that black man was Tutu, who was not even from the WCape! Felt the hurt in his voice.[43]

Tutu, a public personage who held many posts, and had been honored many times over, could scarcely have devoted the time and care to the position that Van der Ross would have done. Such was the nature of affirmative action under the ANC: the politically-connected benefited above all, regardless of qualifications, interest, or results.

Likewise, Rhoda criticized the policy of Black Economic Empowerment (BEE), which tended to reward party insiders with lucrative state contracts, rather than actually uplifting the poor and the bulk of the previously disadvantaged. She described the policy's damaging effect on international investment — and on job growth for the poor:

If you invest your own funds and set up shop in SA, you will struggle to guard your management authority and your money from being stolen by opportunistic BEE front companies, thuggish unions and a gluttonous government. Through BEE, onerous labour laws and the protection of parastatals, the government has established handsome incentives for idleness and expropriation, and destroyed incentives for work and entrepreneurship.[44]

Rhoda frequently complained about "empowerment" deals that essentially shoveled large amounts of cash and equity to ruling party insiders. She explained to a Czech magazine that the early advent of BEE — before it became law — enriched the "few highly qualified black people around," so much so that they were wealthier than white South Africans who had worked a lifetime to build their wealth. "Few would say there was anything wrong with helping black people to become productive, economically active citizens," she wrote. "However, the reality is that black economic empowerment is easily abused" — both by enriching the already "empowered," and by making sure the beneficiaries had close ties to the ANC. The result was inequality — and, often corruption: "Little did

---

43   Rhoda Kadalie. Diary entry, 24 Jan. 2016.
44   Rhoda Kadalie. "Hang signs that say: 'It's poverty and jobs, stupid'."
     Business Day, 16 Nov. 2010.

we know, when apartheid ended in 1994, that by 2005 we would start to despise the very people we had wanted to see in government."[45]

In 2006, Rhoda wrote about her former colleague from the Open Society Foundation, Brigalia Bam, who was linked to a company that received an empowerment contract to run the National Lottery:

> Now that President Thabo Mbeki's term is coming to an end, his cronies are on a feeding frenzy at the trough of black economic enrichment. The National Lottery is known to make a profit of R40m annually, and this is why the vultures swooped in on the prey, which they got by means more foul than fair if the losing consortium Igwija Gaming is anything to go by.

> One name among this lot of "entitlers" worries me immensely, and that is the chairwoman of the Independent Electoral Commission (IEC), Brigalia Bam. She is listed in Empowerdex as the 20th most influential black economic empowerment woman on the JSE. There is no woman more connected to the ruling elite than Brigalia Bam. Her CV on the internet lists her past functions as president of the Women's Development Foundation, vice-chairwoman of the Human Rights Commission and secretary-general of the South African Council of Churches.

> ...

> The internet does not list any of her directorships and I would like to know if she has declared these anywhere, so that one may know how many she holds while also holding down a highly paid constitutional job, one of the most important in this country. And here lies the rub.

> ...

> As chairwoman of the IEC, Bam has many conflicts of interest and I should like to know where she has declared any of these directorships. If she has declared them upfront, even that is not good enough. Politicians and public officials believe that the act of declaring their interests in itself exonerates the conflict of interest, and so they continue with impunity.

> But it is not enough to declare. Bam should resign if her directorships are in conflict with a job that requires the utmost integrity. If these interests are deemed to be more important than her job as chairwoman of the IEC, then she is clearly in the wrong job. Can we be confident that Bam will not rig an election in favour of the ANC with whose interests hers

45   Rhoda Kadalie. "The View from Here." *Business Spotlight*, No. 3 (2005). p. 38.

are firmly enmeshed? What guarantees do we have that as one of the "Queen BEEs", she will exercise her functions without fear or favour, independently and impartially?[46]

The National Lottery deal was only one of countless "empowerment" arrangements that Rhoda ripped apart in her columns, exposing the ANC's self-dealing and leaving no doubt that the corruption many would later attribute to Zuma began in earnest long before.

She summed up her complaints about the ANC's approach to racial redistribution:

> *We have made serious mistakes around affirmative action and employment equity. We are the one country in the world with all the rules in the book around affirmative action, but we implement it wrongly. When we implement affirmative action, we redress the disadvantages suffered by blacks and women, but we do not consider merit and qualification. That's our first mistake. When we appoint blacks, we set them up for failure. We do not train them, and we do not provide them with staff development that will go a long way to assisting affirmative action.*[47]

Ironically, she observed, affirmative action and BEE reinforced racism — not just because they used old racial categories, but because they associated their beneficiaries with failure: "[W]e find that racial prejudices increase because blacks are not delivering."[48]

✳✳✳

Though she was critical of affirmative action and black economic empowerment, Rhoda was adamant about the need to make apartheid's victims whole. One issue in which Rhoda had taken particular interest was land reform and restitution. As part of a family that had been displaced, Rhoda wished to see the issue resolved fairly and quickly.

But like so much else, the effort at land reform and restitution — in District Six, and elsewhere — became bogged down in politics and greed.

In one column in August 2005, she wrote:

---

46   Rhoda Kadalie. "Why IEC's Brigalia Bam shouldn't be playing Lotto - Correction Appended." *Business Day*, 2 Nov. 2006. p. 13.
47   Rhoda Kadalie, quoted by Ryland Fisher. *Race*. Auckland Park: Jacana Media, 2007. p. 107.
48   Ibid.

Remember the time Helena Dolny[49] was unceremoniously booted out of the Land Bank simply for doing her work rigorously?

The reason behind this purge is now obvious. Corrupt deals such as the R800m loan by the bank for a nonagricultural endeavor to Pamodzi Investments — in which two senior African National Congress (ANC) members, secretary-general Kgalema Motlanthe and presidential adviser Manne Dipico, have shares — would never have been allowed under Dolny.

This loan was not intended for agricultural purposes but to facilitate Pamodzi's buyout of Foodcorp, one of Africa's biggest food companies. It represented more than 40% of the Land Bank's reserves and would have seriously compromised its already inadequate servicing of its core business — the desperate need of farmers and community farming groups for money to buy equipment and supplies. Minister [of Agriculture and Land Affairs] Thoko Didiza claims this transaction is a normal Land Bank deal and will not investigate.[50]

She noted: "The ANC has been good at setting up commissions to investigate matters that boost its own, rather than the public's interests."

Rhoda also continued to advocate for human rights in general, despite the ineptitude of the Human Rights Commission, and independent of any political party or controversy. In 2010, with the World Cup tournament drawing thousands of soccer fans to the country, she addressed the sensitive subject of the *abakhwetha*, the young Xhosa men who participated in traditional circumcision rituals, living in tents along the major N2 highway in Cape Town during school holidays for weeks of preparation and recovery. The tents were visible from the roadway that visitors would take from the airport into town; they were also becoming increasingly controversial, as there were reports every year of young men showing up in hospitals with injuries caused by errant circumcisions performed by traditional healers using primitive knives. Rhoda even had an intern at Impumelelo who was to undergo the ritual: though the prospect "terrifie[d]" him, she said, he would not settle for performing the operation in a hospital.[51]

---

49 Dolny was the wife of South African Communist Party stalwart Joe Slovo. She was appointed to the Land Bank but pushed out when she began raising questions about financial mismanagement.

50 Rhoda Kadalie. "Inquiries aplenty, but none into ANC abuses." *Business Day*, 4 Aug. 2005.

51 Rhoda Kadalie. Draft column for *Die Burger*. 21 May 2013. Personal files.

The very subject of the circumcisions was somewhat taboo; at a film screening in the early 2000s about the practice, for example, members of the audience chided the (Xhosa) directors for daring to expose something about their tradition to the wider world. Some argued that the circumcisions should be performed in hospitals; others defended the sacred nature of the traditional ritual.

Though her anthropological training might have suggested that Rhoda should defer to African custom, she took up the issue as a basic violation of the human rights of the young initiates. She wrote:

> What we are witnessing is the tolerance of human rights violations based on the idea that customary practices are "sacred", no matter their deleterious effect. Any customary practice that harms people violates those people's basic human rights and should be outlawed. More seriously, the prevalence of this custom under unhygienic conditions indicates our unwillingness to embrace modernity. The obsession with designer labels, state-of-the-art cellphones and luxury cars among black men contradicts the government's tolerance of a custom enacted under the most inhumane and barbaric conditions.
>
> Black SA's adherence to patriarchal customs that ironically rob the youth of their manhood makes no sense. Could this perhaps explain why gender relations are so fraught with problems and issues of power? Men who feel emasculated often use powerless women to cushion their feelings of inadequacy.[52]

Rhoda saw the problem of circumcision as part of South Africa's larger public health crisis. "That a black-led majority government allows young black men to die year in and year out is unacceptable. By now government should have designed a preventative and enforceable health policy to avoid these unnecessary deaths. Just as there are doctors providing free optometry and cataract surgery, just so, many doctors would volunteer to provide circumcision under pristine surgical conditions. But again, politics trumps black life."[53] She also saw the circumcision debate as a matter of human rights. "Any custom or tradition that hurts a person should be abolished. That is the nub of the issue," she concluded. And instead of

---

52   Rhoda Kadalie. "Tolerance for death in the bush shames SA." *Business Day*, 29 Jun. 2010.

53   Rhoda Kadalie. "Mpumalanga initiate deaths: Politics again trumps black life." PoliticsWeb, reprinted from *Die Burger*, translated from the Afrikaans, 22 May 2013. URL: https://www.politicsweb.co.za/news-and-analysis/mpumalanga-initiate-deaths-politics-again-trumps-b. Accessed on 28 Mar. 2022.

criticizing the affairs of distant countries like Israel, she opined, South Africa should attend to urgent human rights priorities at home.[54]

Rhoda also remained a committed feminist, pushing back against sexism in culture, politics, and the media. Just as she did not hesitate to criticize circumcision rituals in African society, she also criticized rites of passage that applied to women, such as the "reed dance," in which young virgins were summoned to dance half-naked before the Zulu king. She wrote:

As someone trained in anthropology, I understand the need for cultural traditions and the symbolism undergirding customs that often don't make sense to those who don't practice those traditions.

But virginity testing, parading bare-breasted in the presence of male political and cultural leaders, declaring one's availability for marriage, are practices that subordinate women to the demands of men, thus reinforcing patriarchy.

...

What is the significance of a custom if it causes physical harm, humiliation, and promotes subordination?

Her criticism continued her long skepticism of traditional authority, despite her sensitivity, as an anthropologist, to the legitimate concerns of indigenous leaders about cultural continuity.

Rhoda remained a feminist despite her disappointment in the post-apartheid government. For all its promises of women's equality, including quotas for women in its parliamentary caucus and in the executive, the ANC had done little to help women, and much to harm them.

As Rhoda told an audience in Germany in 2003:

Having a high proportion of women in parliament and government has not helped much. Thirty percent of MPs in the ruling party are women, while about 15 women ministers in Cabinet are in key ministries such as housing, mineral and energies [sic], public service, justice, trade and industry, environment, and so on. I am not sure that their presence has made much of a difference to the position of women in SA. We have had two ministers of health, both women doctors who have failed society in combating and preventing the spread of AIDS. Our current minister of health has supported the president to the hilt on his crazy stance that HIV

---

54   Rhoda Kadalie. "Tolerance," ibid.

does not cause AIDS. Her blind loyalty to the president has made her the stumbling block in providing an HIV/Aids programme that will address a pandemic that is spiraling out of control and that affects women in specific ways. What is more, not one woman minister, or speaker of Parliament spoke in support of a rigorous programme to prevent, treat and care for those infected with the virus.[55]

The lesson of the post-colonial world was that unless quotas for women in government were paired "with other strategies that truly advance the position of women, the status of women will hardly change as is obvious in the case of South Africa," she concluded.

Rhoda also remained keenly sensitive to sexism within South Africa's supposedly enlightened media establishment. In 1999, the South African Advertising Standards Authority barred a television advertisement about rape featuring actress Charlize Theron, speaking out against the behavior of men in the country.[56] Rhoda, by then working with Impumelelo, sent a furious letter to the *Cape Argus*:

The advert does not claim that all men are rapists, but it does imply that by their silence, men acquiesce to the crime of rape. ... The strong reaction provoked by Charlize Theron has another dimension, overlooked by many. The majority of South African men cannot deal with a sexy actress who dares to challenge the very basis of male sexuality. It is ok for strident lesbians and feminist [sic] to condemn rape, but for a sexy "bombshell" to do that is to shake the very foundations of male stereotyping of such women as sex objects.[57]

For decades, Rhoda would continue to speak out against the scourge of rape and sexual violence in South Africa, regardless of whom she offended.

In 2003, when writer Chris Barron penned a somewhat harsh article in *Fair Lady* magazine about Helen Suzman, then in her mid-eighties, Rhoda snapped into action, mustering her full arsenal of feminist critiques. Noting that all of Barron's sources were men "not unknown for their chauvinism," Rhoda said that his depiction of her as a cold, "unemotional" politician was "the kind of interpretation that makes feminists balk because it implies that women excel and achieve success

55 Rhoda Kadalie. Speech at the University of Kiel. Kiel, Germany. June 2003.
56 Melanie Aufrichtig. "Charlize Theron in controversial advert." 1999. URL: https://www.youtube.com/watch?v=hNjSDWoktWE. Accessed on 29 May 2022.
57 Rhoda Kadalie. Letter to the *Cape Argus*. 8 Oct. 1999.

at their own peril; that reaching great heights in one's profession, one does so at the risk of losing one's femininity, maternal instincts, and compassion." Rhoda also praised Suzman's ability to marry pragmatic politics with analytical skill.

She concluded:

The Helen that I know is warm, generous, compassionate, witty and extremely funny. I and many others are regular recipients of her largesse and unending generosity. She does, however, not suffer fools gladly and I suspect that those who criticize her harshly fall within that category. I do not expect this kind of uncritical journalism from a journalist of Barron's calibre and his article on Helen reminds me of a feminist quote I read recently:

"Nobody objects to a woman being a good writer or sculptor or geneticist if at the same time she manages to be a good wife, good mother, good looking, good tempered, well groomed, and unaggressive."[58]

It was the first of many tributes Rhoda would offer to Suzman in years to come — and she sent it to Suzman, in a spirit of sisterly solidarity.[59]

Rhoda and Suzman had become close friends since working together on the Human Rights Commission. It was a friendship that lasted a decade and-a-half; they spoke frequently on the telephone, exchanging political gossip and politically incorrect jokes. Suzman became increasingly frail at she reached her late eighties. In 2007, Rhoda recorded in her diary that Suzman called her before undergoing brain surgery to remove a non-cancerous growth: "If anything happens to me, I want you to remember the long interesting life I have had," Suzman told her.[60]

Suzman fractured her hip in late 2008, and her health deteriorated over the following year. Rhoda noted upon learning of Suzman's death on New Year's Day 2009, that they had spoken one last time by telephone the day before: "I told her how much I loved her, that I did not want her to go." Suzman, exhausted, told her: "Go now my love, I am tired and want to sleep."[61] Later, Rhoda recorded what Suzman had told her in a telephone conversation a few days before: "My darling this is it; it is over and I love

---

58   Marya Mannes. *But Will It Sell?*. Philadelphia: Lippincott, 1964. p. 59.
59   See, for example, Rhoda Kadalie. "Suzman's star shone with bright ferocity in a dark chamber of a land unfree." *Cape Times*, 20 Nov. 2007. p. 11.; The 'bright star' whose just and brave light was never dimmed," 2009, ibid.
60   Rhoda Kadalie. Diary entry, 22 Mar. 2007.
61   Rhoda Kadalie. Diary entry, 1 Jan. 2009.

you very much. I am glad to go because this democracy is not what I was hoping for."[62]

Rhoda visits Helen Suzman and her dog in Ilovo, Johannesburg, c. 2007
(Courtesy Rhoda Kadalie)

Later, in an obituary reflecting upon Suzman's death, Rhoda would quip: "At 91, Helen was the youngest friend I had."[63] She had admired Suzman as one of the few South Africans who had pursued democracy for its own sake, and had not been shy to criticize the new order as she had attacked the old. The affection between the two women was clearly mutual, and Suzman left Rhoda R200,000 - a sizable sum at the time — in her will.

In responding to Barron, Rhoda praised Suzman's lifelong fight — not just for liberal principles, but for a better life for the poor. A year later, Rhoda would recall: "Going back to my diary two weeks before she died, I

---

62   Rhoda Kadalie. "Helen Suzman: Obituary." Draft article; notes in margin. 1 Jan. 2009.
63   Rhoda Kadalie. "The 'bright star' whose just and brave light was never dimmed." *Business Day (The Weekender)*, 5 Jan. 2009.

was reminded of her promise to not leave this earth without notifying me and true to her word, she called to say farewell."[64]

She added:

Imbued with a political wisdom rarely seen today, [Suzman] always treated the poor with deep respect, turning her house into one of the country's most efficient advice offices. ... After her resignation in 1989, she continued to help prisoners; help people acquire identity documents; and challenge municipalities to improve services to the poor.

A parliamentarian par excellence, Helen was superb in representing the people to Parliament, and not the other way around. ... She abhorred corruption as much as public service failure. The quintessential liberal, she believed in the power of Parliament, the rule of law, human rights and constitutional democracy. Politically prescient, she foresaw that the African National Congress would regret having enshrined socioeconomic rights in the constitution, as it would become one of the most challenging clauses to uphold.

In her private life, Helen ran her household with military precision. On one occasion, when Helen had the flu, I told Betty, her housekeeper, to keep her under control and in bed, to which Betty replied: [Apartheid-era Prime Minister] John Vorster could not control her; how do you expect me to do it?[65]

Rhoda did her best to keep Suzman's legacy alive in a country eager to honor the ANC's pantheon of heroes and to forget liberals — particularly women — whose principles formed the bedrock of the new constitution and had given South Africa a chance to succeed. When the DA itself, under the leadership of Mmusi Maimane, neglected to observe Suzman's centenary, Rhoda took the opposition party to task, observing wryly: "Our monolithic understanding of history, underpinned by the pernicious tyranny of political correctness, determines who gets memorialised, when and how."[66]

Rhoda also continued to take a strong interest in women's sexual health in the midst of the HIV/Aids pandemic, which persisted alongside the endemic problem of rape. She urged South Africa's leaders to become

---

64   Rhoda Kadalie. "Let us not forget Helen Suzman's great legacy." *Business Day*, 14 Dec. 2010.
65   Ibid.
66   Rhoda Kadalie. "DA must own its history." *The Citizen*, 10 Nov. 2017. URL: https://www.citizen.co.za/news/opinion/1722772/da-must-own-its-history/. Accessed on 13 Apr. 2022.

more outspoken about these problems. The challenges were so great that Rhoda was willing to entertain unconventional approaches. When the mayor of the small town of Ladysmith in KwaZulu-Natal province created a "Maidens Bursary" to provide scholarship funds for girls who remained virgins, human rights groups were outraged. But Rhoda defended the mayor:

The usual arguments against gender inequality, invasion of privacy, discrimination against non-virgins etc are valid. But then a young recipient was interviewed on television and very articulately she extolled her ambitions, claiming that she has seen her mates destroyed by early pregnancies and that she wants the bursary to fulfill her dreams, educate herself, so that she can have a career. Her explanations and those of the mayor, that the incentive is voluntary, and that girls are not compelled to sacrifice their virginity for the sake of the bursary, are as valid and cannot be dismissed as easily.

...

Let me recount one story of the triumph of a young intern who came to work for me and discovered that she was pregnant. With no medical aid, no parental help, no money, she had her baby in one of Cape Town's worst hospitals. Her experience was traumatic and she vowed never to have another child. Not long thereafter, she fell pregnant again. This time I was enraged. I counselled her, explained various options, and she decided to terminate her pregnancy. She enrolled for several courses with the colleges and Cape University of Technology. Today she has several qualifications behind her name; she had a brand new car, she has just bought a house in a middle class residential area, and her son is flourishing at a good school. She is a great mother, wise beyond her years, and ambitious.

There is life after an unwanted baby. Too many of our kids are hobbled by teenage pregnancies when they are still in need of care. That is why, as a feminist, I refuse to criticise the Mayor Mazibuko for her concern because few care about the problem![67]

Privately, Rhoda continued to counsel many young women who came to her for advice. She was, for many, a surrogate mother, the one woman to whom they could turn for advice.

---

67   Rhoda Kadalie. Draft column for *The Citizen*. 29 Jan. 2016. Personal files.

Rhoda would describe the plight of women as her greatest disappointment in the new South Africa. "My Big Issue," she wrote in 2010 for the South African magazine of the same name,[68] "is the South African governments utter failure to improve the situation of poor black women in the country. ... All international indices indicate a decline in the maternal health, infant mortality and life expectancy of women over the past 14 years, and this is an indictment of a country that perennially upholds the slogan 'a non-racial, non-sexist democracy'."[69]

In theory, South Africa had many institutions that could advocate for women. But they had been gutted from within by the ANC and the left. Rhoda wrote:

South Africa is a goldmine for the Gender Commission, the Human Rights Commission and the Women's Ministry to do their work. Yet they are clueless as to how to attack the problem. The "femocrats" who occupy these constitutional agencies earn too much to be of any use and are accountable to no one. Their country reports are shrouded in turgid UN-speak and massaged statistics. The annual 16 days of activism is their futile attempt to combat the violence that has become second nature for men. To date, the campaign has had no effect and women are more brutalised than ever. With the high rates of poverty and unemployment, men will continue to use women as the shock absorbers for their frustrations and emasculation. Nurtured in cultures of patriarchy, there seems to be no way out.

But there is a way out as I have experienced first-hand in my work at UWC over the 21 years. As academic and Gender Equity Officer I engaged the student leaders to work with me in the residences to stamp out sexual violence and harassment. This was accompanied by on-going media campaigns and public debates around policy and implementation. More importantly the University set up a tribunal where cases were heard and where the law was enforced. Many a bright male student was expelled for sexually harassing women and many a professor was disciplined for exploiting female students.

We need "boots on" Commissioners who will sit in magistrate's courts to account how rape cases are processed through the criminal justice system; they need to monitor police stations to see whether or not victims are

---

68   *The Big Issue*, written and edited by professional journalists, is sold by poor and homeless vendors on the streets of South Africa's major cities.

69   Rhoda Kadalie. "Call to women in power: Lead the way in helping SA's girls." *The Big Issue*, Vol. 14 No. 173, 3 Dec. 2010 - 14 Jan. 2011. p. 10.

treated with dignity and respect and whether medico-legal services are provided; they need to ensure that conviction rapes are improved upon from year to year; they need to insist on the provision of sexual offences courts; they need to work with NGOs who engage teachers and principals to include sex education and reproductive health in the curriculum; and they need to advise government how to fund these initiatives.[70]

These were the standards Rhoda had always demanded, and she lamented that Parliament was not holding the government accountable to them.

Rhoda also co-wrote, with her daughter Julia, an electronic short book called *The Politics of Pregnancy*, about fertility, birth control, and the HIV/Aids pandemic in South Africa.[71] They noted that despite the availability of free contraceptives in the new South Africa, sex remained "unsafe" — not just in the sense that participants often chose not to use condoms, but that rape continued to be all too common. "[M]any South Africans lack the freedom and support in their relationships, families and communities that would allow them to make better choices," they observed. In addition to tackling the enduring problem of abusive male behavior, the government ought to seek partnerships with community and civil society organizations active in the field of women's sexual health to replicate "best practices" across the country.

In that spirit, Annie Lennox, the lead singer of the Eurythmics, who took an interest in South Africa, soon befriended Rhoda and worked together with her on an anti-rape campaign. The country, and the world, had been shocked by a series of graphic rapes, including the rape, disembowelment, and murder of 17-year-old Anene Booysen that year. When CNN apparently commented that the Booysen rape had been the "tipping point" on the issue, Rhoda quipped: "How many tipping points do we need?"[72]

Lennox and Rhoda participated together in a silent protest at St. George's Cathedral in Cape Town, and Rhoda helped Lennox launch a petition calling for action against violence targeting women and girls.[73]

70   Rhoda Kadalie. Draft column for *Die Burger*. 12 Feb. 2013. Personal files.
71   Rhoda Kadalie and Julia Pollak. *The Politics of Pregnancy*. Cape Town: Tafelberg, 2013.
72   Rhoda Kadalie, quoted by Mogomotsi Selebi. "Rise in Reported Rapists Despite Heavy Sentences." *Sowetan*, 13 Nov. 2013.
73   Lynley Donnelly. "Lennox calls on SA to fight gender-based violence." *Mail & Guardian*, 2 May 2013.

She continued to use her column to speak out about the "silent epidemic" of rape preying on South African women and girls.[74]

Rhoda watches as Eurythmics legend Annie Lennox signs a petition against rape outside St. George's Cathedral, Cape Town, 2013 (Courtesy Rhoda Kadalie)]

74   Rhoda Kadalie. "A silent epidemic of rape." PoliticsWeb, reprinted and translated from *Die Burger*, 22 Nov. 2011. URL: https://www.politicsweb.co.za/news-and-analysis/a-silent-epidemic-of-rape. Accessed on 26 Mar. 2022.

Rhoda argued repeatedly that the government's failures also represented a failure of South African civil society as a whole — both to hold the ruling party accountable, and to take women's welfare seriously, beyond the reach of politics and the state. Women, she said, had to lead the way themselves — and she was careful to acknowledge those individuals and organizations that were doing so.

***

Rhoda frequently defended the rights of Coloured people, becoming one of the few public intellectuals who dared to do so.

She came from the philosophical school of Black Consciousness, which rejected the idea of a separate Coloured identity as a creation of colonialism and apartheid. Her own grandfather, Clements Kadalie, had advocated for an inclusive "black" identity. But the reality, as she and Jakes Gerwel had agreed, was that Coloured identity was real — and, for Rhoda, worth defending.

"As somebody who fought against that classification, after 1994 people suddenly asserted themselves and their different identities," Rhoda told an interviewer in 2013. "Coloured, in the new South Africa, has become an epithet of pride, where people assert who they are. And suddenly in the new South Africa, the term I most rejected I am almost compelled to appropriate as an assertion that I am part of this new South Africa."[75]

The "Coloured" label, she said, was as much a burden after 1994 as it had been before, because those seen as mixed-race had to fight to assert their legitimacy. She spoke for many in the community who had suffered the burden of apartheid — the forced removals, the disenfranchisement, the dispossession — and yet were treated as second-class citizens by the ANC, which resented the relative privilege of Coloured people in apartheid's old racial hierarchy, believed in the "hegemony" of the country's African majority.

As she told Ryland Fisher in an interview for his book, *Race*, about identity in post-apartheid South Africa:

> I think coloured people have been pathologised pre-1994 and post-1994. It is an easy excuse to discriminate against coloured people. Coloured people were marginalised before 1994. They were co-opted by the apartheid government in several ways ... [b]ut blacks were also

75   Rhoda Kadalie, interview with Abra Barbier. "Rhoda Kadalie on being Coloured in a new South Africa." SABC News, 19 Sep. 2013. URL: https://www.youtube.com/watch?v=fuKjzcFPVIo. Accessed on 28 April 2022.

cooperative. ... The point is that, in the new South Africa, I never thought that I would become a defender of the right of coloured people to exist. ... I think that coloured people are not treated fairly in terms of the new dispensation, in the slicing of the cake.[76]

Though Coloured people benefited from certain privileges under apartheid relative to the black or "African" population — participation in the Tricameral Parliament, for example — she argued that black people, particularly in the Bantustans, had been co-opted even more successfully. "To punish Coloured people for participating in the Tricameral Parliament, is to negate that Africans participated in an apartheid structure, namely the 'homeland' parliaments,"she said.[77] Rather than transcend the labels of the past, the ANC seemed determined to "perfect" the racial divisions that the apartheid regime had introduced. "And I'm annoyed that I am now inserted into a racial hierarchy again."[78]

While she quipped that "being a thoroughbred mongrel is an asset in South Africa's political landscape," she also protested: "Coloured people have never been given power in terms of their own right."[79]

She took particular offense at the ANC applying national radical demographics in its affirmative action policies in Cape Town and the Western Cape, which put local residents at a huge disadvantage in access to government jobs and contracts. She wrote:

Coloured people, once again, find themselves an undercaste — serfs whose station in life is determined not by merit, potential, ability or hard work but by skin colour. Too dark under apartheid, the coloureds are not dark enough for the ANC ...

No wonder coloured people respond with the only power they have in a de facto one-party state - the skilled ones emigrate, depriving the country of desperately needed skills.[80]

To her, the ANC's poor treatment of Coloured people was the ultimate denial of the promise of the "Rainbow Nation."

---

76   Rhoda Kadalie, quoted by Ryland Fisher, ibid. p. 58.
77   Rhoda Kadalie, interview with Business Network Radio, ibid.
78   Ibid.
79   Rhoda Kadalie, quoted by "Why Ryland Fisher says he is a racist." *Sunday Independent*, 8 Jul. 2007. p. 18.
80   Rhoda Kadalie. "ANC rule has again made serfs out of coloureds." *Business Day*, 30 Nov. 2010.

She spoke out when the director general of the labor department, Mzwanele "Jimmy" Manyi, told an interviewer in 2010 that the Western Cape had too many Coloured people. Manyi, who was the government's official spokesperson by the time the remarks emerged in 2011, said that there was an "over-concentration" of Coloured people in the province,[81] adding: "They should spread in the rest of the country ... so they must stop this over-concentration situation because they are in over-supply where they are so you must look into the country and see where you can meet the supply."[82]

To Rhoda, the ANC's approach was simply "ethnic cleansing," not affirmative action.[83] "People have a right to be where they are," she said.[84] She added that Manyi's viewpoint reflected the ANC's failure to reckon with the origins of the Coloured population "as descended from the Khoi and the San, and the slaves who were imported from Madagascar, Indonesia, and elsewhere."

She did not let the DA off the hook, either, castigating the party both for its lapses in serving the Coloured community, and specifically for its mismanagement of the District Six restitution process. In 2011, when restitution had stagnated for years, Rhoda blamed both parties that had governed Cape Town, singling out the DA for particular criticism:

Former claimants expected the DA to tackle District Six head on when they took over both the City and Province and undo the corrupt partnerships and the networks of self-elected representatives that flourished under the ANC and which are deeply embedded within the restitution mafia. Negating the symbolic importance of restoring District Six to the people in a broader integrated model of redevelopment, both the ANC and the DA have failed claimants and the coloured community at large.[85]

---

81   Mzwanele "Jimmy" Manyi, quoted by Solidarity. "Jimmy Many on coloureds in the Western Cape." Solidariteit, YouTube video, 24 Feb. 2011. URL: https://www.youtube.com/watch?v=oBqCD_498hY. Accessed on 28 Apr. 2022.

82   Mzwanele "Jimmy" Manyi, quoted by South African Press Association. "Manyi: 'Over-supply' of coloureds in Western Cape." *Mail and Guardian*, 24 Feb. 2011. URL: https://mg.co.za/article/2011-02-24-coloureds-overconcentrated-in-wcape-says-manyi/. Accessed on 28 April 2022.

83   Rhoda Kadalie. "Jimmy Manyi's ethnic cleansing." PoliticsWeb, reprinted and translated from *Die Burger*, 1 Mar. 2011. URL: https://www.politicsweb.co.za/news-and-analysis/jimmy-manyis-ethnic-cleansing. Accessed on 26 Mar. 2022.

84   Rhoda Kadalie, interview with Business Network Radio, ibid.

85   Ibid.

In a column for *Die Burger*, she blasted the DA for continuing what she called a "corrupt" arrangement between the previous ANC administration of the city and two organizations that, she said, lacked standing to represent the District Six claimants. And she accused the DA-run city — even under her friend Helen Zille — of adopting a patronizing attitude toward the long-suffering, mostly Coloured, families who still awaited restitution.[86]

Rhoda also defended Coloured people against claims by analysts — white and black — that they were racist for voting against the ANC. For example, she attacked a common canard that Cape Town was more "racist" than Johannesburg, the implication being that Coloured people were racist toward black people. While Cape Town had a history of excluding black migrants under apartheid, Rhoda wrote, Cape Town had also provided the foundation for many of the most important movements in the anti-apartheid struggle:

> *Both the Western Cape and Gauteng demand that we understand the different socio-historical and political trajectories of these two provinces before we trade racial insults. It is in the Western Cape that influx control and the pass laws were most viciously enforced against African people. Resistance to these laws generated a series of organisations such as the African People's Organisation, the Non-European Unity Movement, the Black Sash, the Institute of Race Relations, the United Democratic Front and all its hundreds of umbrella organisations – and they all mounted massive campaigns against deportations, detentions and arrests of black people.*
>
> *All of us in the Western Cape, white, black, coloured, and Indian were involved in that struggle. That is why the black middle class in the Western Cape is small unlike Gauteng where the industrial and mining revolutions attracted droves of cheap labour to the burgeoning metropolis. The anti-Cape hot air is a euphemism for being anti-coloured and a negation of their experiences as blacks, under apartheid![87]*

She cautioned her media colleagues to examine their own prejudices: "I, too, do not see coloured people when I go to Gauteng and I too feel alienated

---

86   Rhoda Kadalie. "District Six 'restitution' efforts a disgrace." PoliticsWeb, reprinted and translated from *Die Burger*, 11 Apr. 2012. URL: https://www.politicsweb.co.za/news-and-analysis/district-six-restitution-efforts-a-disgrace. Accessed on 26 Mar. 2022.

87   Rhoda Kadalie. "Why Cape Town is labelled 'racist'." PoliticsWeb, reprinted and translated from *Die* Burger, 27 Mar. 2012. URL: https://www.politicsweb.co.za/news-and-analysis/why-cape-town-is-labelled-racist. Accessed on 26 Mar. 2022.

let alone unwelcome when I visit; and I speak as much for my colleagues as I speak for myself. The point is: based on my experiences alone I dare not make generalisations about Gauteng." She would not tolerate the media ascribing their own racial hangups to opposition-governed Cape Town, or Coloured people in general.

When *Financial Mail* analyst Carol Paton suggested that Coloured voters were more comfortable with the DA because it was led by whites, Rhoda responded:

> *Ms Paton, are you suggesting that coloured people are deeply racist? Do you base this on any poll? Could it be possible that coloured people vote for clean and accountable governance; for service delivery; for an intelligent leadership; and for lack of corruption? Could it be that coloured people are selective about their interests and nonracial, and just as they overwhelmingly voted for the ANC in 1994, they now have voted for a party that has proven that as a government it is serious about addressing the challenges that face SA?*

> *I am coloured and my considerations for voting DA are certainly not racist. Secondly, the DA's leadership is not white only, and that you perpetuate this myth puts you in a class of journalist I have come to despise because of their shoddy research.*[88]

While not denying that some Coloured voters — like any voters — could be susceptible to racial appeals, Rhoda believed that they were a discerning constituency that had learned to be effective by not being loyal to any particular party.

In the 2009 election campaign, when both the incumbent ANC and the surging DA courted the Coloured swing vote in the Western Cape, Rhoda blasted the way Coloured people were being treated as "voting fodder."[89] Responding, perhaps, to the fact that her name had been floated openly as a possible candidate for premier of the province, she commented sardonically: "With the run-up to the election, every political party looks for a coloured leader to lure this group into their trap, and as sure as hell, some or other figure crawls out of the woodwork claiming to represent the interests of the coloured people. ... This routine electoral ploy is an indication of how ignorant politicians are about the coloured people and how they fundamentally misunderstand them. Unpredictable and fiercely

---

88　Rhoda Kadalie. "More to vote than racism." Letter to the editor. *Financial Mail*, 3 Jun. 2011.

89　Rhoda Kadalie. "Election Ploys and Coloured Crises." *Business Day*, 29 Jan. 2009.

independent in their political choices, coloureds remain an enigma to politicians, but this is no excuse."[90]

The ANC in particular had forfeited the trust of Coloured voters, she observed, through its "negation of the role that coloured people played in the anti-apartheid and liberation movements and the close affinity between coloureds and Africans in opposing white minority rule." She also lamented the decline of the outstanding schools that the Coloured community had created, against the odds, under apartheid rule, such has her own alma mater, Harold Cressy. All were victims of the ANC's racial politics and centralized machinery.

Conversely, Rhoda believed that Coloured people had unique leverage in the new South Africa— if they chose to use it. She believed Coloured voters were "supremely placed to safeguard ... democracy by putting a check on the power of the majority"; "steer[ing] clear of race politics and [the] politics of ethnicity"; and becoming a "[p]owerful political force for what is right, just, and lawful."[91]

There were also aspects of Coloured identity that Rhoda celebrated beyond their role in the history and politics of South Africa. "I don't know what it is in Coloured people," she said, "but they have the capacity to laugh at their disaster. And it often turns against them, where they can't be serious enough about the things that hurt. And maybe it's a survival mechanism, this Coloured humor."[92]

***

Vignette: "Coloured Culture" by Rhoda Kadalie

Just before the founding of the Tricameral Parliament in 1983, the apartheid government increasingly wooed coloureds and Indians into their fold to create a bulwark against the African majority. More and more we heard a discourse that implied that there was such a thing as "coloured culture." The intention of the ruling class was to suggest that coloured people were closer to whites socially, culturally, and politically than to Africans.

---

90   Ibid.
91   Rhoda Kadalie. "Bruin Mense Quo Vadis." Notes for a lecture. 30 Aug. 2003.
92   Rhoda Kadalie, interview with Abra Barbier, ibid.

Anti-apartheid coloureds avowedly denied that there was such a thing a "coloured culture" distinct from the rest of South Africans, and the more the National Party pushed the line, the more coloured people denied it.

One day, a friend of mine who taught at St Cyprian's, a girls' school, told me that their schoolgirls had just hosted an Indian cultural evening where Indian culture was on full display – saris, makeup, food, delicacies, and music.

Obviously thrilled at the success of the evening, I asked her, tongue in cheek, "Why don't you host a coloured evening?"

Embarrassed, she responded: "Don't be ridiculous; it's such a stupid thing to say." Rather curious, she nevertheless asked: "By the way, what would you show off at a coloured culture (she could barely utter the words) evening?"

"Oh" I said, "I would serve cabbage stew, cauliflower *bredie* [stew], green jelly and custard, *koeksisters* [fried doughnuts], *samoosas*, and so on."

That was the end of that.

The next day I chatted to our University Chaplain, Colin Jones, a former neighbour and colleague who once lived in District Six and who, incidentally was also a Chaplain of St Cyprian's.

"Colin", I said, "I heard your kids at St Cyprian's hosted an Indian cultural evening last night. Why don't you host a coloured cultural evening?"

Fully aware of the national debate about coloured culture, he played along and jokingly said, "Yes, we would serve cauliflower *bredie*, cabbage stew, curry and rice, green jelly and custard, *koeksisters*, *samoosas* and sago (tapioca) pudding."

"Hey Colin, you've just proved there is such a thing as coloured culture, because that is exactly what I told my friend."

Colin wryly whispered: "Just don't tell anyone."

In the course of the week, I bumped into Prof. Jakes Gerwel and told him my story. Since we often exchanged stories about our families and communities, I knew he would like the St Cyprian's story.

While we kept up the political front of negating the idea of "coloured culture", he said to me "*Kadalietjie* [little Kadalie], *maar net ons weet daar is so 'n ding soos KK* [but only we know there is such a thing as coloured culture]." The abbreviation stood for "kleurling kultuur," i.e. "coloured culture."

"*Jy is die antropoloog en ek die Afrikaans spesialis,*" he continued, "*kom ons versamel voorbeelde van KK en skryf 'n boek, maar dis net tussen ons twee*" [You are the anthropologist and I am the Afrikaans specialist, let's collect examples of KK and write a book, but it's just between the two of us].

Thus began the collection of "coloured memorabilia, cultural artefacts, and vignettes." We gathered explanations for the "passion gap" – reasons for why coloured people extract their front teeth; the idiosyncrasies of the "*Kaapse Klopse,*" the minstrel carnival; coloured gangs on the Cape Flats; coloured colloquialisms; cuisine peculiarities; the consumption of sweet wine out of brown packets; and so on.[93]

Much of this elicited debate, denial, and great laughter. We explored questions of regional differences, since Gerwel came from rural Kommadagga and I from urban District Six; we also talked about generational similarities, and so on.

One day, Prof. Gerwel invited a colleague and me to stop by on our way home from UWC for a cup of tea at his house. Chatting amiably in his living room about our fabled book, I suddenly blurted out loudly: "Jakes, another thing coloured people love is rooibos tea with sugar and condensed milk."

Just then, his wife entered the living room carrying a tray of rooibos tea and condensed milk!

"Fuck you and the book!" he exclaimed.

That was the end of our dive into KK.[94]

***

In advocating for the rights of Coloured people, Rhoda rejected the idea that South Africa's minority groups were to be forever burdened by the apartheid past.

---

93   Editorial note: one such note from these exchanges survives. Gerwel sent Rhoda a handwritten message on official stationery, adding parenthetically: "I wonder what psycho-analysis will make of our early desire to do a collaborative piece on KK?" Jakes Gerwel. Note to Rhoda Kadalie. 27 Oct. Year unknown.

94   On his 60th birthday, Rhoda would teasingly remind Gerwel "to finish his life's work ... to write the definitive KK text and prove contrary to all PC–beliefs, that Coloureds are indeed the stereotype, starting with him and me!!!!!". Rhoda Kadalie. "Tribute to Jakes Gerwel on his 60th birthday." In *Professor Jakes Gerwel: 60 years, marking time....* Commemorative book. 2006. p. 27.

Rhoda: 'Comrade Kadalie, You Are Out of Order!'

In late 2000, a group of left-wing white South Africans produced an apologetic confession, a so-called "Declaration of Commitment," declaring themselves to have been unjust beneficiaries of apartheid. They added: "We therefore believe that it is right and necessary to commit ourselves to redressing these wrongs. We pledge to use our skills, resources and energy...(toward) promoting a non-racial society whose resources are used to the benefit of all its people."[95] They urged other white people to sign as part of what they called the "Home for All" initiative, launching their declaration on December 16, a public holiday known as Reconciliation Day, and once known as Dingane's Day, a celebration of an Afrikaner victory over Zulu warriors. The signatories included several prominent names, including Frederick van Zyl Slabbert, Alex Boraine, and several Constitutional Court judges. The ANC welcomed the gesture as a statement of loyalty to the new South Africa from a group whose members overwhelmingly voted for opposition parties.

But Rhoda dismissed the gesture. It was too late, she said, "to say sorry now."[96] More important, she saw the effort as an attempt to generate political consensus around the ANC, and undermine legitimate criticism: "I think it is a disgraceful declaration. ... It is the resurrection of the sorry ideology which has more to do with making white people feel good than it has for promoting justice. It is also aimed at silencing white people from being critical of the black government. If they want white people to say sorry about the past then, as a black person, I must say sorry about not spending the poverty money or providing the anti-retroviral drugs. It is of no consequence to black people to say sorry. The statement is dangerous."[97]

She appeared on a panel discussion on SABC that month to debate the issue. She made the case that the declaration "stereotype[s] white people" as the oppressors, when there were Coloured and black people who also collaborated with apartheid.[98] And given the compromise at Codesa that ushered in democracy, which accepted that "whites, too, will be part of this new South Africa," there was no use for such apologies. She added:

If white people insist, as that group insists, that white people should say sorry for the past, then I, as a black person today, want to say sorry for

95   Claire Keeton. "White South Africans divided over 'reconciliation' fund." Agence France Presse, 16 Dec. 2000.
96   Rhoda Kadalie, quoted by Hugh Nevill. "White S. African reconciliation bid runs into further trouble." Agence France Presse, 17 Dec. 2000.
97   Rhoda Kadalie, quoted by Barry Streek. "Whites split over guilt trip." Mail & Guardian, 15 Dec. 2000.
98   Rhoda Kadalie. Remarks on Two-way, SABC 1. Dec. 2000.

the fact that we've bungled on the Aids question, we've bungled on the poverty alleviation budget, we've bungled on the service delivery in this country. There are many issues. I think we have a new democracy, we have a black majority government, and we must govern with confidence. Whether whites say sorry or not is immaterial to our transformation. We have to move forward confidently that we can govern.[99]

Similarly, she argued in a debate with fellow black intellectuals at a debate in 2000:

Our victory over apartheid was a victory over white racial minority domination. Whether whites say sorry or not is of no consequence to me. The challenge is for this democratic government, which is led by a black majority, to govern confidently and justly in such a way that those who were victims in the past no longer seek the approval of their former oppressors in order to be human.[100]

She described a return to the fixation on racism as an effort to divert attention from the failures of the post-apartheid government.

Later, she would write in the *Mail & Guardian*:

The declaration simplistically blames the deprivation experienced by most black people mainly on racist attitudes, internalised inferiority, and the failure of white people to take responsibility for the past. The apologists, therefore, call upon their white compatriots to seek absolution and contribute towards a fund that will help empower disadvantaged people.

...

Secondly, to blame everything on race and racism is to fail to acknowledge that this government has done little for the development of black South Africa. To spend R44-billion on arms as a priority, when there are much more urgent developmental needs, is something this so-called concerned group should have been more vocal about. But this group does not want to be seen to be criticising this government as their access to power and resources is dependent on supporting the agenda of this government — a perceptive point made by both Tony Holiday of the University of the Western Cape and Helen Zille, Western Cape MEC for Education, in recent newspaper columns.

---

99 Ibid.
100 Rhoda Kadalie, Goedgedacht Forum, ibid.

Rhoda: 'Comrade Kadalie, You Are Out of Order!'

...

I can only conclude that one of their concerns stems from the overwhelming vote the Democratic Alliance got in the recent elections. The timing of the declaration, its focus on the Western Cape and its campaign slogan, a "Home for All" — as a counter to the implicit assumption that the Western Cape is not a home for all — explain the disquiet of some who attended the ceremony in Cape Town's St George's Cathedral on December 16. Instead of welcoming the DA's advance as a sign of a vibrant and healthy democracy, the declaration is used to put whites on a guilt trip for having chosen to vote the way they did.

...

We must learn to live with the gory side of the negotiations deal struck between the former oppressors and the ANC. Either we (meaning black and white) accept all the weaknesses of the compromises forged at Codesa and get on with our lives. Or we exclude whites from becoming part of this vibrant democratic civil society, and take responsibility for its consequences.[101]

Rhoda urged South Africans not to let race preclude them from voting for the opposition, even if the ANC had once been the party to liberate the country from apartheid.

In November 2000, Rhoda responded to another columnist, Glenda Daniels, who wrote that she was dismayed at the ANC, but could not vote for the opposition, and would therefore sit out South Africa's municipal elections that December.

Daniels had written that while she had been disappointed by President Mbeki's stance on HIV/Aids, the ANC's inaction on Zimbabwe, and attempts generally to reduce every political issue to race, she could not bring herself to vote for the Democratic Alliance. "In my view the Democratic Alliance is a party to protect white privilege, so I couldn't possibly vote for them."[102]

In a speech to the Cape Town Press Club that was partially reprinted in the *M&G*, Rhoda responded:

101 Rhoda Kadalie. "Sorry, This Is Just Another Divisive Fad." *Mail & Guardian*, 5 Jan. 2001.
102 Glenda Daniels. "Give us a good reason to vote." *Mail & Guardian*, 27 Oct. 2000. In David Macfarlane. *Bedside Book 2001*. Johannesburg: M&G Books, 2001. p. 66.

I wish to suggest that Daniels's view, and it is the view of many on the left, is deeply flawed and highly problematic for the development of democracy in South Africa. It is based on a sentimentalism and nostalgia for the sense of common purpose that characterised the liberation movement.

...

Many of my friends admit that they have lost political perspective because of their loyalty to the ANC. Loyalty to the party has taken precedence over loyalty to justice.

As [a] liberation movement, the ANC had the moral high ground. As the majority party in government, it no longer commands that moral high ground and can be found wanting on many levels, because it has reneged on many of its own very noble policies.

...

The Aids debacle and the racism in the media conference are indications that internal democracy is not alive and well in the ANC. Opposition parties, too, can be loyal to democracy, even should they differ on matters of policy. To dismiss them by constantly racialising them is to fail to assess them on merit.

Developing opposition requires that we look past race and look at how opposition as an institution needs to be cultivated and developed. It is customary for the left, after independence, to dismiss opposition and wait for the fateful day until a social democratic/socialist movement is formed to oppose the new government in power. And what happens when nobody is looking is that people vote again and again for the ANC, for sentimental reasons, entrenching their majority and so eroding the possibility of a real opposition developing. The all-inclusive opposition that Daniels is looking for only happens in 20 years' time, as in Zimbabwe, when it is far too late.[103]

To Rhoda, it was clear that South Africa could never succeed if it could not move beyond the racial politics of the past.

---

103   Rhoda Kadalie. "Use your vote to fight a one-party state." Speech to Cape Town Press Club. *Mail & Guardian*, 10 Nov. 2000. URL: https://mg.co.za/article/2000-11-10-use-your-vote-to-fight-a-one-party/. Accessed on 15 Oct. 2021.

Chapter 15:
The Struggle Within

"It was easier to criticize apartheid because it was so blatantly wrong, and was internationally declared a crime against humanity. It may be bold to stand up against a Draconian government, but even more so to stand up against a government you supported, that you voted into power."[1]

Rhoda was a strident critic of the ANC — but remained a member of the party, long after she had condemned it. By the early 2000s, she no longer voted for the ANC, or supported it ideologically; indeed, she openly endorsed the opposition in several elections (see Chapter 16). But she cherished the posture of an internal critic — as a "comrade" who was "out of order," an epithet that had once been flung at her in "struggle" meetings, and which she quickly embraced.

Rhoda wrestled with the ANC while broadly sharing its aspirations of a "better life for all," as its 1994 slogan promised. That meant she soon occupied a unique position in South African politics and media. As she noted in an Afrikaans-language profile in 2009:

"What creates a schizophrenia around me is that I write a political column with one hand and with my other hand I am in charge of a program that rewards excellence in the public sector.

"So we are in fact showing the government the good work they are doing. And the good work they are doing in collaboration with the public sector and civil society. "[2]

That "schizophrenia" allowed Rhoda to emerge as a rare public figure who was willing to criticize the ANC from the perspective of an insider. Though she was initially greeted by vehement denunciation and even social isolation at times, her trailblazing example inspired other critics to emerge, over time, in her wake.

---

1   Rhoda Kadalie, quoted by *The Oprah Magazine*, Jul. 2007, ibid.
2   Rhoda Kadalie, quoted by Murray La Vita. "Rhoda Kadalie: Die vrou wat nie stilgebly het nie." Netwerk 24, 16 Apr. 2022. Translated from the Afrikaans via Google Translate. URL: https://www.netwerk24.com/netwerk24/stemme/profiele/rhoda-kadalie-die-vrou-wat-nie-stilgebly-het-nie-20220416. Accessed on 20 Apr. 2022.

Rhoda: 'Comrade Kadalie, You Are Out of Order!'

Few ANC members dared to disagree openly with their party leadership for the first decade or so after 1994. It was a fear that went far beyond mere party loyalty in the ordinary sense. The ANC had a long history of persecuting its dissidents, and had confessed to the TRC, grudgingly, that it had committed human rights abuses against fellow activists during the anti-apartheid struggle. Mbeki's faction of "exiles" was known to operate in a particularly secretive faction; they were feared and even loathed by fellow party members.

The Afrikaans journalist Murray La Vita asked Rhoda in 2011 if she ever felt afraid:

Is she sometimes scared after writing a column?

"I've never been anxiety-ridden about a column I wrote about. And, in a sense, if you grew up in a religious home ... I'm not afraid of people, I'm not afraid of them. The worst that what they can do to you is kill you. They can not kill your spirit. So, I have no fear of politicians."

She remains silent.

"For the past two months, my ANC friends have been warning me ... friends high up have told me, 'Watch your back. Be careful.' The only thing I worry about in the new South Africa is that ... in the old days we knew about our spy ... now we do not know; it could be anyone."

...

She describes a street confrontation with one of her former comrades as follows:

"He almost slapped me over a column I wrote. He was so furious about it. He admired me, and I taught him on university. He went through cronyism to get where he is today.

"I have experienced many similar incidents. People wrote me off; stopped inviting me to parties ... Yes ... I mean ... I once invited ministers to my house for dinner. Nou is ek persona non grata. They can not even look at me when I walk into a room. They can not even face me. But that's okay.[3]

---

3   Rhoda Kadalie, quoted by Murray La Vita. *Gesprekke Met Merkwaardige Mense*. Cape Town: Tafelberg, 2011. p. 192-3.

Rhoda *was* afraid of retaliation, and at times bitter about her growing isolation from old friends. But she also knew that her growing popularity was the best form of protection — and she believed, perhaps to a fault, in telling the truth as she saw it.

And the more she told the truth, the more liberated she felt. In 2015, she told an audience of American academics and students: "I am qualified to speak about SA in ways that my peers find difficult. ... I no longer subscribe to the dictates and orthodoxies of the liberation struggle and have long ago weaned myself from the jargon of liberation in favor of SPEAKING TRUTH TO POWER."[4]

In 2009, Rhoda was invited to publish a collection of her columns. Tentatively titled "Kadalie 101," the project eventually emerged under the more provocative title *In Your Face*.[5] At the launch for her book, Rhoda praised her sources within the ruling party — "those citizens and whistleblowers who will sacrifice life and limb to put the truth into the public arena." She added:

Many anonymous people here today provided me with undercover information because they are so admirably on the side of right. I wish to thank them deeply. Many encouraged and egged me on when I became so enraged that I could hardly express myself. Many called to compliment me again and again on a column and to give advice. And when I gave up writing for a while, many convinced me that I had a job to do, so I gave in. Even those who stopped greeting me, those who verbally abused me, and those who questioned my credentials, convinced me that speaking truth to power is a powerful weapon of mass empowerment. When I started writing there were very few black critics; in small measure I contributed to the growth of a small pool of insider critics, who have become such a formidable force that Mbeki suggested the Native Club as a counter-revolutionary force to neutralize us![6]

That pool of critics was to grow — and within a few short years, the shortcomings of the ANC would be clear to all.

Even as she criticized the ANC vehemently in her columns, Rhoda refused to sever her ties with it completely. Yet over time, in her writing,

4 Rhoda Kadalie. "Role of the Tabloids in SA." Lecture, Semester at Sea. 14 Sep. 2005. Original emphasis.
5 Rhoda Kadalie. *In Your Face: Passionate Conversations about People and Politics*. Cape Town: NB Publishers, 2009.
6 Rhoda Kadalie. Speech at the launch of *In Your Face*. Wordsworth Books, Cape Town. 7 Apr. 2009.

she began to air public doubts that the ANC could yet be saved from its own poor leadership and failing ideology.

Rhoda signing a copy of In Your Face for her parents, 2009
(Courtesy Rhoda Kadalie)

She became vocal in her opposition to the increasingly imperious attitude of the ruling party, which, she argued, began to exceed that of the National Party at the height of its power. Whereas former President F. W. De Klerk had traveled with only a security vehicle trailing him, for example, ANC ministers moved about the country in motorcades, displacing drivers on their regular commutes and snarling traffic.

Rhoda slammed Mbeki as a "president who commands a lawless cavalcade — that shoves everyone off the road, that blares its sirens all day long, announcing to the unimpressed Capetonians that he is around."[7] In 2002, she was enraged by the ANC's street closures near her office for the annual opening of Parliament. As the *Mail & Guardian* reported:

---

7   Rhoda Kadalie. "Democratic charade misses the point of dialogue." *Business Day*, 9 Feb. 2006. p. 13.

After a row with office workers, police allegedly planted barricades in front of the Institute for Democracy in South Africa (Idasa) building on Spin Street in Cape Town.

Former [human rights] commissioner Rhoda Kadalie is executive director of the Impumelelo Trust, housed in the Idasa building. When she objected to the placing of barricades, she says: "The barricades were deliberately smashed into my face, breaking my spectacles." She says people were not allowed to leave the building for three hours. Kadalie says when people were walking around on the streets again she tried to go to an optometrist, "only to be prevented once again by the police", but only briefly.

"While my glasses were being fixed the police taunted me from outside, shouting all kinds of abuse," says Kadalie.

Once the glasses had been repaired, "three big white men blocked my attempt to go back to my offices, threatening to arrest me and physically manhandling me. I broke free from their grip and ran across to my offices."

Kadalie maintains while she and others were being trapped, workers in an adjacent state building were allowed unhindered access.[8]

Year after year, Rhoda would object to the closing of roads, and the pompous pageantry of the red carpet — "all those politicians who dress up like clowns"[9] — for Parliament's opening. She also mocked efforts to increase salaries for members of Parliament (MPs): "MPs enjoy the shortest work year of all. ... Frankly, many of our MPs are unemployable elsewhere. They wouldn't last a week in a competitive, private sector job."[10]

Though her sentiments were widely shared, even within the ANC, few others were so direct in their criticism. But Rhoda's credentials — her struggle past, her unassailable achievements for women,   and   her grandfather's enduring political legacy — gave her unique authenticity.

Her work on the Human Rights Commission had also sharpened her sensitivity to the consequences of "cadre deployment" — the ANC's policy of bringing public institutions and private corporations under its control

---

8   "No Go for Workers During Parliament's Opening." *Mail & Guardian*, 15 Feb. 2002.
9   Rhoda Kadalie. "Bunch of clowns." Letter to the editor. *Business Day*, 15 Feb. 2006. p. 10.
10   Rhoda Kadalie. "Laughable reasons to fill MPs' pay trough." *Business Day*, 19 Jun. 2008. p. 13.

by appointing loyal party members to positions of influence. She observed that supposedly independent bodies like the Human Rights Commission and the Gender Commission were dominated by "cadre deployed political appointees," rendering them largely ineffective as checks on the ANC's power.[11] (In 2022, the Zondo Commission would officially declare that the ANC's policy of cadre deployment was a violation of the South African Constitution.)

In 2006, Rhoda noted that the office of the Public Protector — like the Human Rights Commission, one of the nominally independent "Chapter 9" institutions in the new Constitution — had been subordinated to the ruling party. After listing a series of corruption scandals that then–Public Protector Lawrence Mushwana had failed to investigate properly, she wrote:

> Mushwana is a master at skirting investigations that implicate the ruling elite. His tenure has been characterised by contempt for the constitution and for his obligation to be independent, impartial and exercise his powers and perform his functions without fear, favour or prejudice.

> As a former ANC MP, Mushwana, like most of the heads of the Chapter 9 institutions who have all been co–opted into uselessness, dares not bite the hand that feeds him. He knows he would be thoroughly neutered should he indict any of them.[12]

Mushwana would later be replaced by a far more independent-minded Public Protector, Thuli Madonsela, who would help expose the corruption of "state capture" under President Jacob Zuma. (Adding insult to injury, Mushwana was appointed chair of the Human Rights Commission, confirming Rhoda's decision to resign over a decade before and to continue her criticism in the years since.) By the time Madonsela took over, factionalism within the ruling party had provided a modicum of internal opposition within the state — not enough to hold the ANC fully accountable, but enough to encourage leaks that shed light on some of the government's misdeeds.

Rhoda also spoke out against the steady decline of the judiciary, both in terms of competence and judicial independence. In its haste to make the bench more racially representative of the country, the ANC appointed some judges before they had the knowledge and experience for their positions, a problem that became apparent in complex commercial

---

11   Rhoda Kadalie, interview with Business Network Radio, ibid.
12   Rhoda Kadalie. "Public Protector is a master at protecting the ANC elite." *Business Day*, 23 Feb. 2006. p. 21.

disputes. Critics also charged that the ANC sought to appoint judges who were ideologically aligned with the ruling party, eroding the hard-fought judicial independence that had been a flickering light of hope during the apartheid years.

The nominally independent Judicial Services Commission (JSC), which recommends judges to the president for appointment, became a vehicle for the ruling party's policy of racial preferences, often turning down applicants with sterling anti-apartheid credentials solely because they were white. In 2012, Rhoda Kadalie co-signed a letter supporting the nomination of experienced attorney Jeremy Gauntlett to the Constitutional Court, after he had been turned down for judicial positions several times.[13] He was, again, denied, confirming suspicions that the JSC was primarily interested in race, gender, and ideological conformity.

Rhoda commented:

The repeated refusal to select [Gauntlett] points to something deeply rotten in an organisation that should epitomise rectitude. ... [T]he JSC shuns excellence at their peril and consciously eschews appointing candidates who have the ability to perform their duty as required by the Constitution. Instead they deliberately choose candidates who are grossly underqualified as long as they are connected and pliable.

Those chosen over Gauntlett included a Mpumalanga attorney who admitted not disclosing to the JSC disciplinary infractions, only having himself argued unopposed cases and delays as an acting judge in writing judgments. So too a state attorney who opened her own law firm a year ago — only to close it a month later (after owning it) to take up an acting appointment. Optimism, uncanny foresight or simply a nod?

The negative effects of their decisions will plague SA for generations to come. This disrespect for excellence is happening everywhere – at our universities, schools, government departments, state enterprises, all in the name of transformation.

The JSC seems to forget that an independent judiciary is critical to the success of a nation. Instead it exploits its immunity from professional critique; it exploits the fact that potential candidates cannot complain because it will be held against them forever; it enjoys creating factions within the legal community to ensure that it can govern through its divide and rule policy; it enjoys playing God by denying people achieving

---

13   Rhoda Kadalie. Open letter in support of Jeremy Gauntlett. *Cape Times*, 20 Nov. 2012. p. 10.

their highest potential, when in fact it is the devil incarnate; and it enjoys
taking revenge against white advocates who are independent and who
dare to deliver judgements that go against the ruling party.[14]

Gauntlett joined a growing list of qualified, brave legal minds, such as
anti-apartheid attorney Geoff Budlender, who were denied a place on the
bench due to the need for "transformation," not just in terms of race but
also in fealty to the ruling party.

Rhoda also took the lead in opposing the advancement of Judge John
Hlophe, judge president of the courts in the Western Cape. He had accused
fellow justices of racism; had been accused of ethical and personal lapses;
and had a penchant for vicious public debates with his critics and rivals.
Rhoda warned that if Hlophe were ever appointed to the Constitutional
Court, his appointment would "destroy the dwindling confidence the
public has in the judiciary."[15] Thanks in part to pressure from Rhoda and
others, he was passed over in favor of Sandile Ngcobo as Chief Justice, and
remained in the Western Cape. Of Hlophe, Rhoda was later to say that he
"demonstrates just how deep the wounds inflicted by apartheid are, that
not even the very privileged and educated among us can overcome them. So
deep is the hurt felt by blacks who now have power that they are prepared
to destroy the institutions that should serve the next generation."[16]

* * *

The problem was not just Mbeki, as Rhoda later wrote, as dissident factions
began to rebel against his authoritarian style. When Mbeki dismissed
then-Deputy President Jacob Zuma in 2005 over allegations of corruption,
he triggered a backlash that finally opened room for debate and criticism
within the ruling party. But Rhoda warned: "In all of this political upheaval,
the ANC's allies should not be let off the hook. Supporting Zuma just to
spite Mbeki is cheap politics par excellence."[17] She warned that the ruling
party had to correct its policies, not its leadership.

---

14   Rhoda Kadalie. "There's something deeply rotten in the JSC." PoliticsWeb,
      reprinted from *Die Burger* and translated from the Afrikaans, 23 Oct.
      2012. URL: https://www.politicsweb.co.za/news-and-analysis/theres-
      something-deeply-rotten-in-the-jsc. Accessed on 26 Mar. 2022.
15   Rhoda Kadalie. Quoted by Robyn Dixon. "THE WORLD; S. Africa's divisive
      jurist; A man as controversial as President Zuma could be appointed by
      him to the nation's highest court." *Los Angeles Times*, 19 Aug. 2009. p. 18.
16   Rhoda Kadalie. "Worse than judges' racist bluster is the silence
      supporting it." *Business Day*, 10 Sep. 2009.
17   Rhoda Kadalie. "More to ANC's grassroots revolt than Zuma's case."
      Business Day, 7 Jul. 2005. Published in Rhoda Kadalie. *In Your Face*. Cape

Those policies — nominally socialist, obsessed with race — were holding the country back — and, ironically, hurting most of the black majority these policies ostensibly were intended to benefit.

Rhoda began to see the state-centered philosophy of the ANC as its fatal flaw, more than the incompetence of its cadres, or even the corruption of its politicians. The problem was within the ANC's beliefs about government: the ruling party could never fulfill all of its promises to the country if it pursued those goals by emphasizing the state and not the private sector.

Meanwhile, Rhoda noted, both Mbeki and Zuma faced little resistance — not only because the political opposition was too weak, but also because the activists and organizations who had built a powerful and vocal civil society in the latter years of apartheid became almost dormant in the post-apartheid era. "Civil society ... became too happy with its new government ... many withdrew from civil society and supported government; at the same time government creamed off the top leadership of civil society incorporating them into government."[18] As a result, it was difficult to hold the ANC accountable, and the only opposition that mattered was within the ruling party itself, whose divisions — often based on ethnicity and class — threatened to destabilize the entire country.

As the fight between the pro-Mbeki and pro-Zuma factions intensified, Rhoda took a cautious approach, warning South Africans not to trust either side, or to take anything at face value. When Zuma, then leading an insurgent campaign within the ANC to dislodge Mbeki, was charged with rape, there were suspicions that he had been set up by Mbeki and his supporters. Rhoda, emphasizing that she did not want Zuma to become president, wrote nonetheless that he deserved to be presumed innocent until proven guilty:

Because JZ [Jacob Zuma] was found to have had a corrupt relationship with [convicted fraudster] Schabir Shaik, and because he is a polygamist and womaniser, his detractors assume him guilty before they have even heard the evidence. That he slept with someone who is HIV-positive, as reprehensible as that might be, does not mean that we have a right to assume that he has raped the woman and therefore has no right to a fair trial.

...

Town: Tafelberg, 2009. p. 112.

18   Rhoda Kadalie. "Introduction" Lecture, Semester at Sea. 10 Sep. 2011.

Rhoda: 'Comrade Kadalie, You Are Out of Order!'

At the University of the Western Cape where I was the gender equity officer I dealt with enough cases where women used claims of rape and sexual harassment claims to get even with their partners. I was called the "gender police" and I feminised our courts substantially.

This does not preclude the fact that in most circumstances of rape women have no protection or defence and that it often happens under violent conditions that are life threatening.

The fact is this alleged rape by JZ of the complainant did not happen under violent circumstances. It happened between two people who know each other. At no stage did the complainant say no and she admitted that JZ might have thought it okay to have sex. There was a policeman on the premises and other people. This complicates the matter even further.

...

JZ's supporters have a right to feel that he has been set up. The linkage with the intelligence ministry is not coincidental. All this does not excuse their behaviour or their harassment of the complainant. But what this whole sorry saga points to is contempt for the rule of law when President Mbeki applies double standards. Mbeki is weakening the constitutional state with his inconsistencies around what gets investigated and what doesn't. Can we blame the masses when they become deeply suspicious of the rule of law?[19]

In her diary, Rhoda also noted a hidden agenda at work. The Director of Public Prosecutions, Bulelani Ngcuka, was married to Deputy President Phumzile Mlambo-Ngcuka. By prosecuting Zuma, she noted, he was "clearing the way for [his] wife's ambitions." She credited columnist David Gleason -- who himself was a player in the ANC's internal struggles[20] — with being the only one to predict Ngcuka's moves and explain his motives ahead of time.

Ultimately, Zuma was found not guilty. He went on to become president of the ANC, then of the country. In that role, he would bring South Africa to new lows in government malfeasance and mismanagement — but by then, even many of his own supporters had abandoned him. As Rhoda had warned: neither faction of the ANC offered a real alternative to failed state-centered policies, racial polarization, and corruption.

---

19   Rhoda Kadalie. "Double standards muddy the waters of Zuma trial." *Business Day*, 6 Apr. 2006. p. 11.

20   Chris Barron. "David Gleason Columnist who became voice of Brett Kebble." *Sunday Times*, 16 Feb. 2014. p. 23.

Ironically, Mbeki's presidency would later come to seem something of a golden age, given the flaws of his successor. But that was no credit to Mbeki, Rhoda argued.

"[T]he moment for greatness was lost under former president Thabo Mbeki's rule," Rhoda lamented. "He boosted the economy with his sound macroeconomic policies, yet his autocratic style of leadership mixed with an unhealthy dose of Stalinist politics sunk his and our fortunes, making way for a successor whom we all knew would wreck the economy."[21]

***

In 2007, with Mbeki's power already on the wane, Rhoda had observed that the ANC was almost beyond salvation — not because the supposedly competent Mbeki was being replaced by the populist Zuma, but because Mbeki's centralized, race-obsessed rule had institutionalized corruption and conformity. She wrote:

> To ensure loyalty, Mbeki has turned a blind eye to the abuse of state resources by those close to him. Key state institutions have been used to hound out of office those who do not toe the line. His selective use of the law has created a groundswell of anger among the masses, with service delivery protests, and rampant crime becoming the order of the day.
>
> ...
>
> Political patronage and cronyism ensure you retain your job, and since material gain is more important than political integrity, politicians acquiesce to the rot that surrounds them.
>
> One reason people can no longer change the ANC from within is that they have indebted themselves to the party financially. Many appear to have skipped rent payments, accepted big salary increases and extra benefits, and used the government as a piggy bank, and are now bound to the party's doctrine lest they step out of line and have their sins exposed.[22]

That pattern would only continue in the Zuma era, with the major difference being that Zuma would partake openly and personally in the corruption that Mbeki had managed, more deftly, at arm's length.

---

21   Rhoda Kadalie. "Spare us the ritual charade ANC." *The Citizen*, 8 Dec. 2017. URL: https://www.citizen.co.za/news/opinion/1752698/spare-us-the-ritual-charade-anc/. Accessed on 13 Apr. 2022.

22   Rhoda Kadalie. "Sick ruling party sits at the heart of SA's malaise." *Business Day*, 6 Sep. 2007. p. 11.

Rhoda: 'Comrade Kadalie, You Are Out of Order!'

Rhoda had no doubt that Zuma was corrupt, but she believed him to be a victim of selective prosecution. When he was accused of rape, Rhoda suspected that he had been framed or set up by Mbeki. As she later recalled:

At the time, I was the only feminist that put my head above the parapet and dared to write a column, even before the court case, pleading with the public, and feminists in particular, to respect the audi alterem partem [hear the other side] rule and give Zuma his day in court and not portray the woman solely as a victim. A series of strange facts emerged from the cross-examination. Yes, Jacob Zuma irresponsibly had unprotected sex with a HIV positive woman; he said stupid things about HIV, her skirt, the shower, etc. But it was clear that the sex was consensual. In her testimony, equally strange revelations were made. That she voluntarily went to his room; that Zuma's daughter was in the house; that she waited until the next day to report despite security on the premises; that she had some dubious history in exile with a series of allegations of rape. To crown it all, she phoned the Minister of Intelligence, Ronnie Kasrils, the next day to report the incident. Strange coincidence? I think not.

Just because we don't like our President, does not mean he has no rights.[23]

Ultimately Zuma was acquitted — though he did not take the trial as a cue to change his behavior.

Likewise on corruption: Zuma was a crook, but if Zuma was to be charged, Rhoda wrote, hundreds of ANC apparatchiks deserved to be charged along with him.[24] With Zuma, at least the voters knew what they were getting: "Zuma's morality gets discussed ad nauseam, yet serial monogamy has become a ruling party sport. Zuma, at least, is a self-declared polygamist, a marital status sanctioned by our constitution," Rhoda observed.[25] Later, she would join in criticism of the president for having an extramarital affair with a younger woman, despite having multiple wives already: "There is a difference between polygamy and screwing around."[26]

---

23   Rhoda Kadalie. Draft column for *The Citizen*. 12 Aug. 2016.
24   Rhoda Kadalie. "Zuma: Zille livid as allies cheer; DA and ID consider launching private prosecution of ANC president." *Cape Argus*, 18 Mar. 2009. p. 5
25   Rhoda Kadalie. "Lessons for Zuma from Polokwane." *Cape Argus*, 27 Dec. 2007. p. 19.
26   Rhoda Kadalie, quoted by *Sunday Tribune*. 7 Feb. 2010.

Though the excesses of the Zuma presidency awakened many South Africans to the rot in the ruling party, Rhoda believed it had taken root under Mbeki, if not before. She wrote in *Die Burger* in 2011:

> *Under former President Mbeki's rule the seeds of corruption took root and the plants now flourish under Zuma. The Stalinist language of the National Democratic Revolution, ANC control of the levers of power, cadre deployment and the Native Club provided fertile ground for crony capitalism through black economic empowerment, nepotism and "tenderpreneurship" to embed themselves firmly within the body politic of South Africa.[27]*

In another column, she opined that the decay had set in even before the ANC had been legalized, and had taken power. It was evident already, she argued, in the lavish lives led by ANC leaders in exile, which shocked ordinary activists and Umkhonto we Sizwe soldiers who had been indoctrinated with communist ideals.[28] In 2017, she wrote:

> *But how did we get here?*
>
> *It started under President Mandela where few would criticise the ANC, even when it was palpably wrong. ...*
>
> *The atmosphere of political correctness at the time was awful for those of us who dared to criticise. White guilt mixed with black entitlement is a toxic cocktail and accounts for where we are today. For example the SACP should never have been as prominent within the party and the cabinet without contesting an election. Today they are Zuma's biggest critics. That is the logical conclusion of corrupt relationships with power whomever wields the rule of power at the time.[29]*

She also observed that "more than a decade into our new democracy, the ANC still clings to its Stalinist discourse of the national democratic revolution (NDR), while the president, the cabinet and deployed cadres

27   Rhoda Kadalie. "The rot set in under Mbeki." PoliticsWeb, reprinted and translated from *Die Burger*, 30 Mar. 2011. URL: https://www.politicsweb. co.za/news-and-analysis/the-rot-set-in-under-mbeki. Accessed on 26 Mar. 2022.

28   Rhoda Kadalie. "When did the ANC lose its moral compass?". PoliticsWeb, reprinted and translated from *Die Burger*, 25 Oct. 2011. URL: https:// www.politicsweb.co.za/news-and-analysis/when-did-the-anc-lose-its-moral-compass. Accused on 26 Mar. 2022.

29   Rhoda Kadalie. Draft column for *Beeld*. 3 May 2017. Personal files.

sport the trappings of the high life, luxury imported cars, mansions and designer clothes."[30]

It was the very idea of the statist, socialist, autocratic NDR that was toxic: "National Democratic Revolutions (NDR) the world over, have failed and except for our partially successful economic policy, this country is ailing because every other aspect of governance is in the mould of the NDR."[31] Rhoda may have been echoing the assessment of provocative liberal writer R. W. Johnson, who took to the pages of *Focus*, the official publication of the Helen Suzman Foundation, to explain the deference that the ANC and other ruling parties in the region showed toward Zimbabwe's self-destructive regime:

> The NLMs [National Liberation Movements] share what can only be termed a common theology. National liberation is both the just and historically necessary conclusion of the struggle between the people and the forces of racism and colonialism. This has two implications. First, the NLMs – whatever venial sins they may commit – are the righteous. They not merely represent the masses but in a sense they are the masses, and as such they cannot really be wrong. Secondly, according to the theology, their coming to power represents the end of a process. No further group can succeed them for that would mean that the masses, the forces of righteousness, had been overthrown. That, in turn, could only mean that the forces of racism and colonialism, after sulking in defeat and biding their time, had regrouped and launched a counter-attack.
>
> Thus it follows that having won, a NLM should stay in power forever. ... The real truth about the NLM governments is that they allow corrupt elites to cling to power indefinitely. [32]

It was this quasi-religious concept of the revolutionary movement that guided the ANC in foreign policy and in dealing with its domestic political

---

30   Rhoda Kadalie. "The ANC needs to learn a new political language." PoliticsWeb, reprinted and translated from *Die Burger*, 31 Jul. 2022. URL: https://www.politicsweb.co.za/news-and-analysis/the-anc-needs-to-learn-a-new-political-language. Accessed on 26 Mar. 2022.

31   Rhoda Kadalie. "Don't blame the constitution for failures of the NDR." PoliticsWeb, reprinted from *Die Burger*, translated from the Afrikaans, 17 Mar. 2012. URL: https://www.politicsweb.co.za/news-and-analysis/dont-blame-the-constitution-for-failures-of-the-nd. Accessed on 28 Mar. 2022.

32   R.W. Johnson. "The Final Struggle Is to Stay in Power." *Focus*, Vol. 25, 1st Quarter (2002). URL: https://hsf.org.za/publications/focus/issue-25-first-quarter-2002/the-final-struggle-is-to-stay-in-power. Accessed on 5 Jul. 20222.

rivals. And it was, Rhoda observed, a far cry from what Mandela's ascent had represented in 1994.

Part of the problem was also the decline of civil society — that constellation of activist groups, academic institutions, faith-based organizations, and media outlets that had banded together to fight apartheid. During the latter years of the "struggle," they had, ironically, flourished. "Sectarian differences were sacrificed in favor fo fighting the common enemy of apartheid ... [and] around the slogan [of a] non-racial, non-sexist SA," she noted in a diary.[33] There had also been "[s]trong international donor support" for various organizations. But after 1994, donors, including foreign governments, pulled funding from activist groups and gave it directly to the new administration. Civil society leaders were recruited by the new ANC government, where they often disappeared into the bureaucracy. They left behind non-governmental organizations that lacked the skills and money to survive; those that did often became dependent on government contracts and lost their political independence.[34] Mbeki's centralized leadership style, and his preference for former exiles in leadership positions, further deepened the crisis in civil society, robbing South Africa democracy of its animating spirit.

Without civil society, Rhoda feared that South Africa would decline into anarchy and authoritarianism, as much of the rest of the continent had done. "Whenever I tell people, especially foreigners from the West, that I am worried about SA," she noted, "their response would be 'You must be patient. It took us hundreds of years to achieve democracy.' My response is: 'It takes 15-20 years to undo democracy in Africa.'"[35]

In 2020, reflecting on the 30 years since Mandela was freed from jail, Rhoda wrote:

> *Dare I say this? Prison saved Mandela from the mess of liberation. He had none of the paranoia, vengefulness and entitlement that subsequent administrations, led by the "exilers", came to epitomise. His regime was truly open, transparent, consultative and embracing. His advisers were from every part of the racial spectrum, and Mandela led with authority because he did not have to prove anything.*
>
> *Thabo Mbeki, on the other hand, suffered from Prince Charles syndrome. Born into succession, Mbeki spent most of his presidential life trying to prove that he could be a president: hence his nasty remarks about not*

---

33   Rhoda Kadalie. Notes at United Nations Global Forum on Reinventing Government. 26-29 Jun. 2007.

34   Ibid.

35   Ibid.

wanting to fill Mandela's "ugly" shoes. His regime was supposed to transform the economy, bolster black economic empowerment, and push for an African renaissance - nothing more than a glorified euphemism for African nationalism.

In contrast, Mandela was much more of a modern constitutional democrat, eschewing any political ideologies, but eager to make the country work. Unlike Mbeki, he was neither a technocrat nor driven by grand schemes that needed to be engineered through parliament.[36]

She observed that while Zuma had enjoyed a brief honeymoon, simply for his success in replacing the autocratic Mbeki, that, too, was coming to a swift end.

For Rhoda, part of what had made the struggle worthwhile — from the heyday of the UDF to the heady early years of the Mandela presidency — had been its tolerance of diversity and dissent. As president, Mandela had exemplified those virtues. When Mandela passed away in 2013, Rhoda recalled:

When former French president François Mitterrand visited South Africa in July 1994, Mandela invited an array of people to the lunch at Constantia Uitsig. We were asked to form a guard of honour as Madiba walked Mitterrand from the lawns to the restaurant, introducing each of us individually. And did he know all of us, not so much for what we did but for our idiosyncrasies. As he approached me, he said to Mitterrand: "Meet Rhoda Kadalie, that troublesome woman!"

When I did become troublesome, Madiba didn't always like it. My exposés of human rights violations in Pollsmoor prison annoyed him as he least needed such negative headlines so early in his presidency. Despite this, he visited the prison with former correctional services minister, Sipho Mzimela, indicating a willingness to clean it up.

...

Known for his stubbornness, he knew equally well that he did not know everything, that his isolation denied him everyday knowledge of what made South Africans tick, the aspects of our socio-cultural life. Hence he made it his business to get to know people.

---

36   Rhoda Kadalie. "Comment: A humanity forged in jail: It may sound sacrilegious but in prison Mandela was spared the paranoia of South Africa's exiles." *Guardian*, 11 Feb. 2010. p. 30

He told Jakes Gerwel in no uncertain terms that UWC should not only remain the home of the Left but also become the home of coloured students primarily, the more Africanised the university became. He went into Mitchells Plain to meet ordinary township folk and when a woman insulted him, Madiba readily forgave her, acknowledging her as a victim of our apartheid past. Similarly, he went into black areas. Not even there was he automatically accepted. Cognisant of the racial and tribal fissures in the country, Mandela actively crossed those divides, culminating in the visit to the wives of apartheid leaders – Betsie Verwoerd and Elise Botha.

Already in prison, Madiba made it his business to understand the Afrikaners and nationalism. His relationship with his warders, and his willingness to forgive and promote his presidency as the era of reconciliation, laid sound foundations for the constitutional democracy we have today.[37]

With Mandela's passing, Rhoda mourned the loss of that spirit of tolerance, reconciliation, and debate from within the ANC and South African politics more generally.

Others felt the same, and began to make those feelings known. In 2005, there was even an effort to relaunch the UDF, and with it the spirit of tolerance and camaraderie within a "progressive" political movement. Rhoda attended the launch at Cape Town City Hall, and was deeply disappointed. "Chaotic ... not mobilised around agreed set of principles," she wrote in her diary. "Every group was clamoring for its voice ... No leadership & control & shifting positions were evident from Podium." She noted that there had been vocal support for Zuma, as well as support for — and attacks on — the Congress of South African Trade Unions (Cosatu). Eventually, she "stormed out," but not before noting with amusement that the participants seemed uncertain whether to sing the country's new, hybrid national anthem, or only the first portion, *Nkosi Sikel' iAfrika*, which had been a struggle anthem. They voted to omit the latter, Afrikaans portion, *Die Stem*, but then sang it anyway, out of habit. The "new UDF" never became a political force, doomed by internal division and public apathy.

Rhoda felt that South Africans themselves were to blame for the spread of corruption, because they had turned a blind eye to it at first, perhaps out of a reluctance to criticize the new government. She told the Parliamentary Institute of South Africa in 2012:

---

37   Rhoda Kadalie. "He wanted to diminish that aura." *Cape Argus*, 14 Dec. 2013.

Once corruption starts, it creates a momentum of its own and becomes an entangled web. That is why we should have been vocal about it from the start. We justified a million; then we justified billions; then we justified BEE[.] I sat next to a businessman at a dinner table once who said, if Mandela were corrupt, he would accept it as he was entitled to it for serving time in jail — and was applauded around the table.[38]

She also noted the fallacy of blaming corruption on the legacy of colonialism and apartheid, rather than blaming the current government. "Because of that attitude," Rhoda concluded grimly, "it is too late to clean out [corruption] because it has seeped into the body politic of the country."[39]

What had once been tacit theft became increasingly brazen. Later, in considering the growing morass of corruption scandals under Zuma, she wrote, somewhat cynically:

I am not as disappointed in the ANC as many of my comrades. I never expected anything better. Having studied liberation movements, I knew what to expect. The ANC's governance was scarily predictable since day 1 and Jacob Zuma is the culmination of a party that has consistently refused to distinguish between party and state; that undermines media freedom; and that has no respect for the rule of law and loyal opposition. Zuma is behaving exactly like he did in exile."[40]

Nevertheless, Rhoda never gave up entirely on the ANC. As late as 2017, she admitted being a member of the party, though she noted: "Just last week I removed my membership card from my wallet because it kept peering out with every payment I made to sales people who looked at me askance."[41]

In July 2006, as Jacob Zuma's lieutenants were preparing to take over the party from Thabo Mbeki, Rhoda proposed an alternative: Cyril Ramaphosa, the trade unionist-turned-businessman whom Mbeki had displaced as Mandela's second-in-command in the early 1990s. Rhoda saw Mbeki's maneuvering against Zuma — his own deputy president of the party and the country — as a way to keep Ramaphosa and his strong domestic constituency at bay.

---

38   Rhoda Kadalie. "Corruption." Speech to Parliamentary Institute of South Africa. 27 Aug. 2012.
39   Ibid.
40   Rhoda Kadalie. Draft column for *The Citizen*. 20 May 2016. Personal files.
41   Rhoda Kadalie. "So what if you fly the old SA flag?" *The Citizen*, 8 Sep. 2017. URL: https://www.citizen.co.za/news/opinion/1644813/not-all-symbols-are-red-flags/. Accessed on 13 Apr. 2022.

In a *Business Day* column titled "Ramaphosa's rich talents equip him for top office," she wrote: "I am glad that Cyril Ramaphosa's name has been added to the list of African National Congress (ANC) presidential hopefuls for 2007. His candidature would be a pleasant neutraliser to the other alternatives, who are too ghastly to contemplate."[42] In answer to potential criticism that his newfound Black Economic Empowerment wealth might be a hindrance, she noted that he had "a proven track record" in the negotiations toward South Africa's new Constitution, untainted by any suspicions of corruption or self-dealing.

She added:

He could defuse the growing tension between divergent views with even a lame joke and have everyone in stitches. He pulled in the expertise and resources of the best constitutional experts into the six theme committees and I shall never forget the flurry of activity, debates, conferences and workshops between the politicians and the nongovernmental organisations trying to get to grips with what a truly representative South African constitution would be, with a Bill of Rights that would be unique to SA.

What this entire exercise demonstrated was the willingness of political actors across wide divisions to work together and reach a compromise. People whom many of us wrote off as dinosaurs were now in the fold and talking to each other. Four months before the May 8 deadline, 68 issues were unresolved and there was great concern that the deadline would not be reached. By April 22 there was no consensus on the death penalty, the appointment of judges and the attorney-general, language, local government, proportional representation and the floor-crossing issue.

By April, there were 298 amendments but the entire process went swimmingly under Ramaphosa's capable leadership, so that by May 8 the text was completed. March 1997 was the culmination of a difficult process, ending with more than 7-million copies of the constitution distributed in 11 languages all over the country.

For these reasons, Ramaphosa is ideally suited to bring that experience to bear on bringing the ANC together again, with its political contenders, into an inclusive society united in its goal to drag SA out of poverty.

42   Rhoda Kadalie. "Ramaphosa's rich talents equip him for top office." *Business Day*, 27 Jul. 2006. p. 13.

As opposed to other politicians who used political office to enrich themselves, Ramaphosa had become wealthy outside of power and would enter the political arena with nobler motives, Rhoda argued. "If he stands for president, we might just be in for one of the most exciting dispensations this country has seen. I am sure the country will rally around him despite some minor misgivings."

That rosy endorsement would later meet hard reality, twelve years later, when Ramaphosa finally took office amid the rubble of the Zuma presidency. Rhoda's optimistic portrayal, however, should be seen in context: while the ANC was mired in a factional battle between the authoritarianism of Mbeki and the populist anarchy of Zuma, much of the country yearned for a viable alternative within the ruling party.

When Zuma shocked Mbeki — and the world — by ousting Mbeki as party leader at the ANC's national conference in the northern city of Polokwane in December 2007, Rhoda celebrated Mbeki's downfall:

> *The peasant usurped the intellectual. Zuma quietly plotted and schemed while Mbeki flew around the world intoxicated by his own greatness. In one fell swoop the street-smart contender took over the entire top six positions in the ANC and most of the national executive. Whereas before, decisions were made by consensus, now members changed their leaders through the ballot box and contested that ballot even within their own ranks - unprecedented stuff for the ANC!*

> *The nation was disturbed at the intolerance of the contenders at Polokwane; at the populist rhetoric that flowed freely; they balked at the constant singing of Zuma's anthem, umshini wami ["My Machine Gun," a violent struggle-era song], in a country desperately trying to shed its violent present; the nation feared a takeover by a man who makes no claim to be what he is not; they were ashamed of the ugly spectacle beamed to the world of a party that, despite invoking the language of unity, of the collective, of consensus, of the national democratic revolution, seemed to behave like an unruly bunch of undisciplined cadres. But were they that? Certainly not.*

> *They were acting out their deep distrust of a ruling clique they had lost faith in; rebelling against a president who thought he could govern without the support of the governed; who thought he knew what was good for us even when he no longer enjoyed our trust.*[43]

---

43   Rhoda Kadalie. "Lessons for Zuma from Polokwane," ibid.

For all of Zuma's obvious flaws, she would later add, he deserved praise for "daring to challenge the autocrat Mbeki."[44] She advised Zuma to heed the lessons of Mbeki's failures:

Beware of double standards because the people will remember. Respect the separation of powers. Do not use the state's resources to enrich the party, friends, family and cronies. Lead by example and adopt serious symbolic gestures to show the masses that state-accumulated wealth is not the driving force for entrée into politics.

Strengthen parliament and restore it to its rightful place; do not take advice from your cronies alone; surround yourself with expert advisors, include those you trust even though you might not like them; speak to the media regularly; read the media regularly; hold regular press conferences; take the public into your confidence. Apply the law fairly to everyone – make this bedrock of our constitution your driving force. In foreign policy, move away from our crippling notion of "exceptionalism" and become part of the modern progressive world and do what is best for the country.

The big policy questions will be easier to deal with. Abandon the anachronistic language of the National Democratic Revolution for modern social democratic policies that will generate growth and development.

Poverty, jobs, unemployment, crime, healthcare, and housing cannot be addressed through backward socialist policies. Use the expertise that exists outside of the party to find collective solutions to our problems. Abandon Affirmative Action and make those with expertise, white and black, work to grow the economy even more, so that the poor will have a stake in the system as much as the rich.

Zuma, you have the world at your feet. Do not throw this opportunity away. You have the chance to make South Africa the definitive democracy in Africa. Seize the day![45]

Even as she wrote those words, however, Rhoda doubted Zuma's ability to deliver. Her concerns only grew in the aftermath of the Polokwane conference. When Zuma and the ANC leadership compelled Mbeki to resign the presidency of the country — exacting revenge for Zuma's own dismissal by Mbeki in 2005 — South Africa was led by a caretaker

---

44   Rhoda Kadalie. "ANC split just a fight among thieves." *Business Day*, 6 Nov. 2008. p. 13.
45   Rhoda Kadalie. "Lessons for Zuma from Polokwane," ibid.

president, Kgalema Motlanthe, who was soft-spoken but widely respected. Unfortunately, Rhoda noted, he did not seem inclined to stop the ANC's gravy train. "The post-Mbeki government continues to recycle thugs and thieves, appointing them to leading positions in the state," she wrote.[46]

***

The trouble, Rhoda argued, lay within the ANC's obsession with power, which not only eroded South Africa's democracy, but made the ruling party less able to deliver on its promises. Earlier in 2007, she had written:

> *The transition from struggle to statehood is the ANC's biggest challenge. Its obsession with power has come to override its revolutionary goal to provide services to all, even if it splits the party asunder. Its intolerance of inter-party political competition and intra-party differences has had deleterious effects on governance at both provincial and municipal levels. The constant factionalism and internal feuding have led to management paralyses in more than 100 municipalities and many provinces are not doing too well either. The ANC's own strongholds, in Limpopo, Free State, Mpumalanga, Western Cape and Eastern Cape, are floundering.*

> ...

> *The ruling party's obsession with absolute control has made it so intolerant of party political competition that service delivery has become the casualty of infighting. If it continues on this path, its political intolerance will eventually destroy it. The ANC should realize that a threat more worrying to its longevity than the looming [Mbeki-Zuma] succession battle is its failure to deliver basic services to the poor.[47]*

Her warnings were to prove prophetic, as ANC-controlled provinces and municipalities largely collapsed over the subsequent decade and a half. Though Zuma was an improvement over Mbeki when it came to HIV/Aids policy, in most other respects his government was even less capable, and more corrupt, than its predecessor.

But Rhoda did not simply blame the ANC. She also lamented the fear and complacency of the South African public — led by the media, but not limited to it. In 2008, she pleaded with her readers:

---

46   Rhoda Kadalie. "More of the same from ANC after Polokwane." *Business Day (The Weekender)*, 26 Mar. 2009.

47   Rhoda Kadalie. ""Intolerant ANC ignores biggest threat to its power." *Business Day*, 17 May 2007.

What's to be done? South Africans need to wake up and smell the coffee. More than ever we need a reinvigoration of civil society organisations, the media, faith-based organisations, women's groups, human rights organisations, and opposition parties who will unite and hold government accountable.

We should jettison those self-serving civic organisations that suck up to government and placate them when they are so obviously out of touch and corrupt.

Big business, too, should cease its deal-making and sycophantic relationship with government and keep its eye on the ball.

In a theme she would explore in dozens of columns, Rhoda identified the willingness of South Africans to tolerate and excuse corruption by their leaders as a key driver in the country's moral decay. Her view was reinforced by an experience she had in Sweden, about which she wrote years later:

I am reminded of my own hubris when I was told the University of Uppsala, Sweden, had decided to confer an honorary doctorate on me in 1999. After the reception we walked towards the parking lot, but my host walked past her car. When I alerted her to that she said: "I am not driving because I drank a glass of wine."

I complained that I would not walk back home in high heels, and that she should just drive, as no one would know. Aghast, she said: "In Sweden, we just don't do that."

Then I saw everyone in their finery either walking home or calling a taxi to take them home.

"We just don't do that" has stuck with me ever since. I realised that in Sweden ethics has become woven into the DNA of the national consciousness. It had become systemic and part of the culture of business, politics (not so much) and daily life – the national fabric.

...

I look forward to the day when we in South Africa can turn to one another and say: "We just don't do that."[48]

---

48   Rhoda Kadalie. "Finding a thread of ethics in our frayed social fabric; We need to change our ways lest the lack of personal, political and corporate

The solutions to South Africa's problems, she believed, were in the hands of South Africans themselves — if they would only summon the courage to do what was right, and to jettison a corrupt and inept ruling party. "SA is more than the ANC. It belongs to all of us," she wrote in 2008. "It is a great country of diverse people with enormous potential; it has an army of nongovernmental organisations and volunteers who are doing what the government should be doing. Yet we are allowing a party bent on controlling all the levers of power to sow the seeds of our destruction."[49]

In a speech to university graduates in 2013, Rhoda emphasized that South Africans needed to embrace the better part of their nature, and set aside the pain and politics of the past. Reflecting on the deaths of young people from Aids, crime, and road accidents, she asked:

Do South Africans have a death wish? Why is life so cheap?

Our desire should be to live, to live life to the full and to create a population that wants to live. The challenge fo us is to remove all the obstacles that destroy our passion and compassion, so that we can live life abundantly, as the Bible says.[50]

The ANC had once removed obstacles to freedom; now it *was* the obstacle.

The problem was not who led the ANC, or even just the ANC – it was the ruling elite itself. The country's leading intellectuals struggled to criticize a ruling party that they credited for ending apartheid — and which increasingly controlled access to wealth and opportunity.

In 2007, at a panel discussion sponsored by the Stellenbosch Business School, Rhoda found herself confronted publicly by business leader and ANC insider Bheki Khumalo, who was close to Mbeki. He addressed Rhoda patronizingly, defending her right (in theory) to criticize the government, but adding — according to Rhoda's notes — that "one does not have to take her seriously."[51] He also proclaimed, curiously, that "we need more Rhoda Kadalies," perhaps hoping to maintain a façade of openness to debate. Rhoda noted in her diary: "I responded to Bheki by welcoming his

integrity becomes second nature, writes Rhoda Kadalie." *Cape Argus*, 14 Nov. 2013. p. 21.

49   Rhoda Kadalie. "Taking the reins of SA back from ANC." *Business Day*, 31 Jul. 2008. p. 13.

50   Rhoda Kadalie. Graduation speech, Cape Peninsula University of Technology. Cape Town, 17 Apr. 2013.

51   Bheki Khumalo, quoted by Rhoda Kadalie. Diary entry, 11 Jul. 2007.

riposte & declaring that I welcome debate which stunned the audience which expected me to fight back."[52]

Rhoda mocked the pretenses of the ANC's alliance partners, Cosatu and the SACP, when they disagreed with the policies or performance of the ruling party: "If the ANC's alliance partners are really as *gatvol* [fed up] as they pretend to be with the ANC, then they should do the honourable thing and break away," she wrote.[53]

Some former Mbeki loyalists did, in fact, break away in piecemeal fashion to form their own splinter parties, such as the so-called Congress of the People (COPE). But Rhoda dismissed their prospects: "The split from the ANC is not, as many think, an opportunity for true opposition. True opposition arises out of principle, values, sound policies, policy differences, and a programme of effective action. Lest we be fooled, this split from the ANC is nothing but a fight among thieves over power, control and spoils at the trough."[54] She also mocked COPE as a party of elitists, reduced to recruiting "Bishops and Vice-Chancellors" rather than political leaders — or, for that matter, voters.[55]

Rhoda's predictions were soon vindicated, as COPE suffered a leadership collapse several months after its first electoral test in the 2009 elections, when it placed third, behind the ANC and the DA. COPE's struggles disproved the claim "that all opposition parties can only come out of the ANC, or forces close to them," she concluded. "This is a myth that has just been proved wrong."[56] She told the Cape Town Press Club in 2009 that "the only good thing about COPE is that they threaten to weaken the hegemony of the ANC."[57] She doubted their commitment to opposition: they were, she suggested, simply "Mbeki's *aanhangers* [hangers-on]."

In 2014, former ANC minister Ronnie Kasrils, a Mbeki loyalist and fellow "exile" who was ousted by Zuma's political insurgency, urged South Africans to vote for any party except the ANC or the DA. Rhoda criticized him for opposing the DA, the only opposition party capable of challenging the ANC for power, and for failing to take responsibility for his role in the

---

52   Rhoda Kadalie, ibid.
53   Rhoda Kadalie. "Gatvol with the ANC." PoliticsWeb, reprinted and translated from *Die Burger*, 6 Jul. 2011. URL: https://www.politicsweb. co.za/news-and-analysis/gatvol-with-the-anc. Accessed on 26 Mar. 2022.
54   Rhoda Kadalie. "ANC split just a fight among thieves." *Business Day*, ibid.
55   Rhoda Kadalie. Draft column. *Business Day*, 26 Feb. 2009.
56   Rhoda Kadalie, quoted by Fiona Forde. "Can there be hope after Cope?" *Sunday Independent*, 12 Jul. 2009. p. 9.
57   Rhoda Kadalie. Speech to the Cape Town Press Club. Cape Town, South Africa. 31 Mar. 2009.

country's political decline: "Claiming that the ANC is off the rails, he still believes that our salvation lies within the party. ... As a staunch Mbeki-ite, Kasrils takes no responsibility for his failure to condemn Mbeki for Zimbabwe, for his denials that HIV causes AIDS, leading to the deaths of thousands of black South Africans in particular, and for his dire foreign policy actions. To wit, the arms deal happened under his watch."[58]

Conversely, Rhoda prized political diversity and competition, seeing them as the salvation of good governance in South Africa and beyond. She criticized emerging ANC dissidents, such as former ANC official Andrew Feinstein and the HIV/Aids activists of the Treatment Action Campaign, for their refusal to back alternatives to the ruling party. "In a country where there is no real political contestation, the sanctification of the ruling party leads to tyranny," she wrote in 2008.[59]

She also mocked ANC leaders who broke with the party after Zuma displaced Mbeki: "These people are not leaving the ANC because of nobler ideals. Having thought Mbeki would make a third term, they realised they had not accumulated enough for their retirement."[60] And reflecting on the demise of democracy in Zimbabwe, and upheavals in Kenya's disputed elections, she wrote in 2008: "The rebirth of competitive party democracy is, therefore, essential to the survival of African good governance."[61] She saw the same worrying tendencies in the ANC that had emerged in Zimbabwe's ruling ZANU-PF: both ruling parties were so convinced of their own right to rule that they had "appropriated the right even to determine what the nature of opposition should be."[62]

***

In September 2006, Rhoda addressed the members of The 1926 Club, an elite debating society that had been founded among the lords of the Rand in Johannesburg in the early twentieth century. Within the private

58 Rhoda Kadalie. "Ronnie Kasrils: Unarmed but still dangerous!". PoliticsWeb, reprinted from *Die Burger* and translated from the Afrikaans, 23 Apr. 2014. URL: https://www.politicsweb.co.za/news-and-analysis/ronnie-kasrils-unarmed-but-still-dangerous. Accessed on 28 Mar. 2022.
59 Rhoda Kadalie. "Analysts need to think past the party." *Business Day*, 17 Jul. 2008.
60 Rhoda Kadalie. "The bitter fuel that is driving 'rebels'." *Business Day*, 23 Oct. 2008. p. 13.
61 Rhoda Kadalie. "States become vampires in Africa." *Business Day*, 3 Jul. 2008.
62 Rhoda Kadalie. "So much for 'new deal' in Zimbabwe." *Business Day (The Weekender)*, 12 Feb. 2009.

confines of their club, away from the political limelight or the reach of the media, South Africa's leaders allowed themselves the luxury of open discussions of some of the most fraught political issues of their day. Their first speaker: Clements Kadalie, who addressed The 1926 Club on the subject of his union, the ICU, in 1926.

Rhoda receives The Citizen's award for "columnist of the year," 2017
(Courtesy Rhoda Kadalie)

In her remarks, titled "The Future of Opposition in SA," Rhoda recounted her grandfather's own political journey.[63] "The qualities of political courage and fearlessness that catapulted Kadalie onto the national stage

---

63   Rhoda Kadalie. "The Future of Opposition in SA." Speech to The 1926 Club. Johannesburg, South Africa. 26 Sep. 2006.

are qualities fast disappearing in our democracy today — and [that] is partly to blame for the political turbulence characterizing our political landscape today." Recalling her warnings in Grahamstown in 2001, Rhoda blamed a growing culture of political intolerance in South Africa for the country's woes. And the answer, she argued, was strong political opposition — not the DA alone, but the variety of parties that had emerged to challenge the ANC's dominance and hold it accountable. "Lest we forget," she observed, "this democracy was forged out of dissent, debate and diversity."

Rhoda valued political diversity. That is partly why Rhoda retained her friendships with people from a variety of political backgrounds, including those whose parties she opposed. These included active members and leaders of the ANC, the DA, and the IFP, among other parties.

Her close friends also included several noted iconoclasts, such as former South African Communist Party activist Tony Holiday, who had worked for the clandestine opposition to apartheid while pursuing a career as a journalist. Holiday, a disheveled, unkempt, and physically awkward man, with a thin tuft of white hair slicked back across a balding pate, knew the country's new leaders — and their dirty secrets. He frequented the city's brothels, and knew Cape Town's drug dealers; many of them gave information to him about their clients. Through his underworld contacts, he had "dirt" on the country's new elite — some of which he shared with Rhoda.

Rhoda, in turn, was a loyal friend to Holiday, though they often disagreed on the issues of the day. Holiday, for example, was vehemently anti-Israel, and used one of his occasional columns in the *Cape Times* to issue an extraordinary call for the South African Zionist Federation, one of the country's oldest Jewish communal organizations, to be banned because of Israel's counter-terror operations.[64] It was the ultimate irony: a member of the once-banned Communist Party was calling for the banning of an organization whose ideas he found objectionable. Rhoda disagreed, but remained friendly with Holiday, to the point of offering him lifts to and from the hospitals during his many bouts of ill health.

When he passed away in 2006, Rhoda penned a stirring obituary that paid tribute to the colorful life of a unique South African character. In her recounting of Holiday's political adventures, she offered a glimpse into the kind of open-minded, irreverent adventurism that was fast fading from South African political life. And she described his alienation from the ANC:

---

64 Tony Holiday. "Local federation promotes Zionism: Patriotism of SA Jews undermined." *Cape Times*, 30 Mar. 2004.

A political prophet not recognized in his own country, Tony understood the ANC like no other. His years in the underground transformed him into one of SA's most astute analysts for which his former comrades often resented him. Truth was the driving force behind his writings which were never meant to spite the ANC but to dialog. Stupidly they dumped him. But it was their loss because Tony would have been the best presidential adviser any president could have had.

Unlike those who used their two days or one week of detention as political credentials, few knew that Tony was in jail for 6 years for his communist beliefs. He denounced communism in an excellent confessional ending his column resignedly: "Today I depart from the closed community of ideas." As a true intellectual he could no longer constrain his thoughts by anachronistic ideologies, yet he remained a leftie.[65]

Rhoda saw Holiday as something of a kindred spirit — a fellow leftist who had fallen out with a corrupt ruling party, a writer who had inspired her own political irreverence. She kept several of his papers with her, even after she left South Africa for the U.S. One such paper, "The Idea of an African University," meditated on the challenge of finding a path between "Eurocentric skeptics" on the one hand, and "Africanist ideologues," on the other. The concluding passage is worth quoting in full:

To achieve this recovery of what colonialism and slavery have interred, a generation of artists, historians, scientists and philosopher[s] that is growing up among us must brave the twin dangers of scientism disguised as science, on the one hand, and superstition parading as African religion on the other. It will have to endure the cynical mockery of Eurocentric skeptics as well as the accusations of disloyalty which Africanist ideologues are bound to heap on it. Above all, this generation of seekers will have to withstand the dark night of intellectual loneliness which travelers towards goals of this sort must inevitably traverse. It will find no companions among the politically orthodox. But there may be those from other cultures, spaces and times, who will join the pilgrimage and, whatever its perils, not betray it.[66]

Rhoda likely identified with that experience of walking through the "dark night of intellectual loneliness"; it was the key to her friendship with Holiday. She, too, was seeking to reconcile idealism and reality in the new

---

65   Rhoda Kadalie. "Tribute to Tony Holiday." July 2006. Unpublished.
66   Anthony Holiday. "The Idea of an African University." *Theoria: A Journal of Social and Political Theory*, No. 100, 202. p. 94.

South Africa, and there were few like her who were prepared to do so with open eyes.

In a *Business Day* column in 2008, Rhoda reflected on the reasons South Africans found it so hard to criticize their new government:

> *When things went awry early on in our democracy, political leaders were often given the benefit of the doubt, the rationale being that since they struggled for a moral cause, they must therefore be highly moral. Hence, the escalating corruption, political intolerance, nondelivery and mismanagement were initially excused as mistakes, committed by infants of democracy. Many comrades refused to see the warning signals, covering up until the festering sores which, like gangrene, became too septic and widespread to cure.*

> *Civic leaders and the media practised the masterful art of self-censorship, and critique was silenced in subtle ways. Sympathisers of the government turned a blind eye, wanting to benefit from government's largesse, cosying up to the ruling elite through acquiescence and tacit support lest they jeopardise their vested interests. White guilt shut up many a critic. ANC supporters, understandably, found it hard to criticise a government they had voted into power. The destiny of the ANC was so deeply wrapped up with their own that they could not be seen to judge a party with which they had become synonymous.[67]*

If the ANC could not be reformed from within, the only answer was to support the political opposition — something many South Africans found hard to do. Many were still sentimentally attached to the ANC; others feared that if they voted for the DA, they would be caricatured as racists, or sellouts.

In the run-up to the 2009 general elections, for example, Archbishop Desmond Tutu said that he would not vote, rather than vote for the opposition, even though he and others were disappointed with the ANC and feared the prospect of electing Zuma president.

As she would later do to Kasrils in 2014, Rhoda blasted Tutu for shirking his democratic duty, in a letter to the editor that appeared in several publications:

---

67   Rhoda Kadalie. "We must shed notion that only ANC can save SA." *Business Day*, 8 May 2008. p. 11.

How undemocratic! Every citizen has a right to vote or not to vote, but one would expect Tutu to encourage voters to use their hard-earned right to vote responsibly, instead of abstaining.

...

Tutu treats the ANC as though it is a church that has strayed off the straight and narrow and he seems to believe that some good can still come out of a party that is corrupt, lawless, and that has consigned thousands to death. He still subscribes to the old school that one has to be loyal to a party, instead of the other way around.[68]

Without a strong and effective opposition, Rhoda argued, the ANC felt free to ignore the voters and to overlook its own failures as it pursued its narrow ideological — and pecuniary — interests.

As she continued to criticize the ANC on ideological as well as political grounds, Rhoda began to be seen by many South Africans as a voice for opposition, and for liberalism — a label she began, carefully, to embrace.

---

68   Rhoda Kadalie. "Not voting makes no sense." Letter to the editor. *Business Day (The Weekender)*, 9 Oct. 2008. p. 10.

Chapter 16:
Opposition

"What we on the left have not learnt is the need for the development of institutional opposition. It is time South Africans learn to vote against corruption and for good governance and effective delivery."[1]

Rhoda was more than an opinion columnist, though that is how much of the public recognized her, as her popularity grew. Through Impumelelo, she continued to help the government strive toward its development goals. And through her writing, she criticized the ruling party and its failures.

She also wrote about the difficult task of political opposition — so effectively, in fact, that many considered her one of the leading voices of the South African opposition, though she never formally joined it.

Rhoda's concern with opposition politics began early in the country's new democracy — even when she was still a loyal member of the ANC, vocally supportive of its policies and goals. She told a BBC forum in 1998, ahead of the country's second democratic elections in 1999:

> I think we need a strong opposition. Because loyal opposition is a foreign concept in Africa. And because the ANC is very strong, it can easily become a law unto itself. And it's very tempted to change the Constitution. So I think we should actually develop strong opposition, especially [since] we have a strong majority party. Because the constitution is about protecting the rights of the individual against the state. Where you have a strong state, it can do with you as you please.[2]

That argument, delivered in front of a live audience, prompted applause.

Rhoda explicitly noted, on that occasion: "I'm not electioneering for anybody." But like many South Africans, she hoped the ANC would be held to less than the two-thirds majority needed to amend the Constitution unilaterally.

By the time the municipal elections of 2000 arrived, Mbeki had been in office for over a year, and had triggered outrage over his policies on Aids and Zimbabwe. Those controversies, and Mbeki's hostility to criticism and dissent, appear to have convinced Rhoda to endorse the opposition openly.

1   Rhoda Kadalie, quoted in Barron, "Obituary," ibid.
2   Rhoda Kadalie, "South Africans Talking," ibid.

While she did not call on South Africans to vote specifically for the newly-formed Democratic Alliance — an uncomfortable marriage between the liberal Democratic Party and its former nemesis, the "New" National Party — she urged them to back opposition parties in general, rather than not voting (see Chapter 14).

In the aftermath of the country's third general election in 2004, Rhoda's voice became particularly important. Despite Mbeki's poor performance and growing concern about government corruption, the ANC won nearly 70% of the vote — giving it the power to change South Africa's constitution unilaterally, if it chose.

In Parliament and the media, there was intense pressure to conform to the ANC's agenda of "transformation." Though the word never appears once in South Africa's constitution, the idea became almost universally regarded as a political imperative. In an idealistic sense, it meant making South Africa's institutions more representative of the country's racial demographics. In practice, it meant allowing the ANC to use race to place its cadres in control of more institutions, especially business, the media, and the judiciary.

Though Rhoda herself had used the word "transformation" in her early feminist writings, she came to dislike the term. "I hate the word 'transformation' because nobody ever says 'from what to what'," she noted.[3]

The ANC's consensus was also notable for whom it excluded. After Leader of the Opposition Tony Leon offered a handshake on the floor of Parliament to Mbeki after he was formally re-elected, a subsequent ANC speaker rebuked Leon sharply: "The contract between us and the masses cannot be supplanted by a handshake. Thank you very much, Mr Leon, your hand must not cross the floor. Keep it to yourself."[4]

Rhoda wrote:

Consensus politics has its place, and has had its place in our history. The constitution is the result of consensus battered out at the Convention for Democracy in SA. With the basics in place, SA should allow and manage its pluralism in all its diversity, in line with constitutional principles.

---

3   Rhoda Kadalie. Response to paper by Xolela Mangcu. Goedgedacht Forum on Racism. Malmesbury, South Africa. 14 Oct. 2000.

4   Sydney Mufamadi. Speech in Parliament. 23 April 2004. URL: https://www.politicsweb.co.za/news-and-analysis/tony-leon-on-mbeki-pahad-kortbroek-and-others. Accessed on 15 Oct. 2021.

Chapter 16: Opposition

It is the task of Parliament, of the opposition, of the media, of business and civil society to hold government accountable, especially with its firmly entrenched majority. Since the ANC has the support of the entire media and controls most state institutions, consensus politics is hardly the only way to go.

...

I would sooner live in a robust, vibrant democracy than in a polity based on consensus where the ruling party reigns and remains supreme. Those who fear criticism should be feared.[5]

Rhoda was not a member of the DA, but her philosophical support for the idea of opposition ran against the consensus of South African politics and punditry.

In fact, behind the scenes, Rhoda had already begun cultivating relationships with the leaders of the DA and other prominent opposition parties.

In the early 2000s, when the Democratic Alliance (DA) was formed between the old liberal "Progs" of the Democratic Party, and the rump of the New National Party, DA leader Tony Leon found himself struggling to navigate the messy politics of the Western Cape. The DA had inherited two difficult leaders in particular: Western Cape Premier Gerald Morkel and Cape Town Mayor Peter Marais, both of whom had been Coloured supporters of the National Party.

The DA was forced to dismiss Marais as mayor for mismanagement. In a series of reshuffles, Morkel briefly became mayor and Marais became premier. Shortly thereafter, the leadership of the New National Party defected to join the ANC, and the DA lost control of the province and the city. It was a bewildering game of political musical chairs.

Rhoda called Leon with unsolicited advice. "I'd like to brief you on Coloured politics in the Western Cape," she offered. "As someone from Johannesburg, you are clearly clueless about Western Cape politics and the importance of self-interest!"

Leon was glad for the straightforward criticism, and invited Rhoda to his office in parliament, which led to a strong friendship with Leon and his family for many years.

---

5   Rhoda Kadalie. "'Consensus politics' just a way to silence dissidents?". *Business Day*, 27 May 2004.

Rhoda with Tony and Michal Leon, c. 2007 (Courtesy Rhoda Kadalie)

Yet there were some interesting twists and turns.

In June 2004, James Selfe, the chair of the Democratic Alliance's governing federal council, and Ryan Coetzee, the CEO of the party itself, arrived discreetly at Rhoda Kadalie's home in University Estate for a meeting at their request.

They had come to ask Rhoda to take over South Africa's political opposition.

It was a stunning offer. Selfe and Coetzee were both trusted lieutenants of then–Democratic Alliance (DA) leader Tony Leon, who also served as Leader of the Opposition in the Parliament of South Africa. Leon had made no indication whatsoever, at least publicly, that he was preparing to quit.

Moreover, the April 2004 election had cemented the DA's position as South Africa's premier opposition party. Its former rival, the New National Party (NNP), had been utterly destroyed at the polls, as voters rejected its alliance with the ruling African National Congress (ANC). A new upstart, the Independent Democrats (ID), led by the volatile Patricia de Lille, a former member of the Pan Africanist Congress who had moved to the political center, only mustered about two percent of the vote — the same as the DA's predecessor, the Democratic Party (DP), had won in 1994, but with poor prospects for growth.

The DA had won over 12 percent of the vote. It was a disappointment for many within the party, who had hoped the party would match its success in the 2000 municipal elections, when it earned over 20% of the nationwide vote. But 12% was still growth from the 1999 total of just under ten percent, and it left the DA's 50-seat parliamentary delegation, which had been increased by floor-crossing, unchanged.

Most agreed that Leon had done well to consolidate the opposition behind the DA, attracting NNP voters who had refused to follow their leaders into political oblivion.

The question, however, was whether the DA could continue to grow, and to grow fast enough to be a real challenge to the hegemony of the ANC, which had won nearly 70% of the vote, enough to surpass the two-thirds majority necessary to change the Constitution unilaterally, virtually at will.

The DA could only grow slightly if it continued to rely on South Africa's minorities— white, Indian, and Coloured. Though it had won more black votes in 2004 than ever before, it still represented a tiny sliver of the black electorate. To grow, the DA needed more black support.

And to do that, the conventional thinking went, the DA needed a black leader. The question was: who could do the job?

The DA's deputy leader, Joe Seremane, was a black anti-apartheid activist who had broken with the ANC after his brother had been tortured and killed in the movement's prison camps during the armed struggle. Seremane was a soft-spoken and genial figure, popular within the DA caucus.

His ethnic background was also fascinating: he was a member of the tiny Lemba minority group, which claims descent from the ancient Israelites. Unlike other such groups, the Lemba have the DNA to prove it: they have sequences in mitochondrial DNA that are typically found among the Cohanim, the Jewish priestly caste.

But there was little faith that Seremane could lead the DA forward. He was too mild to attract popular support, and the party insiders lacked confidence in him.

There were few other black leaders in the party who might have been candidates. Though the party had recruited more black members of Parliament, some were enticed by the ANC — or perhaps bribed — to cross the floor, mouthing the ANC's talking points about the "racist" opposition as they did so.

At Coetzee's direction, the DA had begun a "rebranding" exercise, in which it sought advice from outside the party, including from some of its opponents, particularly black leaders. Quietly, Coetzee and Selfe had also begun searching for a replacement for Leon.

And Rhoda was a favorite to fill the role.

She was black, and female, and politically astute, checking the boxes that the party — and its critics — believed that it needed to fill in order to appeal to black voters. More than that, however, she understood the DA and its role of providing necessary opposition in South Africa's fledgling, one-party-dominant democracy.

She also had unique credibility. She had been part of the anti-apartheid struggle, and had been a member of the ANC, albeit a critical one. She was immune to the charge of racism, flung so easily at the government's critics.

Flattered though she was, Rhoda turned Selfe and Coetzee down, politely. A political party, she told them, required compromises of principle. That was not who she was; she needed to be an independent voice. It would end badly, she said.

Later — without referring to the offer to lead the Democratic Alliance — Rhoda quipped "Frequently I get asked, why I do not enter into politics, and my abiding response is — I have seen it ruin too many of my best friends."[6]

Rhoda kept her meeting with the DA officials a secret. But she would continue to make her mark on opposition politics in South Africa — in the realm of public debate.

***

In early 2005, Rhoda was one of several public figures to be invited to participate in a symposium on liberalism convened by Milton Shain, the director of the Isaac and Jesse Kaplan Centre for Jewish Studies and Research at the University of Cape Town. The symposium was a tribute to Helen Suzman, the Jewish parliamentarian who led a tireless fight against the apartheid regime from inside the political system.

Some of the speakers were past and present political leaders — Tony Leon, Frederick van Zyl Slabbert, and Colin Eglin, the latter a key negotiator for the DP in South Africa's transition. Helen Zille, then a rising star within the DA, was another speaker.

---

6   Rhoda Kadalie. Speech during panel discussion of *Running with Horses* by Allan Boesak. 15 Sep. 2009.

Julia, Rhoda, and Helen Suzman on Human Rights Day, 2005

Others were scholars and observers who were sympathetic to the liberal cause, even if some were also critical of it. Sipho Seepe, a black intellectual who had been one of the foremost critics of President Thabo Mbeki in the South African media, was among the speakers. So, too, was Hermann Giliomee, an Afrikaner historian who, while supportive of South Africa's new democracy, believed that it was fatally flawed because it failed to protect ethnic minorities sufficiently, and had been unduly optimistic about voters' ability to transcend racial boundaries.

Not all of the speakers identified as "liberal," a position associated historically in South Africa with free-market economic philosophies as well as opposition to racial discrimination. Rhoda did not oppose the idea of the welfare state, or state-centered policies. Despite her early exposure to the absurdities of East German communism, and her growing skepticism of socialist economic policy, she remained open to redistributionist policies. In a lecture on the concept of "welfare" in 2014, she would declare: "[W]hile I have many reservations about welfare states, especially for a country with SA's complicated history, I do believe that where we have such high levels of poverty and unemployment, as a society we must be involved as a nation in addressing collectively the sins of the past." That included government — though she was careful to stipulate that "we all have a role to play," especially in civil society.[7] It was in her embrace of civil liberties, and her rejection of identity politics, that Rhoda came closest to endorsing the liberal political model explicitly.

The speeches were held over a series of weeks, following an initial event honoring Suzman on March 21, the anniversary of the Sharpeville massacre, which is observed as Human Rights Day in South Africa.

Rhoda's lecture stands out from the rest. Unlike most of the other participants, she did not dwell on liberalism as an ideology — neither its history in South Africa, nor its uncertain prospects in a country with deep racial, ethnic, and economic divisions.

Instead, she outlined a political philosophy that was not only theoretical, but practical, and which prized the role of opposition — for its own sake.[8]

Rhoda began by describing her sense of disappointment in how opposition was treated in the new South Africa. The "euphoria" of the elections of 1994 and the new constitution of 1996 had yielded to frustration as the ANC had produced one corruption scandal after another, silencing objections from Parliament in every case. Members of Parliament (MPs) of all parties, Rhoda observed, were marginalized when they "dared to do what MPs are supposed to do — ask crucial questions and hold politicians accountable to the electorate." The ANC rejected any checks on its own power, particularly when coming from its political opponents.

But the intolerance toward opposition was not confined to the ruling party, she observed. "I have become impatient with the media and the political elite who deride opposition. In fact, I am convinced that they do so out of a profound ignorance of the meaning of the role of opposition."[9] While the media was regarded by the ANC as too sympathetic to the opposition, many journalists were uncomfortable with the fact that the main opposition party was positioned well to the right of the ANC, and led by a white man who refused to behave deferentially to the new government.

Rhoda took them on: "Many are of the view that true opposition will emerge, in the fullness of time, from the left, and that for the present we

---

7   Rhoda Kadalie. "Welfare Is Everybody's Business!" Speech to ACVV. 12 Sep. 2014.

8   Rhoda Kadalie. "Why Parliamentary Opposition Is Essential to Democracy." *Opposing Voices: Liberalism and Opposition in South Africa Today.* Milton Shain, ed. Jonathan Ball, Cape Town: 2006. 113-130.

9   Rhoda Kadalie. "Why Parliamentary Opposition Is Essential to Democracy." *Opposing Voices: Liberalism and Opposition in South Africa Today.* Milton Shain, ed. Jonathan Ball, Cape Town: 2006. 114.

should be patient as we are merely going through a transition. Needless to say, this view is myopic given what has happened elsewhere in Africa and Eastern Europe." She added — perhaps in a quiet rebuke to Selfe and Coetzee — that "the expectation that some black superwoman will emerge to usurp Tony Leon's position" had "become boring and self-defeating." It was, she said, a surrender to the ANC's insistence on race in politics.

Rhoda then outlined her philosophy of opposition. The ancient Greeks, she noted, believed "inner dialogue and disputation are indispensable to democratic states." That was not because they liked "to sit around and chat," or because opposition was a "regrettable instance of a number of people whose ideas and interests did not coincide with one's own." Rather, "opposition was crucial because without one there could be no dialogue; and without dialogue, one could not begin to approach the truth. No one person and no one party, whatever their credentials, can lay absolute claim to the truth."

Even the Greeks struggled to tolerate opposition: the fate of Socrates was a reminder of the need for checks on the power of the state, which it was the duty of political opposition to defend.

To Rhoda, it was less important that opposition be self-consciously liberal. It had to exist regardless, and be robust enough to present an alternative to the government.

"Some parties offer liberal solutions, others nationalist ones; some socialist and some religious. Some of these are unpopular, impractical, or simply obsolete. Nevertheless it is important that we have these choices."

To Rhoda, diversity and choice were prerequisites for true political freedom.

Labels were never important to Rhoda when it came to opposition politics. What she cared about were courage, and competence.

For example, at the moment when she was becoming a prominent voice among South African liberals, Rhoda retained an openness, in theory, to socialist ideals, even if she was skeptical of socialist policies and politicians. Like her forebear Clements Kadalie, she distinguished socialism or social democracy, and their noble goals, from outright communism and its narrow, revolutionary worldview.

In a column in 2007, Rhoda turned to the prospects of the South African Communist Party (SACP), which co-governed with the ANC. (South Africa could be described as the one country in which the communists won the Cold War: the fall of the Berlin Wall ultimately cleared a path for the SACP to emerge from the underground and eventually join the ANC's governing alliance, together with the trade unions.)

She noted that the SACP's publications still used "the language of my sociology classes of 30 years ago - ideologically intact, and used with great gusto." She added: "All this language is anathema to postmodern societies in which constitutional democracy and some form of capitalism are the only viable ways to lift the poor out of their misery."

Rhoda concluded:

> The astounding thing is that while middle-class socialist politicians live bourgeois lives, travel the world, enjoy the benefits of globalisation, the internet and global information technology, they speak a language out of synch with the modern democratic society that allows them their lifestyles.

> Why can we not speak of a social democratic form of capitalism geared towards socialist ideals as a viable alternative to address poverty and unemployment? Why can the excessive revenue generated by the government not be used to create employment and fulfil some of the socialist goals that most of us share?

> No national democratic revolution or the overthrow of "colonialism of a special type" will provide answers to these problems. They will, I know for sure, make them worse. What political leaders need tons of is common sense.[10]

It was "common sense," rather than ideological coherence, that Rhoda sought.

***

Rhoda never did join the DA in a leadership sense, though she came to support the DA's electoral efforts. She was particularly supportive of the DA in the municipal election of 2006, when the DA nominated its parliamentary spokesperson, Helen Zille MP, as its candidate for mayor of Cape Town.

Like many Capetonians, Rhoda had come to regard the ANC's brief rule as a disaster for the city. The ANC imposed racial quotas in its affirmative action policies that left many local businesses unable to compete for city contracts — but allowed well-connected ANC bigwigs to benefit. The city cut spending on emergency services while spending heavily on projects like the N2 Gateway housing development, which would be visible from a major local highway but would otherwise fail to

---

10   Rhoda Kadalie. *Business Day*, 26 Jul. 2007, ibid.

make a dent in the local housing backlog. And the ANC was perceived to discriminate against Coloured residents, seeing them as less than "African."

Zille, like Rhoda, had begun her political career on the political left. She had been a member of the Black Sash, an organization of women who staged protests against the apartheid government and its treatment of political prisoners. She had then pursued a career as a journalist, working for the *Rand Daily Mail*, and broke the story of Steve Biko's murder by police in 1977. It was in that context that Rhoda and Zille had one of their first meetings: Rhoda noted in her 1984 diary that she had an "interview on beach apartheid" with Helen Zille on Wednesday, the 25th of July.

She had been an enthusiastic supporter of the country's political changes, and its transition from apartheid to democracy. When she became involved in her school's governing board, she was thrilled that the new ANC government was receptive to her community's ideas about education reform.

But Zille was soon disappointed that the ANC effectively outsourced education policy to the South African Democratic Teachers' Union (SADTU). The union protected failing teachers from being disciplined or replaced. It also pushed for aggressive affirmative action policies that encouraged many of the most qualified and experienced white teachers to opt for early retirement. The result was that black students, for whom government schools were the only affordable option, often suffered worse education than had been the case under apartheid.

Zille joined the opposition, and soon found herself as the provincial minister (MEC) for education for the Western Cape. She developed a habit of dropping in on schools unannounced, and found that in many of the poorest schools, neither faculty nor students were bothering to show up on time. Money, she discovered, was not the problem: good management and commitment separated success from failure.

In addition to her sterling résumé, Zille spoke Afrikaans and was working diligently on polishing her Xhosa language skills. She could speak to the DA's traditional supporters, as well as the black constituency it hoped to build.

Rhoda had a long association with Zille, one that preceded Zille's entry into politics. Their paths crossed when Zille was involved in the non-governmental organization (NGO) world, and again when Zille was Director of Public Affairs at UCT. Rhoda was, by then, on the UCT Council, and joined Zille on the board of George Soros's OSF-SA. They also attended the same church, Rondebosch United Church, a Congregationalist-Presbyterian congregation in the academic suburb that is home to UCT.

*Rhoda at her home, after receiving an honorary doctorate from UWC,
with Helen Zille, 2007 (Courtesy Rhoda Kadalie)*

Zille ran locally as the standard-bearer for the DA nationally, under
the slogan: "Stop corruption; start delivery." The ANC, sensing its own
vulnerability, began to use whatever tricks came to hand to discourage
voters from choosing the DA. Rhoda accused the ANC of using government
resources in its campaign — and to rig the election in its favor:

> *I live off De Waal Drive in Cape Town and observed the poster war close
> at hand. I saw people in municipal trucks remove DA posters. I was sent
> photos of these by a parliamentary official who caught them in the act
> and we sent them to the media, all of which refused to publish them,
> except for Business Day, on its back page.*

> *The DA's Gareth Morgan's detailed account in these pages of the ANC's
> abuse of taxpayers' money for election advertisements reminds us
> that the use of state resources undermines democracy by giving unfair
> advantage to the incumbent. While opposition parties are forced to fight
> for the hearts and minds of voters with little more than donations and
> pluck, the ruling party can tap into the state machinery and pass off self-
> promotion as legitimate government communication.*

> *...[T]he ANC dished out food parcels and houses to the poor just before the elections, reinforcing the electorate's perception of the ANC as the party of patronage. Where people are poor and eking out a miserable existence, taking handouts during elections is considered a survival tactic and taking from the government what is rightfully yours anyway.[11]*

Rhoda also complained of bias in the media — not just the SABC, but private outlets like the *Sunday Times*, which she said "flogged us to death with the noble utterances of President Thabo Mbeki" before the election.

These tactics worked to the ANC's advantage in much of the country. But in Cape Town, the ruling party struggled to turn out its vote. It was bedeviled by a massive fire on Table Mountain that was set by a British tourist who tossed a cigarette into the brush, but whose impact was worse because the ANC-led city administration had diverted funds from emergency services to housing construction. Shortly before the election, the city also suffered a massive power outage, thanks to a malfunction at Eskom's nearby Koeberg nuclear power plant — the first of many such outages to follow. These events reinforced a sense that the ANC was incapable of governing — except to toss patronage to its supporters and lucrative contracts to its senior membership.

Change was in the air.

***

On Election Day, the DA won a plurality of the vote in Cape Town. But victory was not certain until Zille managed to assemble a narrow city council majority with an unlikely coalition of smaller parties, shocking the ANC and unseating it in a democratic election for the first time. Patricia de Lille, who had promised voters that her Independent Democrats would not back the ANC, broke her word and threw her party's votes to the incumbent party in a failed attempt to keep the DA out of office. The *Daily Sun* was brutal in its assessment: "Patricia de Liar," its headline read.

Rhoda followed up with a similar verdict: "The significance of this nail-biting contest for mayor in the City of Cape Town is that it exposed the leader of the Independent Democrats (ID) for what she is - egotistical, immoderate and politically irresponsible. ... She tried to outfox the smaller parties by overplaying her hand and lost in a battle where one of her own betrayed her. ... What may seem like courage and principle - a phrase she used ad nauseam throughout the discussions - is stubbornness and a

---

11   Rhoda Kadalie. "ANC 'manipulation' of pre-poll conditions 'real' reason for victory." *Business Day*, 11 Mar. 2006.

failure to compromise when it is the right thing to do. Using this refrain in the negotiations, as though it was a mark of integrity, provoked a rebellion among her gatvol supporters, one of whom remarked: "*Kyk hoe lyk haar principles nou!* [Look what her principles look like now!]"[12]

Rhoda's criticism had a particular edge: she and De Lille had long been friends, and Rhoda had encouraged De Lille to join the DA before De Lille decided to launch her own party instead.[13] (Later, ironically, De Lille *would* join the DA, and served for several years as mayor of Cape Town, before bolting once again, facing accusations of mismanagement. She created another new party and serves, as of this writing, in the ANC's national government.)

Julia and Rhoda with Patricia de Lille, c. 2001 (Courtesy Rhoda Kadalie)

The positive effect of DA governance on Cape Town in 2006 was immediate. Zille replaced many of the ANC's political appointees and restored authority to the city's professional staff. The DA also dropped the ANC's stiff racial quotas for city contracts, which had succeeded only in

12   Rhoda Kadalie. "Hero to zero for media darling Patricia de Lille." *Business Day*, 23 Mar. 2006. p. 11.
13   Donwald Pressly. "Gibson exchanges whip for peace pipe." *Sunday Independent*, 30 Sep. 2007. p. 9.

"empowering" a wealthy group of insiders with ties to the ruling party. As a result of *lowering* racial quotas, the DA managed to *increase* the number of black vendors doing business with the city. Zille also scrutinized funding for the new stadium being built for the 2010 World Cup, insisting the city not be placed in debt.

The ANC panicked. It had never lost power through the ballot box before, and did not want Cape Town to set a precedent, nor to present a clear alternative to ANC misrule in other municipalities. Rhoda exposed the ANC's secret maneuverings in her *Business Day* column:

> *The election is hardly two months past and, shocked by the outcome —
> of more than 60% in Cape Town for the opposition collectively — the
> African National Congress (ANC) is doing everything to undermine the
> coalition and its elected mayor, Helen Zille.*

> *Rumours abound that a senior ANC minister has visited one of the
> smaller parties, offering it all kinds of incentives to break up the coalition.
> Secret meetings are being held between ANC politicians and officials to
> strategise the downfall of the Democratic Alliance (DA) partnership.*

> *On three occasions officials who should be neutral have countermanded
> the decisions of the multiparty government in council. The city asked
> for control of the VIP protection unit to be returned to the councillor
> support department from the city police. This was countermanded by
> city manager Wallace Mgoqi. The city asked for all tender meetings to
> be opened. This was countermanded by Mgoqi's representative, Ike
> Nxedlana, who said publicly that he would refuse to open the meeting
> to the public.*

> ...

> *Mgoqi has flatly refused to go on leave, arriving with burly bodyguards
> at council meetings to intimidate the new council. He continues to sign
> documents on behalf of the city and still enters contracts – all of which
> will be null and void if the city's legal advice turns out to have been right.
> This could cost the city millions. He persists as if the new administration
> does not exist.*

> *Obsessively engaged in toppling a legitimately constituted
> administration, the ANC shows how insecure it is about Zille as mayor.
> Her track record as an efficient, uncorrupt and hardworking politician
> is a direct threat to its record of gross mismanagement under mayor
> Nomaindia Mfeketo who, with Mgoqi, virtually ran the city into the*

ground. More seriously, the message the ANC sends to public officials is: "Play our game and you can reward yourselves as you wish."

...

Having lost the election, the ANC continues to govern through incompetent officials, whose jobs are on the line and who now find it convenient to call it a "racial purge". The ANC has demonised the DA to such an extent that it cannot afford for it to succeed. This is what citizens should be worried about.

Should the ANC lose a national election, the consequences will be too ghastly to contemplate. The ANC believes that it is its revolutionary right to rule in perpetuity and will use Stalinist tactics to squash any political competitor out of existence. The recent Economist Survey on SA echoes these warning signals. It is time to take note.[14]

But the ANC was less concerned about the opinions of the *Economist*. It was obsessed with retaining power.

ANC activists resorted to ever-more desperate tactics to break up the DA's governing coalition. Mayor Helen Zille was also the target of violence: she was pushed down a stairwell in Khayelitsha, and her car was hit by bullets as she visited a township one evening. Zille preferred to downplay these events, rather than create a sense of alarm that would frighten residents and trigger instability within the coalition.

Rhoda was not so constrained. She blasted the ANC — this time, in another letter to the editor of the *Business Day* — for suggesting that Zille, the mayor, needed to inform the ANC ahead of time of her plans to visit a black neighborhood.[15] And she condemned the silence of Idasa and the Human Rights Commission for failing to defend Zille's democratically-elected government against the evident thuggery of the ANC.

Rhoda played a role in the new Cape Town administration, when Zille invited her to chair a commission in April 2007 to review efforts to rename city streets. There was broad public support for renaming roads once named for apartheid leaders — including Oswald Pirow, a notorious Nazi sympathizer whose name graced the street outside Cape Town's new convention center. But other changes favored by earlier city administrations, such as renaming historic Adderley and Wale streets for

---

14   Rhoda Kadalie. "Moves to undermine Cape coalition bode ill for SA." *Business Day*, 20 Apr. 2006. p. 13.
15   Rhoda Kadalie. "Time to stand up." *Business Day*, 26 Apr. 2006. p. 11.

Nelson Mandela and F. W. de Klerk, were viewed as excessive. Critics said the ANC was abusing the issue to distract from its policy failures.[16]

When Helen asked her to chair the commission, Rhoda joked: "You chose the right person, because I don't believe in any of this." To Rhoda, practical achievements were more important than symbolic changes — especially when District Six remained barren, and Cape Town's poor continued to suffer.

The ANC agreed with Rhoda's own assessment of her fitness for the role, declaring: "There is no way that Rhoda Kadalie can exercise an impartial role as chairperson. Apart from the fact that she is a close friend and supporter of Mayor Helen Zille, she is a strident critic of the ANC. Many if not most of the great heroes of the city, a good number of whom paid with their lives in the struggle for democracy, were members of the ANC or the Congress Alliance."[17] In response, Dean Rowan Smith of the city's iconic St. George's Cathedral wrote to the *Cape Times*: "We need more people like Kadalie, who, like [the Biblical prophet] Micaiah, are not afraid to hold an opposing view and to express it, even when it relates to those in power, and that includes all those who hold political office. ... we all need to learn that democracy means defending the right of the other to hold a different view to their own and to have the freedom to express it."[18]

Zille likewise defended Rhoda, and urged her to lead the panel, which considered the issue carefully under her leadership. After 238 suggestions from the public for street name changes, the Kadalie Commission recommended 31 changes in a final report in October 2007. Many of the name changes, ironically, had been made by the ANC. These included renaming J. B. Herzog Boulevard — named for an Afrikaner politician before apartheid — as Nelson Mandela Boulevard, and replacing the Gugulethu road known as "NY 1" (short for "Native Yard 1") with the name Steve Biko Drive.[19]

Looking back on the process, Rhoda observed that it had exceeded her expectations: "We had some people who overwhelmingly rejected the proposed names. Even more interesting was members of political

---

16   The Adderley/Wale change had actually been proposed by Peter Marais, who had been mayor under the previous DA administration, but who had defected to the New National Party.

17   African National Congress, quoted by Anél Powell. "ANC lashes Kadalie for leading street naming panel." *Cape Times*, 13 Jun. 2007. p. 3.

18   Dean Rowan Q. Smith. "Give Kadalie a chance." Letter to the editor. *Cape Times*, 14 Jun. 2007. p. 12.

19   "CT holds back on renaming." News24.com, 24 Mar. 2008. URL: https://www.news24.com/news24/ct-holds-back-on-renaming-20080327. Accessed on 17 Oct. 2021.

parties who rejected names suggested by their own parties. Some families even withdrew the recommendations because of one kind of pressure or another. Some people, including some high-profile politicians, asked questions and opened debate on the matter. I thought the whole process was interesting."

One of the people who had raised questions, she added, had been Nelson Mandela himself. Ever sensitive to the task of reconciliation, the man who had once donned a Springbok jersey at the 1995 Rugby World Cup balked at the idea that a road named for pre-apartheid Prime Minister J.B.M. Herzog would be renamed for him. [20] Rhoda later recalled that when she called Mandela to tell him of the renaming, his answer was: "I shan't replace any former Afrikaner political hero, thank you very much."[21]

The DA-led council took several years to implement the Kadalie Commission's proposals, which had received some opposition from various constituencies in the city. Eventually, after several delays, the DA passed several name changes unanimously in 2010, under Mayor Patricia de Lille, just before the next municipal election, prompting criticism from the ANC, which slammed the changes as an election stunt.[22]

For Rhoda, the experience was an affirmation that symbolic changes could be managed properly, without distracting from more substantive concerns — though she was reminded that even in a city governed by the opposition, the wheels of bureaucracy turned slowly.

***

While broadly supportive of the DA, Rhoda was not shy about her disagreements with the party, either. In the run-up to the 2009 general elections, Zille tried to recruit Rhoda to join the party in a senior position. Rhoda declined, as the *Cape Times* reported:

20   Sipokazi Makoza. "City to change street names next year." *Cape Argus*, 14 Nov. 2007. p. 6.
21   Nelson Mandela, quoted by Rhoda Kadalie. "Comment: A humanity forged in jail: It may sound sacrilegious but in prison Mandela was spared the paranoia of South Africa's exiles." *Guardian*, 11 Feb. 2010. p. 30
22   Babalo Ndenze and Aziz Hartley. "Cape Town streets to get name makeover." *Cape Times*, 10 Dec. 2010. URL: https://www.pressreader.com/south-africa/cape-times/20101210/281487862763930. Accessed on 17 Oct. 2021.

"Anything is possible. But I'm busy running an organisation," said Kadalie, the executive director of the Impumelelo Innovations Award Trust.

Zille said as far as Kadalie was concerned, she had tried to recruit her before the 1999 election.

"I have tried year in and year out to persuade her to enter politics, and every single time she has said no.

"I have to respect that. Rhoda has no specific role in the DA at present," she said.[23]

Rhoda was irritated by the *Cape Times* article, later writing a letter to the editor in which she called it a "non-story":

I told your reporter that Helen has not recruited me recently; I am not being head-hunted; what is this "Rhoda thing"?

...

As promoters of the ANC, the Cape Times continues to try and stir anti-DA publicity and this is one of those stupid attempts that makes no sense. I reassure you, the day I decide to go into politics I will let the world know. There is nothing to be ashamed about, going into opposition politics, because some of my best friends are there! I just don't like lies and to be used to fuel your agenda.[24]

In election after election, Rhoda's name came up as a possible candidate — for mayor of Cape Town, for premier of the Western Cape, or for some other leadership role. Yet Rhoda believed that she could be more effective within the media, and civil society, than within formal politics — and that she could retain her integrity.

Indeed, though Rhoda focused her criticism on the ANC, she also criticized the DA, when warranted. She repeatedly criticized the DA administration of Cape Town, for example, over the destruction of a historic villa in her neighborhood, and over the failure to maintain City Hall, which was a concert venue for the Cape Town Philharmonic Orchestra. She wrote in 2010 that "the entire Philharmonic board finds it hard to believe that, for all the time we have been waiting for the refurbishment of the City

---

23   Babalo Ndenze. "DA hopefuls bitter over speculation Zille will recruit political activist Kadalie." *Cape Times*, 21 Jun. 2010. p.3.

24   Rhoda Kadalie. Letter to the editor. *Cape Times*, 22 Jun. 2010. p. 8.

Hall's toilets, a world-class stadium has been built [for the World Cup]."[25] The city's response was rather laughable: "Rhoda Kadalie alleged that the contractor had "gone AWOL". This is not true. The appointed contractor did not have the capacity to carry out the work and subsequently informed the city that they were abandoning the project – which was beyond the city's control."[26] Later, she wrote to the city to express alarm that City Hall was being used to stage boxing matches, which she feared would risk further damage to the auditorium in which the orchestra performed.[27]

In the 2011 municipal elections, Rhoda voted for the DA, and said so publicly — though she said that she had done so only "grudgingly." She wrote: "On 18th May I grudgingly voted for the DA. My vote in their favour was to foster their continued control of the City of Cape Town and the greater good of the country. On a personal level, however, I have had bad experiences with the party and had very little reason to vote for them."[28] She would voice even more criticisms of the party in the future as it attempted to make its leadership less obviously white — and nearly sacrificed its principles, and its voting base, as a result.

Still, she acknowledged: "Personal sentiments aside, since 2006 the DA has transformed the former ANC-controlled City of Cape Town, a cesspit of corruption, into a model of clean governance."[29] She also praised the provincial government of the Western Cape, which vastly improved under Zille after she took over as premier in 2009. For example, Rhoda lauded Zille's former provincial rival, Theuns Botha, for his performance as provincial health minister, reporting in 2013 that she had seen "remarkable improvements and innovation in the health sector in the Western Cape."[30] A former "Nat," Botha had succeeded simply by focusing on his job, conducting himself without "fuss" or pretense. Rhoda also lauded Anroux Marais, the provincial minister of cultural affairs and

25 Rhoda Kadalie. "Crumbling foundation of citizen participation." *Business Day*, 19 Oct. 2010.
26 Councillor Brett Herron. Letter to the editor. *Cape Times*, 26 Oct. 2020. p. 10.
27 Rhoda Kadalie. Letter to Mayor Patricia De Lille. 5 May 2015. Personal files.
28 Rhoda Kadalie. "Why I grudgingly voted DA." PoliticsWeb, reprinted and translated from *Die Burger*, 24 May 2011. URL: https://www.politicsweb.co.za/opinion/why-i-grudgingly-voted-da. Accessed on 26 Mar. 2022.
29 Ibid.
30 Rhoda Kadalie. "A provincial healthcare system that works." PoliticsWeb, reprinted from *Die Burger*, translated from the Afrikaans, 4 Dec. 2013. URL: https://www.politicsweb.co.za/news-and-analysis/a-provincial-healthcare-system-that-works. Accessed on 28 Mar. 2022.

sport, whom she praised for making her ministry "sexy," and expanding its work to reach disadvantaged communities across the Western Cape.[31]

***

For the next several years, the DA would continue its search for young, talented black leaders. It found them in Lindiwe Mazibuko, who was elected to the post of parliamentary leader in 2011; and in Mmusi Maimane, a dynamic speaker and pastor who was elected to lead the party and became South Africa's first black Leader of the Opposition in 2014. The party also found a winning mayoral candidate for Johannesburg in 2016 in businessman Herman Mashaba. And in Cape Town, the DA made its peace with Patricia de Lille — albeit temporarily — who took over from 2011 to 2018 as mayor.

The challenge in diversifying the party rapidly was that it might lose touch with its core values. In the Mbeki years, the DA had offered a clear alternative to the ANC because it rejected his focus on race, and embraced the free market rather than statist economic policies — albeit with a social "safety net" and enhanced support for state institutions like the police.

The DA's new cohort of black leaders often sought a middle ground between the DA and the ANC on issues like black economic empowerment (BEE), the ruling party's policy of radical distribution of equity in major firms.

Tensions grew within the party, and often erupted around Zille. The woman who led the party to victory in Cape Town, and then in the Western Cape, had a demonstrated record of competent management that set the standard for governance in South Africa. Yet she also had a manner of plain speaking that irritated some of her colleagues. Despite her anti-apartheid credentials and growing fluency in Xhosa, she was cast by the ANC as a racist. Her penchant for commentary on Twitter provided fodder for her critics, much as it would, later, for Donald Trump in the United States.

Rhoda defended Zille from the media's knee-jerk criticism of the opposition. In 2007, as Zille — then a relatively new mayor of Cape Town — was encouraged to take over the national leadership of her party, Rhoda defended Zille from media critics. She wrote: "The media that try to weaken Zille do so at their own, and our, peril. Instead of strengthening democracy by respecting her leadership as she tries to clean up the city, bring back

---

31   Rhoda Kadalie. "Anroux Marais." Post on Facebook, reprinted from *Beeld*, 27 Dec. 2017, translated from the Afrikaans, 1 Jan. 2018. URL: https://www.facebook.com/rhoda.kadalie/posts/10156162601530039. Accessed on 28 Mar. 2022.

good governance and restore the institutional memory that has been lost through rampant affirmative action policies, they cast aspersions on her, because they cannot be seen to be promoting a white woman opposition leader, regardless of her credentials."[32]

While she defended Zille from some criticism, however, Rhoda was perfectly willing to criticize Zille on her own. In 2013, when Zille gave an address to a DA rally in the black township of Alexandria, in Johannesburg, she focused on the party's black leaders, leaving Tony Leon out of her history of the party. Rhoda blasted Zille and the DA on Twitter, accusing Zille of behaving like "Stalin" in ensuring "Tony Leon is airbrushed out of opposition politics."[33]

Zille sought desperately to diversify the party's image. In 2014, she joined forces with Mamphele Ramphele, who had created a new political party the year before called Agang ("Build"). Ramphele had sought to represent a growing faction of ANC voters who were dissatisfied with the corrupt governance of Jacob Zuma, whom Mbeki had dismissed as Deputy President in 2005 over a bribery scandal related to the arms deal, but won elections to lead the party in 2007 and the country in 2009. (Rhoda would later note of Zuma's dismissal: "President Thabo Mbeki will go down in history as someone who fired only one person from his cabinet, and not for mismanagement but for being a political competitor. This when more than half his ministers are incompetent and pose direct threats to the wellbeing of the public."[34])

Ramphele and Zille were two powerful, accomplished women. Ramphele would be the DA's presidential candidate in the 2014 national elections, targeting black voters.

But the arrangement soon fell apart — as Rhoda had long expected that it would. She had long been skeptical of the DA's attempt to recruit black leaders who were not already members of the party. To Rhoda, such efforts smacked of tokenism, and tended to attract poor leaders with troubled pasts. And despite her friendship with, and past support of, Helen Zille, she did not mince words when she disagreed with Zille or her party.

She reflected on the short-lived arrangement with Ramaphele in a column for the *Cape Times*:

32   Rhoda Kadalie. "Hackneyed digs at Zille expose SA's gutless media." *Business Day*, 3 May 2007. p. 13.
33   Rhoda Kadalie, quoted by "Zille 'airbrushed' Leon from DA tribute speech." *Daily Dispatch*, 16 Apr. 2013.
34   Rhoda Kadalie. "A Crime That Many of SA's Ministers Keep Their Jobs." *Business Day* 14 Jun. 2007.

The nuclear fallout over the "crossracial quickie" between Helen Zille and Mamphela Ramphele has been relentless.

Insiders and political pundits alike have roasted the twosome mercilessly, and justifiably so.

...

South Africans yearn for a potent, diverse and united opposition, given their disenchantment with the ANC. With an approaching election they do not want to see an opposition that is wobbly, insecure and one that violates its own principles for the sake of expediency.

Regrettably, as the exemplar of good governance, the DA has not escaped the hubris associated with political aristocracies who believe they have the divine right to make decisions on behalf of the electorate.

...

Parachuting Ramphele into the DA as presidential leader, based on criteria of race, friendship and image, is nothing but a spectacular case of cadre deployment.

Invoking a long-standing friendship as the reason for the relationship of trust was nepotism, pure and simple. One does not appoint one's friends to a presidential position, especially one that is created for them.

Zille stupidly thought that with Ramphele at the helm her party was well on its way to opposition heaven. Not so. Marriages based on lies, looks, ego and debt are sure to implode, as this one did.

She added:

Lastly, the most vexed question I wish to pursue with DA leaders is: why must the presidential candidate be black when the DA owes its strength to the minorities of the country, and the coloureds and whites in particular in the Western Cape? If the criterion of race is central to high-profile political appointments, can the DA please explain why coloured faces are never considered good enough to ascend the throne of presidential leadership but are good enough as voting fodder?

Rhoda's criticism was all the more biting, and credible, because of her long friendship with Zille. The DA leader, however, took Rhoda's criticism in stride. She would later joke that Rhoda could have succeeded at anything "except a diplomatic career."[35]

It was not the first time Rhoda had been vindicated in her feeling that affirmative action appointments in public office rarely succeed, as the DA had learned at great cost. Leaders like Mamphela Ramphele, Joe Seremane, and Lindiwe Mazibuko were widely popular across South Africa, but that did not translate into political strength or effective leadership.

Rhoda was initially hopeful about the young Mazibuko, whom she called "postracial," writing in 2011: "She appeals to a broad spectrum of South Africans because of her leadership qualities, integrity and pleasant disposition. She does not shy away from debate. She gets her hands dirty. She works. Her race is of secondary importance."[36] But Mazibuko clashed with other party leaders, and eventually left politics.

Rhoda was particularly scathing about the elevation of DA leader Mmusi Maimane, a young, charismatic, but inexperienced lay preacher who rose rapidly within the party as he was promoted by Zille and others. She was, initially, alone in her skepticism. She commented on Facebook: "There is a perverse likening of Maimane with [U.S. President Barack] Obama by some DA members. [Obama's slogan] 'Yes we can' is as stupid as [Maimane's slogan] 'Believe in Tomorrow'. Today Obama's ratings are even lower than Bush's and Obama will go down as one of worst US presidents. A portent of things to come for the DA."[37] She was hounded by DA members on Facebook, whom she referred to as "Blue DA lemmings."[38]

She saw Maimaine's elevation as a function of white liberal guilt: "White liberals deal very poorly with intelligent black people, especially those who assert their autonomy and who can think for themselves. Patronizing black people is often easier than treating them as equals."[39] She did not think he would be capable of leading the party to greater levels of black support while retaining the DA's traditional constituency and preserving its values.

35　Helen Zille, quoted by Steven Gruzd. "Remembering Rhoda Kadalie, feisty friend of Israel." *South African Jewish Report*, 30 Jun. 2022. p. 7.

36　Rhoda Kadalie. "Mazibuko's appeal is postracial." *Business Day*, 3 Oct. 2011.

37　Rhoda Kadalie. Post on Facebook, 10 May 2015. URL: https://www.facebook.com/rhoda.kadalie/posts/10153416148875039. Accessed on 28 Mar. 2022.

38　Rhoda Kadalie. Post on Facebook, 10 May 2015. URL: https://www.facebook.com/rhoda.kadalie/posts/10153417508300039. Accessed on 28 Mar. 2022.

39　Rhoda Kadalie. Draft column for *The Citizen*. 15 May 2015. Personal files.

Her warnings would later be vindicated, as Maimane began to push left-wing policies within the DA, such as a controversial embrace of a new Black Economic Empowerment bill in 2013, which the DA initially backed but had to abandon after a backlash from its supporters.[40]

Maimane also began to expel white liberals from the party for minor transgressions. Diane Kohler-Barnard, a news anchor-turned-member of Parliament, found herself targeted by Maimane after she shared a Facebook post whose author praised former apartheid leader P.W. Botha. Rhoda responded to the controversy on Facebook: "Irony of all ironies. When I opposed Mmusi Maimane's appointment as DA leader Diane Kohler Barnard defended this appointment very loyally. You see Diane I have a nose for politics and can separate the wheat from the chaff!"[41]

Zille, who had once supported Maimane's ascent through the ranks, would also find herself in his crosshairs over some of her more provocative tweets. In 2017, for example, before returning from a trip to Singapore, Zille posted several tweets about what she had learned from the success of that small island nation, which embraced the best of the British colonial experience to rise from poverty and obscurity to gleaming prosperity. In one comment, she said: "For those claiming legacy of colonialism was ONLY negative, think of our independent judiciary, transport infrastructure, piped water etc."[42] She thought her remark uncontroversial, but landed in South Africa to discover there were calls for her resignation from office and expulsion from the DA. She eventually apologized, partly to save Maimane the embarrassment of being a black leader in a party under attack for its purportedly retrograde views on colonialism.

Rhoda, who had criticized Zille's hurried efforts to place black leaders in leadership positions, was fully in her corner. She wrote in her *Beeld* column:

> *The Pavlovian response to Helen Zille's tweet is more a commentary on the "enraged", than it is about the tweet. The context of the tweet is extremely interesting – a reaction to her visit to Singapore, a country that was once the poorest in world, is today a leader in the economic world.*

40   Andisiwe Makinana. "EE Bill: Is black the DA's new true blue?". *Mail & Guardian*, 14 Nov. 2013. URL: https://mg.co.za/article/2013-11-14-is-black-the-das-new-true-blue/. Accessed on 31 Mar. 2022.

41   Rhoda Kadalie. Post on Facebook, 3 Oct. 2015. URL: https://www.facebook.com/rhoda.kadalie/posts/10153786417575039. Accessed on 28 Mar. 2022.

42   Helen Zille. *#StayWoke: Go Broke.* Cape Town: Obsidian World Publishing, 2021. p. 97.

Rhoda: 'Comrade Kadalie, You Are Out of Order!'

Her tweet is part of her contemplation on how [former Singaporean leader] Lee Kuan Yew got it right.

...

The venom against her is all the more poisonous because she is white, a woman, and "refuses to know her place", a prerequisite for the McCarthyists who appropriate the right to condemn and stone her in the court of public opinion. Bolstered by a colluding media with their insidious headlines – "Helen Zille and the myth of the White Saviour", "Zille could face career-ending racism charge" - the push for her demise is relentless, regardless of whether the "crime fits the punishment". The party of liberalism has become captive to the tyranny of political correctness.[43]

Rhoda added, in a column in *The Citizen, that* "freedom of speech includes the right to be offended, to be challenged and to be confronted by the facts, regardless."[44] Rhoda did not simply defend Zille's right to free speech, but also the substance of her comment:

In 1995 President Mandela sent a women's delegation to Uganda and Australia to explore how they mainstreamed gender equality through various mechanisms and institutions. On our way we passed through the University of Makerere, once a crown in pre-colonial Uganda's higher education system, reduced to a shell of its former glory after independence. I spoke to someone about it, and he immediately lamented "the departure of colonialism". I had the same reaction on a visit to Nairobi in the early 2000s where community leaders openly claimed that life was better under the colony. And lest these people be accused of the "nostalgia for empire", as so many post-colonial scholars wish to label it, the real concern was the betrayal of post-independence leaders to usher in the constitutional democracies they promised so vociferously during their liberation struggles. Colonialism and apartheid were indeed pernicious systems of subjugation, but those systems also brought development to the colonies, if not for the indigenous peoples, but then certainly for the colonisers, benefiting the colonised by default. It is a

---

43   Rhoda Kadalie. Post on Facebook, reprinted from *Beeld*, translated from the Afrikaans, 22 Mar. 2017. URL: https://www.facebook.com/rhoda. kadalie/posts/10155269350555039. Accessed on 28 Mar. 2022.

44   Rhoda Kadalie. "Hysteria over Zille's colonialism tweet a storm in a teacup." *The Citizen*, 24 Mar. 2017. URL: https://www.citizen.co.za/ news/opinion/1466229/hysteria-over-zilles-colonialism-tweet-a-storm-in-a-teacup/. Accessed on 13 Apr. 2022.

fact that those subjugated benefited from the massive infrastructural development, albeit within systems of oppression and discrimination.[45]

Still, Rhoda pointed out that Zille partly had herself to blame. In a subsequent Facebook post, she noted that "Zille ironically fought tooth and nail to install" Maimane.[46] In return, he had tried to destroy her career and reputation.

While persecuting political incorrectness among white members was thought to be a way of appealing to a broader black electorate, in practice it attracted few black voters while alienating minority voters, leading the DA to a disappointing election result in 2019. Zille would later admit: "I am personally responsible for one of the biggest mistakes in the DA's history, which was supporting Mmusi's candidature for the leadership."[47] Maimane eventually resigned — and Zille would return as chair of the party's Federal Executive.

Meanwhile, the DA faced new opposition from the left, in the form of the quasi-communist, populist Economic Freedom Fighters (EFF), led by the expelled ANC youth leader Julius Malema. Opposition politics became more fraught, not more hopeful. And with its decline the country's hopes, too, were dimmed.

---

45   Rhoda Kadalie, ibid.
46   Rhoda Kadalie. Comment on Facebook, 14 Jun. 2017. URL: https://www.facebook.com/rhoda.kadalie/posts/10155545221805039. Accessed on 28 Mar. 2022.
47   Helen Zille. ibid., p. 125.

Chapter 17:
Community and Civil Society

"[T]he language of music belongs to the human soul; and that is ultimately what the main objective of a university is: to bring out the best in students and help them master various disciplines, whether they originate in Europe, Africa, Asia or America."[1]

Rhoda's influence on South Africa went far beyond politics. She was a *bon vivant*, a patron (or matron) of the arts, and a hostess of innumerable dinner parties.

Her cozy dining room in University Estate included a long window overlooking Table Bay. She had chairs on one side of the table and a long bench on the side by the window, meaning that guests — including those of opposing political persuasions — were sometimes forced to become intimately familiar, like it or not. Rhoda prodded her guests to discuss and defend their views, creating an environment in which the expectation was that people would find a way to get along, regardless of partisan labels and racial or gender identity.

When not fussing over a stove and passing warm Cape Malay dishes through the window that connected the kitchen to the living and dining room, Rhoda enjoyed restaurants, treating herself — and Julia — to meals at the city's top establishments. When she would appear at a table, the room would often erupt in greetings. John Field recalled: "Everyone greeted Rhoda at a meal."[2] Politicians, artists, captains of industry — all were fond of Rhoda, though occasionally wary of her sharp and critical wit. And she would greet the *bergies* outside the restaurant with the same ease.

---

1   Rhoda Kadalie. "Opera clicks with African students." *Business Day*, 31 July 2003. URL: https://web.archive.org/web/20030812043202/ https://allafrica.com/stories/200307310151.html. Accessed on 18 Oct. 2021.

2   Personal communication with the author. 21 Feb. 2022.

Rhoda Kadalie with Julia and sister Judy, c. 2002 (Courtesy Rhoda Kadalie)

Some of Rhoda's friendships suffered as a result of her iconoclastic political views and her forthright columns, which spared neither friend nor foe. As she told the Afrikaans journalist Murray La Vita in 2011:

> *"Patricia (de Lille, ID leader) and I were very close, and I got to know her very well and learned things from her that I did not like, and I wrote a column about it. After that, our friendship was gone.*
>
> *"My friendship with Jakes Gerwel is also gone because I wrote a column about which he was angry."*
>
> *People might think the columns are ad hominem?*
>
> *"Yes, but the best columnists in the world are ad hominem. They take people by surprise!"*
>
> *Are there limits?*
>
> *"I have no limits! I believe in unbridled freedom of speech. And I grant everyone the right to approach me in the same way."*[3]

---

3   Rhoda Kadalie, in Murray La Vita, ibid. p. 192.

Some of those rifts were never mended. Other friendships were on again, off again — as much for personal as political reasons. Rhoda herself knew that she could be tough to get along with — but for those who could ride the ups and downs with her, there was no better friend, and certainly none more honest.

Rhoda was also involved in a variety of civic, business, and academic activities. Unlike many members of South Africa's emerging political and media elite, Rhoda did not seek opportunities for self-enrichment. The ANC's policy of "black economic empowerment" (BEE), which became formalized under President Mbeki, typically involved large companies handling over at least 25% of their shares to "historically disadvantaged individuals," many of whom were senior members of the ruling party. Because these new owners had little money, the purchases were often financed by the companies themselves, draining scarce capital.

Rhoda had contempt for the BEE policy, seeing it as a vehicle for corruption that neglected the more fundamental challenge of building skills and entrepreneurship from the ground up. When she was offered shares in South African companies, she invariably turned them down.

On one such occasion, she was approached by Motty Sacks, the chairman of South African health insurance giant Netcare, to join its board. Sacks clearly coveted Rhoda's reputation for independence and integrity. But after considering the offer, she turned it down. The financial renumeration was not worth the loss of her credibility on the subject of BEE.

Rhoda did serve on other boards. Her sole business interest was a role on the board of a farm, known as the Molteno Brothers Trust, located in the Elgin Valley, near the town of Grabouw, in the Overberg region, just over the mountains east of Cape Town. The Molteno Brothers farm invested a sizable amount of its profits into the training of farmworkers, creating opportunities for them to become self-sustaining and independent. The trust provided clinics, schools, and community development projects, and even granted residential property rights to some farm workers. These were pilot projects aimed at discovering how to make land reform work in South Africa — an urgent necessity after the catastrophe in Zimbabwe, and the failure of early efforts in South Africa.

A ripe apple growing in a hillside orchard on the Molteno Brothers farm, Grabouw, Western Cape

Though she had no farming background, Rhoda had long taken an interest in rural South Africa, and the human rights of farm workers. She recalled in 1998:

> *When I was a Human Rights Commissioner, with the Minister of Land Affairs, I visited several rural areas. And repeatedly, the farm workers would say, apartheid is dead constitutionally, but not on our farms. And so I think on the farms is the place where apartheid is still entrenched, where farmers have absolute power. Despite labor relations, and the Labor Relations Act, and the Equity Bill, people are really treated badly. And I think farmers get away with murder in the way they treat their farmworkers. Literally, with murder.[4]*

Rhoda also had a strong interest in environmental issues and conservation. Through Impumelelo, she had helped fund various environmental projects; in 2004, she would deliver a speech urging South Africans to learn more

---

4   Rhoda Kadalie. "South Africans Talking," ibid.

about "green" issues.⁵ In later years, she would share links on Facebook to various petitions to save South Africa's unique ecosystems and wildlife.

Rhoda drove to the farm in Grabouw regularly, helping to oversee its community development programs, and attending board meetings. In her role, she also helped develop closer relationships between the farm's management and its labor force. She would later describe the board as one of the most exciting she had ever joined. Though she was the only woman on the board, serving alongside seven men, she enjoyed complete equality and power in decision-making, as well as the complete trust of her colleagues.

Despite a steep learning curve, Rhoda found herself developing expertise about the different varieties of apple cultivars, species of protea flowers, and suitable soils (or *terroirs*) for winemaking. She frequently drove home with bushels of apples and other produce to share with family and friends.

She also had a lasting impact on the community of the region through the funding that she provided to worthy social development projects on behalf of the Molteno Brothers trust.

Betsie Ryke, the executive director of the Rural Arts Network, recalled the impact that Impumelelo had on her project, which teaches musical performance skills to disadvantaged and impoverished youth, many of them children of farm workers in the Overberg region of the Western Cape.

Rhoda visited the project in February 2016 in the town of Grabouw, about 90 minutes east of Cape Town, over the Hottentots-Holland Mountains and along the N2 highway. Ryke was very nervous to meet Rhoda, whom she knew would see right through any "window dressing" of the project.⁶ But Rhoda was not only impressed by the marimba and djembe skills of the children: she was also deeply moved by the commitment of the four women — all white — who ran the project.

In a subsequent column, "A flight of white angels," Rhoda praised the women, contrasting their values with those of the student activists running rampant on the country's university campuses at the time, "burning art, smashing pianos and burning down libraries and labs."⁷ She wrote:

This week, I spent an entire day evaluating a rural music and arts project with my team in the farmlands of Grabouw.

5   Rhoda Kadalie, quoted by "'Learn About Green Issues'." *Cape Argus*, 21 Sep. 2004.
6   Interview with Betsie Ryke. 24 Feb. 2022.
7   Rhoda Kadalie. "A flight of white angels." *The Citizen*, 4 Mar. 2016. p. 12.

Rhoda: 'Comrade Kadalie, You Are Out of Order!'

I discovered four white women who, in my estimation, should receive an international award for doing national development work government should be doing. Their commitment makes nonsense of this notion of "white privilege" and "whiteness" in our racist discourse today.

These Mother Theresas share with a dedication unmatched their music and arts expertise with local children.

The first stop was Pineview Primary.

In a small prefab classroom, about 60 kids sang in a choir that could rate with some of the best in SA. The pupils sang passionately while radiating smiles as broad as the ocean.

The relationship between teacher and student was one of trust. They moved from one rendition to the next, showing off their prowess.

Thereafter, we visited another school to witness a teacher instructing kids to reproduce different art forms. As we walked around watching the kids drawing pictures, the range of quality was astounding.

We picked up immediately which kids had perceptual difficulties and which ones excelled. This helped teachers with referrals to social workers.

The next stop was another arts project where the teacher and pupils adorned the art room with mosaic tiles into an aesthetically pleasing space.

There, the teacher demonstrated to young kids how to reproduce a still life by showing them a real "still life" painting and one recreated on the table with vases filled with flowers, surrounded by onions.

The pièce de résistance came at the end of our fieldwork. A visit to a marimba class showed beginners emulating older students with finesse.

Later, five older pupils joined them, hungry and tired from having walked some distance in the heat. They gave a splendid performance, justifying the prize won last year in a national competition.

Betsie, Melissa, Salome, and headmistress Mrs. Du Plooy may be white, but their place in the pantheon of SA's national treasures is etched in the heavens.

Betsie Ryke treasured that column, years later. And Rhoda's sentiments were sincere. Such was the impact the best of the projects had on Rhoda — and the Molteno Brothers Trust, in turn, had a profound impact on its awardees, providing funding that allowed them to continue, expand, and grow.

Rhoda also served on the board of the Cape Town Philharmonic Orchestra and the Cape Town Opera, continuing a lifelong interest in classical music. In fact, the Kadalie family's enthusiasm transcended several generations. As Rhoda was to write on the Cape Town Philharmonic's 100th anniversary in 2014:

> *My father's mother, Molly, lived in Bloemhof Flats with her divorced daughter and bachelor son, Robert, known to us as Uncle Bobby. Uncle Bobby was an irascible man, difficult, and hard to please, unlike his eldest brother, Uncle Alexander, who was refined, gentle, loving, and powerful. My dad, Fenner, was the youngest, a mummy's boy, who loved his mother, and all he wanted to be was a theologian, in reaction to his father, the famous trade unionist, Clements Kadalie, who founded the Industrial Commercial Workers' Union.*
>
> *Both Uncle Alex and Uncle Bobby frequented the City Hall concerts every Thursday since I can recall. Uncle Alex could not attend as regularly as he was a Pastor of the African Methodist Episcopal Church, which posted him to rural areas all over the Cape Province, but whenever he was in Cape Town he would attend. It was he who introduced me to the City Hall concerts and to see the young pianist Marian Friedman, the Eoan Group and the operas they performed in the City Hall. Uncle Bobby, however, attended every week, sat in the same seat, and never missed a concert. Both uncles loved Beethoven and Brahms best, and they both had the best collections of LPs of complete operas, opera stars, concertos, choral music, and all the great symphonies.*
>
> *It was from them that I learnt about Maria Callas, Joan Sutherland, and Beverley Sills and the differences between them; of Verdi, Puccini, and most of all Bellini, not spoken of much in music circles at the time. No brothers could be more different, yet share the love of classical music so deeply. Uncle Bobby was an uncle so judgemental, so critical, so self-important that no one in the family took him seriously. He was difficult to like. Uncle Alex elicited different sentiments. He was much loved and adored by his family, his community and his parish. He was adored for his intellect, for his oratory, which he inherited from Clements Kadalie, and for his compassion. He was the uncle everyone wanted and somehow he knew that together with his daughters, I could be cultivated to love the Arts, and would include a ticket for me as well, when he took his daughters to concerts.*

Rhoda: 'Comrade Kadalie, You Are Out of Order!'

All of this came to an end in the early seventies or late sixties when coloured and black people were suddenly excluded from the concerts. Uncle Bobby was enraged. He felt insulted and became bitter towards every government, since then, regardless. He must have complained about it vociferously, when somehow, he landed up in one of the local newspapers, either the Cape Times or the Argus (I cannot remember but I confirmed this with Uncle Alex's daughter, Yvonne, recently) recalling his long history with the Cape Town Philharmonic Orchestra. It was like a death in the family. This was how people who loved the finer things in life, spent their Thursday evenings. He could not understand why such a simple pleasure could be wrenched from his weekly routine. And since Uncle Bobby loved complaining, this lament died with him when he passed away aged 82 years in 2009.[8]

The orchestra, which performed in the cavernous City Hall, was constantly struggling to find musicians, recruiting among students and members of the various local music academies. But through the efforts of Rhoda and the board, the orchestra managed to maintain a world-class program and to host elite international performers. The orchestra's concerts were a who's who of Cape Town dignitaries, and maintained a loyal following throughout the city, despite a disinterest by the national government in classical music.

Rhoda was similarly interested in the Cape Town Opera. Opera was an art form Rhoda loved — her favorite aria was "Vissi d'arte," the "prayer" from Giacomo Puccini's *Tosca* — and she attended every opera staged in the city. To Rhoda, the interest and success of African students in opera was a rebuke to the essentialist idea that students had to be confined to "African" cultural offerings. She particularly enjoyed watching music students perform, and the sight of black and white students excelling together in a classical genre often thought beyond the ability or interest of black students in particular. She championed the career of soprano Pretty Yende, who came from an obscure town in the impoverished province of Mpumalanga and went on to international stardom. She also found inspiration in music for one of her favorite sayings: "If you want to lead the orchestra, you must turn your back on the crowd."[9]

---

8   Rhoda Kadalie. "The Cape Philharmonic Orchestra's 100th Anniversary." March 2014. Personal files.
9   Rhoda Kadalie. Speech to Ronnie Samaai Music Education Project. Cape Town, South Africa. 26 Nov. 2017.

In a 2003 column titled "Opera clicks with African students," she described the vice-chancellor's concert at the University of Cape Town, which she attended annually:

> *All the opera singers were black except one, and to see them mastering Italian opera, an essentially European genre, with such finesse makes nonsense of Prof William Makgoba's assertion that our universities should become bastions of African essentialism, knowledge and experience, whatever that might mean. "After all," says he, "we have African music, poetry, dance, politics, philosophy, architecture, traditional medicine and so on."*
>
> *I spoke afterwards with the head of the opera school, Dr Angelo Gobbato, to ask him how he was able to transform the opera school from 98% white in the past to 90% black today. His response was enlightening. The admission of a large number of black students was not simply about increasing the head count. It was about acknowledging the strong choral tradition and rich vocal talent in the townships that can actively be incorporated into the opera tradition at UCT.*
>
> *The opera school went into communities to recruit students. The response was overwhelming. At one stage more than 310 came to audition, and bursaries were made available to people with no music training but strong vocal talent.*[10]

This, to Rhoda, was affirmative action at its best, where the idealism of the policy was matched by the result. She also served on the board of the Baxter Theatre, affiliated with — but somewhat independent from — the University of Cape Town. She also donated to the Baxter; to this day, there is a seat in the main auditorium endowed in her daughter's name.

Still, regardless of her love of the arts, Rhoda insisted on the same high standard of accountability in cultural institutions that she demanded from government, the media, and academia. In 2014, she resigned from the board of the Cape Town Philharmonic Orchestra (CPO) over concerns about corruption and nepotism.

As she later recalled, in her typical plain-spoken way: "I was very active in the CPO and worked with the CEO to appoint new staff, help with disciplinary measures, etc. With one appointment I discovered that the CEO used CPO money to fly up a candidate who was clearly under-qualified, and put him in a hotel, for the interview. The interview was a

---

10   Rhoda Kadalie. "Opera clicks with African students." *Business Day*, 2003, ibid.

farce, but it soon transpired that this guy was a gay friend of the gay CEO who enjoyed the largesse of the CPO to visit with his friend in Cape Town.

"I reported this to the Board, who were clearly disgusted, but they refused to do anything about it. Many other issues arose, which led to the appointment of a consultant to investigate tensions within the Board. Nothing came of it and the entire process was a farce, as the consultant was clearly a friend of the Board chairman and other leading lights on the Board. I decided to resign."[11]

Rhoda was also nominated to join the board of the F. W. de Klerk Foundation, which works to support constitutional principles in South Africa. Though he had joined Mandela's first government of national unity, De Klerk had become disillusioned about the direction of South Africa under the ANC, and his foundation existed to support and promote the South African Constitution, and to shore up civil society against the ruling party's hegemony.

The fact that Rhoda joined the board was something of a surprise, given her history of anti-apartheid activism, which included, at times, opposition to De Klerk himself. She had bitter memories of those confrontations, when the National Party had ruled with an iron fist and did all it could to crush the UDF and other allied groups.

When the former president sent her a letter inviting her to join the board, she was doubtful, but consulted her ANC friends, all of whom advised her to join, considering the appointment an accolade. She considered it for some time before agreeing. Among her reasons were the fact that if President Mandela, a political prisoner for 27 years, could accept De Klerk's offer of release from prison to start negotiations toward a new democratic dispensation, then that reconciliatory gesture should count for something. She also came to admire the fact that De Klerk had given up power, something few leaders do in any society, to help Mandela rebuild a South Africa that apartheid had nearly destroyed.

Rhoda also felt deeply that if Mandela could forgive De Klerk, and work across the racial divide toward reconciliation, then all South Africans should work together to overcome differences that persisted among the country's diverse racial groups. And she feared that populist left-wing movements had the potential to destroy South Africa's fragile democracy. It was imperative, she felt, to maintain a strong constitutional barrier to keep political anarchy at bay — and if De Klerk wanted her to join him in that effort, she would do so.

---

11   Personal communication with the author, 1 Feb. 2022.

Rhoda with former South African President F. W. de Klerk and Public Protector Thuli Madonsela, c. 2015 (Courtesy Rhoda Kadalie)

After joining the board in 2014, Rhoda was elevated to the position of deputy chairperson in 2016. She commented: "Joining this board was one of my boldest steps towards reconciliation and today I can happily say that it is one of the most vibrant political boards in the country, where freedom of speech is a reality, where different points of view are entertained, and where we all learn from each other acknowledging our different political trajectories."[12] Through the foundation, she continued to advocate for her views on the importance of free speech and tolerance for political opposition.

Rhoda served on a variety of other boards. In 1999, following her resignation from the Human Rights Commission, she was invited to serve on the Academic Advisory Committee of the Cape Town Holocaust Centre. Cape Town's own Holocaust museum, located on the large Jewish community campus adjacent to the Company Gardens in the center of the city, is small, but unique. Unlike many museums — including the U.S. Holocaust Memorial Museum — it stresses the life of the Jewish

12   Rhoda Kadalie. Post on Facebook, 15 Jul. 2019. URL: https://www. facebook.com/rhoda.kadalie/posts/10154462380280039. Accessed on 28 Mar. 2022.

communities that were destroyed in Europe, before turning to the horror of the death camps. Moreover, it stresses the overall theme of human rights, making the lessons of the Holocaust relevant to South Africans.

Rhoda won numerous awards for her leadership and her writing. In 2007, for example, she was honored by the *Rapport* and *City Press* newspapers as one of South Africa's leading women at their annual "Prestige" award ceremony.[13] Rhoda also continued her feminist advocacy and activism. In 2016, she addressed the anniversary breakfast of the Foundation for Alcohol Related Research (FARR), an organization specifically devoted to helping women struggling with alcohol abuse during pregnancy, which posed the risk of fetal alcohol syndrome for their babies. Ascribing alcoholism among women to "a sense of hopelessness, a lack of self-worth, and an inability to rely on the inner resources God gave us," she praised FARR for its role in teaching basic parenting skills that had been lost in the various social and political upheavals of South African society.[14]

She also continued her scholarship and teaching in the field of women's studies, even when she was no longer at UWC or affiliated with any other university. She participated in the Semester at Sea program, an academic "study abroad" option for American students who traveled around the world on a cruise ship and studied with guest lecturers. In 2011, for example, she taught a course on "Gender Politics in South Africa." Her focus was the familiar tension between "national liberation" and "women's liberation," and the poor performance of the post-apartheid government on women's issues, even with large numbers of women in prominent positions in public life.[15] In one lecture, she concluded:

> [W]omen in senior leadership positions, in business, are complicit in maintaining the status quo, in defending their male comrades who abuse women, in exploiting the poo in order to be rich, in supporting their husbands in corrupt deals. ... Those in power are not going to help bring about a dispensation that respects women and advance[s] their cause.
>
> The sisters must do it for themselves.[16]

---

13   *Rapport* and *City Press*. Program. Prestige Awards 2007.
14   Rhoda Kadalie. Speech to Foundation for Alcohol Related Research. 11 Aug. 2016.
15   Rhoda Kadalie. "Course Outline: Gender Politics in South Africa." Semester at Sea. Feb. 2011.
16   Rhoda Kadalie. "Women and Democracy Ten Years of Democracy from Progress to Consensus." Lecture, Semester at Sea. Feb. 2011.

She continued to call upon women in public life "to unite around gender interests above party loyalties, across the board of women's causes."[17] Rhoda led by example, supporting women in both the ANC and the opposition, holding the government accountable while doing what she could in her own life to advance the interests of South African women, and a variety of other causes.

In virtually every arena of South African life, Rhoda's advice and commentary were sought. She was regarded as both a fighter and a mentor, as well as a rare public figure with authenticity and political credibility.

***

One area in which Rhoda began to have outsized influence was on the topic of Israel. The Israeli-Palestinian conflict became one of the most hotly-debated topics in South Africa after the eruption of the second *intifada* in September 2000, and especially after the United Nations World Conference Against Racism in Durban in August 2001.

Anti-Israel activists had used the Durban conference to advocate for the idea that Israel was the new "apartheid" state, and that it should be treated as apartheid South Africa once was: isolated from the international community, punished with sanctions, and eventually perhaps dismantled.

The issue caught fire in South Africa for a variety of reasons. One was that the South African Muslim community, which had been sidelined during the apartheid era, had become increasingly vocal, and enjoyed influence in the Mbeki administration through the ascent of Essop Pahad and his brother, Minister of Foreign Affairs Aziz Pahad.

Another was that the Israeli-Palestinian issue was a proxy for emerging tensions between the ANC and its trade union allies. For the unions, solidarity with the Palestinians was a way of rallying around a radical cause, and reminding the ANC leaders of their revolutionary roots.

The ANC had closely aligned with the Palestinian cause in exile, when the Palestine Liberation Organization (PLO) — then an internationally-recognized terrorist group — offered weapons, money, and political support to South Africa's liberation movement.

The Israeli government had opposed apartheid at the United Nations, leading to tense relations with the South African government in the 1960s. But after the African and Asian nations, under Soviet influence, moved to isolate Israel, the Israeli government reached out to the South African government, launching a covert relationship that included arms sales

---

17   Rhoda Kadalie, quoted in Neethling, 2010. Ibid.

and even Israeli assistance with the apartheid regime's secret nuclear weapons program.

Israel eventually joined international sanctions against apartheid, and worked to build relations with the post-apartheid government. Mandela was receptive to these overtures, and supported the Oslo Peace Process. But he was also demonstrative in his continuing support for the Palestinian cause, as well as his friendship with controversial Arab figures like Libya's Muammar Ghadafi.

With the new *intifada*, support for the Palestinian cause became a rallying cry throughout the global left, particularly in South Africa. Though South Africa enjoyed a large trade surplus with Israel, the government became increasingly hostile to Israel, spurred on by activists and the media.

Rhoda refused to conform. She saw the Israeli-Palestinian issue as a giant distraction from pressing local issues, such as unemployment, Zimbabwe, and the HIV/Aids pandemic. She described the World Conference Against Racism as having been "a bad thing for the world and South Africa" because it obscured actual racism — such as attacks on white farmers in Zimbabwe — by focusing on, and exacerbating, the Israeli-Palestinian conflict. She concluded: "It generated more race hate than it mobilized against racism."[18]

Moreover, Rhoda had never had much use for the ANC's foreign policy, which stuck to "struggle" alliances and Cold War alignments. Perhaps as a result of her studies in Europe, she believed that South Africa's best hope was to emulate the developed world, and build closer ties to the West, rather than accepting an outdated, structuralist and socialist view that divided the globe into "North" and "South," spurning relations with the capitalist metropoles.

When left-wing pundits attacked countries like Australia, for example — a popular destination for South African emigrants — Rhoda defended it as an exemplar of good governance, economic growth, and good social mores. True, it was a "colonialist-settler" state, one that had an abysmal record in its relations with aboriginal peoples. But if the question was how best South Africans could benefit from Australia, the answer was to learn from its success, not treat it with resentful disdain.

So Rhoda was already outside the ANC's and the left-wing's consensus on international affairs when the Israeli-Palestinian issue flared up. But she also believed — without, as of yet, a deep familiarity

---

18   Rhoda Kadalie, quoted by Ryland Fisher. *Race*. Auckland Park: Jacana Media, 2007. p. 150.

with the details — that Israel could not possibly be in the wrong, at least as portrayed by the South African media.

Rhoda found the analogy to apartheid both offensive, and wrong. But if comparisons were to be made, it was notable that the Palestinians declined to follow the ANC's example of giving up the "armed struggle" when the opportunity for negotiations arose. And despite decades of generous financial support from the Soviet bloc and the United Nations, the Palestinian leadership had done little to build institutions for self-governance.

In October 2001, then-Minister of Water Affairs and Forestry Ronnie Kasrils — the highest-ranking Jew in the South African government, and a leader within the South African Communist Party — circulated a petition, titled "Declaration of Conscience by South Africans of Jewish Descent." It began: "We assert that the fundamental causes of the current conflict are Israel's suppression of the Palestinian struggle for national self-determination and its continued occupation of Palestinian lands."[19] It called on Israel — and only Israel — to resume negotiations with the Palestinian Authority. Kasrils called on South African Jews to sign the document, and join his "Not in My Name" campaign to distance the Jewish community from the Israeli government. In publicly defending the document from his critics, Kasrils portrayed the few hundred signatories as more enlightened and loyal to the new South Africa than the bulk of the 80,000-strong Jewish community and its institutional leaders, who dismissed his efforts.

Rhoda rejected the declaration as another "Home for All" campaign, an attempt to corral minorities into the ANC camp with a simplistic declaration of fealty to the ruling party and its outlook. She described the "Declaration of Conscience" as part of an effort to appeal to Muslim voters in the Western Cape — a key swing vote as the ANC fought the DA for control of the province — and to appeal to Arab States as South Africa sought a seat on the United Nations Security Council.[20]

As she stood up for Israel, and against its detractors, Rhoda was embraced by South Africa's beleaguered Jewish community, who invited her to speak to women's groups and pro-Israel organizations, such as the Women's International Zionist Organization (WIZO). In 2011, she was

---

19   Ronnie Kasrils, et al. "Declaration of Conscience by South Africans of Jewish Descent, 23 October 2001." *Palestine-Israel Journal*, Vol. 8, No. 4, 2001. URL: https://pij.org/articles/1097/declaration-of-conscience-by-south-africans-of-jewish-descent-23-october-2001.   Accessed 22 Mar. 2022.

20   Rhoda Kadalie, quoted by Bram Vermeulen. "Anti-Israel stuk verdeelt joden Zuid-Afrika." *NRC Handelsblad*, 2 Jan. 2002. p. 4.

invited to deliver a lecture at the Jacob Gitlin Library, a small library founded by the South African Zionist Federation and devoted to Jewish topics.

Rhoda began her remarks by describing the anti-Israel stance of the government and the left as a symptom of a greater malady within South African political life. "When it comes to the prevailing anti-Israel climate I get all fired up because it needs pointing out that the destructive obsession with Israel exposes a deeper malaise few dare to tackle head on. It so starkly exposes the deadly cocktail of double standards, hypocrisy and anti-intellectualism that have come to represent public discourse in general and about Israel in particular."[21]

She argued further: "Much of the interest in Israel is insincere and those constantly on the attack are more concerned with resurrecting the dwindling struggle reputations of political has-beens than really helping Israel and the Palestinian Authorities [sic] find lasting solutions." She noted that while there was much that Israel could learn from South Africa's successful transition to democracy, "Two very different conflicts demand two very different solutions." Moreover, it was equally important for Israel and the Palestinians to learn from South Africa's mistakes, she argued: "We failed to create adequate safeguards against the breakdown of our new democracy. ... Our story of triumph could yet become one of tragedy." She concluded that South Africa could best make a contribution not by criticizing Israel as some kind of new apartheid, but rather by preparing Palestinians for statehood.

At the same time that she gained renown within the Jewish community, and in general, for her insights on the Israeli-Palestinian conflict, Rhoda became the object of vicious criticism because of her stance. Rhoda was told more than once that she had fallen under the pernicious influence of her "right-wing" son-in-law, a claim that was racist as well as antisemitic, since it presumed she could not think for herself.

Her own explanation for her views was simpler: her father had always encouraged the family to "pray for the peace of Jerusalem." She could not be anti-Israel after that — and as a devout Christian, raised equally on the Old and New Testaments, she was not going to disavow teachings that were essentially part of her religious beliefs.

In 2010, Rhoda joined a media tour of Israel organized by the Israeli foreign ministry and the South African Jewish Board of Deputies. Her trip emphasized her sense that the Israeli-Palestinian conflict was a complex one, and not easily resolved. "Those who are prejudiced against Israel

---

21 Rhoda Kadalie. "The Clash Between Party and State: SA's Foreign Policy Toward Israel." Jacob Gitlin Library, Cape Town, South Africa. 1 Jun. 2011.

for ideological reasons do us a disservice when they portray the Israeli–Palestinian conflict in black-and-white terms," she wrote.[22]

She vehemently opposed efforts to organize academic boycotts of Israel. When the University of Johannesburg, under Vice-Chancellor Adam Habib, decided to boycott Israel's Ben-Gurion University, she wrote:

> *[The boycott] is politically correct nonsense. Israeli universities do not undermine human rights. Israel is one of the freest democracies in the world and political dissent is widespread on Israeli campuses. Israeli universities have a level of political independence we can only envy in our own universities, which are unduly politically influenced and sickeningly politically correct.*

> *When the University of Johannesburg should be focusing on academic excellence and freedom, or the problems assailing SA, it wastes its time going on a crusade against Israel. There is more academic freedom in Israel than here and while political correctness has become the dictatorship of the left in SA, universities abroad are flourishing. Such sectarian academic boycotts freeze dialogue and communication and expose the narrow-mindedness and the bigotry of those who crusade.*

> *Why not pursue Sudan, Zimbabwe, the Democratic Republic of Congo, Rwanda and Iran with the same vigour? Why the silence against Iran's dictator? Why the silence against President Omar al-Bashir of Sudan? Why has Israel become the whipping boy of leftist academics? The reason, I believe, is because their leftist project internationally and in SA in particular, has failed dismally. South African universities are so low on the academic radar that such a boycott will be laughed out of court. We have more to lose by cutting our ties with universities abroad than they have to gain from us.[23]*

Perhaps most controversially of all, Rhoda repeatedly criticized Archbishop Desmond Tutu, a venerated icon of the anti-apartheid struggle, for his anti-Israel stance, even accusing him of antisemitism. When Tutu backed a cultural boycott of Israel in 2010, asking the Cape Town Opera not to perform a production of *Porgy and Bess* In Israel she called him a "bigot," accusing him of "discrimination against Jews" when there were so many

---

22   Rhoda Kadalie. "Complex crisis most analysts fail to explain." *Business Day*, 6 May 2010.

23   Rhoda Kadalie. "Universities blinded by political correctness." *Business Day*, 5 Oct. 2020.

other states to criticize, and so many problems facing South Africa.[24] Her criticism stirred a media controversy and forced the opera company to respond, promising to work with Palestinian artists while on tour in Israel.[25]

Nor was Rhoda afraid to take on left-wing critics of Israel within the Jewish community. In 2011, when Judge Dennis Davis led an effort to boycott a local lecture by pro-Israel Harvard Law School professor Alan Dershowitz, she responded in a comment on the independent PoliticsWeb site: "When it comes to Israel you and your ilk ... get a hard-on when Israel does anything wrong because Israel gives you a platform for your dwindling struggle reputations here in SA. You guys bore me to tears. It is time you find another issue." She advised Davis to "[g]et a life."[26]

Rhoda in Caesaria, Israel, on a family holiday in 2019
(Courtesy Rhoda Kadalie)

24   Rhoda Kadalie, quoted by Max McLaren and Peter Fabricius. "Furore over Tutu's boycott Israel call." *Cape Times*, 28 Oct. 2010. p. 1.

25   Verashni Pillay. "Israel opera tour goes ahead, with a difference." *Mail & Guardian*, 4 Nov. 2010.

26   Rhoda Kadalie, quoted by Mercury Correspondent. "Life is no Tea Party as 'Rhoda Kadalie' is hard on Judge Dennis Davis." *The Mercury*, 10 May 2011. p. 4.

Rhoda also criticized Israeli leftists who tried to use the apartheid analogy — or, in her view, to exploit it inappropriately. After left-wing *Ha'aretz* columnist Gideon Levy visited South Africa in 2013, he used the apartheid analogy to recommend a single-state solution to the Israeli-Palestinian conflict, whereupon Rhoda penned an angry letter to the editor: "Apartheid was a crime against humanity and fully deserved to be placed in the dustbin of history. Israel, on the other hand, is a vibrant democracy, surrounded by enemies who have never accepted her presence in the neighbourhood. She is occupying territory captured in a legitimate war but should do everything possible to extricate herself from the role of occupier."[27] She added: "Mr Levy's impatience with the two parties' failure to reach a settlement is fully understandable, but his conclusion that "one person, one vote" based on his visit to South Africa, is naive beyond belief!"[28]

When another South African Jewish leftist tried to renounce her Jewish identity as a form of protest against Israel, Rhoda mocked South Africa's obsession with Israel as only she could, calling it a case of "penis envy":

The Left is quick to condemn Israel, when matters at home should shame us into silence.

...

Bashing Israel has become a self-promotion industry and the disinvestment campaign is its marketing tool. We should be attracting Israelis to our shores as the ideal foreign direct investment destination for Israelis.

With its huge growth potential and features that set it apart from other African countries, SA's large Jewish community with its numerous Jewish institutions and a rich cultural life has a vested interest in maintaining cordial relations between the two states.

The book, Start-Up Nation, reveals that the per-capita venture-capital investment in Israel is 2.5 times that in the U.S and 30 times that in Europe. Israel attracts as much venture capital as Britain, France and Germany combined and it has more companies listed on Nasdaq than any other country outside the US and its economic growth has been faster than the average for developed economies in most years since

---

27   Rhoda Kadalie. Letter to the editor of *Ha'aretz*. Unpublished. 26 Apr. 2013. Personal files.

28   Ibid.

1995. Between 1980 and 2000, 7652 patents were registered in the U.S. from Israel.

Is this penis envy or what?[29]

When criticism of Israel crossed the boundary into outright antisemitism, Rhoda was among the first to defend the Jewish community. In 2014, when a leading student activist placed a pig's head in the kosher meat section of a Cape Town supermarket, Rhoda pointed out that the hateful gesture insulted Muslims as well:

So driven by hate is this young leader he thought nothing of violating one of the most sacred taboos of Judaism and, by mistake, also Islam. Palestinian students would be disgusted by this act of "solidarity". And that has always been my point.

Our black shock troopers of the Boycotts, Divestment and Sanctions (BDS) campaign have no idea where Gaza, the West Bank or even Israel are. Not only is this a deeply anti-Semitic act of hate, it is also profoundly barbaric and anti-Islamic.[30]

She blamed the ANC, too: "This climate of hate has been nurtured since the ANC came to power and those former party acolytes who now oppose the ANC are directly responsible for creating an ethos in which these acts of intimidation against South Africa's Jewish community can take place.

In addition, Rhoda also took up the cause of Christian minorities in the Middle East and Africa, often contrasting the world's professed concern for the Palestinians, or for Muslim victims of Western intervention, with the indifference that greeted the persecution of Christians by Islamic extremists. She classified this bias as a form of antisemitism, since it focused on alleged human rights abuses by the Jewish state, while ignoring the rights of Christians in the Arab and Muslim world:

Anything remotely smacking of criticism against Muslims propels the Obama administration, the European Union, the United Nations, the Global Elders, and the Left into action.

---

29   Rhoda Kadalie. "Don't be too quick to condemn Israel." PoliticsWeb, reprinted and translated from the Afrikaans, *Die Burger*, 12 Sep. 2022. URL: https://www.politicsweb.co.za/news-and-analysis/dont-be-too-quick-to-condemn-israel. Accessed 26 Mar. 2022.

30   Rhoda Kadalie. "Pig-headed Cosas act idiotic." *Citizen*, 7 Nov. 2014. p. 12.

Not so with Christians and the question is why. This same group does not hesitate to single out Israel for condemnation and when one country is singled out for censure, as is routinely done then the only explanation can be anti-Semitism. Otherwise how do we explain the double standards?

...

The tyrannical suppression of the freedom of expression, religion and association of Christians in Muslim countries has escaped their censure. This sanitised form of anti-Semitism feeds into the bipolar view of the "West against the Rest".[31]

In March 2008, Rhoda co-authored an essay with her daughter, Julia, for Z Word, a pro-Israel online publication. In it, she and Julia refuted the effort to equate Israel with apartheid South Africa, and explained the virulent tone of the debate in South Africa as the consequence of domestic politics.

Israel is not an apartheid state. ... [R]acism and discrimination do not form the rationale for Israel's policies and actions. Arab citizens of Israel can vote and serve in the Knesset; black South Africans could not vote until 1994. There are no laws in Israel that discriminate against Arab citizens or separate them from Jews. Unlike the United Kingdom, Greece, and Norway, Israel has no state religion, and it recognizes Arabic as one of its official languages.

Whereas apartheid was established through a series of oppressive laws that governed which park benches we could sit on, where we could go to school, which areas we were allowed to live in, and even whom we could marry, Israel was founded upon a liberal and inclusive Declaration of Independence. South Africa had a job reservation policy for white people; Israel has adopted pro-Arab affirmative action measures in some sectors.

Israeli schools, universities and hospitals make no distinction between Jews and Arabs. An Arab citizen who brings a case before an Israeli court will have that case decided on the basis of merit, not ethnicity. This was never the case for blacks under apartheid. Moreover, Israel respects freedom of speech and human rights. Its newspapers are far more independent, outspoken, and critical of the government than our

31   Rhoda Kadalie. "Christians under attack in the Middle East." PoliticsWeb, 17 Jan. 2012. URL: https://www.politicsweb.co.za/news-and-analysis/christians-under-attack-in-the-middle-east. Accessed on 26 Mar. 2022.

newspapers in present-day, post-apartheid South Africa, let alone those of old.

...

On the one hand, the use of the apartheid metaphor is hardly unusual in the South African political context. Almost every political debate is framed in terms of apartheid. The ANC routinely accuses its opponents, often without justification, of having supported apartheid, and opposition parties retort by comparing the ANC to the National Party which designed the intricate apartheid system and ruled the country for five decades. The past is still present in South African political discourse, on Israel and on many other issues as well.

On the other hand, Israel is different. The ANC devotes more attention to Israel than to many domestic issues and conflicts closer to home. It denies that anti-Israel protest is often antisemitic, but on no other issue has the party been more willing to abandon its supposedly non-racial ideals. Party leaders have addressed openly antisemitic rallies; radical sectors of the party have made blatantly antisemitic statements; and ANC election posters have featured blood-drenched Israeli flags.

In truth, the Israel-apartheid analogy is not entirely new. It was first used not by anti-apartheid activists, but the apartheid regime itself, protesting Israel's stance against South Africa at the UN in the 1950s and 1960s. Prime Minister Hendrik Verwoerd, the chief architect of apartheid, threatened South Africa's Jews with a tide of rising antisemitism should they fail to dissent from Israel's foreign policy. The Afrikaans press supported Verwoerd, with many writers and correspondents comparing Zionism with apartheid and complaining that Israel's opposition to the latter was hypocritical.

What the white nationalist right and the black post-colonial left share is distaste for opposition and difference combined with envy of Israel's success. Afrikaners viewed Israel, falsely, as a state of "whites" that had thrived in a sea of "non-white" nations, but which unlike South Africa had largely escaped global condemnation. Today's far-right remnant envies Israel's persistence when Afrikaners have had to give up their own national aspirations.

The ANC looked to Israel as an example of an oppressed people that had overcome racial persecution, enormous political obstacles and military weakness to build a successful, thriving nation. Israel's continued economic achievements, scientific innovation and vibrant culture in the

face of terror stand in stark contrast to the ANC's mismanagement of the
state and economy, which it still blames on the past.

...

South Africa tells Israel that it only has a right to exist — if at all — as a
victim of Nazi oppression, just as the ANC bases its claim to legitimacy,
power and privilege on apartheid. But Israel has moved beyond its past,
while South Africa has failed to use the memory of apartheid to motivate
positive national unity and achievement. No false analogies and no re-
writing of history can mask that.[32]

Likewise, in a tribute to Helen Suzman that was published in *Jewish Affairs*,
a journal published by the South African Jewish Board of Deputies, Rhoda
chastised the South African government, and South African civil society,
for their double standard on Israel:

In July last year [2008] a group of local activists went on a tour of
Israel and the occupied territories to inspect human rights violations
in the region, and the Israeli occupation in particular. They visited one
side of the conflict during their five-day visit and came back smugly
condemning Israel from a dizzy height. Immediately, others got on the
bandwagon, supporting them because it was the politically correct thing
to do. They did not for one moment reflect on why it was important to
see both sides of the conflict, how they could help both the Israelis and
the Palestinians find solutions to it and how we could share some of our
experiences to help two related peoples imagine a future together, just as
we have done. There was no modesty in their condemnation given what
was going on in our country and how ashamed and modest we should be
about the beam in our own eye. Intrinsic to human rights investigations
is the weighing up of all sides, of weighing up one side against another,
as Helen did so adeptly.

...

Let me pose a question to SA: if Israel sent a human rights delegation to
SA, what would it find?

---

32   Rhoda Kadalie and Julia Bertelsmann. "Franchising 'Apartheid': Why
      South Africans Push the Analogy." Z Word, March 2008. URL: https://
      fdocuments.in/reader/full/franchising-apartheid-why-south-
      africans-push-the-analogy. Accessed on 8 Mar. 2022. Footnotes
      omitted.

Rhoda: 'Comrade Kadalie, You Are Out of Order!'

The HR delegation went to Israel at a time when SA was reeling in the aftermath of the embarrassing outbreak of xenophobic violence, in which hundreds were killed simply because they were foreign and black: in a matter of weeks over 32 Somalis were killed for simply being entrepreneurial. Bishop Paul Verryn's church is overflowing with thousands of Zimbabwean refugees, treated like dirt by the very South African regime that is quick to offer condemnation of others.[33]

Rhoda cast Suzman's own defenses of Israel as part of Suzman's long career of "speaking truth to power," and standing up against apartheid. In a context in which many veterans of the struggle were claiming that opposing apartheid then meant opposing Israel today, Rhoda's argument was a crucial dissent.

To Rhoda, there was no contradiction between her support for Israel and her other political stances: defending Israel and the Jewish community dovetailed with standing up against abuses of power. She found a model for her advocacy in the Biblical heroine of Queen Esther, whom she cited in several speeches — both to Christian and Jewish audiences. "Esther was willing to risk her position and her life by speaking truth to power, unlike many in SA.," Rhoda said. "But unlike the toyi-toyi-ing crowd, she was careful, strategic, quiet when necessary and loud when appropriate."[34] Another lesson from Esther: "If you are not causing trouble, you are probably not solving the problem."[35]

Rhoda's effective advocacy, which bravely stood outside the consensus view of the South African media and political chattering classes, soon caught the attention of Professor Milton Shain, head of the Isaac & Jessie Kaplan Centre for Jewish Studies & Research at the University of Cape Town, and one of the world's foremost authorities on antisemitism. Shain had been impressed by Rhoda when, as a member of the South African Human Rights Commission, she had publicly criticized PAGAD for its anti-Israel and antisemitic hate speech (see Chapter 10). That led him to invite her to join a symposium on liberalism in honor of Helen Suzman (see Chapter 13). She was "an appropriate speaker and someone who could cut through the anti-Israel nonsense," Shain later recalled.[36]

---

33   Rhoda Kadalie. "A Bright Star in a Chamber of Darkness: Helen Suzman and Her Legacy." *Jewish Affairs*, Chanukah 2009. pp. 17-18.
34   Rhoda Kadalie. Speech at the University of Stellenbosch Faculty of Theology. June 2013. Personal files.
35   Ibid.
36   Milton Shain. Personal communication with the author. 5 Jul. 2022.

Rhoda speaks at her 60th birthday, as (left to right) journalist
Donwald Pressly, scholar Milton Shain, and fashion legend Cyril Kern —
a close friend of the late Israeli prime minister Ariel Sharon — look on, 2013
(Courtesy Rhoda Kadalie)

It was not Rhoda's first involvement with Jewish institutions. Already, as noted earlier, she had been a member of the advisory board of the Cape Town Holocaust Centre, in recognition of her expertise in the field of human rights. Soon, she was also invited to join the board of the Jewish Museum in Cape Town, an important local cultural and historic institution that welcomes visitors from throughout the world. And she was frequently cited by supporters of Israel, who were grateful that Rhoda, with her "struggle" credentials and moral clarity, had come to their aid.

In 2011, Rhoda was invited to deliver the annual lecture at Cape Town's Jacob Gitlin Library, located on the main campus of the Jewish Museum and named after an early Zionist leader in Cape Town. Her address, titled "The Clash Between Party and State: SA's Foreign Policy towards Israel," wove together Rhoda's criticism of the anti-Israel movement and South Africa's ruling party.

After pointing out the ANC's hypocrisy on human rights, and dismantling several common criticisms of Israel, she observed:

Rhoda: 'Comrade Kadalie, You Are Out of Order!'

The traditional paradigm of support for the Palestinians on [sic] moralistic political pressure on Israel for alleged human rights violations vis à vis the South African experience with Apartheid, is inappropriate at best and infuriating to say that least. To put it more simply, the desire to moralize Israel into submission based on the South African narrative is counter-productive as it just further delays the impact on the Peace Process.

Two very different conflicts demand two very different solutions.

That said I believe it may be useful to Israelis and Palestinians to learn from South Africa's successes. But it is equally important — perhaps more important — for them to learn from our mistakes. Certainly, our transition from a pariah state on the brink of civil war to a non-racial, constitutional democracy was remarkable. Yet we failed to create adequate safeguards against the breakdown of our new democracy.

…

I believe that the most important contribution we can make is to focus on a serious discussion about Palestinian nation-building. From a South African perspective, it is also important to show that people from both communities can get along, and we should help each other build support for peace, and support the many communities who indeed do that.

But the immediate task is to prepare Palestinians for statehood, before that dream dies. It is a task that Palestinians themselves must lead, but to which Israelis can contribute, and which those of us in the rest of the world can support. It is not too late to re-invigorate this process — indeed, if some Palestinians believe this task should be left until the conclusion of the peace process, it will be far too late. The new SA, ironically, and thankfully, inherited quite a modern urban infrastructure from their oppressors but now we see the damage that can be done by a liberation movement that arrives in office without being properly prepared to govern.[37]

Rhoda not only looked beyond the "apartheid" paradigm to discover the lessons that South Africa's "miracle" could offer the Middle East, but also used the debate as an opportunity to examine the flaws in South Africa's own transition.

---

37   Rhoda Kadalie. "The Clash Between Party and State: SA's Foreign Policy towards Israel." 23rd Jacob Gitlin Memorial Lecture. Jacob Gitlin Library, Cape Town. 1 Jun. 2011. Original emphasis.

Rhoda soon befriended several Israeli diplomats, including Ambassadors Ilan Baruch and Dov Steinberg, who sought her advice about navigating South Africa's often impenetrable political world. When Steinberg returned to Israel in 2013, she wrote him a farewell letter. Wishing him well in his future career, she added: "Allow me to apologise for the way members of the ruling party treated you but please know that they are not representative of the vast majority of South Africans who love Israel and who sympathise with its intractable political challenges."[38]

***

Rhoda also became involved in the governance of two of South Africa's most important universities: the University of Cape Town (UCT), and Stellenbosch University.

She had already been involved in the administration at the University of the Western Cape (UWC), launching its Gender Equity Unit. She had taught social anthropology for decades, and written for years. She had also earned academic distinctions for her work, both in academia and in activism. In 1999, she received an honorary doctorate from Uppsala University in Sweden, in recognition of her work in "gender and social transformation."[39] She had developed a strong reputation in Sweden in the early 1990s, when she delivered a paper there criticizing sexual harassment in the anti-apartheid struggle, and the proposal to confer the honor cited her "substantial contributions to the fields of feminist theory, sexual violence against women, women's history in South Africa, and the role of the women's movement in the democratic transformation."[40] Rhoda responded humbly, commenting that "greatness comes too easily to us South Africans," and adding that Sweden had much to teach South Africa about women's equality.[41] She flew to Sweden for the ceremony, where the proceedings were conducted in Latin and accompanied by a string ensemble. She was accompanied by her daughter, Julia, who would also travel with her mother to Canada in 2003 for an award recognizing Rhoda's work on behalf of South African women.[42]

---

38   Rhoda Kadalie. Letter to Ambassador Dov Steinberg. 13 Jun. 2013. Personal files.
39   "Uppsala Grants Honorary Doctorate." *Nordic Business Report*, 7 Jun. 1999.
40   Uppsala University, quoted by Michael Morris. "Swedes To Honour Cape Rights Activist Kadalie." 27 May 1999.
41   Rhoda Kadalie, ibid.
42   Gavin Taylor. "South African women honoured for crusading roles." *Toronto Star*, 11 Aug. 2003.

Rhoda receives an honorary doctorate at the University of Uppsala, Sweden, 1999 (Courtesy Rhoda Kadalie)

Later, Rhoda would also earn an honorary doctorate from UWC, her alma mater, in 2007. She was surprised and delighted when Julia, then a sophomore at Harvard College, interrupted her studies and flew back, unannounced, for just three days to attend the UWC ceremony. Rhoda would also receive an honorary doctorate in 2009 from Stellenbosch. She was also sought after as a graduation speaker. In 2011, she addressed the graduating class of the CTI Education Group, a private college, telling students: "Ask questions, seize opportunities, create your own businesses, challenge the status quo, and do not take no for an answer."[43]

---

43   Rhoda Kadalie. Speech at graduation of CTI Education Group. Cape Town. 11 Mar. 2011.

Rhoda receives an honorary doctorate at the University of Western Cape,
Bellville, 2007 (Courtesy Rhoda Kadalie)

There was a particular irony, however, to Rhoda's appointment in 2004 to the governing council of UCT.[44] It was an institution she had declined to attend in the early 1970s, and which she had been forced to leave due to the political unrest of the early 1980s (see Chapter 4). Her appointment to the UCT council represented the fulfillment of a path that had long been deferred.

It was also a timely assignment. South Africa's universities faced a crisis in the post-apartheid era. On the one hand, they were under tremendous pressure to produce black graduates, who could provide the skills — and the role models — that the country desperately needed. On the other hand, aside from private schools and the best, or "Model C," public schools, few secondary schools were producing black matriculants who could meet the standards of South Africa's best tertiary institutions. Many were in need of remedial education; some struggled through, or opted for basic, generic degrees that offered only minimal additional skills.

The tensions that resulted often led to protests by students. And in the tradition of the anti-apartheid struggle, those protests often took a radical turn, becoming riots that destroyed university property.

Rhoda found the students' behavior unacceptable. As a student in the 1970s, she had faced even greater inequities, and fewer opportunities. But she had worked hard despite racial discrimination and constant unrest. In 1998, she observed: "I think the nice thing about the new South Africa, young people do not have to protest any longer. They can now knuckle down and study because there are people out there fighting to keep democracy on track, fighting to get the best education that we can for you."[45] But students did not seem to understand the chance they had been given. "I find it very disturbing that students are continually destroying their own universities, marching and stampeding around issues that I think are issues we all need to engage in about creating educational privileges for people in South Africa," she said.

Rhoda also opposed the idea that the universities should be primarily responsible for closing racial gaps bequeathed to them by a failing elementary and secondary education system. In a 2009 column titled "Not universities' job to make up for basic education failures," she wrote:

> It is not the job of universities to address a basic education system that will not come right. The government and the university managements know

44 Naledi Pandor. "Appointment on the Council of the University of Cape Town." Letter to Rhoda Kadalie. 7 Jul. 2004.
45 Rhoda Kadalie. "South Africans Talking," ibid.

that, but they continue in their deluded self-righteous and politically correct ways, pursuing remedies that have been proven to fail ...

The transformation agenda at universities amounts to racial bean-counting and perpetuates this scenario, made even more complex by the social engineering thrust upon universities by government. The pressure to fill formerly white universities with black faces is the reason for this.

...

Appointment processes are engineered by those desperate to make politically correct appointments based on race alone, rather than looking at race in conjunction with skills, competence and merit. No wonder many black appointments end in disaster – for institution and candidate.[46]

Rhoda also noted that remedial education at the university level also held women back from advancing, since women were often assigned to undergraduate teaching and to "nurturing" roles.

Her experiences at UWC, her international recognition, and her strong views prioritizing excellence made her a perfect candidate to oversee the country's major universities. Unfortunately, those same qualifications also meant she ran into strong opposition.

At the time Rhoda joined the UCT Council, the university was still thought to be one of the few English-language institutions that had kept its standards high. It was seen as a contrast to the University of the Witwatersrand in Johannesburg, which came under intense pressure to "transform," and hence lowered its admissions standards rapidly. The result was an influx of enthusiastic but often unqualified students.

More ambitious students, especially white students, began flocking across town to the Rand Afrikaans University (RAU), which began offering an English curriculum to the newcomers. The ANC, however, soon ended RAU as a separate institution, merging it into the larger University of Johannesburg.

UCT, shining above the city on the windward slope of Table Mountain, knew that it, too, had to "transform." But it wanted to do so without suffering the fate of the Johannesburg institutions. Rhoda had the right skill set to help with that process: she had worked directly with black and Coloured students at UWC, and was familiar with their needs; yet she had also earned graduate degrees at foreign institutions, and understood the importance of maintaining UCT's world-class reputation. She also

---

46   Rhoda Kadalie. "Not universities' job to make up for basic education failures." *Business Day*, Aug. 27, 2009.

understood the country's new government as few others did, and could help UCT navigate treacherous political debates.

For several years, Rhoda served on the council with pride. But the political pressure from the national government grew, and was soon accompanied by pressure from below. Students began making increasingly vociferous demands for free tuition, as well as for the cultural "transformation" of the university to something that felt less alien to them.

The faculty, many of whom empathized with the students, and viewed their own anti-apartheid activism with nostalgia, found it increasingly difficult to resist the pressures on the institution. In council meetings, Rhoda found she had few allies, save for the brilliant philosophy professor, David Benatar; and a trio of attorneys — Peter Leon (brother of South Africa's opposition leader), Richard Rosenthal, and occasionally Jeremy Gauntlett.

Rhoda found the decisions of the council increasingly unpalatable. On one occasion, Rhoda had participated in the appointment of a lecturer in the department of criminology in the law faculty. There had been several applications, but the selection committee, with support from the dean of the law school, had favored a black candidate who wanted to teach African customary law as an alternative to South Africa's existing legal framework, a hybrid between Roman Dutch law and English common law. Rhoda was appalled that the other members of the committee had voted in his favor; hers was the lone dissenting vote. The dean, noting her displeasure, suggested that a more in-depth review of the candidate be conducted to reassure her that the selection was beyond reproach. Five weeks later, the committee learned that UCT had an open lawsuit against the candidate, who had been appointed to previous positions but had claimed his salary without showing up to teach.

On a subsequent occasion, the vice chancellor and the head of the governing council sought to approve a senior appointment of a black faculty member without revealing who the other two contenders for the job were, defying a statute of the council. Rhoda enlisted Peter Leon and a few other members of the UCT council in objecting. In a meeting to discuss the issue, the university administration persisted in concealing the credentials of the other candidates.

Rhoda simply walked out of the meeting, and never came back. Her departure was, effectively, her resignation letter — though she later resigned formally in September 2007. UCT Council chair Geoff Budlender — a renowned anti-apartheid lawyer who had, ironically, been denied a seat on the Constitutional Court because of his white skin and political independence – wrote to Rhoda that he was "very sorry" she had decided to leave.[47]

These early clashes foreshadowed the upheavals that later were to rock the UCT campus. Already, a "woke" culture had begun to spread across South African campuses, accelerated by local politics. In 2012, the Nelson Mandela Metropolitan University (NMMU) in Port Elizabeth canceled a lecture by Western Cape Premier Helen Zille that was to have been delivered in honor of the late Steve Biko.[48] Zille was targeted despite the fact that it was she who had, as a journalist, exposed the truth behind Biko's death in police custody in 1977.

In 2015, a troubled student dumped human excrement on the statue of Cecil John Rhodes, which stood at the entrance to the upper portion of campus, at the foot of a majestic staircase, overlooking the rugby field, the M3 highway, and the city below. The gesture mimicked the tactics of impoverished township dwellers, who often dumped excrement-filled "honey buckets" in the streets or near the homes of politicians to protest the lack of modern plumbing and sanitation. But this gesture, aimed at a symbol of British colonialism, was not a complaint about poor services but rather a declaration of war against the university and its supposedly "racist" culture.

The "Rhodes Must Fall" movement was born. The radical students demanded the immediate removal of the statue, which was said to be a violent affront to the thousands of black students who had to walk past it every day, to and from their classes.

Rhoda rejected the students' demands as being fundamentally hostile to the very idea of the university:

> *While universities and scholarship are fundamentally about the preservation of heritage, they are also about engaging critically – and sometimes irreverently – with history. A scholarly approach to history is to understand its complexity, not to reduce it to one narrative. Universities preserve both the good and the bad of our heritage so that people can learn from it. But when we dismantle that heritage, there is nothing left to engage, to study, or to lampoon.*

...

---

47 Geoff Budlender. Letter to Rhoda Kadalie. 17 Sep. 2007.
48 Rhoda Kadalie. "South Africa's universities: Bastions of intolerance?". PoliticsWeb, reprinted from *Die Burger* and translated from the Afrikaans, 26 Sep. 2012. URL: https://www.politicsweb.co.za/news-and-analysis/south-africas-universities-bastions-of-intolerance. Accessed on 26 Mar. 2022.

Rhoda: 'Comrade Kadalie, You Are Out of Order!'

If we're going to remove the Rhodes statue, why not reject all of Rhodes' inheritance. There are always positives and negatives to a heritage, but why don't we just demolish the whole damn thing? The entire UCT campus was Rhodes' property. He donated it. Why don't we just bulldoze it? Let's give back his land and his money, and disqualify UCT students from all Rhodes scholarships in future. That would downgrade the institution – appropriately, mind you, to reflect the degraded thinking that takes place there. We're already going to spend millions removing the statue that could be better spent on bursaries and scholarships.

…

The inscription on the statue is the verse titled "Capetown" from a poem by Rudyard Kipling. It reads "Hail! Snatched and bartered oft from hand to hand // I dream my dream, by rock and heath and pine // Of Empire to the northward. Ay, one land // From Lion's Head to Line!" The statue shows Rhodes sitting on his perch, dreaming of a vast British Empire stretching from Cape Town to Egypt. Of course, we know today that that dream was futile. The British lost. Colonialism ended, failed, and was disgraced.

But that's the thing – our students don't get the irony. They don't understand the joke. They don't know how to be irreverent, wry, or witty. Desecration without destruction is too subtle for them. Rather than emulating artist Beezy Bailey and dressing the statue as a young Xhosa initiate [as Bailey had done to the statue of Boer General Louis Botha in front of Parliament] or poking gentle fun at their heritage, our students prefer to emulate ISIS and grab a sledgehammer.[49]

The university authorities capitulated and hastily removed the statue, as a crowd of watching students jeered and pelted it with projectiles.

Rhoda commented on Facebook: "UCT stupidly capitulated to the tyranny of a small mindless mob. Hardly any debate with convocation. If they had any sense they would have put up a statue of Mandela or Steve Biko or Albertina Sisulu next to it. I despair. Students should be encouraged to debate the issue to death or be invited to enter a competition to produce the best essay as to what to do. I despair."[50] She gave full vent to her views

---

49   Rhoda Kadalie. "UCT: An ode to Rhodes." PoliticsWeb, 26 Mar. 2015. URL: https://www.politicsweb.co.za/opinion/uct-an-ode-to-rhodes. Accessed on 26 Mar. 2022.

50   Rhoda Kadalie. Comment on Facebook, 24 Mar. 2015. URL: https://www. facebook.com/rhoda.kadalie/posts/10153303303680039. Accessed on 28 Mar. 2022.

in another, more explicit comment on a television news report about the statue's removal: "Fucking barbaric of the highest order. Not one adult has the balls to discipline and suspend students for vandalism and distributing human excrement. And that little white runt whining on and on about the way the students collected the excrement to explain their pain. Such utter rubbish that TV gives airtime."[51]

Later, Rhoda would argue against the removal of memorials — even offensive ones from the apartheid era. She recalled in a 2017 Facebook post: "Why monuments should not be destroyed. At some ANC celebration in 1994 I was invited to attend in Parliament. I took my daughter who was 7 to the event. I showed her the big portrait of Verwoerd and the apartheid apparatchiks and explained to her that Verwoerd was the architect of apartheid, to which she responded instantaneously - "no wonder he looks like a piggy" - and very loudly!"[52]

But the "Rhodes Must Fall" movement was not satisfied with the removal of a statue or two; it became even more extreme after its initial victory. "Fees Must Fall" was the new rallying cry, demanding free or reduced tuition, as well as other radical changes. In 2016, students who had erected a shantytown on campus known as "Shackville" to protest the lack of available campus housing went on a rampage, ransacking university buildings and even burning art they deemed to be unacceptably "colonial" in nature. Among the destroyed paintings were five by Keresemose Richard Baholo, a black anti-apartheid artist who also happened to have been the first black graduate in fine arts at UCT.[53]

The "Fallist" movement spread across South African university campuses, threatening the fragile edifice of tertiary education in South Africa. Violent attacks were launched on public institutions, including Parliament, and at universities across the country — including at Rhoda's alma mater, UWC, where the violence far exceeded anything that had happened during anti-apartheid riots.

Rhoda blamed the ANC for the chaos on South Africa's campuses: "Somehow the mobs believe that the country's resources are limitless

---

51   Rhoda Kadalie. Comment on Facebook post, 9 Apr. 2015. URL: https://www.facebook.com/rhoda.kadalie/posts/10153341241695039?comment_id=10153342007785039. Accessed on 28 Mar. 2022.

52   Rhoda Kadalie. Comment on Facebook, 20 Aug. 2017. URL: https://www.facebook.com/rhoda.kadalie/posts/10155781705920039. Accessed on 28 Mar. 2022.

53   André Jurgens. "UCT's 'colonial art' faces threat after burning outrage." *Sunday Times* 21 Feb. 2016. URL: https://www.timeslive.co.za/sunday-times/news/2016-02-21-ucts-colonial-art-faces-threat-after-burning-outrage/. Accessed on 26 Mar. 2022.

because the ruling elite behaves as though they are."[54] Rhoda also criticized the extreme demands of the students, whom she believed had taken for granted the academic, financial, and political support for which an earlier generation of students and faculty had struggled. She wrote in a column for *Die Burger* that "the destruction and lack of discipline" of the Fallists "demonstrate that this movement does not know what it wants and what the long-term consequences of their utterly irresponsible demands will achieve."[55] She concluded:

> *That is why thousands of alumni, are simply gatvol with this ahistorical approach of protesters who narcissistically talk about their black pain, ignorant that thousands preceded them to pave the way for them to have access to better opportunities. There are many students who struggle and who are deeply poor, but who excel against all odds. These are the ones who lament this hideous interference with their studies. No one represents them; they are the silent majority whose rights are subordinate to a minority that increasingly looks more criminal.*

As she noted in a comment on her Facebook page:

> *[UCT vice-chancellor] Max Price was extolling the university's massive efforts to accommodate and support black students. When I was a student, one of 9 siblings, my parents could not afford sending us to university. Someone sponsored my education but I charred [worked as a housekeeper] weekends cleaning the home of a white woman and babysat for pocket money. One of my brothers, who is extremely clever, did not qualify for a bursary. He was one of the top matriculants in the country. He was a peer of Zinzi Mandela and the children of other struggle stalwarts who drowned in monetary support from donors locally and abroad. He was nauseated by this knowing how privileged some of his peers were. No one challenges students to work to supplement their income; what about work study on campus; etc etc. What efforts do they [UCT] make to go and assist kids in the townships with their education?[56]*

---

54 Rhoda Kadalie. Draft column for *The Citizen*, 13 Nov. 2015. Personal files.
55 Rhoda Kadalie. "White guilt is going to destroy SA." Reprinted from *Die Burger*, translated from the Afrikaans, 15 Oct. 2016. URL: https://www.facebook.com/rhoda.kadalie/posts/10154739852070039. Accessed on 30 Mar. 2022.
56 Rhoda Kadalie. Post on Facebook, 9 Apr. 2015. URL: https://www.facebook.com/rhoda.kadalie/posts/10153341355635039. Accessed on 28 Mar. 2022.

She also mocked those who wanted Afrikaans removed from university campuses like UWC, where it was the mother tongue of many of the Coloured students:

> *When Afrikaans was forced down our throats by the Afrikaner establishment in the 1970s at UWC, at least we, students, became multilingual and used the very language of "oppression" to liberate ourselves. Yes, we not only shouted "one person, one vote" but also "een boer, een moer." Our cultural activists turned Afrikaans upside down, producing radical plays, poetry and subversive songs in Afrikaans.*
>
> *By using sjamboks [stiff leather whips, commonly used by apartheid-era police] against fellow students, the EFF thinks it will smash its way towards the destruction of Afrikaans. But I have news for the EFF — Afrikaans is as durable as English. As a highly developed minority language, respected globally academically for its rapid scientific and cultural development, it will outlive the EFF and all the barbarians who want to destroy it. If students really want an issue, they could start by pressurising government to put money into the development of black languages just like the Afrikaner establishment is doing with their language and cultural festivals.*[57]

In addition to the excesses of "woke" ideology, Rhoda blamed a left-wing backlash against the Democratic Alliance Students Organisation (DASO), which had won student council elections on a number of campuses, with votes from a predominantly black electorate. She wrote:

> *Students [at UWC] also assaulted a female security officer whom they held at knife-point and another who was held hostage. UWC's fire and medical officer had to be rushed to hospital. The wanton destruction and taunting of police have elicited an un-assuaged anger among many of us who have been central in the formation of UWC as a non-racial, non-sexist institution.*
>
> *...*
>
> *Buses have been torched at UWC; residences set alight; and at Wits and Fort Hare shops were looted and books burned. And so from UCT to Wits protests have spread to other black campuses, either in solidarity with*

---

57   Rhoda Kadalie. "Binging on whingeing." PoliticsWeb, 30 Sep. 2015. URL: https://www.politicsweb.co.za/opinion/binging-on-whingeing. Accessed on 27 Mar. 2022.

the demand for free education or simply because protesting is fun – especially when exams are around the corner.

Initial claims that the free education campaign would be peaceful, were absolute hogwash. Anyone with common sense would have known that the uncompromising brinkmanship and unwillingness to negotiate with university managements like adults would ultimately end in chaos and violence.

...

A direct response to the RhodesMustFall campaign and the dominance of Black Consciousness ideology that spearheaded this movement, it is about political competition with DASO's ascendancy on campuses across the country.[58]

She also argued that at UWC in particular, there were racial tensions between black and Coloured students. While the Coloured students, she said, had ceded leadership roles to African students, the latter had not reciprocated. "African hegemony is increasingly pissing those of us off who believed in majority rule," she wrote, provocatively.[59]

She warned that South African universities were in danger of becoming as intolerant as American campuses, which "have swung so far to the left that they have become intolerant of what they construe to be conservative ideas. The banning of conservative academics has become commonplace, with many universities willfully refusing to protect political speakers considered beyond the pale." And elite universities, she noted, were just as guilty as lower-tier institutions.[60] In that way, she identified the Fallist movement as part of a broader global challenge to academic institutions, and the idea of the West itself.[61]

---

58   Rhoda Kadalie. "The wanton destruction of UWC." PoliticsWeb, 18 Nov. 2015. URL: https://www.politicsweb.co.za/news-and-analysis/the-wanton-destruction-of-uwc. Accessed on 27 Mar. 2022.

59   Ibid.

60   Rhoda Kadalie. "US varsities fail the political test." *The Citizen*, 30 Jun. 2017. URL: https://www.citizen.co.za/news/opinion/1556177/us-varsities-fail-political-test/. Accessed on 13 Apr. 2022.

61   There is some question as to whether "wokeness" is an import from the United States to South Africa, or the other way around. Helen Zille, in her 2021 book *#StayWoke: Go Broke*, argues that wokeness is a foreign concept. But the "Rhodes Must Fall" movement was noted by left-wing activists abroad, and may have helped to inspire a spate of statue-toppling efforts in the United Kingdom and the United States. In today's

There were a few academic leaders in South Africa who stood up to the mob: Jonathan Jansen, the rector of the University of the Free State; and Adam Habib, the vice-chancellor of Wits University. Rhoda had clashed with Habib in the past, particularly over the issue of Israel, when the University of Johannesburg decided to boycott its sister institution in Israel, Ben Gurion University. Years later, when anti-Israel students attacked a concert by a visiting Israeli pianist, and Habib, now at Wits, struggled to restore order, Rhoda gloated: "Habib is now in the hot seat, shouted down by the very thugs who learnt from him. ... An anti-Israel band-wagoner of note, Habib is getting his just desserts."[62] But a few years later, Habib's courage against the Fallists earned her praise. "A committed activist, he has dedicated virtually his whole life to the liberation struggle while many of these young revolutionaries were in nappies," she wrote.[63] In a subsequent column, she added that Habib's "refusal to succumb to hooliganism is informed by his own historic commitment to a transformed SA and his continuing contribution to a democratic and constitutional state."[64] She called him "*the* person of the year" in 2016 (original emphasis).[65] Most administrators, however, capitulated, leaving higher education in disarray.

Rhoda's early warnings had gone unheeded, and South African academia had paid the price for its fear, complacency, and political correctness.

* * *

Long before the orgy of Fallist violence, in 2009 Rhoda joined the governing board of Stellenbosch University, one of the country's remaining Afrikaans-language institutions. It was a move that, she hoped, would allow her to defend the principles of academic excellence that UCT and other tertiary institutions had sacrificed to politics and political correctness.

Whereas UCT was set in the midst of the city, albeit on a mountainside above it, Stellenbosch is a rural campus, an hour's drive away, nestled in the rolling hills of the wine region of the Western Cape. With its Cape Dutch

---

interconnected world, influences flow in both directions, and activists adopt tactics and rhetoric from each other with relative ease.

62   Rhoda Kadalie. Draft column for *The Citizen*. 17 May 2013. Personal files.
63   Rhoda Kadalie. "Binging," ibid.
64   Rhoda Kadalie. "White guilt is going to destroy SA." Post on Facebook, reprinted from *Die Burger*, translated from the Afrikaans, 15 Oct. 2016. URL: https://www.facebook.com/rhoda.kadalie/posts/10154739852070039. Accessed on 28 Mar. 2022.
65   Rhoda Kadalie. Draft column, *The Citizen*. 9 Dec. 2016. Personal files.

buildings and bucolic atmosphere, Stellenbosch resembled an American college town.

Unlike American college towns, which had traditionally been centers of liberal and radical thought, Stellenbosch was a bastion of conservatism for generations. Many of South Africa's leading Afrikaans figures studied there, and the campus, like other Afrikaans universities, had been generally pro-apartheid, in contrast to the more dissenting English institutions.

Post-apartheid, Stellenbosch had mellowed considerably. But it clung to its Afrikaans curriculum, both for reasons of cultural preservation and academic excellence. Because Afrikaans was unpopular among many black students, the linguistic barrier was a deterrent to applications from all but the best matriculants. As such, its standards remained high. Notably, the use of Afrikaans also gave Coloured students a foothold, in theory, that they would not have at elite English institutions, since many spoke it as a first language.

In a lecture on Human Rights Day at Stellenbosch in 2006, Rhoda dealt with the language issue in a nuanced way. The university ought not use language as a barrier to keep out black students and retain the culture of the apartheid past, she argued; but nor should it bow to the whims to students who applied to Stellenbosch knowing full well that the medium of instruction was Afrikaans.

She called for further study into the question of how Afrikaans affected campus life — and for "a multi-dimensional understanding of what it means to be Afrikaans," one that would embrace both black and white speakers, from all over the political spectrum.[66]

Above all, Rhoda hoped that Stellenbosch would hold out against the general decline of other South African universities. In 2013, she would observe: "The problem is not just the poor students; it is also about the quality of the teachers and teaching at schools, colleges and universities. In this, our universities mirror very much what is wrong with the public sector."[67] Stellenbosch, which stood apart from the political and cultural mainstream, had a better chance of success than most.

Over time, however, Stellenbosch faced increasing pressure to add more English classes, thanks to demand from black applicants, who formed a small percentage of the student population, and pressure from

---

66   Rhoda Kadalie, quoted in "Human Rights Day: Stellenbosch has to move away from exclusivity." *Kampus Nuus*, 30 Mar. 2006. p. 3.
67   Rhoda Kadalie. "What's wrong with our universities?". PoliticsWeb, reprinted from *Die Burger*, translated from the Afrikaans. URL: https://www.politicsweb.co.za/news-and-analysis/whats-wrong-with-our-universities. Accessed on 28 Mar. 2022.

the national government. (The Western Cape province was run since 2009 by the DA, which favored protecting Afrikaans institutions, as well as those preserving other official languages.)

Rhoda accepted that, but soon found that even Stellenbosch could not find the courage to challenge the racial dogmas of the new order. When the university faced a decision between two candidates for the position of Dean of Military Science, it had narrowed the search down to two applicants: one, a white applicant from a U.S. military academy who had written twelve books, had published many articles in accredited journals, and had trained at top military institutions throughout the world; the other, Samuel Tshehla, had been the acting dean.

As the *Cape Times* reported the episode:

> *Academic Rhoda Kadalie has resigned from the Stellenbosch University council because she said it was racist in its appointment of a new dean of the Faculty of Military Science, chosen by a two-thirds majority.*
>
> ...
>
> *Kadalie told the Cape Times that Tshehla had been appointed because he was black, despite being unqualified for the position.*
>
> *"Two candidates were discussed. Two candidates were proposed for appointment. And they chose the weaker one. One candidate is head, shoulders and body over the other."*
>
> *Asked whether the council had appointed Tshehla because of his race, Kadalie said: "Yes. Definitely. I understand the need for affirmative action, but you can headhunt someone more appropriate."*[68]

Rhoda's resignation shocked the university, but she was lauded by the public. It was virtually unheard of for a black person — indeed, a black woman — to sacrifice her own position on principle because she believed a white man had been treated unfairly. This was the essence of the "non-racism" to which the new South Africa was theoretically committed, and which it had quickly abandoned.

Tony Leon, with whom Rhoda remained friends, quipped sardonically to her that she was "running out of things from which to resign."[69] But

---

68   Rhoda Kadalie. "Kadalie quits 'racist' university." *Cape Times*, 15 Sep. 2011. URL: https://www.iol.co.za/news/south-africa/western-cape/kadalie-quits-racist-university-1138171. Accessed on 18 Oct. 2021.

69   Tony Leon. Personal communication with the author. 22 Feb. 2022.

others admired her defiance as one South African institution after another bowed before the altar of political correctness.

One observer who was awestruck by Rhoda's defiance was Justa Niemand, the assertive CEO of African Sun Media, a scholarly press affiliated with, but independent from, Stellenbosch University itself. She reached out to Rhoda, shortly after the latter had resigned from Stellenbosch, seeing in Rhoda a kindred spirit of female resistance to the still-powerful male establishment of the Afrikaans-speaking world. The two soon became fast friends, taking holidays together and sharing their daily struggles. Niemand herself would resign in 2019, in protest, from the companies she had founded, exasperated by the constant challenges of operating alongside what she described as the white male-dominated university management. She drew on Rhoda's courage and example in walking away from what she had built up over a period of 16 years, realizing that the rules of engagement with the university were not going to change any time soon.

Rhoda did not need to be involved in the governance of major institutions to have an impact on the lives of ordinary South Africans. She frequently went to great lengths to help people — especially young women, whom Rhoda often mentored. Several of the employees and interns who worked for her at Impumelelo noted how many lessons they had learned from her — about service, about writing, and about life. One former employee made a list for Rhoda of the "firsts" she had experienced while working for Rhoda: "1. My first job, boss, office, business card, paycheck & tax return; 2. My first car; 3. My first office romance; 4. My first work/study adventure; 5. My first publisher." She added that Rhoda had also shown her that "Feminists can be cool," and taught her "The art of profanity."[70]

Often, Rhoda went to extraordinary lengths to help complete strangers. Julia, Rhoda's daughter, recalled an incident when she and her mother were driving in Cape Town during a rainstorm on a Saturday night. They saw a newspaper vendor at a traffic light, selling the new edition of the *Sunday Times*, which went on sale Saturday evenings. He was shivering in the cold, bracing himself against the Cape storm. Rhoda reached into her purse and bought his entire stack of newspapers so that he could go home. Then she and Julia drove around their neighborhood, dropping newspapers on neighbors' doorsteps.

Julia also recalled another case — that of Rhoda's hairdresser. He worked at the salon in the Coloured suburb of Athlone to which Rhoda faithfully went every week to have her hair done by hairdressers for

---

70   Candice Jansen. Letter to Rhoda Kadalie. 8 Aug. 2012.

whom her coarse hair was familiar. Her hairdresser was HIV-positive and contracted full-blown Aids; he began wasting away physically. Rhoda invited him to stay, for free, in the apartment on the ground floor of her house. She nursed him and helped connect him to gay friends of hers who were also doctors and could treat his condition with sensitivity and care.

Initially, Rhoda and Julia expected the hairdresser to stay for his last few months, or weeks, and pass away peacefully. But he rallied and walked out, revived, to resume his life, enjoying several more years before finally passing away when Julia was away at college.

THe hairdresser was not the only person for whom a stay in Rhoda's downstairs flat was life-changing. In the late 1990s, when she was still on the Human Rights Commission, Rhoda took in a troubled teenager named Lisa Sasha Robertson-Smith, who had been the victim of sexual violence. Robertson-Smith would later recall that when Rhoda intervened, "I was at a crossroads in my life where I could go either way. There was a harder path that I could take, and that was the path that I was on."[71]

She would go on to spend a year living with Rhoda and Julia, then entering her own teenage years. "Rhoda showed me my potential," Lisa said, "and she was the first person to have seen any sort of potential in me."

At the time, Lisa was in standard nine, or eleventh grade. She was 15 years old, going on 16. One day, she was walking home from school in the Coloured township where she lived, and she was attacked and raped. Her family was furious, but said that she bore some of the blame, even though she was simply wearing her school uniform: she must have asked for it, they said.

The rapist was eventually caught, and turned out to be a serial offender. Many girls came forward as victims. But Lisa was reluctant to testify. "I didn't want to have anything to do with the case, it was over and done with, I didn't feel the need to want to rehash what I had gone through," she recalled.

Despite her family's unsympathetic reaction to the initial assault, Lisa's mother insisted that she testify against her attacker. Somehow, she came up with the idea of enlisting Rhoda to convince her daughter to go to court. At the time, Rhoda was a highly visible public figure, well known for intervening in human rights abuses, and her mother seemed to believe Rhoda would convince Lisa to testify.

---

71   Lisa Sasha Robertson-Smith. Personal communication with the author. 16 Mar. 2022.

"I had never met Rhoda before in my life," Lisa recalled. "And Rhoda at that point was the Human Rights Commissioner. And we went to Rhoda's office. My mother was more interested in what she wanted. Rhoda pulled me aside, and told my mother she needed to speak to me alone. She told me: 'Ultimately, the decision is up to you.' And I said, 'I don't want to go through with this, I don't want to testify.'"

Rhoda told Lisa's mother that she would have to accept her daughter's decision. They went home, but Lisa never forgot Rhoda's trust in her judgment, and the two stayed in touch through the various tumultuous changes in Lisa's life. At one point, she left home to live with an aunt, but when her aunt emigrated, she had to move back with her mother, who became "physically, emotionally, and mentally abusive." Lisa turned to Rhoda for help, and Rhoda invited her to move in with her in University Estate. To Lisa's surprise, her mother agreed, "and off I went and I stayed with Rhoda."

At first, Lisa recalled, she experienced a profound sense of culture shock. "Coming from the background that I did, the adjustment into — this is going to sound funny — civilized society was not something I was accustomed to," she recalled. "I was accustomed to being devious, doing things behind my mother's back — it didn't matter what I did, I was going to get a beating anyway.

"Rhoda offered a rewards system. The better I did academically, the more freedom I would have. She asked me about my homework, she invested in my projects, asking what I needed, and generally helping me." Rhoda also packed school lunches —"yummy stuff" — for Lisa, who had gone hungry at school for years. And her school immediately noticed a difference in her performance: "The comment from my school was that they could see the difference in me academically."

Rhoda encouraged Lisa in other ways as well. One of her favorite memories, Lisa recalled, was when Rhoda took her and Julia to the Spier wine estate, and to the small town of Darling to watch drag queen Pieter Dirk-Uys — stage name, Evita Perron — perform at his own theater. Lisa so enjoyed the experience that she applied for a job. "I started working on the Spier train after that, and actually earning an income," she recalled. "They said, if you want to continue working, you need to focus academically. And if I stepped out of line, which was quite often, there would be no hidings, there would be things like groundings."

In addition, Rhoda took Lisa along with her daughter to social events in the city, as she hobnobbed with Cape Town's political and cultural elite. "Rhoda showed me a different side of society, where we went to events where your picture was in the paper," Lisa recalled fondly. "Rhoda taught me culture. I came from an area in Cape Town that is known for gangsterism and drugs." At first, Lisa was reluctant to immerse herself in new experiences. But "Rhoda was a person that encouraged me to experience things, try everything at least once."

The good times were not to last, though: Lisa still tested Rhoda's boundaries, taking an interest in boys, and parties, that Rhoda felt was unhealthy, and that set a poor example for Julia. "Things went pear-shaped," Lisa recalled, "when I got given a little bit too much freedom, and I had a diary that I wrote in code. ... Rhoda basically found the diary and what I had written, and felt that I wouldn't be the best of influences on Julia if I continued staying there."

Rhoda decided that Lisa had to leave. "And if I look back in hindsight," Lisa reflected, "I can completely understand where Rhoda was coming from, because having someone like me around her daughter would not have been in Julia's best interests. So I went back to my mother."

Even back at her mother's home, however, Lisa continued to feel Rhoda's influence. "Rhoda asking me to go back to my parents was a huge wake-up call to me," she recalled, because I had been given an amazing opportunity, and because of my shit ways I blew it. And after that I took control of my life, and I went from strength to strength."

Lisa became determined to succeed. Rhoda had shown her that a better life was possible, and she was determined to achieve it. "I didn't have funds to study after school," Lisa said. "So, straight from school, I went into a working environment, and I ended up in a project manager position, overseeing meetings, conferences, and events for some of the biggest companies in the world." Soon, Lisa bought her own home; she bought a second one at the age of 27. She fell in love, married, and built a stable and successful family, raising two children — one boy, and one girl.

"I would regard myself as successful, considering where I come from. It's been a long road, but I believe everything in life happens for a reason. And Rhoda was the major reason. ...

"Rhoda was a strong, single parent that was highly successful, and she did it on her own, through hard work. And she instilled that in me. And Rhoda was the first one that said to me that there's nothing that I can't do, [though] I came from a background where I doubted myself my entire life. And I took that mindset — that I can achieve anything that I put my mind to.

"I am not a feminist in any way or form, but I do believe women like Rhoda, who show the rest of women that we don't have to be docile. We have fought exceptionally hard for quality in the country. I, as a woman, learned that anything a man can do, I can do. And that is the attitude that I carried with me throughout my life.

"I'm the Rhoda for my children. If I look at the way that I chose to parent my children, it was based on the way that Rhoda parented me, where there was time invested as a parent.

"My son is twelve. I say that any girl that ends up marrying him is going to be very lucky, because he's such a sweetheart. My daughter's 18 — she's everything that a mother could ask for."

"And the way that I raised her was what I saw Rhoda do — she always tells her friends that I'm her best friend. We've got a very open relationship. I took the same approach with her: you work hard academically, you get more freedom; you don't get the results, we're going to have a problem," Lisa explained.

"I'm really glad to say that all the people who have had a major [positive] influence in my life have all been female. And it started with Rhoda.

"Rhoda's just an amazing woman. And she's done it all, and she's had it all.

"I think that anybody that doesn't have a Rhoda in their life is missing out."

Rhoda was constantly helping others — often, as in Lisa's case, complete strangers. She would visit elderly neighbors whose children had emigrated and had no one to attend to their well-being. She would check in on former interns and employees. She gave thousands of rands to friends and relatives who asked for help. She would give advice to friends in need — often unsolicited, and usually right.

Chris Mingo also recalled Rhoda's generosity to the people around her — almost to a fault. "She was so generous on a personal level that people took advantage of it." On one occasion, he recalled, she loaned a car registered in Impumelelo's name to the son of a staff member. Years later, when she was preparing to leave for America, Rhoda tried to dispose of the car, only to find it had countless outstanding traffic fines. He credited her with his own personal and professional development: "I am today what I am because of what she taught me."[72]

Most of Rhoda's contributions to others passed quietly, without wider notice or publicity. Rhoda rarely drew attention to them, except when doing so served a larger purpose. In one case, she told the story of a

---

72   Chris Mingo, quoted by Soyiso Maliti. "Tributes stream in for 'fearless' rights champion." *Echo*, 21 Apr. 2022. p.6.

petrol (gasoline) station attendant whom she had helped pursue a career in law:

> *I met Glin [Loggenberg] at the Orange Street Service Station, where I regularly buy groceries and fill my car with petrol. He started off as a petrol attendant, then became cashier, and then was promoted to manager of the store. I used to greet him and have casual chats, and Glin would carry my bags to the car.*
>
> *We started talking politics, and then proceeded to talk about his education. At the time he was studying part-time through Unisa for a BJuris and is now studying for his LLB. As a former academic, I used to encourage him to persevere regardless and kept track of his studies. I shall never forget. Once I promised to buy him a dictionary if he passed his exam. After the exam he told me disappointedly that he had failed. I gave him the dictionary, nevertheless. He could so easily have lied.*
>
> *Last week, his colleagues at the garage asked me to call Glin urgently. When I called him he asked me if I could write a letter of reference for him in support of his application to be candidate attorney for a law firm in Claremont. That request made my day. Glin Loggenberg epitomises the essence of determination to rise above his circumstances. Working long hours, over weekends and studying at the same time was not easy but he persevered regardless.*
>
> *Petrol attendants are the lowest-paid workers in the country, with very little labour legislation to protect them. They work under the most unsafe working conditions in the country but through all of this Glin was focused and determined to succeed."*

Rhoda contrasted Glin's hard work with the selfishness of the country's political class: "I have had the most interesting political discussions with Glin and even encouraged him to go into politics, just to escape his circumstances. He could so easily have become a ward councillor or an MP but Glin had nobler ambitions, to become a lawyer through hard work. Entitlement was not his game."[73]

But her own altruism, and that of countless other South Africans, often seemed swamped by the scale of mismanagement, corruption, and anarchy in South Africa. While the poor continued to suffer, the new governing elite helped itself to lucrative opportunities and junkets at the

---

73   Rhoda Kadalie. "What Glin Loggenberg could teach SA's politicians." *Business Day,* 16 Nov. 2006. p. 19.

taxpayers' expense. After one such episode was exposed — a luxury Cape Town weekend for 75 senior government officials, paid for by the State Information Technology Agency — Rhoda commented: "The vast, vast majority of South Africans live in abject poverty and I am truly astounded that any member of our government can justify accepting a luxury weekend like this, particularly from a company that was set up by the government to provide services for the government."[74]

The one government department that seemed to function effectively was the tax collection agency, the South African Revenue Service (SARS), of which Rhoda wrote that the only reason the ANC did not interfere with its operations was that the government and the ruling party wanted "to extract as much tax from the public as they can."[75]

Rhoda also despaired of seeing progress for women in South Africa, except among those whom she was able to help through Impumelelo or through her own personal intervention. In 2007, looking back at more than a decade since United Nations' Fourth World Conference on Women in Beijing, China — which then-First Lady Hillary Clinton had attended, amid much fanfare — Rhoda declared that South Africa had, if anything, moved backward:

> More than 10 years on, we can justifiably ask what the significance was of convening 40000 delegates to adopt a global platform for action, when conditions for women have since deteriorated and when women in government and Parliament have become as self-serving as the men who govern us; when the maternal mortality rate in sub-Saharan Africa is the equivalent of three jumbo jets going down every day?
>
> Have the strategies advanced in Beijing to improve the status of women had any effect in this country? A critical review of 12 areas of concern discussed at Beijing lamentably show[s] that no such thing has happened. The intention to address certain focal areas needed not only substantial resources but political will, which is a commodity feminists always claim they have in vast amounts.

...

---

74   Rhoda Kadalie, quoted in "South Africa; Officials Riding High on the Hog." *Cape Argus*, 1 Apr. 2007.

75   Rhoda Kadalie. "Tax collection in itself really nothing to crow about." *Business Day*, 8 Mar. 2007. p. 15.

Just last Thursday, [the television show] Top Billing nauseatingly featured the Queen BEE kugels[76] giving a party in honour of President Thabo Mbeki's birthday and repeatedly thanking him, with no irony, for what he'd done for them and for his inclusion of women in the power echelons of society. And they were right – Mbeki did much to empower a small sector of women through black economic empowerment, through access to Parliament through the proportional representative electoral system and through their co-option on the grounds of vested interests.

This image is wonderfully captured by feminists Amina Mama and Pumla Gqola, who say our empowered women "submit to the patriarchal 'cult of femininity'".

Academic theorist Shireen Hassim notes: "Changing inequities in social and economic power will require not just the increased representation of women within the state, but also the increased and assertive representation of poor women within the state, as well as a strong feminist movement outside the state."

For as long as we have the schism between female protest action outside of the state by communities gatvol [fed up] with poor service delivery, and female inaction in Parliament and government where it matters, the gender question will remain that, a question, and the seizure of power, rather than empowerment, a more promising option.[77]

For women (and men) with education and skills, emigration was a more attractive option than waiting for South Africa to become safer, or to provide better opportunities. A year earlier, Rhoda had written a column in which she had warned that the ANC was creating a "new diaspora" of exiles from the country. Just as skilled black South Africans had to leave the country to pursue their careers under apartheid, now skilled white, Coloured, and Indian South Africans were being pushed to seek opportunities elsewhere because of aggressive affirmative action policies.[78]

Rhoda also felt pessimistic about the country's education system, and its ability to train future leaders who could turn South Africa around.

---

76 A "kugel" is a potato or noodle cake, in Yiddish. The term, which has escaped the South African Jewish community and entered wider use, refers to an opulent woman, the South African equivalent of the "Jewish American Princess," but not necessarily in a pejorative way.

77 Rhoda Kadalie. "Sisters in power give ordinary SA women little joy." *Business Day*, 12 Jul. 2007. p. 9.

78 Rhoda Kadalie. "ANC creates new diaspora with race-based laws." *Business Day*, 30 Sep. 2004.

After meeting with a group of top recent graduates from local universities in 2007, she recorded in her diary: "Was astounded at low level of understanding of global and national politics, even though many are extremely bright." She found them insufficiently critical in their thinking — too "sweet" and "syrupy" to challenge the dogmas and the leaders who were failing them.[79]

Rhoda's own daughter, Julia, had begun to look abroad for her education. Rhoda's battles on the UCT council, and the underwhelming experiences of some of her own friends at UCT, motivated her to apply to Harvard University, where she was accepted by late 2004. She began her studies in September 2005, and was instantly exposed to the world's foremost scholars. For example, she was accepted into a small freshman seminar by then-Harvard President Lawrence Summers, who had been President Bill Clinton's treasury secretary.

Following Julia's departure for Harvard, Rhoda returned to the theme of emigration. In a column defending white South Africans who chose to leave the country, she wrote:

> *I am convinced that most whites who leave do not want to go and that they feel driven out by crime and affirmative action. We forget that it is government's duty to create the kind of society in which people want to stay and contribute. And there are many who do stay at great cost to themselves. A sound case for affirmative action can be made when properly applied, but when vacancies in the public sector amount to thousands, government has to find ways to seriously stem the tide of current emigration levels.*
>
> *...*
>
> *Unlike many of us who do not have the option to leave, or who choose the beauty of SA above our safety, others choose life and freedom and I certainly do not blame them for it.*[80]

She concluded: "My daughter is well on her way to becoming a villain." And soon, Rhoda began to contemplate joining her.

---

79   Rhoda Kadalie. Diary entry, 23 Jul. 2007.
80   Rhoda Kadalie. "We cannot dismiss reasons whites give for leaving." *Business Day*, 5 Oct. 2006.

Chapter 18:
Trump

"It is so typical of liberals both here and abroad to point out Donald Trump's flaws and say nothing about Hillary Clinton's corruption. Yet here Zuma's corruption is condemned from the rooftops by the liberals. To them conservative equals evil yet they support liberal policies in SA which mostly align with Republican policies except on some social issues. The lack of intellectual engagement is part of the national dumbing down trend that seems to affect so many."[1]

Of all Rhoda Kadalie's controversial political stances, none puzzled observers — and close friends — as much as her support for U.S. President Donald Trump. Almost uniquely among political observers, Rhoda predicted that he would win the Republican Party's nomination in 2016, as well as the presidency itself. She soon became a vehement defender of the Trump presidency, standing alone against virtually the entire South African media.

To her opponents, Rhoda's affinity for Trump was, by definition, discrediting and disqualifying. But to Rhoda, Trump was a welcome disruptive force who had the potential to reverse the decline of American democracy and western society in general. She reveled in his disdain for the media, his mockery of political correctness, and — above all — his remarkable policy successes, particularly the economic advances made by black Americans during his tenure.

Rhoda possessed an intimate familiarity with American politics and had met many key officials, many with close ties to the Democratic Party. She had visited the United States many times over three decades, usually for academic exchanges, conferences, or meetings with donors. Under the auspices of the Ford Foundation, she had traveled to the U.S. almost every year since 1999 to participate in a program called the International Liaison Group (ILG) for Innovations in Governance and Public Action, which was hosted by Harvard University.

---

1   Rhoda Kadalie. Comment on Facebook, 19 Jun. 2016. URL: https://www. facebook.com/rhoda.kadalie/posts/10154389801720039. Accessed on 13 Apr. 2022.

Rhoda in New York City with the World Trade Center in the background,
c. 1999 (Courtesy Rhoda Kadalie)

The ILG program included participants from the U.S., Mexico, Peru, Chile, Brazil, the Philippines, and China. Each country's delegates would report on their work, and occasionally bring grassroots champions to share their innovations with an academic audience. These examples would often serve as the basis for new theoretical models of best practices that could be used elsewhere around the world

But her ties to the U.S. grew stronger once Julia left to begin her studies at Harvard in September 2005 — a journey that would eventually see Rhoda join her daughter in America.

***

Thanks in no small part to Rhoda's tutelage, Julia had been an outstanding student from the very beginning. She had refused to attend kindergarten, and attended Rhoda's lectures at UWC instead, occasionally interrupting to demand that her mother draw a cat on the chalkboard. Years later, Rhoda's colleagues would remember the charming young girl in the yellow raincoat who made an impression on everyone around her.

Later, Rhoda had enrolled Julia in a Catholic school, and then St. Cyprian's, an all-girls school (see Chapter 7). Julia flourished at St. Cyprian's, where she studied the cello alongside her regular schoolwork. It was a second home for Julia: occasionally, she would stay at the school's boarding facility while Rhoda was overseas.

As she made her way through St. Cyprian's, Julia had expected to apply to the University of Cape Town, perhaps to the medical school, where she imagined she might become an obstetrician. But Rhoda's experience on the UCT council had prompted worries that the quality of education on campus might be declining, and she encouraged Julia to look further afield.

Julia was already well-traveled; she had accompanied Rhoda on trips to the U.S., Canada, Sweden, the United Kingdom, and elsewhere. By 2004, Julia would turn the tables by inviting Rhoda to join *her* in Europe, where she was spending the summer in Germany with her high school sweetheart, Julian Tauschke. Julia also traveled to the U.S. with a teacher, having organized a fundraising trip for a school charity project she had begun called Girl Child in Afrika. The project provided funds for children from disadvantaged backgrounds to study at St. Cyprian's, which had a boarding facility.

While in the U.S., Julia visited several of the elite private schools within the Round Square network, with which St. Cyprian's was affiliated. She also spent several weeks exploring New York City, spending her allowance on classical music concerts. And she visited a South African friend who was studying at Harvard, and decided she would apply there.

Rhoda made no secret of the fact that her daughter was applying abroad, and was proud when Julia was accepted through the college's early admissions program in mid-December 2004. Since the academic year had ended in November, but the American school year would not begin until September, Julia was left with a nine-month gap. Rhoda encouraged her to seek an internship in Parliament.

Though her own political views were still forming, Julia applied to work at the DA — partly at the urging of Minister of Education Kader Asmal, who warned, half-jokingly, that if Julia worked for the ANC, she would "forget to read, write, and spell."

Julia joined Tony Leon's staff in the office of the Leader of the Opposition, working closely with economics researcher Tim Harris, who would go on to be a member of Parliament himself. In addition to meeting her future husband, who worked across the hallway in the speechwriting office, Julia explored an interest in economic policy, and the search for solutions that would expand employment opportunities for South Africa's poor.

After several months of farewells, including a cello concert to raise additional funds for her expenses, Julia left for Harvard. Rhoda suffered through the day of Julia's departure. She grumbled as Julia spent the morning saying goodbye to friends, then bickered with Julia as they packed and rushed through last-minute preparations. Jakes Gerwel — who had always felt warmly toward Julia — showed up to say goodbye, and ended up helping Julia cover her cello case in bubble wrap. Soon, Richard arrived to take Julia to the airport. Rhoda decided not to accompany them, wishing to avoid an emotional scene. But when Julia's luggage would not fit in Richard's car, Rhoda had to drive there anyway. She did not accompany Julia inside. She later wrote in her diary: "When Julia left I felt relieved but empty & unhappy. Bad way to leave but then I thought — if we did not have an argument we would be so sad and weep."[2]

When she arrived at Harvard, Julia continued her interest in economics, and was accepted into a small seminar for first-year students with the president of Harvard, Lawrence Summers, an economist who had been Secretary of the Treasury under President Bill Clinton. She also played cello in the Harvard-Radcliffe Orchestra, and explored a growing interest in Jewish literature, studying with renowned Yiddish scholar Ruth Wisse.

Rhoda's home in University Estate felt empty without Julia — though her boyfriend (the author) visited often, enjoying Rhoda's home cooking in Julia's absence. Rhoda quietly indulged him, though she was unsure where the relationship was heading.

The two lovers were eventually reunited at Harvard, with Rhoda watching from afar. Though she pined for Julia, she had ample responsibilities to keep her busy in South Africa. She continued to grow Impumelelo, helping the government achieve its various policy goals; and she remained one of South Africa's most popular columnists, tearing into the ANC's corruption and mismanagement.

Rhoda also had innumerable family responsibilities, including caring for her elderly parents, and her brother, Paul. Pastor Fenner Kadalie, though semi-retired, continued to work in his church community, preaching to his congregation and delivering meals to poor families on the Cape Flats.

The other Kadalie siblings all remained in Cape Town. Her brother Charles had become something of a local celebrity. As director of street lighting for the city, Charles appeared frequently in local media to explain to an exasperated population how power outages, which were becoming increasingly common, would affect their lives.

---

2   Rhoda Kadalie. Diary entry, 2 Sep. 2005.

*Rhoda with her seven brothers and her sister outside the home of Joan and
Fenner Kadalie, c. 2010. From left to right: Charles, Judy, Rhoda,
Patrick, Fenner, David, Joan, Bruce, Paul, Reuben, Thomas
(Courtesy Rhoda Kadalie)*

Rhoda was also occasionally in touch with her ex-husband's extended
family. Long after the divorce from Richard, when Julia was eleven years
old, "Großmutter" Brigitte Bertelsmann phoned Rhoda to apologize for
her past behavior. South Africa had changed, and she had changed, too.
Rhoda noted in a letter to friends in Germany:

> *Can you imagine my disbelief when she called me on my birthday after
> nine years of silence? In October I went to London, fell on the bus, and
> fractured my spine. When I returned she phoned again to commiserate.
> I then wrote her a letter commending her courage and thanking her for
> breaking the silence after so many years, requesting that we forget the
> past for Julia's sake and remain friends. Since then I have been writing
> to her regularly as though nothing ever happened.[3]*

The two remained in contact, and Rhoda also spoke occasionally to
Richard's other relatives, notably Anchen Dreyer, his former sister-in-
law, who had become a DA member of Parliament.

---

3   Rhoda Kadalie. Letter to Jurgen and Catherine Girgensohn. 4 Jan. 2000.

Other changes were also afoot. Rhoda accepted Julia's conversion to Judaism, which her daughter had begun to explore at Harvard, attending services and lectures at the Harvard Hillel and studying the great works of Jewish literature with Professor Ruth Wisse. It was not easy for Rhoda to understand, at first: Julia had been committed to her Anglican faith, which she had chosen of her own volition in her early teenage years. She had something precious already; why exchange it for something new?

As difficult as any conversion to Judaism is, an Orthodox conversion is even more difficult, with its mandatory Sabbaths, its dietary restrictions, and its modest dress code. Rhoda, ever the feminist, did not want her daughter to accept a stultifying set of old and confusing rules that would limit her expression as a woman — certainly not for the sake of a relationship with a man. But she also respected Julia's freedom and her choices, though she would joke that Julia's newfound faith, together with her mixed-race background, made her a *"gemors"* (a mess)..

Rhoda and Richard attend Julia's graduation from Harvard
in Cambridge, Massachusetts, 2009

In December 2009, Rhoda threw Julia an Orthodox Jewish wedding, renting Premier Helen Zille's official residence, Leeuwenhof. Much to her amusement, the ANC complained about the use of the facility, though it was perfectly legal. Co-operative Governance Minister Sicelo Shiceka warned: "This is the first I've heard of it and I will certainly be following up on it."[4]

The ceremony was conducted by the Orthodox Jewish rabbinate, together with Julia's rabbi from Harvard, and Rhoda had arranged a kosher caterer, though some three-quarters of the guests were not Jewish and had never been to a Jewish wedding in their lives. She also conspired with the groom to subvert, playfully, one of the most tedious South African Jewish wedding traditions: the singing of "Baruch HaBa," a wedding hymn drawn from Psalm 118: 26-29. Rhoda helped arrange for one of Cape Town's traditional Islamic music ensembles, known as the Malay Choirs, to perform the wedding song instead, to the tune of the traditional *Nederlandse* Cape folk song, "Rosa," with Eastern melodies floating above Western chord progressions.

Rhoda embraces Julia at the traditional Jewish bedekin ceremony at Julia's wedding, 2009 (Courtesy Rhoda Kadalie)

---

4   Sicelo Shiceka, quoted by Andisiwe Makinana. "Wedding Bells to Ring at Leeuwenhof." *Cape Argus*, 29 Dec. 2009.

Rhoda embraces Julia's mother-in-law-to-be, Naomi Pollak (née Perkel),
2009 (Courtesy Dave Le)

Julia later graduated from Harvard and worked for the Heritage Foundation,
a conservative think tank in Washington, DC. She also enlisted in the U.S.
Navy Reserve, serving as an Aviation Structural Mechanic at a base in
Coronado, California. As it became clear that Julia was not returning to
South Africa, Rhoda began considering her own future — and paying even
closer attention to American politics.

***

South Africa's own dramatic political decline also sharpened Rhoda's
interest in American politics. While Julia's departure overseas was a "pull"
factor, the collapse of many institutions of governance and civil society in
post-apartheid South Africa was a "push" factor as well.

At first, the election of Jacob Zuma in 2009 was not the disaster that
many, including senior members of the predominantly Xhosa leadership
of the ANC, had feared.

In 2010, South Africa hosted the FIFA World Cup and put on a nearly
flawless tournament — thanks, in part, to some of the reforms that Helen

Zille had insisted on in Cape Town to prevent financial mismanagement. The event, which outshone subsequent World Cup tournaments in Brazil and Russia, marked a high point in post-apartheid South Africa — or, perhaps, a last hurrah.

The Zuma presidency, which had been billed as a working-class populist insurgency, brought about one of the darkest moments in the history of South African labor relations. On August 16, 2012, officers with the South African Police Services fired on striking workers who were protesting at a platinum mine in Marikana, in the North West Province, killing 34 miners and wounding 78 others.[5]

Marikana was the worst abuse of human rights in post-apartheid South Africa — and recalled scenes from the Sharpeville massacre of 1960, a bloody milestone in the struggle against apartheid. But this time, the apartheid regime was not to blame.

Rhoda observed:

Since the retirement of Mandela, South Africa has become a fragile place. The natives (all of us) are restless; citizens are easily provoked; protests erupt in a flash over water, sanitation, housing and potholes; and the ANC Youth League is a semblance of the state of the Party. Increasing vigilantism and necklacing in the townships, the rape of black lesbians, the murder of foreign nationals, road rage, and widespread violence point to a society in deep distress.

We are witnessing chronic break down of authority on all levels; the police are out of control; the highly paid mining and union bosses are out of order; and the unrepresented workers act out when they feel their voices are not being heard. Police action against the protesters was completely out of proportion to their action. Granted, brandishing pangas is illegal but our police should be trained to deal with protests? Where was their riot gear, shields and helmets?

When President Zuma took over from Mbeki, he promised to undo Mbeki's autocratic rule and take the country on a different course. Alas he has failed and continues very much along the same path.[6]

---

5   South African History Online. "Marikana Massacre 16 August 2012." URL: https://www.sahistory.org.za/article/marikana-massacre-16-august-2012. Accessed on 19 Oct. 2021.

6   Rhoda Kadalie. "A society in deep distress." PoliticsWeb, reprinted from *The Citizen*, 26 Aug. 2012. URL: https://www.politicsweb.co.za/news-and-analysis/a-society-in-deep-distress. Accessed on 28 Mar. 2022.

Ironically, trade unionists themselves had launched a violent attack just months before, assaulting DA members who had led a protest march to Cosatu's offices in Johannesburg in May 2012. The trade union later boasted: "In the event the DA did not even reach their destination and beat an ignominious retreat when confronted by the massed ranks of the workers."[7] The breakdown of civility, and law and order, was undeniable.

There were other problems. South Africa's electricity had been among the cheapest in the world when Mbeki took office. A decade later, South Africa was running out of electricity, and major cities were forced to endure rolling blackouts.

The problem was partly due to rising demand, thanks to modest economic growth in the Mbeki years. But the government and the state-run power company, Eskom, had failed to plan for the future. Qualified engineers, often white, had been let go; ruling party cronies had been installed in key positions.

The poor performance of Eskom and other state-owned enterprises — many of which had been considered candidates for privatization at the dawn of the Mbeki era — became a major obstacle to economic growth. The scholar R. W. Johnson observed that the parastatal companies had become "a drain on the productive private sector" as well as the state.[8]

"All of them are badly managed and even Eskom — under apartheid a mighty, profit-making utility which always had a large power reserve — has been reduced to a crippled giant," he wrote in 2015.[9] The parastatals added to the country's debt without improving South Africa's productive capacity. And there was no end in sight.

These problems were not simply the ordinary challenges facing any developing country, nor were they the legacy of apartheid. They were the direct outcome of the ANC's corruption, which Rhoda had warned about for years, and which persisted in the illiberal political culture that the ruling party had created (see Chapter 15).

That corruption achieved new lows under Jacob Zuma, a charismatic yet incompetent leader who had enriched himself through a series of close relationships with avaricious businessmen. The first of these to come to light was Schabir Shaik, whose conviction in 2005 for bribery led Mbeki to dismiss Zuma as deputy president.

---

7   Patrick Craven. "DA beat an ignominious retreat - COSATU." PoliticsWeb, 15 May 2012. URL: https://www.politicsweb.co.za/politics/da-beat-an-ignominious-retreat--cosatu. Accessed on 28 Mar. 2022.
8   R. W. Johnson. *How Long Will South Africa Survive?* London: Hurst & Company, 2015. 147.
9   Ibid, 148.

Zuma also developed close ties to a family of Indian-South African entrepreneurs known as the Guptas. They had arrived in the country during the transition to democracy and set up a legitimate business, trading in computer components. Over time, through donations to the ANC — and direct financial support of ANC politicians — the Guptas gained access to lucrative state contracts.

Once Zuma became president, the Guptas were essentially running the country, interviewing and approving Zuma's appointments to the Cabinet and other positions. South Africans began referring to the arrangement as "state capture," and it took years of investigations to unravel.

The Guptas, in an effort to manipulate their public image, hired the British public relations firm Bell Pottinger to push back. The consultants from the United Kingdom shrewdly observed that the best way to avoid scrutiny in South Africa was to exacerbate racial tensions — and they unleashed a campaign to do exactly that. As the *New York Times* later reported:

> *So Bell Pottinger was retained, and given an assignment that initially sounded benign enough: grass-roots political activism intended to help poor blacks.*
>
> *By the following year, Bell Pottinger was embroiled in a national maelstrom. In TV reports, editorials and public rallies, it stood accused of setting off racial tensions through a furtive campaign built on Twitter bots, hate-filled websites and speeches. All were pushing a highly toxic narrative, namely that whites in South Africa had seized resources and wealth while they deprived blacks of education and jobs. The message was popularized with an incendiary phrase, "white monopoly capital."*
>
> *...*
>
> *When Bell Pottinger's role became public, protesters rallied against the company, both in South Africa and outside the firm's London office. A subsequent investigation by the Public Relations and Communications Association, a trade group in Britain, ended with the ejection of Bell Pottinger.*[10]

---

10   David Segal. "How Bell Pottinger, P.R. Firm for Despots and Rogues, Met Its End in South Africa." *New York Times*, 4 Feb. 2018. URL: https://www. nytimes.com/2018/02/04/business/bell-pottinger-guptas-zuma-south-africa.html. Accessed on 13 Apr. 2022.

The firm eventually went bankrupt. Other firms that were associated with the Guptas — KPMG, McKinsey — also suffered fleeting reputational harm. But the damage the scandal caused to South Africa remained. As Rhoda observed: "What we see on a grand scale is the democratization of corruption, from the highest to the lowest, from so-called prestigious auditing firms to convicted felons."[11]

The DA flourished in the Zuma era, winning new black recruits to the opposition cause. But new political challenges arose from the left, as Julius Malema and his red-beret-wearing EFF party pushed for the forcible transfer of land and wealth from white to black South Africans, which they defined as economic "freedom." Zuma, fearful of being outflanked, introduced a new policy called "Radical Economic Transformation" (RET) Rhoda mocked RET as an empty political exercise, full of bad ideas: "Words such as radical economic transformation are a ruse for radical economic enrichment and point to why all the policy recommendations have been controversial despite a series of degradations to junk status."[12] Regardless, the RET policy failed to mollify Malema and his followers, who brought the tactics of radical protest into the halls of Parliament itself.

A particular low point was Zuma's annual State of the Nation address to Parliament in 2015, which erupted in violence as members of the EFF disrupted the president and were forcibly ejected by police. Television screens went dark as the violent clashes continued in the chamber to which the people's representatives had been elected through the hard-won power of the ballot, the object of decades of struggle against apartheid. The *Sunday Times* lamented in an editorial: "It was hard to believe that South Africa is a functional democracy. ... For a solid hour last night South Africa resembled a messy, dysfunctional state being held together by the security forces."[13]

Rhoda used the occasion to reflect on how far South Africa had fallen. Looking back on the ideals that had motivated her, and other black South Africans, to succeed despite apartheid, she wrote:

That ambition to become "something", despite the many obstacles, was not only personal. It was part of the DNA of the oppressed at the time,

11 Rhoda Kadalie. Draft column for *Beeld*. 20 Sep. 2017. Personal files.
12 Rhoda Kadalie. "Reject destructive ANC policies." 7 Jul. 2017. URL: https://www.citizen.co.za/news/opinion/1562969/reject-destructive-anc-policies/. Accessed on 13 Apr. 2022.
13 *Sunday Times*. "Actions spoke much louder than scripted words last night." Editorial, 13 Feb. 2015. URL: https://www.timeslive.co.za/news/south-africa/2015-02-13-actions-spoke-much-louder-than-scripted-words-last-night/. Accessed on 28 Mar. 2022.

not to let racial oppression, poverty, and gender discrimination define us. Because we were denied quality education, many of us used our bad education to study and to use even the very inferior education thrust upon us to beat the Nationalists at their own game. The motivation was no different to what drove the founding members of the ANC in 1912 to form a political movement of resistance against their colonial oppressors, using their missionary education to chart a new way forward.

...

But where did these ambitions come from?

Our working class parents nurtured them in us. All they wanted was a better life for their children, believing implicitly that education was the ticket out of poverty.

...

Thursday evening killed the ambitions many of our young people might have had to enter into politics. When I ask my daughter if she would ever consider returning to SA, she would mockingly say "You deserve Jacob Zuma, I don't." She implicitly blames us adults (who were all a part of the struggle), for allowing the ANC to sink "below sea level". Frankly, I was not shocked to see Parliament's descent into anarchy on Thursday.

It was the logical outcome of years of abuse against the opposition and criticism. In this, all sectors of society were complicit. Big business for shutting up lest they be restricted from making deals; civil society for acting as apologists for the ANC for at least the first decade of its rule; and the media for behaving like fifth columns, instead of providing us with the unvarnished truth.

What we sowed, we have reaped, and the fruits are rotten![14]

Rhoda recorded the sense of disappointment in the "vampire state" through the eyes of friends from "a rather anaesthetic European country," who had developed a strong interest in South Africa after 1994.

"I saw them again on Friday," she observed in 2014, "after two years and I could see the deep disappointment in their eyes about what they consider to be a national squandering of the country's human and natural

---

14   Rhoda Kadalie. "SONA: What we sowed, we have reaped!". PoliticsWeb, reprinted from *The Citizen*, 20 Feb. 2015. URL: https://www.politicsweb. co.za/opinion/sona-what-we-sowed-we-have-reaped. Accessed on 28 Mar. 2022.

resources."[15] Not only was the government corrupt, but its corruption was tolerated by the citizenry. "The co-optation of the middle classes has become so nauseating that the unravelling of the state cannot be blamed on the Zuma administration alone, but also on all those leaders who have gone before and who have used the state's resources as their personal or party political banks."

When the country could no longer look away from the ANC's venality, exemplified by Zuma using state resources to upgrade his personal homestead of Nkandla, in rural KwaZulu-Natal, Rhoda noted that it had taken several state institutions to overlook the corruption. Citing the damning report of Public Protector Thuli Madonsela, Rhoda noted: "Instead of one appointed entity to see to the security of our presidents, a range of agencies is involved, allowing for much to fall through the cracks ... [S]ome officials clearly complained; others proceeded knowing that in the name of the President, they could milk the system."[16] Corruption was no longer a problem in the system; had, in fact, become the system.

The one center of excellence in the country was the opposition-governed Western Cape, which the ANC coveted but could not win back — not after the DA had established a foothold with a track record of successful, if occasionally troubled, government. As Rhoda observed: "Using language appropriate to the pre-1994 era, it accuses the Democratic Alliance of perpetuating apartheid. It has even threatened 'to liberate' us from DA rule. In a weird sort of a way, the ANC envies the DA-ruled Western Cape. Here things happen; services are rendered; hospitals are built; and schools function better than in any other province."[17] The ANC, she argued, sought to undermine DA governance by any means necessary — encouraging violent "service delivery" protests, for example, or even denying national police resources to the province to drive up the crime rate.[18] The local and provincial governments responded by improving their

15   Rhoda Kadalie. "Life under the vampire state." PoliticsWeb, reprinted from *Die Burger*, translated from the Afrikaans, 11 Sep. 2014. URL: https://www.politicsweb.co.za/news-and-analysis/life-under-the-vampire-state. Accessed on 28 Mar. 2022.
16   Rhoda Kadalie. "A kraal on steroids!". PoliticsWeb, reprinted from *Die Burger*, translated from the Afrikaans, 26 Mar. 2014. URL: https://www.politicsweb.co.za/news-and-analysis/a-kraal-on-steroids. Accessed on 28 Mar. 2022.
17   Rhoda Kadalie. "The ANC comes to Cape Town." PoliticsWeb, reprinted from *Die Burger* and translated from the Afrikaans, 14 Jan. 2015. URL: https://www.politicsweb.co.za/opinion/the-anc-comes-to-cape-town. Accessed on 28 Mar. 2022.
18   Rhoda Kadalie. "The SAPS is useless and the govt doesn't care." PoliticsWeb, reprinted from *Die Burger*, translated from the Afrikaans,

services, and boosting their own police forces. But the Western Cape's endurance simply highlighted the rest of South Africa's failures.

The country whose peaceful transition had once inspired the world, whose leaders once set an example for reconciliation, and which embraced the ideals of constitutional democracy, had begun spiraling downward into corruption, tribalism, and stagnation. "More than learning from our success," Rhoda quipped, "people should learn from our mistakes."[19]

Rhoda's hope for women's progress in South Africa had also been dashed — not just by the endemic culture of rape and violence, not just by the sordid example set by the president, but also by the behavior of female leaders in the ruling party. "In fact some of our worst ministers have been women," Rhoda noted, "not because they are women, but because they are beholden to the party bosses who put them there."[20]

Just as Zuma once replaced Mbeki as ANC president while the latter was still in office, Zuma was defeated in an internal party election in 2017 by his deputy, Cyril Ramaphosa. The following year, the ANC forced Zuma to resign the presidency of the country itself, and Ramaphosa took over.

Rhoda, like many South Africans, had high hopes for Ramaphosa. A trade union activist in the 1980s, he had been eclipsed by Mbeki in the ANC leadership in the early 1990s, thanks to the latter's support among the exiles.

Many who chafed at Mbeki's authoritarian style, particularly on the left, had pined for Ramaphosa's return. In the interim, Ramaphosa had become one of South Africa's new black billionaires, taking advantage of "empowerment" opportunities. However dubious, his business connections suggested he could tackle South Africa's growing economic problems.

But Ramaphosa struggled to turn the country around. Instead, he deferred to radical voices demanding radical land reform, announcing that South Africa would consider seizing white-owned land — so-called "expropriation without compensation."

---

24 Sep. 2014. URL: https://www.politicsweb.co.za/news-and-analysis/the-saps-is-useless-and-the-govt-doesnt-care. Accessed on 28 Mar. 2022.

19   Rhoda Kadalie. "Partnership from a Human Rights Perspective." Speech to Council of World Mission, 15 Oct. 2008.

20   Rhoda Kadalie. "I did not know that we would mess up so badly." PoliticsWeb 2014, ibid.

He only relented — however briefly — after a critical tweet by U.S. President Donald Trump in August 2018.[21] And Trump, while reviled by the South African intelligentsia, had begun to pique Rhoda's interest.

* * *

Rhoda had been a keen observer of American politics for many years, and especially since Julia left for the U.S. In 2003, she had publicly criticized the Iraq War, as well as the erosion of civil liberties under anti-terror legislation such as the U.S.A. Patriot Act. She devoted an entire column to criticizing the American "paranoia" about security that had complicated international air travel across the world. But she was never given to knee-jerk anti-American sentiment, or the habitual attacks on President George W. Bush that were the common currency of South African pundits at the time. She studied American politics through a careful analytical lens, sharpened by her experiences in South Africa.

In 2008, Barack Obama's victory in the presidential election thrilled many observers, especially in South Africa, where the election of America's first black president had acute symbolic resonance. CNN's coverage, available on regular South African television, was glowing. Even leading figures in the DA, like Helen Zille, openly admired Obama. To the South African opposition, the fact that a member of a racial minority had won a democratic election was a source of inspiration.

Rhoda made that point herself: "Perhaps the prospect of Helen Zille ascending the throne like Barack Obama as someone from a minority group is more imminent than we think," she wrote hopefully.[22] But she was also more skeptical of Obama than Zille and many in the DA were. "One cannot help but feel a bit queasy about the hagiography," she observed, after he won.[23]

Part of the problem, to Rhoda, was that many of Obama's far-left policies echoed those of the ANC. She had already made up her mind about him long before he ran for president. When Obama visited South Africa in 2006, as a Senator from Illinois, he paid a luncheon visit to the Cape

---

21 Rhoda Kadalie. "Rhoda Kadalie: South Africa Walks Back Land Reform Proposal After Trump Tweet." Breitbart News, 31 Aug. 2018. URL: https://www.breitbart.com/politics/2018/08/31/rhoda-kadalie-south-africa-walks-back-land-reform-proposal-after-trump-tweet/. Accessed on 19 Oct. 2021.

22 Rhoda Kadalie. "The bitter fuel that is driving 'rebels'." Business Day, ibid.

23 Rhoda Kadalie. "Foreign ironies and Cape changes." Business Day, 20 Nov. 2008. p. 11.

Town Club, an elite social group that brought together the city's leaders and its opinion-makers. Rhoda declined to attend, and believed strongly that South Africans of all political persuasions — including the DA — were starstruck by the future president solely because of his race.[24]

In visits to the U.S., Rhoda had been impressed by the vigor of Obama's campaign. But she was also willing to be critical of his performance in office, as few South Africans were, and she predicted many of his policy failures.

When Trump announced his candidacy in June 2015, famously descending the escalator in Trump Tower in New York, few political pundits gave him a chance of winning: they treated his campaign as a vanity project at best, a joke at worst.

But Rhoda was impressed by Trump's swashbuckling style and political incorrectness. "America needs a *skollie*," she said, using the South African slang for "gangster." She viewed Trump as many Americans did: an antidote to a moribund political establishment that had become corrupt and that seemed unwilling to confront chronic problems. At the very least, Trump would shake things up.

Not that Rhoda was uncritical of Trump: she often felt he was his own worst enemy. She was particularly critical of his language toward women. But to Rhoda, it was neither difficult nor unusual to support a politician while also speaking plainly about his or her flaws.

In 2015, during a visit to the Los Angeles area, where Julia and the author, by then Rhoda's son-in-law, had settled, Rhoda attended one of the early Republican presidential primary debates, hosted by CNN and held at the Ronald Reagan Presidential Library in Simi Valley, California. The author, as an editor at Breitbart News, a conservative news website, had helped arrange press credentials for her to cover the debate for readers of the *Citizen* in South Africa.

---

24 Later, Rhoda had direct access to the views of the American opposition to Obama: Julia and her fiancé (this author) had volunteered for Obama's Republican opponent, Senator John McCain of Arizona.

In 2009, they became more directly involved in politics, through a series of unusual circumstances. That spring, they attended a lecture at Harvard by Congressman Barney Frank, a Democrat who chaired a powerful financial committee during the global financial crisis, which he blamed on Republicans. When her fiancé (i.e. the author) asked Frank how much responsibility he himself had for the meltdown, the congressman exploded in anger.

The exchange was captured by a local television news crew, and went viral. Republicans from Illinois, the author's home state, urged him to run for Congress against incumbent Congresswoman Jan Schakowsky. Though unsuccessful, the campaign, with Julia's help, energized a dormant community of conservative activists in the Chicago suburbs.

Rhoda enjoyed the spectacle of the event, and the sheer scale of it, with hundreds of journalists working frantically to file stories in the media room outside the debate hall itself.

Rhoda and the author in the media filing center at the Republican presidential primary debate, Ronald Reagan Presidential Library, Simi Valley, California, 2015 (Courtesy Rhoda Kadalie)

At one point in the debate, CNN moderator Jake Tapper prompted former Hewlett Packard CEO Carly Fiorina, the only woman among the main contenders for the Republican nomination, to respond to one of Trump's barbs in the press:

> *In an interview last week in Rolling Stone magazine, Donald Trump said the following about you. Quote, "Look at that face. Would anyone vote for that? Can you imagine that, the face of our next president?" Mr. Trump later said he was talking about your persona, not your appearance. Please feel free to respond what you think about his persona.*

There was general laughter in the hall. Fiorina took the opportunity to attack Trump: "I think women all over this country heard very clearly what Mr. Trump said."

Rhoda, taking notes, exclaimed: "Good!" She was glad that Fiorina had taken Trump to task. But the exchange did not change her feelings about Trump's campaign. She later wrote:

To most South Africans the Republican Party in the USA personifies evil. Socially conservative on same sex marriage, abortion, affirmative action, and gay rights, the Grand Old Party is considered anathema, even to our conservatives. But upon closer scrutiny, within the party there are opposing views on these issues and on the economy, foreign policy, education, health-care, and even social policies, SA's conservatives and some liberals concur with Republican policies. They are either uninformed or hypocritical or both and largely ignorant of their own party's policies.

...

I have had the privilege of attending the CNN Republican Presidential Debate at the Reagan Library in Simi Valley California on the 16th September. This was the real deal – democracy at work with the intensive grilling of candidates who covet the throne. CNN's Jake Tapper was ruthless with his no-holds barred interrogation, and although his agendas were as transparent as CNN's carefully selected audience, the debate was nevertheless exciting. The Republican candidates displayed a diversity of opinion that is often suppressed by the mainstream media, eager always to portray them as a monolithic group, thereby perpetuating old hackneyed stereotypes.

The biggest casualty of this demonization is democracy. Instead of treating opposition as legitimate, the Obama administration assumes a moral authority over this 'demon' by increasingly using his 'executive powers' to push through ideologically loaded and partisan policies (regarding foreign affairs, immigration, defence, human rights and health-care) instead of consulting with Congress. In this regard America's democracy is on a slippery slope, but debate still matters. Every utterance from prospective candidates is analysed and scrutinised to the extent that some candidates have already been squeezed out of the race by public opinion. Polls are conducted every day with the public to see how they rate candidates. In this respect, the USA's democracy still works, unlike ours, where the restrictions on power have been eroded by a liberation party intent on ruling "until Jesus comes."[25]

---

25   Rhoda Kadalie. Draft article for *The Citizen*. 25 Sep. 2015. Personal files.

As the debates continued, and the 2016 primary votes began, Trump defied the pundits and became his party's nominee, much to the chagrin of the media, which projected its disdain for the Republican candidate across the world.

As Rhoda's views on Trump became known, friends and commentators in South Africa were incredulous. Some challenged her directly: Tony Leon, for one, bet Rhoda one thousand rand that Trump would lose. Others cut ties with Rhoda entirely, and even some who stayed in touch felt a growing distance. Journalist Marianne Thamm, for one, would later confess that she "did not understand" Rhoda's views on U.S. politics.[26] Thamm came up with her own theory, based on notes she later discovered in the margins of Rhoda's copy of Christopher Hitchens's book on the Clintons, *No One Left to Lie To*, which Thamm had forgotten to return. She wrote:

> Paging through the Hitchens book this weekend Rhoda suddenly speaks out to me from the margins. Her handwriting is clear cursive, urgent, in black pen at first, later blue.
>
> On page 48 is an account of Clinton's response in 1998 to Native American poet Sherman Alexie who had complained about the living conditions of first nations.
>
> That day, writes Hitchens, Clinton "announced that his grandmother had been one-quarter Cherokee. This claim, never advanced before, would, if true, have made him the first Native American president".
>
> In cursive Rhoda wrote obliquely in the margin, "Race manipulator of note!"
>
> On the first page of chapter one, titled Triangulation, Rhoda has underlined the sentence "manipulation of populism by elitism".
>
> That is how Hitchens, Trump, Kadalie and Pollak view/viewed the democratic political establishment. Essentially. At its heart.
>
> Rhoda underlined Hitchens' take on philosopher Hannah Arendt's assessment that Stalinism among intellectuals could be attributed to one annihilating tactic.

---

26   Marianne Thamm. "Rhoda Kadalie, friend and mentor, political provocateur and groot bek." Daily Maverick, 17 Apr. 2022. URL: https://www.dailymaverick.co.za/article/2022-04-17-rhoda-kadalie-friend-and-mentor-political-provocateur-and-groot-bek/. Accessed on 20 Apr. 2022.

"Stalinism replaced all debate about the merit of the argument, or a position, or even a person, with an inquiry about motive...When the finger points at the moon, the Chinese say, the idiot looks at the finger."

Rhoda tried not to look at the finger.[27]

Barron came to similar conclusions: "[Rhoda] hated political correctness and identity politics, ...She loved that Trump gave them both the middle finger. ... She saw in Trump someone brash and outspoken enough to take on the wokish tide, and she identified with that."[28]

Rhoda herself told an interviewer for the Afrikaans press in 2018: "I think Trump is hysterical! He challenged the establishment. The irony is that the left wanted to maintain the status quo of the establishment. It makes them right, it makes them conservative!"[29] As to the charge that she had become "right-wing," Rhoda laughed it off:

"I no longer believe in left and right. I believe the world is divided into open and closed societies, and I believe the self-righteous left wing has self-righteous evangelicals who will condemn you to hell if you do not live up to their values and standards."

Similarly, she reckons the label "alt right" is a stupid name that has no basis in history.[30] "If people are going to call me alt right, then I am going to call them alt stupid. Alt delete!"

She laughed. "I have never been right-wing! Do you know what the problem is? People do not distinguish between being right-wing and being right!"[31]

Though fully aware of Trump's checkered history with women, Rhoda pointed out that the Clintons were no better. "Was Hillary a feminist?" she asked, rhetorically.[32]

---

27   Ibid.
28   Barron, "Obituary," ibid.
29   Rhoda Kadalie, quoted by Willemien Brümmer. "Rhoda: 'SA wil my nie laat gaan nie'." *Netwerk 24*, 16 Apr. 2022. Translated from the Afrikaans by Google Translate. URL: https://www.netwerk24.com/netwerk24/stemme/profiele/rhoda-sa-wil-my-nie-laat-gaan-nie-20220416. Accessed on 20 Apr. 2022.
30   The "alt-right" was a movement of right-wing activists who did not fit into conventional Republican politics. Some had extreme views; many supported Trump.
31   Ibid.
32   Ibid.

Rhoda: 'Comrade Kadalie, You Are Out of Order!'

When the election results rolled in on the morning of November 9, 2016, only Rhoda was not surprised Trump had won. She told South African website News24 that Trump's win was a "victory for good over evil":

Academic and founder of the University of the Western Cape's gender equity unit, Rhoda Kadalie, on Wednesday hailed US president elect Donald Trump's victory as "good for the world".

Speaking to News24, Kadalie was vociferous in her support for the controversial Republican candidate.

He beat out Democrat rival Hillary Clinton on Wednesday.

"All I want to say is that 'I told you so'. For the world's sake I'm glad that Trump has won."

She said people had "dumped on" her for supporting Trump.

"They vilified and demonised him and they took their news from CNN and the New York Times, which both support the Clinton Foundation."

Kadalie described Clinton as "pure evil".

"Hillary is pro-big capital and Wall Street and this is everything the Americans hate. She is pure evil and she is corrupt to the core.

"She is the equivalent of Jacob Zuma. She has her Guptas and she got her money from crooks and convicted felons," Kadalie said.[33]

South Africans, like many Americans, were shocked; Rhoda's critics were aghast.

And Leon, to Rhoda's enduring irritation, never made good on his R1000 wager.

***

In the months and years that followed, Rhoda elaborated on the reasons for Trump's victory, and the successes of his administration. Her arguments reflected her own feelings of frustration with South Africa's stagnation.

In January 2017, for example, shortly after Trump's inauguration, she described his victory, and the unexpected triumph of Brexit in the

---

33   "Trump win a victory of good over evil - Kadalie." News24.com, 9 Nov. 2016. URL: https://www.news24.com/News24/trump-win-a-victory-of-good-over-evil-kadalie-20161109. Accessed on 8 Mar. 2022.

United Kingdom, as "retaliation from citizens that feel governed by elites, who have reduced their role of self-governance and self-determination."[34] She also criticised the media for their knee-jerk opposition to Trump: "The plethora of analyses of Trump's rise is so flawed and biased that evidence to the contrary does not seem to bother pundits and the media. Every word of Trump is dissected, emblazoned across pages, and embellished when Obama said much worse."[35]

She also praised Trump's achievements in fighting crime:

> *The media, the political elite, and the ruling party love to ridicule President Donald Trump but when he got into power he immediately clipped the wings of the notorious [El Salvador] MS-13 gang that flourished under Obama's rule and terrorised US citizens.*
>
> *Heavily tattooed, the motto "Kill, Rape, Control" emblazoned across their bodies, they grew and grew the more the police ignored them.*
>
> *When Trump took over, he decimated the gang, knowing that unless the police demonstrated a show of strength, MS-13 would flourish. He pushed stringent law enforcement measures against illegal immigration and aggressive and ongoing prosecution of offenders. He did the same with Black Lives Matter.*[36]

The contrast to South Africa's own failure to fight crime, she wrote, was glaring.

Rhoda's prescience about the 2016 election, and her unique ability to explain the Trump administration, provided a boost to her South African audience, particularly at her new perch at Naspers, the consortium of Afrikaans-language newspapers.

After the *Cape Times* had decided to edit her columns more aggressively, removing some of her more controversial views, Rhoda made the switch to Afrikaans, writing a syndicated column that appeared in the daily *Die Burger* and for the weekly *Rapport*, both of which enjoyed national circulation. (She had endured a similar dispute with her editors at the *Business Day*, who refused to publish a column in which she attacked Mbeki

---

34   Rhoda Kadalie. "Trump, Brexit sagas show cracks in left-wing liberalism." *The Citizen*, 27 Jan. 2017. URL: https://www.citizen.co.za/news/opinion/1409647/trump-brexit-sagas-show-cracks-in-left-wing-liberalism/. Accessed on: 13 Apr. 2022.
35   Ibid.
36   Rhoda Kadalie. "Mbalula's police lose gang battle war." *The Citizen*, 20 Oct. 2017. URL: https://www.citizen.co.za/news/opinion/1696157/mbalulas-police-lose-gang-battle-war/. Accessed on 13 Apr. 2022.

acolyte Ronald Suresh Roberts[37]; she eventually settled on publishing a shorter version as a letter to the editor of the *Mail & Guardian*.[38]) Rhoda would often post English versions of her Afrikaans articles on PoliticsWeb, a website founded by former DA researcher James Myburgh, as well as on Facebook, the social media platform that came to play an increasingly important role in Rhoda's political engagement with the public. She also wrote columns for several years for *The Citizen*, the English-language tabloid that had once been supported clandestinely by the apartheid government, and was the sole outlet willing to take an openly pro-DA line. The paper was, ironically, popular with black readers because of its extensive sports coverage, especially of horse racing. In 2015, she would be named its "Columnist of the Year."

Her clashes with the *Cape Times* had been more than editorial in nature. The paper was part of the Independent Media group, which had been bought by a black economic empowerment firm, Sekunjalo, chaired by doctor-turned-entrepreneur Iqbal Survé. In 2014, Survé had resigned from three boards at the University of Cape Town, accusing the institution of a "lack of transformation."

In January 2015, Rhoda wrote a letter to the Mail & Guardian that was published under the title, "Iqbal Survé wasn't pushed, he jumped."[39] In it, she speculated that Survé had been asked to leave the university due to the controversy over Sekunjalo's purchase of Independent Media.

Survé, furious, sued Rhoda for defamation, asking R1 million in damages. Rhoda decided to fight back. In a memorandum to her lawyers, Rhoda explained:

> When I wrote this it was purely speculative given the course of events in the media. But I also knew as a former member of Coucil [sic] that the rash of negative media pertaining to the Independent Media would make Surve's board memberships at UCT untenable – given their stance on media and academic freedom. When I enquired about statistics demonstrating strides within UCT's transformation agenda, my official source incidentally told me that "Surve was asked to resign at the next

---

37   Rhoda Kadalie. Diary entry, 5 Jul. 2007.
38   Rhoda Kadalie. "Roberts's disservice to Mbeki." Letter to the editor. *Mail & Guardian*, 15 Jun. 2007. URL: https://mg.co.za/article/2007-06-15-july-6-to-12-2007/. Accessed on 14 Oct. 2022.
39   Rhoda Kadalie. "Iqbal Survé wasn't pushed, he jumped." *Mail & Guardian*, 30 Jan. 2015.

meetings of the UCT organisations of which he was a member." According to other sources, he apparently did so before those bodies met.[40]

The lawsuit generated a few media headlines in Survé's favor, but ultimately came to naught: he quietly dropped the case, perhaps intimidated by Rhoda's ability to attract offers of help from high-level senior counsel.[41] Later, Rhoda triumphantly quoted Survé's defunct summons against her, noting that he had claimed she disturbed his "mental tranquility."[42]

Now writing largely for an Afrikaans audience, Rhoda felt a greater sense of freedom: the Afrikaans press was not entirely free of political correctness and the pressure to conform, but self-flagellation was less of a cultural tradition than it was within the English-speaking media.

She also found she was able to play one outlet off against the other to ensure that her voice would be heard. For example, when the editor of the *Beeld*, Adriaan Basson, criticized her views on the subject of farm murders, and refused to print her reply, she turned to *The Citizen*, which was only too happy to oblige:

There is nothing worse than an Afrikaner who reckons he is more left-wing than the communists in the ANC. I don't mind criticism, but I do mind when Basson tries to portray me as an ignoramus for daring to deviate from the research of the SA Institute of Race Relations. Unlike journalists who accept research results as gospel, I dare to question even the SAIRR's assertions that farm murders are tantamount to pure criminality. To assert I have based my column on no evidence is to undermine my ability to assess events independent of the SA Institute of Race Relations, whose research I question. They must explain to me how they distinguish between general criminality and criminality of a special type.

Since Basson will not enter into a debate, here are some of the questions I should like to pose to Basson, which are also of relevance to the SAIRR. Did the SAIRR conduct victim surveys? If so, how big was the sample? Have they investigated any murders of black farmers – if there are any?

---

40   Rhoda Kadalie. Response to Combined Summons, Case No. 13229/15. 16 Aug. 2015. Personal files.

41   News24. "Survé sues political commentator for 'defamatory' letter." News24.com, 04 Aug. 2015. URL: https://www.news24.com/News24/Surve-sues-political-commentator-for-defamatory-letter-20150804. Accessed on 20 Oct. 2021.

42   Rhoda Kadalie. Comment on Facebook, 1 Jul. 2019. URL: https://www.facebook.com/rhoda.kadalie/posts/10157547817040039. Accessed on 28 Mar. 2022.

Did they interview the murderers? Did they make a thorough study of the nature and patterns of the crime and the modus operandi? Did they consider the notion of genocide based on international human rights law? Does Basson know the distinction between "volksmoorde" and "plaasmoorde"? I think not.

So when Basson says: "I will not publish your ad hominem attack on me in Beeld. There is nothing in your "uncensored" reply that gives me comfort about a factual bedrock on which your wild assertions are based", I am simply puzzled why some editors of Afrikaans papers are loathe to admit farm murders are crimes of race hate and/or revenge for land dispossession?[43]

There was no escaping the pressure of political correctness, but Rhoda found a way to connect to her readers — even if she had to jump frequently between rival publications to do so.

Rhoda's columns were also the one place in the South African media where readers could encounter a supportive view of Donald Trump — one that highlighted his policy successes, celebrated his attacks on the political establishment, and defended him from attacks such as the phony "Russia collusion" narrative, which played out endlessly on CNN and elsewhere.

Her views were controversial, and even cost her several friendships. Not that Rhoda was averse to such feuds. A few years before, she had been an active member of a private society called the "Politically Incorrect Group" (PIG), an informal group of disillusioned ANC members, former members of other political parties, academics, intellectuals, and media pundits. According to journalist Donwald Pressly, it was journalist Barry Streek who created PIG, and Pressly himself who gave the group its name and its humorous acronym.[44] Rhoda had been an early and enthusiastic member, but she lost interest in the group over time, as she felt it to be less politically incorrect than advertised. (She also believed that someone had leaked the substance of confidential discussions from PIG, despite the fact that Chatham House rules of confidentiality without consensus had applied.[45])

In many ways, Rhoda's support for Trump was simply a continuation of her trademark iconoclasm.[46] In 1996, she had told *Femina* magazine: "I'm a puritan. I'm often too honest for my own good, and I stick to my

---

43   Rhoda Kadalie. "Open letter to an editor." *The Citizen*, 6 Feb. 2015. p. 12.
44   Donwald Pressly. Personal communication with the author. 23 Feb. 2022.
45   Personal communication with the author. January 2022.
46   Rhoda Kadalie, quoted by Sharon Sorour, p. 74, ibid.

convictions even if it means I'll be unpopular." Supporting Trump was certainly unpopular, especially in a South African context. But the more criticism Rhoda received, the more she dug in — even at times, at the cost of friendships.

***

Rhoda began to devote more attention to social media, which produced new opportunities for debate — and for arguments. She had joined Facebook in 2007, largely to keep up with Julia's exploits at Harvard, and to stay in touch with family and friends. The platform proved particularly popular with South Africans, many of whom have connections that extend across a worldwide diaspora of emigrants.

But in addition to exchanging photos of family events, posting updates about Impumelelo events, sharing video of meaningful church services, and gushing over the latest South African opera stars, Rhoda found Facebook congenial as a political medium. She could react instantly to news as it happened — without the burden, or the benefit, of an editorial process.

In August 2013, for example, Rhoda posted a comment about the Gender Commission:

> *The moribund Gender Commission declares that they will enforce pay parity for women! How about dealing with the dismal position of women in society; the lack of jobs, domestic and sexual violence, femicide, correctional rapes, etc. Pay parity is easy when you do not even begin to address the things that matter. You fat cat commissioners of course would like pay parity, so that you are even more privileged. Close down that Commission and get involved in some structural interventions that matter and that will make a difference. I am sick of the verbiage of these Commissions. They are as useless as the Women's Ministry – co-opted, silent and ineffectual!*[47]

Her post elicited several comments, all approving. Rhoda commented humorously on her own post: "Shall we set up the Commission to abolish All Commissioned [sic]?"[48]

---

47 Rhoda Kadalie. Post on Facebook, 9 Aug. 2013. URL: https://www.facebook.com/rhoda.kadalie/posts/10151866394610039. Accessed on 28 Mar. 2022.
48 Ibid., comment.

She also used Facebook to complain about South Africa's frequent interruptions in basic services, especially electricity and water. During an episode of "load-shedding" by Eskom in 2014, for example, she posted: "We are in darkness in more ways than one!"[49] In another blackout that same year, she quipped: "Can anyone explain why those arseholes who are running Eskom deserve salaries of R8 million? Shouldn't we as taxpayers shed some of the load they steal from us while providing no services?"[50] She delved further into the substance of her complaints, in a later episode: "Eskom's inability to plan for the future smashes small businesses such as hairdressers, laundromats, car mechanics, Internet cafes, bakeries, etc. These people work hard to make a living unlike Eskom managers and directors who earn big bucks regardless. I spoke to Athlone hairdressers today and they just looked depressed as they called customers to cancel. This is their daily income and there is no compensation from Eskom for reducing their livelihoods."[51] The following year, she was more concise: "I know swearing is bad but when will this fucking loadshed end!"[52]

In another post, she mocked the government and the media for obsessing about racism in the face of urgent service delivery problems. In September 2014, she posted: "SA is bizarre or maybe the media is - after showing water cut offs in Johannesburg and residents complaining about a lack of water, the next news item is about 2 students at Stellenbosch University who painted their faces black with a university follow up "for a plan of action" to address this incident!!!! How about a plan of action to provide water!!!!"[53] In a comment, she added: "What SA needs is bold leadership. Those who lead us today are spineless, politically correct, and simply boring. Where are the courageous, the bold, and the unconventional. Nowhere!!! I despair."[54]

---

49 Rhoda Kadalie. Post on Facebook, 6 Mar. 2014. URL: https://www.facebook.com/rhoda.kadalie/posts/10152362014605039. Accessed on 28 Mar. 2022.

50 Rhoda Kadalie. Post on Facebook, 2 Nov. 2014. URL: https://www.facebook.com/rhoda.kadalie/posts/10152926238460039. Accessed on 28 Mar. 2022.

51 Rhoda Kadalie. Post on Facebook, 22 Nov. 2014. URL: https://www.facebook.com/rhoda.kadalie/posts/10152968239655039. Accessed on 28 Mar. 2022.

52 Rhoda Kadalie. Post on Facebook, 22 May 2015. URL: https://www.facebook.com/rhoda.kadalie/posts/10153447695730039. Accessed on 28 Mar. 2022.

53 Rhoda Kadalie. Post on Facebook, 23 Sep. 2014. URL: https://www.facebook.com/rhoda.kadalie/posts/10152826070460039. Accessed on 28 Mar. 2022.

54 Ibid., comment.

She also complained about the lack of customer service in the private sector during the Christmas holiday season, when South Africans traditionally take extended vacations: "Jonathan Jansen rightly said in one of his speeches 'South Africans are wired for laziness.' Most South Africans have left work already for the big break when officially it is the 23rd and unofficially the 15th December. I can get nothing done. Email is not working and IT staff not available. Needed cupboards made and at beginning of November people stopped taking on jobs. Productivity will remain low. It is not just the public sector that shuts down but businesses too. I despair."[55]

Not all of her comments on Facebook were complaints. In fact, most of Rhoda's posts were positive, especially those she published about Impumelelo projects and events. In March 2016, she wrote effusively: "I have the best job in SA. Rewarding social innovation and best practice I get to see the best SA has to offer across the racial and cultural divide. And I get to meet jazz art performer Sbonakaliso Ndaba who dedicates her life to teaching young people fusion and a mix of dance forms. They sing well too - to make one weep with joy."[56] Her words were accompanied by photographs of dancers from Indoni, Balu Nivison's awards-winning dance project. She also praised the work of South Africans whom she admired — such as her former tenant, journalist Marianne Thamm, for whom Rhoda retained deep respect despite their growing political differences.[57]

She frequently praised politicians — both DA and ANC — who performed well. Of Western Cape provincial minister Alan Winde, she said: "Alan Winde MEC of Economics and Tourism is the coolest politician in the country. The first Thursday of every month he invites the public to his "open house" to network with likeminded entrepreneurs and display their wares. Today the theme was Saving Water. There were many water saving innovations. WHY DONT [sic] ALL MINISTERS DO THAT????". [58]

---

55   Rhoda Kadalie. Post on Facebook, 11 Dec. 2015. URL: https://www.facebook.com/rhoda.kadalie/posts/10153915585860039. Accessed on 28 Mar. 2022.

56   Rhoda Kadalie. Post on Facebook, 10 Mar. 2016. URL: https://www.facebook.com/rhoda.kadalie/posts/10154114554645039. Accessed on 28 Mar. 2022.

57   Rhoda Kadalie. Post on Facebook, 14 Jun. 2016. URL: https://www.facebook.com/rhoda.kadalie/posts/10154376692445039. Accessed on 28 Mar. 2022.

58   Rhoda Kadalie. Post on Facebook, 2 Mar. 2017. URL: https://www.facebook.com/rhoda.kadalie/posts/10155198761255039. Accessed on 28 Mar. 2022.

In July 2017, she praised ANC parliamentarian Makhosi Khoza for defying her party and calling on President Zuma to resign, calling her a "hero of defiance."[59] (She later criticized Khoza as having "Stockholm syndrome" for failing to break with the ANC itself.[60]) In December 2017, after Cyril Ramaphosa was elected president of the ANC, Rhoda — who had become a frequent critic of his — nonetheless celebrated his victory, posting a photograph of a drink at sunset and commenting: "Here's to Cyril Ramaphosa. Well done on a difficult campaign. [61]Change is always good."

Rhoda also waded into controversial subjects, such as race and crime. When Olympic and Paralympic sprinter Oscar Pistorius was given bail after being arrested for the murder of his girlfriend (for which he was later convicted), Rhoda claimed he was being treated better than ordinary black defendants: "Today I mourn for all black murderers who could not afford legal defense to get them off the hook as easily."[62]

In commenting on an article that referred to R62 billion lost in the "black hole" of irregular spending, Rhoda savored the double entendre of the phrase "black hole": "Is this not good enough reason to vote the ANC out of office. Are they the black hole this article speaks about?"[63]

It was the kind of racial joke that only she could get away with, but as Facebook began tightening its rules on "offensive" content, Rhoda would increasingly find her content censored online. She was among those suspended from Facebook in the wake of the January 6 riot at the U.S. Capitol, for reasons that were never made clear to her. As Rhoda joked in a comment, she had been suspended by Facebook "for two days because "I called a bitch a bitch!!!".[64]

---

59   Rhoda Kadalie. "In case you missed it, Makhosi Khoza is a hero of defiance." *The Citizen*, 21 Jul. 2017. URL: https://www.citizen.co.za/news/opinion/1580039/in-case-you-missed-it-makhosi-khoza-is-a-hero-of-defiance/. Accessed on 13 Apr. 2022.

60   Rhoda Kadalie. "Makhosi Khoza and co have Stockholm syndrome, sorry to say." *The Citizen*, 15 Sep. 2017. URL: https://www.citizen.co.za/news/opinion/1654393/anc-captures-its-members/. Accessed on 13 Apr. 2022.

61   Rhoda Kadalie. Post on Facebook, 18 Dec. 2017. URL: https://www.facebook.com/rhoda.kadalie/posts/10156123722280039. Accessed on 28 Mar. 2022.

62   Rhoda Kadalie. Post on Facebook, 12 Sep. .2014. URL: https://www.facebook.com/rhoda.kadalie/posts/10152801799090039. Accessed on 28 Mar. 2022.

63   Rhoda Kadalie. Post on Facebook, 27 Nov. 2014. URL: https://www.facebook.com/rhoda.kadalie/posts/10152980680780039. Accessed on 28 Mar. 2022.

64   Rhoda Kadalie. Comment on Facebook, comment. 13 Jan. 2022. URL: https://bit.ly/3EhuS9u. Accessed on 28 Mar. 2022.

Occasionally, like many social media users, Rhoda aired personal grievances that might have been better left to private life. "Blood relatives are not chosen hence no compulsion to love them when they behave like barbarians," she said in one provocative post, during a fight with her mother.[65] She would also debate vigorously, and sometimes too venomously, with friends in the comments sections. These virtual clashes often created, or exacerbated, real-world splits with friends and family. She experimented, too, with Twitter, but found herself banned from the platform for using what Silicon Valley's censors considered offensive language.

But Rhoda persisted in her social media commentary, finding Facebook to be a platform with unique advantages.

***

Rhoda loved to talk about politics — both South African and American — on Facebook. Her writing reflected her frustration — and fascination — with events and personalities.

In the early stages of the 2016 election, she took an interest in a variety of candidates, including not only Trump and Fiorina, but also Bernie Sanders, of whom she wrote on Facebook: "Senator Bernie Sanders is the first honest socialist liberal I have heard in the Democratic Party in the USA ever. No wonder his support base is growing. I hope he defeats the devious money grabbing Hillary Clinton."[66]

A repeated theme in Rhoda's commentaries was to dispute those South Africans who praised Clinton, whom Rhoda regarded as corrupt, or who compared Jacob Zuma to Donald Trump. If anything, Rhoda opined, Zuma paralleled the Clintons. In a Facebook post in 2016, for example, she excoriated South African liberals who were keen to trash Trump: "It is so typical of liberals both here and abroad to point out Donald Trump's flaws and say nothing about Hillary Clinton's corruption. Yet here Zuma's corruption is condemned from the rooftops by the liberals. To them conservative equals evil yet they support liberal policies in SA which mostly align with Republican policies except on some social issues.

---

65   Rhoda Kadalie. Post on Facebook, 22 Jul. 2015. URL: https://www.facebook.com/rhoda.kadalie/posts/10153607028260039. Accessed on 28 Mar. 2022.

66   Rhoda Kadalie. Post on Facebook, 5 Jul. 2015. URL: https://www.facebook.com/rhoda.kadalie/posts/10153567339095039. Accessed on 28 Mar. 2022.

The lack of intellectual engagement is part of the national dumbing down trend that seems to affect so many."[67]

In another post, she took issue with commentators who claimed that both Hillary Clinton and Donald Trump were equivalent members of the American elite. "What people fail to realise is that Donald inherited money and became a successful businessman," Rhoda wrote. "The Clintons claimed that when they left the White House they were "dead broke." So where did the wealth come from? From deals with fraudsters and dictators from Russia to the Middle East to Rwanda to Kazakstan etc. which coincided with her term is as Secretary of State." She concluded: "[W]hen Zuma does this everyone calls for his head. Will someone explain the difference."[68]

Later, days before the U.S. presidential election, she reiterated the point: "Hillary becomes rich through pay to play politics. Trump is rich from building businesses yet the latter is more condemned. When Zuma steals our money to enrich himself the entire nation goes *bedonderd* [crazy]. There is no logic here."[69]

When Trump won, Rhoda was exultant. "Those whom hillary [sic] Clinton called deplorable have spoken. Government for and by the people," she proclaimed on Facebook.[70] She added, with considerable glee: "When will the media examine themselves for being so spectacularly wrong instead of still pummeling Trump. They were so palpably stupid. Polls polls lies and statistics."[71] She mocked journalists who had predicted an American economic collapse with Trump's victory, pointing to the soaring stock market. And against those who accused her of reading conservative media, she declared defiantly: "They are right. I read and listen to opposition media. And thats [sic] what I do the world over."

She wrote for *The Citizen*:

67   Rhoda Kadalie. Post on Facebook, 19 Jun. 2016 .URL: https://www.facebook.com/rhoda.kadalie/posts/10154389801720039. Accessed on 28 Mar. 2022.
68   Rhoda Kadalie. Post on Facebook, 31 Jul. 2016. URL: https://www.facebook.com/rhoda.kadalie/posts/10154510081130039. Accessed on 28 Mar. 2022.
69   Rhoda Kadalie. Post on Facebook, 3 Nov. 2016. URL: https://www.facebook.com/rhoda.kadalie/posts/10154805277870039. Accessed on 28 Mar. 2022.
70   Rhoda Kadalie. Post on Facebook, 9 Nov. 2016. URL: https://www.facebook.com/rhoda.kadalie/posts/10154822067155039. Accessed on 28 Mar. 2022.
71   Rhoda Kadalie. Post on Facebook, 9 Nov. 2016. URL: https://www.facebook.com/rhoda.kadalie/posts/10154823574495039. Accessed on 28 Mar. 2022.

I rejoiced in this victory because Trump's triumph was possible because he blew the cover of the almighty crooked and prejudiced media. He called them out where they were openly partisan and he dared "talk back" in a society, smothered in politeness, but expert at backstabbing. ... Like a master chess player, he knocked them over one by one and the more he unmasked the hypocrisy and partisanship, the more the ESTABLISHMENT attacked him, the more voters were drawn to his side. He defied political correctness, which has become a weapon of tyranny amongst the intolerant LEFT.

This election also demonstrated the deeply flawed nature of polling, how samples are drawn, who draws them, and how conventional methodologies of polling hardly hold any water, with social media, a formidable competitor. Social media, despite Zuckerberg, Google, and Twitter's pro-Clinton bias, demonstrated the power of citizen democracy and participation. Politics is no longer as predictable as it once was. The pundits and chattering classes are not to be trusted. Prejudice trumped the need for thorough academic analysis as the "power of the movement" swept America. And the failure of the media to conduct in-depth and honest reporting and investigative journalism is a serious indictment if ever there was one.

...

The media are weighed in the balance and found wanting. They need an overhaul or a massive purge because with both Brexit and the American election, we have seen that the Fourth Estate is not to be trusted. Fact-checkers are a joke and pollsters are off the wall. My experience of the media throughout this entire election is captured in Will Roger's [sic] statement: "All I know is just what I read in the papers, and that's an alibi for ignorance."[72]

But the fight was only beginning: Rhoda would be attacked, not celebrated, for her prescience.

Some of the attacks on Rhoda became more personal: in South Africa as in the United States, Trump supporters were often treated as fair game for abuse on social media. Anti-Trump views were not confined to the left: some of Rhoda's friends from the DA criticized her as well. Rhoda responded:

---

72   Rhoda Kadalie. Draft column for *The Citizen*. 11 Nov. 2016. Personal files.

Just because I think Obama wasn't a good president I get labeled very arrogantly by DA members who defected from the ANC and DA supporters generally and disillusioned ANC members as being rightwing. This from people who live opulent lives in SA's elite suburbs and who know nothing about my life and what I do and where I come from. Political arrogance is the hallmark of these liberals who think they are Left but who have no capacity for self reflection or analysis or to open themselves up to evidence that challenge their partisanship. They so easily label others to make themselves feel great because their choices have so obviously failed or not lived up to expectations.[73]

Rhoda spoke out against George Soros, her former benefactor, for his role in funding radical left-wing groups that were leading the so-called "resistance" to Trump. She wrote:

Anti-Fascist Action movements, Black Lives Matter, Media Matters, among other left-wing groups, are supported financially to undermine a political regime that refuses to be beholden to Wall Street.

To boot, the mega-wealthy George Soros has been accused of funding many of the recent antidemocratic and anti-Trump protests, many of which turned violent.

As a former recipient of his largesse, I am appalled to see what happens under the guise of "open society", often in alliance with other big donors.[74]

She also opposed feminists who protested against Trump, such as those who participated in the Women's March in several major U.S. cities on the day after Trump's inauguration. She wrote:

The Washington women's march after Trump's inauguration was the most egregious display of the mindless emotional responses to a Republican backlash. It displayed the most fundamental ignorance of Dem supporters about the role of opposition in any democracy; the legitimacy

---

73 Rhoda Kadalie. Post on Facebook, 1 Jan. 2017. URL: https://www.facebook.com/rhoda.kadalie/posts/10155010213140039. Accessed on 28 Mar. 2022.

74 Rhoda Kadalie. "A government that refuses to be controlled is treated like the enemy by the rich." *The Citizen*, 13 Oct. 2017. URL: https://www.citizen.co.za/news/opinion/1687391/a-government-that-refuses-to-be-controlled-is-treated-like-the-enemy-by-the-rich/. Accessed on 7 Apr. 2022.

of a president elected by the people and for the people; and that opposition is a constitutional mechanism to hold governments accountable.[75]

To South African feminists who questioned Rhoda's view, she replied: "They are glaringly oblivious of their own undemocratic stances of opposing Trump when they supported the Clintons and their sordid lives."[76]

While Trump's detractors in South Africa tried to link him to Zuma, to Rhoda, the more obvious parallel was between the Democratic Party and the ANC. As she commented on Facebook in February 2017: "We always speculate about what would happen should the ANC lose. If you want to know check the Total and Relentless Onslaught against Trump from the Dems, the media, academia, Silicon Valley, and Hollywood in the USA. They are probably worse than the ANC would be. The establishment must have a lot to hide."[77]

As she participated in these debates, Rhoda had an experience common to many Americans in an age of online vitriol: she lost friends, including many she had known for decades. Some attacked her in the comments on her posts about Trump; others simply "un-friended" her. On one occasion, Rhoda took offense at a comment by Lorna Levy, the wife of former ANC exile Leon Levy, about Rhoda's role as a board member of the F.W. de Klerk Foundation. When Rhoda countered by recalling human rights abuses by the ANC during its fight against apartheid, Levy wrote back: "I suppose supporting Trump hits some high moral note." She pleaded with Rhoda: "Remember our good days. I've got such a lovely speech you once made about Leon and I at our wedding anniversary party. I must show it to you some day."

---

75 Rhoda Kadalie, "Trump, Brexit sagas show cracks in left-wing liberalism," *The Citizen*, ibid.
76 Rhoda Kadalie. Post on Facebook, 21 Jan. 2017. URL: https://www.facebook.com/rhoda.kadalie/posts/10155071905220039. Accessed on 28 Mar. 2022.
77 Rhoda Kadalie. Post on Facebook, 6 Feb 2017. URL: https://www.facebook.com/rhoda.kadalie/posts/10155127433270039. Accessed on 28 Mar. 2022.

*Rhoda sports an iconic "Make America Great Again" (MAGA) hat,
a common symbol of Trump supporters (Courtesy Rhoda Kadalie)*

Rhoda replied: "Likewise I only have respect for you and Leon and hate it when you try to cast aspersions on my character. It is completely unnecessary and ruins the long valuable relationship we have."[78] That seemed to settle the spat, but other disagreements festered — especially over Rhoda's evident support for Trump.

While many liberal English-language politicians and pundits struggled to understand Trump's victory, or inveighed against it, there was considerable interest among Afrikaans readers in Trump. That was not because they shared the "white nationalist" views that were falsely ascribed to him by the left-leaning U.S. media — and which they would not have discovered in Rhoda's columns, anyway. Rather, it was because

---

78   Rhoda Kadalie and Lorna Levy. Comment on Facebook, comments, 1 Aug. 2017. URL: https://www.facebook.com/rhoda.kadalie/posts/10155727081395039. Accessed on 28 Mar. 2022.

Trump had dared to stand up to accusations of racism in advocating for America's national interests. Rhoda would also maintain that many Afrikaners were more well-read than her English-speaking audience.

For millions of Afrikaners, marginalized in a country that they had done so much to build, silenced by presumptions of racism, and saddled with collective guilt, Trump's example also suggested that they, too, might yet transcend their troubled past and rekindle some semblance of national greatness, this time in multiracial form, despite the country's sense of decline.

But Rhoda's happiness at Naspers was to be short-lived. A young *Rapport* journalist who often approached Rhoda for comment on current affairs had spoken informally to one of the staff at Impumelelo while Rhoda was abroad, who innocently suggested that Rhoda might be considering leaving the country.

The news made major headlines the next day. For Rhoda — a household name in South Africa — to be considering emigration was a major blow to her millions of fans.

At that stage, Rhoda had not, in fact, been considering emigration. Her elderly parents were shocked by the news, as was her staff and the board of Impumelelo, and she threatened to sue *Rapport* over the report.

But once the subject had been broached, Rhoda began to consider it more carefully. Julia had already given birth to two children — Rhoda's only grandchildren: a girl, Maya Hannah, in 2012; and a boy, Alexander Caleb, in 2015.

Rhoda holds newborn granddaughter Maya Hannah, February 2012, Santa Monica, California

Rhoda holds one-year-old Alexander Caleb, September 2016, Santa Monica, California

Julia had also joined the U.S. Navy as a reservist, training as a helicopter mechanic and becoming a naturalized U.S. citizen. She had enrolled in graduate studies at the Rand Corporation, where she also worked as a researcher. It was clear that Julia would not be returning to Cape Town: South Africa was too small, and the world too wide.

There was, briefly, a chance that Julia and her family might return to South Africa — at least for a brief sojourn. Once Trump won, rumors began to circulate in the media that Rhoda's son-in-law (the author) might be appointed U.S. ambassador to South Africa. Though these reports, too, were speculative, they were taken seriously enough that the South African left mobilized to oppose the appointment.

Nic Wolpe, son of Harold and Anna Marie Wolpe, who chaired the Liliesleaf Trust, a non-profit organization devoted to preserving the memory of the anti-apartheid struggle, used a fundraising visit to the U.S. to lobby Congress against the hypothetical ambassadorship.

"I told them quite candidly that sending someone like Joel Pollak as ambassador to South Africa would send relations between South Africa and the US back to the dark ages," he told Independent Media.[79] The reason? The potential ambassador's supposedly "extreme rightwing views," of which no examples were given, other than assertions that he opposed the "values of our Struggle for liberation."

The "dark ages," so to speak, seemed to have arrived, regardless. One day, Rhoda entered the U.S. consulate in Cape Town, to launch her application for a green card.

79   Shannon Ebrahim. "Disquiet over possible U.S. ambassador to SA." *The Mercury*, 23 Mar. 2017. URL: https://www.pressreader.com/south-africa/the-mercury-south-africa/20170323/281556585650193. Accessed on 20 Oct. 2021.

Chapter 19:
America

*"Am gonna spend the rest of my life with the Adorables
in Santa Monica."[1]*

Rhoda was in no great hurry to leave South Africa. She was still deeply enmeshed in the country's politics; she was still running Impumelelo; and she was still doting on her aging parents, now well into their eighties. They, too, were still active: Fenner and Joan continued their ministry to the poor, and were frequently seen in Bonteheuwel and other townships, conducting services and providing food to needy residents.

*Joan and Fenner serving soup to needy township residents, c. 2010
(Courtesy Rhoda Kadalie)*

---

1   Rhoda Kadalie. Comment on Facebook, 2 Jan. 2018. URL: https://www.facebook.com/rhoda.kadalie/posts/10156165251600039. Accessed on 13 Apr. 2022.

Rhoda: 'Comrade Kadalie, You Are Out of Order!'

At Christmas in 2011, Pastor Kadalie was on a stepladder in his home, hanging decorations, when he slipped and fell. He broke several ribs and was hospitalized for several weeks.

The fall had affected his heart. A cardiologist recommended heart surgery, suggesting that Fenner's "clean" lifestyle of abstinence from alcohol and smoking would make the procedure relatively easy. But a few days after the operation, despite the care of doctors and the prayers of the whole community, he passed away, on July 11, 2011 — after his whole family, with the exception of Rhoda, had visited the night before.

Rhoda had felt strongly that the constant visits from relatives and parishioners were not good for her father, so she had planned to visit on her own the following day, at lunchtime. Sadly, that visit was not to be — though Rhoda would cherish the fact that she had visited him the Sunday before his death.

On that occasion, Rhoda had brought her father — an avid reader of Sunday newspapers — the day's news, and a few snacks. She spent time with him, reading the papers together and discussing politics. When the cardiologist made his rounds, Rhoda commented: "What did you do to my dad? Look at him? He never looked so good, and I fear he will outlive me." The doctor agreed, mentioning that Fenner's post-operative recovery had been astounding.

That night, Rhoda attended an opera at Cape Town's Artscape theater. She did not enjoy it, and when she left, she called her siblings, who were all at the hospital. She castigated her mother for allowing the whole family, as well as the parish, to visit Fenner *en masse*.

To her great regret, he died that night — and Rhoda was in a state of disbelief for days, given how good her father had looked on her visit the previous Sunday. She had been very close to her father; before being hospitalized, *he* had visited *her* every Sunday, usually after dropping her brother Paul at his home. Fenner also called Rhoda almost every night before going to bed. She felt his passing with particular intensity as a major loss in her life.

The entire city mourned. Fenner Kadalie's funeral was a massive, day-long affair at Cape Town's City Hall, with seemingly endless hymns, and prayers, and sermons. He had touched the lives of thousands of people directly, and many more indirectly. Tributes poured in from politicians and community leaders. Julia, who was then several months pregnant, flew to Cape Town to join her family and to comfort Rhoda.

Rhoda speaks at the funeral for her father, Pastor Fenner Christian Kadalie,
at Cape Town City Hall, 2011 (Courtesy Rhoda Kadalie)

For Rhoda, the trauma of Fenner's death did not end with his passing.
Twelve months after the funeral, Rhoda and her mother visited the
Plumstead Cemetery to plan the headstone for Fenner's grave. When they
arrived, they were informed by gravediggers that Fenner had not been
buried in the allotted grave, but in an irregular plot that could neither
have a headstone nor accommodate an additional grave for Joan when she
passed away.

The news came as a shock to Joan, who had trusted the manager
of the Burial Society implicitly. He had, after all, been a colleague of her
husband as a member of the committee of the burial society, and had
promised to take charge of the funeral. But to reduce costs, he had placed
Fenner — the very pastor who had started the Burial Society, and who had
hired the manager to succeed him — in the wrong plot.

Rhoda posted mournful photos of the grave on Facebook, together
with an acerbic caption that blamed the Burial Society — and some of
her siblings:

Rhoda: 'Comrade Kadalie, You Are Out of Order!'

My father was a pastor on the Cape Flats. When he died in 2011 my mother put a beautiful marble tombstone on his grave where she would also be buried. My mother and I chose the tombstone and it gave her much pleasure to have it installed. When she died 8th December the pastor siblings had the stone removed to have her buried in the same grave. They did not have the stone professionally removed as we were led to believe and on a recent visit we discovered a grave that was busy collapsing. When we called the undertaker that they chose he said that he had the tombstone and would install it in two weeks. Today my sister and my mother's friends found the tombstone on someone else's grave, the engraved pillars with my father's name had been hacked off.[2]

Thoroughly enraged, Rhoda snapped into action. She contacted the officials in charge of the cemetery and helped Joan write a formal letter of complaint demanding an exhumation. "Given my husband's position in the community and given that he recently received the national Order of the Baobab from President Zuma for his philanthropic work in Cape Town's townships for over 50 years it is unacceptable for him to be in a grave that cannot accommodate a tombstone."[3] She contacted her siblings, too, some of whom advised her not to rock the boat. She nevertheless proceeded with threats of a lawsuit against the Burial Society.

A few months later, Rhoda and the family were granted exhumation rights, but only after the grave had dried out in summer, given the high water table at the Plumstead Cemetery. Waiting for that moment caused Joan untold anxiety. She felt robbed: her husband had not only passed away in sudden fashion, but seemed to have been cheated of his final rest.

Julia had visited in 2011 to attend Fenner's funeral; at the end of 2013, she returned for a holiday visit with her family. There were happy reunions, and the extended Kadalie clan made their acquaintance with Maya, nearly two years old, who delighted in singing, dancing, and playing with Rhoda.

---

2   Rhoda Kadalie. Post on Facebook, 9 Jul. 2016. URL: https://www. facebook.com/rhoda.kadalie/posts/10154445981965039. Accessed on 28 Mar. 2022.

3   Letter from Joan Kadalie to Cheryl Wyngard. 19 Jul 2012.

Four generations of Kadalie women: Rhoda (seated) with mother Joan, daughter Julia, and granddaughter Maya, Cape Town, 2013 (Courtesy Rhoda Kadalie)

Rhoda plays with Maya on Clifton Beach, Cape Town, 2013

*Julia and Rhoda sing and dance with Maya in Rhoda's living room,
University Estate, 2013*

But after a few short weeks, Julia returned to Los Angeles, leaving Rhoda alone in the house on Fryde Street. And a year later, Joan reported that she had not been feeling well. She had always suffered from mild hypochondria, and was constantly seeing doctors in her later years; she had even had her knees replaced, in what Rhoda suspected was an unnecessary surgery. But this time, Joan's suspicions were well-founded — though rather shocking: she had advanced lung cancer, despite never having smoked a day in her life.

The prospects for recovery were dim; surgery would not solve the problem, and Joan did not want to endure the rigors of chemotherapy. So she simply decided to endure the progression of the disease, first staying with Rhoda in the apartment at her house, then returning to her own home in Athlone.

She passed away there after several months, suffering quietly but living out her last days in the home she and Fenner had filled with memories, photographs, and the bric-a-brac of decades.

With her parents gone, Rhoda began to consider her own future. She felt somewhat alienated from some of her siblings, who had became embroiled in disagreements over Joan's estate and the ownership of her home. Moreover, Rhoda was alone in the house in University Estate, leaving the apartments empty after a succession of tenants. She did not feel safe: crime remained high in South Africa, and she felt she was a potential target, as a single woman on her own.

She had already endured several attempted burglaries and muggings, including an incident in which she had fought off a mugger near the University of Cape Town in 2003.[4] But once she was alone at home, she felt even more vulnerable. One night in May 2014, a burglar entered while Rhoda was in her bed, and began rummaging through the house. Thankfully, he left her alone, but departed with the new iPad that Julia had bought her.

Rhoda recounted the chilling experience in her diary:

> I went to bed at 2 am, struggling to refine a column. Before I went to bed I heard Paul [her brother] shuffling downstairs. At 3:50 am I woke up to the sound of creaking floor boards. I lay immobilised for at least 3 mins as the sounds became more and more real. I got up walked to the passage & saw a man in a crouched position on the carpet in the foyer of the sitting room. He wore a khaki beanie and khaki-ish jersey. I screamed, he ran to my bedroom, I smashed the door in his face! Pushed the panic button; opened the door again realising that the door key was on the outside. Face to face with him, I grabbed the key, smashed the door in his face & locked myself inside the bedroom. I opened my bedroom window, contemplating to jump but I knew I would damage my legs for life so I screamed Help! At least 20 times until I saw windows going on and people appearing. Marthine [a neighbor] shouted to me to throw out the key. I shouted that key was in the sitting room. Giving intruder a lot of time to plan his escape. He knew police could not get in. By some adrenaline rush I remember that my spare key was in my bag. I threw it out the window & neighbors police & Chubb [private security], piled in. The intruder had come in through kitchen window. He escaped thru kitchen window again. Police shouted loudly that they would not search area, had no torch, were just useless. They told me that 40 mins before a similar incident happened at 88 Ritchie Street where an 11 yr old boy was terrorised by "cat burglar." The guy is an absolute pro — did not disturb the scale, walked past me while I was asleep, etc. Whole experience reduced me to jelly, a dysfunctional pulp.

It was not the last burglary Rhoda would experience. Her car and her office were both broken into in her last years in South Africa. Living alone was no longer a safe proposition — not in the country South Africa had become, at least not for a middle-aged woman on her own.

---

4   Rhoda Kadalie. Diary entry, 18 Oct. 2003.

Rhoda also dearly missed her daughter, and the growth of her grandchildren, whom she only saw once a year. When Julia graduated with a Master of Philosophy from the Pardee Rand Graduate School in Santa Monica, California, Rhoda yearned to be there to celebrate: "Congratulations darling Julia. Regrets for missing so many milestones in your wonderful life. You are simply the best any mother could want," she posted on Facebook.[5] The thought of missing more of those milestones was too heavy a burden to bear. She knew she played a unique role in South African politics, but as she commented in August 2017, on a post full of photos of her grandchildren playing at a birthday party: "Leaving these kids behind for SA's toxic politics is not worth it."[6]

It was time to move on.

Rhoda put her house on the market, but no one wanted to match her price, or come anywhere near it. Then, suddenly, a realtor who was looking for a house for clients who were interested in the neighborhood heard from some of Rhoda's neighbors that she had been looking to sell. He called Rhoda — but since she did not know him, she did not trust him. A few months later, he called again, asking to see the house. She relented — and when he came to see the house, he found it ideal. His clients paid the asking price.

Rhoda packed up the home she once fought to keep, placing her most prized possessions in storage, sorting through years of files, books, pamphlets, and newspaper clippings that she had stored in the crawl space adjacent to the apartment and the garage.

She commented on Facebook on February, 26, 2016: "Have sold the love of my life and moved out today to live a simpler life. Sad but glad cos that house was too big for me alone."[7] She added: "The best is that two sweet brothers bought the house and I felt happy to release it to them. I chose my successors with care. I feel happily unburdened. That house was ginormous for me alone."[8]

5   Rhoda Kadalie. Post on Facebook, 19 Jun. 2016. URL: https://www.facebook.com/photo/?fbid=10154389839670039. Accessed on 28 Mar. 2022.

6   Rhoda Kadalie. Comment on Facebook, 1 Aug. 2017. URL: https://www.facebook.com/rhoda.kadalie/posts/10155727289935039. Accessed on 28 Mar. 2022.

7   Rhoda Kadalie. Post on Facebook, 26 Feb. 2016. URL: https://www.facebook.com/rhoda.kadalie/posts/10154085092900039. Accessed on 28 Mar. 2022.

8   Ibid., comment.

She moved into an apartment behind a friend's house in Pinelands for several months before finding an apartment in a complex in the leafy suburb of Newlands.

The next challenge was Impumelelo. Rhoda did not want the institution, which she had spent fifteen years building, to fall into disrepair. She considered several options for its future. The first was an attempted partnership with the Bertha Center, part of the University of Cape Town. But as Chris Mingo recalled,[9] while UCT was eager to exploit Impumelelo's years of careful research and case studies, it was less interested in a working partnership to continue Impumelelo's investment in community organizations. The same was true at Rhoda's alma mater, UWC, which lacked the "vision," in Mingo's words, to guide the project.

Eventually, Rhoda reached an agreement with Stellenbosch University to absorb Impumelelo into its organizational structure. She moved Impumelelo's offices to the relative calm and quiet of Stellenbosch, leaving behind the bustle of the Idasa building at the corner of Spin Street and Parliament Street.

Through Impumelelo, Rhoda had made a profound contribution to the building of a new South Africa. As much as she loved the organization, she let it go.

It was later to die what Mingo called a "tragic death,"; in Mingo's version of events, Stellenbosch proved to be just like the other contenders in its willingness to exploit Impumelelo's research without adopting its stewardship of community organizations. It was a "*regte* [real] *Broederbond* setup," Mingo recalled, alluding to the secret Afrikaner society that wielded power behind the scenes under apartheid. The old network, he claimed, would not tolerate the autonomy the organization needed to function, leading it to it eventually being incorporated into another, more established charity, the Community Chest.

In some ways, South Africa was not ready for Impumelelo. "It was leaps and bounds ahead" of thinking about development projects, Mingo recalled. "She was ahead of her time. She was a visionary — bloody hell!"

***

Rhoda was restless, in semi-retirement. Her application for a green card had been delayed by politics. In 2012, facing re-election, President Obama had launched a new program called Deferred Action for Childhood Arrivals (DACA), which allowed illegal aliens who had been brought to the country

---

9   Chris Mingo, ibid.

as children to apply for protection from deportation. Republicans were furious, claiming that Obama had exceeded his constitutional authority, abusing his power of prosecutorial discretion to circumvent Congress.

Some 800,000 people applied to DACA, clogging the bureaucratic machine. Many immigrants who were trying to enter the country legally had to endure lengthy delays.[10]

Eventually, Rhoda's green card was approved. But it never arrived: months after the government had dispatched it to Rhoda, at Julia's address, it was missing.

During a visit to the U.S., Rhoda went to U.S. Citizenship and Immigration Services (USCIS) to inquire about the missing document. An agent, stamping her documents, whispered that a criminal syndicate was suspected of stealing green cards from envelopes in the mail.

Finally, a replacement arrived. And in late 2017, Rhoda began making preparations to leave Cape Town — her birthplace, her home — for the last time.

Still, leaving was not easy. "South Africa does not want me to retire," she quipped.[11] She added: "I am now at the end of my career. My attitude is been there, done that. So, now my attitude is you can not return, it's retirement. In anthropology, I taught my students about rites of passage. It's a French phrase, the *rites de passage*, and I came to a point where I admit Santa Monica is my departure hall."[12]

In a coincidental irony, Rhoda's mentor, former UWC Rector Dick van der Ross, passed away in December 2017, weeks before she was due to leave the country. She attended his memorial service, and noted on Facebook: "A Vice-Chancellor par excellence Uncle Dick. Was an honour to have you as a colleague and boss. Today you brought together UWC alumnae from far and wide to honour you. You will leave a big void in our lives but an even bigger legacy by which we can celebrate your life and leadership."[13]

---

10   Julia Preston. "Program Benefiting Some Immigrants Extends Visa Wait for Others." *New York Times*, 8 Feb. 2014. URL: https://www.nytimes.com/2014/02/09/us/program-benefiting-some-immigrants-extends-visa-wait-for-others.html?hp&_r=2. Accessed on 21 Oct. 2021.
11   Rhoda Kadalie, quoted by Brümmer, ibid.
12   Ibid.
13   Rhoda Kadalie. Comment on Facebook, 22 Dec. 2017. URL: https://www.facebook.com/rhoda.kadalie/posts/10156134603145039. Accessed on 28 Mar. 2022.

There were innumerable going-away parties and toasts to Rhoda, thrown by heartbroken friends who understood why she was leaving but were distraught to see her go. Balu Nivison, speaking for many in Rhoda's close-knit circle, was "devastated" when Rhoda left.[14] Her voice in South African politics seemed irreplaceable; she remained dear to so many, through all the ups and downs of her relationships with friends and family.

Her colleagues, while sad to see her go, understood her desire to be near family. And some also understood that she had outgrown the country — a country that seemed to be stagnating, politically and otherwise. Mingo declared: "South Africa was not ready for someone of Rhoda's character, and will never be, simply because of who she is, and her integrity."

Rhoda wrapped up her affairs by resigning from the many boards and organizations on which she had served: the Hugo Lambrechts Music Centre Trust, the Cape Town Holocaust Centre Board of Trustees, the Board of the South African Jewish Museum, the Molteno Brothers Trust, and others. Of the latter, she wrote: "The 16 years spent with this highly effective and well-run organisation has [sic] probably been one of the most enlightening and edifying experiences of any I have had in my long career that spans several academic positions, board memberships, and various professions."[15]

She penned a similar letter of resignation to Impumelelo. She wrote:

I leave Impumelelo with great sadness not only for the enormous resources we have built up over the decades, but also for the formidable network of award-winning social entrepreneurs that have become friends and partners of Impumelelo. To extricate myself from that network is indeed difficult and sad. I wish to thank the Board of Trustees for their sterling support to me as executive director and my colleagues since inception. To the Impumelelo team I owe a deep sense of gratitude for making my success also their success.[16]

Rhoda also sent several farewell messages to friends and colleagues, which provoked a wave of responses, many of them raw in their sense of loss about her impending departure.

She wrote, for example, to Marianne Thamm, her former tenant and dear friend, whose adopted daughters had been the flower girls at Julia's

---

14   Balu Nivison. Interview 28 Feb. 2022.
15   Rhoda Kadalie. Letter of Resignation as Trustee from Molteno Brothers Trust. 6 Jan. 2018. Personal files.
16   Rhoda Kadalie. Letter of Resignation as Executive Director from the Impumelelo Social Innovations Centre. 15 Oct. 2017. Personal files.

wedding. Hinting at some of their emerging political differences Rhoda said: "My emigration deadline looms but before I go let me thank you for being a friend, mentor, and sparring partner second to none over the many years I have known you. ... You are part of Julia and me and even if you want to dump us, you are stuck somewhere in our hearts and history!" She added: "I leave having contributed at least a millionth to the downfall of Zuma. Under Cyril things will improve despite the challenges and the ANC's antediluvian rhetoric and backwardness. Anything is better than Zuma so things are looking up."[17]

Rhoda with journalist and friend Marianne Thamm at
Rhoda's 60th birthday party, 2013 (Courtesy Rhoda Kadalie)

Thamm replied:

My heart breaks to lose you physically in this space. You have contributed so, so much to what and who we are. I have always loved you dearly even when we might have disagreed. You are principled and fearless, you are a pioneer ... you are a wonderful mother and I understand that you must now go and be a wonderful grandmother. This country is the poorer for our losing you. You have been an inspiration and a mentor as

---

17   Rhoda Kadalie. Letter to Marianne Thamm. 20 Jan. 2018.

well as a friend and while we may not have seen enough of each other your presence was always reassuring for me.

I shall miss you ... and shall continue to be inspired by your bravery. One day, if either of my gorgeous daughters becomes a writer, which I pray they do not, I will urge them to write about you.

Love to all, look after yourself and bon voyage on this new and exciting journey in your life.[18]

John and Anne Field, who had been the Kadalie family's neighbors in Mowbray, and who had been surrogate parents to Rhoda even after the forced removals, wrote:

We have both been extremely proud of all that you have achieved and what you have become and it has been a pleasure knowing you and your family. You have always been very generous towards us and we were always very grateful that we could entrust our children to you and know that they were well cared for and loved. Thank you for all that you did for us and for all the things that you have given to us.

You will be greatly missed by your many friends and admirers in Cape Town. Whenever and wherever we were with you people would come up to you and greet you with affection. We shall miss you Rhoda and wish you everything of the best in the new phase of your life. Stay in touch and let us know how you get on in America. Please send us your contact details when you have them.[19]

Many mourned the loss of Rhoda's voice in South African politics, in which she had played a crucial role as one of the few people courageous and credible enough to criticize the post-apartheid government, creating room for more timid voices.

As Freddie Engelbrecht later recalled: "She is a well-balanced person, she's knowledgeable, she's very intelligent, she's fearless. ... Politicians perceived her as a troublemaker. ... She was passionate about the work she was doing, and tried to assist people. She wrote many articles ... she is a decent woman. Whether she was with Impumelelo, or an activist, it was always about service delivery to the most vulnerable, and to the poor people. I was under the impression that she will be the

---

18   Marianne Thamm. Letter to Rhoda Kadalie. 21 Jan. 2018.
19   John and Anne Field. Letter to Rhoda Kadalie. 15. Jan. 2018.

president of the country, but unfortunately she went to the USA to ... be a good grandmother."[20]

Christina Teichmann of the liberal Konrad Adenauer Stiftung, a German public policy group promoting classical liberal principles, wrote to Rhoda:

While I fully understand your motivation – to be close to your family and lovely grandchildren – I always saw and still see you as an integral part of SA 's vibrant civil society.

You will be missed very much – not only by your friends but also by people who might have differed with you in the past.

Your frank and outspoken personality has always made an impact in debates and inspired me personally.

The combination of a sharp mind and a genuine care for others is rare.[21]

One friend predicted that Rhoda would have the same impact on American politics that she had on South African politics:

You will be missed for your sharp, incisive, sometimes too straight-forward tongue or pen ... that was far mightier than the sword.

...

The Americans are going to love you ... hate you and enjoy you ... their gain. Your family [are] going to enjoy ... the wise words of grandma. Mum who has transcended culture, race ... gender and class ... a true human being![22]

Rhoda was not so sure: she was exhausted from decades of work, and simply wanted to retire to become what she called a "brain dead" grandmother.[23]

Those who had benefited from Rhoda's support and guidance in social development projects were particularly pained by her departure. At a special gathering in the farming community of Grabouw, among those who had benefited from Rhoda's stewardship of the Molteno Brothers' philanthropic grants, Betsie Ryke offered a tribute to Rhoda, in which she recalled Rhoda's visit to the Rural Arts Network:

---

20 Engelbrecht, ibid.
21 Christina Teichmann. Letter to Rhoda Kadalie. 15 Jan. 2018.
22 Linda de Vries. Letter to Rhoda Kadalie. 12 Jan. 2018.
23 Rhoda Kadalie, quoted by Brümmer, ibid.

Her response to me after the visit made for one of the most special memories that I will always treasure and carry in my heart and will stand out forever. Here I was — a white woman, and even worse, an Afrikaans woman — coming from a privileged background versus Rhoda, a liberal political activist that has been wronged and oppressed by the system for years, and she makes me feel appreciated and validated. Especially in a time when the cultural group that I belong to, were made to feel useless, disposable and to be blamed for all that goes wrong in this country.

...

You have been a wonderful mentor, critic, friend, and soulmate to so many in this room.[24]

For Rhoda, the feeling was mutual. She wrote a parting note to Betsie in response:

My emigration deadline looms and while I'm preparing everything for freighting let me thank you for the wonderful friendship we have developed and enjoyed over the few years I know you. You have become a true and loyal friend that I shall miss enormously. Your energy and commitment laced with your contrarian humour attracted me to you so that I feel I'm losing a sister on my way out the country. So if you need some intelligent conversation with a brain-dead granny please write.

...

May God bless you richly in your service to Grabouw's children. There is no greater privilege than to serve our children.[25]

Rhoda penned a similar heartfelt note to Justa Niemand in Stellenbosch:

Before I leave I must thank you for initiating a conversation with me sometime ago that blossomed into a very special friendship of mentorship, support, understanding and love over the short period I have gotten to know you. Already a deep bond exists that is irreplaceable, forged by similar origins, similar job experiences, similar irritations and dissimilar tastes! You were led to find me by Divine providence.

---

24   Bestie Ryke. Speech in honor of Rhoda Kadalie, as prepared for delivery. January 2018.
25   Rhoda Kadalie. Letter to Betsie Ryke. 14 January 2018.

Rhoda: 'Comrade Kadalie, You Are Out of Order!'

Wie sal ek bel om te ontlaai? Om te skinder? Om net plain nasty te wees[26] without being judged? I shall miss you enormously and I hope distance will be no barrier.

She was leaving, too, the memories of friends past, who had shaped her life in South Africa, of whom there would be few reminders in the U.S. One was Dr. Katherine Chubb, a young radical intern who had died tragically in April 1994 in Windhoek, Namibia. Another was Beverly Knipe, a young scholar who died suddenly in 2011. There were too may such stories — too many people, especially women, gone before their time. Their passing made Rhoda keenly aware that life was short. Not that she wanted to live forever: she often said she preferred to die at 70 than to spend decades in old age. But time was short, and she wanted to be with Julia, and the babies.

She told the Afrikaans press, with typical dark humor: "I really wanted to enjoy our democracy, just for a few years. Zuma and Thabo did not allow us to enjoy our democracy. I remember the euphoria of 1995 and 1996, and it soon seeped away.

"But I am also leaving South Africa on a positive note. I think things are going to get better.

"Nothing is worse than Zuma."[27]

And then, at the end of January, Rhoda boarded a flight, and left South Africa. And for the first time, when she landed at LAX, she breezed through immigration, green card in hand.

***

Rhoda settled quickly into life in the U.S. She moved into the Pollak home, a four-bedroom, garden-level condominium near downtown Santa Monica, a picturesque town on the Pacific coast, surrounded by Los Angeles on three sides.

"Granny Rhoda" took up residence in the guest room, where Maya, nearly six years old, had slept. She moved in together with her two-and-a-half-year-old brother, Alexander, though they spent hours with Rhoda in her room, and especially in her bed, watching television together. Rhoda kept a set of paints handy, and prodded the children to produce endless pictures of princesses and dragons. She reveled in her role as an "anarchist" granny, teaming up with the children at times to upset the

---

26   [Whom should I call to unburden myself? To gossip? Just to be nasty]
27   Rhoda Kadalie, quoted by Brümmer, ibid.

household order established by their parents. Rhoda and the children invented a game called "sockey hockey," which involved whacking a ball of socks with sticks across the living and dining room, glass vases and lamps be damned. In one prank, Rhoda wrapped Alexander entirely in toilet paper and let him loose in the hallway. "I'm the grandmother rolling around on the ground, I take my grandson on excursions nearby. I am the grandmother who plays rough and dirty," she observed.[28]

The children delighted in the presence of their grandmother, who could be strict as she oversaw math homework and piano lessons, but brought an irreverent and spontaneous delight to life in a household with busy parents.

Rhoda kept a letter Maya wrote her, complete with hearts and stick-figure self-portraits:

Dear grany

thank you for bieing the best grany in the whole intier world. every thing you do helps me lern.

you alwase stik up for me. and you help me with my math, Play with me and wosh my hair properly. and do everything that helps our family.

ador and Love Maya

heartface

Young Alexander's sentiments were similar. She walked him to the local park, teaching him to play soccer among the homeless people lounging in the shade, noting that Alexander displayed an early preference for kicking with his left foot. She indulged his minor acts of disobedience: the two of them were kindred rebel spirits.

Two things were markedly different from life in Cape Town. One was that Rhoda was actually able to walk around outside — whether to go to the grocery store, or to church nearby, or to take the children to the park.

Walking in her neighborhood in Cape Town had been nearly impossible. The streets of University Estate, on the slope of Devil's Peak, were so steep, and so high above the rest of the town, that walking was simply difficult.

Moreover, South Africa had become too dangerous for many people, especially women, to feel safe walking down the street, even in a residential neighborhood. One night, a man scaled the highest wall of her house in

---

28   Ibid.

Cape Town and broke in at 4:00 a.m. She believed that it was a miracle she survived that ordeal unscathed. It was one of the most important experiences in influencing her decision to leave the country.

Rhoda had bought a car, a Subaru sedan, on a previous visit. But she decided not to drive, and found that she did not miss doing so.

The other major difference was the availability of water. Rhoda had left Cape Town during the worst drought in its history, when the city was close to running out of water. For months, she was aghast at the water profligacy of Californians, who lived in an equally arid climate.

When she wanted to go somewhere, and Julia had the car, Rhoda found it easy to take the bus, or the new Santa Monica train, or — if all else failed — an Uber or a Lyft. The Los Angeles Philharmonic Orchestra also ran its own system of shuttle buses from all points in the city to the Walt Disney Concert Hall. Rhoda attended concerts frequently, as well as performances at the Los Angeles Opera. She also enjoyed taking the bus from Santa Monica to Venice Beach, where L.A.'s most interesting characters could be found on any given afternoon.

She negotiated the delicate balance of a religious household with members of two different faiths. At Christmas, she decorated her bedroom with a small Christmas tree, and hung stockings on the faux fireplace. She also mastered the Jewish dietary laws of *kashrut*, shopping for kosher-certified products and keeping dishes for dairy and meat separate. "My daughter respects who I am and I respect who they are," she said. "I keep the Sabbath with them whenever I want and on Sundays I go to a Baptist church. We are a happy, confused family of hybrids."[29]

Rhoda had developed late-night habits, and maintained that rhythm in her new surroundings, following late news broadcasts on the television that Julia had installed in her room. When the children were not watching their own programs, the channel was set to Fox News, where Rhoda followed American politics with interest.

Speeches by President Donald Trump, which often aired in full, were a highlight. Rhoda enjoyed his audacious wit, and the rowdy spectacle, though she would also offer critiques of his performance. The grandchildren were divided over Trump. Maya, who had "voted" for Trump in a preschool election, loved him. Alexander, a contrarian by nature, declared himself a Democrat — though he giggled at Trump's antics.

In 2019, Rhoda and the children attended a speech by Trump, in person, accompanying the author to the annual leadership conference of the Republican Jewish Coalition in Las Vegas, Nevada. Trump and Vice

29   Ibid.

President Mike Pence both addressed the meeting, which was opened to the public in a ballroom at the Venetian hotel, and turned into a rally-style event.

Rhoda in a family photograph, Will Rogers State Historic Park,
Los Angeles, 2016 (Courtesy Trisha Jochen)

The children endured several warmup speakers, growing increasingly bored, until Trump finally appeared. Shortly after he began speaking, a group of anti-Israel protesters, one wearing a swastika, leapt to their feet and stood atop their chairs, shouting, three rows in front of the children. Security arrived and dragged the protesters away. The children were frightened by the commotion, until Trump joked about the hecklers: "Go home to mommy!" The crowd laughed, and so did they; it was a comment Alexander would repeat for months afterwards.

Rhoda enjoyed taking care of the children, often picking Maya up from the nearby public school, and volunteering at Alexander's Jewish preschool, run by the family's rabbi and his family. For the benefit of friends in South Africa, she posted an account of one of her trips, via Uber, to preschool with Alex:

Black Uber driver: what part of India are you from?

Me: I'm not Indian. I'm South African classified coloured under apartheid.

Rhoda: 'Comrade Kadalie, You Are Out of Order!'

Driver: why do you say that? You're definitely Indian. If not then you must have Indian blood.

Me: my paternal grandfather was a Malawian who married a Malay woman from the Cape. My maternal grandfather was white who married a brown woman like me.

Driver: I studied anthropology and would love to trace your family tree. So why are you here?

Me: I've emigrated from SA a year and a half ago. My daughter lives here and won't return to SA. I have two grandchildren.

Uber driver: what does she look like.

Me: she's a mongrel like me. Her father is German. Her husband is White American from Chicago.

By this time we're almost at Alexander's preschool.

Uber driver: whoa I'm dying to see what that grandson looks like.

We get into the car.

Uber driver: wow he's white and blonde BUT I love the curly hair. The curly hair is proof of mixed ancestry.

We reach our destination and the uber driver anthropologist regrets the end of the conversation.

So it goes every day. Guessing where I'm from![30]

On weekend nights, Rhoda was often a babysitter, allowing the grateful parents to escape to a local pub or restaurant.

Julia, who had begun teaching economics part-time at Pepperdine University, soon found a new job as a labor economist with a local startup company that specialized in matching job-seekers with employers. She continued her Navy reserve duty, and the family, with Rhoda in tow, occasionally accompanied her on weekend trips to San Diego, staying at local hotels.

But the condominium began to feel crowded, with three adults and two children in four small bedrooms — one of which was used as

---

30   Rhoda Kadalie. Comment on Facebook, 15 Aug. 2019. URL: https://www. facebook.com/rhoda.kadalie/posts/10157670680080039. Accessed on 28 Mar. 2022.

an office. Julia found a home in Pacific Palisades, a picturesque coastal neighborhood, just north of Santa Monica.

Rhoda assembles a construction set in the new family home in
Pacific Palisades, California, c. 2020

The home included a semi-detached wing with two bedrooms and a separate bathroom, which became Rhoda's new residence. Outdoors, there was plenty of yard space, where Rhoda taught the children to play catch, and tennis; and tended a vegetable patch with her son-in-law. And just down the street, Rhoda made a rare find: a corner store that stocked South African goods, run by a fellow immigrant, an Indian South African named Ronny Naidoo.

"We've just moved from Santa Monica to Pacific Palisades. I went exploring and down the road I discovered Ronnie's [sic] store. Guess what I found? Ronnie [sic] is a SA and stocks rooibos tea, Mrs Balls, Tex and Cadbury chocolates, marmite, etc etc," she posted exuberantly on Facebook, together with a photo of Ouma Rusks, a familiar South African breakfast staple.[31]

Retirement was looking good.

***

From a distance, Rhoda continued to write columns for a South African audience. Having lost faith long before in the established English-language media, including the left-leaning upstart known as the Daily Maverick, she had begun writing for the Afrikaans-language online publication, Maroelamedia. Her work was admired — though locals still missed her voice as an active participant in public affairs.

"We need people who are not scared to talk," Robert Goff recalled later.[32] "We need people who are straight-on, head-on, who say it as it is." Rhoda was one of the few such people in South Africa, he noted with regret.

Rhoda continued to comment, from afar, on South African affairs. Noting the emergence of a new academic discipline at UCT, she quipped: "UCT is offering a MPhil [Master of Philosophy] in Justice and Inequality. Are political slogans becoming disciplines? Isn't this just plain old sociology?"[33] She continued her lifelong interest in political puns, both about South Africa and the U.S. "Remember when Mugabe insulted gays. Activists picketed 'To Mugay or not to Mugaybe.' Another said "Zimbabwe needs a Queen," she wrote in one post.[34] In another, she captioned a photo of former U.S. President Barack Obama and Canadian Prime Minister Justin Trudeau, who had recently admitted wearing "blackface" costumes as a student: "Black Facade and Black Face (Obama and Trudeau)."[35]

As disillusioned as many South Africans became with their politics in the years of "state capture," Rhoda was encountering her own

31 Rhoda Kadalie. Comment on Facebook, 9 Nov. 2019. URL: https://www.facebook.com/rhoda.kadalie/posts/10157924183410039. Accessed on 28 Mar. 2022.
32 Robert Goff. Interview 25 Feb. 2022.
33 Rhoda Kadalie. Comment on Facebook, 6 Sep. 2019. URL: https://www.facebook.com/rhoda.kadalie/posts/10157728717090039. Accessed on 28 Mar. 2022.
34 Rhoda Kadalie. Comment on Facebook, 6 Sep. 2019. URL: https://www.facebook.com/rhoda.kadalie/posts/10157727385140039. Accessed on 28 Mar. 2022.
35 Rhoda Kadalie. Comment on Facebook, 16 Oct. 2019. URL: https://www.facebook.com/rhoda.kadalie/posts/10157846849095039. Accessed on 28 Mar. 2022.

disappointment in the U.S. She watched the impeachment of President Trump with great consternation in late 2019 and early 2020. She could not understand how, in a supposedly advanced democracy, which South Africa had sought to emulate, the legislature could be allowed to abuse its power and pursue the removal of a president with no regard for due process. She noted on Facebook: "SA is without electricity. The USA has electricity but political madness of epic proportions in Congress!"[36]

The Democratic Party presidential primary was also a frequent topic of conversation in the household, as a field of left-wing contenders vied for the favor of the party base, embracing outdated socialist policies and divisive identity politics — both of which were failing in South Africa.

And then, suddenly, in March 2020, everything came to a screeching halt. The coronavirus pandemic arrived from China and began to spread rapidly. President Trump, under mounting pressure to take drastic action, shut down international travel and urged Americans to stay home when possible, promising that the pause would only need to last "fifteen days to slow the spread."

A few days later, the governor of California shut down the state's economy. The mayor of Los Angeles required residents to wear masks at all times — even outside. As a beautiful spring blossomed outside, the world retreated into a fearful hibernation.

For Rhoda, the lockdown was intolerable. She was suddenly cut off from the things she most enjoyed, and the opportunity to socialize. Tickets to the symphony, or to the theater, were suddenly useless. Even casual conversations with neighbors became impossible: in the early weeks of the pandemic, people would avoid one another, even walking down the street.

Eventually, Rhoda refused to wear a mask when walking outside. Sometimes, strangers would scold her: in left-wing Los Angeles, support for draconian coronavirus policies was strongest — boosted, in part, by a sense that compliance was a form of political resistance to Trump.

The entire experience reinforced a sense of isolation. The one bright spot was the opportunity to spend time with the grandchildren, whose schools were closed. While their parents were preoccupied with work, Rhoda would supervise the children's math and reading lessons from their Kumon tutoring program. She also kept them entertained with endless art projects, or baking, or games of basketball in the driveway. They could not visit their friends, but they could play with their grandmother.

---

36   Rhoda Kadalie. Comment on Facebook, 12 Dec. 2019. URL: https://www.facebook.com/rhoda.kadalie/posts/10158030655525039. Accessed on 28 Mar. 2022.

*Rhoda works on a column while supervising the
children attending school remotely, via Zoom, 2020*

While many children struggled with the restrictions of the pandemic, Maya and Alexander thrived in their new home, thanks to Rhoda's fortuitous intervention.

At the end of May, riots broke out in cities and towns across the U.S., in the wake of the murder of a black man, George Floyd, in an encounter with police in Minneapolis, Minnesota. The unrest was partly an expression of legitimate outrage, but soon became a destructive free-for-all, fueled in part by frustration with the coronavirus lockdowns, but also by the country's toxic, divisive political environment.

Rhoda's initial response to Floyd's death was the same as that of millions of people: "Police officer Derek Chauvin living up to his chauvinist swine name," she said on Facebook.[37] But she was shocked by the looting and violence that swept the nation, starting in Minneapolis and spreading rapidly to other cities — including Los Angeles.

---

37   Rhoda Kadalie. Comment on Facebook, 29 May 2020. URL: https://www.facebook.com/rhoda.kadalie/posts/10158639389385039. Accessed on 28 Mar. 2022.

*Rhoda teaches Alexander to paint, one of their
favorite pandemic pastimes, 2021*

Rhoda and the family watched in horror on live video as their former neighborhood in Santa Monica was ransacked by looters, as police did nothing. In the weeks that followed, on occasional errands to Santa Monica, the children would be shocked by the graffiti and the boarded-up buildings.

Even Pacific Palisades was threatened. In early June, fearing the spread of riots, the mayor of Los Angeles called out the National Guard. They took up positions in the upscale central area of Pacific Palisades, known as the "village," where Rhoda had frequently taken the bus to shop before the pandemic. High-end stores boarded up their windows; armored personnel carriers were parked on Sunset Boulevard.

Meanwhile, the "mostly peaceful protests," as Democrats and some news networks called them, continued across the country. The mobs defaced or tore down statues and monuments— including monuments to those who had fought slavery. In Philadelphia, a statue of abolitionist Matthias Baldwin was defaced in red with the word: "colonizer." Rhoda, aghast, responded on Facebook: "Looters in Philadelphia vandalized the statue of famous abolitionist Matthias Baldwin, who employed black people when many were enslaved. No cure for stupid."[38]

Rhoda felt as if she were watching a repeat of the worst days of the unrest in South Africa. The difference: the United States had democracy, and a constitution; it had even elected a black president, twice. To her, the outrage felt artificial, an overreaction fueled by politics, and the manic desire of Democrats to be rid of Donald Trump — by force, if necessary.

Her comments on social media became more and more dismissive of the Black Lives Matter movement. She was especially opposed to the ritual confessions that police, politicians, and other authority figures were expected to make, denouncing their own "white privilege" and "taking a knee" with the crowd. When the movement reached beyond the issue of police brutality, and engulfed the broad sweep of American history, she had seen enough. When the Museum of Natural History in New York decided to remove a statue of Teddy Roosevelt — ironically, one of the founders of the American Progressive movement — she wrote: "This enrages me. The mob determines whose history is acceptable and whose not. Worse they're an uneducated mob of knuckleheads and everyone kowtows to these idiots who firstly need a f*cking bath!"[39]

When she finally penned a column about the unrest for South African readers in Maroelamedia, she could still barely contain her alarm:

Current events in the USA have left a diehard protest-pickled person like me, speechless. As someone bred by UWC and UCT, I thought I had seen it all. I have worked in the heart of Cape Town Adderley Street for decades where protests from PAGAD to COSATU were commonplace. I have seen and participated in many protests. I have witnessed looting, arson and vandalism of every size and shape. Fees/RhodesMust Fall campaigns revolted me. I have borne the brunt of the Thought Police in academia, the media and the many committees on which I served, but I have never felt silenced in the country of my birth. By the time I left SA to settle in the USA in 2018, I never thought that soon I'd witness a Cultural Revolution in the Land of the Free.

George Floyd's tragic death at the hands of a white cop unleashed a sinister backlash that has caused death, destruction, carnage and

38 Rhoda Kadalie. Comment on Facebook, 12 Jun. 2020. URL: https://www.facebook.com/rhoda.kadalie/posts/10158688860360039. Accessed on 28 Mar. 2022.

39 Rhoda Kadalie. Comment on Facebook, 22 Jun. 2020. URL: https://www.facebook.com/rhoda.kadalie/posts/10158718657455039. Accessed on 28 Mar 2022.

mayhem the likes [of which] the USA had never seen before. The unfortunate shooting of Rayshard Brooks on the 12 June, added fuel to the fire. Santa Monica where I lived until a few months ago is a cozy little coastal town of intimacy and flair. But two weeks ago, it lost its virginity. Boarded up after looters arrived targeting the attractive stores on Third Street Promenade, smashing everything in sight, it is unrecognisable. As the looters moved further away from the ocean, the destruction morphed into pure wantonness as young boys grabbed electric guitars and other expensive musical instruments in broad daylight from music stores. Unaffordable designer sneakers and jewellery suddenly seemed valueless as marauding savages moved from one store to the next stealing whatever their hearts desired. They smashed the Kumon School attended by my grandchildren; they looted the store next to my grandson's pre-school. No one stopped them. No one investigated who these kids were, obviously transported into neighbourhoods where they did not live.

My grandchildren could not internalise what they saw in the town of their birth, where their happiest memories were nurtured.

How does one explain to children the carnage?

…

Black Lives Matter, Antifa and other radical groups were spoiling for a fight a long time ago but their bête noire, pun intended, President Donald Trump, gave them no reason to rebel, what with a soaring economy and low unemployment figures, the most they could do was call him the usual – racist, misogynist, bigot, Hitler, Nazi, etc. He was the first President in recent decades to craft policies to improve the lives of African Americans, not least The First Step Act, targeting criminal [justice] reform, providing funding for historically black colleges/universities, reducing unemployment to the lowest rate for African Americans, and creating opportunity zones for black people and so on. The substantial increase in black support for him in the upcoming election has so rattled the Democrats that when the dreaded video of Floyd's murder went viral, they rejoiced. With their armed wing of extremists, they finally found their cause.

…

The sudden and groundswell support for BLM and their surrogates was music to the ears of the Democrat. And as a decades-old race-hustling party, they embraced these guerrillas with open arms, who are just so much better at using race to put every sane person on edge. It matters not that current statistics prove that considerable police reform had taken place over the past decades. ... And by the way, President Trump today (16 June) just signed an executive order on additional police reform. But then, logic and rationality were never the hallmarks of revolutionaries.

...

With their newfound power, BLM squeezed white guilt to the maximum, witnessed on our television screens as white supplicants sought the forgiveness of the guerrilla warlords, demonstrating BLM's supernatural powers against which not even the Catholic clergy can compete.

...

The more people genuflect before BLM, the more repressive their Cultural Revolution. Intoxicated by the smell of power, they view their purges as righteous, jettisoning reason and rationality as easily as underwear. Neighbours who self righteously post their BLM posters on their fences feel virtuous; social media warriors brand their sites with the ubiquitous black box; conservative news websites are censored and some shut down in cooperation with Google; and no longer are those who dare to dissent persecuted but also those who refuse to speak are branded equally guilty with epithets like "silence is violence."

Hitler's Brown Shirts as well as Mao's Red Guards, reincarnated as BLM and Antifa, are destroying historical relics, artifacts, and cultural and religious sites with impunity. Bizarrely, their Marxist strategy to mobilise all the levers of cultural power to attack the levers of state power has worked, and broadly supported by the illiberal left. They are immune from criticism and anyone who dares do so, is accused of hate speech; worse, many have lost their jobs for daring to expose BLM for the farce that it is, not least academics, purged for simply calling out their tyranny. Former Guardian journalist, Melanie Philips, eloquently calls this, the 'totalitarianism of virtue". With the millions of dollars thrown at them by the virtue-signalling celebs and big business, BLM now behaves like the very guerrillas they have always aspired to be. The barbarians are inside the gates, they're large and in charge.[40]

---

40   Rhoda Kadalie. Column, Maroelamedia, reprinted in Post on Facebook, translated from the Afrikaans, 22 Jun. 2020. URL: https://www.facebook.com/rhoda.kadalie/posts/10158728240580039. Accessed on 28 Mar. 2022.

Chapter 19: America

Rhoda was not only angry at the tactics used by the protesters and rioters; she was also contemptuous of their claims to be the representatives of an oppressed population. From her perspective, as someone who came of age during apartheid, nothing Americans were experiencing could remotely compare.

She posted on Facebook:

I have travelled to the USA regularly over 30 years and have now lived here since 2018. True to form the Democrats resurrect racial politics months prior to every election to the point of nausea. Their slavish instruments BLM and white-dominated Antifa play the race card dangerously close to destroying the glue that keeps the United States of America together. Highly paid, these champagne socialists have nothing to complain about, except act out their nihilism for having achieved nothing in their lives.

Yesterday I was at a party where I told local friends that these anarchists have no idea what systemic racism is, that their struggle, in fact, hankers after segregation again.

I began to tell them about my experience of racial discrimination in SA where it was systemic. They were shocked, had no idea what the substance of apartheid was, and how it permeated every aspect of our lives.

1. *I went to five different schools because of the Group Areas Act.*

2. *At age seven I was kicked out of a park across [from] our home that was suddenly declared for "Whites Only."*

3. *In the 1970s my father's City Mission in Smart Street, District Six and its other branches were demolished by the apartheid government, as part of the policy to remove 66 000 people classified coloured from prime property reserved for white People.*

4. *My father's entire parish was forcibly removed.*

5. *All my maternal and paternal kin were forcibly removed.*

6. *In 1971 my family was evicted from Mowbray an area declared for White People only.*

7. *In 1971 I attended a university designated for coloured people by law, because UCT demanded a full length photograph of myself for my application to study physiotherapy. I refused and went to the "coloured" university, UWC, under protest.*

8. *In 1982 I left SA to go to Namibia to marry a white man because it was illegal to do so in SA. I returned to a house we bought in a "Grey Area" defying the Group Areas Act, the Mixed Marriages Act and the Immorality Act. The police called immediately to notify that they had a copy of our marriage certificate. I was constantly in defiance of the Separate Amenities Act, and a range of other laws, where I was thrown off beaches, not allowed in certain theatres, restaurants, government offices etc.*

9. *My little sister and I were shown back counters of fast food kiosks, etc. because of our colour.*

10. *After our involvement in politics the police called us into head office for questioning for having broken the Mixed Marriages Act.*

11. *I gave birth to my daughter in a segregated hospital.*

I MENTION THIS MERELY TO REMIND ADHERENTS OF BLM THAT LIFE IN THE USA IS A FAR CRY FROM WHAT PEOPLE ENDURED FOR DECADES UNDER SYSTEMIC RACISM IN SA.

THE USA IS THE LAND OF OPPORTUNITY. I HAVE NEVER SEEN A COUNTRY OF SUCH INNOVATION, RESOURCES, WEALTH, PROMISE, PROGRESS, OPULENCE, DIVERSITY, CULTURAL AND ENVIRONMENTAL RESOURCES. WITH ALL ITS FLAWS, AND THERE ARE MANY, IT EXPLAINS WHY THE WORLD EMIGRATES TO ITS SHORES. SHOUTS OF RACISM AROUND EVERY TURN IS [sic] THE LAST REFUGE OF THE SCOUNDREL AND ARE USED TO KEEP BLACK PEOPLE IN A PERMANENT STATE OF VICTIMHOOD AND WOUNDEDNESS. THE EASIEST WAY TO TRANSFORM THESE NIHILIST ACTIVISTS IS TO DUMP THEM FOR A WEEK IN A SOUTH AFRICAN TOWNSHIP SO THEY CAN SEE REAL POVERTY, HUNGER AND CRIME.[41]

She followed the ongoing presidential election, too, with increasing alarm, peppering her daughter and son-in-law with questions. Why were the American media censoring news about Biden family scandals? Why were debate moderators so biased in favor of Democrats? Why didn't the U.S. have an independent electoral commission, as South Africa did, to monitor the voting process and certify the results?

---

[41]   Rhoda Kadalie. Comment on Facebook, 6 Jul. 2020. URL: https://www.facebook.com/rhoda.kadalie/posts/10158771546600039. Accessed on 28 Mar. 2022. Original emphasis.

Increasingly, Rhoda pushed back against the mainstream tide, and soon found herself caught in the expanding web of social media censorship. The algorithms of Facebook seemed to become more sensitive to her posts, over time, as one suspension led to another; sometimes she was banned for words and phrases that seemed innocuous to her. After she referred to Black Lives Matter as "trash" in August 2020, she was suspended for a day. Upon her return, she was indignant. "BIG BROTHER FB BANNED ME FOR 24 HOURS. NOT EVEN UNDER APARTHEID WAS I CENSORED!" she proclaimed.[42]

In a September 2020 update for Maroelamedia, she commented on the many lines of attack against Trump undertaken by Democrats and the American media:

The Democrats and their Cultural Czars are united in their determination to rid the country of the Orange Man. The Russian Collusion charges proved untrue; the Mueller Investigation failed; the Ukraine debacle was a hoax; and the Impeachment Trial was the biggest farce of the century, so whoever you are, dig and dig, until you find something that sticks.

Terrified that Orange Man will reveal more and more skeletons from the Democrat closet, the panic in Washington DC is palpable. Trump's opponents are dropping one bombshell after another as a last ditch effort to make him disappear. The more popular the president, the more hysterical the plots and the polls. The more robust his achievements, the more frantic the efforts to dig up dirt.

Regardless, the Democrats continue. Why? They know that the lapdog mainstream media (MSM) will do their bidding. The MSM no longer report news; they manufacture news. They play an active role in dividing the country into two opposing factions exposing this democracy for what it has become – a bastion of dead liberalism, the language of loyal opposition, even deader. [43]

Day by day, Rhoda's respect for American democracy continued to decline. What she saw was a version of what she thought she had left behind: a corrupt ruling elite, a complicit media, and a populace unable to take

---

42   Rhoda Kadalie. Comment on Facebook, 27 Aug. 2020. URL: https://www.facebook.com/rhoda.kadalie/posts/10158921725445039. Accessed on 28 Mar. 2022.
43   Rhoda Kadalie. Column, reprinted from Maroelamedia, translated from Afrikaans, 22 Sep. 2020. URL: https://www.facebook.com/rhoda.kadalie/posts/10158992587475039. Accessed on 28 Mar. 2022.

control of its own destiny. In fact, she wrote, "South Africa CAN TEACH AMERICA A THING OR TWO ABOUT ELECTIONS!"[44]

With much of the Los Angeles area still subject to strict coronavirus lockdowns, and with the media reflecting an urgent anti-Trump bias, Rhoda felt isolated, even though her family generally agreed with her views, and had even defiantly posted yard signs for Donald Trump on their fence and lawn — one of which was stolen in broad daylight.

One day, however, a neighbor offered a quiet signal of solidarity:

Flowers from a stranger who knocked on our door today thanking us for our courage for displaying a Trump sign. COURAGE - In the Land of the Free where people are terrified to disclose whom they are supporting. In this leftwing suburb where we live, the silent majority is rearing their scaredy little heads honking their car hooters in solidarity with us. A neighbour going for a walk told me that she is a Closet Republican so she admires us for being open about our support. Nothing grates [on] me more than political harassment, intimidation and intolerance. In this culture of fear, I bet that if I were unaffiliated, I would deliberately vote for Trump just to defy the lefty fascists, the Cancel Culture, the Wokerati![45]

The neighbor left a note for Rhoda: "I drove by and saw your Trump flags & signs and want to thank you for standing up in this town! ... Your courage was noticed and very much appreciated." While Rhoda was delighted to find a new comrade, she felt intensely frustrated that in a supposedly free country, the mere act of supporting an incumbent president required an unusual degree of bravery.

When Trump lost, Rhoda felt more than a sense of dismay: she simply did not accept the result as credible. She laid out her reasoning in a detailed column on November 6, shortly before the news networks declared Biden the winner:

The November 3 election has just passed, but is inconclusive. The Mail-in Ballot system confirms every suspicion Trump and the general public might have had as to the reliability of this exercise. But the capacity for cheating is why Democratic leaders pushed for this form of voting so vociferously. It was the nexus at which COVID-19 and Mail-in Ballots

44 Rhoda Kadalie. Comment on Facebook, 31 Oct. 2020. URL: https://www.facebook.com/rhoda.kadalie/posts/10159089394555039. Accessed on 28 Mar. 2022.

45 Rhoda Kadalie. Comment on Facebook, 25 Oct. 2020. URL: https://www.facebook.com/rhoda.kadalie/posts/10159073834765039. Accessed on 28 Mar. 2022.

would meet, changing the face of American elections. Biden's message of COVID-19 deaths was used to justify balloting by mail.

On election night as the votes were counted and called, suddenly, when Trump's votes started surging in Pennsylvania, Michigan, Nevada and Wisconsin, election officials incredulously called it a night. Immediately thereafter Trump went on the news declaring that he would file a lawsuit to block any votes that came in afterwards. Sure as hell, votes curiously came in on the morning of November 4, and suddenly Trump and Biden were neck and neck. Trump's lawyers appeared on television informing the nation that they were investigating illegal ballot votes, voter fraud, and opaque vote-counting practices ...

If Trump loses, it will be a stolen election in full view of the public. ... The larger-than-life rallies in support of Trump, boat flotillas and vehicle caravans that stretched up to 91 miles long attested to his popularity.

Should Trump lose, America will, alas, go back to its usual, fetid, Washington, DC swamp politics.[46]

Like millions of Americans, she believed that something had gone terribly wrong. "Protesters can be forgiven for thinking that they have been robbed of an election," she would write. "It was as transparent in its fraud as it was opaque in achieving it."[47] She regarded the new Biden administration with contempt.

*** *

The controversy over the 2020 presidential election continued into the new year. Rhoda, like many Trump supporters, hoped that the contested result would at least be investigated, if not overturned. But the Supreme Court declined to hear constitutional challenges to the voting process in Pennsylvania, and Trump's campaign struggled to marshal evidence to convince federal judges in other states.

46   Rhoda Kadalie. "2020 USA election: How did it come to this?" Litnet. com, 6 Nov. 2020. URL: https://www.litnet.co.za/2020-usa-election-how-did-it-come-to-this/?fbclid=IwAR3VUfLeKBSDdBe7y339FKd_EqXI_q7wPzgcOi83RYnEggoGjqWBaqga72A. Accessed on 28 Mar. 2022.
47   Rhoda Kadalie. "Die raadsel van Biden se oorwinning." Maroelamedia, 21 Dec. 2020. Translated from the Afrikaans. URL: https://maroelamedia. co.za/debat/meningsvormers/die-raaisel-van-biden-se-oorwinning/. Accessed on 18 Jun. 2022.

Trump called for a rally on January 6, 2021, to "Stop the Steal." The idea, according to Trump's trade advisor Peter Navarro, had been to bring thousands of protesters to Capitol Hill as a show of public support for efforts by some Republicans in Congress to reject the certification of the results and send the vote back for reconsideration in several states.[48]

But things went badly awry. As Trump addressed thousands of supporters a mile from the Capitol, a much smaller group pushed through barricades and past Capitol Police, and entered the building. Security had been light, as congressional leaders — particularly Speaker of the House Nancy Pelosi (D-CA) — felt that a National Guard presence, requested by the administration, would be a bad look, given the Democrats' complaints about the use of the military to calm riots in the nation's capital the summer before.

The Capitol riot resulted in the death of one trespassing Trump supporter, who was shot by a plainclothes police officer as she tried to crawl through a broken window into the chamber of the House of Representatives, as members of Congress cowered in fear. (Four other deaths, including those of three protesters and one police officer, were not directly caused by the violence.) Trump had to be pressured by his allies into delivering a public statement calling on his supporters to leave the building. When Congress reconvened, under Vice President Mike Pence, it certified Joe Biden as the winner of the election — not just as a constitutional formality, but as a statement of defiance against the mob.

Rhoda offered her South African readers a sober assessment of the aftermath:

Democrats have threatened retribution to those who supported Trump and are calling for re-education and deprogramming camps. The party that pretends to stand for dignity and unity, doxxes Trump supporters; their names are emblazoned across social media by the hysterical media, seeking revenge against those who "enabled" him. Not skipping a heartbeat, histrionic Pelosi announced Impeachment. Majority Leader Chuck Schumer called for Trump's forceful removal from office. The Wall Street Journal's entire board called for his resignation. Big Tech, at the urging of the self righteous Michelle Obama, join hands with powerful political forces to ban Trump and his followers, Facebook promising to cancel Trump for life. Publisher Simon and Schuster initiates the

---

48   Grace Panetta. "Former White House advisor Peter Navarro says Mike Pence hung up on him as he was pitching a plan to steal the 2020 election." Business Insider, 5 Jan. 2022. URL: https://www.businessinsider.com/peter-navarro-says-mike-pence-hung-up-on-his-election-stealing-pitch-2022-1. Accessed on 28 Mar. 2022.

cancelling of Republican Josh Hawley's book, ironically titled, The Tyranny of Big Tech. Prominent Republicans are put on a No-Fly list and already ordinary conservative citizens are thrown off airplanes in a country where flying has become a mode and means of production. And so it goes.

The Reign of Terror has begun. The crackdown on civil liberties is unprecedented. Robespierre rejoices in his grave because the left has resurrected his spirit. If one thinks China has a state-run media; America has a media-run state.

...

As shocking as the storming of the Capitol was, and as tragic as the deaths of five people are, it revealed serious fault lines between the governed and those who govern. The latter was enraged that their inner sanctum was desecrated. The word "mob" came to take on a new meaning – the dregs of society who dared to encroach on their safe space. Far removed from the people, one member summed up the divide succinctly when she exclaimed on TV, something like: "I didn't know the enemy is within." If anything, they should have understood the anger of the people. Disenfranchised, discredited and vilified for four years, the people have just had enough, the very words with which Trump opened his speech. During the summer BLM and Antifa destroyed 1500 businesses, destroyed cities and 30 people were killed during their violent riots, all lauded by senior Democrat politicians, Senator Kamala Harris insultingly raising funds to bail out all the rioters. Add to that the thousands and thousands of businesses shut down due to coronavirus, then one can understand the anger. Covid lockdowns, the destruction of small businesses while big businesses are thriving, and the tyranny of Democrat mayors and governors in policing their every move vis coronavirus, have all disempowered citizens so much that Trump seemed to be the only hope of protecting them against the bulwark of tyranny.

Senior Democrat politicians and media czars egged on the riots, yet they call the breaching of the building an "insurrection":

- *"Who says protests have to be peaceful?" CNN's Chris Cuomo;*

- *"There needs to be unrest in the streets." Congresswoman Ayanna Pressley.*

- *"Protesters should not let up." Senator Kamala Harris.*

- *"I just don't know why there [aren't] uprisings all over the country. Maybe there should be." Speaker Nancy Pelosi.*

- *"You get out and create a crowd and you push back on them and you tell them they are not welcome anymore, anywhere." Congresswoman Maxine Waters.*

Democrat-inspired riots led to the tearing down of statues, burning of books, including the Bible, banning of movies, art and music, censoring speech, cancelling people, suppressing freedom of speech and thought, and punishing dissenting voices. This is what Communists do, and America is well on their way there.

Apropos the storming of the Capitol: if you think South Africa has a Third Force, the USA with its powerful institutions, has a Third, Fourth, and Fifth force![49]

She also fought back against what she felt was a gross distortion of Trump and his administration in the South African media. In January 2021, she wrote a lengthy reply to an Afrikaans-language column by South African political scientist Amanda Gouws, which several friends had sent to her. Though Rhoda had once referred to Gouws as a fiend,[50] and had also spoken at the University of Stellenbosch at Gouws's invitation,[51] Rhoda had clashed with Gouws more recently, in 2017, when Gouws backed the "Women's March" against the newly-inaugurated President Trump.[52]

Four years later, Gouws described Biden's inauguration as the "*einde van die destruktiewe regering van Donald Trump*" [end of Donald Trump's destructive government] and a "*kollektiewe sug van verligting*" [collective sigh of relief]. She had also described Rhoda as "*verregs*" — "far-right."[53]

Taking exception to the latter, Rhoda outlined Trump's many achievements in office, deriding Gouws's lack of knowledge or, at best,

49   Rhoda Kadalie. "Capitol Hill — uit 'n ander hoek." Maroelamedia, reprinted in Post on Facebook, translated from the Afrikaans, 18 Jan. 2021. URL: https://bit.ly/3WKFftL. Accessed on 28 Mar. 2022.

50   Rhoda Kadalie. "Role of the Tabloids in SA." Lecture, Semester at Sea. 14 Sep. 2005.

51   Amanda Gouws. Email to Rhoda Kadalie, 17 Mar. 2003.

52   Rhoda Kadalie. "En Obama kry geen kritiek?" *Beeld*, 8 Feb. 2017. URL: https://www.netwerk24.com/Netwerk24/en-obama-kry-geen-kritiek-20170207. Accessed on 19 Jun. 2022.

53   Amanda Gouws. "Menings moet op feite berus." *Die Burger*, 25 Jan. 2021. URL: https://www.netwerk24.com/netwerk24/stemme/menings/menings-moet-op-feite-berus-20210125. Accessed on 27 May 2022.

curiosity. She added: "If you think Trump Derangement Syndrome is bad, then Rhoda Kadalie Derangement among SA's media elite is even worse."

She targeted Gouws's "punchline":

Dis wel moeilik om te verstaan dat iemand wat haarself vir die bevryding van vroue en spesifiek swart vroue beywer het, Kamala Harris die Demokrate se 'aanvalshond' wat bereid is om haar siel te verkoop, noem, of verregse standpunte ondersteun.[54]

[It's hard to understand that someone who has campaigned for the liberation of women and specifically black women, calls Kamala Harris the Democrats' 'attack dog' who is willing to sell her soul, or support far-right views.]

Rhoda replied:

Gouws behoort teen hierdie tyd te weet dat ek, as 'n feminis, haar verknegting aan identiteitspolitiek en haar oortuiging dat alle swart vroue in wese engele is, verwerp. ... Te danke aan my pigment is wit skuld nie my probleem nie. Dit is 'n siekte wat ongelukkig die politieke liggaam besmet het tot op 'n pad waar daar geen omkeer is nie. Deur swart mense oor te laat aan 'n permanente stand van slagofferskap, walg Gouws se rasse-deurdrywing 'n mens.

[Gouws should know by now that, as a feminist, I reject her obsession with identity politics and her belief that all black women are essentially angels. ... Thanks to my pigment, white guilt is not my problem. It is a disease that has unfortunately infected the body politic to a point where there is no turning back. By leaving black people to a permanent state of victimhood, Gouws's racial drive disgusts one.][55]

---

54   Ibid.
55   Rhoda Kadalie. "In reaksie op Amanda Gouws se 'Menings Moet Opp Feite Berus'." Maroelamedia, 28 Jan. 2021. Translated from the Afrikaans via Google Translate. URL: https://maroelamedia.co.za/debat/meningsvormers/in-reaksie-op-amanda-gouws-se-menings-moet-op-feite-berus/. Accessed on 17 Aug. 2022. Rhoda's original English draft was slightly different: "Gouws should know by now, that as a feminist I repudiate her enslavement to identity politics and her belief that all black women are intrinsically angels. ... To the woke Amanda Gouws blackness equals goodness. Thanks to my pigment, white guilt is not my problem. It is a disease that regrettably consigns blacks to a permanent state of victimhood, enhancing the power of race hustlers like Gouws." Post on Facebook, 28 Jan. 2021. URL: https://www.

Rhoda continued to criticize the new Biden administration, and to defend Trump's record in her Maroelamedia column. She exulted in the failure of the Democrats' second attempt to impeach Trump — a pointless effort, since he was already out of office, though conviction would have barred him from running again. And she warned about the expansion of the "cancel culture," through which dissidents — including Trump himself — were censored by social media companies, the news media, and the entertainment industry. "In many dictatorships, government censors people through a network of intelligence operatives and spies. In America the very powerful private sector does it, actively encouraged by the government," she noted.[56]

She wondered openly how Americans tolerated the increasing tide of repression:

> *The question remains, why is the USA acquiescing to this epoch of destruction when McCarthyism in the 1950s and the Weather Underground in the late 1960s nearly destroyed America's body politic. People were blacklisted, ostracised, kicked out of jobs for being labelled communist. More curiously, why is America allowing itself to be sucked, yet again, into another vortex of tyranny and socio-political authoritarianism when it knows the end result will only lead to further division?*[57]

In pushing back against cancel culture, Rhoda also noted that it was being promoted by a vast and well-funded network of left-wing organizations, with an intellectual base in American universities and a firm foothold in the corporate world.

The radicalism of the ascendent left prompted Rhoda to take a second look at socially conservative ideas she had once written off, in South Africa, as the outdated traditions of a calcified, patriarchal elite. Though a lifelong champion of gay and lesbian rights, for example, Rhoda detected a more ambitious agenda on the American left, which was to destroy the family unit itself. She wrote:

facebook.com/rhoda.kadalie/posts/10159325822515039. Accessed on 17 Aug. 2022.

56   Rhoda Kadalie. "Daar lê donker Dae vir Amerika voor." Maroelamedia, reprinted in Post on Facebook, translated from the Afrikaans, 19 Feb. 2021. URL: https://maroelamedia.co.za/debat/meningsvormers/daar-le-donker-dae-vir-amerika-voor/?fbclid=IwAR1RSBZo1R7cb-v3v3BV GRv6AGIzVXtPdxzrW7BNQYgJoqoCrhJ499kMQtY. Accessed on 28 Mar. 2022.

57   Rhoda Kadalie. "BLM, Critical Race Theory & Marxism." Unpublished essay. 7 Jul. 2021. Personal files.

> *The destruction of the family is directly linked to BLM's elevation of queer and trans people to the top of the totem pole; the banning of gender-specific nouns and pronouns attest to their attempts at destroying the family; people are cancelled for stating that reproductive functions are peculiar to women; children are taught about homosexuality and transgenderism at school. No longer are these issues the preserve of parents, but teachers have now become crusaders for BLM's sexual revolution.*[58]

This was, she argued, of a piece with the left's effort to throw open the country's borders to uncontrolled migration, to elevate race to the forefront of national consciousness, and to overthrow capitalism itself. In another column, she blamed BLM for having unleashed a crime wave on the country by describing police as racist and likening the U.S., a country that "won a war against slavery," to "an apartheid segregationist state". "[H]istory has proven disastrous consequences for countries adopting such primordial practices," she warned, no doubt reflecting on her familiar South African experience.[59]

Politics slowly receded for Rhoda, however. The children went back to school, part-time: Rhoda often fetched them on foot, as the school was literally next door. Stores reopened, without requiring masks, for a precious few months, before imposing mask and vaccine mandates. The city hummed back to life.

Rhoda ventured out into the newly-opening world. She studied for her driver's test; she took the bus around the city again. After a visit to Santa Monica's waterfront, she posted on Facebook: "*So lyk dit op Santa Monica strand* [This is what it looks like on the Santa Monica beach]. The iconic Pier with its Ferris wheel, a pastor holding a service on the beach, people surfing and bathing, loads of yachts in the background and a garbage bin praising God. More diverse you haven't seen yet the Mainstream Media talks about race and white supremacy all day long."[60]

---

58   Rhoda Kadalie. "'N Kansellasie-tsoenami tref Amerika." Maroelamedia, reprinted in Post on Facebook, translated from the Afrikaans, 19 Mar. 2021. URL: https://maroelamedia.co.za/debat/meningsvormers/n-kansellasie-tsoenami-tref-amerika/?fbclid=IwAR03dPSkEdoirL-SYS1ohphbYx_mcM3aFBt5El3c_1w1IU8Y_yVT4U5-Bg0. Accessed on 28 Mar. 2022.

59   Rhoda Kadalie. "BLM en die tragiese gevolge." Maroelamedia, translated from the Afrikaans, 4 Jun. 2021. URL: https://maroelamedia.co.za/debat/meningsvormers/blm-en-die-tragiese-gevolge/. Accessed on 27 May 2022.

60   Rhoda Kadalie. Comment on Facebook, 6 Jun. 2021. URL: https://www.facebook.com/rhoda.kadalie/posts/10159652867310039. Accessed on

Though not anti-vaccine, Rhoda — like many American conservatives — was skeptical of the Biden administration's efforts to promote COVID-19 vaccination through mandates on government employees and private businesses, some of which were ultimately defeated through the courts. She was incredulous at the administration's reluctance to investigate the origins of the coronavirus pandemic in China, calling it a new form of "denialism" akin to that of Thabo Mbeki on HIV/Aids.[61] And she mocked the media, especially its attempt to cover for Biden's failures.

Rhoda even excoriated more conservative outlets, such as the *Wall Street Journal*, which had never been particularly warm to Trump, and which claimed that Republicans' sweeping victory in the 2021 "off-year" elections, including the governorship of Virginia, showed the benefit of having Trump off the ballot. "The WSJ is but one example of how the mainstream media misled the public for four years about Trump, judging him on his looks, his language, and his demeanor, rather than his accomplishments. He wasted no time in implementing policies he promised his voters during his campaign unlike Biden who has broken many of his promises," she declared in November 2021.[62]

Despite her ongoing disappointment with American democracy, which seemed to have adopted South Africa's worst tendencies and "woke" taboos, she also applied for citizenship, and began studying for her naturalization test. She watched online lectures — notably those of conservative historian Victor Davis Hanson — and took copious notes; she read all she could about the Founding Fathers and the U.S. Constitution.

In July 2021, Julia returned home from the hospital with the family's third child — a daughter, Amira Leah. Rhoda moved back into grandmother mode, helping Julia change and bathe the baby, savoring the simple joy of a new child in the home.

At the same time, the house was beginning to feel small, and crowded. Rhoda began considering a move. Julia, with the benefit of a large raise at work, found an apartment for her mother just two blocks away, in a complex at the edge of nearby bluffs, overlooking the Pacific Ocean. Rhoda visited the apartment, and loved it.

---

28 Mar. 2022.

61   Rhoda Kadalie. "Die sirkus agter die virusgordyn." Maroelamedia, reprinted in Post on Facebook, translated from the Afrikaans, 25 Jun. 2021. URL: https://bit.ly/3WLOfPc. Accessed on 28 Mar. 2022.

62   Rhoda Kadalie. "Die twyftelagtige mag van VSA se hoofdstroommedia." Maroelamedia, reprinted in Post on Facebook, translated from the Afrikaans, 6 Dec. 2021. URL: https://bit.ly/3Eim2IQ. Accessed on 28 Mar. 2022.

Rhoda in her new apartment with members of the Pollak family, 2021

But she did not feel well. She had a persistent pain in her shoulder, and her chest. One evening, while walking around the neighborhood and chatting to a friend on the phone, she found that she was suddenly out of breath.

She went to the hospital for a chest X-ray, which suggested that a large mass had formed in her right lung. But the doctors did not seem inclined to react. Rhoda, worried, asked for a CT scan, to check for cancer. The hospital suggested that its first available appointment was in October; Rhoda insisted on an earlier appointment.

The only available appointment was September 15, which also happened to be the day Rhoda was moving into her new apartment. So she spent the day packing boxes with Julia, directing movers, and stressing about appliances — then arrived at the hospital at 10:00 p.m. for her CT scan.

The doctor called her early the next morning with alarming news. It appeared that she had a large tumor in her lung, and possible tumors elsewhere. There would need to be tests to determine the precise nature of the problem, and the treatment. But the danger was real and imminent.

Eventually, Rhoda was diagnosed with small cell lung cancer — a disease that typically afflicts heavy smokers. Rhoda had never smoked in her life; hers was one of the small percentage of spontaneous cases. One possible factor was that she had been present in Europe during the Chernobyl disaster in 1986, which spread radiation throughout the continent. Regardless of the cause, the prognosis was poor: the five-year survival rate was three percent. There was almost no hope of a recovery.

Rhoda accepted the diagnosis with equanimity. Months of suspicion had been confirmed; the task now was to live as well as possible, in between tests and treatments. Her new apartment was ideal, she felt: it allowed her to manage her illness privately, while still entertaining the family on short daily visits. Alexander, in particular, enjoyed visiting his grandmother on his own, eating cookies, watching television, and playing on the plush carpets.

She woke up daily to spectacular views of the ocean; in the afternoon, ocean breezes blew through the apartment; at night, owls called to each other from eucalyptus trees.

Many of her boxes had been retrieved from storage. Inside were a lifetime of treasures: portraits of her parents, and grandparents; photographs with Nelson Mandela; her honorary doctorate from Uppsala; rare lithographs by African artists.

There were also books, and papers — a small library of rare Africana: books about South African history; once-banned communist pamphlets advertising the achievements of post-colonial African states; programs from international women's conferences; carefully-maintained files from her time on the Human Rights Commission; letters and correspondence from cherished friends; newspaper clippings of important political events, and columns; all that she had preserved from her home in University Estate, liberated once again. She went through it all, at leisure, reflecting on a life of change, and defiance, and celebration: a life well-lived.

Centuries of South African history lined her shelves; photographs of old "struggle" friends, and Impumelelo colleagues, found a home on her walls; and the sounds of her favorite classical music pieces filled the apartment on her old stereo, which was finally put to use once again.

There was a guest room with two beds, for the older children; they would make new memories with her there, thoughts they would take with them, forever.

Rhoda savored the sweeping views of the Santa Monica Bay, with surfers in the foreground, and cargo ships in the far distance. It reminded her of the view from the dining room, in Cape Town, with sailboats and ships bracing against the whitecaps of Table Bay. The sun dipped toward the horizon on warm winter evenings, the wide sky a kaleidoscope of colors. At night, she waited for the waxing moon to cast its brilliant light over the rippled surface of the water.

"I feel as if I've come full circle," Rhoda told Julia. She was, finally, home.

Epilogue

Rhoda Kadalie passed away peacefully in the early hours of April 16, 2022,
with her sister, Judy, by her side, and her daughter, Julia, nearby.

The day before, on Good Friday, during a visit by a pastor from the
local hospice, the nurses overseeing Rhoda's care had alerted Julia and
the family that Rhoda's oxygen levels had dropped and her breathing had
slowed. She had not spoken for three days; it seemed she might be about
to pass away.

Julia played some of Rhoda's beloved Gospel albums on the stereo
in the apartment. As the voice of Mahalia Jackson resounded through the
apartment, Rhoda's breathing and heartbeat stabilized, leaving all around
her smiling. She would spend her last day on earth in that state of spiritual
contemplation and delight.

In the hours after Rhoda passed away, Julia and Judy watched the
sunrise from Rhoda's balcony, and embraced, and wept.

The previous months had been a terrible ordeal.

Rhoda's doctors had missed the diagnosis at first, losing six precious
weeks in which she might have been treated. The hospital where she was
treated, which she had once regarded highly, was overwhelmed by the
ongoing coronavirus pandemic, and she was frustrated by the poor care
she received, as well as the bewildering fights that emerged over payment
and insurance.

Rhoda kept her illness a close secret, shared with only a few
friends. She did not want people fussing over her; she also held out hope
that she would, somehow, recover.

---

1 Rhoda Kadalie. "DA must own its history." *The Citizen*, 2017, ibid.
2 Rhoda Kadalie. Facebook post, 21 Feb. 2022. URL: https://www.facebook.
   com/rhoda.kadalie/posts/10160166332180039. Accessed on 15 July 2022.

She began an immediate course of chemotherapy. Rhoda lost her hair over several weeks, but felt that her physical condition was improving. She prepared a sumptuous Christmas dinner for her family, and joined the children on a three-day visit to the Legoland theme park in early January. A scan showed that her tumor had shrunk from six centimeters to two centimeters, and that there had been no spread to her brain, her liver, or her bones.

Rhoda was optimistic, and hoped to live long enough to see Maya celebrate her bat mitzvah two years later, or at least to see Amira turn two years old, some eighteen months hence.

Rhoda, resting after cancer treatment, exchanges smiles with six-month-old granddaughter Amira while on holiday at Legoland, California, 2022

In mid-January, Rhoda joined her family on a weekend visit to Lake Arrowhead in the San Bernardino mountains, where fresh snow graced the surrounding peaks. She rested in the mountain lodgings as the children ventured into the snow at a nearby Big Bear ski resort. But she began to feel weak, and to lose her appetite. When she ate, she struggled to keep her food down. She would continue to feel ill for several weeks, and began losing weight rapidly, at a rate of several pounds per week.

Epilogue

A scan in February revealed that the tumor had come back — with a vengeance. It had grown dramatically, to seven centimeters, and spread to her liver and her brain. Rhoda was hospitalized, and treated with radiation, which all but eliminated the tumor in her lung and slowed the growth of the tumors in her brain. Her appetite finally recovered. But her liver could not be irradiated. And in the interim, Rhoda had lost the strength to walk.

Rhoda was transferred to a rehabilitation facility, where her room was swiftly decorated with drawings and letters from her grandchildren. But after 48 hours, she insisted on being taken home. Though Rhoda's insurance would not cover the cost of home health care, Julia ensured that her mother's wishes were fulfilled, ordering an ambulance to transport Rhoda back home. And for the last several weeks of her life, Rhoda could, at least, rest in her own bed, surrounded by her books, her photographs, and her grandchildren, who climbed into bed beside her to watch television, until the Saturday before she died.

Once she accepted that she would not recover, Rhoda finally told her siblings about her illness. They were in shock, and called frequently to speak with her. Her brother, Pastor Charles Kadalie, prayed with her and read Psalms with her. His daughter, Robyn, Rhoda's only other relative in the U.S., traveled from Kentucky to spend a weekend with Rhoda. The timing was fortuitous: the day after Robyn returned home was the last day Rhoda was able to speak to anyone.

Alexander, all of six years old, wrote Rhoda one last hopeful note, accompanied by a drawing of her painting with the children — one of their frequent pastimes together:

to granny rhoda

Dear granny I hope you get better soon and I love you so much. Love Alex.

Rhoda acknowledged the letter with a nod, but did not have the strength to respond.

She had not been spared the suffering she had feared. But she had been surrounded by love until the end.

***

When Rhoda first received her diagnosis, I knew that I had to write this book, and so did she. Somehow, she found the strength to work on it with me, even as she endured the travails of a terrible disease and its debilitating treatment.

I wanted to record the details of Rhoda's extraordinary, colorful life — to give coherence to her story, which had been scattered among so many columns and speeches; to preserve the precious insights she possessed into South African history, and politics in general.

What I discovered in the course of writing Rhoda's biography was how close she and I had become, not just emotionally but also intellectually.

I found in Rhoda a true comrade, in the classical sense: one who had made the shift from left to right, as I had, but whose journey was so much more significant because she had actually participated in, and helped to lead, a struggle for liberation; and had sacrificed so much by questioning its leaders, and following her principles to their surprising conclusions in the years that followed.

Rhoda's life was the answer to the question that had once motivated my renewed interest in South Africa, after growing up as an American: were the ideals of constitutional democracy truly universal? Could they succeed outside of a western context, in a society still wounded by past conflict and hatred, and marred by deep economic inequality? Or were radical alternatives, such as socialism, the only solution?

And where did I fit into all of this, as a white, western, Jewish male? Did "social justice" demand some form of self-negation? Or could I reconcile my identity with my ideals?

Rhoda's commitment to her principles allowed her to see past identity politics, and beyond utopian ideals, and to focus on the human lives affected by concrete political outcomes. And her experiences in proximity to power — especially on the South African Human Rights Commission — convinced her that what was more urgent than the revolutionary ideals she hoped to achieve were the basic principles she wished to preserve.

It is liberating to discover, through Rhoda's difficult journey, that the ideals upon which western civilization is based are still worth defending — though we ourselves have often failed to adhere to them, and are perhaps unworthy of them. Rhoda was a revolutionary because of the society into which she was born. Though she rarely used the term herself, she became something of a liberal — in the American sense, a conservative — because she discovered, after the revolution, that while the old order had failed to live up to the principles it had sometimes proclaimed, they were still worth preserving.

Critics often struggled to understand Rhoda's political transition. To Rhoda, there was no "transition": she fought for freedom throughout her life, particularly for women, whose oppression was overlooked in the old South African order and the new. Her conservative values, which became more pronounced later in her life, had always been latent, shaped by her

Christian upbringing — and though she argued for reform within the church, she never abandoned her faith. The political turning points in her life were more like inflection points than wholesale changes: they were moments that accelerated her momentum in a direction she was already moving. These included: the discovery in 1986 that she had been targeted by the anti-apartheid struggle in Europe; the death in 1993 of American scholar Amy Biehl; her resignation in 1997 from the South African Human Rights Commission; the bizarre saga in 2000 of President Thabo Mbeki's denialism on HIV/Aids; the DA's secret offer of leadership in 2004, and Donald Trump's election in 2016. The latter confirmed that Rhoda's keen political instincts were not confined to her familiar South African context.

Her detractors wondered — openly, at times — if her views were in fact being shaped by some man in her life: her husband, her son-in-law, the leader of the opposition. Rhoda was her own woman. She lived a truly examined life, one in which she questioned everything and everyone. Certainly she was influenced by her friends and loved ones, but she also influenced them in turn. In revisiting her life's work, and re-reading so much of what she wrote, I came to appreciate just how much she had influenced me, and guided my own political transition.

She was that guide for countless people whose lives she touched.

Rhoda's lasting impact on South Africa and the world is best summarized by a series of contradictions.

She fought apartheid, but opposed the post-apartheid government. She criticized that government, yet tried to help it achieve its socioeconomic goals. She focused on socioeconomic rights, but rejected socialism and looked to the private sector. She was a black feminist, and a Trump supporter. She was a committed Christian, and beloved by the Jewish community, which admired her and was grateful that she supported Israel. She believed in non-racialism, yet savored being Coloured.

Rhoda was one of a few leading South African figures to have experienced racism directly, and brutally, who could yet transcend the politics of race, clinging instead to the principles and institutions that might ensure justice for all. It was as if she had put western civilization to the test, examined its flaws, and decided that, on balance, its ideas and traditions were not only worth defending, but were urgently needed. The endurance of freedom depended as much on the preservation of what was right and necessary in our institutions as much as on overthrowing what had been proven wrong and prejudicial.

While arguing for reforms in public policy, she never lost sight of the solitary man — or woman — who was to be the beneficiary, and the agent, of social progress. In her life and her writing, Rhoda — uniquely among

South African intellectuals — connected the great themes of South Africa's political liberation with the personal strivings of the South African people.

Another way Rhoda's impact could be measured was in how dearly she was missed in the country she left behind. "Come back; we need you!" was a repeated refrain on social media and in the comments section of columns she continued to dispatch back to South Africa after she left. Hers was a rare voice, in every way.

She could criticize the new government because she had been a victim of the old; she could attack its corruption in her columns because she was trying to help it achieve its development goals in her daily life. She had authority because she had independence and integrity.

Her strong sense of personal integrity would not allow her to benefit unjustly from her race, or her gender. She had fought for the freedom to live as a South African — not as a black, or Coloured, or female South African.

Smuts Ngonyama, a spokesman for President Mbeki, famously explained his own participation in a lucrative "empowerment" deal in 2004 by declaring: "I did not struggle to be poor."[3]

Rhoda had not struggled to be wealthy; she had struggled to be free, and to free others. Freedom could not be compromised.

Rhoda refused to see in the self-enrichment of a few any kind of symbolic victory for the many — especially when the empowerment deals soaked up scarce capital that could have created jobs, or when affirmative action destroyed the public services upon which the poor, in particular, depended.

She knew that socialism, and identity politics, were the path to ruin, even if cloaked in the romantic rhetoric of liberation. "The point is delivery, not the race of the deliverer," she wrote.[4] Her stubborn insistence on principle embarrassed and frustrated former comrades; it was the rock on which friendships were dashed.

Rhoda understood, far sooner than most, that the ANC's "national democratic revolution" was incompatible with constitutional democracy.

And she warned an increasingly "woke" America: lest you be tempted by post-apartheid South Africa's radical political example, you will suffer the same fate.

---

3   Smuts Ngonyama, quoted by "ANC leaders did not win struggle on their own." *Sowetan*, 28 Jun. 2007. URL: https://www.sowetanlive.co.za/news/2007-06-28-anc-leaders-did-not-win-struggle-on-their-own/. Accessed on 29 Mar. 2022.
4   Rhoda Kadalie. "The point is delivery, not the race of the deliverer." *Business Day* 17 Mar. 2005.

In the last years of her life, Rhoda also brought the joy of being South African — and the experience of being Coloured — with her to the United States. Dinners cooked for grandchildren were fragrant, sweet curries, garnished by Mrs. Ball's chutney, followed by sago pudding for dessert.

When discussing American politics, Rhoda peppered her observations with Afrikaans slang, and obscure profanities; savoring Trump's jokes, even while mocking his rhetorical excesses.

Rhoda personified her people: you could take the Coloured out of South Africa, but you could never take the essential "*fok julle*" out of the Coloured — the determination to live, guilt-free, as one was made.

I am here; I am a strange mix, and yet more than the sum of my parts; and fuck you if you don't like it, especially if you can't take a joke.

$$* * *$$

Rhoda's irreverence was central to her approach to politics. Her central political creed was tolerance — not a meek kind of tolerance among anodyne alternatives seeking consensus, but a robust tolerance among rambunctious, rowdy rivals.

In her mind, South Africa's most important political achievement was not the first fully democratic election in 1994, nor the adoption of a new constitution in 1996, but the emergence of the United Democratic Front in 1983, when a hodgepodge of opposition groups stood up to the apartheid regime. There was a joy in their defiance, and a solidarity.

As HIV/Aids activist Zackie Achmat observed later: "[T]he 80s represented enormous sexual and personal freedom and racial mixing and it is the clampdown of the ANC's Stalinism that killed that."[5] It was in the uprising itself that Rhoda and her fellow activists found their voices, and nurtured the democratic values they hoped would guide their future society. At the time, South African politics was still repressive, and violent, but it would never again feel quite so alive.

Like Clements Kadalie, Rhoda rejected the dogmas of both left and right. Like Clements Kadalie, she focused on the concerns of the black majority, but not to the point of racial essentialism; she emphasized pragmatic reform over revolutionary utopia; and she insisted on the importance of merit as a foundation for progress.

Rhoda also emulated her father, Pastor Fenner Kadalie, who not only preached to the communities of District Six and the displaced communities of the Cape Flats, but who devoted his energies to improving

---

5   Zackie Achmat, ibid., 30.

their lives, especially the lives of the poor. For Fenner Kadalie, the needs of the present could not wait for political solutions, or government interventions. Though poor himself, he established his City Mission to provide for the community, largely through its own resources.

Like her father and her grandfather, Rhoda struggled against an unjust regime without bending to the dogma of its opponents.

She did not place her faith in strictly political change — neither through the liberation offered by the ANC, nor the liberalism offered by the leading opposition party. And she measured politicians by their practical achievements — whether they improved the lives of the governed — rather than by the quality of their sentiments. Hence her respect for Trump, whose accomplishments shone despite his rhetoric.

Even as an ANC member, Rhoda wanted the South African government to have strong opposition, because she believed that the ANC would then be more successful in its objectives. She likened parliamentary opposition to a soccer match: "The stronger the opposing side, the more proficiently the defending team is likely to play."[6]

Opposition parties, in her vision, would not only hold the government accountable, but would also — ideally — offer alternative policies. To play that constructive role, it was important that opposition be as effective — and diverse — as possible: voters should not be denied any option, she believed.

Conversely, Rhoda believed, being a citizen in a democracy meant coming to terms with diversity. One did not have to agree with one's opponents; one could even hate them and what they stood for; but one still had to engage, to cooperate, even to socialize together.

Rhoda was best known for attacking corruption — regardless of the culprit, whether it was the ruling ANC; the old white elite, as exemplified in the Steinhoff accounting fraud scandal; or the establishment media. No one — not even friends and allies — was spared. As Edwena Goff would later recall, Rhoda was a fierce debater, one who arrived at arguments in command of the facts, and who rarely contradicted herself. Yet she could embrace and defend her own convictions without losing sight of other people as individual human beings.

In her own life, she exemplified principles of unimpeachable integrity. She had many offers to seize the spoils of struggle, as so many others had done. She turned down requests to join corporate "empowerment" boards; she declined most political appointments; she walked away from powerful positions rather than betray her principles.

---

6   Rhoda Kadalie. *Opposing Voices*, 117.

Epilogue

Throughout her life, Rhoda had friends across the political spectrum. She prized those friends best able to handle the differences that would inevitably erupt. And she used wit and laughter to transcend those differences: "She was one of the cleverest, funniest people I've ever met," Balu Nivison said.[7]

To experience the world with Rhoda was to see it as few did, or could.

Rhoda's life is a lesson in *how to live, politically*: to seek truth everywhere, encourage debate, and celebrate difference — with a sense of righteous indignation against injustice, but always with a sense of humor, wherever possible.

She was also willing to learn, and to change her views, over time. Once a Marxist, she observed in 2015: "In global politics today, the difference is no longer between Left-wing and Right-wing, as politicians would like us to believe, but between Open and Closed societies."[8]

She was also an exemplary mother, who raised Julia with a love of books, a passion for music, and a desire to improve the world. Rhoda's Impumelelo colleagues recall their amazement when she brought Julia to work, and she sat reading books while Rhoda attended to her duties. Chris Mingo gave credit to Rhoda for exposing his own children to books and encouraging her to excel at school.

Moreover, Rhoda was a mentor to countless people — especially women — struggling to find their way in the new South Africa. Many of the women whose careers she helped felt an almost maternal bond to Rhoda: "She felt like a link to my mother," Nivison said.

"I wish she were my mother," Terri Felix told me.[9]

✳✳✳

Rhoda continued writing, even after she was diagnosed with cancer.

In her 2022 diary, which was largely filled with medical appointments and notes on her daily symptoms, Rhoda sketched the outline of what might have been one of her last essays, had she been able to muster the strength to write it: "Similarities between Democrats & ANC."[10] (The Democrats had the "Deep State," the ANC had "state capture"; Democrats "hate the people/voting fodder," while the ANC "Hate the masses.")

---

7   Balu Nivison. Interview 28 Feb. 2022.
8   Rhoda Kadalie. Draft article for PoliticsWeb. 1 May 2015. Personal files.
9   Terri Felix. Interview 23 Feb. 2022.
10   Rhoda Kadalie. Diary entry, 31 Dec. 2021.

She had also contemplated other projects: in 2020, she prepared notes for a proposal for PragerU, the online education resource created by conservative radio host and scholar Dennis Prager. Rhoda wanted to launch a magazine on conservative women, titled "Conservative Women: the Story Behind the Story." The project would "explore how the personal is political, the challenges they face, their obstacles faced, victories achieved. The magazine will focus on reviews, interviews, will invite letters, personal photographs, anecdotes, poems, contributions, etc". She made a list of potential women to be included, including several well-known political figures and television pundits.[11]

Rhoda's last column, on Democrats' cynical effort to push "voting rights" as a theme in a midterm election year, would appear in Maroelamedia on 26 January 2022.[12] She told me, from her bed in the rehabilitation center she briefly stayed in before returning home from the hospital, that she had another column in her mind — perhaps the one outlined in her diary — but did not have the ability to write it, nor the stamina to dictate it.

By then, we were as close as we had ever been, all past quarrels forgotten and forgiven. Rhoda could be tough to get along with, at times; almost everyone who knew her, and loved her, had experienced some tumultuous feud or another.

My wife and I joked, in a moment of dark humor toward the end of Rhoda's battle, that Rhoda would plan to pass away deliberately on my birthday, April 25, just to haunt me. But Rhoda's at-times brittle demeanor was also an outcome of the circumstances that had shaped her, and sprang from the personal integrity she defended at all costs.

Beyond that toughness, Rhoda was an exceptionally kind and warm person, with a great capacity for love and nurturing. She was also a sensual woman, who appreciated beauty and enjoyed romance, when it came along. She was a struggle heroine; she was also a beloved mother and grandmother. She fought valiantly against cancer, and retained her wit and humor throughout her battle, even on the hardest days.

One day, after a morning of fussing by nurses and caregivers, all of whom were female, she summoned me to her room, in her apartment. I arrived, eager to be helpful. "Yes, Rhoda?"

---

11   Rhoda Kadalie. Diary entry, 11-12 Dec. 2020.
12   Rhoda Kadalie. "Hoekom die Democrate die John R Lewis-wet probeer wegsteek." Maroelamedia, 26 Jan. 2022. URL: https://maroelamedia. co.za/debat/meningsvormers/hoekom-die-demokrate-die-john-r-lewis-wet-probeer-wegsteek/. Accessed on 30 May 2022.

"I just wanted to see what a man looked like," she joked, and dismissed me.

Known as a fighter, Rhoda also had an incredible capacity for love. She adored classical music, and opera; she was equally fascinated by the simple beauty of a sunset, or the call of an owl, or the silhouette of a hawk outside her window. She gave generously to complete strangers; she had a natural rapport with children. And she quietly nurtured a deep connection to God.

That faith allowed her to face death with courage. Asked in 2012 about what she believed would happen after death, Rhoda replied simply: "I believe that I shall be reunited with my Creator."[13] She also felt she had fulfilled her purpose. Her greatest achievement she said, was "[r]aising my daughter to be the most loving and lovable person on the planet."[14] Her only regret was that she would not live to see her grandchildren grow. But she had spent four precious years with them — years that, had she not moved, would have included two years of forced isolation during the coronavirus pandemic.

In the last year of her life, before she knew she was ill, Rhoda applied for U.S. citizenship. She dutifully studied for the citizenship test, memorizing facts about American history and the U.S. Constitution. She passed easily, and awaited her formal invitation to a swearing-in ceremony.

Somehow, like her green card, her application for citizenship seemed to become lost in the bureaucratic machine. She waited, and waited, and as she fought her battle with cancer, we wondered if, and when, the final approval would arrive.

A few days after she passed away on April 16, 2022, a letter arrived for Rhoda: an order to appear for her swearing-in as a U.S. citizen, at 10:00 a.m. on April 25th, 2022.

She remained, despite herself, a South African. As she told an Afrikaans newspaper shortly before she left for the U.S.: "*SA wil my nie laat gaan nie.*"

South Africa will not let me go.[15]

Nor can I.

---

13   Rhoda Kadalie. Questionnaire. Draft responses. 3 Oct. 2012. Personal files.
14   Ibid.
15   Rhoda Kadalie, quoted by Willemien Brümmer. "Rhoda: 'SA wil my nie laat gaan nie'," ibid.

Rhoda on her balcony on her last birthday, September 22, 2021

Appendix:
'We Don't Do That'

This address, delivered by Rhoda Kadalie at a conference on business ethics in 2013,[1] is one of many speeches and interviews given by Rhoda Kadalie in her lifetime, but perhaps the one that best expresses her approach to politics, and her signature issue — corruption. She connects abstract principles to personal choices, excoriating South Africa's post-apartheid elite — but giving her audience a way to make a positive contribution.

President Obama's campaign slogan was: "Yes, we can." And President Zuma's campaign slogan is: "Yes, we ... Nkan-dla."

[Laughter]

Today I want to start off with three anecdotes, and they are all linked to a common theme.

When my brother turned 50, he decided to have his birthday party at the Grand West Casino. My daughter, who was 12 at the time, resolutely said: "This is a Christian family. They go to a gambling casino for a party — I am not going. I've just done a project on gambling, and its effects on the poor, and so I don't care if I stay alone at home."

I was gobsmacked that my daughter could cite statistics about the effects of gambling on society, and how it exacerbates the poverty of the poor.

I had no option but to respect her wishes, and I stayed at home with her.

Similarly, not so long ago, I went to the Africa Innovations Awards event at one of our prestigious business schools. The businessman who sponsored the event is involved in what I consider to be a lot of government scandals, and I wrote to the business school expressing my disappointment, asking them how they could reconcile teaching business ethics when they accept sponsorship from someone who is tainted.

Needless to say, I got no response.

In a society riddled with corruption, from the legislature to big business to municipalities, one is confronted with this ambivalence all the time.

---

1   Rhoda Kadalie. "We Just Don't Do That." Speech to EthicsXChange, Fugard Theatre, Cape Town, 5 Nov. 2013. URL: https://www.youtube. com/watch?v=CyDswWDV6WA&t=3s. Accessed on 1 May 2022.

I'm reminded of my own hubris when I was told by the University of Uppsala in Sweden that they decided to confer an honorary doctorate on me in 1999. So off I toddled to Sweden for the ceremony, and it lasted four hours, in Latin. Afterwards, we drove to a castle for a spectacular celebration, which ended in a ball.

After the reception, we walked to the parking lot, and my host walked past her car. And I said to her, "Frieda, you're walking past your car." And she said: "I had a glass of wine, and we don't drive."

At the time, I was a Human Rights Commissioner, and I said to her: "Hey, just drive — nobody will know. I'm not going to walk in my high heels."

And she turned to me, aghast, and said: "In Sweden, we just don't do *that*."

When I turned around, I saw everyone in their finery, either walking home or calling a taxi to take them home.

"We just don't do *that*" — stuck with me ever since.

I realized that in Sweden, ethics has become woven into the DNA of the national consciousness. It had become systemic, and it was part of the culture of business, politics, and daily life. It was part of the national fabric. It was part and parcel of their DNA.

So these anecdotes remind me of what Oprah [Winfrey] once said: "Real integrity is doing the right thing, knowing that nobody's going to know whether you did it or not."

So the question is: Why are we South Africans not like the Swedes? Why are we not as innocent as my daughter, who at an early age knew what was right and wrong? Why do universities teach business ethics, yet take money from tainted people?

Unlike Sweden, in South Africa the culture of impunity has seeped into public life. It has become part of the moral code of the president, of members of Parliament — remember the travel scandal? — the police, big business, government, universities, and so on.

Just this morning, on the news, President Zuma said there's nothing wrong with taking a billion, [and] giving it to an NGO of which his cousin is the head. That was headline news today.

So we have one law for politicians, and another for ordinary citizens. Politicians can steal billions and remain unpunished, while a poor woman who shoplifts will go to jail.

So once this happens, everyone will try to cheat, and beat the system, and get away with it. Everyone loses respect for the rule of law, and government becomes lax about reinforcing it.

The going mantra in the whole world and in South Africa in particular: "Ag, it's just human nature." But you know what? Human nature has proven to be untrustworthy at the best of times. And that is why we need checks and balances to keep us on the right road.

The Constitution, the law, regulations, and moral ethical codes, stemming from our faith or morality, are meant to keep us on the straight and narrow. And that is why we have a Constitution: it's to protect the governed from those who govern. And we often forget why we have a Constitution.

Now, ethical behavior, at the best of times, is difficult, and it has dire consequences for those who want to do the right thing.

Point number one: it takes courage to be ethical.

Consequences of ethical behavior can be dire. Whistleblowers are treated like lepers in our society, and many also disappear from the public domain, and some die in obscurity.

The guys who exposed our Speaker of Parliament, who is now the national chairman of the ANC, he exposed her for acquiring a fraudulent [driver's] license. His name was John Miller. He died in penury, while her career just mobilized upward and upward.

It is particularly hard when one sees how the corrupt are being rewarded with promotions and so on, while those with integrity are punished.

There is no bigger challenge than knowing the difference between what you have a right to do, and what is *right* to do.

Secondly, being ethical, being honest, is unpopular.

Taking an ethical stance can make you deeply unpopular. By standing up for what is right, one unwittingly becomes a conscience, a goody-two-shoes, and so one. You are excluded from invitation lists. People give you a wide berth. They gossip and discuss your life. And they quietly wish you would just go away.

Being unpopular in a sea of corruption is not necessarily a bad thing. But it can be painful.

But we need to know, and I heard this quote from someone: "If someone wants to lead the orchestra, they must turn their back on the crowd."

Honesty is never seen to be sitting astride the fence.

Another challenge to unethical behavior is that our vested interests — people's personal, vested interests, especially in government — are often passed off as the national interest.

And my question to government is: who determines what is in the national interest?

When Thabo Mbeki said HIV does not cause Aids, was that his own vested interest, or was it in the good of the nation?

South Africa is in trouble because of those who put their vested interests above those of the nation. They also have the cheek to treat their vested interests as those of the nation. And those of us who dare to criticize: if you are white, you are called disloyal, a racist; if you are black, you are called a traitor, and unpatriotic.

But I wish to argue that the highest form of patriotism is to be critical, is to ask questions, and to demand loyalty.

And then, lastly: unethical behavior is unsustainable.

It is simply unsustainable. It is costly, it drains the country of its resources, it makes people unhappy, and it digs a hole that pulls everyone into it.

The financial crisis in western capitalism was due to the unbridled accumulation of wealth by the wealthy with no checks and balances. The collapse of Wall Street, Lehman Brothers, the big banks, Fannie Mae and Freddie Mac — was due largely to unethical behavior that had become systemic.

Here in South Africa, debt is increasing because we spend more than we have. Corruption is out of control. And whereas in the past, we were shocked by the theft of a million, now a billion does not even shock us.

South Africa needs a moral truth commission. It was Jacob Zuma and Thabo Mbeki who started the "moral regeneration project." And it failed, because moral regeneration cannot be promoted by moral degenerates.

[Applause]

Unless we change our ways, the lack of personal, political, and corporate integrity will become second nature to South Africans and, indeed, the world. Worse, it will be passed on from generation to generation, and we simply cannot afford to continue on this path.

In conclusion, I look forward to the day that we in South Africa turn to one another and say: "We just don't do *that*."

Maybe we could start right here, now, by altering the phrase to: "*I* just won't do *that*."

Thank you.

Made in the USA
Las Vegas, NV
13 February 2023

67466326R00339